AUSTRALIA TOURING ATLAS

Mobile
Navigation

GPS

Maps & Guides

Prepared to explore.

www.hemamaps.com

CONTENTS

NATIONAL PARKS   iv

QUEENSLAND   1

Queensland Key Map   1
Brisbane CBD   2
Brisbane Throughroads   3
Brisbane Suburbs, Queensland   4
Brisbane Suburbs, Queensland   6
Brisbane Region, Queensland   8
Brisbane Region, Queensland   10
South-East Queensland   12
Central-East Queensland   14
North Queensland   16
Cairns Region, Queensland   18
Cape York, Queensland   19
Outback Queensland   20
South-West Queensland   22
Gold Coast Region, Queensland   24

NEW SOUTH WALES   25

New South Wales Key Map   25
Sydney CBD   26
Sydney Throughroads   27
Sydney Suburbs, New South Wales   28
Sydney Suburbs, New South Wales   30
Sydney Region North, New South Wales   32
Sydney Region South, New South Wales   34
Central-East New South Wales   36
North-East New South Wales   38

North-West New South Wales   40
South-West New South Wales   42
South-East New South Wales   44
Hunter Valley Region, New South Wales   45
Canberra CBD (ACT)   46
Canberra Throughroads (ACT)   47
Australian Capital Territory   48

VICTORIA   49

Victoria Key Map   49
Melbourne CBD   50
Melbourne Throughroads   51
Melbourne Suburbs, Victoria   52
Melbourne Suburbs, Victoria   54
Melbourne Region, Victoria   56
South-West Victoria   58
Great Ocean Road, Victoria   60
North-West Victoria   62
Eastern Victoria   64
Gippsland Region, Victoria   66

TASMANIA   67

Tasmania Key Map   67
Hobart CBD   68
Hobart to Port Arthur, Tasmania   69
Southern Tasmania   70
Central Tasmania   72
North-East Tasmania   74
North-West Tasmania   76
Flinders & King Islands, Tasmania   78

MIRRANPONGA PONGUNNA LAKE, NT. PHOTO: SILKE NAWROCKI

SOUTH AUSTRALIA 79

South Australia Key Map	79
Adelaide CBD	80
Adelaide Throughroads	81
Adelaide Suburbs, South Australia	82
Adelaide Suburbs, South Australia	84
Adelaide to Barossa Region, South Australia	86
Fleurieu Peninsula, South Australia	87
Adelaide & Surrounds, South Australia	88
North-East South Australia	90
North-West South Australia	92
Central-East South Australia	94
Central-West South Australia	96
South-East South Australia	98

WESTERN AUSTRALIA 99

Western Australia Key Map	99
Perth CBD	100
Perth Throughroads	101
Perth Suburbs, Western Australia	102
Perth Suburbs, Western Australia	104
Perth Region, Western Australia	106
South West & South Coast, Western Australia	108
South-West Western Australia	110
Central-West Western Australia	112
The Pilbara, Western Australia	114
The Kimberley, Western Australia	116
Central-East Western Australia	118
South-East Western Australia	119

NORTHERN TERRITORY 120

Northern Territory Key Map	120
Darwin CBD	121
Darwin Throughroads	122
Darwin Region, Northern Territory	123
The Top End, Northern Territory	124
Central Northern Territory	126
Southern Northern Territory	128

INDEX	130
STRIP MAPS	150
LEGEND	152
QUICK FIND DISTANCE CHART	BACK COVER

National Parks

THE MOSS GARDEN, CARNARVON GORGE NATIONAL PARK (12 A4).

LEGEND

- ▲ Camping Area
- 🏕 Bush Camping
- ⛲ Picnic Area
- 🔥 Fireplace/Barbecue
- 🚻 Toilets
- 🚿 Showers
- 🚰 Drinking Water
- 🚶 Walking Trail
- 🏠 Ranger Station
- 🚙 4x4 Advisable
- 🚐 Caravan Sites
- $ Camping Fees Apply
- $ Entry Fees Apply
- * Parks not shown on map

QUEENSLAND

Ph 13 74 68 www.nprsr.qld.gov.au

Park	Ref
Auburn River	13 C10
Bendidee	13 H8
Blackbraes	17 H9
Blackdown Tableland	15 H8
Bladensburg	20 E7
Boodjamulla (Lawn Hill)	16 G1
Bowling Green Bay	17 H13
Brampton Islands	15 C8
Bribie Island	9 F10
Bulburin	15 J11
Bunya Mountains	13 E11
Burleigh Head	11 H13
Burrum Coast	13 A12
Byfield	15 G10
Camooweal Caves	16 J1
Cania Gorge	15 K11
Cape Hillsborough	15 C8
Cape Melville	19 H6
Cape Palmerston	15 E9
Cape Upstart	17 J13
Capricorn Coast *	15 G11
Capricornia Cays	15 J13
Carnarvon (Mt Moffatt & Carnarvon Gorge)	12 A4
Carnarvon (Salvator Rosa & Ka Ka Mundi)	14 K6
Castle Tower	15 J11
Cedar Bay	19 K7
Chillagoe-Mungana Caves	17 E9
Coalstoun Lakes*	13 C1
Conondale	8 D6
Conway	15 C8
Crater Lakes*	18 G4
Crows Nest	8 J2
Culgoa Floodplain	12 K2
Currawinya	23 G11
Curtain Fig*	18 G4
Curtis Island	15 H11
D'Aguilar	8 G7
Daintree	17 C10
Dalrymple	17 J11
Danbulla	18 F4
Davies Creek	18 E3
Dawes	15 K11
Deepwater	15 J12
Diamantina	20 F5
Dinden	18 E4
Djiru	18 K6

Park	Ref
Dryander	14 B7
Errk Oykangand (Mitchell-Alice Rivers) (CYPAL)	19 K2
Eungella	14 D7
Eurimbula	15 J12
Expedition	12 B6
Family Islands *	17 F11
Fitzroy Island	18 E6
Flinders Group	19 H5
Forest Den	21 D10
Fort Lytton	7 A13
Forty Mile Scrub	17 F10
Frankland Group	18 F7
Girramay	17 F11
Girraween	13 K11
Girringun	17 G11
Glasshouse Mountains	9 E8
Gloucester Island	17 J14
Goodedulla	15 G9
Good Night Scrub	13 B11
Goold Island	17 F11
Great Sandy (Cooloola)	13 D13
Great Sandy (Fraser)	13 B13
Green Island	18 D6
Hinchinbrook Island	17 G12
Homevale	14 D7
Hope Islands*	
Idalia	21 H9
Isla Gorge	12 A7
Jardine River	19 C2
Keppel Bay Islands	15 G11
Kirrama	17 F11
Kondalilla	9 C8
Koombooloomba	18 K4
Kroombit Tops	15 J11
Kuranda	17 D10
Kurrimine Beach	18 J7
Kutini-Payamu (Iron Range)	19 E4
Lake Bindegolly	23 E10
Lamington	11 J10
Lindeman Islands	15 C8
Lizard Island	19 H7
Lochern	21 G8
Magnetic Island	17 H12
Main Range	10 F4
Mapleton Falls	9 C8
Mariala	21 K10

MAIN RANGE IN KOSCIUSZKO NATIONAL PARK (44 E2)

PHOTO: PAUL SINCLAIR © DESTINATION NSW

Park	Ref
Turtle Group	19 H7
Undara Volcanic	17 G9
Venman Bushland	3 J7
Welford	21 H8
White Mountains	17 K10
Whitsunday Islands	15 B8
Woondum	13 D13
Wooroonooran	18 G5
Woowoonga	13 B12

NEW SOUTH WALES

Ph 1300 361 967 www.environment.nsw.gov.au/nationalparks

Park	Ref
Millstream Falls*	18 J3
Minerva Hills	14 J6
Molle Islands*	15 B8
Moogerah Peaks	10 G6
Moorrinya	14 D2
Moreton Island	9 H12
Mount Archer	15 H10
Mount Barney	10 J6
Mount Cook*	19 K7
Mount Etna Caves*	15 G10
Mount Hypipamee	18 G3
Mount Walsh	13 C12
Mowbray	18 B3
Mudlo	13 C12
Munga Thirri (Simpson Desert)	20 G1
Newry Islands	15 C8
Noosa	13 D4
Northumberland Islands*	15 D9
Nuga Nuga	12 A5
Orpheus Island	17 G12
Oyala Thumotang (CYPAL)	19 F2
Paluma Range	17 H11
Percy Isles	15 E10
Poona	13 C13
Porcupine Gorge	17 K9
Ravensbourne	8 K3
Repulse Island*	15 C8
Rinyirru (Lakefield) (CYPAL)	19 J5
Rundle Range	15 H11
Russell River	18 F6
Smith Islands	15 C8
South Cumberland Islands	15 C9
Southwood	13 G8
Springbrook	11 H11
St Helena Island	11 A11
Sundown	13 K10
Tamborine	11 F11
Teerk Roo Ra (Peel Island)	11 B12
Tewantin	9 A9
The Palms*	13 F12
Three Islands*	19 J7
Thrushton	12 G3
Tregole	12 D2
Tully Falls	18 J4
Tully Gorge	18 J5

Park	Ref
Abercrombie River	36 H6
Arakoon	39 H12
Barakee	37 A11
Barrington Tops	37 C10
Basket Swamp	39 C10
Ben Boyd	44 J5
Biamanga	44 H5
Bimberamala	44 E5
Bindarri	39 G12
Biriwal Bulga	37 A12
Blue Mountains	34 E5
Bongil Bongil	39 G12
Booderee (Commonwealth Territory)	44 D6
Boonoo Boonoo	39 B10
Booti Booti *	37 C13
Border Ranges	39 A12
Bouddi	33 J13
Bournda	44 H5
Brindabella	44 D2
Brisbane Water	33 J11
Broadwater	39 C13
Budawang	44 D5
Budderoo	44 B6
Bundjalung	39 D13
Bungonia	36 K7
Butterleaf	39 D10
Capertee	37 E7
Capoompeta	39 D10
Carrai	39 H10
Cascade	39 F12
Cataract	39 B11
Cathedral Rock	39 G10
Cattai	35 B8
Chaelundi	39 F11
Clyde River *	44 E5
Cocoparra	43 E10
Conimbla	36 G4
Conjola	44 D6
Coolah Tops	36 A7
Coorabakh	37 B13
Cottan-Bimbang	39 K10
Crowdy Bay	37 B14
Culgoa	41 A11
Deua	44 E5
Dharug	33 J10
Dooragan	37 B14

HOPETOUN FALLS IN GREAT OTWAY NATIONAL PARK, VICTORIA (59 J9).

Park	Ref
Dorrigo	39 G11
Dunggir	39 H11
Eurobodalla	44 F6
Fortis Creek	39 D12
Gardens of Stone	36 F7
Garigal	29 D12
Georges River	30 F6
Gibraltar Range	39 D10
Goobang	36 D3
Goolawah	39 J12
Goulburn River	36 C7
Gulaga	44 G5
Gundabooka	41 D9
Guy Fawkes River	39 E10
Hat Head	39 J12
Heathcote	35 G10
Jerrawangala	44 C6
Jervis Bay	44 C7
Kamay Botany Bay	35 E12
Kanangra-Boyd	34 G3
Kinchega	42 B3
Kings Plains	39 D8
Koreelah	39 A11
Kosciuszko	44 E2
Kumbatine	39 J11
Ku-ring-gai Chase	35 A11
Kwiambal	38 C7
Lane Cove	29 G9
Limeburners Creek	39 K12
Livingstone	43 H12
Macquarie Pass*	44 B6
Mallanganee	39 C12
Marramarra	33 K10
Mebbin	39 A13
Meroo	44 E6
Middle Brother	37 B13
Mimosa Rocks	44 H5
Monga	44 E5
Mooball	39 A13
Morton	44 C6
Mount Imlay	44 J4
Mount Kaputar	38 F5
Mount Nothofagus	39 A11
Mount Pikapene	39 C11
Mount Royal	37 C10
Mummel Gulf	39 J9
Mungo	42 D5
Murramarang	44 E6
Murray Valley	43 J8
Mutawintji	40 F3
Myall Lakes	37 D13
Nangar	36 F4
Nattai	34 J6
New England	39 G11
Nightcap	39 B13
Nowendoc	37 A11
Nymboi-Binderay	39 F11
Nymboida	39 E11
Oolambeyan	43 G8

Park	Ref
Oxley Wild Rivers	39 H9
Paroo-Darling	40 E5
Popran	33 H11
Ramornie	39 E11
Richmond Range	39 B12
Royal	35 F11
Saltwater	37 C14
Scheyville	35 B8
Seven Mile Beach	44 C7
South East Forest	44 H4
Sturt	40 B1
Sydney Harbour	29 H14
Tallaganda	44 D4
Tapin Tops	37 B12
Thirlmere Lakes	34 J7
Timallallie	38 H3
Tomaree	37 E12
Tooloom	39 A11
Toonumbar	39 B12
Towarri	37 B9
Turon	36 F7
Ulidarra	39 F12
Wadbilliga	44 G4
Wallarah	33 E14
Wallingat	37 C13
Warra	39 F10
Warrabah	38 G7
Warrumbungle	38 J3
Washpool	39 D11
Watagans	33 D11
Weddin Mountains	36 H3
Werakata	33 C11
Werrikimbe	39 J10
Willandra	43 C8
Willi Willi	39 H11
Woko	37 B11
Wollemi	37 E8
Wollumbin	39 A13
Woomargama	43 J12
Wyrrabalong	33 G13
Yanga/Murrumbidgee Valley	42 F6
Yarriabini	39 H12
Yengo	33 E1
Yuraygir	39 E13

AUSTRALIAN CAPITAL TERRITORY

Ph 13 22 81 www.tams.act.gov.au

Park	Ref
Namadgi	48 A2

PHOTO: © ISTOCK.COM/SARA WINTER

VICTORIA

Ph 13 19 63 www.parkweb.vic.gov.au

Park	Ref
Alfred	65 G12
Alpine	64 F5
Baw Baw	64 H4
Brisbane Ranges	56 D2
Burrowa-Pine Mountain	65 B8
Chiltern-Mt Pilot	64 B5
Churchill	57 E9
Cobboboonee	58 G3
Coopracambra	65 F12
Croajingolong	65 H12
Dandenong Ranges	57 D10
Errinundra	65 F11
French Island	57 J10
Grampians	58 C6
Great Otway	59 J9
Greater Bendigo	59 A12
Hattah-Kulkyne	62 C5
Heathcote-Graytown	59 A14
Kara Kara	59 B8
Kinglake	64 G1
Lake Eildon	64 F3
Little Desert	62 K1
Lower Glenelg	58 G2
Lower Goulburn	63 H13
Mitchell River	64 G7
Mornington Peninsula	56 J6
Morwell	64 K4
Mount Buffalo	64 D5
Mount Eccles	58 G4
Mount Richmond	58 H2
Murray – Sunset	62 C2
Organ Pipes	56 B6
Point Nepean	56 J5
Port Campbell	59 J8
Snowy River	65 F10
Tarra Bulga	64 K5
Terrick Terrick	63 H10
The Lakes	65 J8
Wilsons Promontory	66 J5
Wyperfeld	62 F3
Yarra Ranges	64 G3

TASMANIA

Ph 1300 135 513 www.parks.tas.gov.au

Park	Ref
Ben Lomond	75 G10
Cradle Mt - Lake St Clair	72 D7
Douglas-Apsley	75 H13
Franklin-Gordon Wild Rivers	70 A5
Freycinet	69 A7
Hartz Mountains	71 G10
Kent Group*	
Maria Island	69 F5
Mole Creek Karst	74 G3
Mount Field	71 C9
Mount William	75 B14
Narawntapu	77 G13
Rocky Cape	76 E7
South Bruny	71 J13
Southwest	70 G7
Strzelecki	78 D5
Tasman	69 K3
Walls of Jerusalem	73 E9

SOUTH AUSTRALIA

Ph (08) 8204 1910 www.environment.sa.gov.au/parks

Park	Ref
Belair	86 J3
Canunda	98 J5
Coffin Bay	88 F2
Coorong	89 K10
Flinders Chase	88 K4
Flinders Ranges	95 E9
Gawler Ranges	88 A2
Innes	88 H5
Kati Thanda-Lake Eyre	90 G7
Lake Torrens	94 C7
Lincoln	88 G3
Malkumba-Coongie Lakes	91 D12
Mount Remarkable	88 B7
Murray River	89 F12
Naracoorte Caves	98 H6
Nullarbor	96 E2
Onkaparinga River	87 C5
Vulkathunha-Gammon Ranges	95 C10
Witjira	93 A14

DOVE LAKE AND CRADLE MOUNTAIN IN CRADLE MOUNTAIN–LAKE ST CLAIR NATIONAL PARK, TASMANIA (72 D7).

PHOTO: © ISTOCK.COM/TSKB

National Parks

WESTERN AUSTRALIA

Ph (08) 9219 9000 www.dpaw.wa.gov.au

Park	Map Ref
Avon Valley	106 D4
Badgingarra	112 H5
Beelu	106 E4
Blackwood River	108 E2
Boorara Gardner	108 H6
Bramley	108 E2
Cape Arid	111 G14
Cape Le Grand	111 G13
Cape Range	114 D2
Collier Range	115 H8
D'Entrecasteaux	108 H4
Dirk Hartog Island	112 A1
Drovers Cave	110 A1
Drysdale River	117 C12
Fitzgerald River	111 H8
Francois Peron	112 A2
Geikie Gorge	117 G10
Gloucester	108 G6
Goldfields-Woodland	111 B10
Goongarrie	113 G12
Gooseberry Hill*	106 E5
Greater Beedelup	108 F5
Greenmount	103 D12
Gull Rock*	109 J13
Helena	106 E5
John Forrest	106 D4
Kalamunda	106 E4
Kalbarri	112 D3
Karijini	115 E8
Karlamilyi (Ruddal River)	115 D13
Kennedy Range	114 H4
Korung*	106 E5
Lake Muir	109 G8
Leeuwin-Naturaliste	108 C1
Lesmurdie Falls	101 G7
Lesueur	112 G4
Millstream-Chichester	114 C6
Mirima (Hidden Valley)	117 D14
Mitchell River	117 C10
Moore River	106 A2
Mount Augustus (Burringurrah)	114 G6
Mount Frankland North	109 H8
Mount Frankland South	109 J8
Mount Lindesay*	109 J10
Murujuga	114 B5
Nambung	110 A2
Neerabup	106 C2
Peak Charles	111 F11
Porongurup	109 H13
Purnululu	117 G13
Scott	108 F2
Serpentine	106 G4
Shannon	108 G7
Stirling Range	109 F13
Stokes	111 G11
Tathra	112 G5
Torndirrup	109 K13
Tuart Forest	108 C3
Tunnel Creek	117 F9
Walpole-Nornalup	109 K8
Walyunga	106 C4
Wandoo	106 E6
Warren	108 G5
Watheroo	112 G5
Waychinicup	110 J7
Wellington	108 B5
West Cape Howe	109 K12
William Bay	109 K10
Windjana Gorge	117 F9
Wolfe Creek Crater	117 J13
Yalgorup	106 H2
Yanchep	106 C2

NORTHERN TERRITORY

Ph (08) 8999 4555 or (08) 8951 8250 www.parksandwildlife.nt.gov.au;
Dept of Environment (Kakadu & Uluru) www.environment.gov.au/parks

Park	Map Ref
Barranyi (North Island)	125 H13
Charles Darwin	122 G4
Elsey	124 G7
Finke Gorge	128 G6
Garig Gunak Barlu	124 A5
Iytwelepenty/Davenport Range	127 J10
Judbarra/Gregory	124 H4
Kakadu (Comm. Terr.)	123 D5
Keep River	126 A1
Limmen	125 G10
Litchfield	123 F1
Mary River	123 B3
Nitmiluk (Katherine Gorge)	123 H6
Uluru-Kata Tjuta (Comm. Terr.)	128 J4
Watarrka (Kings Canyon)	128 G5
West MacDonnell	128 F6

KATHERINE GORGE IN NITMILUK NATIONAL PARK, NORTHERN TERRITORY (123 H6).
PHOTO: SANDRA NEIL

WHITEHAVEN BEACH, WHITSUNDAY ISLAND (15 B8)   PHOTO: © ISTOCK.COM/SAM VALTENBERGS

Queensland Government Disclaimer
Contains data provided by the State of Queensland (Department of Environment and Resource Management) [2010]. In consideration of the State permitting use of this data you acknowledge and agree that the State gives no warranty in relation to the data (including accuracy, reliability, completeness, currency or suitability) and accepts no liability (including without limitation, liability in negligence) for any loss, damage or costs (including consequential damage) relating to any use of the data. Data must not be used for direct marketing or be used in breach of the privacy laws.

Distances are shown in kilometres and follow the most direct major sealed route where possible.

	Birdsville	Brisbane	Bundaberg	Cairns	Charleville	Goondiwindi	Longreach	Mackay	Mount Isa	Rockhampton	Roma	Toowoomba	Townsville	Winton
Bamaga	2709	2681	2444	1008	2637	2727	2132	1747	2265	2081	2369	2719	1359	1957
Birdsville		1575	1743	1687	841	1506	699	1492	680	1380	1109	1453	1339	741
Brisbane			366	1673	734	347	1164	937	1807	603	466	122	1325	1339
Bundaberg				1452	908	591	1044	697	1687	363	640	408	1085	1219
Cairns					1626	1722	1147	736	1190	1070	1358	1708	348	972
Charleville						592	514	1049	1157	848	268	612	1278	689
Goondiwindi							1106	986	1749	652	358	225	1374	1281
Longreach								793	643	681	698	1042	773	175
Mackay									1224	334	781	972	388	916
Mount Isa										1324	1341	1685	906	468
Rockhampton											560	638	722	856
Roma												344	1010	873
Toowoomba													1360	1217
Townsville														598
Winton														

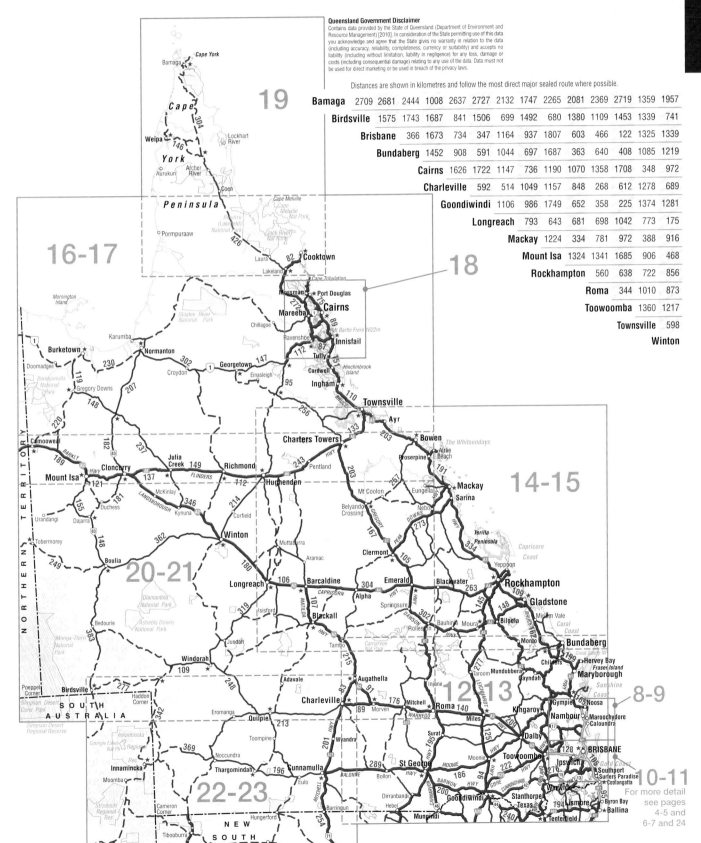

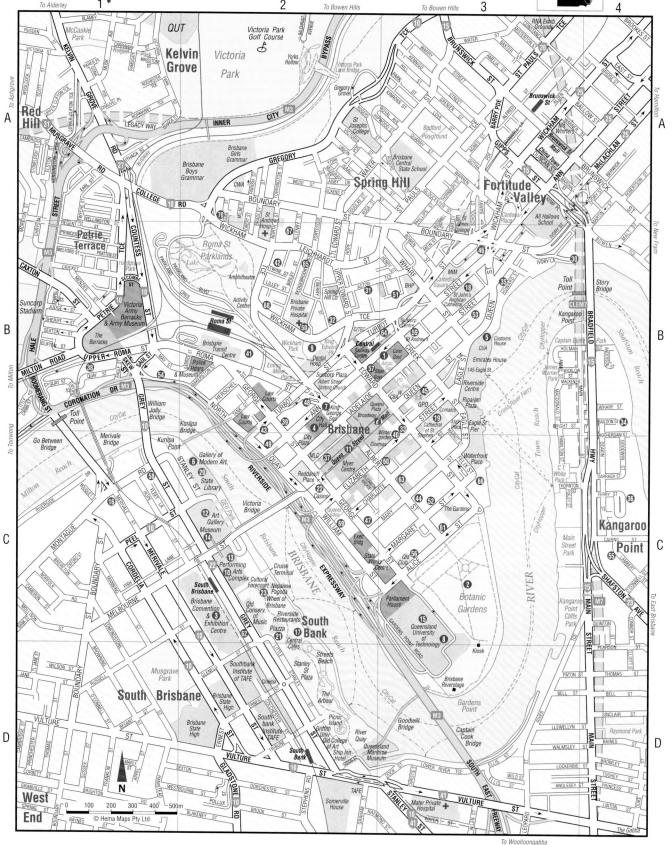

Places of Interest

1. Anzac Memorial B3
2. Botanic Gardens C3
3. Brisbane Convention & Exhib Ctr C2
4. City Hall B2
5. Customs House B3
6. Gallery of Modern Art C2
7. King George Square B2
8. Old Government House C3
9. Old Windmill Observatory B2
10. Performing Arts Complex C2
11. Queen Street Mall C2
12. Queensland Art Gallery C2
13. Queensland Cultural Centre C2
14. Queensland Museum C2
15. Queensland University of Technology C3
16. Queensland Theatre Company C1
17. South Bank C2
18. St John's Cathedral B3
19. St Stephen's Cathedral B3
20. State Library of Queensland C2
21. Suncorp Entertainment Piazza C2
22. Treasury Casino C2
23. Wheel of Brisbane C2

Accommodation

30. Adina Apartment Hotel Brisbane B3
31. Astor Apartments, The B2
32. Astor Metropole Best Western Hotel, The B2
33. Base Brisbane Embassy B3
34. Bridgewater Apartments B4
35. Brisbane Marriott Hotel B3
36. Central Dockside Apartments C4

37. Chifley at Lennons, The C2
38. City Backpackers B1
39. George Williams Hotel B2
40. Hilton Brisbane B3
41. Holiday Inn Hotel Brisbane B2
42. Hotel Grand Chancellor B2
43. Hotel Ibis Brisbane B2
44. iStay River City C3
45. Manor Apartment Hotel, The B3
46. Mantra on Queen B3
47. Marque Hotel, The C2
48. Mercure Brisbane King George Square C2
49. Mercure Hotel Brisbane C2
50. Metro Hotel Tower Mill B2
51. Novotel Brisbane B3
52. Oaks 212 Margaret C3
53. Oaks Aurora B3

54. Park Regis North Quay B1
55. Point Hotel, The C4
56. Quay West Suites Brisbane C3
57. Rendezvous Hotel B2
58. Riverside Hotel C1
59. Rothbury Heritage Apartment Hotel B3
60. Royal Albert Hotel C3
61. Royal on the Park C3
62. Rydges South Bank Hotel C2
63. Sebel Brisbane, The C3
64. Sofitel Brisbane Central B3
65. Spring Hill Centrepoint B2
66. Stamford Plaza Brisbane C3
67. Summit Apartments, The B2
68. Terraces on Wickham B2
69. Treasury Casino & Hotel C2
70. Watermark Hotel Brisbane A2

Symbol	Legend		Symbol	Legend
	Freeway			Ferry Route
	Major Road			Major Building
	Minor Road			Govt Building
	Lane / Path			Theatre/Cinema
	Railway, Station			Shopping
	Busway			Hospital
	CLEM7 Tunnel (Toll)			Mall
	Post Office			
	Accredited Information			

© Hema Maps Pty Ltd

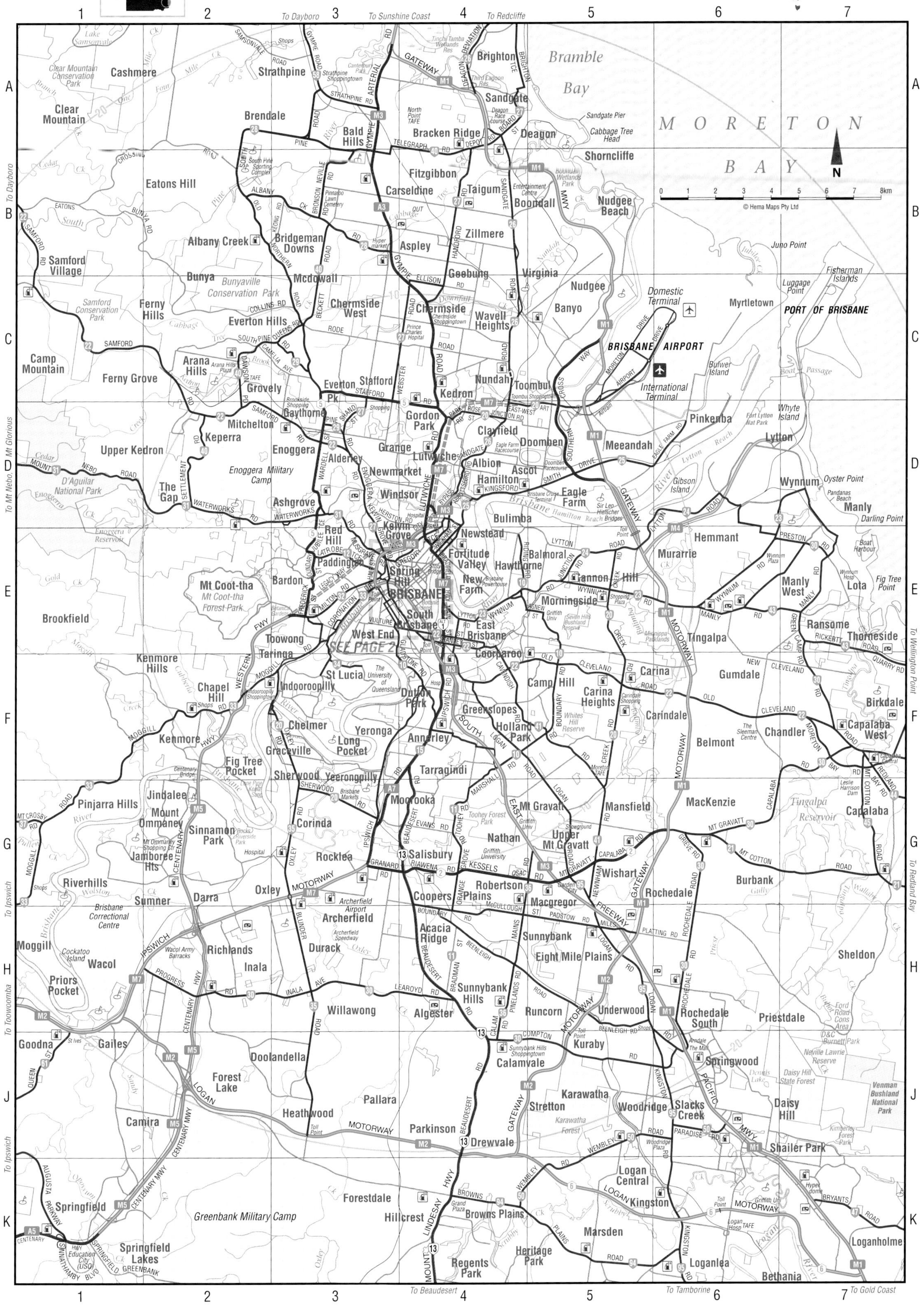
To Dayboro
To Sunshine Coast
To Redcliffe
Bramble Bay
MORETON BAY
N
0 1 2 3 4 5 6 7 8km
© Hema Maps Pty Ltd
Cashmere
Strathpine
Clear Mountain
Brendale
Bald Hills
Bracken Ridge
Brighton
Sandgate
Deagon
Shorncliffe
Eatons Hill
Fitzgibbon
Carseldine
Taigum
Boondall
Nudgee Beach
Albany Creek
Bridgeman Downs
Aspley
Zillmere
Samford Village
Bunya
Mcdowall
Geebung
Virginia
Nudgee
Ferny Hills
Everton Hills
Chermside West
Chermside
Wavell Heights
Banyo
Domestic Terminal
Myrtletown
PORT OF BRISBANE
BRISBANE AIRPORT
International Terminal
Camp Mountain
Arana Hills
Ferny Grove
Grovely
Everton Pk
Stafford
Nundah
Kedron
Toombul
Mitchelton
Gaythorne
Keperra
Gordon Park
Clayfield
Pinkenba
Lytton
Upper Kedron
Enoggera
Alderley
Grange
Lutwyche
Albion
Doomben
Meeandah
D'Aguilar National Park
Enoggera Military Camp
The Gap
Newmarket
Hamilton
Ascot
Wynnum
Windsor
Ashgrove
Eagle Farm
Gibson Island
Manly
Bulimba
Red Hill
Kelvin Grove
Newstead
Hemmant
Paddington
Spring Hill
Fortitude Valley
Balmoral
Murarrie
Bardon
Mt Coot-tha
BRISBANE
New Farm
Hawthorne
Cannon Hill
Morningside
Manly West
Lota
Brookfield
South Brisbane
East Brisbane
Tingalpa
Ransome
Thorneside
West End
SEE PAGE 2
Toowong
Taringa
Coorparoo
Kenmore Hills
St Lucia
Dutton Park
Camp Hill
Carina
Carina Heights
Gumdale
Chapel Hill
Indooroopilly
Greenslopes
Carindale
Birkdale
Chelmer
Yeronga
Holland Park
Belmont
Chandler
Capalaba West
Kenmore
Long Pocket
Graceville
Annerley
Fig Tree Pocket
Tarragindi
Sherwood
Yeerongpilly
Jindalee
Pinjarra Hills
Moorooka
Mt Gravatt
Mansfield
MacKenzie
Capalaba
Mount Ommaney
Sinnamon Park
Corinda
Nathan
Upper Mt Gravatt
Jamboree Hts
Rocklea
Salisbury
Wishart
Burbank
Riverhills
Sumner
Darra
Oxley
Archerfield
Robertson
Coopers Plains
Macgregor
Rochedale
Acacia Ridge
Sunnybank
Eight Mile Plains
Moggill
Wacol
Richlands
Inala
Durack
Sheldon
Priors Pocket
Willawong
Algester
Sunnybank Hills
Runcorn
Underwood
Rochedale South
Priestdale
Goodna
Gailes
Kuraby
Calamvale
Springwood
Doolandella
Forest Lake
Karawatha
Stretton
Woodridge
Slacks Creek
Daisy Hill
Pallara
Heathwood
Camira
Parkinson
Drewvale
Shailer Park
Logan Central
Springfield
Forestdale
Kingston
Greenbank Military Camp
Hillcrest
Browns Plains
Marsden
Loganholme
Springfield Lakes
Heritage Park
Regents Park
Loganlea
Bethania
To Beaudesert
To Tamborine
To Gold Coast
To Ipswich
To Toowoomba
To Mt Nebo, Mt Glorious
To Wellington Point
To Redland Bay

To Mount Mee

D'AGUILAR RANGE

Laceys Creek

Dayboro

Rush Creek

Narangba
New Settlement

Kurwongbah

Samsonvale

D'Aguilar National Park

Whiteside

Lake Samsonvale

Joyner

North Pine Dam
Bullocky Rest

Tenison Woods Mtn

Mt Samson

D'Aguilar Nat Park

Mt D'Aguilar

Cedar Creek

Mt Kobble

State Forest

Cashmere

Mount Samson

Closeburn

Clear Mountain

State Forest

Warner

Mt Glorious

Mt Lawson

Yugar

Draper

Eatons Hill

Eatons Crossing

D'Aguilar RANGE

Mt Nebo

Highvale

Samford Valley Country Club

House Mountain Range

Samford Valley

Samford Village

Albany

Bunya

Ferny Hills

D'Aguilar Nat Park

Wights Mountain

Camp Mountain

Samford Conservation Park

SAMFORD

Arana

Jollys Lookout

Dr Red Vineyard

Camp Mountain Recreation Area

Ferny Grove

Upper Kedron

D'Aguilar Nat Park

Bellbird Grove

D'Aguilar National Park

D'Aguilar Nat Park

RANGE

Enoggera Reservoir

D'Aguilar NP

The Gap

Brisbane Forest Park Info Centre

Gold Creek Reservoir

To Esk

8 9 9 10 11 12 13 14

To Sunshine Coast

Deception Bay

Scarborough

Deception Bay

Redcliffe

Kippa-Ring

Margate

Dakabin

Mango Hill

Kallangur

Clontarf

Woody Point

Petrie

Murrumba Downs

Griffin

Clontarf Point

Lawnton

Wyllie

Bray Park

Strathpine

Brighton

MORETON

Brendale

Bald Hills

Bracken Ridge

Sandgate

Deagon

Shorncliffe

BAY

Bridgeman Downs

Fitzgibbon

Carseldine

Taigum

Boondall

Nudgee Beach

McDowall

Aspley

Geebung

Zillmere

Virginia

Nudgee

Everton Hills

Chermside West

Chermside

Wavell Heights

Banyo

Northgate

Domestic Terminal

PORT OF BRISBANE

Stafford Hts

BRISBANE AIRPORT

Myrtletown

Oxford Park

Everton Park

Stafford

Kedron

Nundah

Toombul

International Terminal

Grovely

Woolowin

Kalinga

Eagle Jcn

Pinkenba

Mitchelton

Gaythorne

Grange

Hendra

Doomben

Eagle Farm

Lytton

Keperra

Enoggera

Wilston

Clayfield

Albion

Ascot

Hamilton

Wynnum

Ashgrove

Newmarket

Windsor

Breakfast Ck

Balmoral

Lindum

Hemmant

Red Hill

Kelvin Grove

Newstead

Bulimba

Wynnum West

Manly

SEE PAGE 2

To Western Fwy

To Gold Coast

Queensport

Colmslie

Murrarie

© Hema Maps Pty Ltd

0 1 2 3 4 5 km

N

To Esk · **To Dayboro**

N

0 1 2 3 4 5 km

© Hema Maps Pty Ltd

D'AGUILAR

RANGE

D'Aguilar National Park

D'Aguilar Nat Park

D'Aguilar NP

Jollys Lookout

Dr Red Vineyard

Camp Mountain Recreation Area

Upper Kedron

Bellbird Grove

The Gap

Enoggera Reservoir

Enoggera Reservoir

Lake Manchester

Lake Manchester

Gold Creek Reservoir

Upper Brookfield

Brookfield

Kenmore Hills

Chapel Hill

Moggill Conservation Park

Kenmore

Mount Crosby

Pullenvale

Jindalee

Kholo

Karana Downs

Karana Downs

Pinjarra Hills

Westlake

Mount Ommaney

Sinnamon Park

17 Mile Rocks

Bellbowrie

Riverhills

Middle Park

Jamboree Hts

Chuwar

Karalee

Barellan Point

Moggill

Sumner

Darra

Brisbane Correctional Centre

Warrego Hwy

Darren

Tivoli

North Tivoli

Ivoli Hill

Riverview

Moggill Ferry

Priors Pocket

Cockatoo Island

Wacol

Richland

Brassall

North Ipswich

Basin Pocket

Moores Pocket

Dinmore

Bundamba

Ipswich

Redbank Plaza

Redbank

Goodna

Gailes

Ellen Grove

Wulkuraka

Coalfalls

Woodend

East Ipswich

North Booval

Ebbw Vale

Wolston Park

Waterford

Leichhardt

Sadliers Crossing

West Ipswich

Ipswich

Newtown

Eastern Heights

Booval

Bergins Hill

Silkstone

New Chum

Collingwood Park

Carole Park

Camira

Churchill

Raceview

Blackstone

Redbank Plains

Bellbird Park

Ipswich Racecourse

Yamanto

Flinders View

Swanbank

Redbank Plains

Springfield

Springfield

Brookwater

Loamside

Deebing Creek

Ripley

Augustine Heights

Brookwater

Springfield Central

Springfield Lakes

Deebing Heights

Education City (USQ)

To Toowoomba, Esk

To Warwick

To Warrill View

8 9 To Sunshine Coast 10 5 11 To Sunshine Coast 12 13 14

Grovely · Keperra · Mitchelton · Gaythorne · Enoggera · Stafford · Gordon Park · Woolowin · Kalinga · Eagle Junction · Clayfield · Hendra · Doomben · Eagle Farm · Pinkenba · Lytton · Whyte Island · Moreton Bay · Wynnum · Oyster Point · Manly · Lota

Enoggera Military Camp · St Johns Wood · Ashgrove · Dorrington · Newmarket · Wilston · Windsor · Albion · Ascot · Hamilton · Meeandah · Gibson Island · Indum · Manly West

Ithaca · Jubilee · Red Hill · Kelvin Grove · Newstead · Bulimba · Balmoral · Hawthorne · Colmslie · Queensport · Murarrie · Hemmant · Wynnum West · Manly West

Bardon · Paddington · Milton · Spring Hill · Fortitude Valley · New Farm · Tenerife · Morningside · Seven Hills · Cannon Hill · Wakerley · Ransome

Mt Coot-tha · Rainworth · Torwood · Auchenflower · BRISBANE · Kangaroo Point · Merthyr · Richmond · Carina · Tingalpa · Carina Heights · Gumdale

Toowong · West End · South Brisbane · East Brisbane · Coorparoo · Camp Hill · Carindale · Belmont · Chandler · Capalaba West

Taringa · St Lucia · Highgate Hill · Woolloongabba · Buranda · Stones Cnr · Greenslopes · Holland Park · Mt Gravatt East · The Sleeman Centre

Indooroopilly · Ironside · Dutton Park · Fairfield · Annerley · Yeronga · Ekibin · Wellers Hill · Holland Park West · Mt Gravatt · Mansfield · MacKenzie

Jay Park · Chelmer · Long Pocket · Graceville · Tennyson · Yeerongpilly · Moorooka · Nathan Hts · Toohey Forest Park · Upper Mt Gravatt · Wishart · Rochedale · Burbank · Sheldon

Fig Tree Pocket · Sherwood · Corinda · Rocklea · Salisbury · Nathan · Robertson · Macgregor · Rochedale

Oxley · Archerfield · Coopers Plains · Sunnybank · Eight Mile Plains · Underwood · Rochedale South · Priestdale

Durack · Inala · Archerfield Airport · Acacia Ridge · Sunnybank Hills · Runcorn · Kuraby · Springwood · Daisy Hill

Doolandella · Willawong · Algester · Calamvale · Karawatha · Woodridge · Slacks Creek · Shailer Park

Forest Lake · Heathwood · Larapinta · Parkinson · Stretton · Karawatha Forest · Logan Central · Meadowbrook · Tanah Merah

Forestdale · Hillcrest · Browns Plains · Heritage Park · Marsden · Kingston · Loganlea · Bethania

Greenbank Military Camp · Regents Park · Boronia Heights

To Beaudesert 10 11 To Tamborine 12 To Gold Coast 13 14

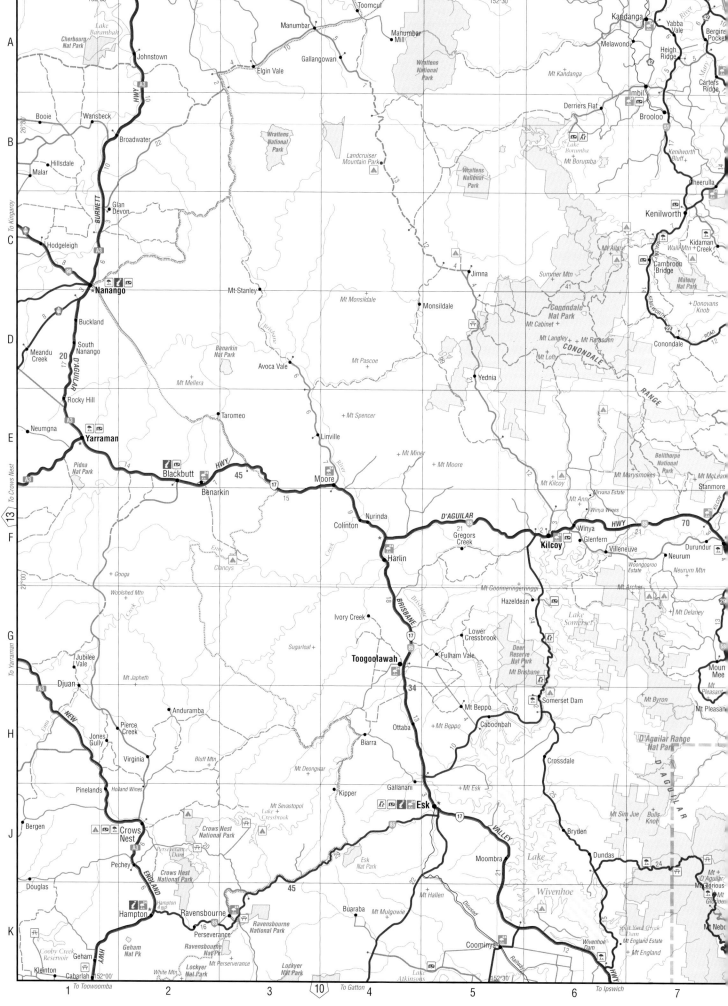

8 13 9 10 11 12 13 14

153°00' 153°30'

Pomona
Yurol
Cooroy
Tewantin
Noosaville
Noosa Heads
Eerwah Vale
Doonan
Eumundi
Mt Eerwah
Weyba Downs
Noosa National Park
Great Sandy Nat Pk
Lake MacDonald
Laguna Bay
Noosa Head
Alexandria Bay
Sunshine Beach
Sunrise Beach
Castaways Beach
Marcus Beach
Belli Park
North Arm
Peregian Beach

29°30'

SOUTH

Cooloolabin Dam
Cooloolabin
Yandina
Wappa Dam
Ferntree Creek Nat Park
Mt Coolum Nat Park
Coolum Beach
Point Arkwright
Mt Coolum

Sunshine

Mapleton National Park
Conners Knob
Mapleton Falls Nat Park
Mapleton
Obi Obi
Nambour
Flaxton
Woombye
Kondalilla Nat Park
Palmwoods
Witta
Montville
Lake Baroon
Maleny
Wootha
Bald Knob

Maroochy River
Bli Bli
Marcoola
Sunshine Coast Airport
Mudjimba

Coast

Maroochydore
Alexandra Headland
Underwater World
Buderim
Mooloolaba
Mountain Creek
Buddina
Warana
Forest Glen Deer Sanct.
Tanawha
Mooloolah River National Park
Bokarina
Kawana Waters
Wurtulla
Currimundi

PACIFIC

Eudlo
Mooloolah
Palmview
Aussie World Ettamogah Pub
Sunshine Coast Turf Club
Dicky Beach
Shelley Beach

Glass House Mtns NP
Candle Mtn
Boroobin
Landsborough
Mt Mellum
Australia Zoo
Golden Beach
Caloundra
Pelican Waters

OCEAN

Peachester
Cedarton
Beerwah
Mt Coochin
Campbellville
Coochin Creek

Glass House Mountains
Mt Beerwah
Coonowrin Nat Park
Mt Tibrogargan
Woodford
Beerburrum
Mt Beerburrum
Long Is
Thooloora Is
Wild Horse Mountain lookout

Bribie Island State Forest

Bribie Island National Park

Bribie Island

D'Aguilar
Delaneys Creek
Bracalba
Donnybrook
Pumicestone Channel

Bribie Island National Park

27°00'

Glass House Mountains National Park
Elimbah
Meldale
Toorbul
Banksia Beach
Bellara

Wamuran
Wamuran Basin
Moodlu
Caboolture Aerodrome
Ningi
Bellara
Woorim

North Pt
Cape Moreton

Mt Mee
Bellmere
Caboolture
Godwin Beach
Sandstone Point
Bongaree
Skirmish Pt
Woody Bay
Bald Pt
South Pt

Comboyuro Pt
Bulwer

Rocksberg
Morayfield
Beachmere

Moreton Island National Park

Oceanview Estates
Ocean View
Upper Caboolture
Burpengary
Narangba
Deception Bay

Deception

Cowan Cowan

Moreton Island

Dayboro
Deception Bay
Oyster Pt
Rothwell
Scarborough Pt
Scarborough
Osborne Pt

SEE PAGES 4-5

Ferry

Tangalooma

Kurwongbah
Dakabin
Kallangur
Redcliffe Pt
Redcliffe
Margate
Margate Beach

Tangalooma Pt

Mt Kobble
Petrie
Griffin
Woody Point
Woody Pt

MORETON

Samsonvale
Lawnton
Bramble

Ferry

Mt Lawson
Cedar Creek
Cashmere
Strathpine
Brighton
Bay
Sandgate
Cabbage-Tree-Head
Shorncliffe
Nudgee Beach
Juno Point

BAY

Mount Samson
Bracken Ridge

Samford Valley
Albany Creek
Carseldine
Boondall
Aspley
Nudgee
Mud Island
Kooringal
Campbell Pt
Reeders Pt

Mt Nebo
D'Aguilar Range Nat Park
Camp Mountain
Brisbane Forest Park
Ferny Grove
Keperra
Chermside
Kedron
BRISBANE AIRPORT
Domestic
International
Fort Lytton Nat Pk
Fisherman Islands
St Helena Island
St Helena Island Nat Pk
Lytton
Whyte Pt
Green Island

Moreton Bay Marine Park

Amity Pt
Amity
North Stradbroke Island

The Gap
Everton Park
Stafford
Doomben
To Brisbane
Naree Budjong Djara NP

153°30'

© Hema Maps Pty Ltd

0 5 10 15km

N

A
B
C
D
E
F
G
H
J
K

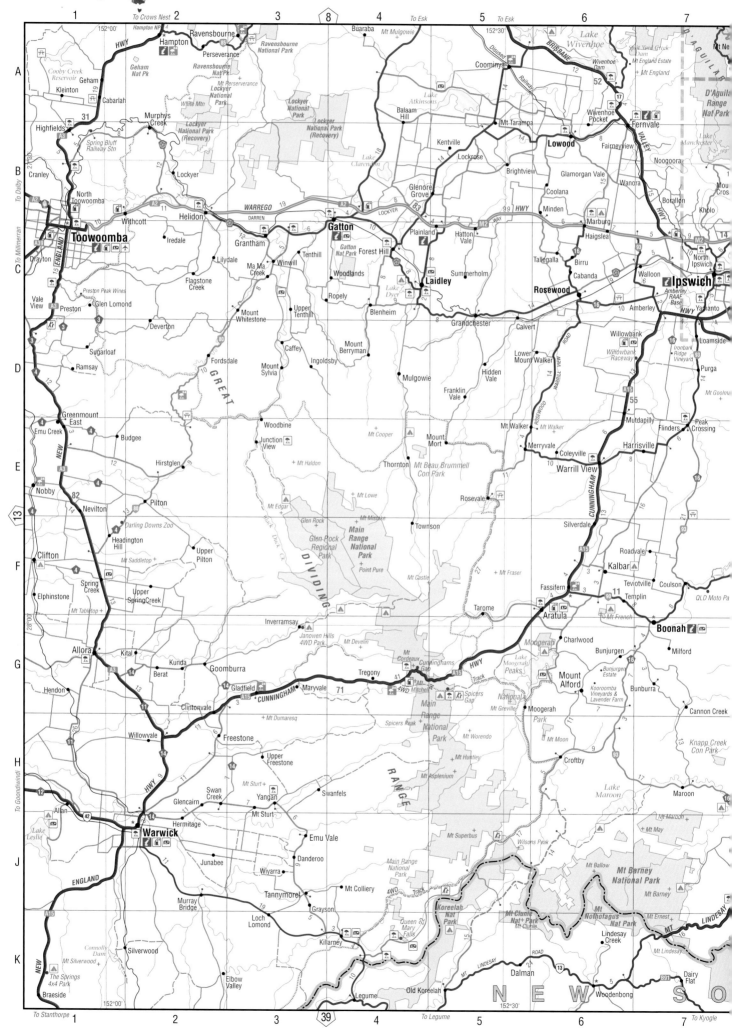

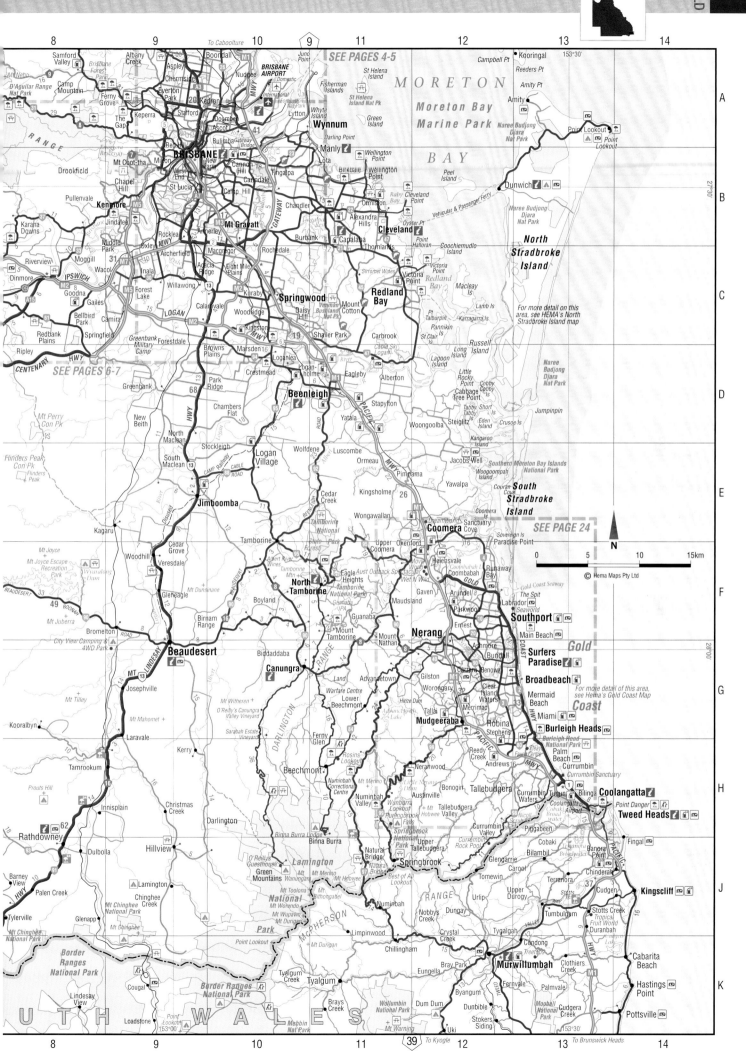

SEE PAGES 4-5

MORETON

Moreton Bay
Marine Park

BAY

North
Stradbroke
Island

SEE PAGES 6-7

For more detail on this
area, see HEMA's North
Stradbroke Island map

Naree
Budjong
Djara
Nat Park

South
Stradbroke
Island

SEE PAGE 24

N

0   5   10   15km

© Hema Maps Pty Ltd

Gold

Coast

For more detail of this area,
see Hema's Gold Coast Map

Border
Ranges
National Park

SOUTH WALES

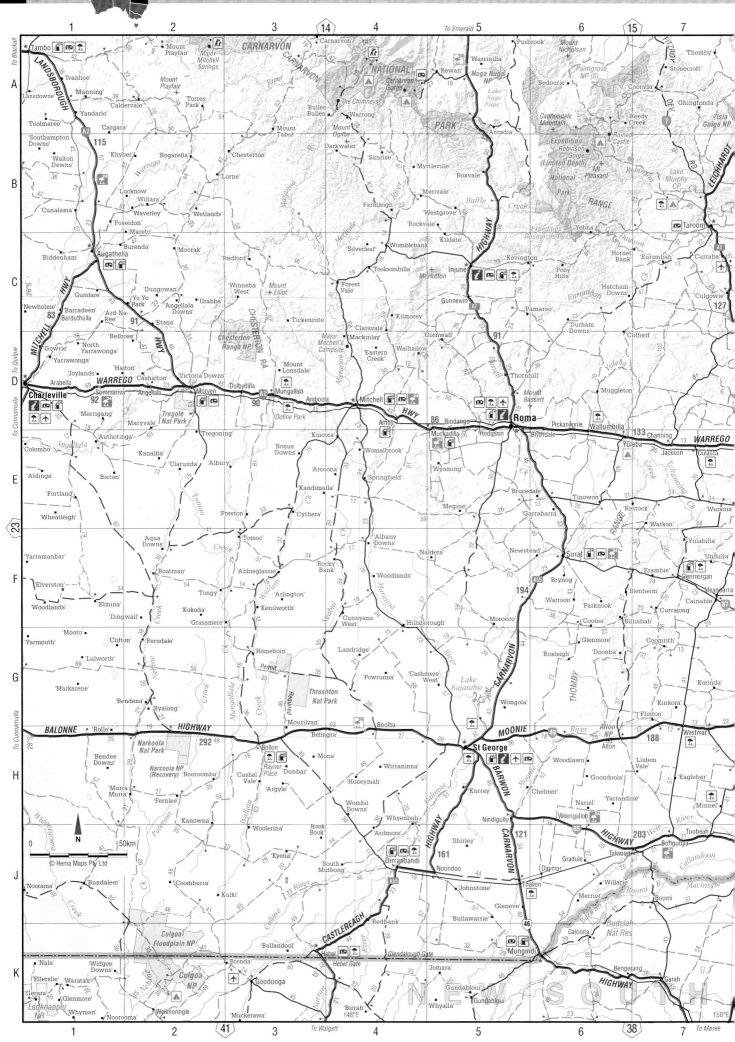

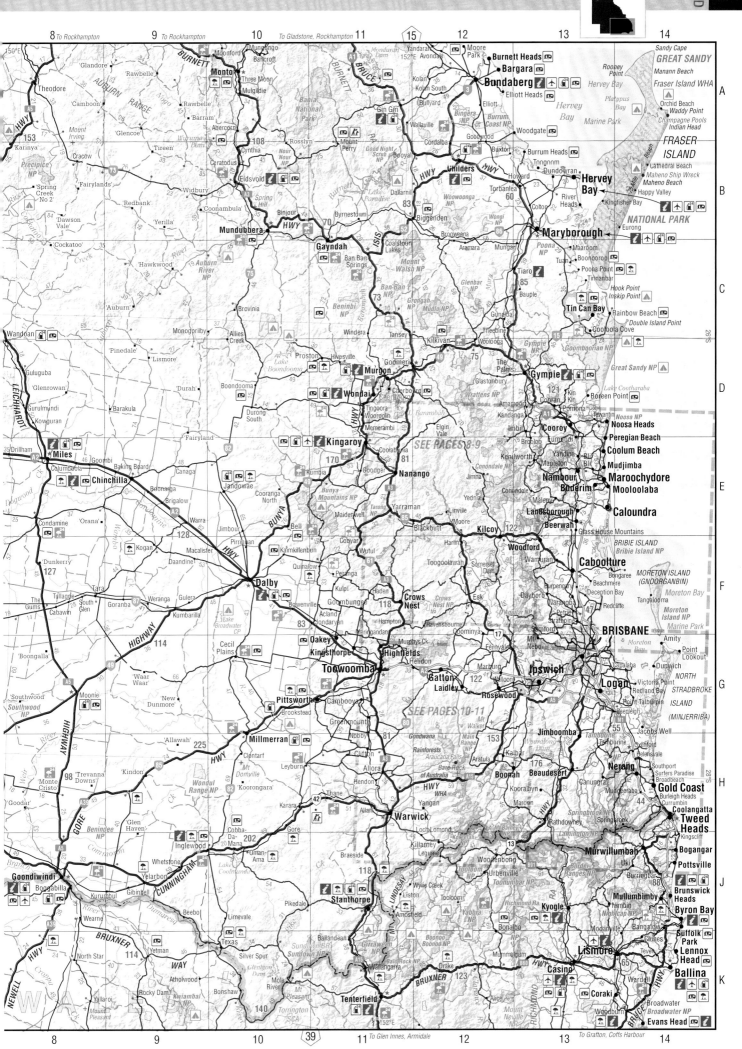

GREAT SANDY
Sandy Cape
Manann Beach
Rooney Point
Fraser Island WHA
Hervey Bay

A

Orchid Beach
Waddy Point
Champagne Pools
Indian Head

FRASER ISLAND

Cathedral Beach
Maheno Ship Wreck
Maheno Beach
Happy Valley
Kingfisher Bay

B

NATIONAL PARK
Eurong

Hook Point
Inskip Point

C

Rainbow Beach
Double Island Point
Goofoola Cove

Burnett Heads
Bargara
Bundaberg
Elliott Heads
Burrum Heads
Hervey Bay

Monto
Three Moon
Mulgildie

Gin Gin

Childers

Maryborough

Mundubbera
Gayndah
Ban Ban Springs

Tin Can Bay

D

Gympie

Murgon
Wondai
Goomeri

Boreen Point

Noosa Heads
Peregian Beach
Coolum Beach
Mudjimba

E

Kingaroy
Nanango

SEE PAGES 8-9

Cooroy

Nambour
Maroochydore
Mooloolaba

Caloundra

Landsborough
Beerwah

F

Miles
Chinchilla

Dalby

Yarraman

Kilcoy
Woodford

Caboolture

BRIBIE ISLAND
Bribie Island NP

Crows Nest

MORETON ISLAND
(GNOORGANBIN)
Moreton Bay
Marine Park

BRISBANE

G

Oakey
Kingsthorpe
Toowoomba

Highfields
Helidon

Ipswich

Logan

NORTH STRADBROKE ISLAND
(MINJERRIBA)

Gatton
Laidley
Rosewood

Pittsworth

SEE PAGES 10-11

Jimboomba

Millmerran

Nerang

H

Boonah
Beaudesert

Gold Coast

Tweed Heads

Goondiwindi
Boggabilla

Inglewood

Warwick

Murwillumbah

Bogangar
Pottsville

J

Stanthorpe

Kyogle

Mullumbimby
Byron Bay

Texas

Tenterfield

Casino
Coraki

Lismore

Suffolk Park
Lennox Head

Ballina

K

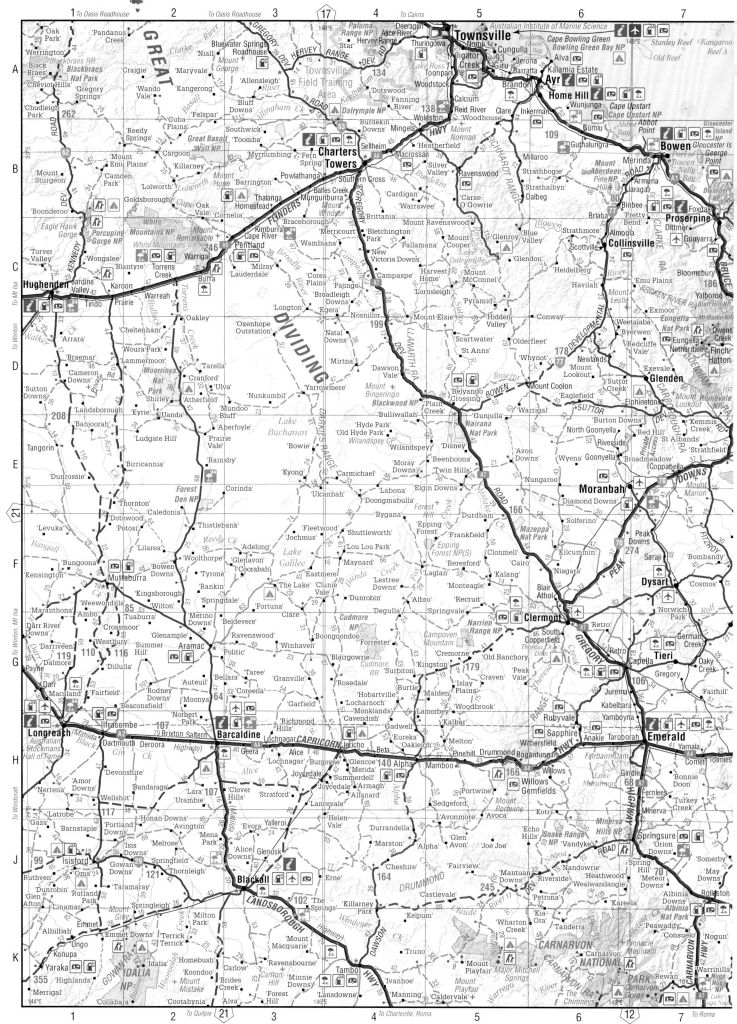

Great Barrier Reef
Coast Marine Park

C O R A L

S E A

S O U T H

N

0 50 100km

© Hema Maps Pty Ltd

150°E 152°E

20°S

Tideway Reef
Square Reef
Hunt Reefs

Hayman Is
Hook Is
Border Is
Airlie Beach
Whitsunday Island
Shutehaven
Cannonvale
Hamilton Island
Conway NP
Conway Beach
Lindeman Island
Lindeman Islands NP
Shaw Is
Whitsunday Islands NP
Repulse Bay
Laguna Quays
Midge Point
Blacksmith Is
Linne Is
Goldsmith Is
Rabbit Is
Wigton Is
Calder Is
Newry Is
Calen Seaforth
Cockermouth Is
Brampton Is
Scawfell Is
St Bees Is
Cape Hillsborough NP
Kuttabul
Bucasia
Shoal Point
Farleigh
Eimeo
Mirani Marian
Slade Point
Walkerston
Mackay
Bakers Creek
Sandringham Bay
Eton
Homebush
Grasstree Beach
Prudhoe Is
Campwin Beach
Sarina
Digby Is
Hotspur Islets
Pine Peak Is
Epsom
Koumala
Ince Bay
Cape Palmerston
Middle Island
Herald Reef Prong
Nebo
Koumala South
Ilbilbie
Cape Palmerston NP
Smythe Shoals
North East Island
Orkabie
Carmila
West Hill Is
South Island
Percy Isles NP
Heralds Prong No.2 Reef
Yeppara IP(S)
Carmila West
Carmila Beach
Flaggy Rock
Poynter Is
Marble Is
High Peak Is
Cockenzie
Elalie
Aquila Is
North Point
Great Barrier Reef
Collaroy
Wild Duck Is
Quail Is
Hexham Is
Cheviot Is
Coast Marine Park
Morpeth
Cardowan
Kalarka
Clairview
Long Is
Stanage
Arthur Point
Cape Townshend
Rookwood Outstation
The Alps
Croydon
Broad Sound
St Lawrence
Collins Is
Leicester Is
Townshend Is
Reef Point
Batheaston
May Downs
Mackenzie Ck
Wumalgi
Mount Wellington
Shoalwater Bay
Pearl Bay
Perforated Point
Port Clinton
Cape Clinton
PACIFIC
Junee NP
Ogmore
Bowman
Kooltandra
Freshwater Bay
Cliff Point
Cape Manifold
Middlemount
Junee
Marlborough
Princhester
Byfield NP
Byfield
Stockyard Point
Nine Mile Beach
Little Corio Bay
Great Barrier Reef
Barwon Park
Apis Creek
Devlin
Kunwarara
Sandy Point
Capricorn International Resort
North Keppel Island
OCEAN
Royles
Mount Gardiner
Kaiuroo
Burkan
Goodedulla National Park
Yaamba
The Caves
Yeppoon
Mt Etna Caves NP
Cawarral
Keppel Bay Islands NP (Scientific)
Great Keppel Island
World Heritage Area
Guthrie Shoal
Douglas Shoal
Ridgelands
Parkhurst
Emu Park
Tryon Is
Curragh
Taunton NP(S)
Rockhampton
Kabra
Keppel Sands
North West Is
Wilson Island Reef
Channel
Melmoth
Stanwell
Wycarbah
Gracemere
Flat Top Range RR
Wistari Reef
Heron Island
TROPIC OF CAPRICORN
Blackwater
Parnabal
Bluff
Boolburra
Goowarra
Westwood
Godango
Bouldercombe
Bajool
Marmor
Port Alma
Curtis Island CP
Cape Capricorn
Heron Is Reef
Dingo
Triphinia
Edungalba
Mount Morgan
Raglan
Rundle Range NP
CURTIS ISLAND
Masthead Is
Duaringa
Dululu
Wowan
Deeford
Ambrose
Yarwun
Curtis Island NP
Black Head
Southend
North Point
Hoskyn Islands
Blackdown Tableland NP
Eastbrook
Mount Larcom
Gladstone
Capricornia Cays NP(S)
South Blackwater
Spring Hill
Woorabinda
Perch Creek
Kokotungo
Lancefield
Mount Harper
Calliope
Boyne Island
Tannum Sands
Fairfax Islands
Lady Musgrave Island
Taylors Creek
Black Mtn
Baralaba
Goovigen
Jambin
Dan Taragoola
Barmundu
Benaraby
Iveragh
Turkey Beach
Eurimbula RR
Round Hill Head
Lady Elliot Island
24°S
Conomara
Mimosa Park
Mount Cooper
Bindawalla
Castle Tower NP
Bororen
Miriam Vale
Nagoorin
Eurimbula
Seventeen Seventy
Rocky Point
Agnes Water
Herald Patches A
Goomally
Barranga
Kroombit
Amys Peak
Bulburin
Deepwater NP
Planet Downs
Bauhinia Downs
Biloela
Thangool
Ubobo
Many Peaks
Bulburin NP
Buljyan
Winfield
Berajondo
For more detail on this area, see HEMA's Fraser Island map.
Moura
Banana
Dawes
Cania Gorge NP
Tops NP
Dawes NP
Rosedale
Norval Park
Littabella NP
Long Shoal
Purbrook
Mount Nicholson
Kianga
Junedale
Glandore
Moonford
Bancroft
Mungungo
Kalpowar
Warro NP
Watalgan
Miara Moore Park
Woongarra Marine Park
FRASER ISLAND
Sandy Cape
Palmgrove NP
Thomby
Stonecroft
Rawbelle
Monto
Three Moon
Mulgildie
Bania NP
Yandaran
Avondale
Burnett Heads
Bargara
Rooney Point
GREAT SANDY
Bedourie
Coorada
Theodore
Camboon
Rawbelle
Gin Gin
Kolan South
Bundaberg
Elliott Heads
Hervey Bay
Fraser Island WHA
Marine Park
NAT PARK
Bullyard
Elliott
Platypus Bay
Orchid Beach

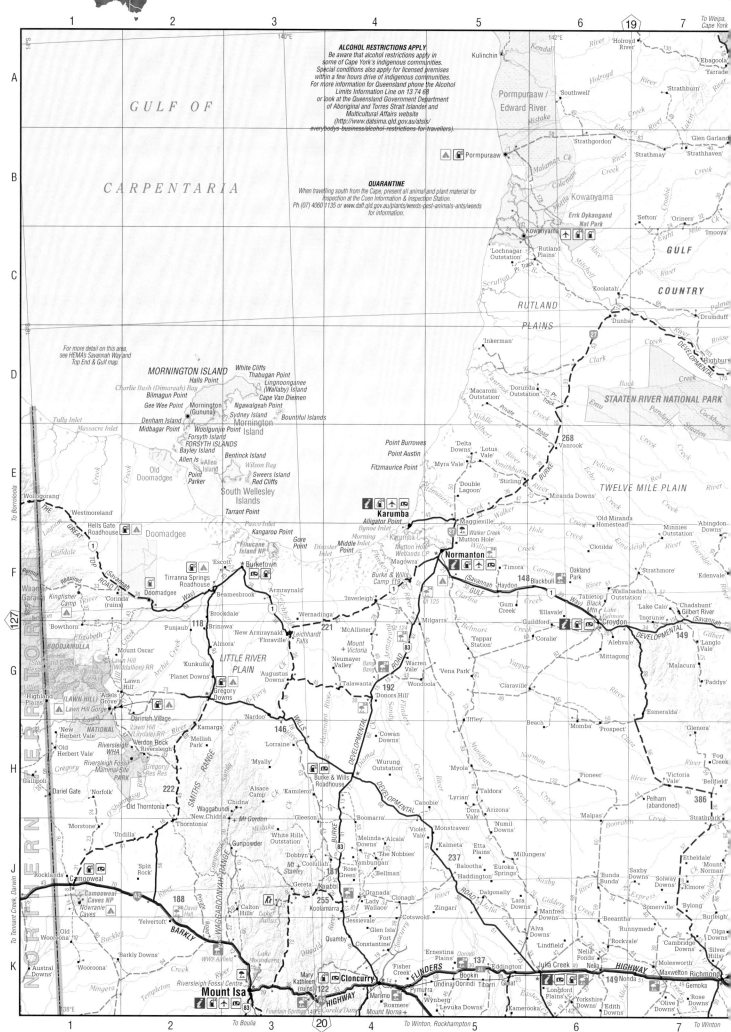

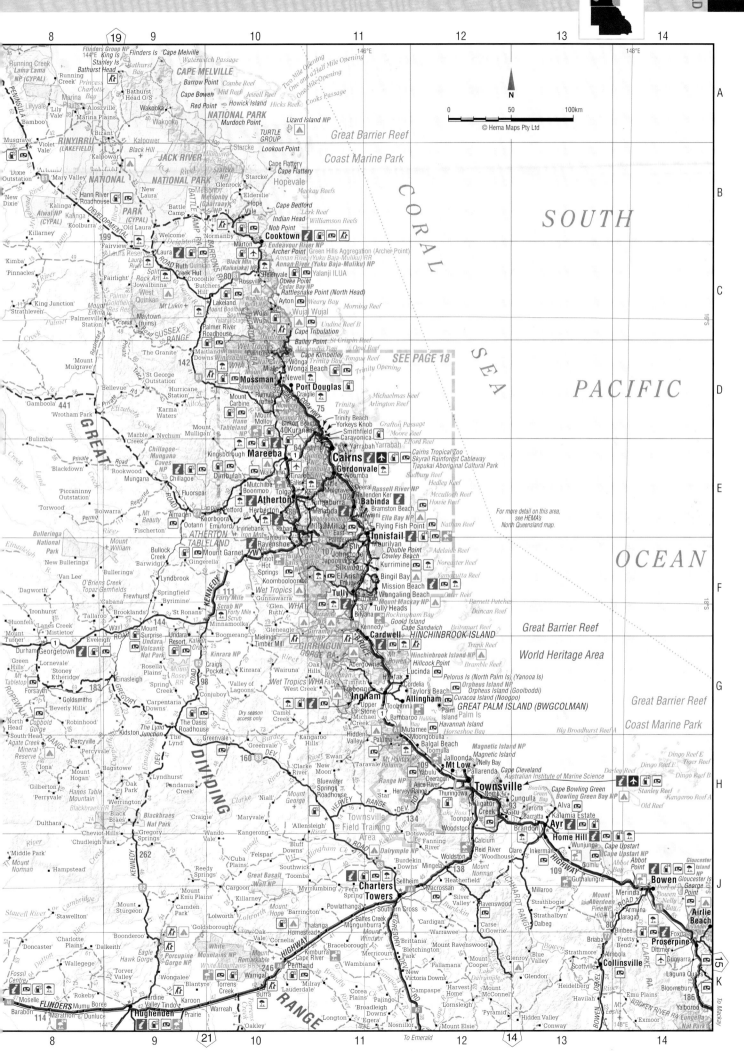

Cairns Region, Queensland

N

0   10   20km

Grid references (top): 1 2 3 4 5 6 7
To Cape Tribulation

Oceans / Seas:
SOUTH PACIFIC OCEAN
CORAL SEA
Trinity Bay
GREAT BARRIER REEF
Great Barrier Reef Coast Marine Park
Grafton Passage
Trinity Opening

National Parks & Ranges:
MOUNT WINDSOR NP
DAINTREE NATIONAL PARK
MOUNT LEWIS NATIONAL PARK
Mount Spurgeon NP
KURANDA NATIONAL PARK
Hann Tableland National Park
DINDEN NATIONAL PARK
Little Mulgrave National Park
Grey Peaks National Park
Bellenden Ker National Park
Russell River National Park
Wooroonooran National Park
Gadgarra National Park
Eubenangee Swamp NP
Ella Bay National Park
Koombooloomba National Park
Tully Gorge National Park
Japoon National Park
Djiru National Park
Clump Mtn NP
Frankland Group NP
Fitzroy Island NP
Green Island NP
Upolu Cay NP
Michaelmas Cay NP
Barnard Is Group NP
North Barnard Islands Reef
South Barnard Islands Reef
Atherton Tableland

Towns & Localities:
Mossman
Port Douglas
Craiglie
Newell
Miallo
Wonga
Cooya
Mount Carbine
Brooklyn
Rumula
Julatten
Mount Molloy
Yalkula
Mareeba
Biboohra
Kuranda
Kowrowa
Koah
Smithfield Heights
Caravonica
Redlynch
Cairns
Yarrabah
Woree
White Rock
Edmonton
Kamma
Gordonvale
Aloomba
Babinda
Mirriwinni
Bramston Beach
Atherton
Yungaburra
Tolga
Kairi
Herberton
Wondecla
Malanda
North Johnstone
Topaz
Bartle Frere
Jogg
Innisfail
Flying Fish Point
Wangan
Mourilyan
Etty Bay
East Palmerston
South Johnstone
Mena Creek
Moresby
Ravenshoe
Millaa Millaa
Tumoulin
Mount Garnet
Innot Hot Springs
Silkwood
Japoon
Japoonvale
Jaffa
Old Silkwood
El Arish
Kurrimine
Kurrimine Beach
Bingil Bay
Mission Beach
Wongaling Beach
South Mission Beach
Tully
Cardstone
Koombooloomba
Dingo Pocket
Feluga
Midgenoo
Dimbulah
Chircan
Mutchilba
Tabacum
Lemonside
Piemonte
Irvinebank
Herberton
Kalunga
Tirrabella
Gunnawarra
Brownville

Highways / Roads:
CAPTAIN COOK HWY
KENNEDY HWY
MULLIGAN HWY
PALMERSTON HIGHWAY
BRUCE HIGHWAY
PETFORD ROAD
HERBERTON ROAD
GREAT DIVIDING RANGE
Malbon Thompson Range
Bellenden Ker Range
Walter Hill Range
Table Top Range

Route markers: 17 81 27 1 A1

Water features:
Lake Mitchell
Lake Tinaroo
Lake Morris
Lake Barrine
Lake Eacham
Barron River
Mitchell River
Russell River
Liverpool Creek
South Johnstone River
Tully River
Walsh River
Herbert River

To Lakeland
To Chillagoe
To Georgetown & The Lynd Junction
To Cardwell

TORRES STRAIT

SOUTH

PACIFIC

OCEAN

Great Barrier Reef

World Heritage Area

Coast Marine Park

ARAFURA SEA

ENDEAVOUR

Mabuiag Island
Aipus Island
Mabuiag Island
Orman Reefs
Widul Island
Yam Island
Basilisk Passage
Zagai Island
Cumberland Passage
Meer (Mer,maer) Island
Mer Reserve

Badu (Mulgrave) Island
Badu Island
Talab Island
Sassie Island
Sassie Island Reefs
Coconut Island
Bet Reef
Vigilant Channel
Derder Reef
Gebar Reef

Kubin
St Pauls
St Pauls
Moa (Clarke) Island
The Three Sisters
Bet, Poll, Aureed, Roberts and Saddle Islands

Warral (Hawkesbury) Island
Long Reef
North Torres Reef
Yule

Wednesday (Maururra) Is
Kagar Reef

Hammond Island
Hammond (Keriri) Is
Thursday (Waiben) Is
Wasaga
Horn (Narupai) Is
Mt Adolphus
Kai-damun Reef

Muralug
Prince of Wales (Muralag) Island

Van Spoult Head
New Mapoon
Seisia
New Mapoon
Injinoo
Bamaga
Umagico
Bamaga Injinoo
Somerset (ruins)
Cape York
Wyborn Reef
Sharp Point
Turtle Head Island
Furze Point
Newcastle Bay

Cowal Creek
Jardine River RR
Ussher Point

Vrilya Point
JARDINE RIVER NATIONAL PARK
Orford Bay
Orford Ness
Wilds Shoal
Olinda Entrance

Injinoo Lands
Eliot/Twin Falls
Fruit Bat Falls
Denham Passage
False Orford Ness
Hunter Point
Wizard Reef
Raine Island NP(S)
Raine Island

Heathlands Resources Reserve
BAMAGA ROAD
Captain Billy Landing
North Channel
Bowles Reef

Old Mapoon
Red Cliffs
Double (Etatapuma) Point
Round Point
Cockburn Reef
Blackwood Channel
Ashmore Banks
Sir Charles Hardy Islands Reef

Cullen Point
Mapoon
Red Beach
Bramwell Roadhouse
'Bramwell Station Tourist Park'
338
Ethel Islet
Cape Grenville
Mason Reef
Nomad Reef
Wreck Bay
Black Rock Entrance
Mantis Reef

'Bertiehaugh'
Weipa / Napranum
96
BATAVIA NATIONAL PARK (CYPAL)
Bolt Head
Gallon Reef
Great Detached Reef

Duyfken Point
'Myerfield'
Billys Lagoon
Moreton Telegraph Station
Batavia 'Downs'
'Bromley'
Mosquito Point
Fair Cape
Kennedy Hill
Temple Bay
Weymouth Bay
Bunker Reef
Curd Reef
Eel Reef
Quoia Island Entrance
Providential Channel

Weipa
Evans Landing
Napranum
Batavia
Wattle Hill
Kutini-Payamu
Iron Range
NP (CYPAL)
Portland Roads
Cape Griffith
Chili Beach
Cape Weymouth
Lockhart River
Lloyd Bay

Wooldrum Point
Boyd Point
'York Downs'
144
Cape
Lockhart River
Cape Direction
Round Point
Night Island
High Boat Entrance
Tijou Reef

Albatross Bay
Pera Head
Thud Point
False Pera Head
'North Camp'
31
'Merluna'
PENINSULA
EMBLEY RD
Weipa
RA
Bare Rock
Eve Peak
Bobardt Point
Cape Sidmouth

Archer Bay
Wutan
Wallaby Island
Aurukun
OYALA THUMOTANG
York NATIONAL PARK
117
Archer River Roadhouse
Cone Peak
Friendly Point
Blanchard Reef
Ogilvie Reef
Campbell Point
Magpie Reef
Lutton Reef

Cape Keerweer
'Kendall River'
'Rokeby'
'Merapah'
Quarantine Checkpoint (CYPAL)
Mt Croll
KULLA (McIlwraith Range) NP (CYPAL)
Silver Plains
Silver Plains
Colmer Point
Roberts Point
Hedge Reef
Corbett Reef
Grub Reef
Melville Passage
Wilson Reef
Scooterboot Reef

Kulinchin
Peninsula
'Holroyd River'
130
Coen
Mount White
Port Stewart
Evanson Point
Claremont Point
Flinders Group NP
King Is
Clack Reef
Pipon Is

Pormpuraaw / Edward River
'Southwell'
'Strathburn'
Running Creek
Lama Lama NP (CYPAL)
'Running Creek'
Princess Charlotte Bay
Stanley Is
Bathurst Head
Flinders Is
Cape Melville
CAPE MELVILLE
Barrow Point
Combe Reef
Waterwitch Passage

Pormpuraaw
'Strathgordon'
'Bamboo'
'Musgrave'
'Glen Garland'
'Strathmay'
'Strathhaven'
Violet Vale
RINYIRRU (LAKEFIELD)
'Lily Vale'
Marina Plains
Aloszville
'Bathurst Head O/S'
Wakooka
Bathurst Bay
Cape Bowen
Red Point
Howick Island
Hicks Reef
NATIONAL PARK
Murdoch Point
Lizard Island NP
TURTLE GROUP

'Dixie Outstation'
'Mary Valley'
NATIONAL PARK
Bizant
Kalpower
Black Hill
JACK RIVER NATIONAL PARK
Lookout Point
Cape Flattery
Cape Flattery
Hopevale

'New Dixie'
Hann River Roadhouse
'Kalinga'
'Koolburra'
'Lakefield'
Kalinga
PARK (CYPAL)
'Old Laura'
'New Laura'
'Battle Camp'
Starcke
Melsonby (Gaarraay) NP
'Glenrock'
Starcke NP
'Starcke'
Mackay Reefs
Lark Reef
Cape Bedford
Indian Head
Williamson Reefs

Kowanyama
'Sefton'
'Oriners'
'Killarney'
199
'Fairview'
'Welcome'
Normanby
Marton
Cooktown
Endeavour River NP
Archer Point

'Lochnagar Outstation'
'Rutland Plains'
'Imooya'
'Kimba'
'Pinnacles'
GULF COUNTRY
'King Junction'
Laura
Laura Reserve
Split Rock Art
Crocodile
'Butchers Hill'
West Quinkan
Lakeland
Mt Boorah
Rossville
Helenvale
Obree Point
Cedar Bay NP
Rattlesnake Point (North Head)
Ayton
Weary Bay
Wujal Wujal

RUTLAND PLAINS
'Koolatah'
'Strathleven'
'Palmerville Station'
Mount Emma
Ngalba Bulal NP
Annan River (Yuku Baja-Muliku) NP
Yalanji ILUA

Errk Oykangand Nat Park
'Lochnagar Outstation'

For more detail on this area, see HEMA's Cape York map.

QUARANTINE
When travelling south from the Cape, present all animal and plant material for inspection at the Coen Information & Inspection Station. Ph (07) 4060 1135 or www.daff.qld.gov.au/plants/weeds-pest-animals-ants/weeds for information.

N

0   50   100km

© Hema Maps Pty Ltd

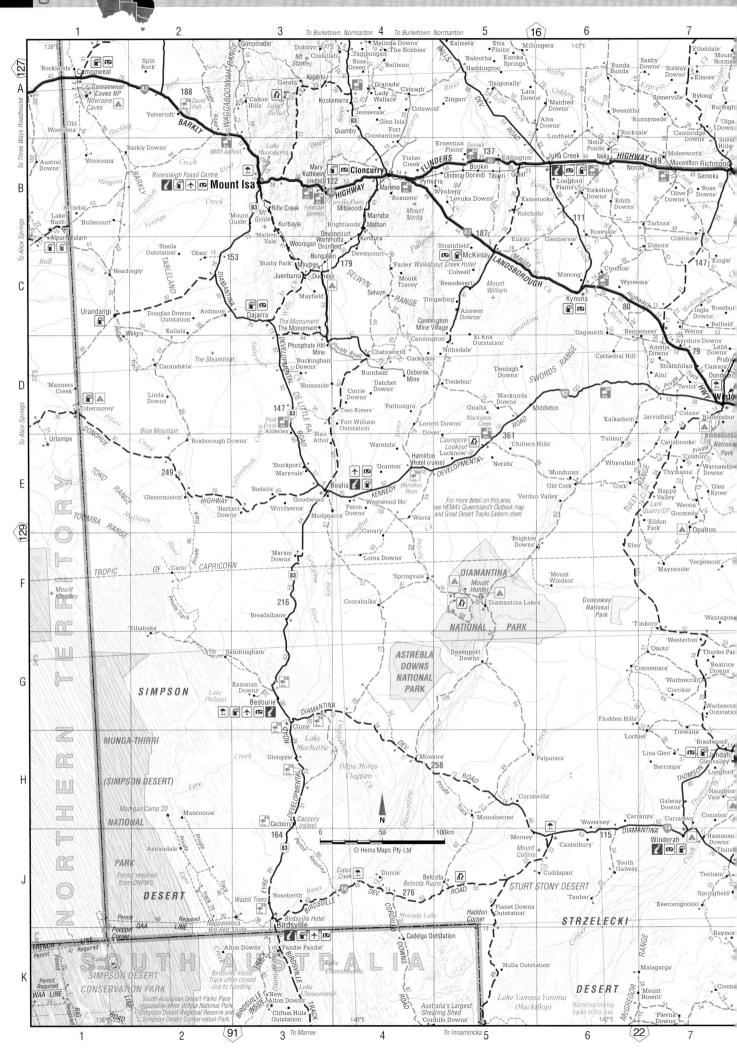

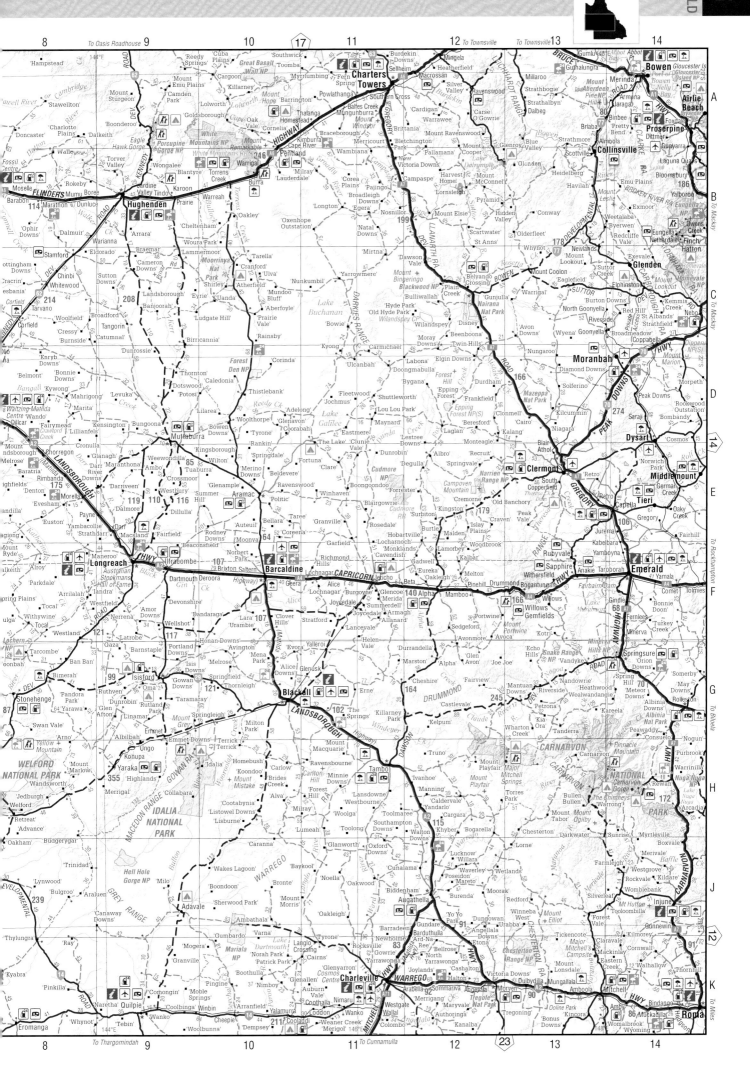

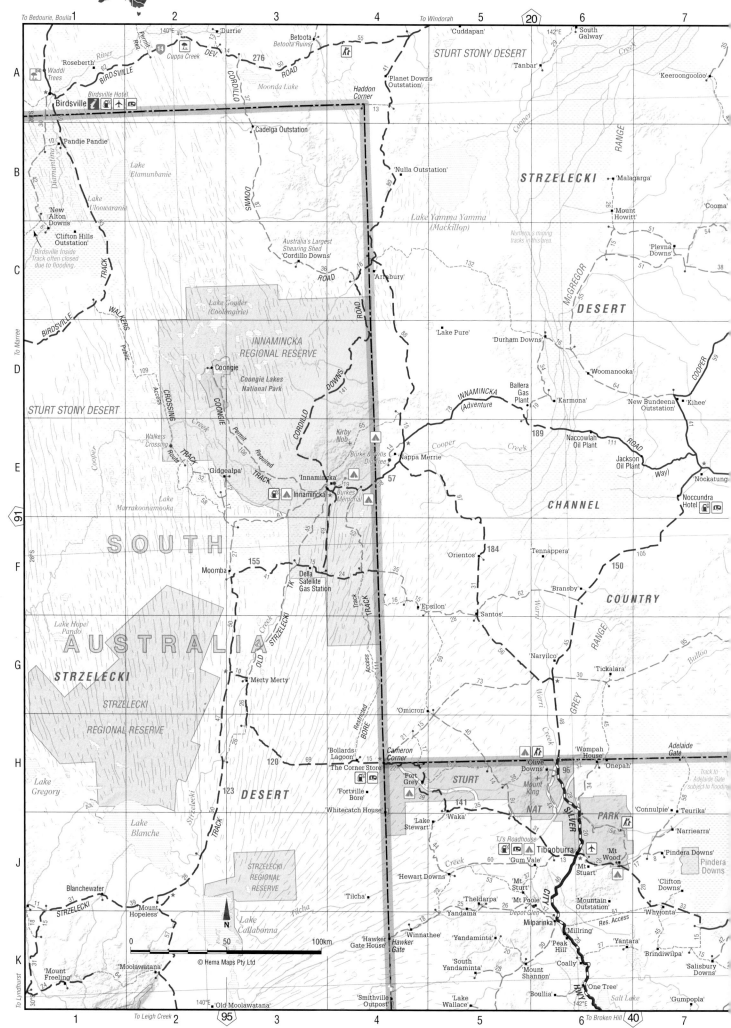

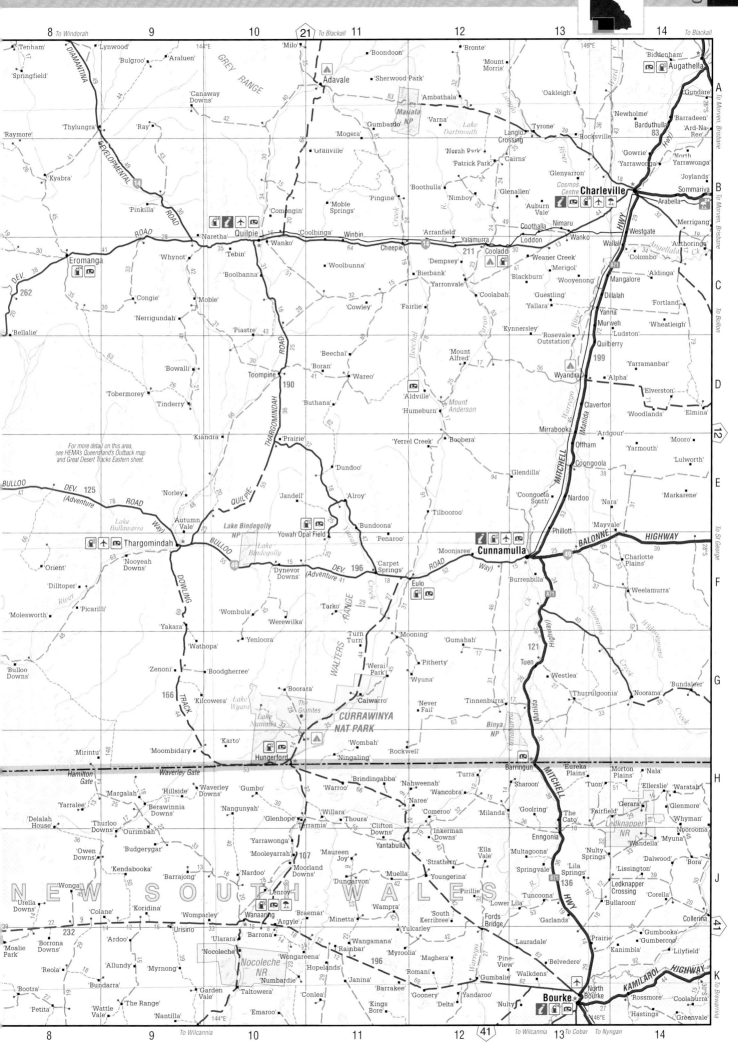

To Windorah | 8 | 9 | 10 | 21 | To Blackall | 11 | 12 | 13 | 14 | To Blackall

'Tenham' 'Lynwood' 'Milo' 'Boondoon' 'Bronte' 'Biddenham' Augathella

'Springfield' 'Bulgroo' 'Araluen' 148°E 'Mount Morris' 'Gundare'

'Raymore' Thylungra 'Ray' 'Canaway Downs' Adavale 'Sherwood Park' 'Oakleigh' Newholme' 'Barradeen' 'Ard-Na-Ree'

Barduthulla 83

'Kyabra' 'Pinkilla' 'Ambathala' 'Varna' 'Gumbardo' NP Lake Dartmouth Langlo Crossing Tyrone Rocksville 'Gowrie' 'North Yarrawonga' 'Joylands'

Manala 'Mogera' 'Norah Park' 'Cairns' 'Glenyarron' 'Yarrawonga'

ROAD Naretha Quilpie 'Comongin' 'Moble Springs' 'Pingine' 'Boothulla' 'Nimboy' 'Glenallen' Auburn Vale' Cosmos Centre Charleville Sommariva

Eromanga 'Whynot' 'Tebin' 'Coolbinga' Winbin Cheepie 'Arranfield' Yalamurra Loddon Wanko Westgate Arabella 'Merrigang'

'Congie' 'Boolbanna' 'Woolbunna' 'Dempsey' Cooladdi 'Weaner Creek' Nimaru Wallal 'Authoringa'

'Nerrigundah' 'Moble' 'Bierbank' 'Yarronvale' 'Blackburn' Merigol 'Wooyenong' Mangalore 'Colombo' 'Aldinga'

'Piastre' 'Cowley' 'Fairlie' 'Coolabah' 'Guestling' 'Yallara' Dilalah 'Fortland'

'Bowalli' Toompine 'Beechal' 'Boran' 'Wareo' 'Mount Alfred' 'Rosevale Outstation' Yanna Murweh Quilberry 'Wheatleigh'

'Tobermorey' 'Tinderry' 'Buthana' 'Aldville' 'Humeburn' 'Mount Anderson' Wyandra 'Alpha' 'Yarramanbar' 'Ludston' 'Elverston'

'Kiandra' 'Prairie' 'Yerrel Creek' 'Boobera' Mirrabooka 'Ardgour' 'Woodlands' 'Elmina'

'Norley' 'Jandell' 'Dundoo' 'Alroy' 'Glendilla' Offham 'Mooro' 'Yarmouth' 'Lulworth'

BULLOO DEV. ROAD (Adventure Autumn Vale' Lake Bindegolly NP Yowah Opal Field 'Bundoona' 'Tilbooroo' 'Penaroo' 'Coongoola South' Coongoola Nardoo 'Nara' 'Markarene'

Thargomindah 'Nooyeah Downs' BULLOO 49 'Dynevor Downs' Lake Bindegolly DEV. 196 Carpet Springs Moonjaree' Cunnamulla 'Mayvale' Phillott BALONNE HIGHWAY 'Charlotte Plains'

'Orient' 'Dilltoper' 'Picarilli' 'Wombula' 'Werewilka' 'Tarko' Eulo Burrenbilla 'Weelamurra'

'Molesworth' DOWLING 'Yakara' 'Yenloora' WALTERS RANGE 'Mooning' 'Gumahah' Tuen 121 'Thurrulgoonia' 'Noorama' 'Bundaleer'

'Bulloo Downs' 'Wathopa' 'Turn Turn' 'Werai Park' 'Pitherty' 'Wyuna' 'Never Fail' Tinnenburra Binya NP Westlea

'Zenoni' 'Boodgherree' 166 'Kilcowera' Lake Wyara The Granites 'Caiwarro' CURRAWINYA NAT PARK Lake Numalla

'Mirintu' 'Moombidary' 'Karto' 'Wombah' 'Ningaling' 'Rockwell' Barringun 'Eureka Plains' 'Morton Plains' 'Nala'

Hamilton Gate Hungerford Waverley Gate 'Turra' 'Sharoon' 'Tuon' 'Ellerslie' 'Waratah'

'Margalah' 'Hillside' 'Waverley Downs' 'Gumbo' 'Brindingabba' 'Nahweenah' 'Wancobra' 'Goolring' MITCHELL 'Gerara' 'Glenmore' 'Whyman'

'Yarralee' 'Berawinnia Downs' 'Nangunyah' 'Glenhope' 'Willara' 'Naree' 'Comeroo' Milanda The Cato' Fairfield' Ledknapper NR 'Noorooma'

'Delalah House' 'Thurloo Downs' 'Ourimbah' Terramia 'Thoura' 'Clifton Downs' 'Inkerman Downs' Enngonia 'Wandella' 'Myuna'

'Owen Downs' 'Budgerygar' 'Yarrawonga' 107 'Mooleyarrah' 'Maureen Joy' Yantabulla 'Ella Vale' 'Multagoona' 'Nulty Springs' 'Lila Springs' 'Dalwood' 'Bora'

'Kendabooka' 'Barrajong' 'Nardoo' 'Moorland Downs' 'Dungarvon' 'Strathern' 'Youngerina' 'Springvale' Ledknapper Crossing 'Lissington' 'Corella'

NEW SOUTH WALES 'Wonga' 'Lenroy' 'Muella' 'Pirillie' 'South Kerribree' Tuncoona 136 'Bullaroon'

'Urella Downs' 'Colane' 'Koridina' Wanaaring 'Braemar' 'Wampra' Fords Bridge 'Garlands' Collerina

'Borrona Downs' 232 'Ardoo' Urisino 'Argyle' 'Minetta' 'Yulcarley' Lower Lila 'Lauradale' 'Prairie' 'Gumbooka' 'Gumbercoo' 'Lilyfield'

'Moalie Park' 'Reola' 'Allundy' 'Myrnong' 'Ularara' 'Barrona' 'Wangamana' 'Rainbar' 'Myroolia' 'Maghera' 'Pine-View' 'Belvedere' KAMILAROI HIGHWAY 'Kanimbla'

'Bootra' 'Bundarra' 'Garden Vale' Nocoleche NR 'Numbardie' 'Wongareena' 'Hopelands' 196 'Romani' 'Gumbalie' North Bourke 'Walkdens' 'Rossmore' 'Coolabura'

'Petita' 'Wattle Vale' 'Nantilla' 144°E 'Taltowera' 'Conlea' 'Barrakee' 'Goonery' 'Yandaroo' 'Delta' 'Nulty' Bourke 'Hastings' 'Greenvale'

'Kings Bore' 46°E

To Wilcannia | 8 | 9 | 10 | 11 | 12 | 41 | 13 | To Cobar | To Nyngan | 14

For more detail on this area, see HEMA's Queensland's Outback map and Great Desert Tracks Eastern sheet.

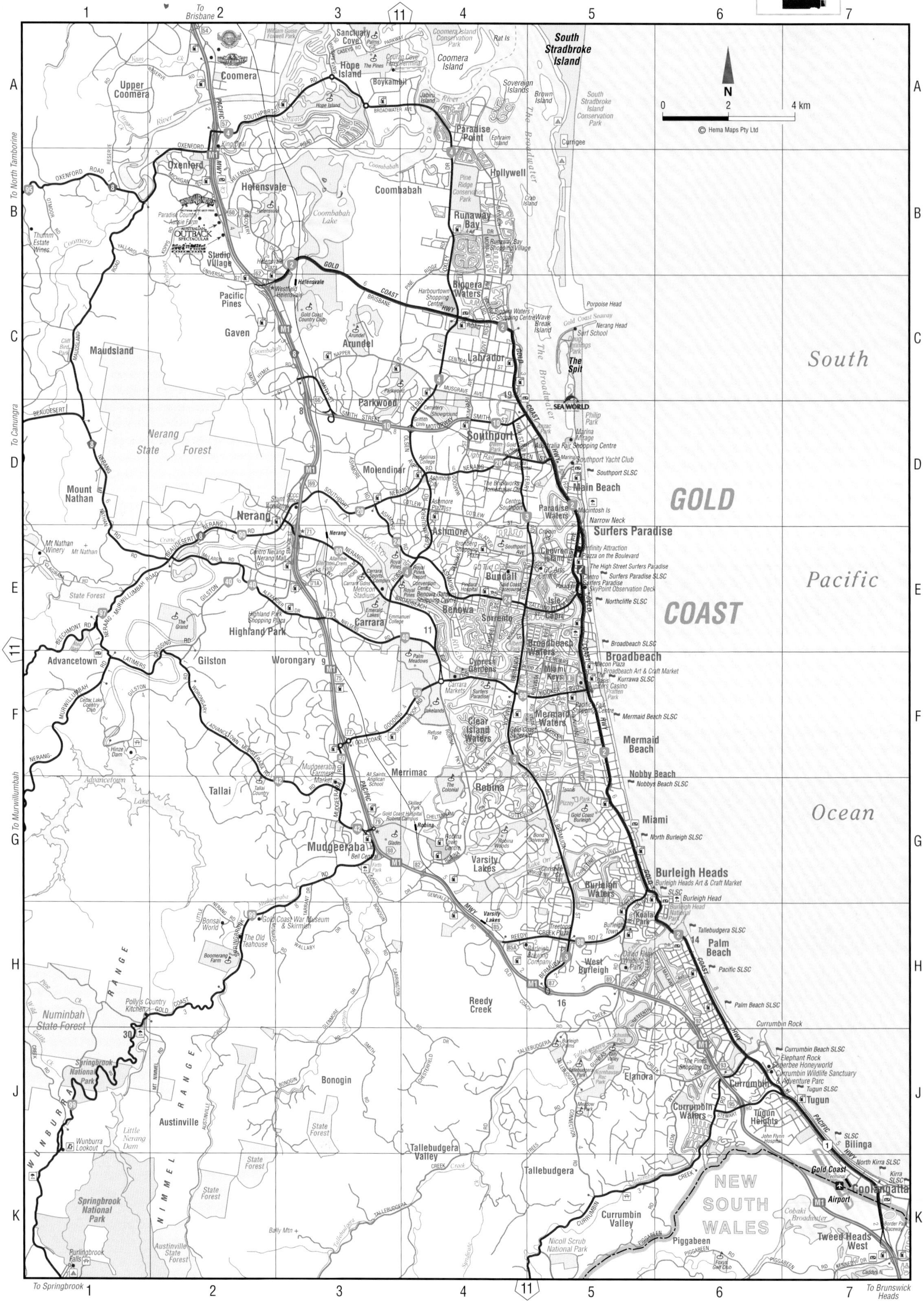

GOLD

COAST

South

Pacific

Ocean

Grid reference numbers (top and bottom): 1 2 3 4 5 6 7

Grid reference letters (sides): A B C D E F G H J K

0 2 4 km
© Hema Maps Pty Ltd
N

To Brisbane
To North Tamborine
To Canungra
To Beaudesert
To Murwillumbah
To Springbrook
To Brunswick Heads

Place names:

Upper Coomera, Coomera, Hope Island, Sanctuary Cove, Boykambil, Coomera Island, Coomera Island Conservation Park, Rat Is, South Stradbroke Island, South Stradbroke Island Conservation Park, Brown Island, Sovereign Islands, Paradise Point, Ephraim Island, Hollywell, Oxenford, Helensvale, Coombabah, Pine Ridge Conservation Park, Runaway Bay, Crab Island, Currigee, Pacific Pines, Coombabah Lake, Biggera Waters, Wave Break Island, Porpoise Head, Gaven, Arundel, Labrador, The Spit, The Broadwater, South, Nerang State Forest, Parkwood, Molendinar, Southport, Philip Park, Marina Mirage, Sea World, Maudsland, Mount Nathan, Mt Nathan Winery, Mt Nathan, State Forest, Ashmore, Main Beach, Paradise Waters, Narrow Neck, Nerang, Molendinar, Gold, Surfers Paradise, Chevron Island, Benowa, Bundall, Sorrento, Isle of Capri, GOLD COAST, Pacific, Advancetown, Highland Park, Gilston, Carrara, Worongary, Broadbeach Waters, Cypress Gardens, Miami Keys, Broadbeach, Mermaid Waters, Mermaid Beach, Clear Island Waters, Nobby Beach, Nobbys Beach SLSC, Tallai, Merrimac, Robina, Miami, Mudgeeraba, Varsity Lakes, Burleigh Waters, Burleigh Heads, Burleigh Head, Bonsai World, The Old Teahouse, Boomerang Farm, Gold Coast War Museum & Skirmish, Koala Park, Tallebudgera SLSC, Palm Beach, Numinbah State Forest, Reedy Creek, Bonogin, Currumbin Rock, Currumbin Beach SLSC, Elephant Rock, Currumbin Wildlife Sanctuary, Elanora, Currumbin, Tugun, Springbrook National Park, Purlingbrook Falls, Wunburra Lookout, Little Nerang Dam, Austinville, Austinville State Forest, Tallebudgera Valley, Tallebudgera, Currumbin Waters, Tugun Heights, John Flynn Hospital, Bilinga, Kirra SLSC, North Kirra SLSC, Gold Coast Airport, Currumbin Valley, NEW SOUTH WALES, Piggabeen, Nicoll Scrub National Park, Cobaki Broadwater, Coolangatta, Tweed Heads West, Border Park Raceway

THE THREE SISTER, BLUE MOUNTAINS (34 E4) PHOTO: © ISTOCK.COM/TOMOGRAF

NEW SOUTH WALES
key map

	Albury	Armidale	Bathurst	Broken Hill	Canberra	Dubbo	Goulburn	Grafton	Lismore	Mildura	Newcastle	Port Macquarie	Sydney	Tamworth	Wagga Wagga
Albury															
Armidale	993														
Bathurst	547	446													
Broken Hill	981	1119	832												
Canberra	1133	263	810	340											
Dubbo	475	775	206	446	537										
Goulburn	410	89	1155	174	721	362									
Grafton	809	641	899	1314	742	195	1188								
Lismore	134	943	775	1048	1448	876	329	1322							
Mildura	1576	1442	859	801	807	296	810	1247	617						
Newcastle	1188	628	479	358	428	448	1094	355	398	721					
Port Macquarie	251	1411	397	248	600	603	671	1276	578	235	944				
Sydney	382	159	1029	759	610	205	403	289	1177	196	529	562			
Tamworth	414	272	283	1132	444	310	619	331	703	1004	432	115	878		
Wagga Wagga	752	465	847	624	564	1224	1075	265	411	243	890	320	857	126	
Wollongong	400	492	78	460	237	964	837	688	134	481	224	1255	274	607	526

Distances are shown in kilometres and follow the most direct major sealed route where possible.

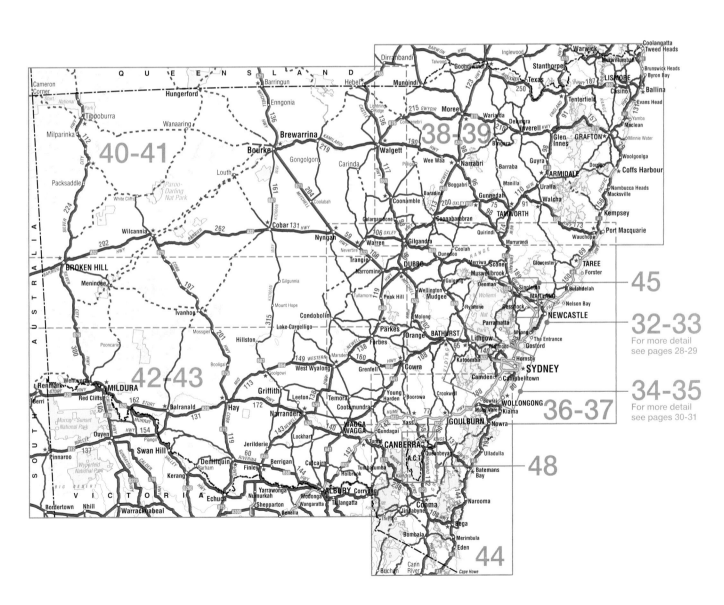

32-33 For more detail see pages 28-29

34-35 For more detail see pages 30-31

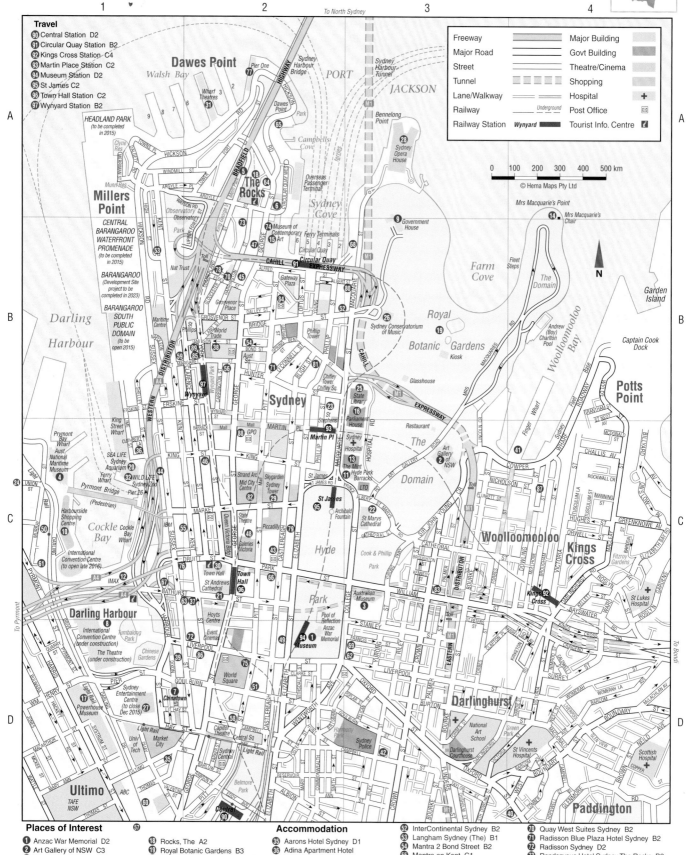

90 Central Station D2
91 Circular Quay Station B2
92 Kings Cross Station C4
93 Martin Place Station C2
94 Museum Station D2
95 St James C2
96 Town Hall Station C2
97 Wynyard Station B2

Places of Interest

1 Anzac War Memorial D2
2 Art Gallery of NSW C3
3 Australian Museum C3
4 Australian Nat. Maritime Museum C1
5 Bridge Climb Sydney A2
6 Cadmans Cottage A2
7 Chinatown D1
8 Darling Harbour D1
9 Government House B3
10 Harbourside Shopping Centre C1
11 Hyde Park Barracks C3
12 LG IMAX Theatre Sydney C1
13 Mint, The C3
14 Mrs Macquarie's Chair A4
15 Museum of Contemporary Art B2
16 Parliament House B3
17 Powerhouse Museum D1
18 Rocks, The A2
19 Royal Botanic Gardens B3
20 SEA LIFE Sydney Aquarium C1
21 St Andrews Cathedral C2
22 St Marys Cathedral C3
23 St Stephens Church B2
24 Star, The C1
25 State Library of NSW B3
26 Sydney Conservatorium of Music B3
27 Sydney Entertainment Centre D1
28 Sydney Opera House A3
29 Sydney Tower Eye & SKYWALK C2
30 Sydney Town Hall C2
31 Wharf Theatres A2
32 WILD LIFE Sydney Zoo C1

Accommodation

35 Aarons Hotel Sydney D1
36 Adina Apartment Hotel Harbourside C1
37 Adina Apartment Hotel Sydney B2
38 Amora Hotel Jamison Sydney B2
39 APX Apartments Darling Hbr D1
41 Arts Hotel D4
41 Blue Sydney C4
42 Cambridge Hotel Sydney D3
43 Castlereagh Boutique Hotel C2
44 Four Points by Sheraton Sydney C1
45 Four Seasons Hotel Sydney B2
46 Grace Hotel Sydney (The) C2
47 Harbour Rocks Hotel (The) B2
48 Hilton Sydney C2
49 Hyde Park Inn D2
50 Ibis Sydney Darling Harbour C1
51 Ibis Sydney World Square D2
52 InterContinental Sydney B2
53 Langham Sydney (The) B1
54 Mantra 2 Bond Street B2
55 Mantra on Kent C1
56 Menzies Sydney (The) B2
57 Mercure Sydney D1
58 Metro Hotel Sydney Central D2
59 Napoleon on Kent B1
60 Novotel Sydney Central D1
61 Novotel Sydney on Darling Harbour C1
62 Oaks Hyde Park Plaza D3
63 Oaks Maestri Towers C1
64 Old Sydney Holiday Inn A2
65 Park Hyatt Hotel Sydney A2
66 Park Regis City Centre C2
67 Parkroyal Darling Harbour C1
68 Pullman Quay Grand Sydney Harbour B3
69 Pullman Sydney Hyde Park Hotel D3
70 Quay West Suites Sydney B2
71 Radisson Blue Plaza Hotel Sydney B2
72 Radisson Sydney D2
73 Rendezvous Hotel Sydney The Rocks B2
74 Russell Hotel B2
75 Rydges World Square Sydney D2
76 Seasons Harbour Plaza Sydney C1
77 Sebel Pier One Sydney (The) A2
78 Shangri-La Hotel Sydney B2
79 Sheraton on the Park C2
80 Sir Stamford at Circular Quay B2
81 Sofitel Sydney Wentworth B2
82 Swissotel Sydney C2
83 Sydney Boulevard Hotel (The) C3
84 Sydney Harbour Marriott Hotel B2
85 Travelodge Wynyard B2
86 Waldorf Apartment Hotel (The) D2
87 Waldorf Woolloomooloo Waters C4
88 Westin Sydney (The) C2
89 York by Swiss - Belhotel (The) B2

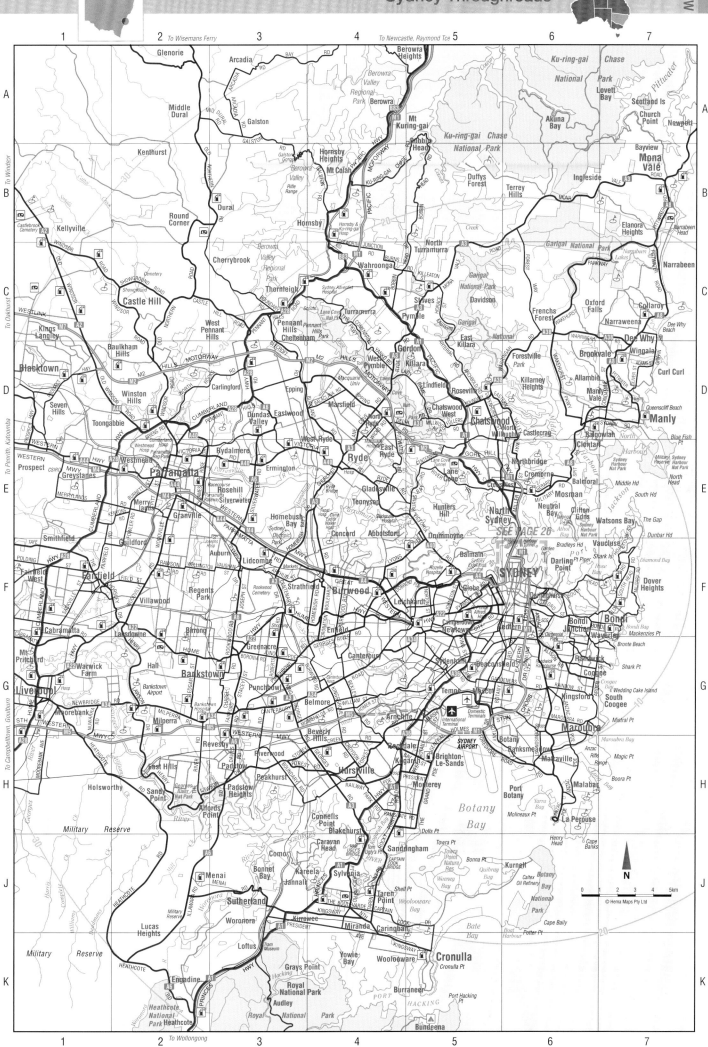

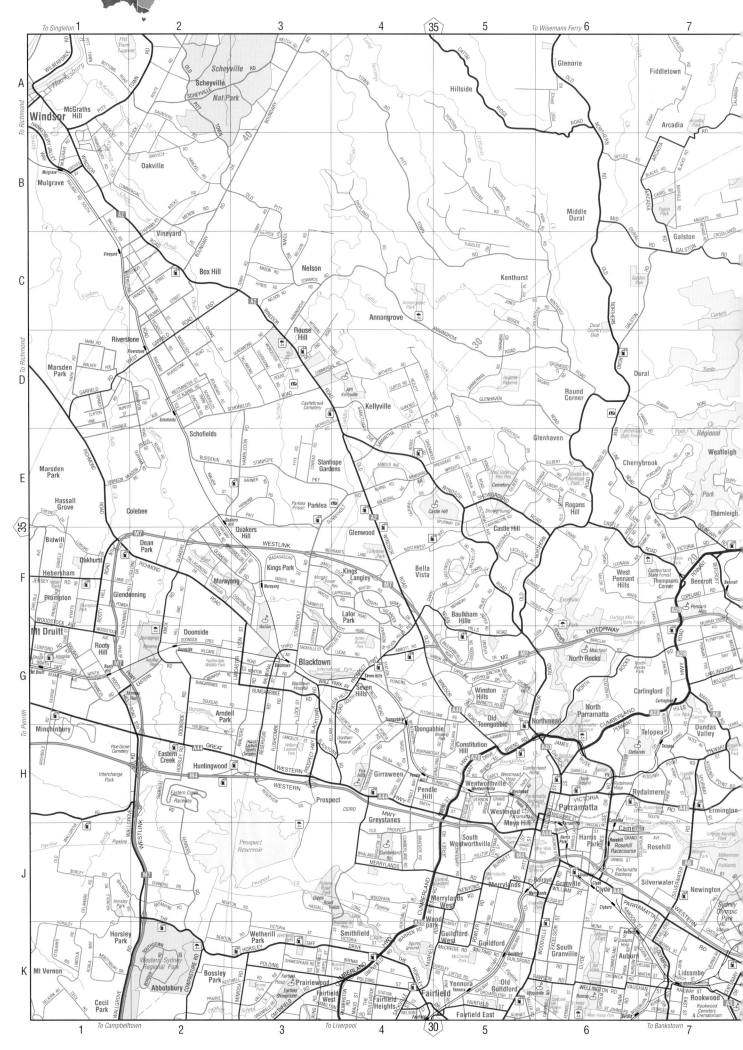

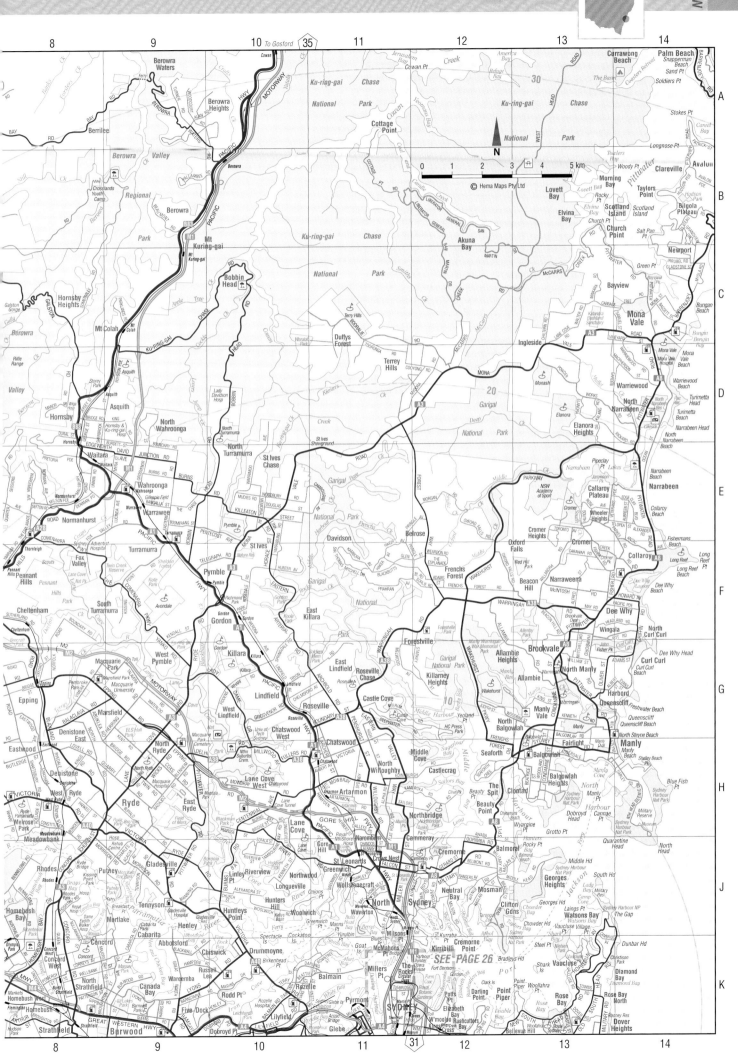

SEE PAGE 26

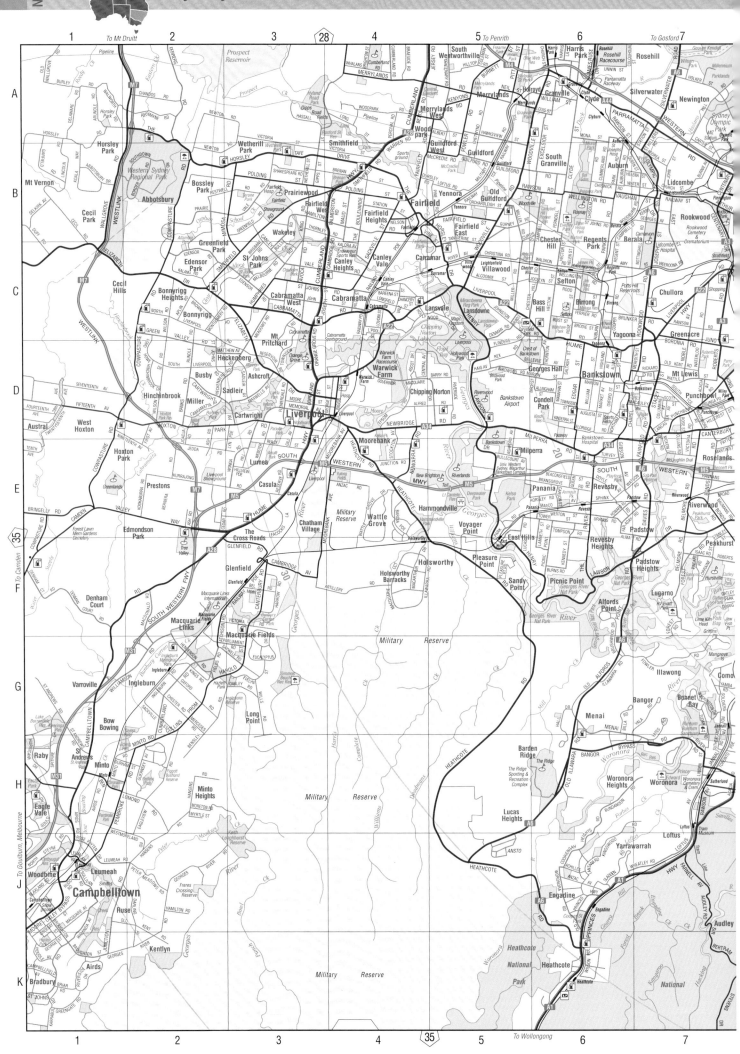

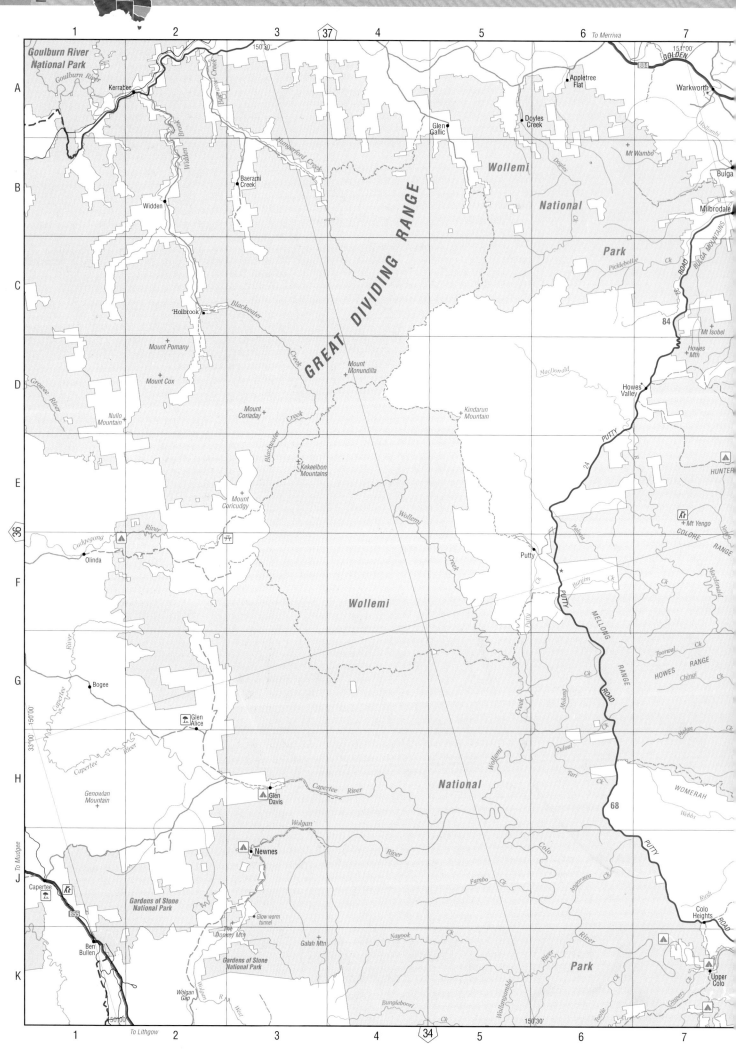

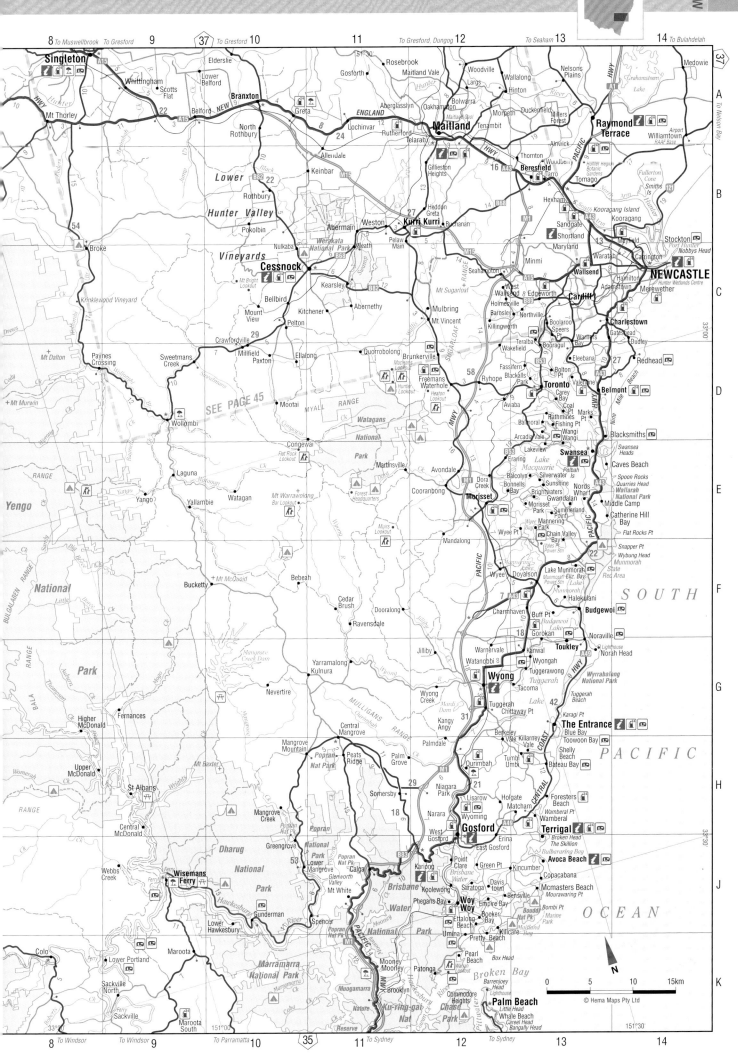

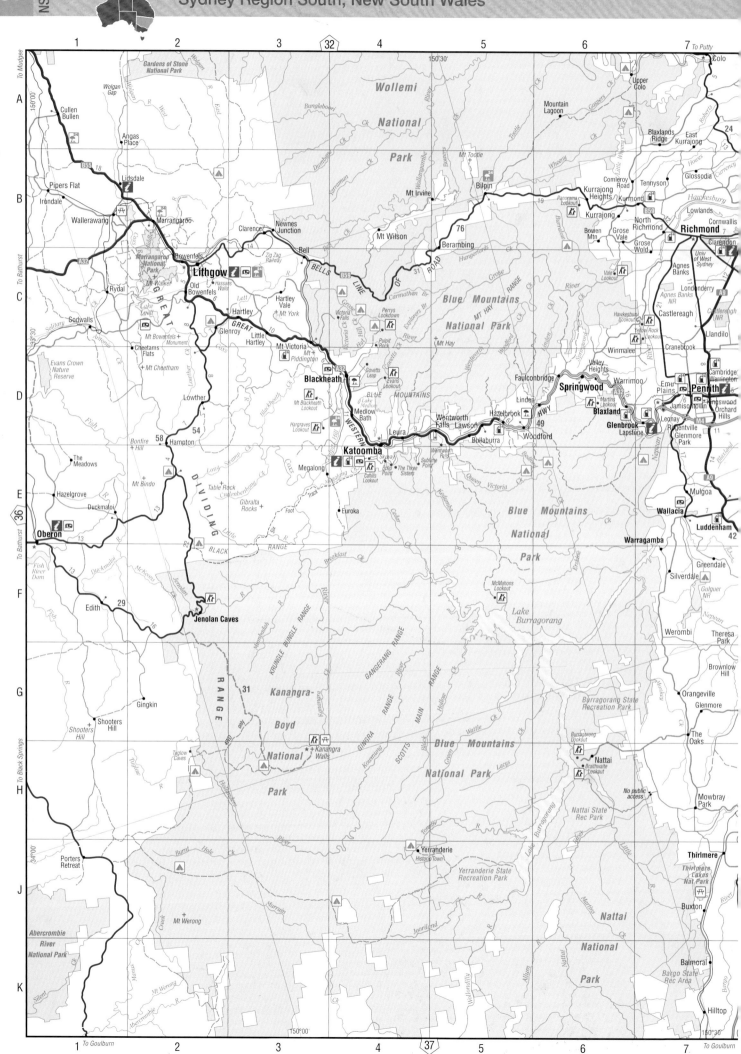

151°30'

8 9 33 10 To Gosford 11 12 13 14

To Wisemans Ferry

SOUTH

PACIFIC

OCEAN

TASMAN

SEA

To Kiama, Moss Vale

151°00'

34°30'

SEE PAGES 28-29

SEE PAGES 30-31

151°30'

34°00'

Broken Bay

Pearl Beach
Patonga
Mooney Mooney
Brooklyn
Commodore Heights
Palm Beach
Little Head
Whale Beach
Careel Head
Bangally Head
Clareville
Avalon
Bilgola
Newport
Bungan Head
Bayview
Mona Vale
Warriewood
Turimetta Head
Narrabeen Head
Narrabeen
Narrabeen Lakes
Collaroy
Long Reef Pt
Dee Why
Dee Why Head
Curl Curl
Queenscliff
Manly
Sydney Harbour National Park
North Head
South Head
The Gap
Watsons Bay
Vaucluse
Dover Heights
North Bondi
Bondi
Bronte
Clovelly
Gordons Bay
Coogee
Maroubra
Boora Pt
Little Bay
La Perouse
Cape Banks
Kamay Botany Bay National Park
Kurnell

Windsor
Hornsby
Castle Hill
Blacktown
Parramatta
Ryde
Nth Sydney
SYDNEY
Strathfield
Burwood
Bankstown
Liverpool
Hurstville
Sutherland
Cronulla
Bundeena
Royal National Park
Campbelltown
Camden
Picton
Menangle
Appin
Helensburgh
Stanwell Park
Coalcliff
Clifton
Scarborough
Wombarra
Coledale
Austinmer
Thirroul
Bulli
Woonona
Bellambi
Corrimal
Towradgi
Fairy Meadow
North Wollongong
WOLLONGONG
Port Kembla
Unanderra

N

0 5 10 15km

© Hema Maps Pty Ltd

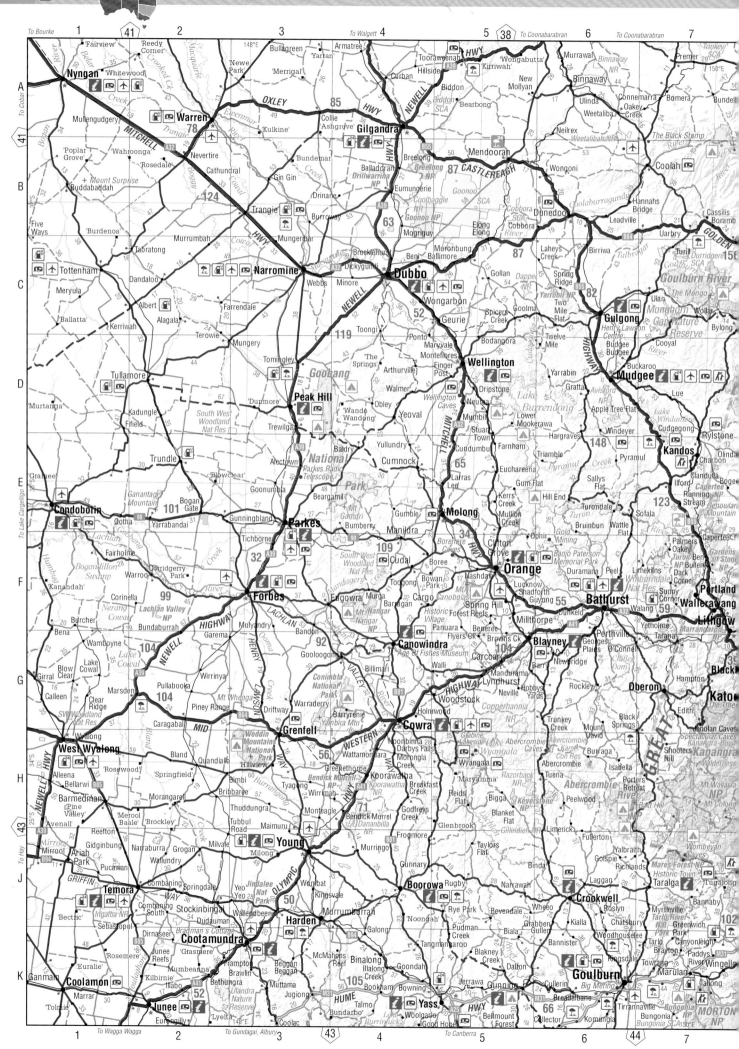

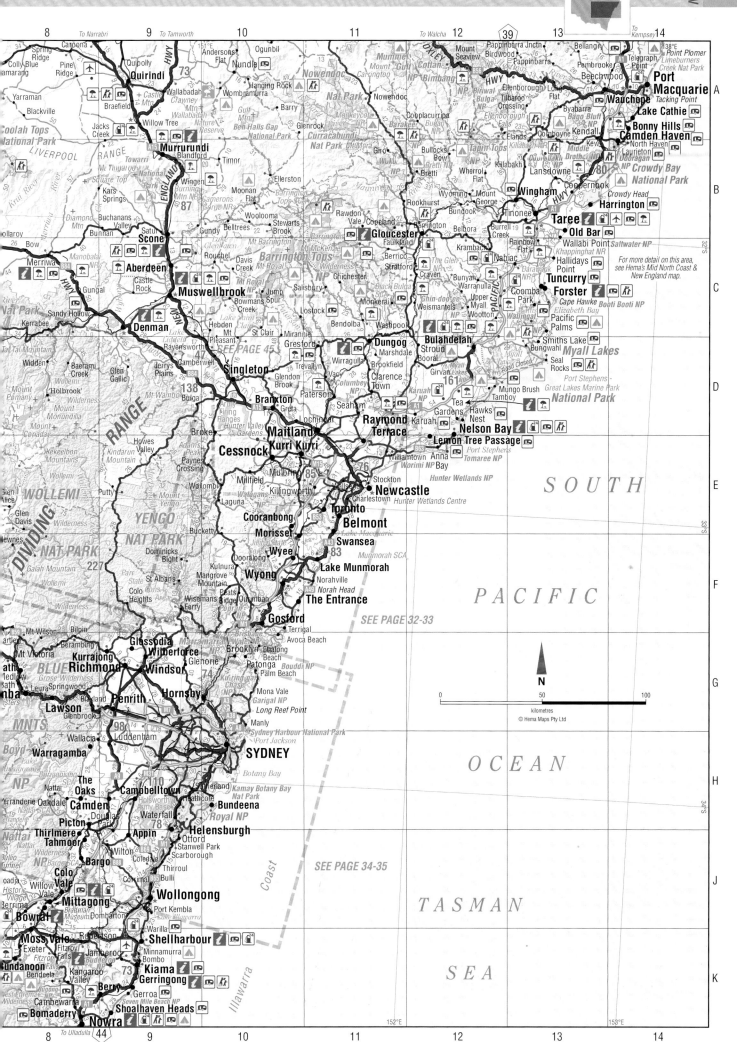

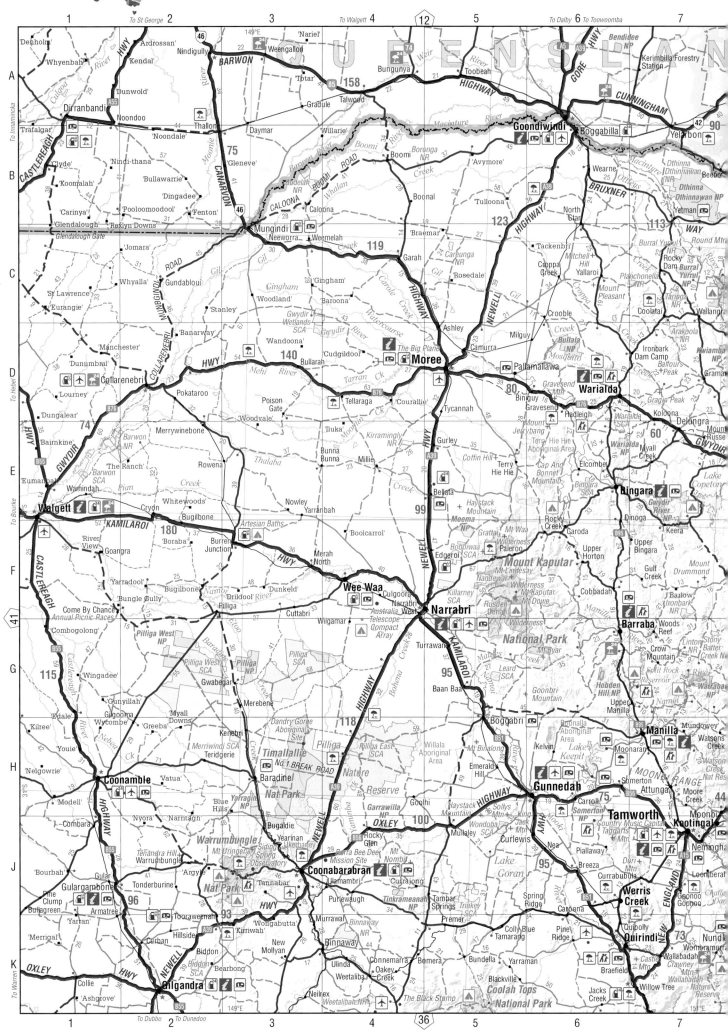

Map grid references (top)
8 13 9 10 To Toowoomba, Brisbane 11 12 To Brisbane 11 13 14

Place names and map labels

Coolangatta
Tweed Heads
Fingal Head
Chinderah
Kingscliff
Bogangar
Hastings Point
Pottsville
New Brighton
Brunswick Heads
Byron Bay
Suffolk Park
Bangalow
Cape Byron Marine Park
Lennox Head
Ballina
Empire Vale
Wardell
Broadwater
Broadwater National Park
Evans Head

Murwillumbah
Mullumbimby
Nimbin
Dunoon
Clunes
Lismore
Wollongbar
Alstonville
Coraki
Woodburn

Warwick
Killarney
Braeside
Legume
Woodenbong
Urbenville
Kyogle
Casino
Bonalbo
Tabulam

Stanthorpe
Ballandean
Wyberba
Boonoo Boonoo NP
Drake
Mallanganee
Mallanganee NP

Texas
Limevale
Mole River
Tenterfield
Bungulla
Billyrimba
Baryulgil
Harwood
Iluka
Yamba
Angourie
Woolweyah
Maclean

Ashford
Torrington
Stannum
Bolivia
Emmaville
Deepwater
Gibraltar Range NP
Glen Elgin
Cangai
Junction Hill
Grafton
Ulmarra
Tucabia
Brooms Head

Inverell
Sapphire
Glen Innes
Stonehenge
Bald Knob
Nymboida
Waterview Heights
Coutts Crossing
Minnie Water
Wooli

Gilgai
Tingha
Ben Lomond
Wandsworth
Llangothlin
Guyra
Glencoe
Red Rock
Corindi Beach
Arrawarra
Woolgoolga
Sandy Beach
Emerald Beach
Moonee Beach

Bundarra
Wongwibinda
Dorrigo
Coramba
Korora Bay
Coffs Harbour
Sawtell

Torryburn
Armidale
Hillgrove
Metz
Wollomombi
Wollomombi Falls
Bellingen
Urunga
Valla Beach
Hyland Park

Uralla
Kentucky
Bowraville
Nambucca Heads
Scotts Head
Stuarts Point

Walcha
Macksville
Warrell Creek
South West Rocks
Arakoon

Bendemeer
Woolbrook
Kempsey
Gladstone
Hat Head
Hat Head National Park
Crescent Head

Oxley Wild Rivers NP
Frederickton
Kinchela
Trial Bay

Nowendoc
Port Macquarie
Wauchope
Lake Cathie
Bonny Hills
Camden Haven
North Haven

Point Plomer
Telegraph Point
Tacking Point
Limeburners Creek Wilderness

SOUTH PACIFIC OCEAN

Great Dividing Range
New England Highway
Oxley Highway
Pacific Highway
Gwydir Highway
Bruxner Highway

N
0 25 50
kilometres
© Hema Maps Pty Ltd

154°E
29°S
30°S
31°S

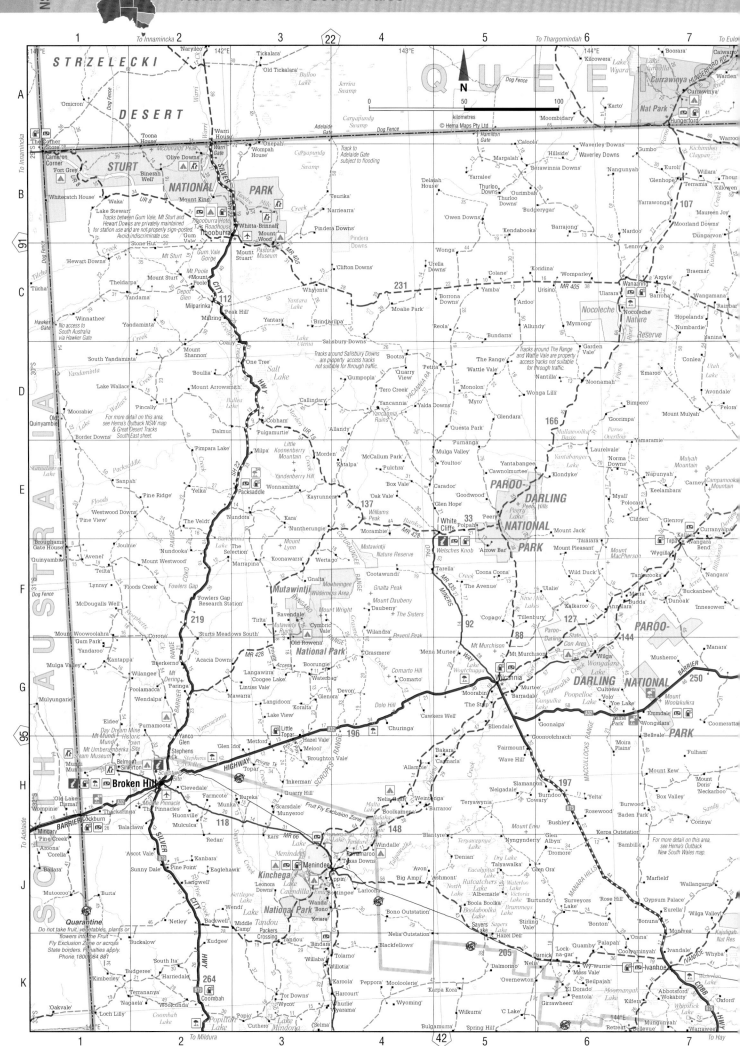

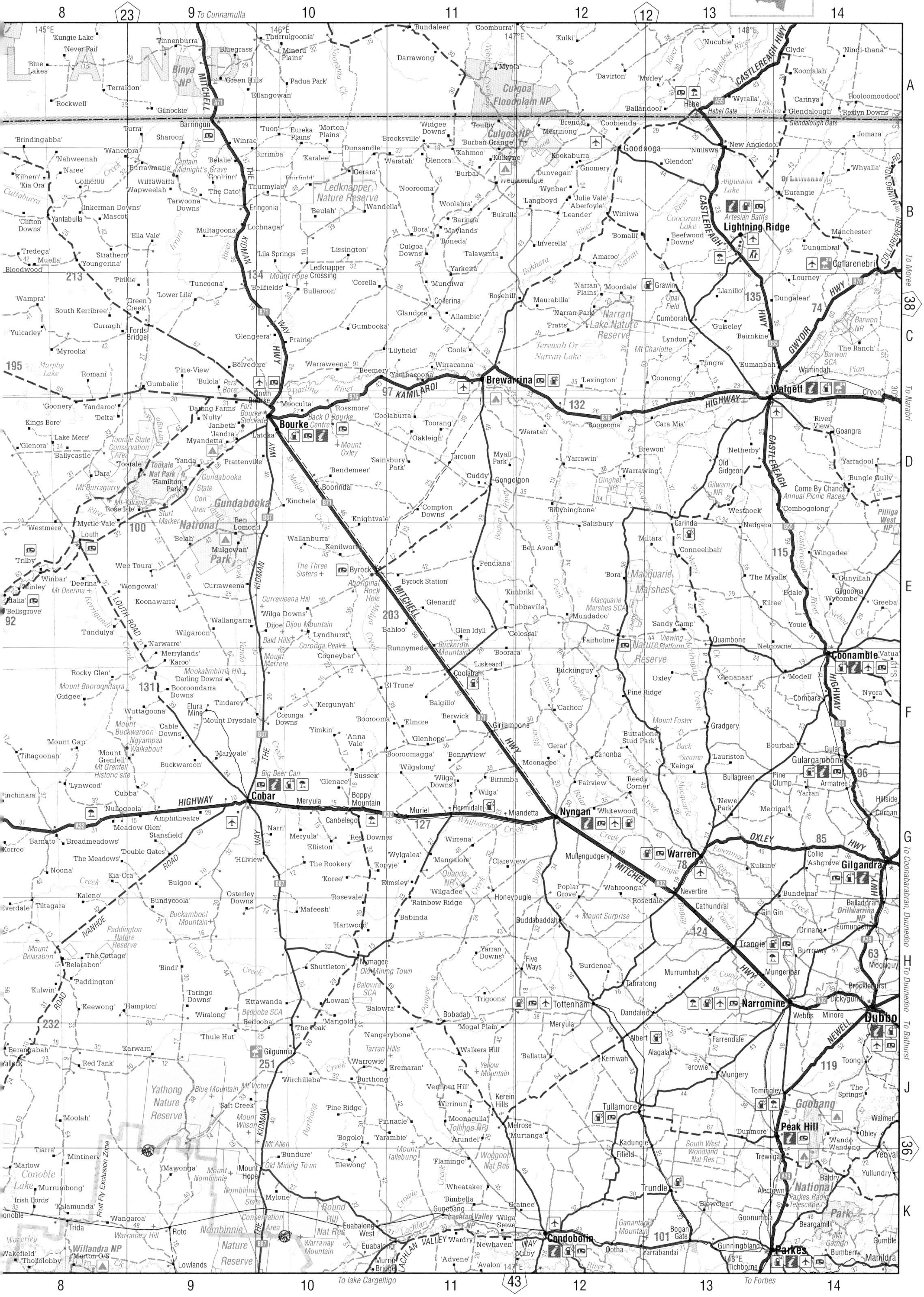

Map grid references

Major towns:
- Lightning Ridge
- Brewarrina
- Bourke
- Walgett
- Cobar
- Nyngan
- Warren
- Coonamble
- Gulargambone
- Gilgandra
- Narromine
- Dubbo
- Peak Hill
- Parkes
- Condobolin
- Tottenham
- Tullamore
- Trangie
- Nevertire
- Goodooga
- Collarenebri

Highways and roads:
- CASTLEREAGH HWY
- MITCHELL HWY
- KIDMAN WAY
- KAMILAROI HIGHWAY
- GWYDIR HWY
- OXLEY HWY
- NEWELL HWY
- THE NORTH WAY
- IVANHOE ROAD
- SOUTH ROAD

National Parks and Reserves:
- Binya NP
- Culgoa Floodplain NP
- Culgoa NP
- Ledknapper Nature Reserve
- Narran Lake Nature Reserve
- Toorale State Conservation Area
- Toorale Nat Park
- Gundabooka National Park
- Gundabooka State Con Area
- Macquarie Marshes
- Macquarie Marshes SCA
- Yathong Nature Reserve
- Willandra NP
- Nombinnie Nature Reserve
- Paddington Nature Reserve
- Goobang National Park
- Pilliga West NP
- Drillwarrina NP
- Beckooba SCA
- Balowra SCA
- South West Woodland Nat Res
- Woggoon Nat Res

To Cunnamulla · To Moree · To Narrabri · To Coonabarabran Dunnedoo · To Dunnedoo · To Bathurst · To Lake Cargelligo · To Forbes

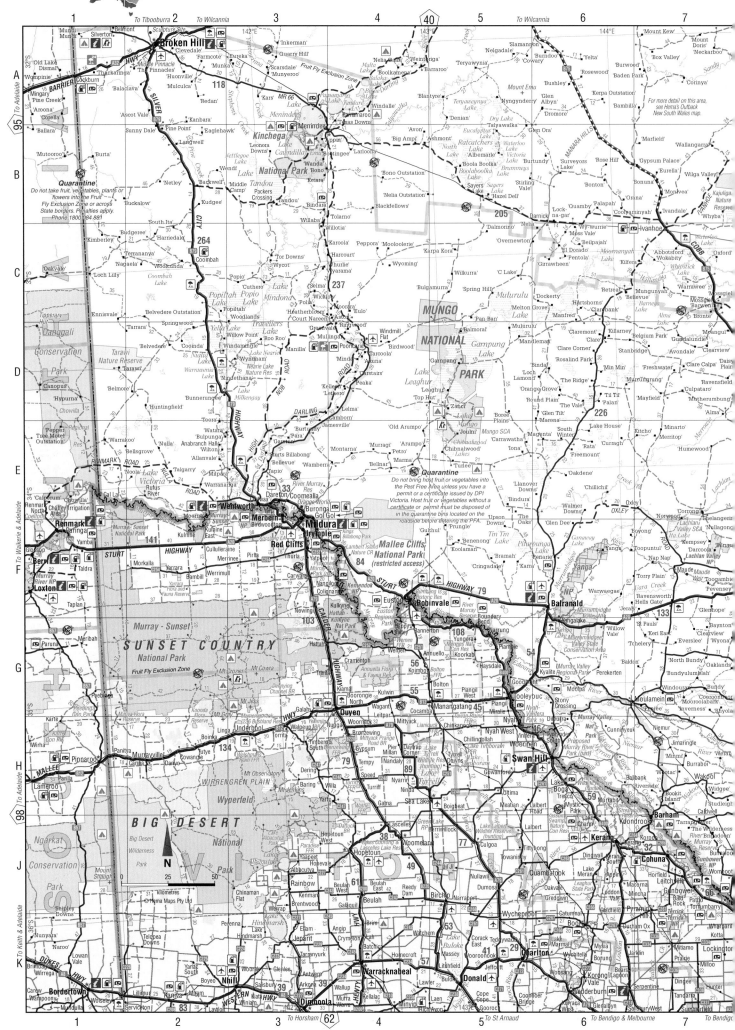

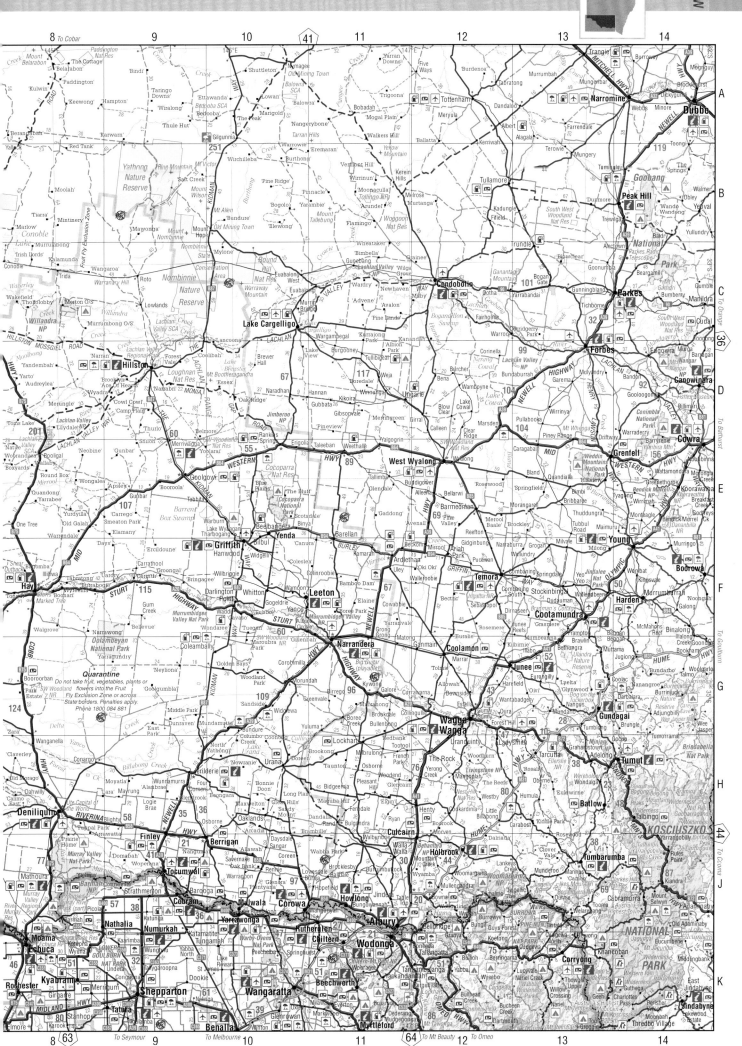

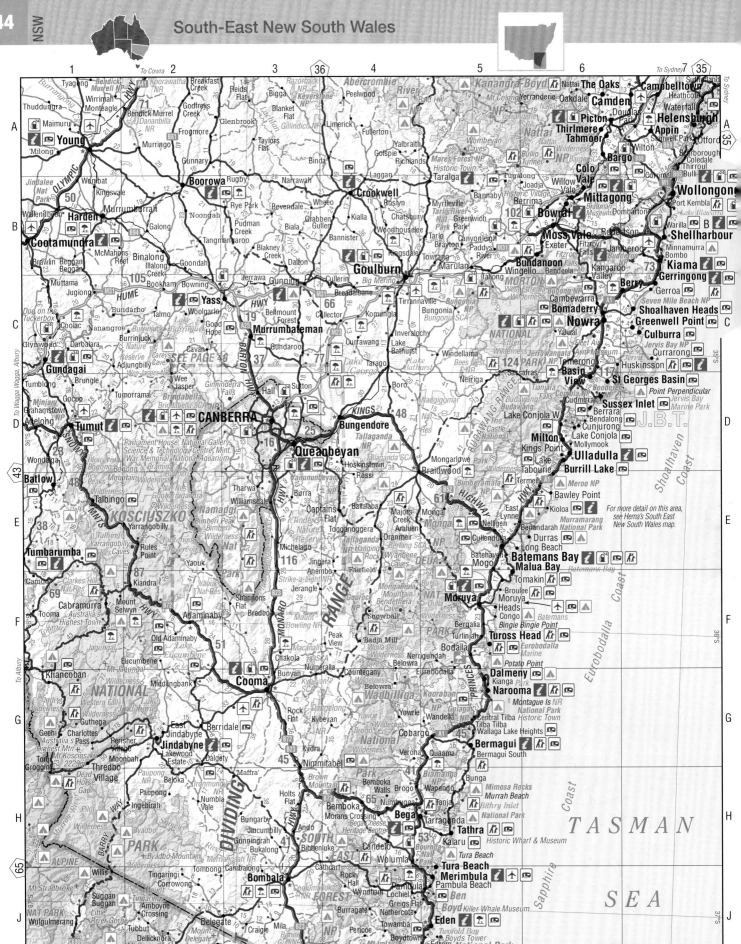

WILLIAMS RANGE
'Brooklyn'

N

0   2.5   5   10km
© Hema Maps Pty Ltd

151°10'E   151°20'E   151°30'E   151°40'E

Bowmans Creek
Dellhurst
Brownmore
Goorangoola
Dawsons Hill
Big Black + Jack Mountain
Bonnington Park
Halton
Lostock
Elwari + Mountain

A

Mount Butterwicki
Lake Saint Clair
Lostock Dam
Ravensworth State Forest
Greenland
St Clair
Mount Rivers
Coulston
Allynbrook
Durham Vale
BINGLEBURRA ROAD

B

Mount Olive
Mirannie
Gresford
East Gresford
Glendonbrook Wines
Mount Richardson
Falbrook
Mount Pleasant
Tyraman
Lewinsbrook
Mount Ararat

C

Oak Park
Westbrook
Ingar
Mirannie Mountain
ROAD
Torryburn
Trevallyn
Hilldale
NORTH COAST RAILWAY

Obanvale
Glendon Brook
GLENDONBROOK ROAD
80
Mount Breckin
Vacy
Mount Johnstone
Mount Douglas
Martins Creek

D

NEW
Rixs Creek
Singleton
Tulky Hill
Tangory Mountain
MOONABUNG RANGE
39

A15
ENGLAND

E

Mount Thorley
20
GOLDEN
B84
HIGHWAY
A15
Belford National Park
Fairview Wines
ELDERSLIE
Mount Hudson
Jacobs Hill
Rosebrook
Paterson
TOCAL ROAD

F

Branxton
NEW
Lower
Belford
Pierre's Wines
Tranquil Vale
Winders Hill
Mindaribba
Woodville
Wallalong
North Rothbury
Greta
A49
Lochinvar
Windella Downs
Bolwarra Heights
Hinton

G

BROKE ROAD
Army Baldwins Hill Firing Ranges
Lucy's Run Winery
Red Hill
M15
ENGLAND
26
HUNTER
NORTH
RAILWAY
Maitland
Morpeth
Broken View Estate
Windsor's Edge
Madigan Vineyard
Tatler Wines
Keinbah
Bishop Grove Wines
39
East Maitland
Thornton

Broke
Binnorie Dairy Cheese Tasting
Rothvale Vineyard and Winery
Worthington's Vineyard
Rothbury
Majors Lane Wines
Bishops Hill
EXPRESSWAY
Gilleston Heights
HIGHWAY
Beresfield

H

Oakvale Winery
Glandore Estate Wines
Hunter Valley
Pokolbin
Tempus Two
Allandale Winery and Vineyards
Werakata National Park
Loxford
Heddon Greta
Hunter Valley Gardens
Ernest Hill Wines
Hunter Valley Zoo
Potters Brewery
Lindeman's Hunter Valley
Tinklers Wines
Nulkaba
Neath
Kurri Kurri
Buchanan
MOTORWAY
A1
Stockrington
Hunter Wetlands National Park

J

Cedar Creek Stonehurst Cottages and Wine
Kelman Vineyard
MAITLAND ROAD
Cessnock
ABERDARE ST
Vineyards
Tallavera Grove Vineyard
Bimbadeen Lookout
Millbrook Estate Winery
Mount Baker
29
Millfield
Pelton
Kitchener
Abernethy
Werakata National Park
Pelaw Main
STANFORD ROAD
Mount Sugarloaf
Seahampton
Minmi
West Wallsend
B89
Wallsend
Edgeworth

K

Wollombi Village Vineyard
Wollombi
Yango State Forest
Corrabare State Forest
Watagan State Forest
Sweetmans Creek
Paxton
Ellalong
Quorrobolong
Brunkerville
Watagans National Park
Mount Vincent
Heaton State Forest
Mulbring
FREEMANS DRIVE
PACIFIC
Killingworth
Estelville
Cardiff
A15
NEWCASTLE LINK RD
Lake Macquarie

To Barton Hwy, Federal Hwy, Yass, Goulburn, Sydney

Australian National Botanic Gardens

CSIRO

Black Mountain Tower

Australian National University

Acton

To Weston Creek, Belconnen

Springbank Island

Acton Peninsula

Spinnaker Island

Blue Gum Point

Lake Burley Griffin

Attunga Point

Stirling Park

West Basin

Hospital Point

National Museum of Australia

Captain Cook Memorial Water Jet

Commonwealth

Nerang Pool

Central Basin

Regatta Point

Commonwealth Park

Gallipoli Reach

Reid

Campbell

Russell

Kings Park

Aspen Island

National Carillon

National Library of Australia

Commonwealth Place

High Court of Australia

Parkes

National Gallery of Australia

Questacon

Treasury Building

National Rose Garden

National Portrait Gallery

Parkes Place

Senate Rose Garden

Old Parliament House

Govt House

Federation Mall

National Archives of Australia

Kings Ave Bridge

Grevillea Park

Yarralumla

Mountbatten Park

Deakin Oval

To Weston Creek

Deakin

Church of England Girls Grammar

To Red Hill

Capital Hill

Parliament House

Senate House of Reps

Prime Minister's Lodge

Forrest

Forrest Primary School

Jewish Memorial Centre

Forrest Tennis Club

York Park Sports ground

Dept of Prime Minister & Cabinet

Foreign Affairs & Trade

Barton

Centenary House

Nat Press Club

York Park

Edmund Barton Building

John Gorton Building

Robert Garran Offices

Bowen Park

Telopea Park HS

Old Powerhouse Old Kingston Bus Markets

Rowing Clubs

Kingston

To Cooma, Queanbeyan

To Canberra Airport, Queanbeyan

Legend

Major Building	
Govt Building	
Accommodation	
Shopping	
Post Office	
Embassy	
National Highway	A23
Tourist Route	2
Cycleway	
Picnic Area	

N

0 100 200 300 400 500m
© Hema Maps Pty Ltd

Places of Interest

1. ACT Legislative Assembly A3
2. Acton Ferry Terminal B2
3. Acton Park B2
4. Albert Hall C2
5. Aust. and New Zealand Memorial B4
6. Australian Army National Memorial A4
7. Australian Hellenic Memorial A4
8. Australian National Botanic Gardens A1
9. Aust. National Korean War Memorial B4
10. Australian National University A2
11. Aust. Service Nurses National Mem B4
12. Aust. Vietnam Forces National Mem B4
13. Australian War Memorial A4
14. Black Mountain Tower A1
15. Blundell's Cottage B4

16. Canberra Centre A3
17. Canberra Institute of Technology B3
18. Canberra Museum & Gallery A3
19. Canberra Olympic Pool B3
20. Canberra Sthn Cross Yacht Club C2
21. Canberra Theatre Centre A3
22. Capital Hill D2
23. Captain Cook Memorial Water Jet B3
24. Casino Canberra A3
25. Civic Square A3
26. Commonwealth Park B3
27. Commonwealth Place C3
28. CSIRO Discovery Centre A1
29. Dendy Cinemas A3
30. Glebe Park A3
31. Gorman House Arts Centre A3
32. High Court of Australia C3

33. Jolimont Tourist Centre A3
34. Kings Park C4
35. Museum of Australian Democracy C3
36. National Capital Exhibition B3
37. National Carillon C4
38. National Convention Centre B3
39. National Film & Sound Archive A2
40. National Gallery of Australia C3
41. National Library of Australia C3
42. National Museum of Australia B2
43. National Portrait Gallery C3
44. National Rose Garden C3
45. Old Parliament House C3
46. Palace Electric Cinema B2
47. Parliament House D2
48. Prime Minister's Lodge D2

49. Questacon-Nat. Science & Tech. Ctr C3
50. RAAF Memorial B4
51. RAN Memorial B4
52. Rats of Tobruk Memorial B4
53. Regatta Point Jetty B3
54. School of Art A2
55. School of Music A2
56. St John's Schoolhouse Museum B4
57. Stage 88 Music Bowl B3
58. Stirling Park C1
59. Telopea Park D3

Accommodation

61. Bentley Suites Canberra D3
62. BreakFree Capital Tower B2
63. Canberra City YHA A3
64. Comfort Inn Downtown A3

65. Crowne Plaza Canberra A3
66. Forrest Hotel & Apartments D3
67. Hotel Kurrajong Canberra D3
68. Hyatt Hotel Canberra C2
69. Kingston Court Serviced Apartments D4
70. Medina Executive James Crt Canberra A3
71. Novotel Canberra A3
72. Olims Canberra Hotel A4
73. QT Canberra A2
74. Quest Canberra A3
75. Rydges Capital Hill D3
76. Telopea Inn on the Park D3
77. The Brassey of Canberra D3
78. The York Canberra D4
79. University House at ANU A2
80. Waldorf Apartment Hotel Canberra A3

Parkhurst Wines
Brindabella Hills Winery
Ginninderra Falls
Wallaroo
Woodstock Nature Reserve
Pine Ridge 656m
Lower Molonglo Nature Reserve
Murrumbidgee River Corridor
Stony Creek Nature Reserve
Uriarra
Mt Stromlo 782m Forest
Stromlo Forest
Weir
Cotter Dam
To Cotter Dam
Murrumbidgee River Corridor
COTTER RD
Paddy's River
Paddys Range
Bullen Range
Murrumbidgee River Corridor
Red Rocks Gorge
Nature Reserve
Bullen Range
Kambah Pool
McQuoid Ck
Namadgi National Park
To Tidbinbilla Nature Reserve
Tidbinbilla
Murrumbidgee River Corridor
Paddy's

To Yass To Young, Gundagai To Gundaroo
Hall
Cemetery
Kinlyside
Casey
Ngunnawal
Amaroo
Forde
Canberra Nature Park
Goorooyarroo 765m
To Goulburn, Moss Vale
Harcourt Hill 693m
Nicholls
Federation Square
Gungahlin Market
GUNGAHLIN
Palmerston
Harrison
Throsby
Fraser
Dunlop
Charnwood
Flynn
Spence
Crace
Franklin
Mulanggari
Kenny
Rifle Club & Range
FEDERAL HWY
NSW
Macgregor
Melba
Evatt
Giralang
Canberra Nature Park
Gungahlin Cemetery
Crematorium
Transmitting Stations
Latham
Mckellar
Holt
Kippax Fair
Florey
Lawson
Kaleen
Mitchell
Downer
Watson
Majura
Mt Majura Vineyard
Higgins
Scullin
BELCONNEN
Page
Belconnen Town Centre
University of Canberra
Fern Hill Technology Park
Exhibition Park
Canberra Racecourse
Canberra Inst of Tech
Mt Majura 888m Park
Hawker
Macquarie
Weetangera
Bruce
Calvary Hospital
Canberra Inst of Tech
Lyneham
Dickson Centre
Dickson
Hackett
Canberra Nature Park
Majura Field Firing Range
Aranda
Cook
Canberra Nature Park
743m Mt Painter
O'Connor
Turner
Ainslie
Mt Ainslie 843m
Black Mtn 812m
CSIRO
Australian National University
Acton
Braddon
Australian War Mem
Campbell
SEE PAGE 46
Canberra International Airport
Fairbairn
Burley Griffin
National Museum of Australia
Scrivener Dam
Yarralumla Government House
Yarralumla
Griffin
Russell
Australian Defence Force Academy
Duntroon Royal Military College
Pialligo
Lake Burley Griffin
Capital Hill
Parkes
Barton
Kingston
Pialligo
Fairbairn
Pine Forest
Air Disaster Memorial
Deakin
Red Hill 720m
Manuka
Forrest
Fyshwick
Oaks Estate
Hospital
Cotter Centre
Canberra Police College
Curtin
Hughes
Nature Park
Red Hill
Griffith
Narrabundah
Symonston
Crestwood
Holder
Weston
Weston shops
Narrabundah Hill 691m
Duffy
Rivett
Stirling
Lyons
Woden Plaza
Cemetery
Phillip
Woden Hospital
Garran
O'Malley
Geoscience Australia
Harman
HMAS Harman
Queanbeyan West
QUEANBEYAN
WESTON CREEK
Chifley
WODEN VALLEY
Karabar
Waramanga
Chapman
Pearce
Fisher
Mawson
Isaacs
Farrer
Torrens
Kambah
Mt Arawang 764m Park
Mt Taylor 856m
Neighbour Hill 702m
Forster Hill 688m
The Village
Jerrabomberra
783m Jerrabomberra Hill
Jerrabomberra Mountain Res
Gale
Wanniassa
Fadden
Macarthur
Hume
Googong
Oxley
Monash
Gowrie
Gilmore
Pemberton Hill 878m
TUGGERANONG
Greenway
Isabella Plains
Richardson
Chisholm
Tuggeranong Siding
Bonython 660m
Barneys Hill
Calwell
Tuggeranong Hill 855m Nature
Theodore
Enchanted Hill 955m
Gordon
Conder
Rob Roy Nature Reserve
Banks
To Tharwa To Tharwa To Cooma

N
0 1 2 3 4 5 km
© Hema Maps Pty Ltd

1 To Yass 2   3   To Yass 4 44 5   6   7 To Goulburn

+ Doctors Hill

NEW

SOUTH

WALES

Brindabella

National

Park

Lake George

Purrorumba Mtn +

Sutton

Ginninderra Falls
Ginninderra Ck

Woodstock NR

Gungahlin

Canberra Nature Park

Ginns Gap

Federal HWY

Gundaroo RD

Yass RD

MACS REEF RD

BUNGENDORE RD

Devils Peak

+ Mt Blundell

Lower Molonglo NR

Belconnen

Lake Ginninderra

+ Mt Majura

Goorooyarroo NR

NORTON RD

+ Mt Coree

Stony Creek Nature Reserve

Stromlo

City

CANBERRA

Capital Hill

Mt Ainslie +

Canberra Nature Park

Mt Black Mtn +

Majura Firing Range

Cotter Dam

Mt Stromlo Observatory

Stromlo Forest

Lake Burley Griffin

RAAF Fairbairn

Canberra Airport

Kowen Pine Forest

Molonglo Gorge NR

Uriarra Forest

Pierces Creek Forest

Weston Creek

Woden

Hindmarsh

Red Hill +

Fyshwick

Molonglo River

KINGS HWY B52

+ Bulls Head

Bullen Range Nature Reserve

Canberra Ave

Burbong

Cuumbeun NR

Stony Creek NR

Brindabella

BRINDABELLA RANGE

+ Cotter Hill

Tuggeranong

Queanbeyan

Cuumbeun NR

Balcombe Hill +

Bimberi Nature Reserve

+ Mt Aggie

Bendora Dam

Tidbinbilla Nature Reserve

Tidbinbilla Visitor Centre

Canberra Deep Space Communication Complex

Lake Tuggeranong

Erindale

Isabella

Hume

Australian Railway Historical Society heritage rail trips

+ Mt Jerrabomberra

AUSTRALIAN

Mt Franklin

Gibraltar Falls

Murrumbidgee Corridor

Lanyon Homestead

Rob Roy Nature Reserve

Googong Reservoir

Mt + Molonglo

SEE PAGE 47

CAPITAL

Mt Ginini +

Corin Dam

Tharwa

Royalla

Googong Hill

London Bridge

44

Mt Gungera

Namadgi

Namadgi Visitor Centre

Lobb Hill

Burra Creek Nature Reserve

Yunununbeyan Nat Park

Bimberi Nature Reserve

APOLLO RD

Burra

Yunununbeyan SCA

TERRITORY

Williamsdale

Kosciuszko

National

Bimberi Peak

Coronet Peak

National

Park

Naas

Rocky Crossing

Mt Burra +

NEW

SOUTH

WALES

Tantangara Reservoir

Mt Murray +

Mt Bullongong +

Mt Michelago

Horseshoe Hill +

Park

+ Mt Kelly

Nursery Hill +

Glendale Crossing

Mt Yarara +

Tinderry Nature Reserve

Mt Morgan +

Half Moon Peak

Yankee Hill +

Booths Hill +

BOOTHS RANGE

Tinderry Peak +

TINDERRY

Scabby Range Nature Reserve

+ Mt Scabby

+ Mt Gudgenby

Michelago

Boolboolma Crossing

Mt Ash Hill +

Sentry Box Rock

+ Shanahans Mtn

CLEAR RANGE

+ Mt Holland

Jingera

Burnt School NR

Yaouk Peak +

Yaouk Nature Reserve

Clear Hill +

Mt Clear +

Anembo

Strike-a-light NR

RANGE

Black Cow Peak

BOBOYAN DIVIDE

Colinton
+ Mt Colinton

N

Wallaby Hill +

Mt Wangrah +

Jerangle

Bugtown

Shannons Flat

44

To Adaminaby To Cooma

To Cooma

0 2 4 6 8 10km

© Hema Maps Pty Ltd

Whinstone Hill +

key map

TWELVE APOSTLES, GREAT OCEAN RD (60 H6)

PHOTO: © ISTOCK.COM

Distances are shown in kilometres and follow the most direct major sealed route where possible.

	Ballarat	Bairnsdale	Bendigo	Echuca	Eden (NSW)	Geelong	Hamilton	Horsham	Melbourne	Mildura	Shepparton	Swan Hill	Traralgon	Wangaratta	Warrnambool
Albury	428	333	310	245	542	372	608	524	305	624	178	403	456	77	601
Ballarat		410	118	201	693	88	180	188	116	449	240	307	287	359	173
Bairnsdale			447	578	283	366	590	598	294	859	511	636	123	410	552
Bendigo				92	730	206	298	214	153	426	122	189	324	230	291
Echuca					787	298	390	306	204	379	68	157	405	176	383
Eden (NSW)						649	873	881	577	1127	794	919	386	619	835
Geelong							233	276	72	537	260	395	273	308	186
Hamilton								128	296	436	420	487	497	532	111
Horsham									304	308	336	403	505	444	239
Melbourne										579	188	342	201	236	258
Mildura											447	220	780	555	547
Shepparton												225	389	108	413
Swan Hill													543	333	480
Traralgon														437	459
Wangaratta															532
Warrnambool															

62-63

64-65

58-59

60-61

66

56-57

For more detail
see pages 52-53
and 54-55

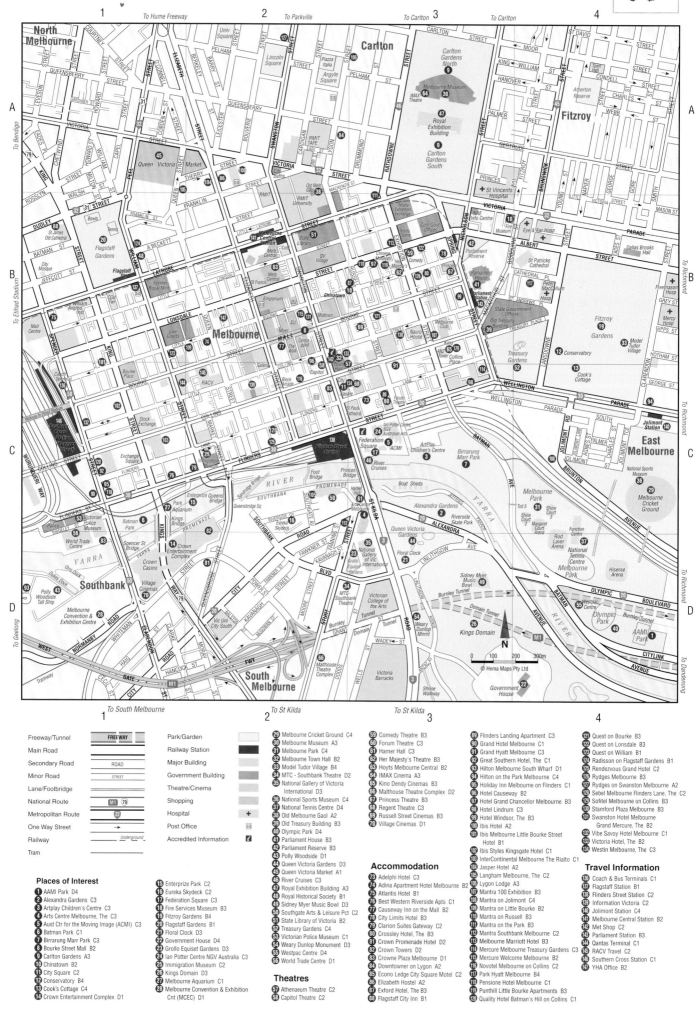

Legend

Freeway/Tunnel	FREEWAY
Main Road	
Secondary Road	ROAD
Minor Road	STREET
Lane/Footbridge	
National Route	M1 (79)
Metropolitan Route	(22)
One Way Street	
Railway	Underground
Tram	

Park/Garden	
Railway Station	
Major Building	
Government Building	
Theatre/Cinema	
Shopping	
Hospital	+
Post Office	
Accredited Information	

Places of Interest

1. AAMI Park D4
2. Alexandra Gardens C3
3. Artplay Children's Centre C3
4. Arts Centre Melbourne, The C3
5. Aust Ctr for the Moving Image (ACMI) C3
6. Batman Park C1
7. Birrarung Marr Park C3
8. Bourke Street Mall B2
9. Carlton Gardens A3
10. Chinatown B2
11. City Square C2
12. Conservatory B4
13. Cook's Cottage C4
14. Crown Entertainment Complex D1
15. Enterprize Park C2
16. Eureka Skydeck C2
17. Federation Square C3
18. Fire Services Museum B3
19. Fitzroy Gardens B4
20. Flagstaff Gardens B1
21. Floral Clock D3
22. Government House D4
23. Grollo Equiset Gardens D3
24. Ian Potter Centre NGV Australia C3
25. Immigration Museum C2
26. Kings Domain D3
27. Melbourne Aquarium C1
28. Melbourne Convention & Exhibition Cnt (MCEC) D1
29. Melbourne Cricket Ground C4
30. Melbourne Museum A3
31. Melbourne Park C4
32. Melbourne Town Hall B2
33. Model Tudor Village B4
34. MTC - Southbank Theatre D2
35. National Gallery of Victoria International D3
36. National Sports Museum C4
37. National Tennis Centre D4
38. Old Melbourne Gaol A2
39. Old Treasury Building B3
40. Olympic Park D4
41. Parliament House B3
42. Parliament Reserve B3
43. Polly Woodside D1
44. Queen Victoria Gardens D3
45. Queen Victoria Market A1
46. River Cruises C3
47. Royal Exhibition Building A3
48. Royal Historical Society B1
49. Sidney Myer Music Bowl D3
50. Southgate Arts & Leisure Pct C2
51. State Library of Victoria B2
52. Treasury Gardens C4
53. Victorian Police Museum C1
54. Weary Dunlop Monument D3
55. Westpac Centre D4
56. World Trade Centre D1

Theatres

57. Athenaeum Theatre C2
58. Capitol Theatre C2
59. Comedy Theatre B3
60. Forum Theatre C3
61. Hamer Hall C3
62. Her Majesty's Theatre B3
63. Hoyts Melbourne Central B2
64. IMAX Cinema A3
65. Kino Dendy Cinemas B3
66. Malthouse Theatre Complex D2
67. Princess Theatre B3
68. Regent Theatre C3
69. Russell Street Cinemas B3
70. Village Cinemas D1

Accommodation

73. Adelphi Hotel C3
74. Adina Apartment Hotel Melbourne B2
75. Atlantis Hotel B1
76. Best Western Riverside Apts C1
77. Causeway Inn on the Mall B2
78. City Limits Hotel B3
79. Clarion Suites Gateway C2
80. Crossley Hotel, The B3
81. Crown Promenade Hotel D2
82. Crown Towers D2
83. Crowne Plaza Melbourne D1
84. Downtowner on Lygon A2
85. Econo Ledge City Square Motel C2
86. Elizabeth Hostel A2
87. Exford Hotel, The B3
88. Flagstaff City Inn B1
89. Flinders Landing Apartment C3
90. Grand Hotel Melbourne C1
91. Grand Hyatt Melbourne C3
92. Great Southern Hotel, The C1
93. Hilton Melbourne South Wharf D1
94. Hilton on the Park Melbourne C4
95. Holiday Inn Melbourne on Flinders C1
96. Hotel Causeway B2
97. Hotel Grand Chancellor Melbourne B3
98. Hotel Lindrum C3
99. Hotel Windsor, The B3
100. Ibis Hotel A2
101. Ibis Melbourne Little Bourke Street Hotel B1
102. Ibis Styles Kingsgate Hotel C1
103. InterContinental Melbourne The Rialto C1
104. Jasper Hotel A2
105. Langham Melbourne, The C2
106. Lygon Lodge A3
107. Mantra 100 Exhibition B3
108. Mantra on Jolimont C4
109. Mantra on Little Bourke B2
110. Mantra on Russell B3
111. Mantra on the Park B3
112. Mantra Southbank Melbourne C2
113. Mercure Melbourne B3
114. Mercure Melbourne Treasury Gardens B4
115. Mercure Welcome Melbourne B2
116. Novotel Melbourne on Collins B3
117. Park Hyatt Melbourne B4
118. Pensione Hotel Melbourne C1
119. Punthill Little Bourke Apartments B3
120. Quality Hotel Batman's Hill on Collins C1
121. Quest on Bourke B3
122. Quest on Lonsdale B3
123. Quest on William B1
124. Radisson on Flagstaff Gardens B1
125. Rendezvous Grand Hotel C2
126. Rydges Melbourne B3
127. Rydges on Swanston Melbourne A2
128. Sebel Melbourne Flinders Lane, The C2
129. Sofitel Melbourne on Collins B3
130. Stamford Plaza Melbourne B3
131. Swanston Hotel Melbourne Grand Mercure, The B2
132. Vibe Savoy Hotel Melbourne C1
133. Victoria Hotel, The B2
134. Westin Melbourne, The C3

Travel Information

135. Coach & Bus Terminals C1
136. Flagstaff Station B1
137. Flinders Street Station C2
138. Information Victoria C2
139. Jolimont Station C4
140. Melbourne Central Station B2
141. Met Shop C2
142. Parliament Station B3
143. Qantas Terminal C1
144. RACV Travel C2
145. Southern Cross Station C1
146. YHA Office B2

To Sunbury 1   2   To Seymour 3   4   5   6   To Kinglake 7

MELBOURNE

Greenvale
Bulla
Somerton
Coolaroo
Westmeadows
Keilor North
Melbourne Airport Terminal
AIRPORT
Tullamarine
Broadmeadows
Campbellfield
Thomastown
Epping
Mill Park
Plenty
Hurstbridge
Diamond Creek
Kangaroo Ground
Research
Greensborough
Eltham
Bundoora
Watsonia
Macleod
Kingsbury
Fawkner
Reservoir
Preston
Coburg
Keilor
St Albans
Essendon
Braybrook
Ardeer
Sunshine
Brooklyn
Thornbury
Heidelberg
Northcote
Brunswick
Doncaster
Templestowe
Park Orchards
Warrandyte
Mitcham
Ringwood
Carlton
Kew
Balwyn
Box Hill
Blackburn
Fitzroy
Collingwood
Hawthorn
Camberwell
MELBOURNE
Richmond
Bayswater
South Melbourne
Toorak
Burwood
Mt Waverley
Glen Waverley
Scoresby
Port Melbourne
Prahran
Armadale
St Kilda
Caulfield
Chadstone
Burwood East
Wheelers Hill
Newport
Williamstown
Altona
Altona Meadows
Altona Bay
Elwood
Brighton
Point Ormond
McKinnon
Oakleigh
Clayton
Monash University
Springvale
Noble Park
Dandenong North
Dandenong
Doveton
Moorabbin
Sandringham
Cheltenham
Black Rock
Mentone
Dingley Village
Braeside
Keysborough
Dandenong South
Mordialloc
Bangholme
Lyndhurst
Edithvale
Chelsea
Carrum
Carrum Downs
Seaford
Skye
Cranbourne
Frankston

PORT PHILLIP BAY

Hobsons Bay
Point Cook
Cheetham Wetlands
Picnic Point
Ricketts Point
Beaumaris Bay

N

0   3   6km

© Hema Maps Pty Ltd

CityLink & EastLink Tollways
For information on passes and e-TAGs visit
www.citylink.com.au
www.eastlink.com.au

Spirit of Tasmania
For more information on the ferry from Melbourne to Devonport
Ph 1800 634 906
www.spiritoftasmania.com.au

To Kyneton
To Ballarat
To Geelong
To Lilydale
To Emerald
To Warragul
To Koo-wee-rup
To Mornington

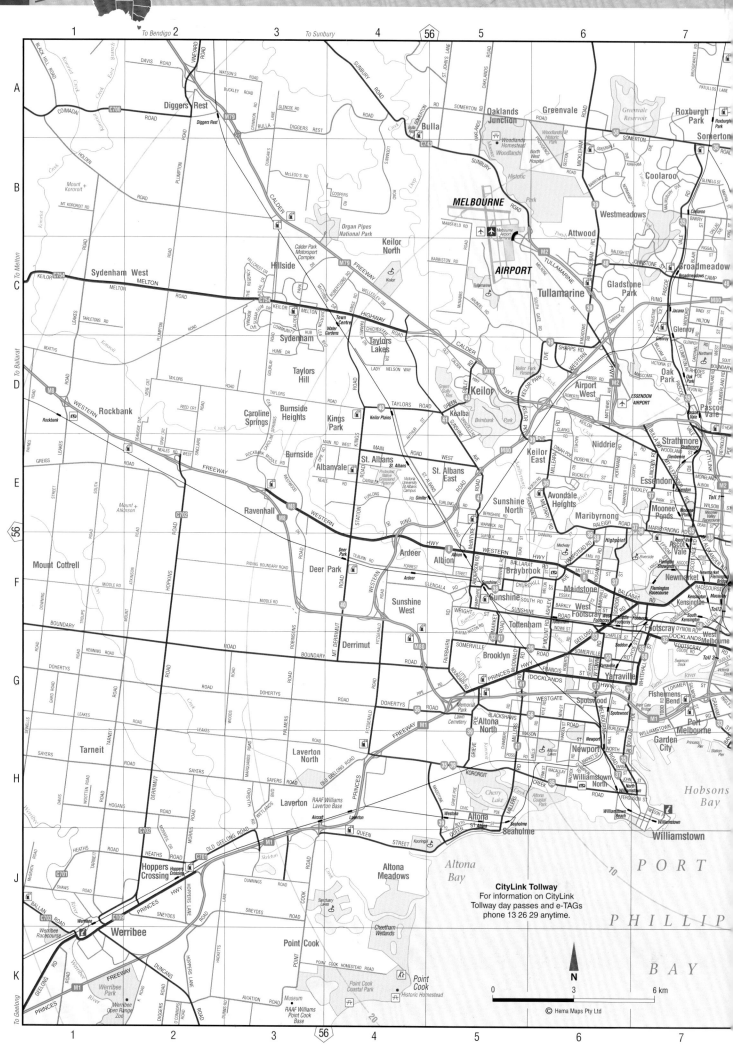

CityLink Tollway
For information on CityLink
Tollway day passes and e-TAGs
phone 13 26 29 anytime.

© Hema Maps Pty Ltd

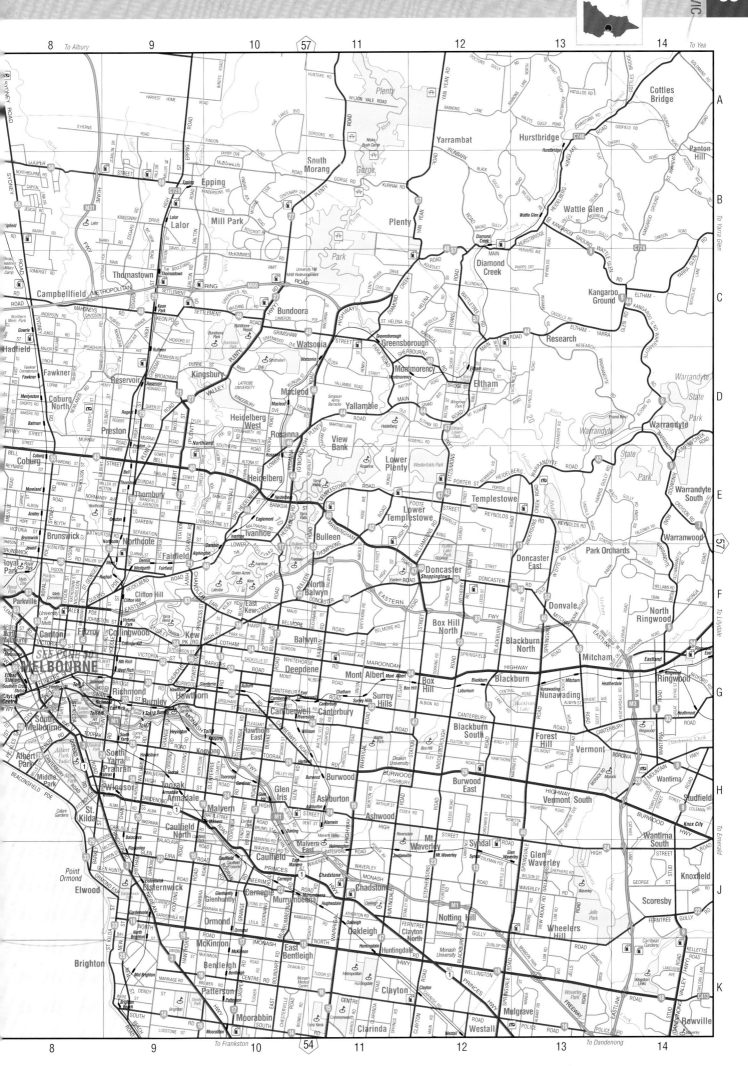

Map grid references (top)
1 2 3 53 4 5 To Melbourne 6 7 To Melbourne

To Melbourne

CityLink Tollway
For information on CityLink
Tollway day passes and e-TAGs
phone 13 26 29 anytime.

N

0   3   6 km

© Hema Maps Pty Ltd

10

20

30

40

PORT

PHILLIP

BAY

Ricketts Point

Beaumaris Bay

Daveys Bay

Half Moon Bay

Schnapper Point

56

57

Place names
Brighton
Hampton
Sandringham
Picnic Point
Black Rock
Beaumaris
Mentone
Mordialloc
Aspendale
Edithvale
Chelsea
Bonbeach
Carrum
Patterson Lakes
Seaford
Frankston
Moondah Beach
Mount Eliza
Mornington

Glenhuntly
Carnegie
Murrumbeena
Ormond
McKinnon
Bentleigh
East Bentleigh
Patterson
Moorabbin
Highett
Cheltenham
Cheltenham North
Heatherton
Kingston
Parkdale
Braeside

Oakleigh
Notting Hill
Wheelers Hill
Clayton North
Huntingdale
Clayton
Clarinda
Clayton South
Springvale
Westall
Mulgrave
Dandenong North
Noble Park
South Springvale
Dingley Village
Keysborough
Braeside Metropolitan Park
Bangholme
Chelsea Heights
Dandenong
Dandenong South
Carrum Downs
Skye
Frankston North
Langwarrin
Baxter

Monash University
Monash Medical Centre
Mordialloc Airport
Sandown Racecourse
Springvale Crematorium

To Rosebud
To Rosebud
To Hastings

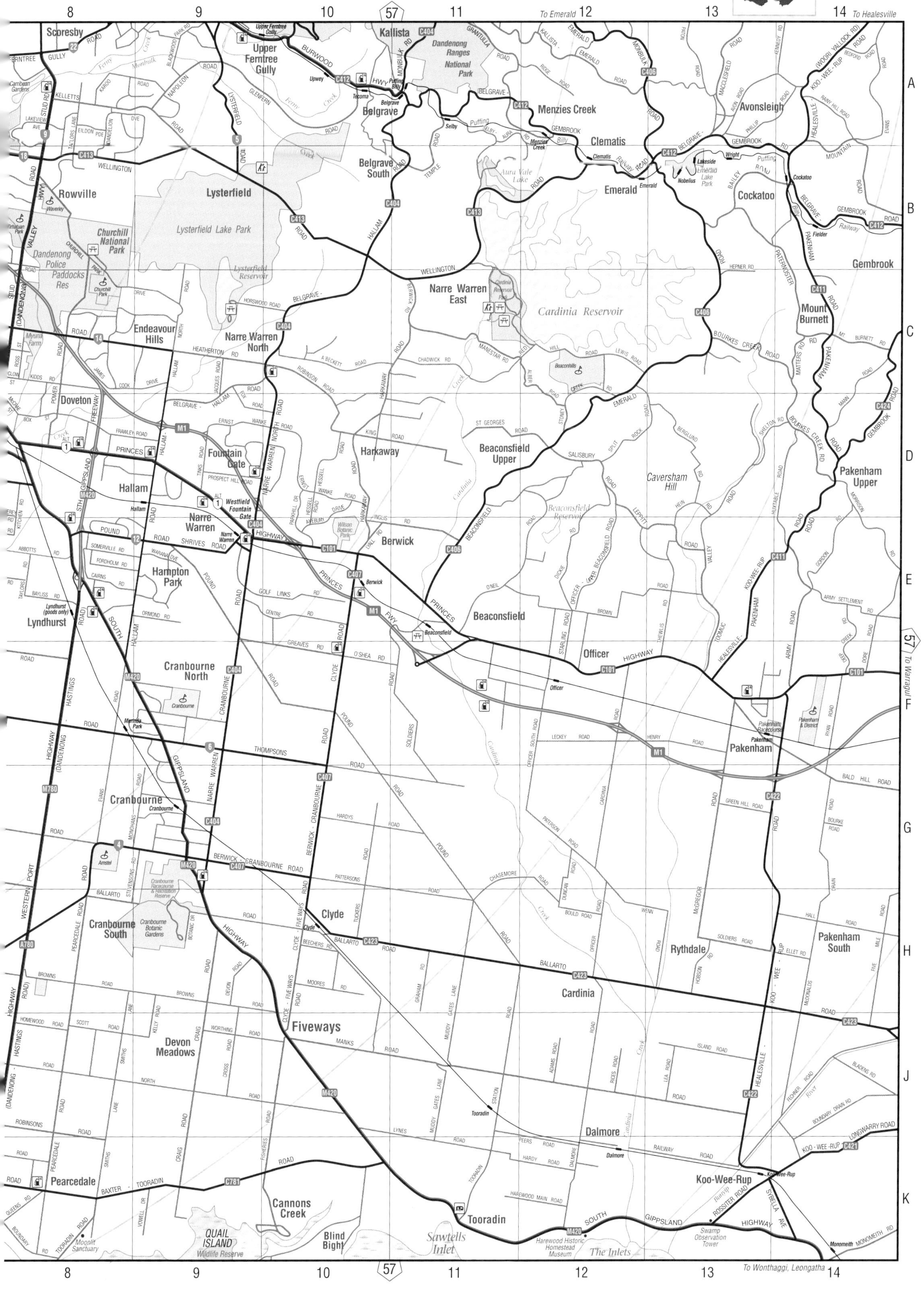

Grid references (top): 8 9 10 11 12 13 14 To Healesville
57 To Emerald To Emerald

Rows: A B C D E F G H J K

Place names and labels:

Scoresby
Ferntree Gully
Upper Ferntree Gully
Upper Ferntree Gully
Kallista
Dandenong Ranges National Park
Upwey
Tecoma
Belgrave
Belgrave South
Menzies Creek
Selby
Puffing Billy
Clematis
Emerald
Lakeside
Emerald Lake Park
Nobelius
Wright
Avonsleigh
Cockatoo
Carabean Gardens
Rowville
Lysterfield
Lysterfield Lake Park
Lysterfield Reservoir
Churchill National Park
Dandenong Police Paddocks Res
Myuna Farm
Narre Warren East
Cardinia Reservoir
Mount Burnett
Gembrook
Endeavour Hills
Narre Warren North
Harkaway
Beaconsfield Upper
Caversham Hill
Beaconsfield Reserve
Pakenham Upper
Doveton
Fountain Gate
Hallam
Westfield Fountain Gate
Narre Warren
Berwick
Beaconsfield
Officer
Pakenham
Hampton Park
Cranbourne North
Cranbourne
Merinda Park
Pakenham Racecourse
Pakenham & District
Lyndhurst
Lyndhurst (goods only)
Amstel
Cranbourne
Cranbourne South
Cranbourne Botanic Gardens
Cranbourne Racecourse & Recreation Reserve
Clyde
Rythdale
Pakenham South
Devon Meadows
Fiveways
Cardinia
Pearcedale
Moonlit Sanctuary
Cannons Creek
Tooradin
Dalmore
Koo-Wee-Rup
Quail Island Wildlife Reserve
Blind Bight
Sawtells Inlet
Tooradin
Harewood Historic Homestead Museum
Swamp Observation Tower
The Inlets
Monomeith

Road / route labels (selection):
M1, M420, M780, A780, C101, C404, C406, C407, C411, C412, C413, C422, C423, C424, C781, C413
Princes Highway, Princes Fwy
Gippsland Highway
South Gippsland Highway
Western Port Highway
Hastings Highway
Ballarto Road
Healesville - Koo-Wee-Rup Road
Koo-Wee-Rup Road

To Emerald
To Healesville
To Waragul
To Wonthaggi, Leongatha

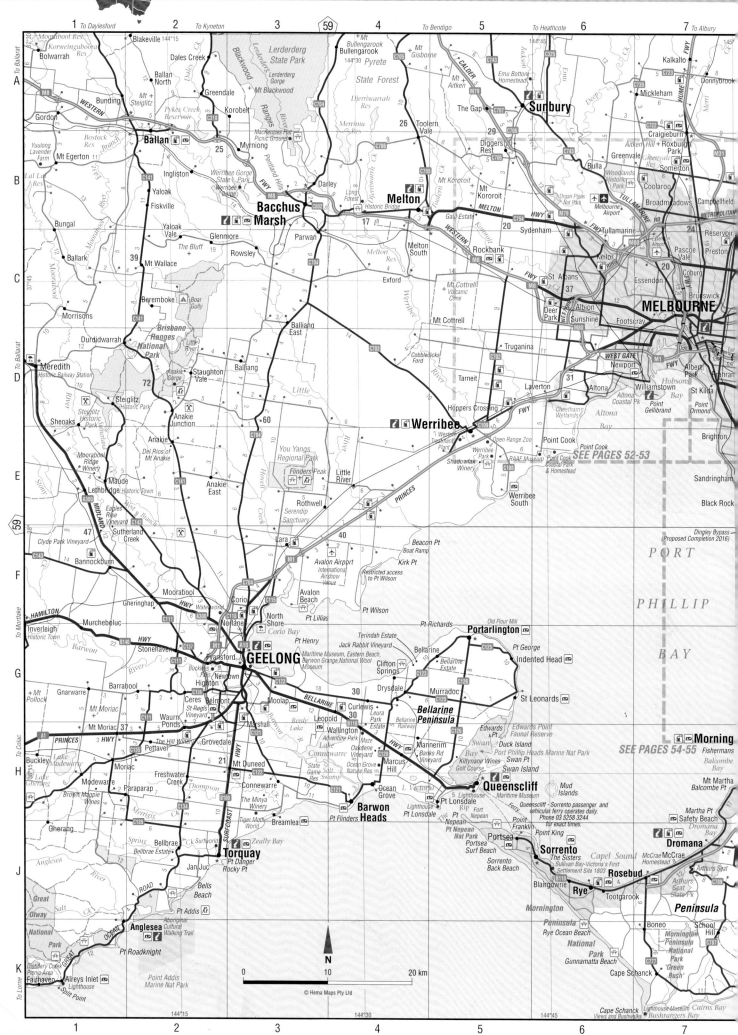

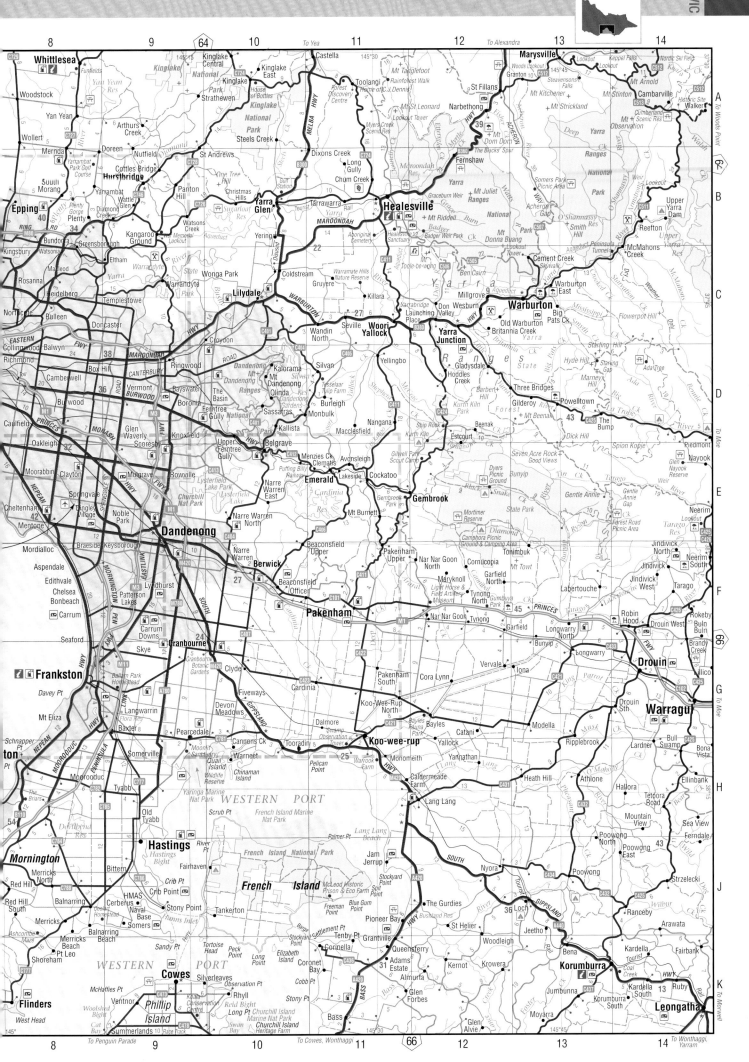

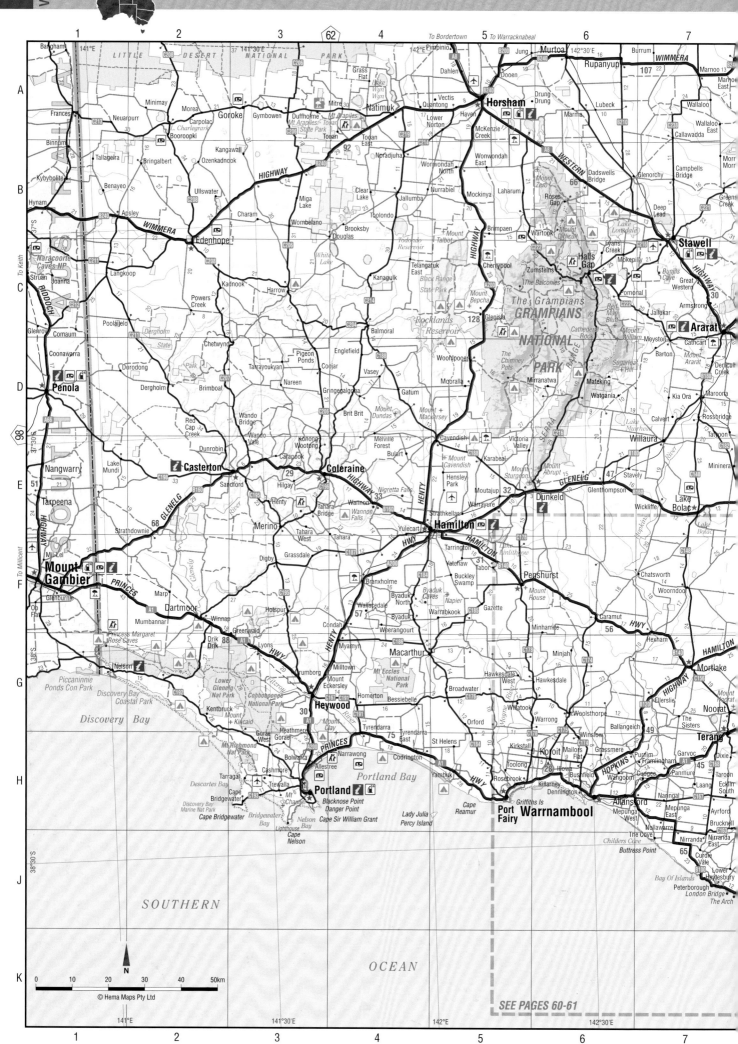

SEE PAGES 60-61

© Hema Maps Pty Ltd

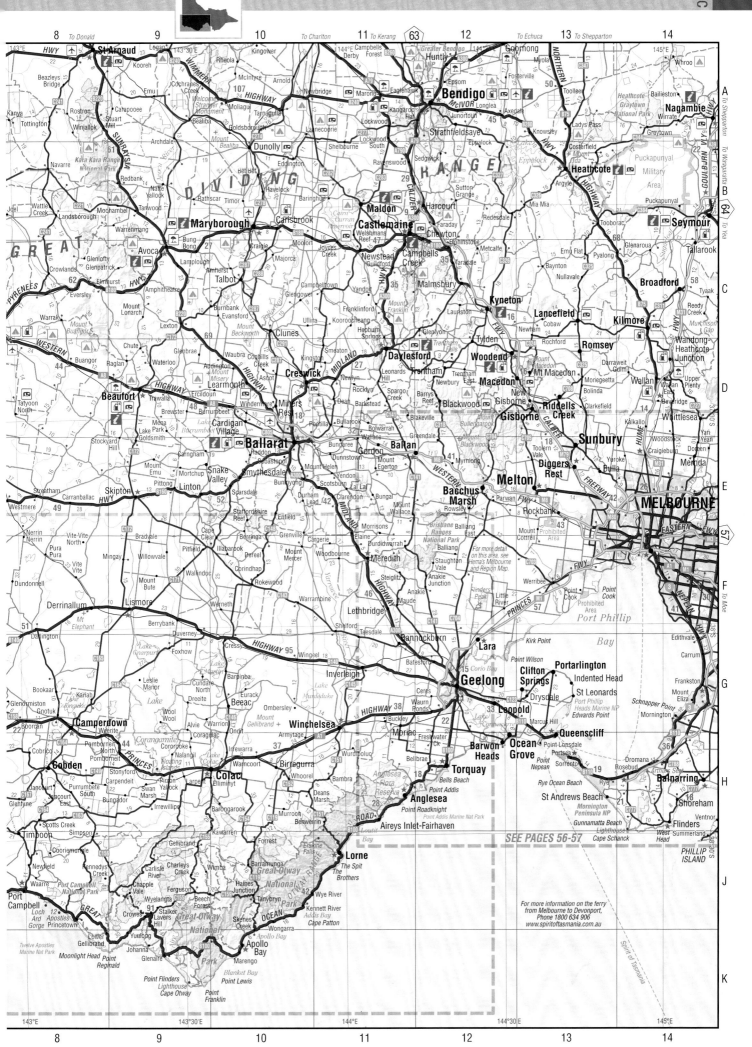

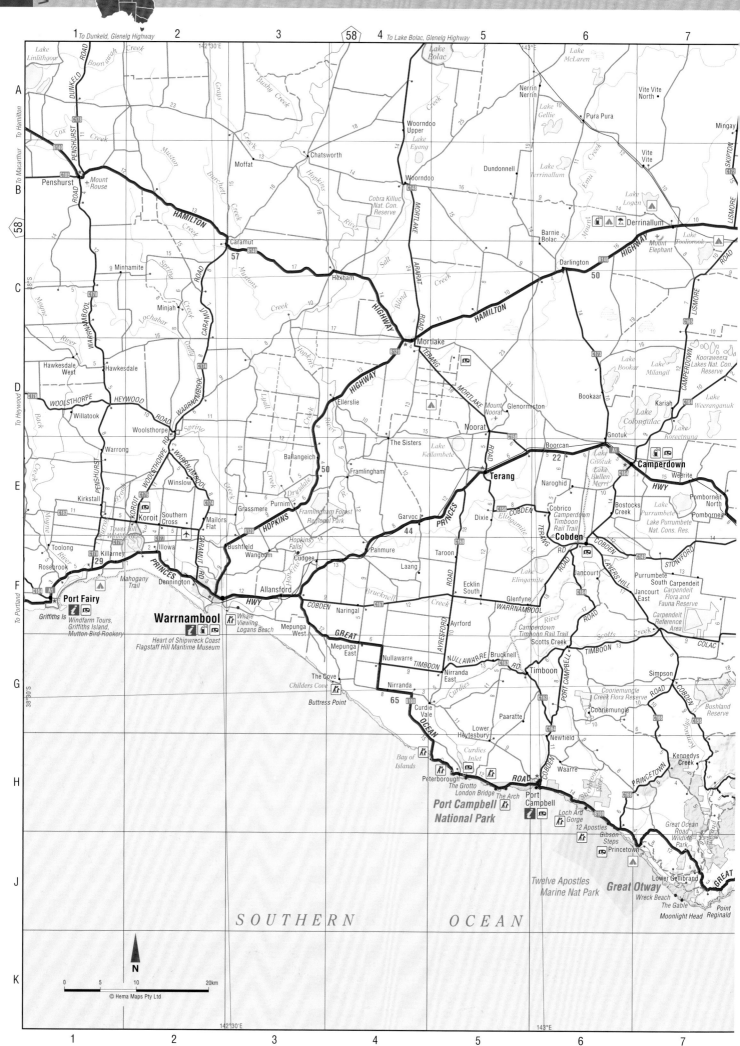

To Skipton · To Skipton · To Scarsdale, Ballarat · 59 · To Ballarat · To Ballarat · To Ballan · To Bacchus Marsh

8 9 10 11 12 13 14

143°30'E

A
Brisbane Ranges National Park
Mannibadar
Staffordshire Reef
Enfield State Park
Morrisons
Balliang
Balliang East
Bradvale
Berringa
Grenville
Cape Clear
Elaine
Durdidwarrah
Willowvale
Mount Mercer
Cargerie
Woodbourne
Stony Creek Reference Area
Staughton Vale
Pitfield
Illabarook
Dereel
Meredith
Reilly
ROKEWOOD
SKIPTON
BALLARAT
MIDLAND
GEELONG

B
Mount Bute
Wallinduc
Rokewood
Steiglitz Park
Steiglitz
Anakie Junction
Anakie
SCARSDALE
Wilgul
Werneth
Warrambine
Sheoaks
You Yangs Regional Park
Flinders Peak
LISMORE
Karinghi Chain

C
HAMILTON
Lismore
Berrybank
Lethbridge
Maude
Sutherland
BALLAN
Duverney
Cressy
Shelford
Teesdale
45
Bannockburn Recreation Reserve
Bannockburn
Lara
Corio
56
HIGHWAY
Foxhow
Lake Rosine
Wingeel
94
HAMILTON
Inverleigh Flora Reserve
Gheringhap
Batesford
Corio Bay
Lake Gnarpurt
Lake Weering
18
Lake Corangamite

D
Lake Martin
Barpinba
Cundare North
Eurack
Ombersley
Wildlife Reserve Lake Murdeduke
Inverleigh
PRINCES
Gnarwarre
Waurn Ponds
Geelong
Ceres
Grovedale
Bellarine Peninsula Rail Trail
Leslie Manor
Lake Cundare
Beeac
Mount Gellibrand
Moriac
38
Connewarre
Wildlife Reserve

E
Wool Wool
Warrion
Ondit
Winchelsea
HIGHWAY
Buckley
Freshwater Creek
22
Connewarre
Dreeite
Alvie
37
Wurdiboluc Res.
Wurdiboluc
Recreation Reserve
Lake Modewarre
Bellbrae
Breamlea
Coragulac
Cororooke
Irrewarra
Warncoort
Dinny Goonan Wines
Torquay
Jan Juc

F
46
Stonyford
Pirron Yallock
PRINCES
Elliminyt
Colac
Birregurra
Whoorel
Deans Marsh
Wensleydale
Anglesea Flora Reserve
17
Anglesea
Point Roadknight
Point Addis Marine Nat Park
Swan Marsh
Larpent
Lake Colac
COLAC
FORREST
Bambra
Blakes Estate Vineyard & Winery
Bells Beach
Point Addis
Bungador
Irrewillipe
Barongarook
Murroon
Gosling Creek Winery
28
Aireys Inlet-Fairhaven

G
Kawarren Regional Park
Kawarren
Old Beechy Rail Trail
Forrest
Benwerrin
Erskine Falls
Loutit Bay
SEE PAGES 56-57
Carlisle River
Carlisle State Park
Barramunga
Erskine Falls
Great Otway
Lorne
The Brothers
The Spit
Sheoak Falls

H
Mt MacKenzie
Crinoline Creek Flora and Fauna Res.
Charleys Creek
Wimba
Old Beechy Rail Trail
Haines Junction
Cumberland
Great Otway NP
Wye River
Chapple Vale
Ferguson
Beech Forest
Tanybryn
43
Kennett River
Addis Bay
Wyelangta
Otway Fly
Carisbrooke Falls
Stalker
Hopetoun Falls
Cape Patton

J
92
Crowes
Lavers Hill
Mariners Falls
Skenes Creek
Wongarra
Yuulong
Melba Gully
Great Otway
Apollo Bay
Apollo Bay Museum, Shell Museum, Glow Worm Tours
Johanna
OCEAN
NP
Marengo
ROAD

K
National Park
Stony Creek Reference Area
Blanket Bay
Point Flinders
Lighthouse
Cape Otway
Point Franklin
Point Lewis
TASMAN SEA

144°E
38°30'S
143°30'E 144°E

8 9 10 11 12 13 14

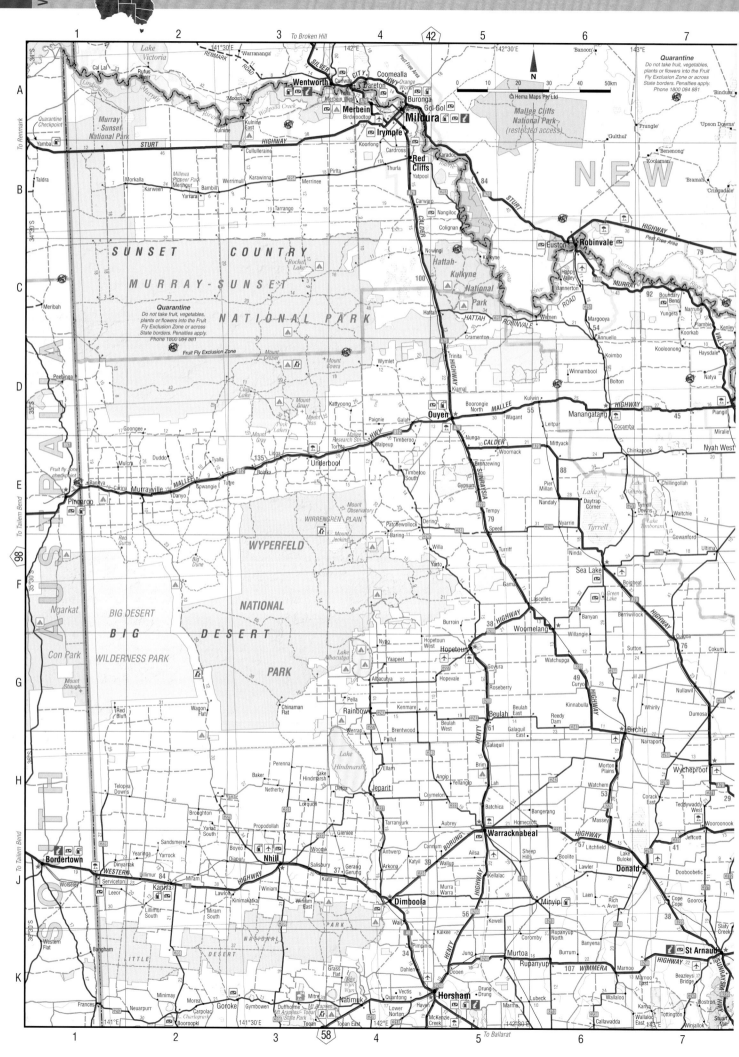

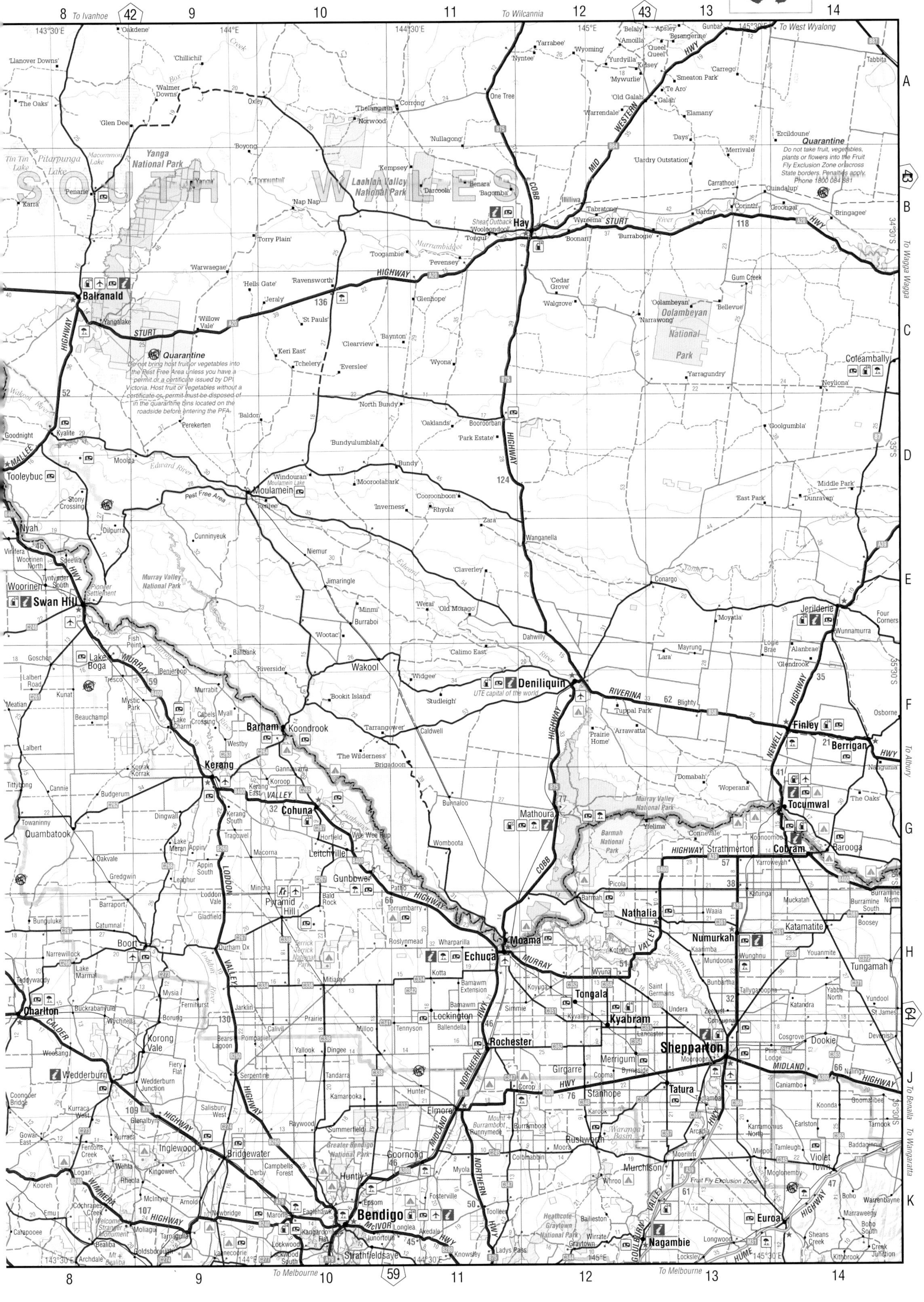

SOUTH WALES

MALLEE

Quarantine — Do not take fruit, vegetables, plants or flowers into the Fruit Fly Exclusion Zone or across State borders. Penalties apply. Phone 1800 084 881

Quarantine — Do not bring host fruit or vegetables into the Pest Free Area unless you have a permit or a certificate issued by DPI Victoria. Host fruit or vegetables without a certificate or permit must be disposed of in the quarantine bins located on the roadside before entering the PFA.

Balranald · Hay · Deniliquin (Ute capital of the world) · Moulamein · Tooleybuc · Swan Hill · Lake Boga · Barham · Koondrook · Kerang · Cohuna · Quambatook · Charlton · Wedderburn · Gunbower · Leitchville · Pyramid Hill · Echuca · Moama · Mathoura · Nathalia · Numurkah · Tocumwal · Cobram · Barooga · Strathmerton · Finley · Berrigan · Jerilderie · Coleambally · Tongala · Kyabram · Shepparton · Tatura · Rochester · Lockington · Rushworth · Murchison · Nagambie · Euroa · Violet Town · Bendigo · Huntly · Bridgewater · Inglewood · Tungamah · Katamatite

Yanga National Park · Lachlan Valley National Park · Oolambeyan National Park · Murray Valley National Park · Barmah National Park · Greater Bendigo National Park · Heathcote-Graytown National Park

Fruit Fly Exclusion Zone

To Ivanhoe · To Wilcannia · To West Wyalong · To Wagga Wagga · To Albury · To Benalla · To Wangaratta · To Melbourne

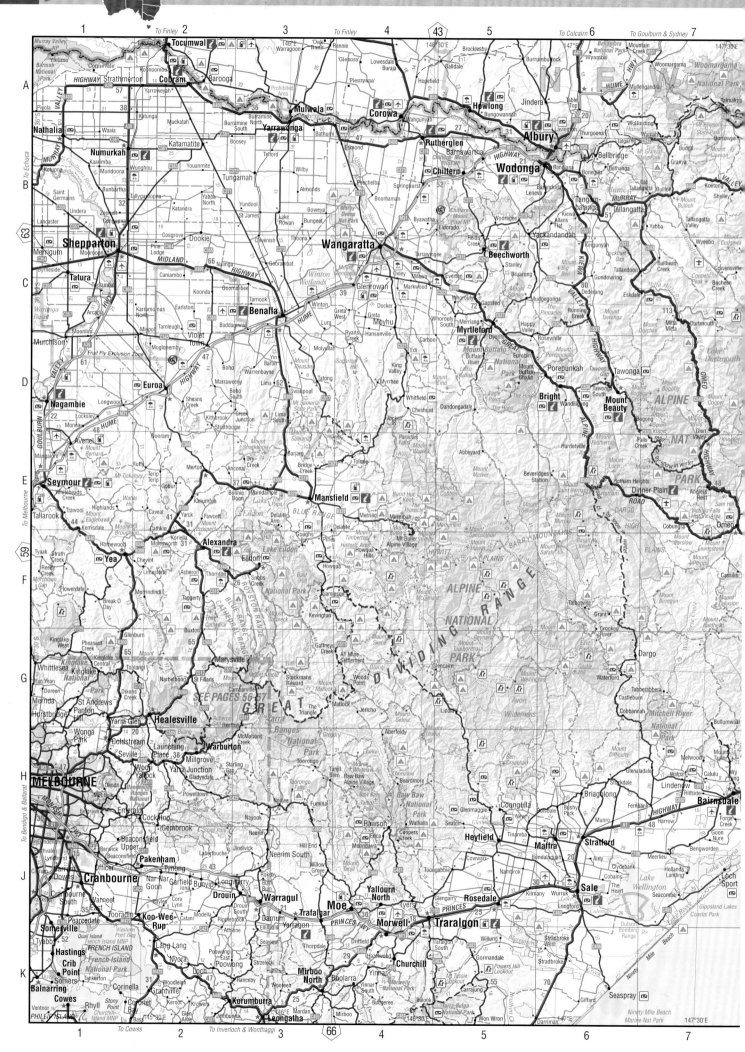

To Holbrook 8 | 9 | 10 To Tumut 44 | 11 To Canberra 12 | 13 To Braidwood 14

NEW SOUTH WALES

Tumbarumba
Mannus
Munderoo
Lankeys Creek
Ingellic
Walwa
'The Glen'
Ournie
Ikes Mountain
'Camoo'
Cabramurra
Mount Selwyn
NAMADGI NP
Jingera
Anembo
Jerangle
Strike-a-Light NP
Tallaganda National Park
Mongamula Mountain
DEUA NATIONAL PARK

Burrowa-Pine Mountain
Guys Forest
Cudgewa North
Tintaldra
Tooma
Adaminaby
Old Adaminaby
Yaouk NR
Mt Dowling NR
Bredbo
Peak View
Bodalla
Nerrigundah

KOSCIUSZKO NATIONAL PARK
Lake Eucumbene
Eucumbene
Middlingbank
51
Kybeyan
Chakola
Numeralla
Cooma
Bunyan
Countegany
Belowra

Corryong
Khancoban
Towong
Thowgla
Biggara
Thowgla Upper
Nariel
Lucyvale
Berringama
Cudgewa
Geehi
Guthega
Charlottes Pass
Perisher Village
Berridale
East Jindabyne
Jindabyne
Lakewood Estate
Dalgety
Rock Flat
Kydra
Cobargo
Quaama
Verona
Bermagui
Bermagui South

Nariel Creek
Wabba Wilderness Park
Willow Crossing
Nariel
Mount Kosciuszko 2229m
Charlottes Pass
Thredbo Village
Tom Groggin
Dead Horse Gap
Beloka
Paupong
Nimmitabel
Holts Flat
Brown Mountain
Bemboka
Bemboka Walls
Numbugga
65 Morans Crossing
Bega
Tarraganda
Kooraban National Park
Gulaga NP
Beauty Point
Koorraban
Wadbilliga National Park

ALPINE NATIONAL PARK
Sassafras Gap
Mount Sassafras
Mount Pinnibar
Paupong NR
Numbla Vale
Bungarby
Jincumbilly
Gumningrah
Bukalong
Bibbenluke
Ando
Cathcart
Candelo
Wolumla
53
Tura Beach
Katungal
Tathra
Mirimbula
Merimbula
Pambula
Pambula Beach
Haycock Point

The Pilot
Mount Hope
Byadbo Mountain
Willis
Ingebirah
Tingaringi
Tombong
Corrowong
Cambalong
Rocky Hall
Wyndham
Lochiel
Nethercote
Greigs Flat
Ben Boyd National Park

Mount Pendergast
Mount Cobberas
Mount Stradbroke
Mount Wombargo
DIVIDING
Delegate
Bendoc North
Craigie
Mila
Bendoc
Lower Bendoc
Pericoe
Towamba
Eden
Edrom
Boydtown
Kiah
Boyds Tower
Green Cape
Lighthouse
Disaster Bay

GREAT
Benambra
Hinnomunjie
Mount Tambo
Mount Shaw
Amboyne Crossing
Mount Tingaringy
Tubbut
Dellickabra
Bonang
Mount Delegate
Mount Bendoc
Nungatta
85
SOUTH EAST FOREST NATIONAL PARK
Burragate
Mount Imlay National Park
Timbillica
Wonboyn Lake
Bittangabee Bay
Lighthouse
Cape Howe

McMillans Lookout
Tongio
Tongio West
Swifts Creek
Doctors Flat
Brookville
Ensay North
Ensay
Ensay South
Stirling
Timbarra
Murrindal
Reedy Flat
Snowy River National Park
Mount Bowen
Mount Jersey
Errinundra National Park
Goongerah
Errinundra
Combienbar
Cooracombra National Park
Chandlers Creek
Wroxham
Wangarabell
Mount Buckle
Maramingo Hill
Genoa
109
Gipsy Point
Genoa Peak
Mallacoota
Gabo Island
Nadgee Nature Reserve
Newtons Beach
Mallacoota Lookout

Tambo Crossing
68
Buchan
Bachan Central
Buchan South
Mount Tara
Raymond Falls
Stringer Knob
Mount Pinnak
Mount Jack
Mount Kuark
Club Terrace
Lind National Park
Noorinbee
Noorinbee North
Alfred National Park
Princes Highway
Bastion Point
Cape Howe Nat Park
Little Rame Head

Mount Welcome
Deptford
Double Bridges
Clifton Creek
Sarsfield
Bruthen
Mossiface
Tambo Upper
Swan Reach
Nowa Nowa
Wairewa
Tostaree
59
Waygara
Orbost
Bete Bolong
Brodribb River
Newmerella
Tabbara
Cabbage Tree Creek
Bellbird Creek
Bemm River
Tonghi Creek
Cann River
Tamboon
Murrungowar
Rainforest Walk
Mount Everard
Croajingolong National Park
Sandpatch Point
Little Rame Head

Lucknow
Nicholson
Kalimna West
Metung
Paynesville
Eagle Point
Jones Bay
Lake King
Raymond Is
Lakes Entrance
Lake Tyers
Lake Tyers Beach
Marlo
Point Ricardo
Cape Conran
Pearl Point
Cape Conran Coastal Reserve
Sydenham Inlet
Tamboon Inlet
Point Hicks Lighthouse
Point Hicks Marine Nat Park
Petrel Point
Rame Head
Wingan Inlet

The Lakes National Park
Ninety Mile Beach

PRINCES HIGHWAY

SEA

TASMAN

N
0 10 20 30 40 50km

© Hema Maps Pty Ltd

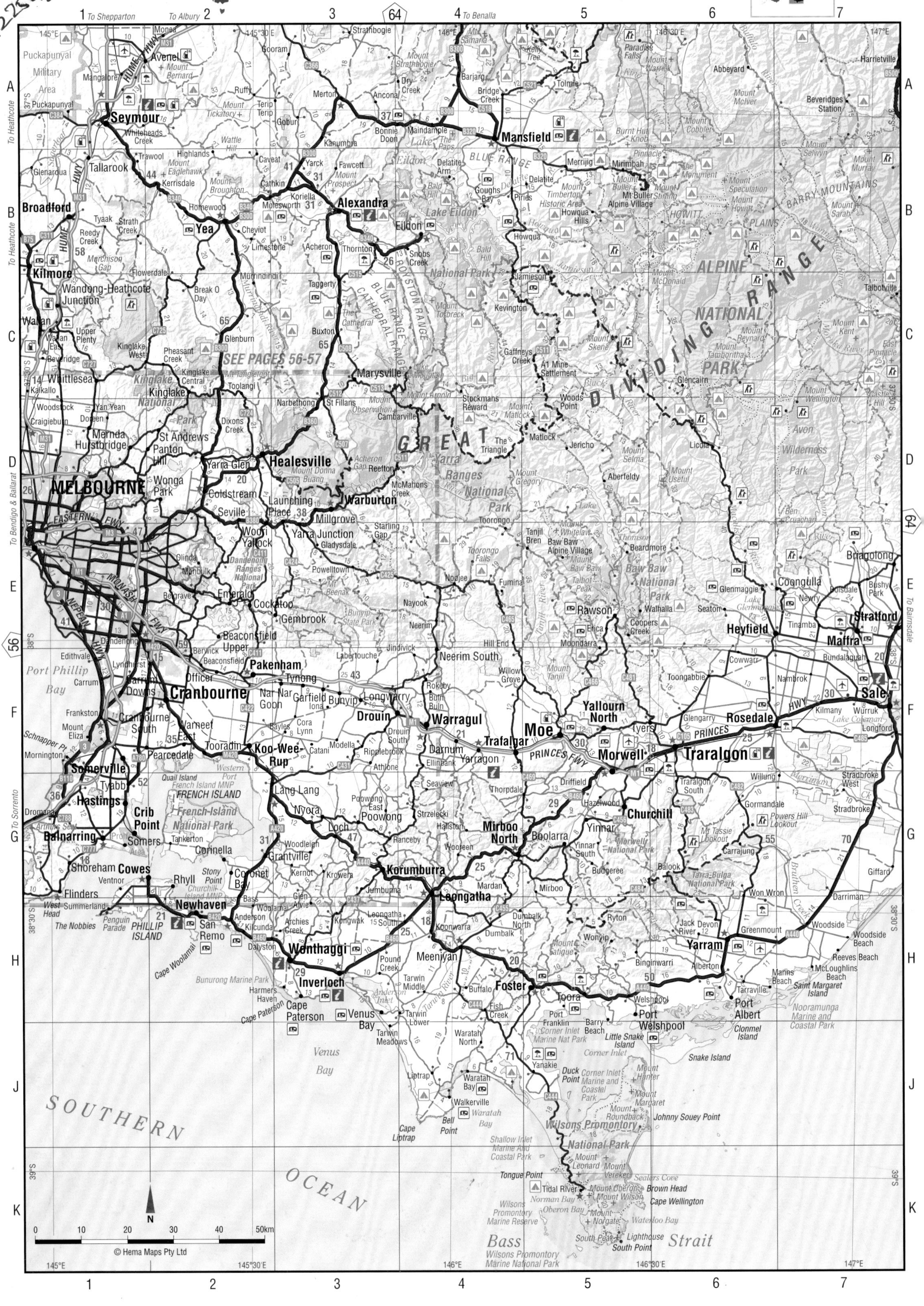

95225548

SEE PAGES 56-57

Map grid references: 1–7 (columns), A–K (rows)

Directional notes:
- To Shepparton
- To Albury
- To Benalla
- To Heathcote
- To Sorrento
- To Bendigo & Ballarat

Major places and labels:

Puckapunyal Military Area, Puckapunyal, Mangalore, Avenel, Mount Bernard, Seymour, Whiteheads Creek, Trawool, Glenaroua, Tallarook, Kerrisdale, Highlands, Mount Eaglehawk, Mount Broughton, Ruffy, Gooram, Merton, Ancona, Strathbogie, Dry Creek, Maindample, Barjarg, Bridge Creek, Mount Samaria, Tolmie, Kelly Tree, Paradise Falls, Abbeyard, Harrietville, Mount McIver, Beveridges Station, Mount Cobbler, Mount Selwyn, Mount Murray

Broadford, Strath Creek, Tyaak, Reedy Creek, Merchison Gap, Kilmore, Wandong-Heathcote Junction, Wallan, Yea, Cheviot, Homewood, Molesworth, Yarck, Cathkin, Caveat, Terip Terip, Gobur, Karumba, Bonnie Doon, Delatite Arm, Bald Hill, Goughs Bay, Merrijig, Mirimbah, Pinnacle, Mt Buller, Alpine Village, Mount Stirling, Mount Howitt, Mansfield, Delatite, Historic Area, Howqua, Howqua Hills, Mount Speculation, Mount Sarah, Barry Mountains, Howitt Plains

Kilmore, Upper Plenty, Beveridge, Whittlesea, Kinglake West, Glenburn, Limestone, Acheron, Thornton, Snobs Creek, Eildon, Lake Eildon, National Park, Jamieson, Howqua, Mount Torbreck, Kevington, Mount McDonald, Alpine National Park, Mount Kent, East Pinnacle, Castle Hill

Kalkallo, Woodstock, Doreen, Mernda, Hurstbridge, St Andrews, Panton Hill, Kinglake, Kinglake Central, National Park, Toolangi, Narbethong, St Fillans, Marysville, Cambarville, Mount Observation, Stockmans Reward, Woods Point, A1 Mine Settlement, Gaffneys Creek, Mount Skene, Mount Bennison, Glencairn, Aberfeldy, Mount Wellington, Avon Wilderness Park, Mount Useful

MELBOURNE, Yarra Glen, Healesville, Coldstream, Seville, Launching Place, Millgrove, Warburton, Woori Yallock, Yarra Junction, Gladysdale, Powelltown, Reefton, McMahons Creek, Mount Donna Buang, Great Dividing Range, Yarra Ranges National Park, The Triangle, Matlock, Jericho, Mount Selma, Licola, Ben Cruachan, Briagolong

Olinda, Monbulk, Belgrave, Emerald, Cockatoo, Gembrook, Nayook, Neerim, Toorongo, Noojee, Toorongo Falls, Tanjil Bren, Baw Baw Alpine Village, Mount Baw Baw, Baw Baw National Park, Talbot Peak, Rawson, Erica, Walhalla, Seaton, Coopers Creek, Glenmaggie, Lake Glenmaggie, Newry, Boisdale, Bushy Park, Stratford, Coongulla

Dandenong, Beaconsfield Upper, Berwick, Labertouche, Jindivick, Neerim South, Willow Grove, Hill End, Moondarra, Toongabbie, Cowwarr, Heyfield, Maffra, Tinamba, Bundalaguah

Frankston, Carrum, Garfield Downs, Officer, Pakenham, Tynong, Longwarry, Rokeby, Bunyip, Drouin, Warragul, Yallourn North, Tyers, Glengarry, Traralgon, Rosedale, Sale, Kilmany, Wurruk, Longford, Lake Coleman

Mornington, Mount Eliza, Schnapper Pt, Cranbourne South, Clyde, Warneet, Tooradin, Koo-Wee-Rup, Nar Nar Goon, Garfield, Iona, Cora Lynn, Bayles, Catani, Modella, Ripplebrook, Athlone, Darnum, Ellinbank, Yarragon, Trafalgar, Moe, Morwell, Driffield, Hazelwood, Thorpdale, Traralgon South, Willung, Gormandale, Stradbroke West, Stradbroke

Somerville, Tyabb, Hastings, Crib Point, Somers, Tankerton, Corinella, Quail Island, French Island, French Island National Park, Lang Lang, Nyora, Loch, Poowong, Poowong East, Strzelecki, Hallston, Ranceby, Woorarra, Mirboo North, Yinnar, Boolarra, Budgeree, Churchill, Yinnar South, Morwell National Park, Mt Tassie Lookout, Powers Hill Lookout, Carrajung, Balook, Tarra-Bulga National Park

Balnarring, Shoreham, Cowes, Rhyll, Ventnor, Newhaven, San Remo, Dalyston, Wonthaggi, Inverloch, Anderson, Kilcunda, Archies Creek, Woolamai, Glen Alvie, Bass, Kernot, Krowera, Jumbunna, Kongwak, Leongatha South, Korumburra, Woodleigh, Grantville, Coronet Bay, Stony Point, Churchill Island, Phillip Island, Penguin Parade, The Nobbies, West Summerland Head, Cape Woolamai

Flinders, Arthurs Seat, Dromana, Blairgowrie, Cape Paterson, Venus Bay, Harmers Haven, Bunurong Marine Park, Anderson Inlet, Tarwin Lower, Tarwin Meadows, Waratah North, Liptrap, Walkerville, Waratah Bay, Cape Liptrap, Bell Point, Leongatha, Koonwarra, Dumbalk North, Dumbalk, Meeniyan, Buffalo, Fish Creek, Foster, Toora, Port Franklin, Corner Inlet Marine National Park, Barry Beach, Little Snake Island, Snake Island, Welshpool, Port Welshpool, Clonmel Island, Binginwarri, Wonyip, Ryton, Alberton, Yarram, Devon, Jack River, Greenmount, Won Wron, Giffard, Woodside, Woodside Beach, Reeves Beach, Manns Beach, McLoughlins Beach, Saint Margaret Island, Darriman, Tarraville, Port Albert, Nooramunga Marine and Coastal Park

Wilsons Promontory National Park, Corner Inlet Marine and Coastal Park, Duck Point, Yanakie, Mount Hunter, Mount Margaret, Mount Roundback, Johnny Souey Point, Shallow Inlet Marine and Coastal Park, Tongue Point, Mount Leonard, Sealers Cove, Tidal River, Norman Bay, Mount Oberon, Brown Head, Cape Wellington, Mount Wilson, Oberon Bay, Mount Norgate, Waterloo Bay, Wilsons Promontory Marine Reserve, South Peak, Lighthouse, South Point

SOUTHERN OCEAN, Port Phillip Bay, Venus Bay, Bass Strait

Scale: 0 10 20 30 40 50km

N

© Hema Maps Pty Ltd

WINEGLASS BAY, FREYCINET NATIONAL PARK (69 B7) PHOTO: ROB BOEGHEIM

key map

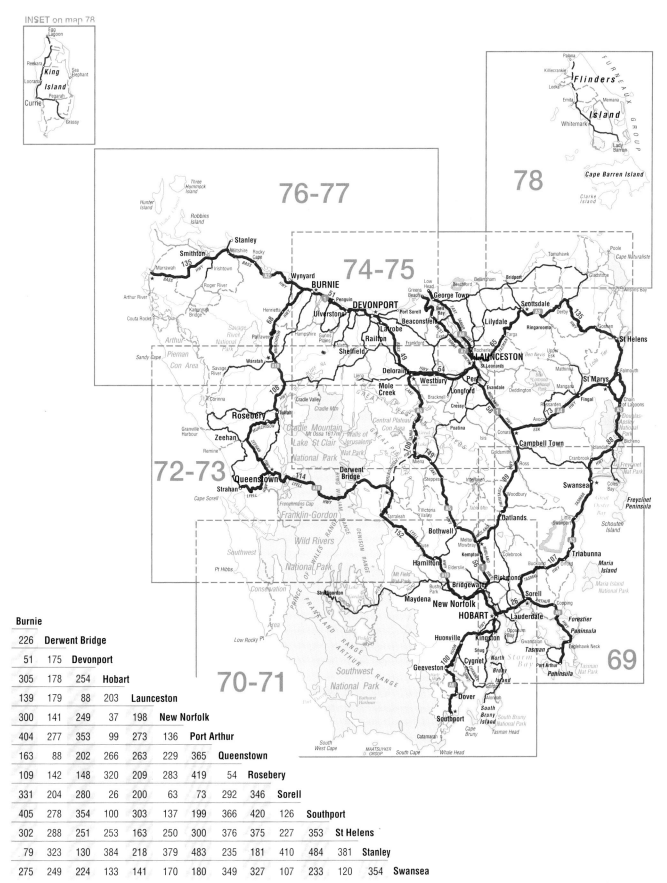

Burnie												
226	Derwent Bridge											
51	175	Devonport										
305	178	254	Hobart									
139	179	88	203	Launceston								
300	141	249	37	198	New Norfolk							
404	277	353	99	273	136	Port Arthur						
163	88	202	266	263	229	365	Queenstown					
109	142	148	320	209	283	419	54	Rosebery				
331	204	280	26	200	63	73	292	346	Sorell			
405	278	354	100	303	137	199	366	420	126	Southport		
302	288	251	253	163	250	300	376	375	227	353	St Helens	
79	323	130	384	218	379	483	235	181	410	484	381	Stanley
275	249	224	133	141	170	180	349	327	107	233	120	354	Swansea

Distances are shown in kilometres and follow the most direct major sealed route where possible.

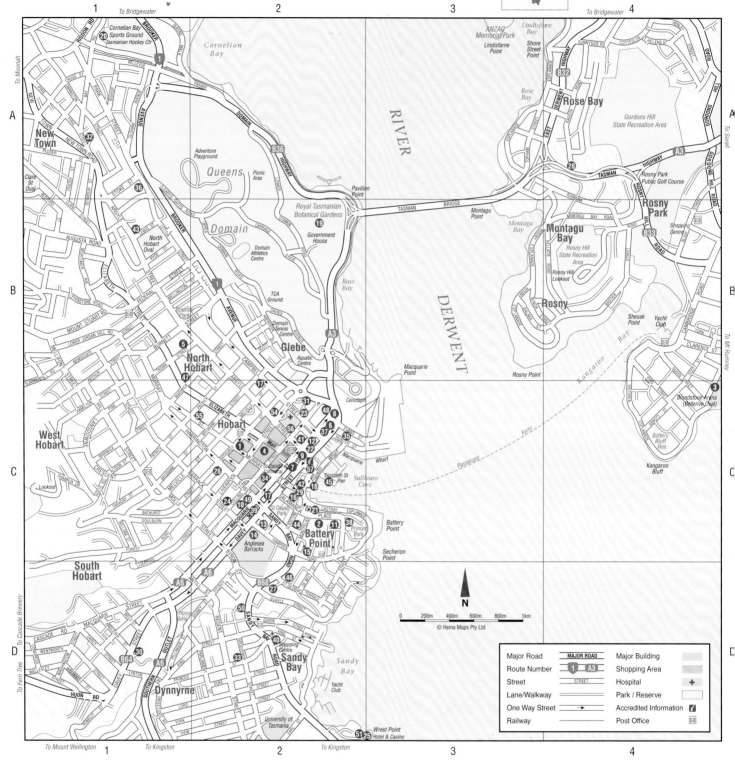

Places of Interest

1. Allport Library & Museum of Fine Arts C2
2. Battery Point Area C2
3. Blundstone Arena C4
4. Cat & Fiddle Arcade C2
5. Designed Objects Tasmania B1
6. Federation Concert Hall C2
7. Franklin Square C2
8. Gasworks Cellar Door C2
9. Hobart Town Hall C2
10. International Wall of Friendship C2
11. Kelly Steps C2
12. Maritime Museum of Tasmania C2
13. Markree House Museum & Gardens C2
14. Military Museum of Tasmania C2
15. Narryna Heritage Museum C2
16. Parliament House C2
17. Penitentiary Chapel Historic Site C2
18. Peppermint Bay Cruises C2
19. Royal Tasmanian Botanical Gardens B2
20. Runnymede A1
21. Salamanca Market (Saturday) C2
22. Tasmanian Museum & Art Gallery C2
23. Theatre Royal C2
24. Village Cinemas C2
25. Wrest Point Casino D2

Accommodation

26. Best Western Hobart C2
27. Blue Hills Motel D2
28. City View Motel A4
29. Customs House Waterfront Hotel C2
30. Davey Place Holiday Town Houses D1
31. Fountainside Hotel C2
32. Graham Court Apartments A1
33. Grosvenor Court Apartments D2
34. Hadleys Hotel C2
35. Henry Jones Art Hotel C2
36. Hobart Tower Motel A1
37. Hotel Grand Chancellor C2
38. Lenna of Hobart C2
39. Macquarie Manor C2
40. Mayfair Plaza Motel D2
41. Montgomery's Hotel Hobart C2
42. Quest Waterfront C2
43. Rydges Hobart B1
44. Salamanca Inn C2
45. Somerset on the Pier C2
46. St Ives Motel Apartments D2
47. The Lodge on Elizabeth B1
48. The Old Woolstore C2
49. Travelodge Hobart C2
50. Woolmers Inn D2
51. Wrest Point Hotel Casino D2

Services

54. Police Headquarters C2
55. Post Office C2,D2
55. RACT C2
56. Royal Hobart Hospital C2
57. Tasmanian Visitor Information Centre C2

Grid references (top): 1 2 3 4 5 6 7

To Launceston, Campbell Town · To St Marys

A
Great Western Tiers Cons Area · Isis Hills · Goldsmith · York Lagoons · Cygnet River 148° · Waters Meeting · Apslawn Forest Reserve · Apslawn · Wineries · Llandaff · Cape Lodi · Courland Bay · Butlers Point · FREYCINET NATIONAL PARK
Macquarie Tier · Macquarie River · HIGHWAY · Gilbert Dick Hills · Meetus Falls · Wye River State Reserve · Moulting Lagoon Game Res · 42°

B
Lake Sorell · Knobby Ridge · Tunbridge Tier Conservation Area · Tunbridge · Woodbury · Pringle Hills · The Peppermints · Nicholsons Tier · Big Blue Tier · Lake Leake · 71 · Cranbrook · Lost Falls Forest Reserve · Eastern Tiers Forest Reserve · Waterloo Pt · Point Bagot · Swansea · East Coast Heritage Museum · Kate's Berry Farm & Winery · Hepburn Point · Coles Bay · Coles Bay Conservation Area · The Nuggets · Cape Tourville · Swanwick · Friendly Beaches · Friendly Point
Ross · Tasmanian Wool Centre · Mona Vale · Agyle Plains · Grange Hills · Moulting Lagoon
42°30'

C
Dogs Head Tier · Wild Pig Tier · Lake Crescent · Woodbury · Antill Ponds · Black Tier · Faddens Tier · Conservation Area · Colonels Hills · Tooms Lake · Diamond Tier · Nature Reserve · Buxton River Forest Reserve · Spiky Bridge · Webber Point · Shelly Point · Mayfield Bay · Weatherhead Point · Buxton Point · Boags Point · Great Oyster Bay · Slaughterhouse Bay · Schouten · The Hazards · Fleurieu Point · Refuge Is · Wineglass Bay · Cape Forestier · Promise Bay · Mt Freycinet · Gates Bluff · Freycinet Peninsula · Baldys Bluff · Cape Degerando · Schouten Island · Cape Baudin · Cham Locker Bay · Cape Sonnerat
Oatlands · Callington Mill · Lake Dulverton · York Plains · Pawtella · Lemont · Nala · Andover · 50 · Seaford Point · 77 · 28

D
Lower Marshes · Spring Hill · Jericho · Stonor · Mt Seymour · Baden · Whitefoord · Stonehenge · Buckland Military Prohibited Area · Pig Tier · Little Swanport · Little Swanport Museum · Pontypool · Ravensdale · Point Bailly · Grindstone Point · Middle Bluff · Île Des Phoques · The beautiful beach of **Wineglass Bay** in Freycinet National Park is one of the state's most recognised locations. The park offers superb scenery in which go to hiking, camping, boating and rock climbing, and birdlife and wildflowers are abundant. The Coles Bay harbour is picture-postcard material when the Hazards glow pink in the late-afternoon sun.
Parattah · Tiberias · Lake Tiberias Game Reserve · Rhyndaston · Tunnack · Woodsdale · 42°30'

E
Kempton · Quoin Mountain · Springhill Bottom · Dysart · Native Corners · Colebrook · Levendale · Gravelly Ridge Cons Area · Prosser · Discus Hills · Ryton Hills · Prosser Bay · Shelly Beach · Spring Beach · Orford · Double Creek · Lords Bluff · Louisville · Cape Bougainville · Pt Home LO Lighthouse · Marine Res · Île Du Nord · Cape Boullanger · Darlington ruins · Fossil Bay · Triabunna · MIDLAND · TASMAN HWY
42°30'

F
Black Brush · Brighton · Bagdad · Mangalore · Pontville · Campania · Rekuna · Enfield · Zoodoo Wildlife Park · Historic Town · Runnymede · Buckland · Tasmanian Bushland Garden · Mt Morrison FR · Nelsons Tier · Nugent · Three Thumbs State Reserve · Rheban · Spinning Gum Conservation Area · Booming Bay · Mount Maria · Maria Island · Bishop and Clerk · Maria Island Great Walk · MARIA ISLAND NATIONAL PARK · Mistaken Cape · Cape Des Tombeaux · Point Mauge · Riedle Bay · Shoal Bay · Oyster Bay
Rogerville Wildlife Sanctuary · Tea Tree · Bonorong Wildlife Park · Richmond · Orielton · Pawleena · Kellevie · Woodvine NR · Marion Bay · 57

G
Claremont · Berriedale · Glenlusk · Glenorchy · MONA · Collinsvale · Bridgewater · Gagebrook · Old Beach · Grasstree Hill · Dulcot · Risdon Vale · Cambridge · Midway Point · Sorell · Lewisham · Penna · Forcett · Copping museum · Bream Creek · Marion Bay Lookout · Point Du Ressac · Cape Peron · Hellfire Bluff · Cape Bernier Nat Res · Barren Head · Cape Maurouard · **Maria Island** has a stunning coastline of tall cliffs and pristine beaches, lots of wildlife, and some interesting historic buildings at the former penitentiary in Darlington. The Painted Cliffs, a string of naturally sculpted sandstone walls with surreal colour patterns, are at the south end of Hopground Beach.
Otago · Risdon · Lindisfarne · Wineries · 26 · ARTHUR · Dodges Ferry · Carlton · Connellys Marsh · Dunalley · Bangor Point · Long Spit · Cape Paul Lamanon · Visscher Island · Cape Frederick Hendrick · Kelly Islands

H
Fern Tree · Mt Wellington Lookout · Cascade Brewery · HOBART · Sandy Bay · Bellerive · Howrah · Rokeby · Lauderdale · Mays Point · Sandford · Cremorne · Pipe Clay Head · Seven Mile Beach · Park Beach · Primrose Sands · Primrose Pt · Frederick Henry Bay · Lime Bay State Res · Sloping Island · Dunalley Bay · Murdunna · Norfolk Bay · Coal Mines Historic Site · Humper Bluff · **Forestier** · High Yellow Bluff · **Peninsula** · Cape Surville · Deep Glen Bluff · Macgregor Peak · Yellow Bluff Ck Forest Reserve · 73 · HUON · Neika · Leslie Vale · Taroona · Shot Tower · Gellibrand Point

J
Longley · Ridgeway · Kingston · Blackmans Bay · Opossum Bay · South Arm · Cape Direction · Iron Pot · Betsey Is · Cape Contrariety · Clifton Beach · Saltwater River · Premaydena · Koonya · Taranna · Nubeena · Oakwood · **Tasman Peninsula** · Thumbs Point · Eaglehawk Neck · Officers Quarters & Dog Line · Tasman Blowhole · Tasman Arch · Devils Kitchen · Waterfall Bay · O'Hara Bluff · Hippolyte Rocks · Australian Antarctic Division · Margate · Snug · Electrona · Coningham · Killora · Bull Bay · Outer North Head · Roaring Beach Bay · 43° · The Tasman Peninsula offers phenomenal coastal scenery with towering dolerite cliffs and pinnacles. No visit to Tasmania is complete without a trip to the former convict settlement at Port Arthur – Australia's most famous convict settlement.

K
Woodbridge · Kettering · Oyster Cove · Barnes Bay · Yellow Bluff · North Bruny · Flowerpot · Middleton · Gordon · Birchs Bay · Great Bay · Variety Bay · Variety Point · **Bruny Island** · Storm Bay · Two Island Bay · Curio Bay · White Beach · Wedge Is · Wedge Bay · Highcroft · Stormlea · Palmers Lookout · **Port Arthur** · Convict Ruins · Mt Raoul · Maingon Bay · Maingon Blowhole · Black Head · Cape Pillar · Cape Raoul · Tasman Island · Tasman Island Lighthouse · 148° · **TASMAN NATIONAL PARK** · Munro Bight · Cape Hauy · Fortescue Bay · D'Entrecasteaux Channel · Isthmus Bay · Cape Queen Elizabeth · 147°30' · 148°30'

N · 0 10 20km · © Hema Maps Pty Ltd

SEE PAGE 68

To Derwent Bridge — To Devonport, Launceston — To Oatlands, Launceston — 73 — 69

HOBART

Major towns and localities:
Bothwell, Kempton, Hamilton, Ouse, Strickland, Black Bobs, Wayatinah, Osterley, Lower Marshes, Parattah, Jericho, Stonor, Mt Seymour, Baden, Whitefoord, Stonehenge, Woodsdale, Tunnack, Levendale, Rhyndaston, Colebrook, Runnymede, Campania, Richmond, Orielton, Pawleena, Sorell, Midway Point, Dodges Ferry, Seven Mile Beach, Park Beach, Carlton, Lauderdale, Cremorne, Clifton Beach, Cambridge, Bellerive, Howrah, Rokeby, Kingston, Blackmans Bay, Margate, Snug, Kettering, Woodbridge, Birchs Bay, Middleton, Gordon, Cygnet, Geeveston, Dover, Southport, Hastings, Franklin, Huonville, Ranelagh, New Norfolk, Maydena, Westerway, Gretna, Bushy Park, Plenty, Hayes, Brighton, Pontville, Bridgewater, Old Beach, Claremont, Glenorchy, Collinsvale, Berriedale, Granton.

MOUNT FIELD NATIONAL PARK
Mt Field National Park is one of the most popular and heavily visited parks in Tasmania. Its biggest draw is Russell Falls, and in winter there's occasional skiing up on the alpine plateau.

SOUTH BRUNY NATIONAL PARK — Bruny Island, Adventure Bay, Alonnah, Lunawanna, Cloudy Bay, Cape Bruny, Cape Bruny Historic Lighthouse, Fluted Cape, Captain Cook Monument, Cookville, Cape Connella, South Bruny.

HARTZ MTNS NATIONAL PARK — Hartz Peak, Federation Peak, Lake Picton, Lake Riveaux.

Storm Bay — Frederick Henry Bay — D'Entrecasteaux Channel — Huon River — Derwent River

Mt Wellington Lookout, Cascade Brewery, MONA, Taroona, Shot Tower, Australian Antarctic Division, Gellibrand Point, Opossum Bay, South Arm, Iron Pot, Betsey Is, North Bruny, Trumpeter Bay, Variety Bay, Great Bay, Neck Beach, Simpsons Bay, Isthmus Bay, Adventure Bay, Mangana Bluff.

TASMAN SEA

South East Cape — The South East Cape is the southern most point of mainland Tasmania.

Cockle Creek, Catamaran, Recherche Bay, Whale Sculptures, Gordon, Southport Lagoon, Ida Bay, Lune River, Moonlight Flats, Moores Garden, Precipitous Bluff, South Cape, Whale Head, Soldier Bluff, Shoemaker Point.

MAATSUYKER GROUP — Flat Top Island, Round Top Island, Louisa Island, De Witt Island, Maatsuyker Island.

Lake Daphne, Wylds Craig, Vale of Rasselas, Gordon Range, Mount Dawson 1050, Mount Wright 1108, Mount Anne, Eve Peak 1358, Mt Eliza 1289, Lake Judd, Lake Timk, Lonely Tarns, Mount Picton, Mount Mueller 1245, Snowy Range, Tiger Range, Weld Ridge, Picton Range, Ironbound Range, New River Lagoon, Mount La Perouse 1161, Adamsons Peak 1226, Mesa 1012, Gibraltar, Dividing Valley.

SEE PAGE 69

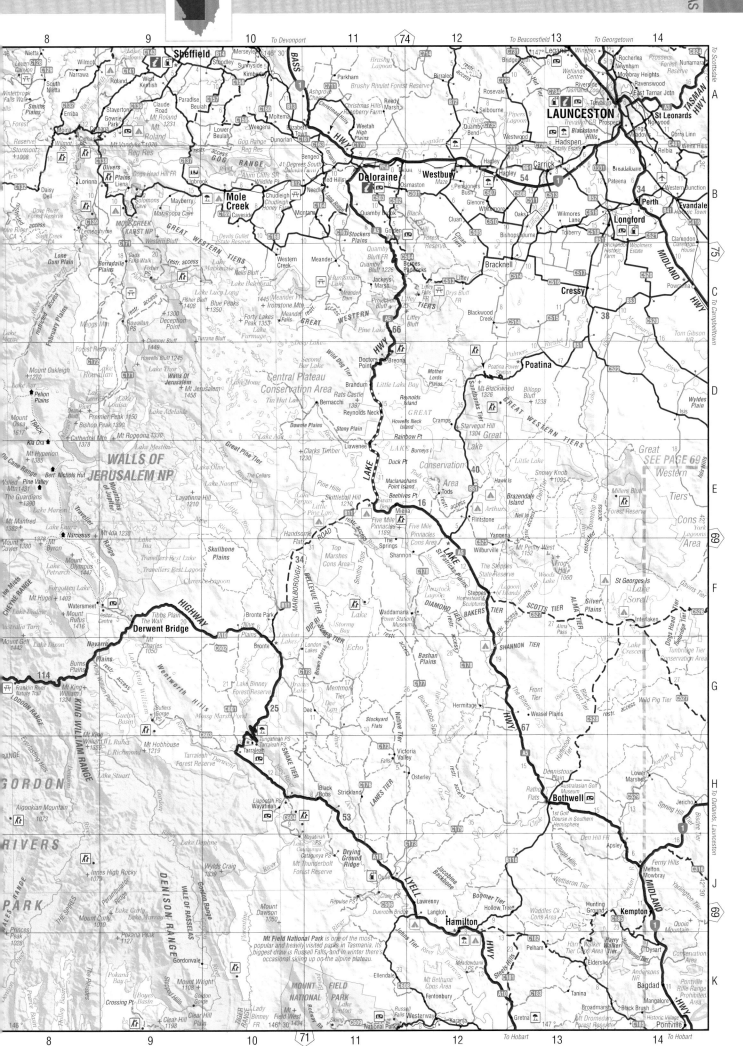

To Scottsdale

8   9   To Devonport   10   11   **74**   12   To Beaconsfield   13   To Georgetown   14

Nietta
Leven
C128
C129
South Nietta
Narrawa
Wilmot
Sheffield
Merseylea
Roland
Kimberley
Parkham
Birralee
Legana
Winkleigh
Prossers Forest Reserve
Nunamara
C824

Winterbrook Falls Walk
Smiths Plains
Forest
C132
Erriba
Gowrie Park
West Kentish
Claude Road
Paradise
Beulah
Ashgrove
Christmas Hills Raspberry Farm
Reedy Marsh
Bridgenorth
Grindelwald
Wetlands Centre
Riverside
Tasmania Zoo
Rocherlea
Newnham
Mowbray Heights
Ravenswood
East Tamar Jctn

Moina
Cethana
Staverton
Cradle Mtn Cethana
Mt Roland 1231
Beulah
Moltema
Weegena
Weetah High Plains
Selbourne
Westwood
LAUNCESTON
Trevallyn SR
Prospect
Corra Linn
White Hills

Daisy Dell
Lorinna
Olivers
Plains
Liena
Igbrook
41 Degrees South Salmon Farm
Alum Cliffs SR Wildlife Pk
Osmaston
Hagley
Hagley
Carrick
54
Breadalbane
Relbia
Pateena
Western Junction

Mole Creek
Mayberry
Matakoopa Cave
Chudleigh
Chudleigh Honey Farm
Caveside
Montana
Deloraine
Quamby Brook
Glenore
Whitemore
Oaks
Toberry
Wilmores Lane
Longford
Clarendon House
Perth
Evandale
Historic Town

MOLE CREEK KARST NP
Lemonthyme
GREAT
WESTERN
TIERS
Western Bluff
Meander
Quamby Bluff FR Quamby Bluff 1226
Berges Paddocks
Cluan
Bishopsbourne
Clarendon
Brickendon Historic Farm
Woolmers Estate

Lone Gum Plain
Borradaile Plains
Gads Falls Walk
Fisher PS
Lake Mackenzie
Nells Bluff
Liffey
Liffey Falls
Drys Bluff
Blackwood Creek
Cressy
Powranna
C520

Pedmary Plains
Fisher Bluff 1408
Lake Lucy Long
Lake Balmoral
Huntsman Lake
Jackeys Marsh
Meander Dam
Projection Bluff
66
Liffey Bluff
38
Tom Gibson NR

Lake Merel
Mount Oakleigh +1270
Lake Rowallan
Rowallan PS
Deception Point
Blue Peaks +1300
Forty Lakes Peak 1353
Meander Falls
Pine Lake
Doctors Point
Breona
Poatina Power Station
Poatina
C522
Wyldes Plain
Isis

Dove River Forest Reserve
Walls Of Jerusalem +Mt Jerusalem 1458
Howells Bluff 1245
Clumner Bluff 1449
Second Bar Lake
Wild Dog Tier
Brandum
Little Lake Bay
Mother Lords Plains
Mt Blackwood 1326
Sandbanks Tier
Starvegut Hill 1304
Billopp Bluff +1238
GREAT WESTERN TIERS

WALLS OF JERUSALEM NP
Mount Ossa 1617
Mt Hyperion +1385
Kia Ora
Cathedral Mtn 1378
Mt Rogoona 1330
Lake Meston
Clarks Timber 1230
Liawenee
Rats Castle 1397
Bernacchi
Reynolds Neck
Reynolds Island
GREAT
Cramps
Starvegut Hill
Great
Snowy Knob +1095
Millers Bluff

Mt Manfred 1382
Lake Marion
Lake Adelaide
Pine Valley
Lake Olive
The Cellars
Dowrie Plains
Stony Plain
Rainbow Pt
Duck Pt
LAKE
Burneys Pt
Conservation
40
Little Lake
Brazendale Island
York Lagoons
SEE PAGE 69
Western Tiers

Mt Cuvier 1380
Narcissus
Mt Byron
Mt Ida 1238
Lake Ina
Pine Hills
Lake Fergus
Skittleball Hill 1210
Maclanaghans Point Island
Beehives Pt
16
Tods Corner
Tods
Hawk Is
Arthur
Area
Neil St
Yangena
Mt Penny West 1152
Cons Area

Cheyne Range
Mt Hugel +1403
The Mists
Lake Lindee
Travellers Rest Lake
Skullbone Plains
Handsome Flat
Five Mile Pinnacles 1189
Five Mile Pinnacles Cons Area
The Springs
Shannon
Wilburville
A5
Flintstone
The Steppes State Reserve
Lagoon of Islands
St Georges Is

Mt Manfred
Watersmeet
Mount Rufus 1416
Tibbs Plain
The Wall
Bronte Park
Nive
B11
Top Marshes Cons Area
Smiths Tops
Lake
Waddamana
Waddamana Power Station Museum
BAKERS TIER
Illetts Tier
Scotts Tier
C527
Alma Tier
Silver Plains
Lake Sorell
Interlaken
Dots Head
Tunbridge Tier
C526

Australia Tarn
Mt Gell 1442
Derwent Bridge
Navarre
Mt Charles 1050
London Lakes
London Plains
Bronte
Brown Marsh
Echo
Stormy Bay
Bashan Plains
C178
Hermitage
SHANNON TIER
19
Front Tier
The Bitters
Weasel Plains
Wild Pig Tier
C527

114
Franklin River Nature Trail
Loddon Range
King William Range
Burns Plains
Lake King William
Mt King William I 1324
Lake Binney Forest Reserve
C173
Bronzes Lake
Mentmore Tier
Dee Lgn
Native Tier
Stockyard Flats
C177
Black Bobs Spur
The Bitters
67
Dennistoun Plain
Lower Marshes
C528

Gordon
Algonkian Mountain 1073
Mt King William II 1355
Mt Hobhouse 1219
Tarraleah Forest Reserve
Tarraleah
25
Tungatinah PS
Tarraleah PS
Dee
Snake Tier
Victoria Valley
Falls
Osterley
Australasian Golf Museum
Bothwell
A5
Ratho Flats
Lake Crescent
Lower Marshes
C529
Jericho

Innes High Rocky +1079
Wylds Craig 1339
Black Bobs
Strickland
Lames Tier
Wayatinah PS
Liapootah PS
Wayatinah
C604
53
Catagunya PS
Mt Thunderbolt 1050
Drying Ground Ridge
A10
C173
Ouse
Jacobins Backbone
Hamilton
1st Golf Course in Southern Hemisphere
C179
Den Hill FR
Apsley
Ferny Hills
Melton Mowbray
C316

Lake Dobson
Mount Curly 1010
Perambulator Ridge
Lake Curly
Lake Murray
Pokana Peak 1127
Mount Dawson 1050
Repulse PS
Clony PS
Dunrobin Bridge
Langloh
Boomer Tier
Hollow Tree
Waddles Ck Cons Area
Hunting Ground
Rough Plains
Wetheron Tier
Yadlington Tier
Kempton
Quoin Mountain
Dysart

DENISON RANGE
VALE OF RASSELAS
Gordonvale
Mt Field National Park is one of the most popular and heavily visited parks in Tasmania. Its biggest draw is Russell Falls, and in winter there's occasional skiing up on the alpine plateau.
Ellendale
Mt Bethune Cons Area
Fentonbury
C182
Pelham
C181
Meadowbank PS
Harry Walker Tier Cons Area
Elderslie
Broadmarsh
Andersons NR
Conservation Area
Bagdad

THE SPIRES
Boyes Basin
Pokana Bay
The Pleiades
Crossing Pt
Stepped Hills
Gordon Gorge
Mt Wright 1108
MOUNT FIELD NATIONAL PARK
Lake Fenton
Mt Field West 1434
Lady Binney
Skiing
Russell Falls
Westerway
Karanja
Gretna
Mt Dromedary Forest Reserve
Pontville
Pontville Rifle Range Prohibited Area
Historic Village

Clear Hill 1198
Gordonvale
C609
National Park
LYELL HWY
C183
Broadmarsh
C185

8   9   10   **71**   11   To Hobart   12   13   To Oatlands, Launceston   14   To Hobart

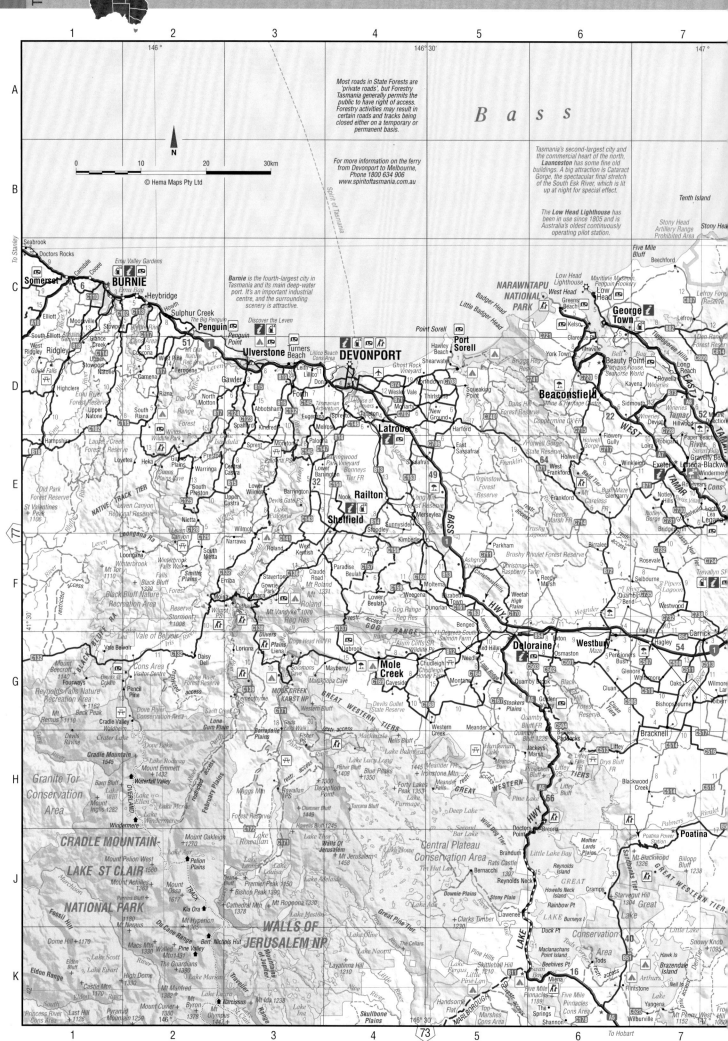

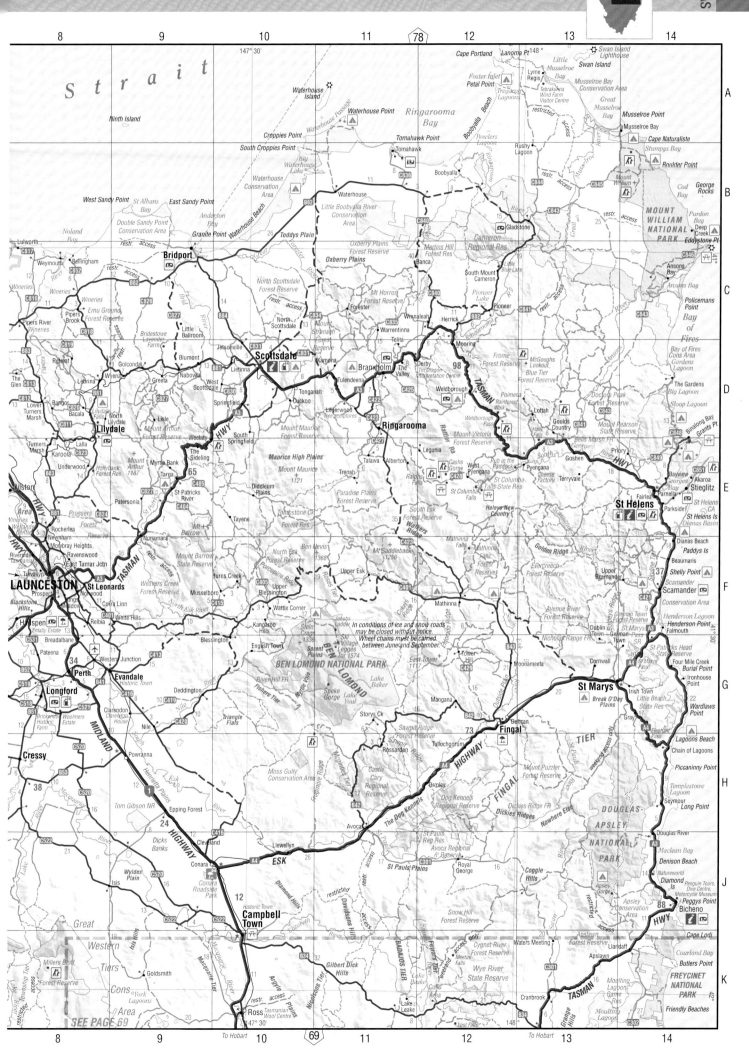

78

| | 1 | 2 | 3 | 4 | 5 | 6 | 7 |

144° 30'   145°   145° 30'

A

B

Three Hummock Island State Reserve
Albatross Is   Cape Keraudren   North West Cape   Cape Rochon
Coulomb Bay   **Three Hummock Island**
Cape Adamson   *East Telegraph Bay*
B a s s
Cuvier Point   *Cuvier Bay*
Black Pyramid

40° 30'

C

Wallaby Point   **Hunter Island**   Cave Bay
Hunter Island Conservation Area
Steep Is
Perigo Point   Cape Buache
Bird Is   Stack Is   Walker Island
Weber Point   *Hunter Passage*
Trefoil Is   Woolnorth Point

Stanley sits at the base of a distinctive, 150m-high volcanic plug called Circular Head but better known as the Nut. For a panoramic view, visitors can climb the Nut or take the chairlift.

D

The Doughboys   Woolnorth'   *Boullanger Bay*   **Robbins Island**   Guyton Point
Cape Grim   Tarkine road   Montagu Is   Robbins   Cape Elie   North Point   Highfield Historic Site
Valley Bay   Kangaroo Is   Stony Point   Half Moon Bay   West Point   Highfield Point
Wind Farm (Tours from Smithton)   *Passage*   Shipwreck Point   The Nut Chairlift   The Nut
Flat Topped Bluff   Swan Bay Plain   *Big Bay*   Perkins Island   *Perkins Bay*   Beach   Stanley Seaquarium
Bluff Point   *Studland Bay*   Montagu   West Montagu   Scopus   Duck Bay   Anthony   Beach   Stanley Historic Town   Seal Cruises
Dodgers Point   Harcus Plain   18   Tatlows Folly   Sawyer Bay   Colvine Point   Port Latta   Crayfish Creek   Rocky Cape Beach
S O U T H E R N   Jims Plain   *Thorpes Plain*   Smithton   Mella   Smokers Bank   North Forest   Wilshire   *B A S S*   Hellyer   Rocky Cape NP
Preminghana   *Montagu Plains*   Broadmeadows   13   Scotchtown   Pribeena   Forest   Black River   South Forest   Montumana
C215   *Ann Bay*   *Seventeen Mile Plain*   Christmas Hills   16   Irishtown   Menghan   Shakespeare Hills Forest Reserve   Mawbanna
Green Point   *Bond Tier Forest Reserve*   *Thorpes Plain*   Jones Plain   9   Alcomie   Lileah   Shakespeare Hills Regional Reserve   Rulla

E

F

West Point   Marrawah   C213   Redpa   Togari   *Hopeless Plains*   Eurebia   Lileah   Dip Range   Mibena
BASS   Brittons Swamp   *Waratah Plain*   Edith Creek   Nabageena   Gibson Plains   Dip Falls Big Tree
West Point State Reserve   Dismal Swamp FR   *Plains Creek Forest Reserve*   Allendale Gardens   C218   C219   Meunna Hills
Mawson Bay   Tarkine Forest Adventures   **HIGHWAY**   Duffs Flat   Junction Plain   Roger River   Duck River Forest Reserve   Meunna
Bluff Hill Point   *Richardsons Flats*   Montagu Swamp Forest Reserve   Roger River West   Trowutta   Dip River Forest Reserve
Cruises   *Warra Creek Forest Reserve*   Tayetea Bridge (rebuilt)   CAMPBELL RANGE
Arthur River   Edge of the World Viewing Platform   Gardiner Pt   *Arthur*   Lovells Creek Forest Reserve   Celery Top Pine Forest Walk   C218   *Wynsmith Hills*   Pruana

G

41°   *Dunns Plain*   Milkshake Hills FR   West Takone
Wuthering Heights Plain   Kanunnah Bridge   Lake Chisholm FR   *Holder Plains*
Sundown Point   Ballour Track Forest Reserve   Trowutta Forest Reserve   Luncheon Hill Forest Reserve   Rapid River Bridge
Nelson Bay   17   Julius River Forest Reserve   C218

H

Couta Rocks   17   *Sumac Forest Reserve*   *Dempster Plains*   Wes Beckett Forest Reserve   DONALDSON   SAVAGE   SAVAGE RIVER
Rebecca Creek Forest Reserve   RIVER   Arthur River Forest Reserve
Temma   Balfour   NATURE   REC
Hazard Bay   permit required   Contact Arthur River Parks & Wildlife Service on (03) 6457 1225 regarding permits and 4WDing in the conservation area.   AREA   REGIONAL   NATIONAL PARK
Ordnance Point   ARTHUR-   Deep Gully Forest Reserve

J

O C E A N   Kenneth Bay   PIEMAN   C249
Sandy Cape   66   Magnet Ra
Mount Norfolk   *Magnet*   **Waratah** Heritage Mining Town

41° 30'   CONSERVATION   RESERVE   44   Luina   16   Knole
Meredith Range   C247   *Regional Reserve*   Wombat Hill   *Netherby*
AREA   Badger Plains   Savage River   Long Plains   C249   145°

144° 30'   72   145°   145° 30'

| | 1 | 2 | 3 | 4 | 5 | 6 | 7 |

84

8 9 10 11 12 13 14

A

B

Strait

146° 146° 30'

N

0   10   20   30km

© Hema Maps Pty Ltd

C

D

E

Most roads in State Forests are 'private roads', but Forestry Tasmania generally permits the public to have right of access. Forestry activities may result in certain roads and tracks being closed either on a temporary or permanent basis.

For more information on the ferry from Devonport to Melbourne, Phone 1800 634 906 www.spiritoftasmania.com.au

The **Low Head Lighthouse** has been in use since 1805 and is Australia's oldest continuously operating pilot station.

40° 30'

Sisters Is
Sisters Beach
Sisters Creek
C233
Flowerdale
Myalla
Moorleah
Lapoinya
Detention Falls Conservation Area
C229 C235
Upper Calder
C237
Calder
Oldina
Preolenna
Kellatier
Yolla
C236
Takone
Henrietta
Forest Reserve
Tewkesbury
Oonah
C101
C103
Hampshire
Hellyer Gorge
62
Patrawe
Hellyer Gorge State Reserve
MURCHISON
restricted access
Gatcomb Plain C618
Guildford
Fingerpost
Plain
A10
Mt Pearse 1001
Pearsefield Plain
Hatfield
Plain
Surrey Hills
Murrays Plain
Hatfield River Forest Res
C132
Mount Beecroft 1140

Boat Harbour Beach
Boat Harbour
Lobster Ponds
HWY
Wynyard
Seabrook
Doctors Rocks
Camdale
Cooee
Somerset
C230
C110
Upper Mount Hicks
Lower Mount Hicks
B26
C238
C235
Upper Hicks
Elliott
A10
Mooreville
South Elliott
Ridgley
B18
Glance Creek
C114
Upper Stowport
West Ridgley
East Yolla
Gude Falls
HIGHWAY
Highclere
C102
Upper Natone
C115
Loyetea
Laurel Creek Forest Reserve
Heka
Old Park Forest Reserve
St Valentines Peak 1106
NATIVE TRACK TIER
Leven Canyon Regional Reserve
Loongana Ra
Loongana
Winterbrook Falls Walk
Mt Tor 1110
Black Bluff 1339
Black Bluff Nature Recreation Area
Reserve
BLACK BLUFF RA
Stormont 1008
Wilmot
C139
Lea
Vale of Belvoir
Vale Belvoir
C132
Iris
Daisy Dell
Dove River Forest Reserve
Cons Area Visitor Centre
146°

Table Cape
Penguin Tours
BURNIE
Emu Bay
Emu Valley Gardens
Heybridge
Howth
Sulphur Creek
Penguin
C102
C119
Stowport
Camena
C117
West Pine
Natone
Ferndene
B17
Riana
North Motton
South Riana
Dial Range
Abbotsham
C124
C123
Spalford
Forest Res
C115
Wings Wildlife Park
Gunns Plains
Gunns Plains Cave
South Preston
Central Castra
Warringa
B15
Lower Wilmot
Upper Castra
Nietta
C128
C129
Narrawa
C141
Roland
West Kentish
C132
Smiths Plains
Staverton
C136
Gowrie Park
Mt Roland 1231
Mt Vandyke 1070 Reg Res
Cethana
Meina
Olivers
Plains Liena
Lorinna
Mayberry
Marakoopa Cave
Dogs Head Hill FR
King Solomons Cave
146° 30'

F

G

H

J

K

Discover the Leven
Penguin Point
Turners Beach
Ulverstone
Gawler
Leith
Lillico
Forth
C145
Eugenana
Moorleah
Sprent
Moreton
Paloma
Kindred
Melrose
Isandula
Preston
Paloma PS
Barringwood Vineyard Park
Lower Barrington
Barrington
Devils Gate PS
Lake Paloma
Paradise
Beulah
Claude Road
Lower Beulah
Weegena
Dunorlan
Bengeo
Gog Range Reg Res
GOG RANGE
Alum Cliffs SR Wildlife Pk
Chudleigh
Mole Creek
Needles
C164

DEVONPORT
Don
Tasmanian Arboretum
C132
Spreyton
Tarleton
C148
House of Anvers
Moriarty
C702
Latrobe
Harford
East Sassafras
Sassafras
Bonneys Tier FR
C153
Nook
Railton
Sheffield
Studley
Sunnyside
Merseylea
Kimberley
C156
Ashgrove Cheese
C157
C159
Moltema
Elizabeth Town
C161
Weetah
High Plains
HWY
41 Degrees South Salmon Farm
Alum Cliffs SR
Red Hills
Chudleigh
Deloraine
Osmaston
C163
C170
Exton
B54
B12
C503
C502
Westbury
Pensioners Bush

Point Sorell
Hawley Beach
Shearwater
Port Sorell
Ghost Rock Vineyard
Northdown
Wesley Vale
Thirlstane
New Ground
C740
C706
Squeaking Point
C708
Harford
Holwell Gorge State Reserve
Franklin
64
Holwell
Frankford
West Frankford
Winkleigh
Reedy Marsh FR
C714
Birralee
Brushy Lagoon
Parkham
Brushy Rivulet Forest Reserve
B72
Christmas Hills
Raspberry Farm
Maze
Meander
River

NARAWNTAPU NATIONAL PARK
Badger Head
Little Badger Head
Greens Beach
West Head
Kelso
Clarence Pt
York Town
Beaconsfield Mine & Heritage Centre
Dans Hill Forest Reserve
Coppermine Ck FR
C721
C741
Beauty Point
Platypus House
Seahorse World
Bell Bay
Flowery Gully
Holwell Gorge
C715
C717
Mt Careless
B71
Careless FR
restr access

Low Head Lighthouse
Maritime Museum, Penguin Rookery
George Town
Itraville
74
To Launceston

62
Racecourse Plain

32
49
1
Long Plain
BASS
Virginstow Forest Reserve
To Launceston

Hatfield
8 To Rosebery, Queenstown 9 10 74 11 12 13 To Hobart 14

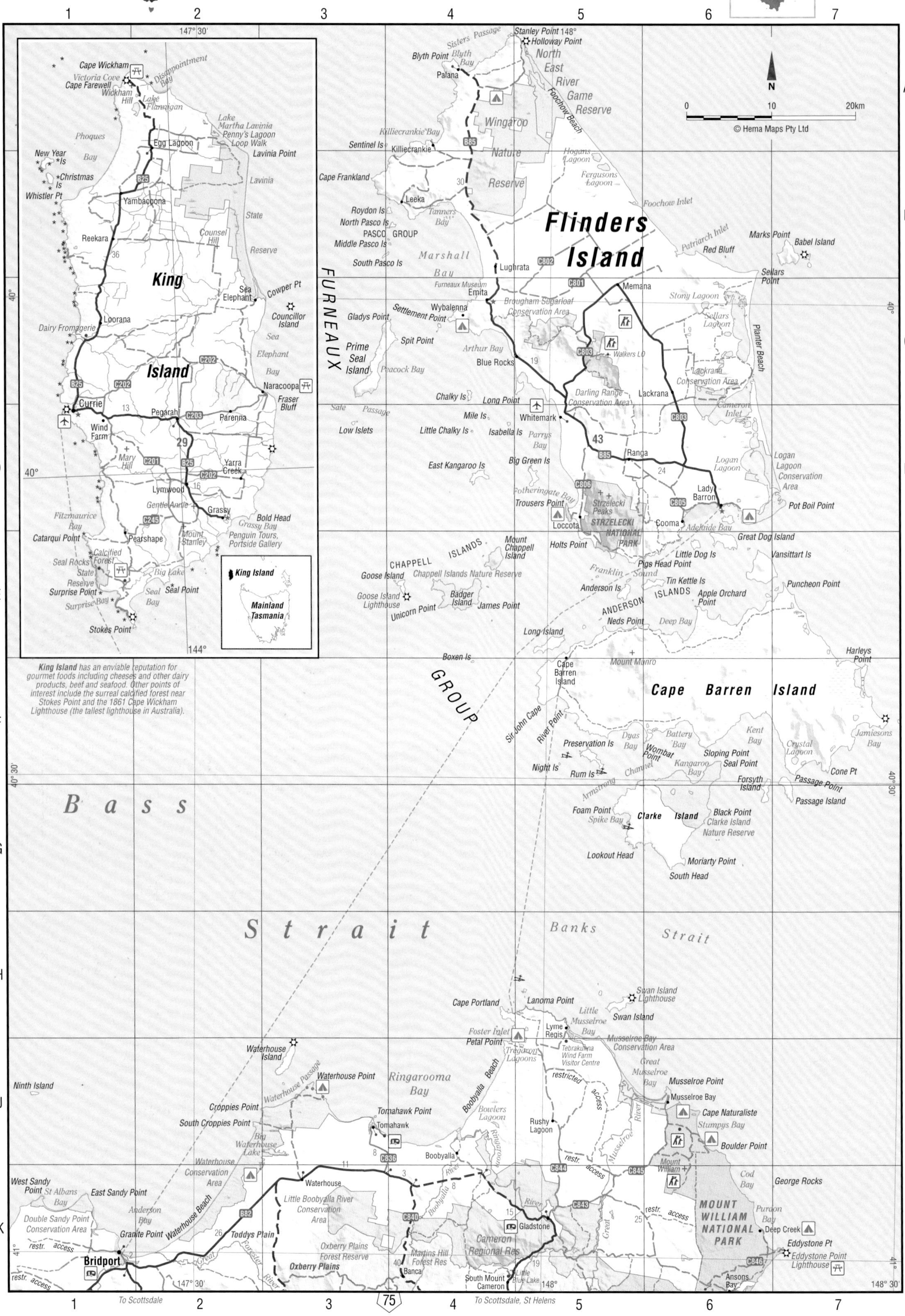

© Hema Maps Pty Ltd

N

0 10 20km

Flinders Island

King Island

FURNEAUX

Cape Barren Island

GROUP

CHAPPELL ISLANDS

ANDERSON ISLANDS

Bass Strait

Banks Strait

King Island inset labels:
Cape Wickham, Victoria Cove, Cape Farewell, Wickham Hill, Disappointment Bay, Lake Flannigan, Phoques Bay, New Year Is, Christmas Is, Whistler Pt, Egg Lagoon, Lake Martha Lavinia, Penny's Lagoon, Loop Walk, Lavinia Point, Yambacoona, Reekara, Counsel Hill, Lavinia, State Reserve, Sea Elephant, Cowper Pt, Councillor Island, Dairy Fromagerie, Loorana, Sea Elephant Bay, Naracoopa, Fraser Bluff, King Island, C202, Currie, Wind Farm, Pegarah, Parenna, C203, Mary Hill, C201, B25, C202, Yarra Creek, Lymwood, Gentle Annie, Grassy, Bold Head, Grassy Bay, Penguin Tours, Portside Gallery, Mount Stanley, Fitzmaurice Bay, Catarqui Point, Pearshape, C245, Seal Rocks State Reserve, Calcified Forest, Surprise Point, Surprise Bay, Big Lake, Seal Bay, Seal Point, Stokes Point

King Island inset location map: King Island, Mainland Tasmania

King Island has an enviable reputation for gourmet foods including cheeses and other dairy products, beef and seafood. Other points of interest include the surreal calcified forest near Stokes Point and the 1861 Cape Wickham Lighthouse (the tallest lighthouse in Australia).

Flinders Island labels:
Blyth Point, Blyth Bay, Palana, Stanley Point, Holloway Point, North East River Game Reserve, Foochow Beach, Sisters Passage, Wingaroo, Killiecrankie Bay, Sentinel Is, Killiecrankie, Leeka, Cape Frankland, Hogans Lagoon, Fergusons Lagoon, Foochow Inlet, Roydon Is, North Pasco Is, PASCO GROUP, Middle Pasco Is, South Pasco Is, Tanners Bay, Patriarch Inlet, Marks Point, Red Bluff, Babel Island, Sellars Point, Marshall Bay, Lughrata, Furneaux Museum, Emita, Memana, Stony Lagoon, C802, C801, Gladys Point, Settlement Point, Wybalenna, Brougham Sugarloaf Conservation Area, Sellars Lagoon, Prime Seal Island, Spit Point, Arthur Bay, Blue Rocks, C803, Walkers LO, Lackrana Conservation Area, Peacock Bay, Chalky Is, Long Point, Mile Is, Whitemark, Darling Range Conservation Area, C803, Cameron Inlet, Planter Beach, Low Islets, Little Chalky Is, Isabella Is, Parrys Bay, 43, Ranga, B85, 24, Logan Lagoon, Logan Lagoon Conservation Area, East Kangaroo Is, Big Green Is, Lady Barron, Pot Boil Point, Fotheringate Bay, Trousers Point, C806, Strzelecki Peaks, STRZELECKI NATIONAL PARK, Cooma, Adelaide Bay, C805, Great Dog Island, Loccota, Holts Point, Mount Chappell Island, Pigs Head Point, Little Dog Is, Vansittart Is, Franklin Sound, Tin Kettle Is, Apple Orchard Point, Puncheon Point, CHAPPELL ISLANDS, Goose Island, Chappell Islands Nature Reserve, Anderson Is, Deep Bay, Goose Island Lighthouse, Badger Island, James Point, Neds Point, Long Island, Unicorn Point, Harleys Point, Boxen Is, Mount Munro, Cape Barren Island, Jamiesons Bay, Sir John Cape, River Point, Preservation Is, Dyas Bay, Battery Bay, Kent Bay, Crystal Lagoon, Cone Pt, Night Is, Wombat Point, Kangaroo Bay, Sloping Point, Seal Point, Forsyth Island, Passage Point, Passage Island, Rum Is, Armstrong Channel, Foam Point, Spike Bay, Clarke Island, Black Point, Clarke Island Nature Reserve, Lookout Head, Moriarty Point, South Head

Bottom mainland labels:
Cape Portland, Lanoma Point, Swan Island Lighthouse, Swan Island, Little Musselroe Bay, Musselroe Bay Conservation Area, Musselroe Point, Waterhouse Island, Foster Inlet, Petal Point, Lyme Regis, Tregaroola Lagoons, Tebrakunna Wind Farm Visitor Centre, Great Musselroe Bay, Musselroe Bay, Cape Naturaliste, Stumpys Bay, Waterhouse Point, Ringarooma Bay, Boobyalla Beach, Bowlers Lagoon, Rushy Lagoon, Boulder Point, Ninth Island, Croppies Point, South Croppies Point, Big Waterhouse Lake, Tomahawk Point, Tomahawk, C636, Boobyalla, restricted, C844, Mount William, C845, West Sandy Point, St Albans Bay, East Sandy Point, Anderson Bay, Waterhouse Conservation Area, Little Boobyalla River Conservation Area, Waterhouse, C840, C843, Cod Bay, George Rocks, MOUNT WILLIAM NATIONAL PARK, Purdon Bay, Double Sandy Point Conservation Area, Granite Point, Toddys Plain, Oxberry Plains Forest Reserve, Oxberry Plains, Gladstone, Cameron Regional Res, Deep Creek, Eddystone Pt, Bridport, Banca, Martins Hill Forest Res, South Mount Cameron, Ansons Bay, C846, Eddystone Point Lighthouse

REMARKABLE ROCKS, KANGAROO ISLAND (88 J5)   PHOTO: © ISTOCK.COM/YEKORZH

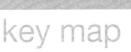

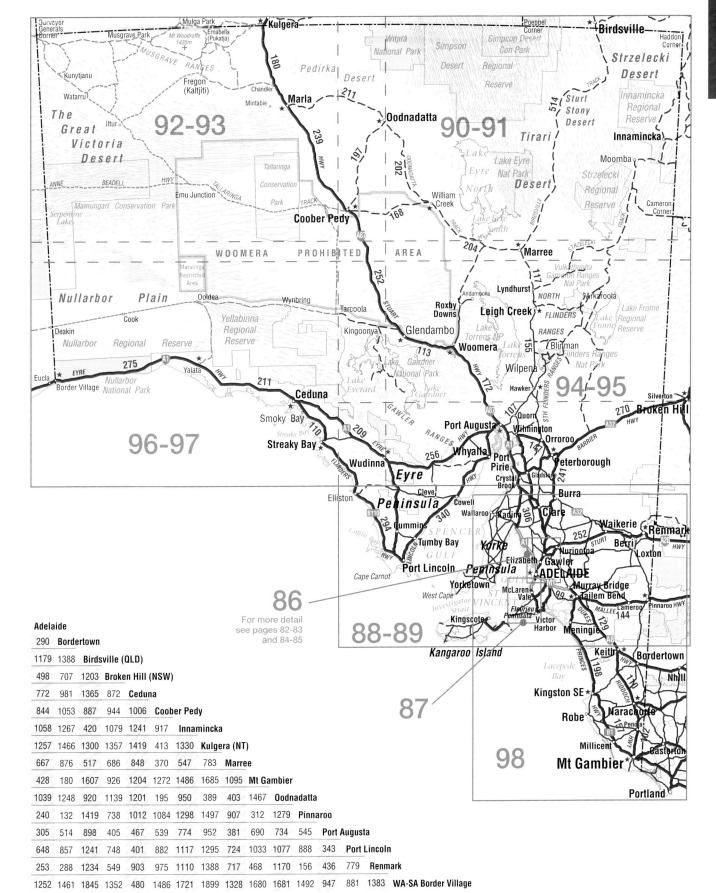

SOUTH AUSTRALIA

key map

Adelaide

290	**Bordertown**													
1179	1388	**Birdsville (QLD)**												
498	707	1203	**Broken Hill (NSW)**											
772	981	1365	872	**Ceduna**										
844	1053	887	944	1006	**Coober Pedy**									
1058	1267	420	1079	1241	917	**Innamincka**								
1257	1466	1300	1357	1419	413	1330	**Kulgera (NT)**							
667	876	517	686	848	370	547	783	**Marree**						
428	180	1607	926	1204	1272	1486	1685	1095	**Mt Gambier**					
1039	1248	920	1139	1201	195	950	389	403	1467	**Oodnadatta**				
240	132	1419	738	1012	1084	1298	1497	907	312	1279	**Pinnaroo**			
305	514	898	405	467	539	774	952	381	690	734	545	**Port Augusta**		
648	857	1241	748	401	882	1117	1295	724	1033	1077	888	343	**Port Lincoln**	
253	288	1234	549	903	975	1110	1388	717	468	1170	156	436	779	**Renmark**
1252	1461	1845	1352	480	1486	1721	1899	1328	1680	1681	1492	947	881	1383	**WA-SA Border Village**

Distances are shown in kilometres and follow the most direct major sealed route where possible.

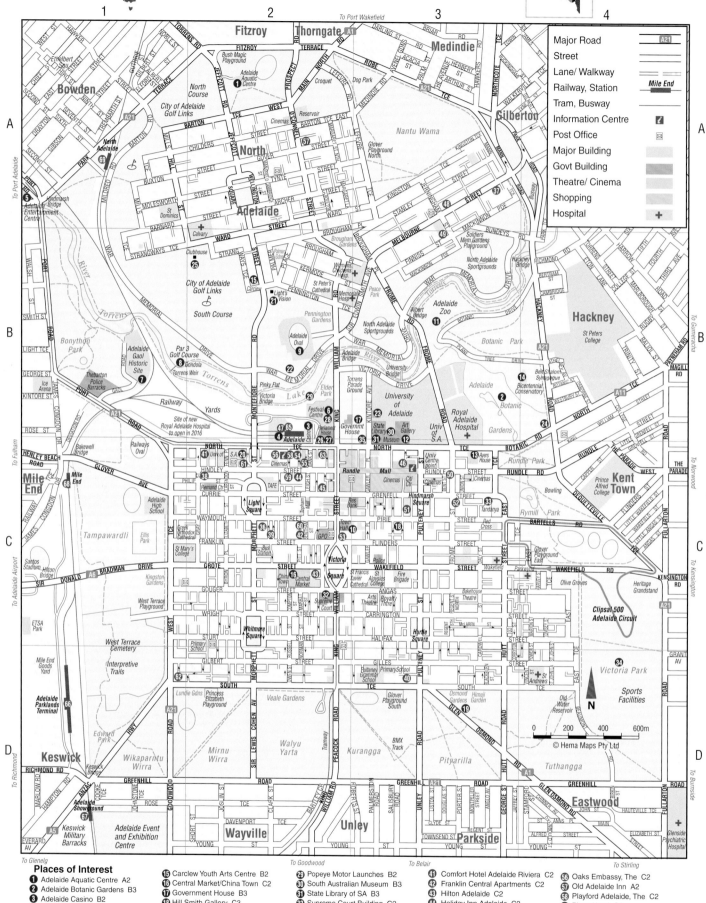

Places of Interest

1 Adelaide Aquatic Centre A2
2 Adelaide Botanic Gardens B3
3 Adelaide Casino B2
4 Adelaide Convention/Exhibition Ctr B2
5 Adelaide Entertainment Centre A1
6 Adelaide Festival Centre B2
7 Adelaide Gaol Historic Site B1
8 Adelaide Gondola B1
9 Adelaide Oval B2
10 Adelaide Town Hall C2
11 Adelaide Zoo B3
12 Art Gallery of South Australia B3
13 Ayers House C3
14 Bicentennial Conservatory B4

15 Carclew Youth Arts Centre B2
16 Central Market/China Town C2
17 Government House B3
18 Hill Smith Gallery C3
19 Himeji Japanese Garden D3
20 Jam Factory Craft & Design Centre C2
21 Light's Vision B2
22 Memorial Drive Tennis Courts B2
23 Migration Museum B3
24 National Wine Centre of Australia B4
25 North Adelaide Golf Links B2
26 Old Parliament House – Museum B2
27 Parliament House B2
28 Performing Arts Collection of SA B2

29 Popeye Motor Launches B2
30 South Australian Museum B3
31 State Library of SA B3
32 Supreme Court Building C2
33 Tandanya National Aboriginal
   Cultural Inst C3
34 Victoria Park Raceway D4
35 War Memorial B3

Accommodation

36 Adelaide Central YHA C2
37 Adelaide Meridien A3
38 Breakfree Adelaide C2
39 Cannon Street Backpackers C2
40 Chifley on South Terrace, The D3

41 Comfort Hotel Adelaide Riviera C2
42 Franklin Central Apartments C2
43 Hilton Adelaide C2
44 Holiday Inn Adelaide C2
45 Hotel Grand Chancellor Adelaide C2
46 Hotel Richmond C3
47 InterContinental Adelaide C2
48 Majestic Minima Hotel A3
49 Majestic Old Lion Apartments B3
50 Majestic Roof Garden Hotel C3
51 Mantra Hindmarsh Square C3
52 Mantra on Frome C3
53 Medina Grand Adelaide Treasury C2
54 Mercure Grosvenor Hotel Adelaide C2
55 Motel Adjacent Casino C2

56 Oaks Embassy, The C2
57 Old Adelaide Inn A2
58 Playford Adelaide, The C2
59 Plaza Hotel C2
60 Rendezvous Allegra Hotel C2
61 Rockford Hotel C2
62 Rydges South Park Adelaide D1
63 Stamford Plaza Adelaide C2

Railway Stations

65 Adelaide B2
66 Adelaide Parklands Terminal D1
67 Adelaide Showground D1
68 Mile End C1
69 North Adelaide A1

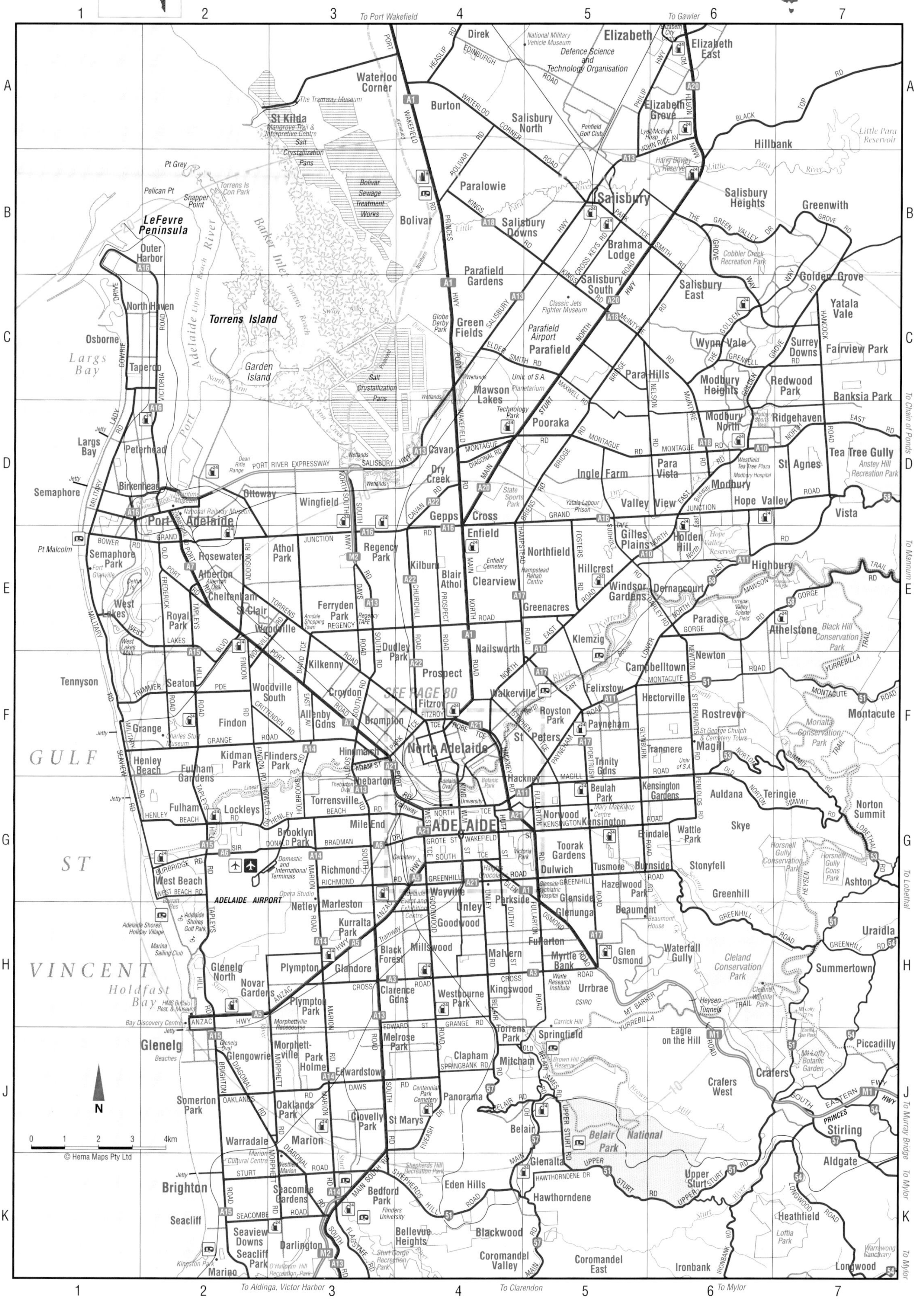
To Port Wakefield
To Gawler
Direk
Elizabeth
Elizabeth East
Elizabeth Grove
Defence Science and Technology Organisation
National Military Vehicle Museum
Waterloo Corner
Burton
Salisbury North
Hillbank
Little Para Reservoir
St Kilda
The Tramway Museum
Mangrove Trail & Interpretive Centre
Salt Crystallization Pans
Pt Grey
Pelican Pt
Snapper Point
Torrens Is Con Park
LeFevre Peninsula
Outer Harbor
Barker Inlet
Bolivar Sewage Treatment Works
Bolivar
Paralowie
Salisbury
Salisbury Heights
Greenwith
Salisbury Downs
Brahma Lodge
Cobbler Creek Recreation Park
Parafield Gardens
Salisbury South
Salisbury East
Golden Grove
Yatala Vale
North Haven
Torrens Island
Green Fields
Classic Jets Fighter Museum
Parafield Airport
Parafield
Wynn Vale
Surrey Downs
Fairview Park
Osborne
Largs Bay
Taperoo
Garden Island
Mawson Lakes
Para Hills
Modbury Heights
Redwood Park
Banksia Park
Pooraka
Modbury North
Ridgehaven
Peterhead
Cavan
Dry Creek
Ingle Farm
Para Vista
Modbury
St Agnes
Tea Tree Gully
Semaphore
Birkenhead
Ottoway
Wingfield
Gepps Cross
Valley View
Hope Valley
Vista
Port Adelaide
Pt Malcolm
Semaphore Park
Rosewater
Athol Park
Regency Park
Enfield
Northfield
Gilles Plains
Holden Hill
Highbury
Alberton
Cheltenham
Kilburn
Blair Athol
Clearview
Hillcrest
Windsor Gardens
Dernancourt
West Lakes
St Clair
Royal Park
Ferryden Park
Greenacres
Paradise
Athelstone
Woodville
Dudley Park
Nailsworth
Klemzig
Black Hill Conservation Park
Kilkenny
Prospect
Newton
Tennyson
Seaton
Woodville South
Croydon
Campbelltown
Hectorville
SEE PAGE 80
Fitzroy
Walkerville
Felixstow
Montacute
Allenby Gdns
Brompton
Royston Park
Rostrevor
Grange
Findon
North Adelaide
St Peters
Payneham
Magill
Morialta Conservation Park
GULF
Henley Beach
Fulham Gardens
Kidman Park
Flinders Park
Hindmarsh
Thebarton
Hackney
Trinity Gdns
Tranmere
Beulah Park
Kensington Gardens
Auldana
Teringie
Norton Summit
Fulham
Lockleys
Torrensville
Mile End
ADELAIDE
Norwood
Kensington
Skye
Brooklyn Park
Toorak Gardens
Erindale
Wattle Park
ST
West Beach
Richmond
Dulwich
Tusmore
Burnside
Stonyfell
ADELAIDE AIRPORT
Netley
Marleston
Wayville
Unley
Parkside
Glenside
Hazelwood Park
Greenhill
Ashton
Beaumont
Kurralta Park
Goodwood
Glenunga
Adelaide Shores Holiday Village
Black Forest
Millswood
Malvern
Fullarton
Myrtle Bank
Glen Osmond
Waterfall Gully
Uraidla
VINCENT
Holdfast Bay
Glenelg North
Plympton
Glandore
Clarence Gdns
Westbourne Park
Kingswood
Urrbrae
Cleland Conservation Park
Summertown
Novar Gardens
Plympton Park
Torrens Park
Springfield
Eagle on the Hill
Glenelg
Morphett-ville
Park Holme
Melrose Park
Clapham
Mitcham
Piccadilly
Glengowrie
Edwardstown
Crafers
Crafers West
Somerton Park
Oaklands Park
Panorama
Clovelly Park
St Marys
Belair
Belair National Park
Stirling
Warradale
Marion
Glenalta
Aldgate
Brighton
Seacombe Gardens
Bedford Park
Eden Hills
Hawthorndene
Upper Sturt
Seacliff
Flinders University
Heathfield
Seaview Downs
Bellevue Heights
Blackwood
Seacliff Park
Darlington
Coromandel Valley
Coromandel East
Ironbank
Longwood
Marino
To Aldinga, Victor Harbor
To Clarendon
To Mylor
To Chain of Ponds
To Mannum
To Lobethal
To Murray Bridge
0 1 2 3 4km
© Hema Maps Pty Ltd

Adelaide Suburbs, South Australia

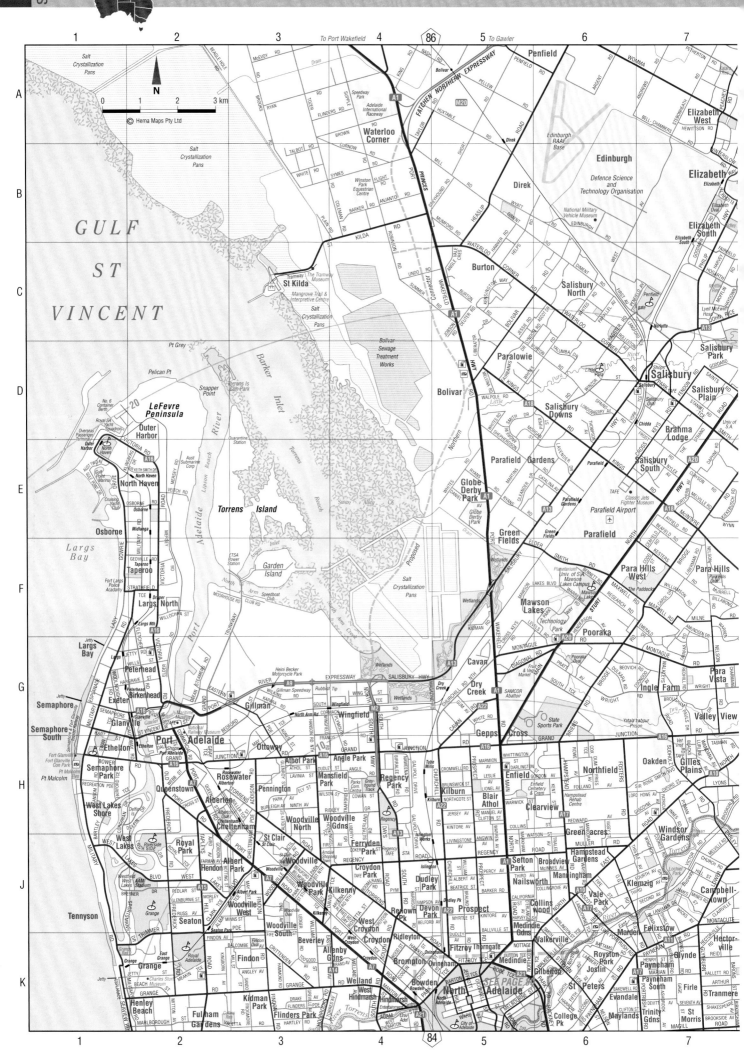

8 9 10 86 To Gawler 11 12 13 14

To Gawler

A

Davoren Park
Munno Para Shopping Centre
ULEY
CRAIGMORE
VINEY DR
GAWLER
TOOLUNGA RD
Toadcote Creek
Para Wirra
PLUM QUARRY RD
South Para Reservoir

Smithfield
Broadmeadows
ADAMS
ULEY
ULEY
MILES RD
SCRUB
Humbug Scrub Wildlife Sanctuary
Recreation
Mount Crawford Forest
Red Gum Flat

Elizabeth North
Elizabeth Downs
Craigmore
FRITH RD
Smith
Creek
FRANK BARBER
Malcolm

B

Womma
A20
Elizabeth Park
YORKTOWN
TURNER DR
SEABOROUGH RD
ULEY
TOP
TYEKA DR
ONE TREE HILL ROAD
CORNISHMANS
HUMBUG RD
TAYLOR RD
KERSBROOK RD
Humbug Scrub
BASSET RD
Mount Crawford Forest

Elizabeth East
Adam Ck
BLACK
GULF VIEW DR
GOULD RD
JOHNSON
One Tree Hill
HARVEY RD
KELLY HILL RD
SAMBEL RD

Elizabeth Grove
Little Para Reservoir
PRECOLUMB
KARWIN
One Tree Hill RD
SHEOAK RD

C

Hillbank
A20
BLACK
TOP
GOULD RD
Gould Creek
Gould Creek
Little
SHILLABER
Sampson Flat
KERSBROOK RD
DEVIL'S GULLY
To Lyndoch

Elizabeth Vale
Para River
Rifle Range Lookout
WILLIAMS
HILL
HANNAFORD HUMP RD
Mount Crawford Forest
RAKE
STONE QUARRY
B31

D

THE GROVE
Salisbury Heights
TARGET HILL
GREEN VALLEY
IMMANUEL RD
GOLDEN GROVE RD
Greenwith
Little Tree
BURG
AIRSTRIP
MILLAR RD
MOUNT GAWLER RD
KENT RD
KERSBROOK
WATTLE
HILL
WELSH RD
HILL

E

Salisbury East
Cobbler Creek Recreation Park
Golden Grove Village Shops
Golden Grove
GREENWITH RD
SEAVIEW
Upper Hermitage
Lower Hermitage
RICHARDSON
ADELAIDE GULLY
LYNDOCH RD
GLOVER RD
Kersbrook
MAIDSTONE
LEVETT RD

86

Wynn Vale
Surrey Downs
Yatala Vale
VALE
NORMAN RD
ANGWORI RD
WARNER
BURNS
CHECKER
Cemetery
B58

F

Modbury Heights
Redwood Park
Fairview Park
Tea Tree Gully
Banksia Park
GRENFELL
MILNE
Gould Res
RANGE RD
Inglewood
CHAPMAN
ADELAIDE RD
MANNUM RD
FIDDLERS
B10
Mount Crawford Forest
Torrens
Talunga Winery
To Gumeracha

G

Modbury North
A10
Ridgehaven
St Agnes
Westfield Tea Tree Plaza
Modbury
Angove Con Park
WHITING RD
HANCOCK
Tea Tree Gully
Houghton
BLACKHILL
A11
Anstey Hill Recreation Park
Vista
Millbrook Reservoir
Chain of Ponds
B10
Chain of Ponds Winery
Cudlee Creek Con Park
B58

H

Holden Hill
A18
Hope Valley
Hope Valley Reservoir
Higher combe Municipal Park
Paracombe
Gorge Wildlife Park
Cudlee Creek
GORGE RD
Mount Crawford Forest
LANGLEY
B58

Highbury
MAWSON
GORGE RD
Torrens River
B58
Kangaroo Creek Reservoir
HEYSEN TRAIL
CUDLEE CREEK RD
LOBETHAL

J

Newton
Thorndon Park Reservoir
Black Hill Conservation Park
YURREBILLA
Castambul
Montacute Conservation Park
Kangaroo Creek
Mount Crawford Forest
MAWSON TRAIL
CROFT RD
BERRY

Rostrevor
Wadmore Park
MONTACUTE RD
Montacute
Moralta Conservation Park
Sixth Creek
HEYSEN
EDWARDS
MAGPIE CASTLE RD
NEUDORF

K

Magill
Uni of SA
Woodforde
HEYSEN TRAIL
SUMMIT RD
Cherryville
Mount Crawford Forest
PLUMMERS RD
MARSHALL RD
ADELAIDE
LOBETHAL
To Lobethal

10km radius from GPO

8 9 85 11 12 13 14

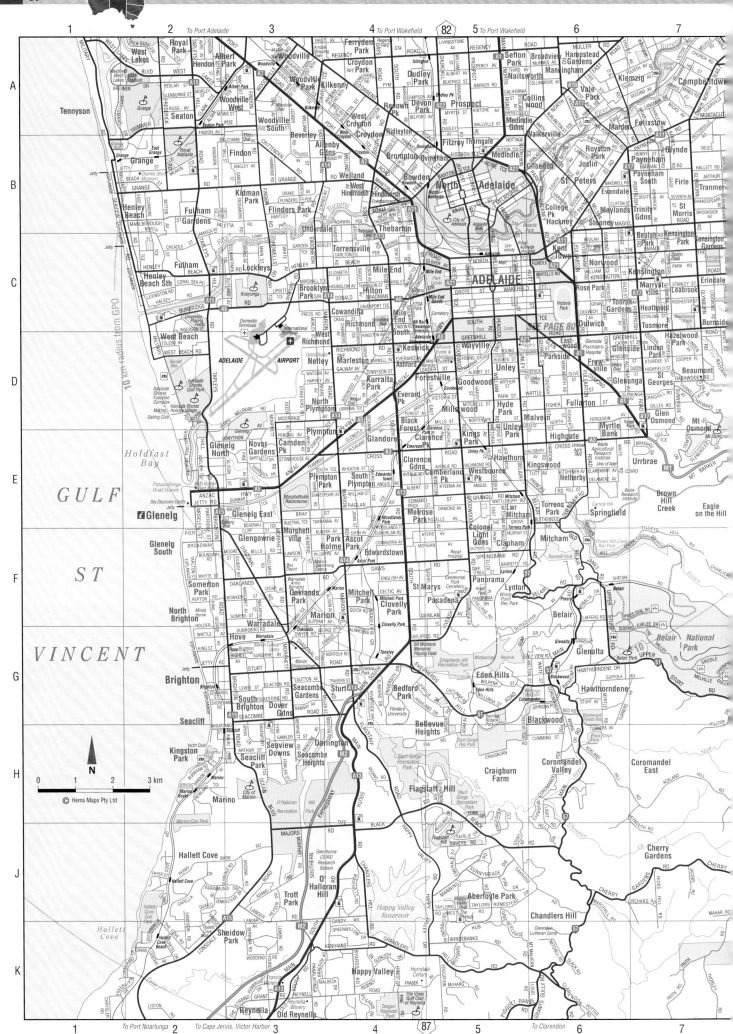

To Cudlee Creek

8 9 10 83 11 12 13 14

Castambul

Athelstone

Black Hill Conservation Park

Montacute

Montacute Conservation Park

Mount Crawford Forest

Newton

Mawson Trail

Mount Crawford Forest

Nootrovor

Woodforde

Magill

Cherryville

Marble Hill

Forest Range

Lenswood

Auldana

Teringie

Norton Summit

Marble Hill Nat Trust Reserve

Kenneth Stirling Con Park

Rosslyn Park

Wattle Park

Skye

Horsnell Gully Conservation Park

Horsnell Gully Con Park

Stonyfell

Ashton

Lobethal

Adelaide - Lobethal

Greenhill Recreation Park

Greenhill

Uraidla

Carey Gully

Kenneth Stirling Conservation Park

Waterfall Gully

Cleland Conservation Park

Cleland Wildlife Park

Summertown

Oakbank Racecourse

Yurrebilla

Leawood Gardens

Mt Lofty 727m

Eurilla Con Park

Piccadilly

Mt Lofty Botanic Garden

Woodhouse Scout Camp

Kenneth Stirling Conservation Park

Mt George

Greenhill

Oakbank

Balhannah

Crafers West

Crafers

Mt Lofty

Mt George Conservation Park

Mt Barker Junction

Stirling

Verdun

Onkaparinga

Balhannah

Upper Sturt

Aldgate

Bridgewater

Hahndorf

Upper Sturt

Heathfield

Warrawong Sanctuary

Mylor Conservation Park

Hahndorf Oval

Littlehampton

Ironbank

Heathfield

Longwood

Mylor

Mylor Parklands

Totness Recreation Park

Blackwood

Scott Creek

Bradbury

Biggs Flat

Mt Barker

To Tailem Bend

Scott Creek Conservation Park

Echunga

Echunga

Dorset Vale

Mt Bold

8 9 10 11 87 12 13 89 14

To Strathalbyn, Goolwa

Adelaide to Barossa Region, South Australia

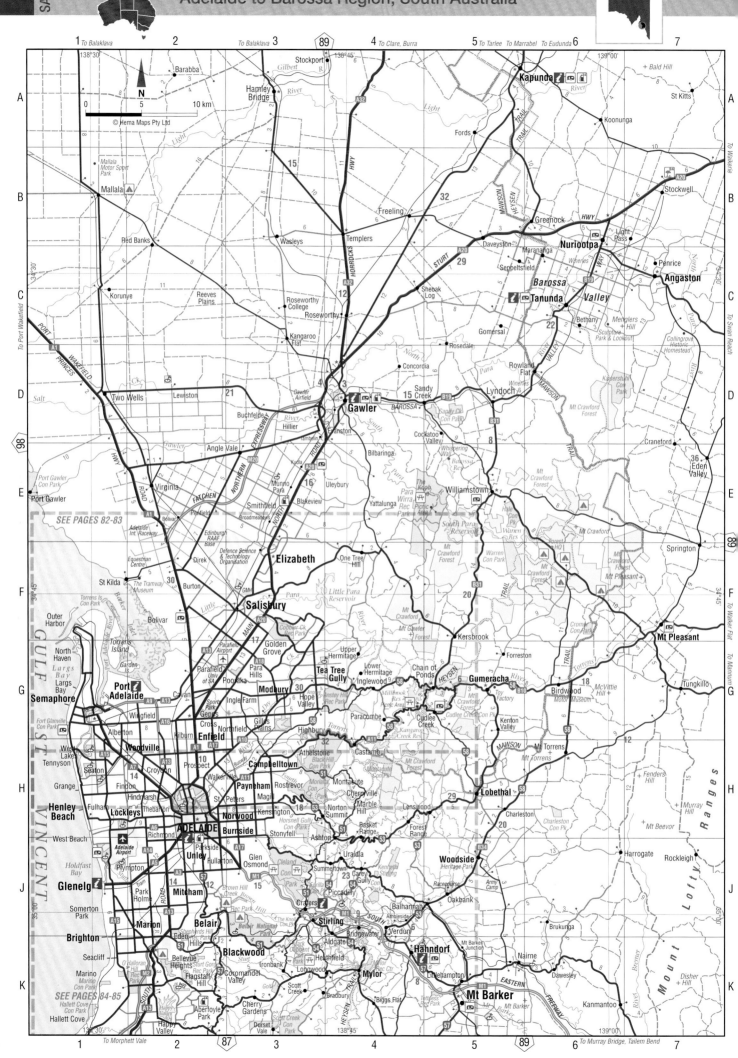

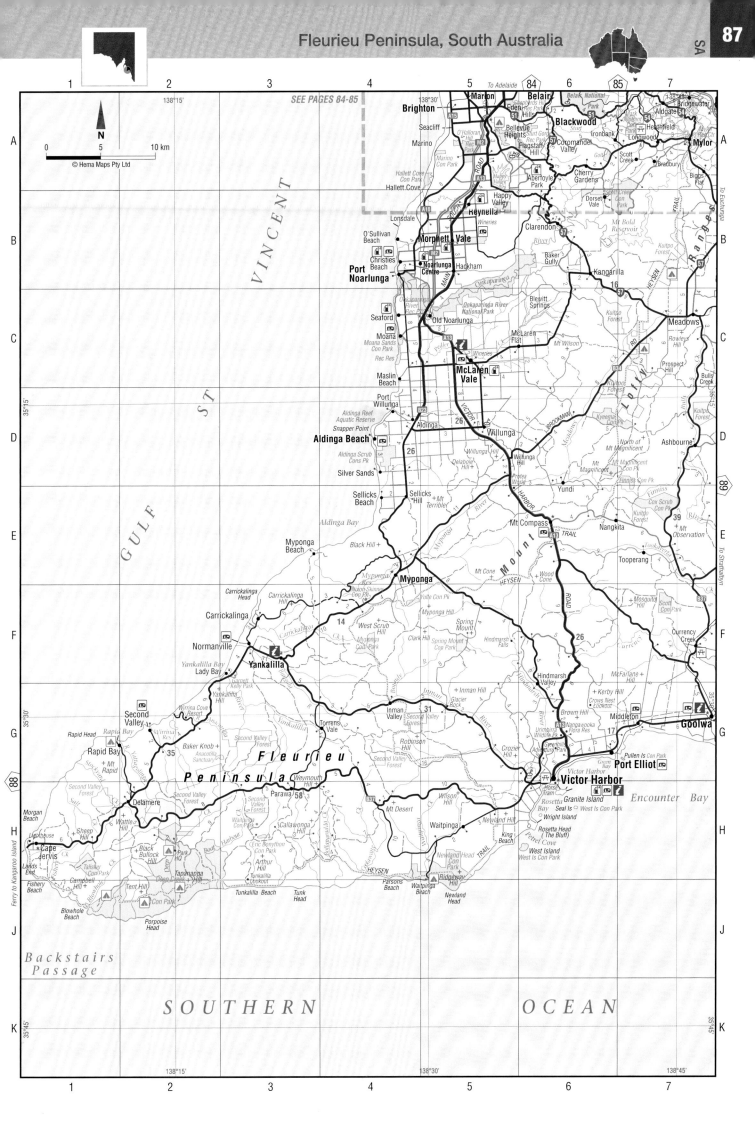

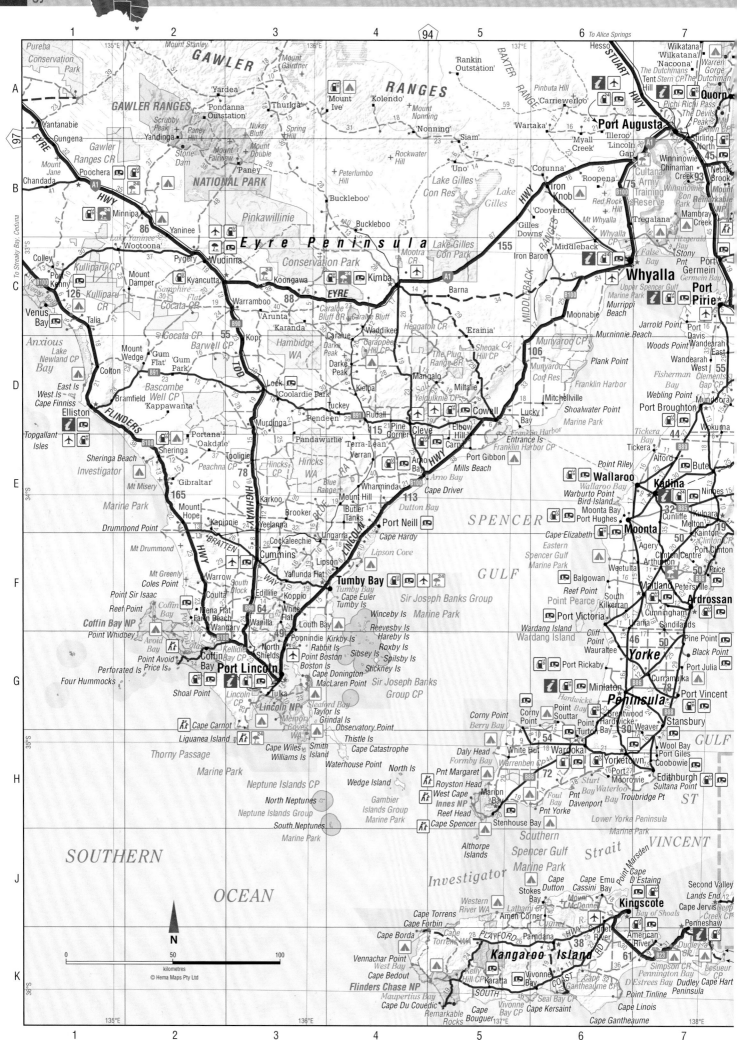

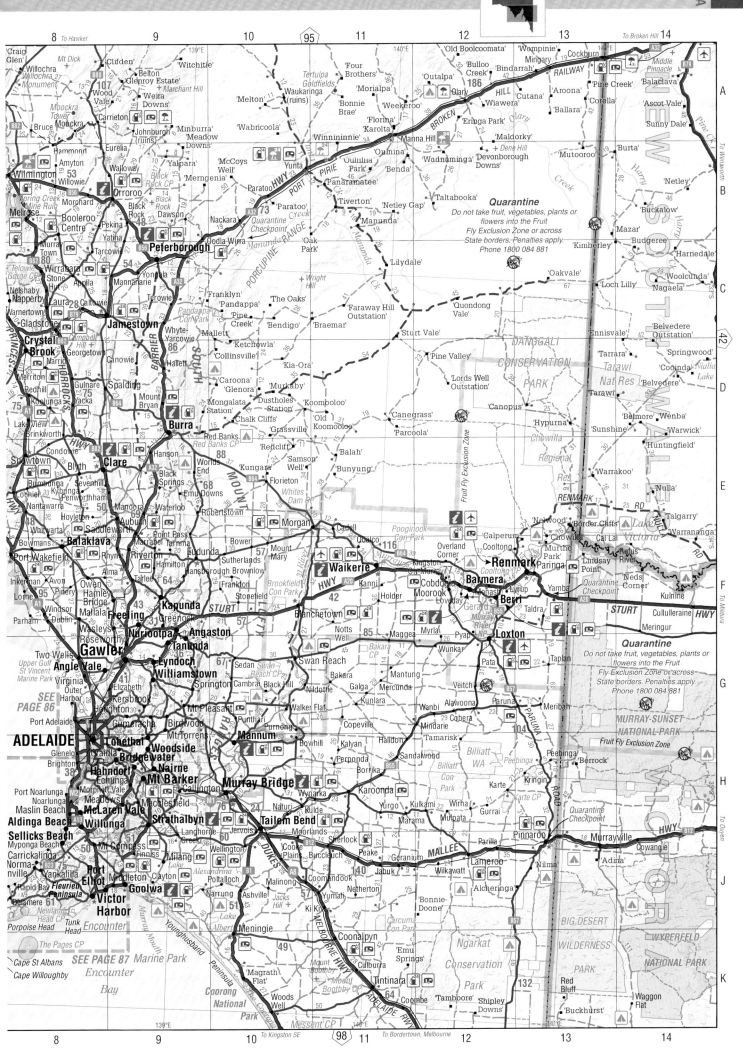

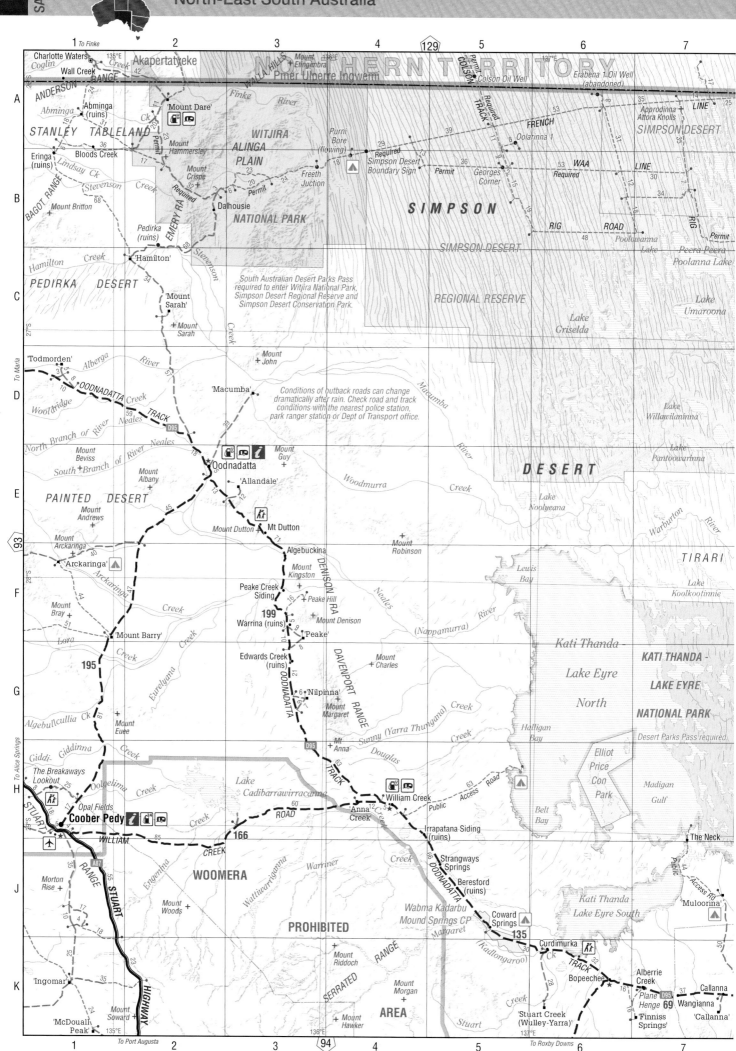

Charlotte Waters
Coglin
Wall Creek
135°E
Akapertatyeke
42
To Finke

ANDERSON RANGE
Abminga
Abminga (ruins)
24
31
'Mount Dare'

NORTHERN TERRITORY

Mount Etingimbra
136°E
Pmer Ulperte Ingwemi

WALL HILLS
Finke River

COLSON
Colson Oil Well
137°E
Erabena 1 Oil Well (abandoned)

Permit
TRACK
Required

A

STANLEY TABLELAND
Eringa (ruins)
6
36
Bloods Creek
16
17
Lindsay Ck
Mount Hammersley
Mount Crispe
Stevenson
68
WITJIRA
ALINGA
PLAIN
Purni Bore (flowing)

FRENCH
39
53
11
Oolarinna 1
8

Approdinna
Attora Knolls
35
14
LINE
25
SIMPSON DESERT
35
17

B

BAGOT RANGE
Mount Britton
Creek
EMERY RA
Required
Dalhousie
Pedirka (ruins)
Hamilton Creek
'Hamilton'
34
Stevenson Creek
20
24
23
3
6
Permit
Freeth Juction
18
Required
29
Simpson Desert Boundary Sign
Permit
36
Georges Corner
15
2
53
Required
WAA
LINE
12
30
34
18

S I M P S O N
SIMPSON DESERT
RIG
ROAD
48
Poolowanna
Lake
RIG
Permit
Peera Peera Poolanna Lake

C

PEDIRKA DESERT
'Mount Sarah'
Mount Sarah
Creek
South Australian Desert Parks Pass required to enter Witjira National Park, Simpson Desert Regional Reserve and Simpson Desert Conservation Park.
REGIONAL RESERVE
Lake Griselda
Lake Umaroona

D

To Marla
'Todmorden'
Alberga River
3
8
10
OODNADATTA Creek TRACK
D95
Wooldridge
Neales
59
North Branch of River Neales
'Macumba'
Mount John
Conditions of outback roads can change dramatically after rain. Check road and track conditions with the nearest police station, park ranger station or Dept of Transport office.
Macumba River
Lake Willawilanima
Lake Pantoowarinna

E

93
PAINTED DESERT
Mount Beviss
South Branch of River Neales
Mount Albany
45
Mount Andrews
Mount Arckaringa
40
'Arckaringa'
18
Oodnadatta
Mount Guy
'Allandale'
13
12
Mount Dutton
Mt Dutton
DESERT
Woodmurra Creek
Lake Noolyeana
Warburton River
Lewis Bay
TIRARI
Lake Pantoowarinna

F

Mount Bray
44
51
Arckaringa Creek
17
'Mount Barry'
Algebuckina
Mount Kingston
Peake Creek Siding
19
Peake Hill
199
Warrina (ruins)
9
5
'Peake'
DENISON RA
Mount Denison
Neales River
(Nappamurra)
Lake Koolkootinnie

G

195
Eureiyana Creek
Mount Euee
Edwards Creek (ruins)
12
6
'Nilpinna'
Mount Margaret
OODNADATTA
DAVENPORT RANGE
Mount Charles
Mount Robinson
Sunny (Yarra Thungana) Creek
Kati Thanda - Lake Eyre North
KATI THANDA - LAKE EYRE NATIONAL PARK
Desert Parks Pass required

H

To Alice Springs
Giddi
Giddinna Creek
The Breakaways Lookout
25
Opal Fields
Coober Pedy
17
STUART
Oolgelima Creek
Lake Cadibarrawirracanna
Mt Anna
D95
TRACK
William Creek
Anna Creek
63
Access Road
Public
Halligan Bay
Belt Bay
Madigan Gulf
Elliot Price Con Park

J

RANGE
Morton Rise
10
4
STUART
WILLIAM
85
CREEK
166
WOOMERA
Mount Woods
Engenina Creek
Wattuwarrigana
ROAD
60
Warriner
Irrapatana Siding (ruins)
Strangways Springs
66
OODNADATTA
Beresford (ruins)
Wabma Kadarbu Mound Springs CP
Margaret
Coward Springs
135
Kati Thanda - Lake Eyre South
The Neck
Muloorina
'Callanna'

K

'Ingomar'
35
HIGHWAY
A87
55
23
Mount Soward
135°E
Mount Riddoch
PROHIBITED
Mount Morgan
AREA
Mount Hawker
Mount Woods
SERRATED RANGE
Stuart Creek (Wulley-Yarra)'
137°E
Curdimurka
TRACK
32
Bopeechee
Plane Henge
69
D95
Finniss Springs'
Alberrie Creek
16
Wangianna
Callanna
37

To Port Augusta
136°E
94
To Roxby Downs

8 9 10 11 12 13 14

QUEENSLAND

To Bedourie
To Windorah

MUNGA - THIRRI (SIMPSON DESERT) NATIONAL PARK
Permit required from QNPWS.

Nappanerica 'Big Red' Dune
Birdsville
Birdsville Hotel

'Planet Downs Outstation'

Poeppel Corner

South Australian Desert Parks Pass required to enter Witjira National Park, Simpson Desert Regional Reserve and Simpson Desert Conservation Park.

Lake Thomas

'Alton Downs'
'Pandie Pandie'

STURT STONY DESERT

Moomba Lake
Cadelga Outstation
Haddon Corner

CONSERVATION PARK

Lake Uloowaranie
Lake Etamunbanie

161

N
0 50 100
kilometres
© Hema Maps Pty Ltd

Kuncherinna No 1 Oil Well Site

STURT STONY DESERT

Birdsville Inside Track often closed due to flooding.

Australia's Largest Shearing Shed 'Cordillo Downs'

'Arrabury'

Koonchera Dune (Southern End of Dune)

Poolyeruninna Lake

'Clifton Hills'
Warburton Crossing

315

Lake Goyder (Coolangirie)

INNAMINCKA

22

Malkumba-Coongie Lakes National Park
Coongie

For more detail on this area, see HEMA's Great Desert Tracks Eastern sheet.

Coongie Lakes

Mulga Bore

Mt Gason Bore

STRZELECKI

REGIONAL RESERVE

142

Patchawara Bore

Lake Warrandirinna

Walkers Crossing

'Kalamurina'
'Cowarie'
Lake Howitt

Burke & Wills Dig Tree

'Nappa Merrie'

Gypsum Cliff

Lake Marrakodondmooka
'Gidgealpa'
'Innamincka'
Innamincka
Burkes Memorial

DESERT

Kalamurra Lake

'Mungerannie'

Cooper

Moomba

154

Della Satellite Gas Station

Innamincka Bore No 3

Lake Kittakittaooloo

'Mulka'

Lake Mulapula
Lake Puntawolona
Cooper Creek

Lake Hope or Pando

Innamincka Bore No 2

'Epsilon'

Lake Florence

'Etadunna'
Flood Bypass Only

STRZELECKI REGIONAL RESERVE

'Merty Merty'

Bore Track
Access along Bore Track from Bollards Lagoon is no longer permitted.

'Omicron'

202

Dulkaninna
Lake Gregory
Mount Flint

DESERT

Bollards Lagoon
Cameron Corner
'Fortville House'
Dog Fence

The Corner Store
'Fortville Bore'
Fort Grey
STURT NP
'Whitecatch House'
'Waka'

'Clayton'
River
Lake Harry

Lake Blanche

122

'Tilcha' (ruins)
Lake Stewart
'Hewart Downs'

Lake Harry
Mount Playford

Dog Fence

For more detail on this area, see HEMA's Flinders Ranges map.

'Murnpeowie'
Blanchewater
STRZELECKI

STRZELECKI REGIONAL RESERVE

Marree
Mundowdna

'Mount Hopeless'

Lake Callabonna

NEW SOUTH WALES

To Lyndhurst
To Lyndhurst
To Thoobura

95

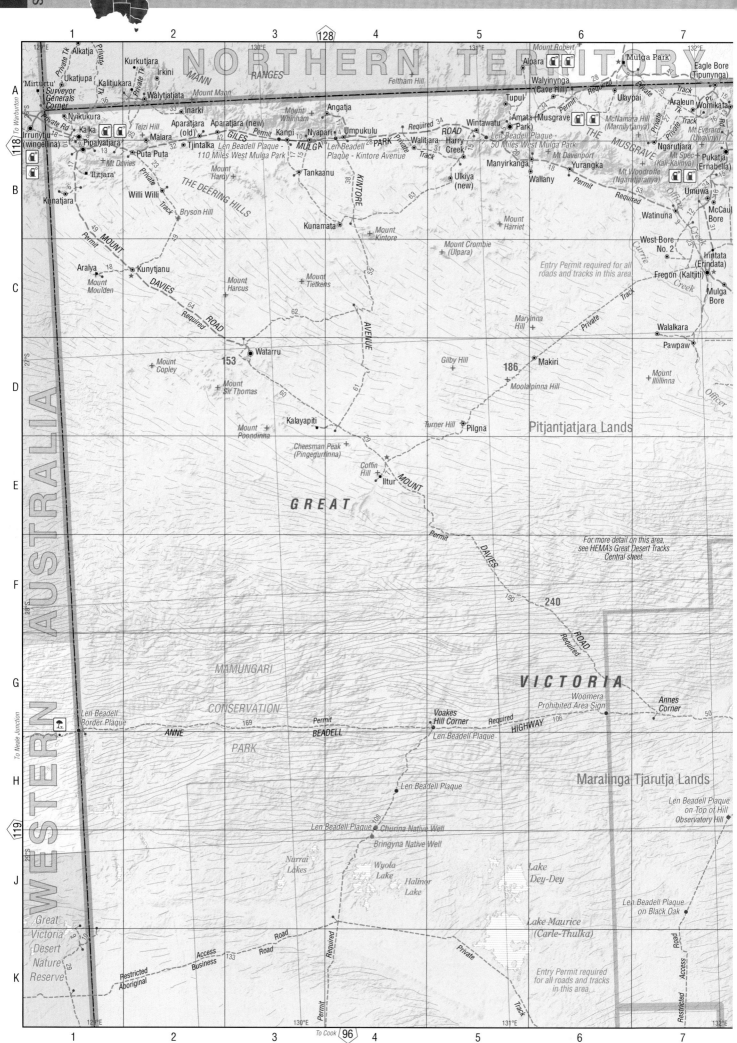

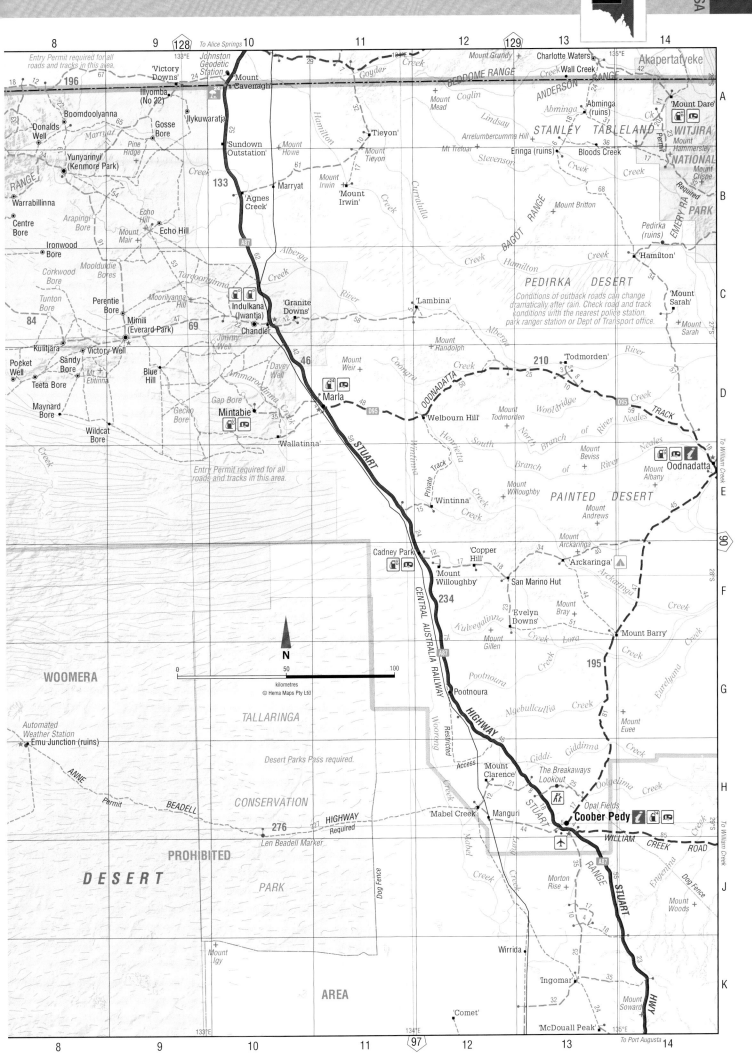

Entry Permit required for all
roads and tracks in this area.

196

To Alice Springs

'Victory Downs'
Johnston Geodetic Station
Illyomba (No 22)
Ilykuwaratja
Mount Cavenagh
Gosse Bore
Donalds Well
Boomdoolyanna
Yunyarinyi (Kenmore Park)
Pine Ridge
'Sundown Outstation'
Mount Howe
133
Centre Bore
Warrabillinna
Arapingi Bore
Echo Hill
Mount Mair
Echo Hill
Ironwood Bore
Mooulduldie Bores
Moorilyanna Hill
Marryat
'Agnes Creek'
Mount Irwin
'Mount Irwin'
'Tieyon'
Mount Tieyon
Corkwood Bore
Perentie Bore
Tunton Bore
Indulkana (Iwantja)
'Granite Downs'
Chandler
84
Mimili (Everard Park)
69
Jimmy Well
46
A7
Kulitjara
Victory Well
Mt Etitinna
Sandy Bore
Blue Hill
Davey Well
Ammaroodinna Creek
Mount Weir
Marla
48
Pocket Well
Teeta Bore
Gap Bore
Gecko Bore
Mintabie
Maynard Bore
Wildcat Bore
'Wallatinna'
STUART
'Welbourn Hill'
210
'Todmorden'
OODNADATTA
Mount Randolph
Coongra Creek
Alberga Creek
Mount Todmorden
Mount Beviss
Neales River
TRACK
D95
Oodnadatta
Mount Albany
PAINTED DESERT
Mount Willoughby
Henrietta Creek
Mount Andrews
'Wintinna'
Private Track
Mount Arckaringa
Arckaringa
90
Cadney Park
'Copper Hill'
'Mount Willoughby'
San Marino Hut
234
'Evelyn Downs'
Mount Bray
Mount Gillen
'Mount Barry'
195
Pootnoura
HIGHWAY
Algebullcullia Creek
Mount Euee
Eurelyana Creek

WOOMERA

Automated Weather Station
Emu Junction (ruins)
ANNE
BEADELL
Permit
HIGHWAY
Required
'Mount Clarence'
The Breakaways Lookout
Oolgelima Creek
Giddinna
Restricted
Access
'Mabel Creek'
Manguri
Opal Fields
Coober Pedy
TALLARINGA
Desert Parks Pass required.
276
Len Beadell Marker
CONSERVATION
Dog Fence
STUART
RANGE
WILLIAM
CREEK
ROAD
PROHIBITED
PARK
Morton Rise
DESERT
Mount Igy
Wirrida
STUART HWY
'Ingomar'
Mount Woods
AREA
'Comet'
'McDouall Peak'
To Port Augusta

N
0   50   100
kilometres
© Hema Maps Pty Ltd

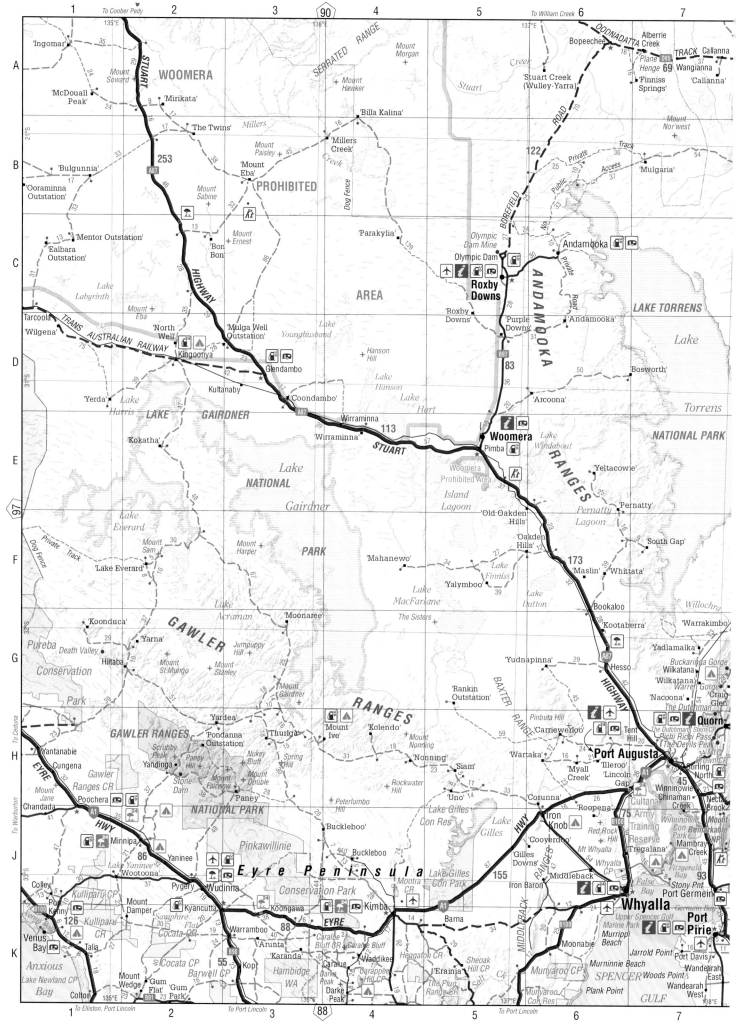

SA

To Birdsville

STRZELECKI
REGIONAL
RESERVE

'Hewart
Downs'

Marree
'Mundowdna'

Murnpeowie
Blanchewater
STRZELECKI TRACK
'Mount Hopeless'

'Tilcha'
(ruins)

To Innamincka

Lake
Callabonna

Tilcha Creek

Winnathee

Hawker
Gate

Hawker
Gate House

No access to
South Australia
via Hawker Gate

'Wilpoorinna'

Mount
Distance

Mt Frooling

Mt Livingston
Mt Neil

Petermorra Creek

Mount
Yerila

'Moolawatana'

FLINDERS

RANGES

Boolkaree

Yandaminta
Ck

Witchelina
Farina (ruins)
Farina Historic Ruins

'Mount
Freeling'

Mt Crocker

Smithville
Outpost

Ochre Cliffs
Lyndhurst
'Avondale'

'Umberatana'

Arkaroola
Village
Arkaroola

'North
Mulga'

152

'Moorabie'

Lake Wallace

'Border Downs'

40

'Myrtle
Springs'

Mount
Burr

'Mount
Lyndhurst'

VULKATHUNHA
GAMMON RANGES
NATIONAL PARK

'Yankaninna'
Benbonyathe Hill

'Turleys House'

Packsaddle Ck

Copley
'Depot
Springs'

'Owieandana'

'Wooltana'

Leigh Creek

North
Moolooloo

Mt Serle
Angepena
Nepabunna
Iga Warta

Mt
McKinlay

Balcanoona

Italowie
Gorge

'Wertaloona'

Lake
Frome

Lake Frome

N

kilometres
© Hema Maps Pty Ltd

'Pine
View'

'Westwood
Downs'

'Broughams
Gate House'

'Quinyambie'

'Avenel'

Joulnie

Teilta

Ediacara
Con Park

Mount
James

Beltana
Roadhouse
(closed)

Manners
Well

Mt
Wallace
Commemorative
Plaque

100

Regional Reserve

'Lynray'

'Nilpena'

'Warraweena'
Nantawarrinna

'Moorillah'
Nuccaleena
Historic Site

Old Fencers
Camp

'McDougalls
Well'

'Mount
Woowoolahra'

Mount
Woowoolahra

Parachilna
Motpena

'Narrina'
'Moolooloo'
Mt Lucius

Mulga
View

Aboriginal Dreaming Site -
Mt Chambers

'Gum Park'

Corona

Angorichina
Village
Oratunga
Nildottie Gap

Kantappa

'Commodore'

Blinman
'Gum
Creek'

'Wirrealpa'

Balcoracana
Creek

'Mulga
Valley'

Wilangee

Brachina
Gorge

Great Walls
of China
Flinders
Ranges NP

Benagerie

'Eldee'

Purnamoota
Day Dream
Mine Historic
Town Site

Parachilna
Gorge

Bunyeroo
Gorge

Drapanulna
Bunkers
Con Res

'Frome
Downs'

Dog Fence

'Edeowie'

'Moralana'

Edeowie
Gorge
Upalinna
Wilpena

Willow
Springs

'Martins
Well'

'Benagerie'

'Mooleulooloo'

Nine
Mile

'Merna
Mora'

Wilpena
Pound
Rawnsley
Park

Sacred
Canyon
'Prelinna'

'Erudina'

'Mulyungarie'

'Yarramba'

Steam
Museum

Silverton
Sculpture Site
Acacia Site

'Lake
Torrens'
'Mernmerna'

'Curnamona'

'Stratheam'

Kalkaroo

'Mundi
Mundi

Broken Hill

'Wallerberdina'
Hookina

Arkaba
Glen
Lyle
Glen Oak

'Warcowie'

'Willipa'

270

'Killawarra
Outstation'

'Kalabity'

Old Lake Dismal

Wild
Dog Glen

Hawker
Mt Ernest

'Holowiliena'
'Bibliando'

'Glenorchy'

'Boolcoomata'
'Old Boolcoomata'

Wompinie

'Pine Creek'

Balaclava

'Partacoona'
Wilson

'Worumba'

'Baratta'
(ruins)

Orama
Hill

'Holowiliena
South'

'Nillinghoo'

'Mount
Victor'

'Plumbago'

'Bimbowrie'

Mingary
Cockburn

RAILWAY

'Aroona'

'Corella'

'Ascot Vale'

'Buckaringa'
'Springfield'

Kanyaka (ruins)
Gordon (ruins)

Cradock

'Milang'

Koonamore

'Bulloo
Creek'

'Outalpa'

186

'Bindarrah'

Middle
Pinnacle

'Sunny Dale'

Willow
Glen
Wyacca Pioneer Monument

109

Mt Dick
Clifden

Witchitie

BROKEN

Olary

HILL

'Cutana'

'Ballara'

Willochra
Willochra
Monument

Belton
'Glenroy Estate'

Marchant Hill

Waukaringa
(ruins)

'Morialpa'

Weekeroo

Eringa Park

107

Wood
Vale

'Weira
Downs'

'Melton'

'Bonnie
Brae'

'Florina'
'Karolta'

Manna Hill

'Maldorky'

Mutooroo

'Burta'

'Netley'

Moockra
Tower

Carrieton
Johnburgh
(ruins)

Minburra
'Meadow
Downs'

'Winnininnie'

'Oulnina'

'Devonborough
Downs'

Bruce
Moockra

Hammond
Amyton

Eurelia

'Wabricoola'

'McCoys
Well'

Yunta

'Oulnina
Park'

'Benda'

'Wadnaminga'

'Buckalow'

Wilmington
Willowie

Walloway

'Yalpara'

'Merngenia'

Paratoo

PIRIE

'Panaramitee'

'Taltabooka'

Mazar

'Budgeree'

Morchard

Orroroo

Black
Rock CP

Black
Rock
Dawson

PORT

'Paratoo'

Tiverton

'Netley Gap'

Manunda

Quarantine
Do not take fruit, vegetables, plants or
flowers into the Fruit
Fly Exclusion Zone or across
State borders. Penalties apply.
Phone 1800 084 881

'Kimberley'

'Harriedale'

Spring Creek
Mine Ruin

Melrose

Pekina
Yatina

Nackara
Quarantine
Checkpoint

'Oak
Park'

Lilydale

Booleroo
Centre

Oodla Wirra

Tarcowie

Peterborough

54

'Oakvale'

'Loch Lilly'

'Woolcunda'

'Nagaela'

Murray
Town

Wirrabara

Yongala

Franklyn
'Pandappa'

'Quondong
Vale'

'Belvedere
Outstation'

Telowie
Gorge CP

Appila
Caltowie

Terowie

'Pine
Creek'

'The Oaks'

'Faraway Hill
Outstation'

DANGGALI
CONSERVATION
PARK

Tipperary Hut

'Springwood'

Nelshaby
Napperby

Laura

Whyte-
Yarcowie

Mallett

'Bendigo'
'Braemar'

'Sturt Vale'

Ennisvale

'Tarrara'

'Cooinda'

Gladstone
Warnertown

Jamestown
86

'Collinsville'

'Ketchowla'

'Pine Valley'

Tarawi
Nat Res

Crystal
Brook

Narridy
Merriton

Campbell
Hill
Georgetown

Canowie

Hallett

BARRIER

'Kia-Ora'

To Adelaide

To Burra, Adelaide

To Wentworth

To Tibooburra

To Cobar

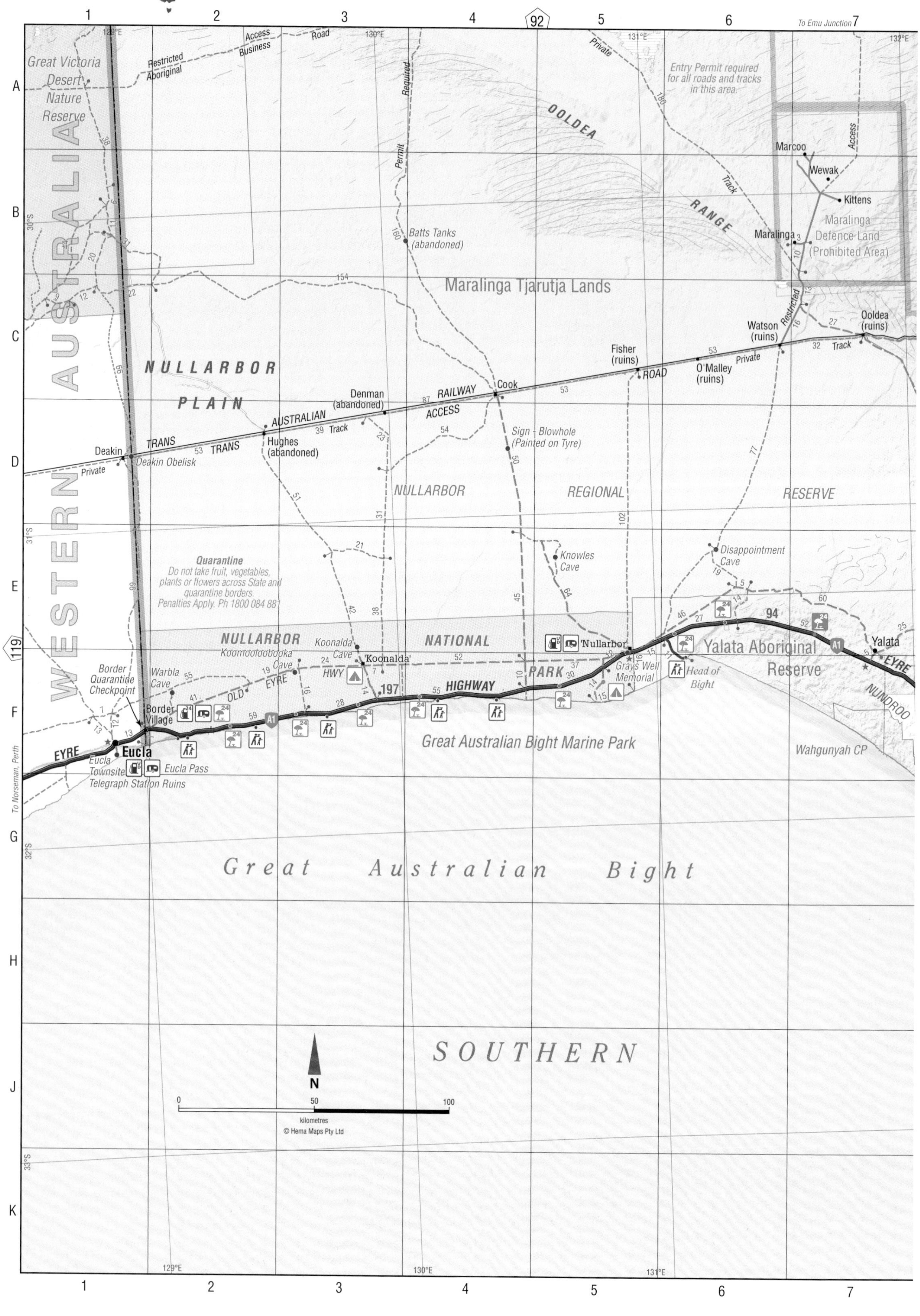
Great Victoria Desert Nature Reserve
Restricted Aboriginal
Access Business Road
Permit Required
Private
Entry Permit required for all roads and tracks in this area.
OOLDEA RANGE
Track
Access
Marcoo
Wewak
Kittens
Maralinga
Maralinga Defence Land (Prohibited Area)
Batts Tanks (abandoned)
Maralinga Tjarutja Lands
Restricted
Watson (ruins)
Ooldea (ruins)
Track
Fisher (ruins)
O'Malley (ruins)
Private
ROAD
NULLARBOR PLAIN
Cook
RAILWAY
ACCESS
Denman (abandoned)
AUSTRALIAN
Track
TRANS
Hughes (abandoned)
Deakin
Deakin Obelisk
Private
Sign - Blowhole (Painted on Tyre)
NULLARBOR REGIONAL RESERVE
WESTERN AUSTRALIA
Quarantine
Do not take fruit, vegetables, plants or flowers across State and quarantine borders.
Penalties Apply. Ph 1800 084 881
Knowles Cave
Disappointment Cave
NULLARBOR NATIONAL PARK
Koonalda Cave
Koomooloobooka Cave
'Koonalda'
'Nullarbor'
Yalata Aboriginal Reserve
Yalata
EYRE
NUNDROO
Grays Well Memorial
Head of Bight
Border Quarantine Checkpoint
Warbla Cave
OLD EYRE HWY
HIGHWAY
Border Village
Eucla
Eucla Townsite
Telegraph Station Ruins
Eucla Pass
To Norseman, Perth
Great Australian Bight Marine Park
Wahgunyah CP
Great Australian Bight
SOUTHERN
N
0 50 100
kilometres
© Hema Maps Pty Ltd
To Emu Junction
92
119
197
94
A1
129°E
130°E
131°E
132°E
30°S
31°S
32°S
33°S

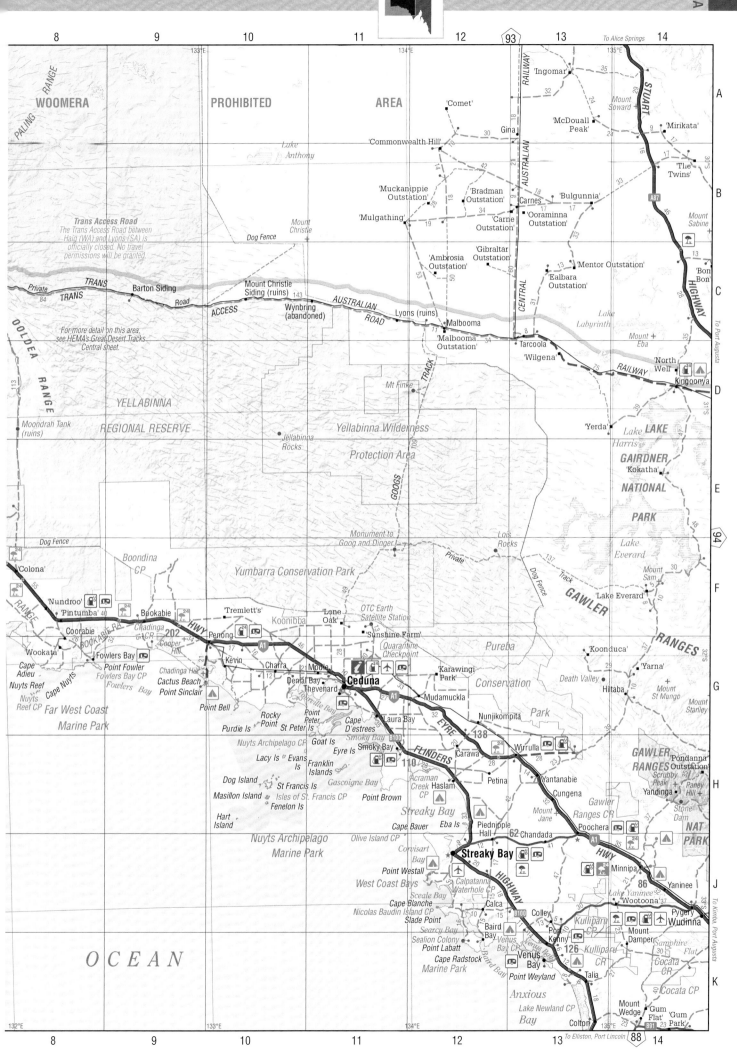

WOOMERA   PROHIBITED   AREA

131°E   134°E   135°E

'Ingomar'

'Comet'   Mount
'McDouall   Soward
Peak'   'Mirikata'

Lake   'Commonwealth Hill'   Gina
Anthony   'The
Twins'
30°S

Mount   'Muckanippie   'Bradman   'Bulgunnia'
Christie   Outstation'   Outstation'
'Mulgathing'   Carnes
'Carne   'Ooraminna
Outstation'   Outstation'   Mount
Sabine

Dog Fence   'Gibraltar
'Ambrosia   Outstation'
Outstation'   'Bon
'Ealbara   Bon'
'Mentor Outstation'
Outstation'   13

Trans Access Road
The Trans Access Road between
Haig (WA) and Lyons (SA) is
officially closed. No travel
permissions will be granted.   CENTRAL

Private   TRANS   Barton Siding   Mount Christie   HIGHWAY
84   Siding (ruins)   143   AUSTRALIAN
TRANS   ACCESS   Road   ROAD   Lyons (ruins)
Wynbring
(abandoned)   Malbooma   Lake
For more detail on this area,   Labyrinth
see HEMA's Great Desert Tracks   'Malbooma
Central sheet.   Outstation'   Tarcoola   Mount
'Wilgena'   Eba   'North
Well'
75   RAILWAY   Kingoonya

Moondrah Tank   'Yerda'   Lake   LAKE
(ruins)   YELLABINNA   Harris
REGIONAL RESERVE   Yellabinna Wilderness   GAIRDNER
Jellabinna   'Kokatha'
Rocks   Protection Area   NATIONAL

Mt Finke
PARK

Dog Fence   Monument to   Lois   Lake
Goog and Dinger   Rocks   Everard   Mount
'Colona'   Private   Sam
Boondina   'Lake Everard'
'Nundroo'   CP   Yumbarra Conservation Park   Dog Fence   Track   137
'Pintumba'   GAWLER
Coorabie   Bookabie   OTC Earth   'Koonduca'
'Tremlett's'   'Lone   Satellite Station   Pureba   RANGES
Chadinga   Koonibba   Oak'   'Yarna'
'Wookata'   Fowlers Bay   CR   202   HWY   Penong   'Sunshine Farm'   Death Valley   Hiltaba
Cooper   Kevin   Quarantine   Mount
Fowlers Bay   Hill   Charra   Checkpoint   'Karawingi'   Pureba   St Mungo   Mount
Cape   Point Fowler   Chadinga Hill   Moule   Park'   Conservation   Stanley
Adieu   Cactus Beach   Dental Bay   Ceduna   Mount
Nuyts Reef   Point Sinclair   Thevenard   Mudamuckla   Park   GAWLER   Pondanna
Nuyts   RANGES   Outstation
Reef CP   Far West Coast   Point Bell   Rocky   Point   Laura Bay   Nunjikompita   Scrubby   Paney
Marine Park   Point   Peter Is   Cape   Carawa   Wirrulla   Peak   Hill
Purdie Is   St Peter Is   D'estrees   Smoky Bay   138   Yandinga
Goat Is   Eyre Is   FLINDERS   Petina   Gawler   Stone
Lacy Is   Evans   Franklin   110   Vantanabie   Ranges CR   Dam
Dog Island   Is   Islands   Gascoigne Bay   Acraman   Haslam   Cungena   NAT
St Francis Is   Creek   Petina   Mount   Poochera   PARK
Masillon Island   Isles of St Francis CP   Point Brown   CP   Jane   Chandada
Hart   Fenelon Is   Streaky Bay   Cape Bauer   Eba Is   Piednipple   62   A1
Island   Hall
Nuyts Archipelago   Olive Island CP   Mount   Minnipa   86
Marine Park   Corvisart   Streaky Bay   Jane   Yaninee
Bay   Lake Yaninee
Point Westall   Calpatanna   Wootoona
West Coast Bays   Waterhole CP   Chandada   Mount
Cape Blanche   Scale Bay   Calca   Colley   Damper   Sapphire
Nicolas Baudin Island CP   B100   Pygery   Flat
Slade Point   Searcy Bay   Baird   Port   Kulliparu   Mount   Wudinna
Bay   Sealion Colony   Bay   Kenny   126   CP   Cocata
OCEAN   Point Labatt   Venus   Venus   Kulliparu   CR   Cocata CP
Cape Radstock   Bay   Point Weyland   Bay CP   CR
Marine Park   Point Labatt   Talia   Mount
Anxious   Wedge   'Gum
Lake Newland CP   Colton   Flat'   'Gum
Bay   B91   Park'

132°E   133°E   134°E   135°E   To Kimba, Port Augusta

8   9   10   11   12   13   14
To Elliston, Port Lincoln   88

SPENCER GULF

NEW SOUTH WALES

SOUTHERN OCEAN

Investigator Strait

GULF ST VINCENT

Kangaroo Island

ADELAIDE

SEE PAGE 86

SEE PAGE 87

Wallaroo
Kadina
Moonta
Moonta Bay
Port Hughes
Ardrossan
Yorke Peninsula
Yorketown
Kingscote
Edithburgh
Stansbury
Port Vincent
Minlaton

Snowtown
Clare
Burra
Balaklava
Gawler
Kapunda
Angaston
Nuriootpa
Tanunda
Lyndoch
Williamstown
Angle Vale
Virginia
Elizabeth
Mt Pleasant
Mannum
Murray Bridge
Tailem Bend
Hahndorf
Mt Barker
Woodside
Nairne
Lobethal
Bridgewater
Strathalbyn
McLaren Vale
Willunga
Aldinga Beach
Sellicks Beach
Normanville
Yankalilla
Victor Harbor
Goolwa
Port Elliot
Middleton
Clayton

Waikerie
Morgan
Renmark
Berri
Loxton
Barmera
Cobdogla
Moorook
Blanchetown
Swan Reach
Pinnaroo
Murrayville
Lameroo
Keith
Bordertown
Nhill
Tintinara
Coonalpyn
Meningie
Coorong National Park

MURRAY-SUNSET NATIONAL PARK

BIG DESERT WILDERNESS PARK

WYPERFELD NATIONAL PARK

LITTLE DESERT NATIONAL PARK

Kingston SE
Robe
Beachport
Millicent
Mount Gambier
Port MacDonnell
Penola
Naracoorte
Casterton
Edenhope
Nhill
Kaniva
Heywood
Portland

Encounter Bay

Quarantine
Do not take fruit, vegetables, plants or flowers into the Fruit Fly Exclusion Zone or across State borders. Penalties apply. Phone 1800 084 881

N

kilometres
0   50   100

© Hema Maps Pty Ltd

PURNULULU NATIONAL PARK (117 G13) PHOTO: © ISTOCK.COM/SARAH WINTER

Distances are shown in kilometres and follow the most direct major sealed route where possible.

1400	1000	113	1546	958	3575	1892	865	799	476	1276	358	2594	**Albany**
3223	609	2217	1048	1654	1049	842	2314	1992	2703	1457	2592		**Broome**
1593	1800	178	1347	723	3372	1693	770	600	669	1077			**Bunbury**
2344	862	899	1237	815	2438	634	1459	477	1600				**Carnarvon**
924	2108	737	1655	1049	3684	2268	389	1275					**Esperance**
1867	1327	422	964	338	2983	1093	982						**Geraldton**
909	1719	596	1266	660	3295	1879							**Kalgoorlie**
2788	238	1515	631	1219	1867								**Karratha**
4206	1590	3198	2029	2635									**Kununurra**
1569	1059	563	606										**Mount Magnet**
2175	453	1169											**Newman**
1445	1622												**Perth**
2628													**Port Hedland**
													WA-SA Border Village

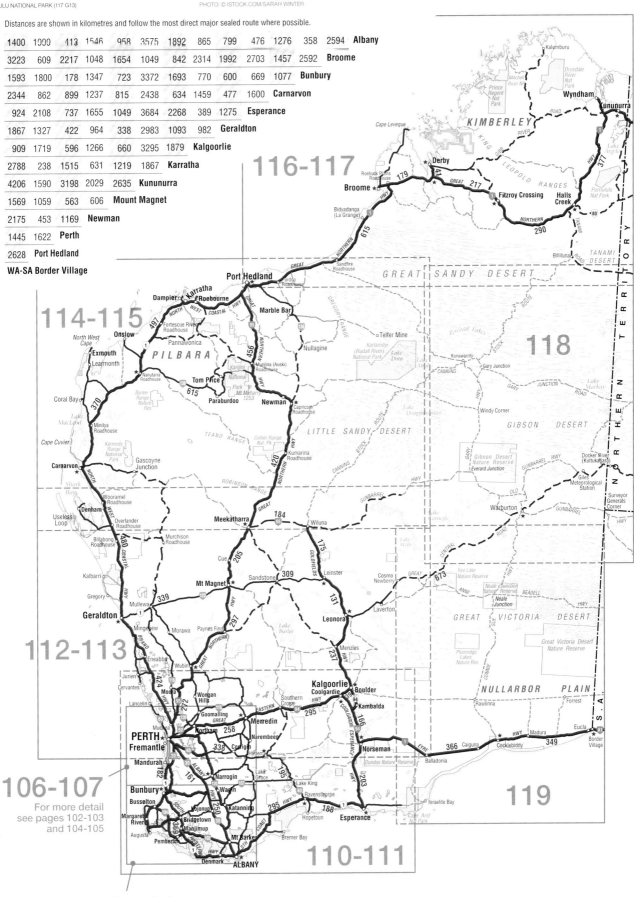

106-107

For more detail
see pages 102-103
and 104-105

112-113

114-115

116-117

118

119

110-111

108-109

Perth CBD

Map Labels

Northbridge · West Perth · Perth · East Perth · Wellington Square · Kings Park · South Perth · Swan · Perth Water · River · Heirisson Island · The Narrows · Milyu · Nature Res · Windsor Park · Sir James Mitchell Park · Lake Vasto · Queens Gardens

To Edgewater · To Bayswater · To Riverdale · To Fremantle · To Victoria Park · To Kwinana

Legend

Freeway/Tunnel	FREEWAY
Main Road	
Secondary	ROAD
Road/Minor Road	STREET
Lane/Footbridge	
Metropolitan Route	22
One Way Street	
Railway	Underground

Park/Garden · Railway Station · Major Building · Government Building · Theatre/Cinema · Shopping · Post Office · Accredited Information · 24hr Fuel

Points of Interest

1 Art Gallery of Western Australia A3
2 Barracks Archway B1
3 Cloisters, The B2
4 Deanery, The B3
5 Government House B3
6 Hay Street Mall B2
7 His Majesty's Theatre B2
8 Horseshoe Bridge B2
9 King Street Arts Centre B2
10 Kings Park B1
11 Kings Park Lookout C1
12 Langley Park C3
13 Murray Street Mall B2
14 NIB Stadium A4
15 Old Council House B3
16 Old Court House B3
17 Old Mill C1
18 Old Perth Boys School B2
19 Old Perth Observatory B1
20 Parliament House B1
21 Perth Arena A2
22 Perth Concert Hall B3
23 Perth Convention Exhibition Ctr B2
24 Perth Inst of Contemporary Arts A3
25 Perth Mint B4
26 Perth Town Hall B3
27 Perth Zoo E2
28 St George's Cathedral B3
29 St Mary's RC Cathedral B3
30 Scitech Discovery Centre A1
31 State Library of Western Aust A3
32 State War Memorial C1
33 Swan Bells C2
34 Wellington Square B4
35 Western Australian Museum A3

Accommodation

38 Aarons All Suites B3
39 Aarons Hotel Perth B3
40 Adina Apartment Hotel Perth B2
41 Citadines St Georges Terrace Perth B2
42 Comfort Hotel Perth City C4
43 Comfort Inn Wentworth Plaza Hotel Perth B2
44 Criterion Hotel B3
45 Crowne Plaza Perth C4
46 Duxton Hotel Perth, The B3
47 Four Points by Sheraton Perth A2
48 Globe Backpackers and City Oasis Resort B2
49 Goodearth Hotel C4
50 Grand Central Backpackers B3
51 Holiday Inn Perth City Centre B2
52 Hotel Ibis Perth B2
53 Hyatt Regency Perth C4
54 Ibis Styles Perth A3
55 Kings Perth Hotel B3
56 Mantra on Hay C4
57 Mantra on Murray B2
58 Marque Hotel Perth B1
59 Melbourne Hotel, The B2
60 Mercure Hotel, The B3
61 Mounts Bay Waters Apartments B1
62 New Esplanade Hotel Perth, The B2
63 Novotel Perth Hotel Langley C3
64 Parmelia Hilton Perth Hotel B2
65 Perth Ambassador Hotel C4
66 Perth City YHA B3
67 Quest West End B2
68 River View on Mount Street B1
69 Rydges Perth B2
70 Seasons of Perth B3
71 Sheraton Perth Hotel C3
72 Sullivans Hotel C1
73 Travelodge Perth Hotel B3

Travel Information

75 City West Train Station A1
76 Claisebrook Train Station A4
77 East Perth Train Station A4
78 Elizabeth Quay Station B2
79 McIver Train Station B3
80 Perth Train Station B3
81 Perth Underground Station B2
82 Perth Visitor Centre B2
83 RAC Office A1
84 Roe Street Temporary Bus Station A2
85 Wellington Street Temporary Bus Station A2

© Hema Maps Pty Ltd

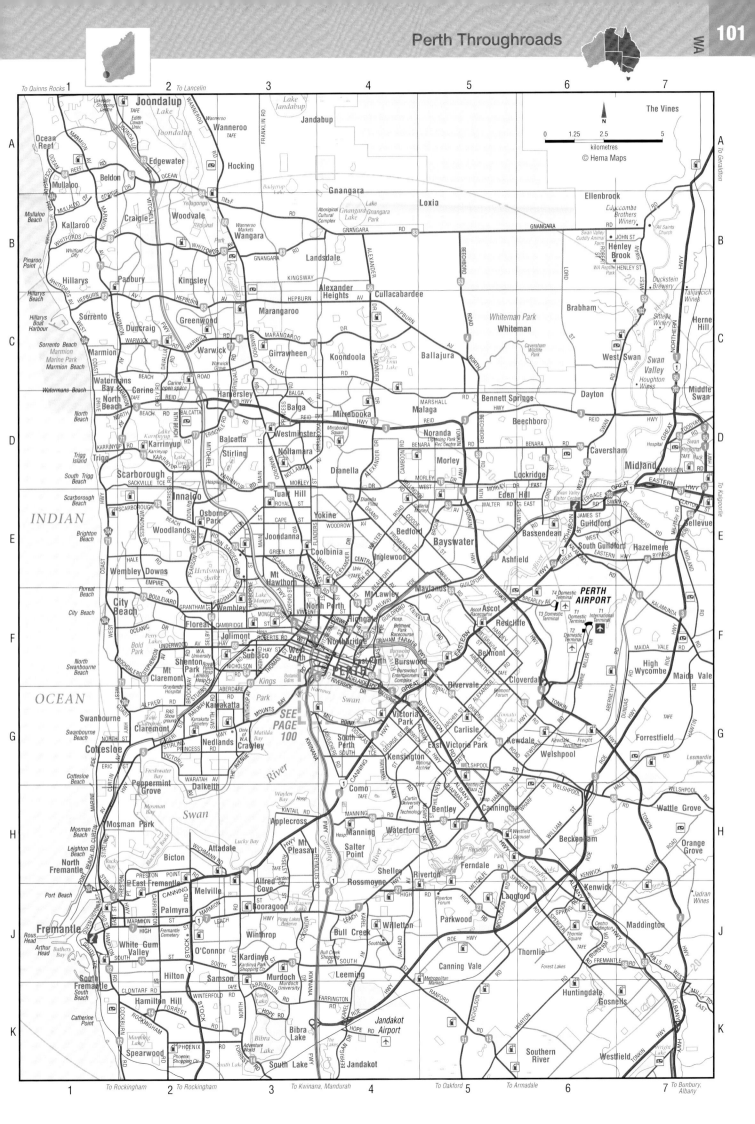

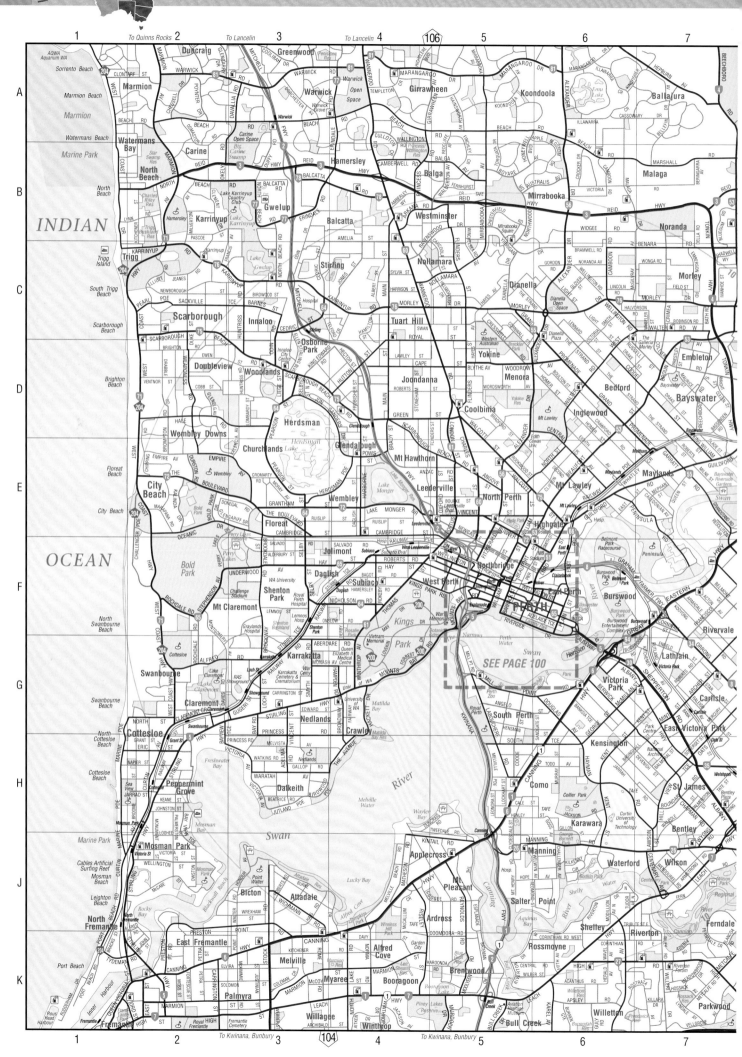

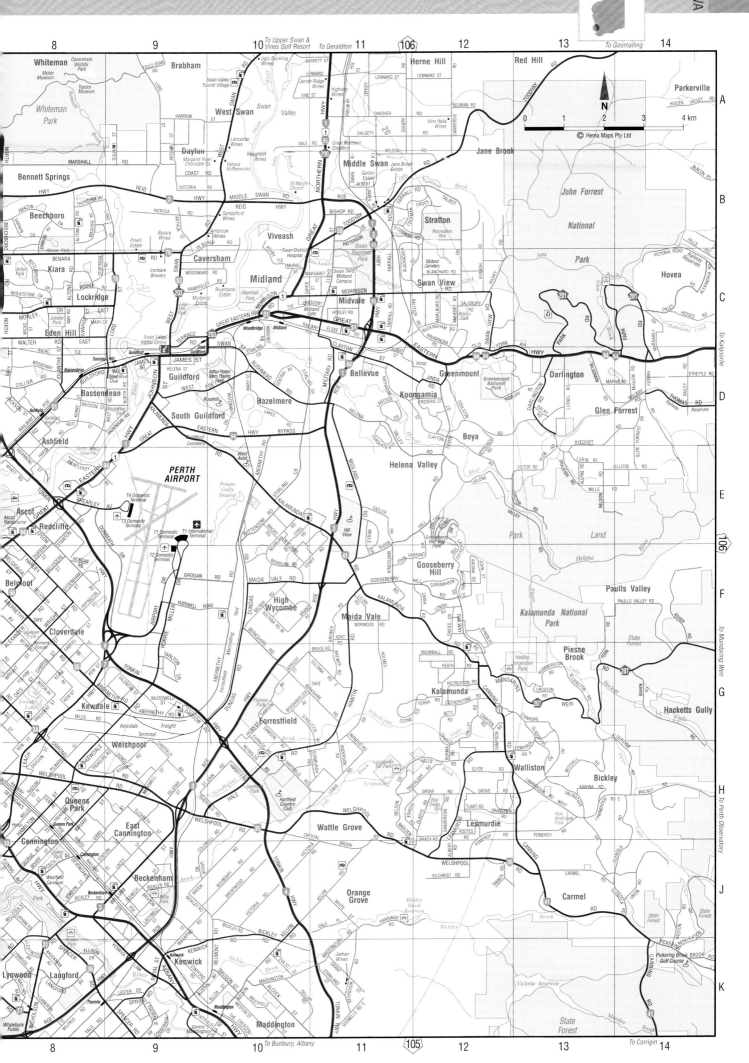

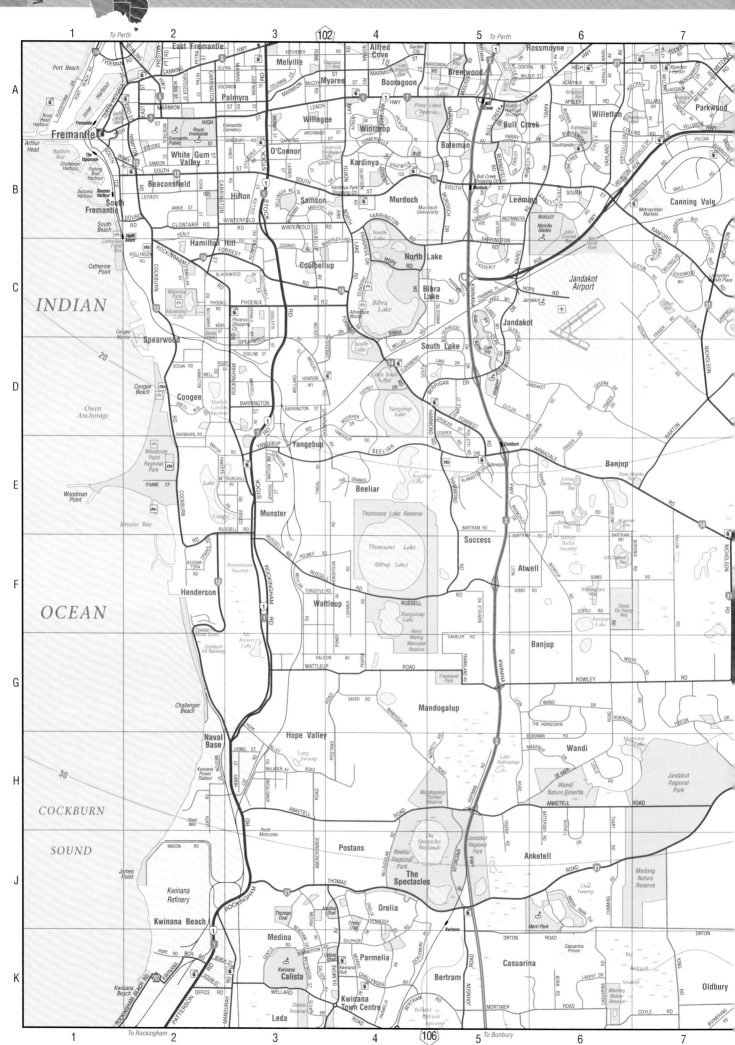

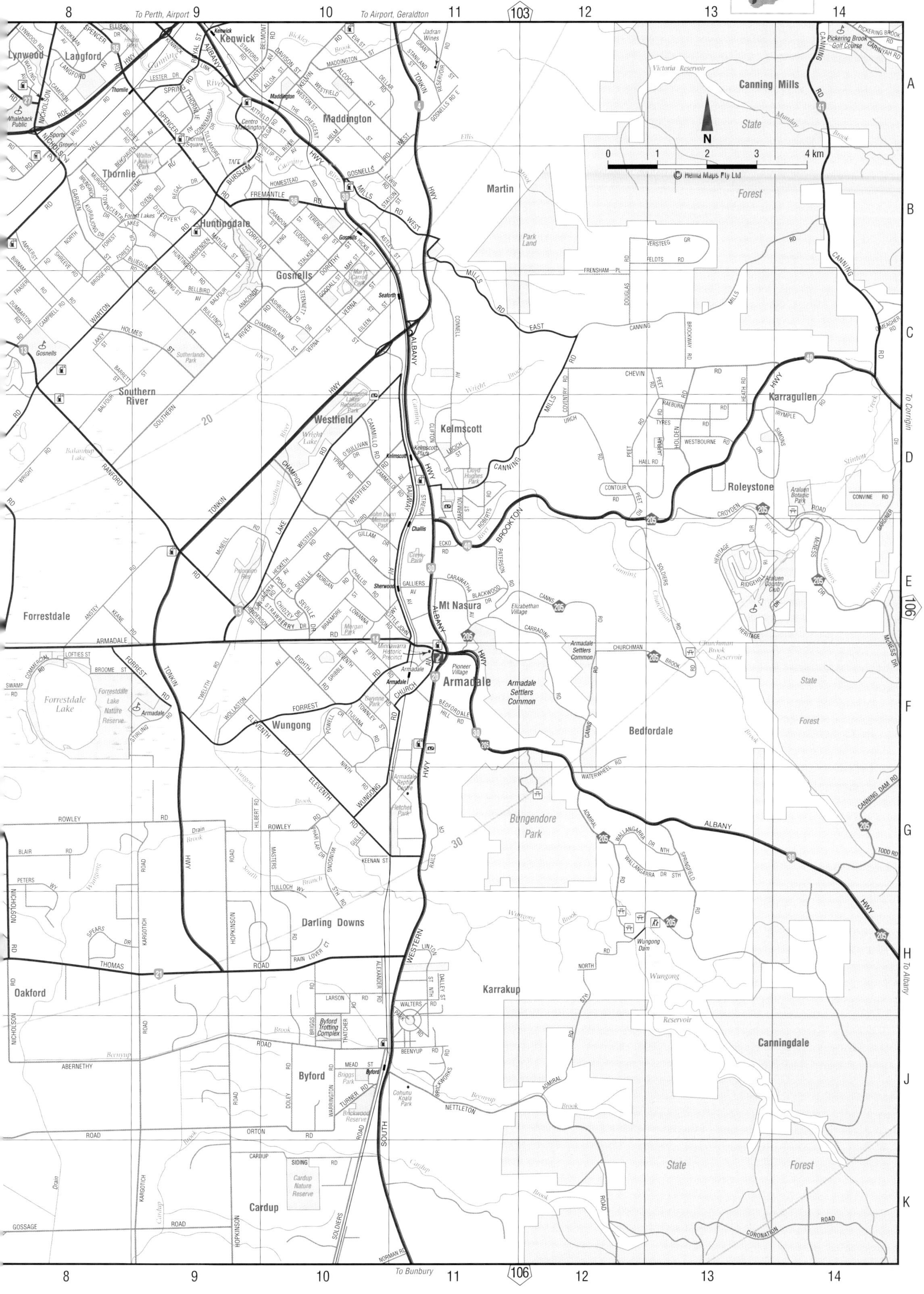

8 To Perth, Airport 9 10 To Airport, Geraldton 11 103 12 13 14

Lynwood Langford
Kenwick
Thornlie
Whaleback Public
Sports Ground
Maddington
Huntingdale
Gosnells
Southern River
Westfield
Kelmscott
Martin
Park Land
Canning Mills
State Forest
Victoria Reservoir
Kelmscott Plaza
Lloyd Hughes Park
Karragullen
Roleystone
Araluen Botanic Park
Araluen Country Club
Forrestdale
Armadale
Minnawarra Historic Precinct
Mt Nasura
Elizabethan Village
Armadale Settlers Common
Pioneer Village
Bedfordale
Wungong
Forrestdale Lake
Forrestdale Lake Nature Reserve
Bungendore Park
State Forest
Darling Downs
Wungong Dam
Oakford
Karrakup
Canningdale
Byford
Byford Trotting Complex
Cohunu Koala Park
Brickwood Reserve
Cardup
Cardup Nature Reserve
State Forest

To Bunbury 106
To Corrigin
To Albany

0 1 2 3 4 km
N
© Hema Maps Pty Ltd

A B C D E F G H J K

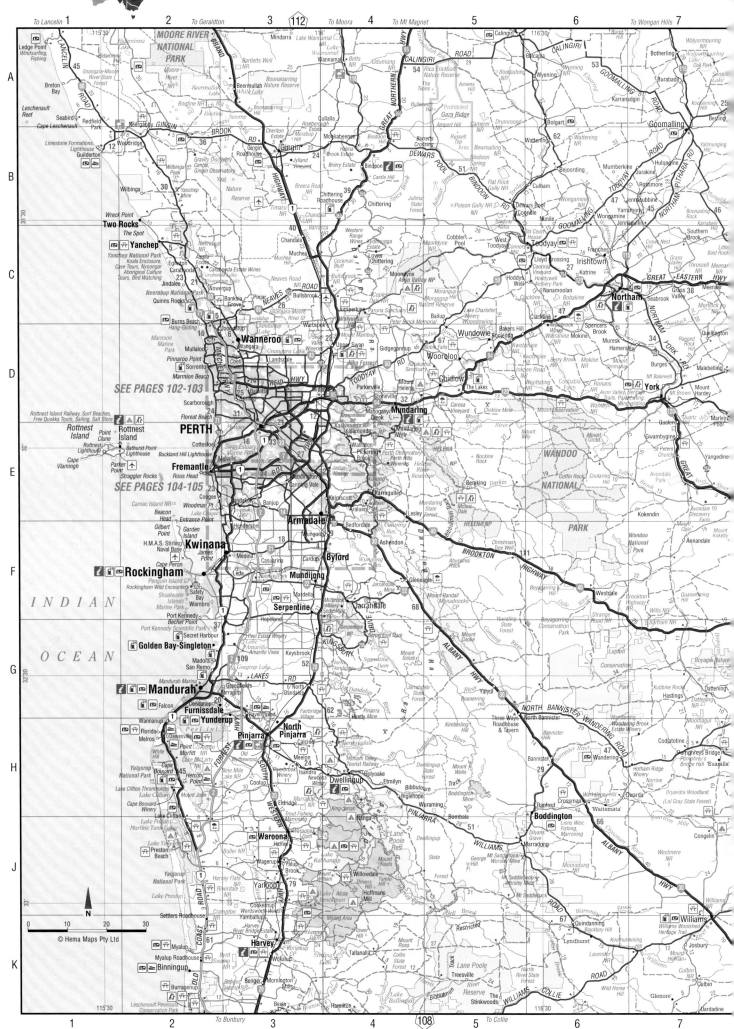

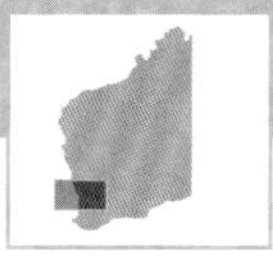

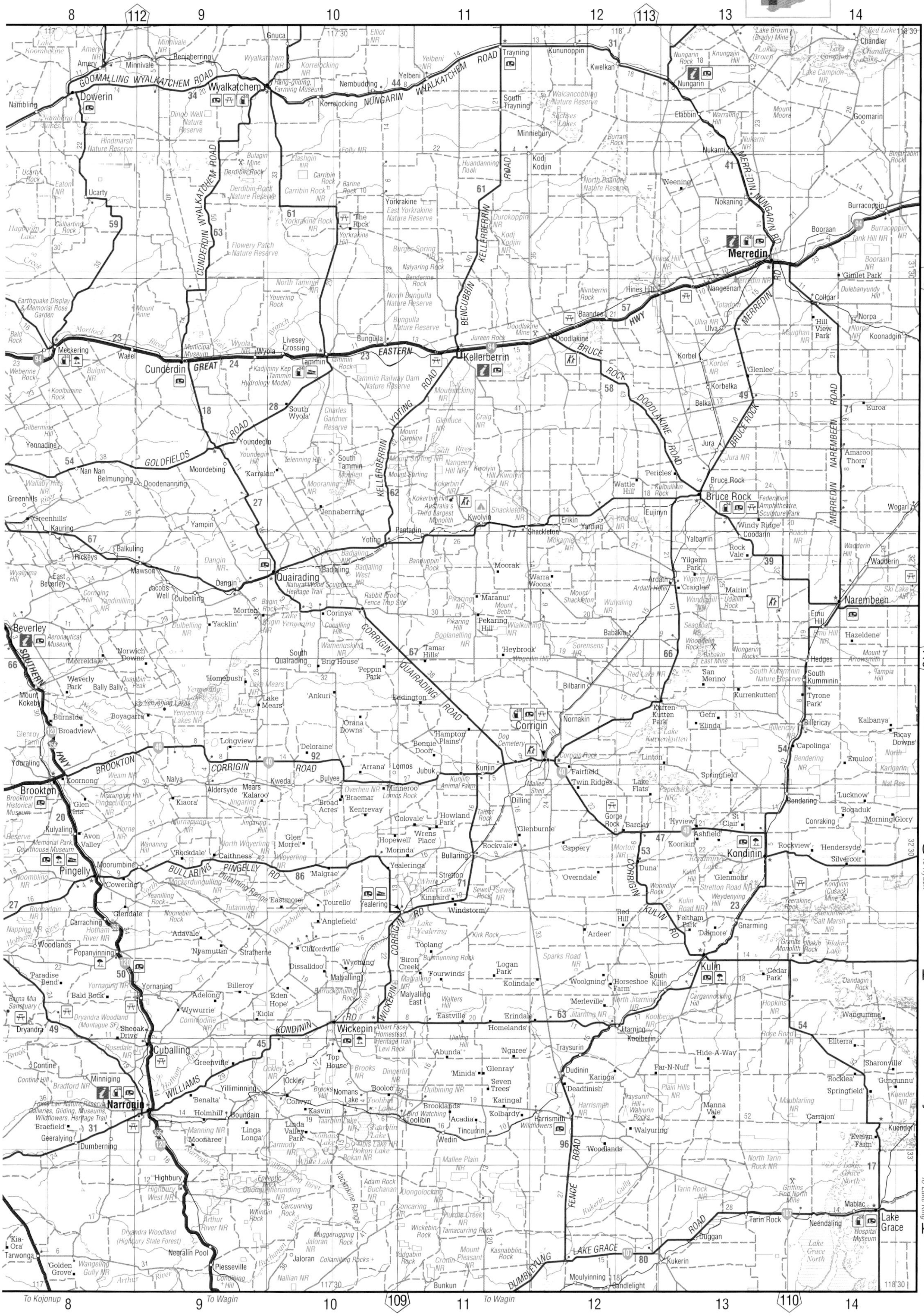
8
9
10
11
12
13
14
A
B
C
D
E
F
G
H
J
K
Dowerin
Wyalkatchem
Nungarin
Merredin
Kellerberrin
Cunderdin
Meckering
Quairading
Bruce Rock
Narembeen
Beverley
Corrigin
Brookton
Pingelly
Kondinin
Kulin
Wickepin
Cuballing
Narrogin
Lake Grace
GOOMALLING WYALKATCHEM ROAD
NUNGARIN WYALKATCHEM ROAD
GREAT EASTERN HWY
GOLDFIELDS ROAD
BRUCE ROCK DOODLAKINE ROAD
CORRIGIN QUAIRADING ROAD
BROOKTON CORRIGIN ROAD
BULLARING PINGELLY RD
SOUTHERN HWY
KONDININ RD
WILLIAMS
LAKE GRACE DUMBLEYUNG
FENCE ROAD
To Kalgoorlie
To Hyden
To Lake King
To Kojonup
To Wagin
112
113
110
109

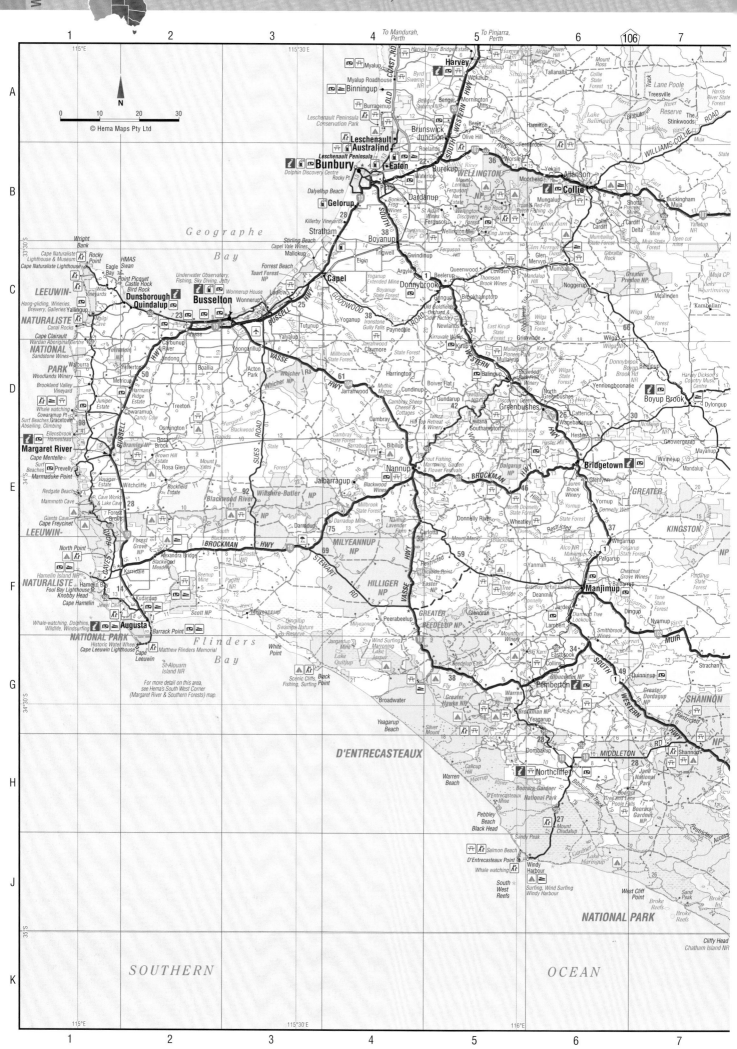

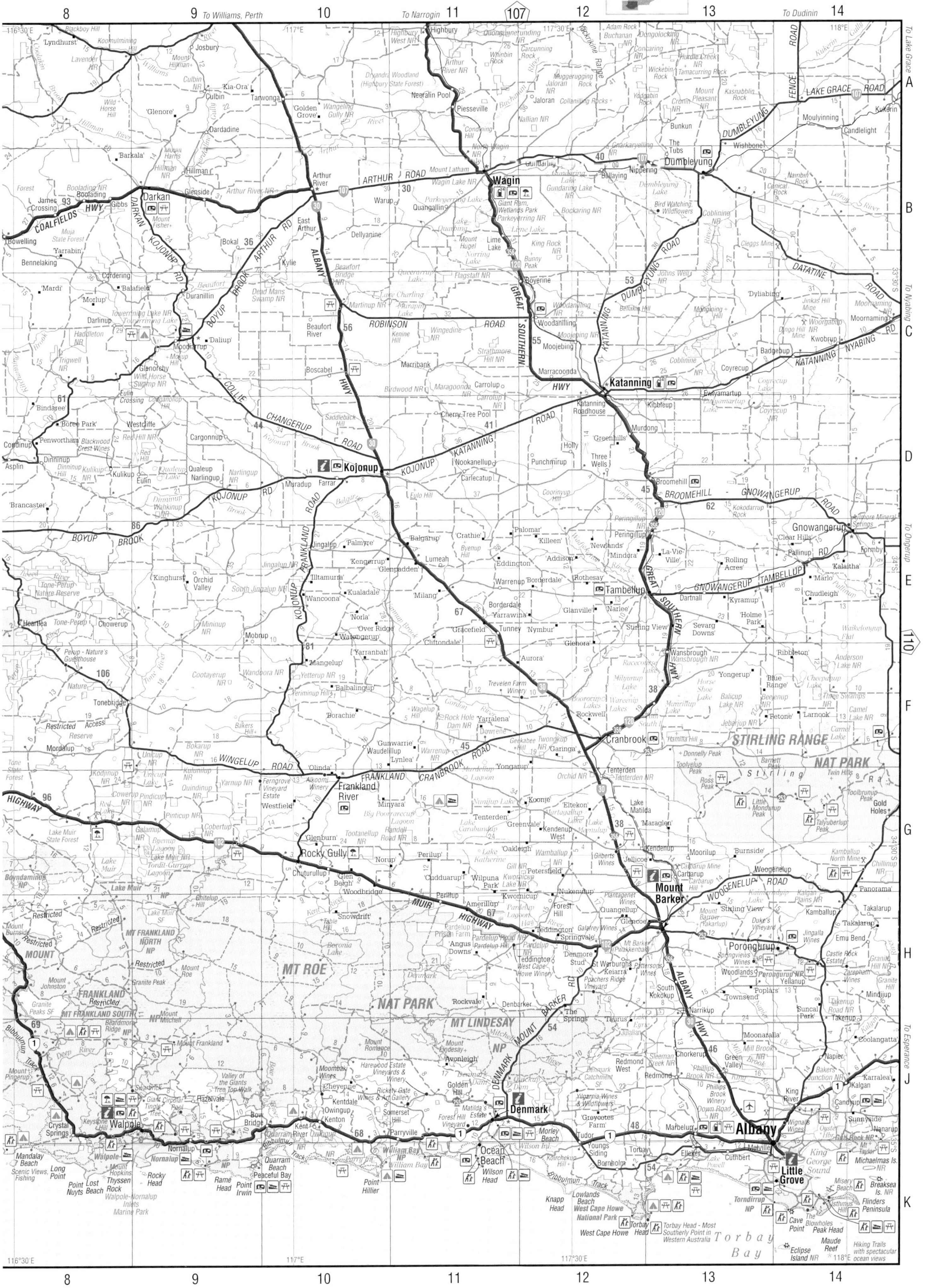

To Williams, Perth — To Narrogin — To Dudinin — To Lake Grace

Wagin
Dumbleyung
Darkan
Katanning
Kojonup
Frankland River
Rocky Gully
Cranbrook
Tambellup
Gnowangerup
Mount Barker
Porongurup
Walpole
Denmark
Ocean Beach
Albany
Little Grove

STIRLING RANGE NAT PARK
MT ROE NAT PARK
MT FRANKLAND NATIONAL PARK
MT FRANKLAND NORTH NP
MT FRANKLAND SOUTH NP
MT LINDESAY NP
WEST CAPE HOWE NATIONAL PARK
Torbay Bay
King George Sound

COALFIELDS HWY
ALBANY HWY
GREAT SOUTHERN HWY
KATANNING NYABING ROAD
DUMBLEYUNG ROAD
DATATINE ROAD
GNOWANGERUP ROAD
TAMBELLUP
COLLIE KOJONUP RD
ARTHUR ROAD
ROBINSON ROAD
CHANGERUP ROAD
KOJONUP RD
FRANKLAND NR
BOYUP BROOK
WINGELUP ROAD
CRANBROOK RD
MUIR HIGHWAY
DENMARK MOUNT BARKER ROAD
WOOGENELUP ROAD
SOUTH COAST HIGHWAY

116°30'E — 117°E — 117°30'E — 118°E
32°30'S — 33°S — 33°30'S — 34°S — 34°30'S

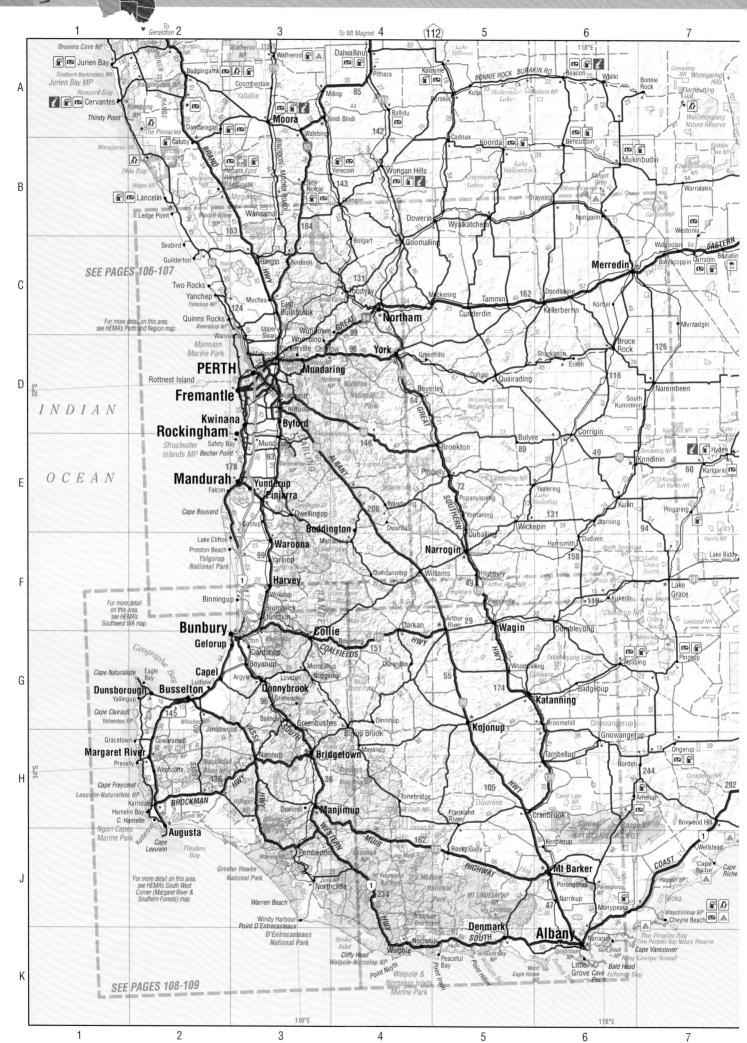

SEE PAGES 106-107

SEE PAGES 108-109

SOUTHERN OCEAN

8 9 10 113 11 To Leonora 12 13 14

To Leonora

122°E Pinjin
QUEEN VICTORIA SPRING NATURE RESERVE

Bungalbin Hill
'Yindi'
Lake Rebecca

Bardoc 'Mount Vetters'
Mount D'Carnage
Ora Banda
Broad Arrow
Gindalbie

Clear & Muddy Lakes Nature Reserve
'Credo'
'Carbine'
Kanowna'
Bullock Holes TR
Mount Charles

Ex Credo

MOUNT MANNING - HELENA & AURORA RANGES CONS PARK
Jaurdi Cons Park
Jaurdi Hill
Kundana
Kanowna
'Hampton Hill'
Mount Turner
Cundeelee Mission
Cundeelee (abandoned)

Lake Deborah East
Koolyanobbing
'Jaurdi'
Kalgoorlie-Boulder
Kurrawang
'Perkolilli'
Bulong
Curtin
Lake Yindarlgooda
Wallaby Rocks Timber Reserve
Permit Required

Lake Baladjie
'Carinta'
Mt Burges 'Mt Durgee'
Coolgardie
Bonnie Vale
Golden Ridge
'Avoca Downs'
Karonie
Chifley
Emu Rocks TR

Bullfinch
'Bullabulling'
Bullabulling
Mount Marion
Kambalda West
'Woolibar'
'Mount Monger'
'Cowarna Downs'
TRANS ACCESS ROAD
Coonana
Coonana

Southern Cross
HIGHWAY
Boorabbin NP
Boorabbin
94
Goldfields Woodlands CP
Kambalda
Kambalda NR
Kambalda
Lake Lefroy

Moorine Rock
Yellowdine
Koorarawalyee
Goldfields Woodlands NR
Scahill Timber Res
'Mandilla'
Roysalt
Yalca Hill
'Madoonia Downs'

109
Marvel Loch
Goldfields Woodlands NP
Widgiemooltha
166
'Mareil'
Mount Morgan

Mount Hampton
Mount Hampton NR
Neendojer Rock NR
JILBADJI NATURE RESERVE
TRACK
Cave Hill
94
Higginsville
Lake Cowan

HOLLAND
Mount Holland
Mount Day
Iragul
ROAD
Mount Thirsty
Wingarnie
Pioneer
Mount Pleasant
'Fraser Range'
32°S

HYDEN
Norseman
Mt Norcott
Woolyeenyer Hill
EYRE
Wyalinu Hill
'Southern Hills'
108 HIGHWAY
To Adelaide

Wave Rock
Lake Carmody
Lake Hurlstone NR
Holt Rock
Mount Stewart
Lake Johnston
BREMER RANGE
Mount Gordon
Bromus
Dundas Rocks
OLD COACH/TELEGRAPH ROAD
179
119

124
Varley
Mt Vernon
Mt Sheridan
Hatter Hill
Frank Hann National Park
NORSEMAN ROAD
Lake Sharpe
Peak Charles
1 Gilmore
Lake Dundas
DUNDAS NATURE RESERVE

Newdegate
Lake Ace NR
Lake King
LAKE KING
113
Three Star Lake
Lake Tay
Peak Charles Nat Park
Salmon Gums
202
BALLADONIA ROAD
Tower Peak

115
Lake King
Lake King NR
'Karak Park'
Pallarup NR
Pyramid Lake
'Kappi Ki'
Griffiths NR
Grass Patch
Kau Rock Nature Reserve
Beaumont Nature Reserve
PARMANGO ROAD
128

Breakaway Ridge NR
Dunn Rock Nature Reserve
40
Cheadanup NR
Cascade
'Clare Downs'
Scaddan (abandoned)
Truslove Townsite NR
Burdett South NR
Muntz Nature Reserve
CAPE ARID NP

Lake Magenta
LAKE MAGENTA NAT RES
71
Phillips River
Oldfield River
Young River
Lort River
'Lauriana'
'Zeehan'
Gibson
'Warrawoona'
Condingup
FISHERIES ROAD
Boyatup
Mount Baring

Ravensthorpe
184
Munglinup
1 59
Fairfield'
18
Esperance
'Gerbryn'
'Peak Downs'
Hammer Head
Mount Arid
Sandy Bight

HIGHWAY
Fitzgerald
Maydon
Kundip NR
'Nurragi'
Jerdacuttup Lakes NR
'Dalyup Park'
Butty Head
Rossiter Bay
North East Point

Jerramungup
FITZGERALD RIVER NATIONAL PARK
Mount Drummond
Annie Peak
Hopetoun
Lake Shaster NR
Stokes Inlet
Stokes NP
Shoal Cape
West Group
Observatory Point
Esperance Bay
Cape Le Grand
Mississippi Point
Cape Le Grand NP
Cape Arid
34°S

Point Ann
West Mt Barren
Point Charles Bay
RECHERCHE ARCHIPELAGO NATURE RESERVE

Gairdner
Point Hood
Bremer Bay
Bremer Bay
Point Henry
ARCHIPELAGO OF THE RECHERCHE

SOUTHERN OCEAN

N

0 50 100 km
© Hema Maps Pty Ltd

120°E 122°E
8 9 10 11 12 13 14

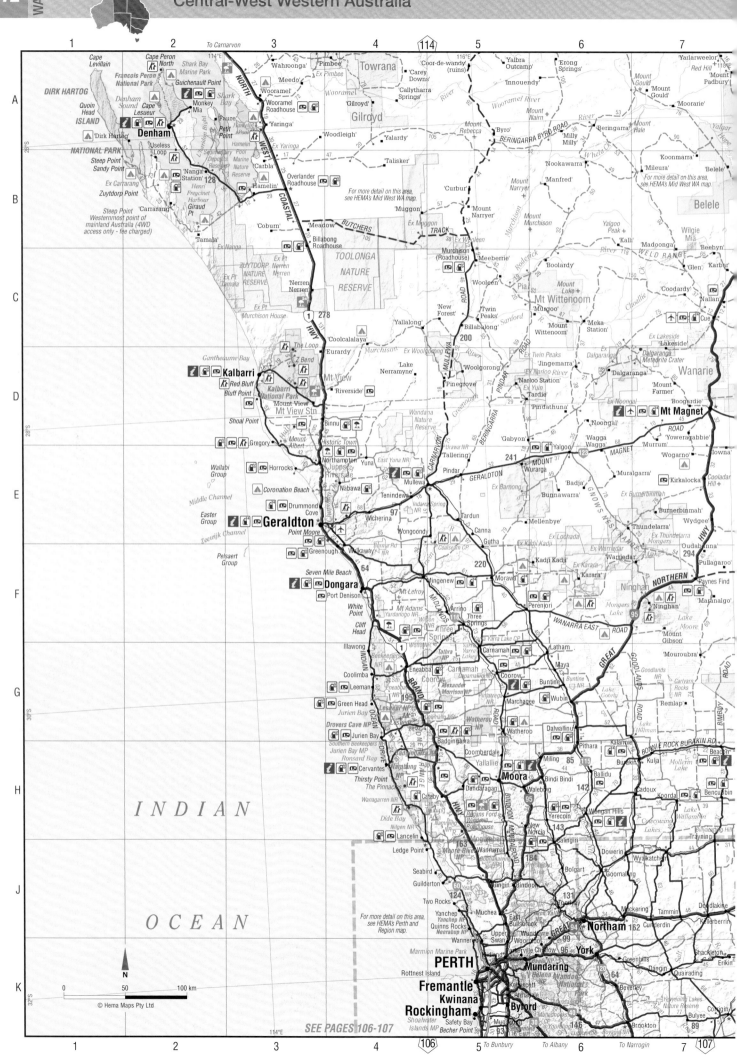

SEE PAGES 106-107

© Hema Maps Pty Ltd

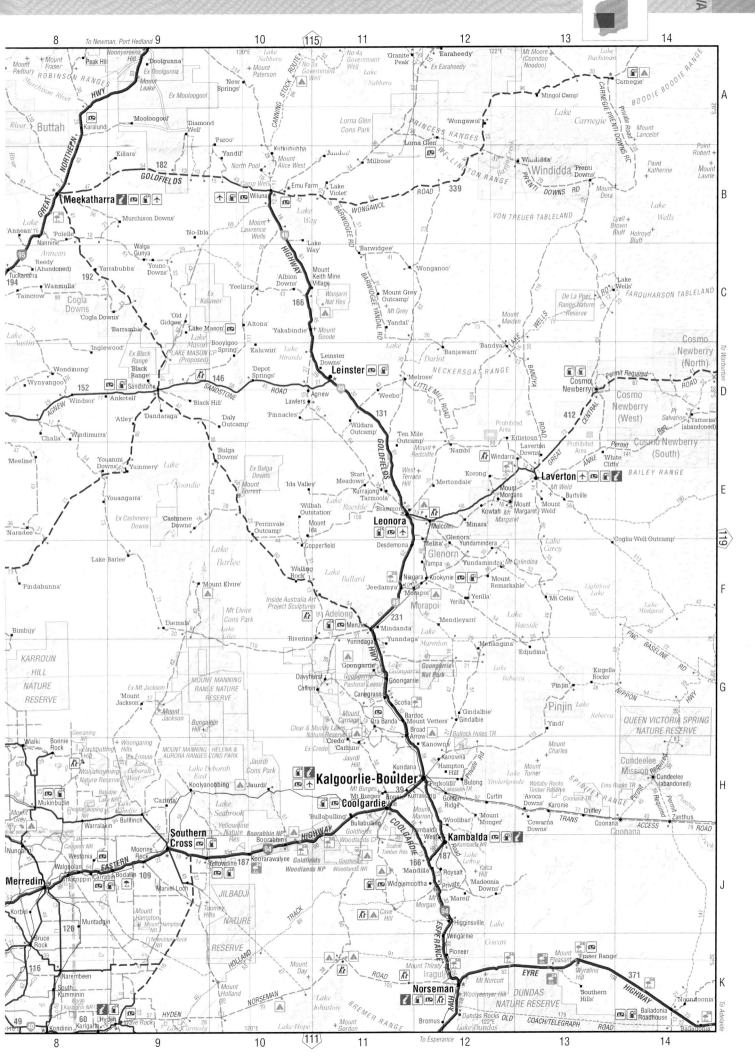

To Geraldton | To Murchison Roadhouse

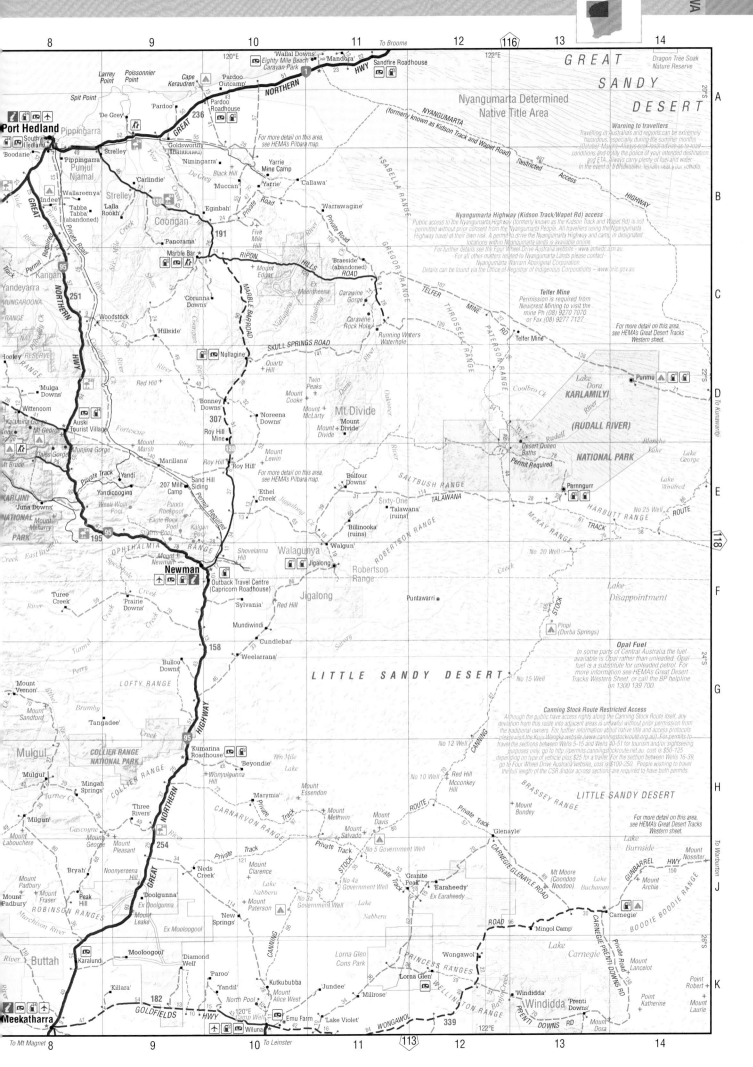

1   2   3   4   5   6   7

A

B

INDIAN

C

OCEAN

D

E

F

G

H

J

K

N

0   50   100 km

© Hema Maps Pty Ltd

120°E

14°S

16°S

18°S

20°S

122°E

*Scott Reef
Nature Reserve*

Fraser Inlet

*Lalang-garram
/ Camden Sound
Marine Park*

BUCCANEER ARCHIPELAGO

Yampi Sound

Cockatoo
Koola

*Strickland
Bay*

Cone Bay

Cape
Leveque
One Arm Point
(One Arm Point)
Bardi

Sunday
Island

Cygnet Bay
Bygnunn
Willie Pt

*Compass
Hill*
'Kimbolton'

Thomas Bay
Lombadina
Lombadina Point
Chilli Creek

Emeriau
Point
Cape
Borda

Cascade Bay

Cunningham
Point

*King
Sound*

Pender Bay

*Lacepede
Islands*

Sandy
Point
Middle Lagoon

Maddarr

La-Djardarr Bay

Cornambie Point

Beagle Bay

Bobieding

*Disaster
Bay*

Point
Torment

Stokes Bay

Lacepede Channel

Beagle
Bay

Malaburra

Christine
Point

Bungarun

Cape
Baskerville

Carnot
Bay

'Country
Downs'

Mount
Jowlaenga
Mount
Jowlaenga

Fraser

River

Derby

'Birdwood
Downs

Cape
Bertholet

Coulomb Point
James Price Point

*Coulomb Point
Nat Reserve*

217

Reeves Hill

Boab Prison Tree

41

Quondong Point

*Rowley Shoals
Marine Park*

Cape Boileau

Willie Creek Pearl Farm
Waterbank

'Kilto'

Bedunburra

Yeeda

Roebuck Plains
Roadhouse

180

Willare Bridge
Roadhouse

Cable Beach
Broome

Gantheaume Point
Entrance Point

Roebuck Bay

'Roebuck
Plains'

Roebuck
Plains

'Yakka
Munga'

'Udialla'

Udialla
Springs

Mt Anderson
Moun
Anderson

HIGHWAY

Thangoo

Private

Track

(No Access)

*Frome
Rocks*

Bush Point
Cape Villaret

'Barn Hill
Outstation

'Dampier Downs
Outcamp'

*Near
Hill*

'Dampier
Downs'

Babrongan
Tower

Mowla
Bluff

Cape Latouche Treville
Port Smith
Port Smith

'Shamrock'

Mount
Alexander

False Cape Bossut
Lagrange Bay
Bidyadanga (Lagrange)

Injudinah

Mowla
Bluff

Mount
Collins

Mt +
Jarlema

Cape Bossut
Admiral Bay
'Frazier Downs'

366

EDGAR   RANGE

*Mowla
Bluff*

Geoffroy Bay
Cape Jaubert
Desault Bay
Cape Missiessy

Frazier Downs

'Nita
Downs'

*Eighty Mile
Beach
Marine Park*

*Private
Track*

'Anna
Plains'

*Ex Anna
Plains*

GREAT

Eighty Mile Beach

NORTHERN

'Wallal
Downs'

'Mandora'

*Dragon Tree Soak
Nature Reserve*

For more detail on this area,
see HEMA's Pilbara map.

Eighty Mile Beach
Caravan Park

Sandfire
Roadhouse

Nyangumarta Highway (Kidson Track/Wapet Rd) access
Public access to the Nyangumarta Highway (formerly known as the Kidson Track
and Wapet Rd) is not permitted without prior consent from the Nyangumarta People.
All travellers using the Nyangumarta Highway travel at their own risk.
A permit to drive the Nyangumarta Highway and camp in designated
locations within Nyangumarta lands is available online.
For further details see the Four-Wheel Drive Australia website – www.anfwdc.asn.au.
For all other matters related to Nyangumarta Lands please contact
Nyangumarta Warrarn Aboriginal Corporation.
Details can be found via the Office of Registrar of Indigenous Corporations – www.oric.gov.au

Larrey
Point
Poissonnier
Point
Cape
Keraudren
'Pardoo
Outcamp'

Spit Point

'Pardoo'
Pardoo
Roadhouse

236

GREAT

'De Grey'

Port Hedland
Pippingarra
52
'Boodarie'
South Hedland
'Strelley'

Goldsworthy
(abandoned)

120°E

(formerly known as Kidson Track
Restricted

NYANGUMARTA

Access

NYANGUMARTA

HIGHWAY

and Wapet Rd) Access

122°E

Nyangumarta Determined
Native Title Area

To Karratha

1   2   3   4   115   5   6   7

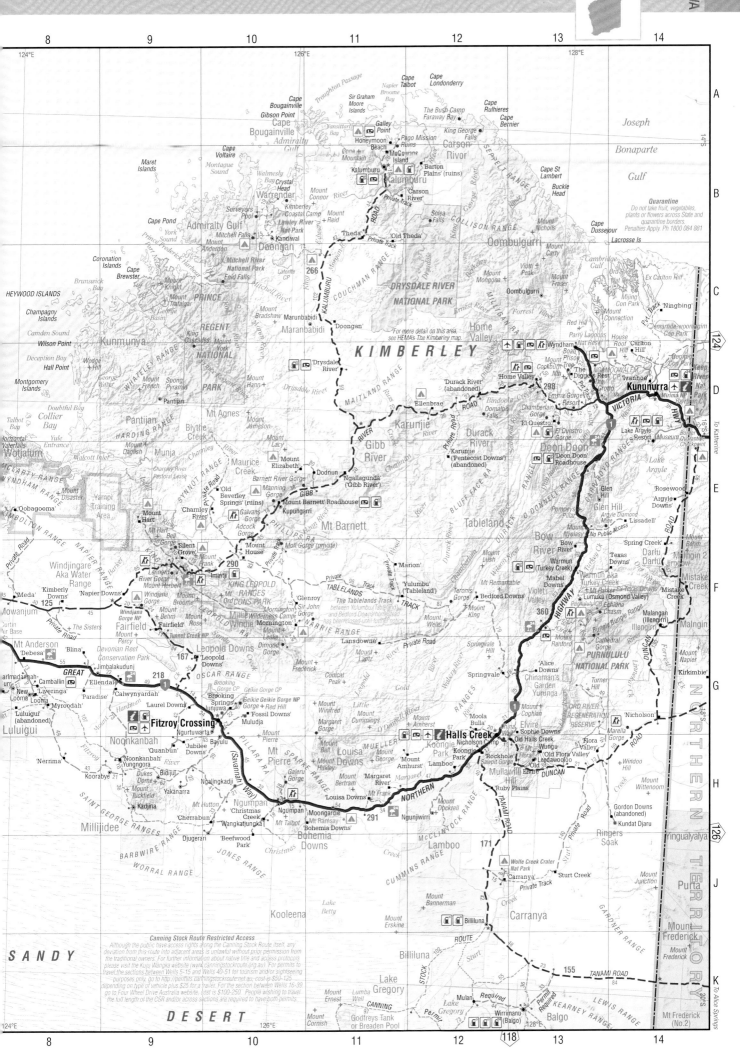

8 **9** **10** **11** **12** **13** **14**

124°E 126°E 128°E

A

B

C

D

E

F

G

H

J

K

Joseph Bonaparte Gulf

Cape Talbot
Cape Londonderry
Cape Rulhieres
Cape Bernier

Cape Bougainville
Gibson Point
Cape Bougainville

Cape Voltaire

Maret Islands

Cape Pond

Admiralty Gulf

Troughton Passage
Vansittart Bay
Napier Broome Bay
Sir Graham Moore Islands

Galley Point
Honeymoon Beach
Cone Mountain
Pago Mission Ruins
McGowans Island
Kalumburu

King George Falls
The Bush Camp Faraway Bay
Barton Plains' (ruins)
'Carson River'

Cape St Lambert
Buckle Head
Cape Dusséjour
Lacrosse Is

Quarantine
Do not take fruit, vegetables, plants or flowers across State and quarantine borders. Penalties Apply. Ph 1800 084 881

Cambridge Gulf

CARSON RIVER

COLLISON RANGE
Solea Falls
Oombulgurri

Mount Nichols

Ord River Dam
Ex Carlton Hill
Ningbing
Ivanhoe
Keep River Nat Park

SEPPELT RANGE

Coronation Islands
Cape Brewster
HEYWOOD ISLANDS
Champagny Islands

Brunswick Bay

York Sound
Prince Frederick Harbour
St George Basin
Mount Trafalgar
Mount Waterloo

Surveyors Pool
Crystal Head
Kimberley Coastal Camp
Lawley River Nat Park
Kandiwal
Mitchell Falls
Mount Anderson

'Theda'
'Old Theda'

KALUMBURU ROAD

Private Track
Private Track

DRYSDALE RIVER NATIONAL PARK

Mount Connor
Mount Reid

Mount Mohgona
Viotti Peak
Mount Fraser

Mijing Con Park
Mount Connection

For more detail on this area, see HEMA's The Kimberley map.

Home Valley

Parry Lagoons
Red Hill
House Roof Hill
'Carlton Hill'
Goodie Con Park
Jemanda-woongoon Con Park

Wilson Point
Deception Bay
Hall Point
Camden Sound
Doubtful Bay
Montgomery Islands

Kunmunya

WHATELEY RANGE

PRINCE REGENT NATIONAL PARK

Enid Falls
266
Mitchell River

Laterite CP

Mount York
King Cascades

Mount Hann

KALUMBURU
COUCHMAN RANGE

Marunbabidi

Marunbabidi

'Doongan'

KIMBERLEY

Drysdale River
'Home Valley'

MICHIGAN RANGE

Ernest River
Forrest River

Wyndham
Boab Prison Tree
Copkburn Nth
The Diggers Rest
Ngamoowalem CP
Grotto

Kununurra
Mirima NP

Durack River (abandoned)

MAITLAND RANGE

KARUNJIE RANGE

102

Doongan'

Collier Bay
Talbot Bay
Yule Entrance
Walcott Inlet
Horizontal Waterfalls
Wotjalum

HARDING RANGE

Pantijan

Mount French
Spong Pyramid

Mount Daglish
'Oobagooma'

Munja

Pantijan'

Mt Agnes

Mount Jameson

Mount Lacy

GIBB RIVER ROAD

Karunjie
Gibb River

'Ellenbrae'

Durack River

Oomatoo Falls

El Questro
El Questro Gorge

DURACK

Bindoola Falls
Chamberlain Gorge
Emma Gorge Resort

298

Ivanhoe
Museum
Lake Argyle Resort

VICTORIA HWY

Lake Argyle

Rosewood
'Argyle Downs'

Blythe Creek

Charnley River
Charnley River Pastoral Lease

Maurice Creek
SYNNOT RANGE

Mount Elizabeth
Barnett River Gorge
Manning Gorge

Dodnun
GIBB
Ngallagunda ('Gibb River')

Mount Barnett' Roadhouse

Mt Barnett
Kupungarri

Galvans Gorge
Adcock Gorge

PHILLIPS RA

Tableland

O DONNELL RANGE

Doon Doon
'Doon Doon' Roadhouse

CARR BOYD RANGE

Glen Hill
Glen Hill
Argyle Diamond Mine
No Public Access
'Lissadell'

Spring Creek

Mount Behn
'Darlu Darlu'

Mangin 2
Jimow

WYNDHAM RANGE
IMBOLTON RANGE

'Mount Disaster'

Yampi Training Area

'Mount Hart'
Mt Hart
Bell Gorge
'Silent Grove'

Old Beverley Springs' (ruins)
'Charnley River'

'Mount House'

'Marion'
'Yulumbu' ('Tableland')

Pompeys Pillar

Bow River
'Bow River'

Mount Nyulasy

Texas Downs

Violet Valley

Warmun (Turkey Creek)

Mt Parker
Lumuku (Osmond Valley)

Malangan (Illengirri)
Illengirri

Mistake Creek
'Mistake Creek'

Malngin

'Meda'
'Kimberly Downs'
'Napier Downs'

125

Mowanjum
Curtin Air Base

NAPIER RANGE

KING LEOPOLD RANGES

Windjana River Gorge
Lennard Gorge

Mount Frank
290

Imintji

KING LEOPOLD RANGES NAT CONS PARK

Moll Gorge (private)

TABLELANDS

'Yulumbu' ('Tableland')

The Tablelands Track between Yulumbu (Tableland) and Bedford Downs homestead has been reclosed until further notice.

Mt Remarkable
Terong Gorge
'Bedford Downs'

Mabel Downs

Warmun
Turkey Creek

Ex Texas Downs

360

Osmond IDR
Panton Chasm

Cathedral Gorge
BUNGLE BUNGLE RANGE

Mistake Creek
Malngin

Windjingare Aka Water Range

Windjana Gorge NP

Mount Broome
Mount Bell

Windjana Gorge

'Napier Downs'

The Sisters

Fairfield
Mount Percy

'Fairfield'

Tunnel Creek NP

Mount Rose

Mille Windie
Mornington Wilderness Camp
'Mornington'
Sir John Gorge
NARRIE RANGE

'Glenroy'

'Lansdowne'

Mount Wells

Mount King

Springvale Hill

Private Road

'Ord'
Mount Ranford

PURNULULU NATIONAL PARK

'Alice Downs'
Chinaman's Garden
Yurunga

Turner Hill

Mount Napier

'Kirkimbie'

Mt Anderson
'Debesa'
'Blina'

Jimbalakudunj

Camballin

GREAT
218
167

Leopold Downs

OSCAR RANGE

Leopold Downs

Devonian Reef Conservation Park

Dimond Gorge

Mount Frederick

Conkat Peak

Gold
Leopold

Springvale

Mount Coghlan

Mount Coghlan

ORD RIVER REGENERATION RESERVE

'Nicholson'

Marella Gorge

Gordon Downs (abandoned)

New Looma
Looma
'Liveringa'
'Paradise'
'Calwynyardah'

'Laurel Downs'

Brooking Springs
Brooking Gorge
Junjuwa

Geikie Gorge NP
Red Hill
'Fossil Downs'
Muludja

Mount Winifred

Little Gold

Mount Cummings

Mount Amherst

'Moola Bulla'

Halls Creek
Nicholson Camp
Old Halls Creek

Sophie Downs
Elvire
'Old Flora Valley'
Leedawooloo

Flora Valley
Wungu

Windoo Hill

Mount Wittenoom

'Luluigui' (abandoned)

Luluigui

Fitzroy Crossing

Ngurtuwarta

Noonkanbah

FITZROY RIVER

'Quanbun'
'Jubilee Downs'
Bayulu

'Nerrima'
'Noonkanbah'
'Yungngora'

Dukes Dome
Bidijul

Kooraybe

Mount Tuckfield
Yakanarra

SAINT GEORGE RANGES

Kadjina

'Cherrabun'

Millijidee

MT PIERRE

SPARKE RANGE

PILLARA RA

Mount Bertram
Mt Frank

Galeru Gorge

Mount Ball
Mount Huxley

Mount George

'Margaret River'

'Margaret River'

'Louisa Downs'

Mount Pierre

NORTHERN

Louisa Downs

MUELLER RANGE

'Lamboo'

Koongie Park

Koongie Park

Rockhole
Sawpit Gorge

Mullawilli Hill
Ruby Plains

'Sturt Creek'

MCCLINTOCK RANGE

Mount Dockrell

TANAMI ROAD

Ngunjiwirri

'Nerrima'

Djugerari

'Beefwood Park'

BARBWIRE RANGE

Ngalingkadji
Wangkatjungka

JONES RANGE

Ngumpan
Moongardie
Mt Ramsay
'Bohemia Downs'
Mt Talbot

291

'Christmas Creek'

WORRAL RANGE

Christmas Creek

Bohemia Downs

CUMMINS RANGE

Lamboo

Mount Bannerman

Ringers Soak

Yingualyalya

Purta

NORTHERN TERRITORY

Kooleena

Lake Betty

Mount Erskine

Mount Cornish

Mount Ernest
Lumba Well

Lake Gregory

CANNING STOCK ROUTE

Godreys Tank or Breaden Pool

Billiluna

Carranya

Wolfe Creek Crater Nat Park

'Carranya'

'Sturt Creek'

Private Track

Mount Junction

Mount Frederick
Mount Frederick

SANDY DESERT

Mulan
Lake Gregory

Wirrimanu (Balgo)

Permit Required
Permit Required

STOCK ROUTE

KEARNEY RANGE

LEWIS RANGE

GARDNER RANGE

155
TANAMI ROAD

84

Balgo

Mt Frederick (No.2)

To Alice Springs

To Katherine

8 **9** **10** **11** **12** **13** **14**

124°E 126°E 128°E

118

GREAT SANDY DESERT

N

0   50   100 km

© Hema Maps Pty Ltd

Warning to travellers
Travelling in Australia's arid regions can be extremely hazardous, especially during the summer months (October-March). Always seek local advice as to road conditions and notify the police of your intended destination and ETA. Always carry plenty of fuel and water. In the event of a breakdown, remain near your vehicle.

Canning Stock Route Restricted Access
Although the public have access rights along the Canning Stock Route itself, any deviation from this route into adjacent areas is unlawful without prior permission from the traditional owners. For further information about native title and access protocols please visit the Kuju Wangka website (www.canningstockroute.org.au). For permits to travel the sections between Wells 5-15 and Wells 40-51 for tourism and/or sightseeing purposes only, go to http://permits.canningstockroute.net.au, cost is $50-125 depending on type of vehicle plus $25 for a trailer. For the section between Wells 16-39, go to Four Wheel Drive Australia website; cost is $100-250. People wishing to travel the full length of the CSR and/or across sections are required to have both permits.

For more detail on this area, see HEMA's Great Desert Tracks Western sheet.

Opal Fuel
In some parts of Central Australia the fuel available is Opal rather than unleaded. Opal fuel is a substitute for unleaded petrol. For more information see HEMA's Great Desert Tracks Western Sheet, or call the BP helpline on 1300 139 700.

For more detail on this area, see HEMA's Great Desert Tracks Western sheet.

Bililuna
Lake Gregory
To Halls Creek

GREAT SANDY DESERT

Mount Ernest
Lumba Well
Mount Cornish
Godfreys Tank or Breaden Pool
Mount Elliott
Mount Stewart

Mulan
Lake Gregory
Wirrimanu (Balgo)
Balgo
Kearney

Ngulupi
Mt Frederick (No.2)
Central Desert
Mangkururrpa

Yagga Yagga
Lake Dennis
Yiningarra

Percival Lakes
Percival Lakes
Tobin Lake
Waddawalla Well

No 45 Well
617

Lake White
Lake Wills
STANSMORE RANGE
SYDNEY MARGARET RANGE
WILBRUNGA RANGE
NORTHERN

Minjoo Well
Kunawarritji
Restricted Access
Dunda Jinnda (No 30) Well
Tabletop
STOCK
Lake Auld
Lake George
CANNING
Separation Well
Gary Junction

Mount Russell
Ngaanyatjarra Central Australia
Ngaanyatjarra Aka Maruwa
Lake Mackay
Lake Mackay

KIWIRRKURRA ROAD
Veevers Meteorite Crater
GARY HIGHWAY

GARY
Jupiter Well
JUNCTION
Permit Required
ROAD
Kiwirrkurra
Mount Webb
Gunbarrel Ration Truck
Len Beadell Plaque - Original Site Of Ration Truck
Mount Tietkens
'Ininti'
Mount Lindsay
Walungurru (Kintore)
Permit Required

Ngaanyatjarra Kiwirrkurra
Permit Required
GARY JUNCTION ROAD
KINTORE RANGE

TERRY RANGE
TALAWANA
Midway Well
TRACK
TROPIC OF CAPRICORN
Windy Corner

Ngaanyatjarra

Lake Macdonald

GIBSON DESERT
Ngaanyatjarra Kurlkuta

Eagle Dragoon Drillhole No. 1
HIGHWAY

Lake Hopkins

Tjukurla
HAASTS BLUFF
Haasts Bluff

Mount Madley
EAGLE
GARY
McPhersons Pillar
Ngaanyatjarra Clutter Buck Hill
Patjarr (Karilwara)
Permit Required

Mount Destruction
Mount Barlee
Mount Harris

Mount Cox
YOUNG RANGE
GIBSON DESERT
NATURE RESERVE
Tsakalos Hills
ALFRED AND MARIE RANGE

Karrku
Mount Forrest
Yirrirra
Mount Butthfield
Private

Walu

Mungilli Reserve
Charles Knob
Everard Junction
Mount Gordon
Access
Permit Required

Lapaku
Mount Russell
Kutjuntari
Track
Docker River (Kaltukatjara)
Tjuntinanta
Karukaki
Tjunti

'Mungilli' (abandoned)
Mungilli
HIGHWAY
Mount Everard
BROWN RANGE
126
Permit Required

Warakurna
Giles Meteorological Station
101
Mount Sargood
Lasseters Cave
TJUKARURU RD
DEARING RANGE

GUNBARREL
Mount Nossiter
Mt Johnson
Mangkili Claypan NR
Mount William Lambert
HUNT
(EAGLE HIGHWAY)

Wannan
Warakurna Roadhouse
CENTRAL
ROAD
Mount Deering
CAVENAGH RANGE
Petermann
BLOODS RANGE

Len Beadell Monument
Len Beadell Marker
Permit
Required
Jackie Junction
'Kurrkarturtu'
227

Mount Rawlinson
JAMIESON RANGE
Private Track
'Ngaturn'
Mantamaru (Jamieson)
'Pirntirri Mulari'
Mt Daisy Bates
Warlpakupa
Mt Gosse
Mt Le Hunte

Mount Beadell
SUTHERLAND RANGE
HEATHER
Lake Breaden
Permit Required
GREAT

Blackstone (Papulankutja)
'Arnold Creek'
Tammy Mirturtu
Ukatjupa
Irkini
Mount Cockburn
Walytjatjara

Ngaanyatjarra Tjirrkarli
Tjirrkarli
Mt Allott
Mt Worsnop
Warburton
'Pulpapunka Outstation'
Waratjara
Mt Cuanthus
'Anumarrapirti'
Mt Atoyslus
Irrunytju (Wingellina)
Kalka
Pipalyatjara
Mt Davies
Tjintalka

Square Hill
Lake Gillen
OIL
Ngaanyatjarra
Warburton
'Beal Outstation'
Axe Hill
Mt Eveline
Mt Squires
BARROW RANGE
Ngaanyatjarra Central Reserve
'Tjatara'
Willi Willi
Aparatjara (Old)
Kupuru

Point Robert
Mount Laurie
Mount Smith
Mount O'Loughlin
ERNEST GILES RANGE
DAVID CARNEGIE RANGE
ROAD
Kanpa
245
ROAD
Kunmarara Bore
Kunatjara
'Pirrilyungka'
Kunytjanu

Tjukayirla Roadhouse
CENTRAL
Baker Road
Ngaanyatjarra Yapuparra
Hanns Tabletop Hill
Ryans Bluff
Mount Irving
Sykes Bluff
Kampurarr Pirti
Aboriginal Business Road
Warutarri
Mt Lindsay
Pitjantjatjara Lands
Mount Sir Thomas

Lake Throssell
GREAT
GREAT VICTORIA DESERT
To Laverton
CONNIE SUE
SOUTH AUSTRALIA

To Alice Springs

1 2 3 118 4 To Warburton 5 6 7

124°E 126°E 128°E

GREAT VICTORIA DESERT

Kampurarr Pirti • 'Pirrilyungka'

Lake Wells
Lyell + Brown Bluff
Holroyd Bluff

Ngaanyatjarra Yapuparra

Permit Required

Baker Lake

Ngaanyatjarra Central Reserve

'Lake Wells'

FARQUHARSON TABLELAND

Hanns Tabletop Hill
Ryans Bluff
+ Mount Irving
Sykes Bluff

De La Poer Range Nature Reserve

Cosmo Newberry (North)

Lake Throssell

Tjukayirla Roadhouse

CENTRAL

Point Lihan

Saunders + Point

SAUNDERS RANGE

Permit Required

YEO LAKE NATURE RESERVE

Yeo Lake
Yeo Station (abandoned)

Light Aircraft Wreck

Restricted

28°S 92

Cosmo Newberry

Cosmo Newberry (West)

Yamarna (abandoned)

Permit Reg.

Pt Salvation

ANNE

Neale Junction

NEALE JUNCTION

CONNIE

HIGHWAY

Ilkurlka (Roadhouse)

Len Beadell Border Plaque

Prohibited Area

'White Cliffs'

BAILEY RANGE

Cosmo Newberry (South)

Cosmo Newberry (East)

BEADELL

NATURE RESERVE

ANNE BEADELL HIGHWAY

Lake Rason

For more detail on this area, see HEMA's Great Desert Tracks Western sheet.

Jubilee Lake

GREAT VICTORIA DESERT

113

'Coglia Well Outcamp'

PLUMRIDGE LAKES NATURE RESERVE

Tjuntjuntjara (Closed Community)

Aboriginal

Permit Required

Lightfoot Lake

Lake Minigwal

RASON LAKE ROAD

HWY

GREAT VICTORIA DESERT

NATURE RESERVE

30°S

'Kirgella Rocks'

NIPPON

CABLE HAUL ROAD

BASELINE

PNC HWY

Yakadunia Yackadunyah

96

Lake Rebecca

QUEEN VICTORIA SPRING NATURE RESERVE

SUE

Sleeper Camp

Decoration Cave

'Premier Downs' (abandoned)

NULLARBOR PLAIN

Trans Access Road
The Trans Access Road between Haig (WA) and Lyons (SA) is officially closed. No travel permissions will be granted.

Cundeelee Mission

Cundeelee (abandoned)

'Seemore Downs'

'Kinclaven'

Forrest

Coonana NR
Emu Rocks

SPINIFEX RANGE

Zanthus

'Kanandah'

913 Mile

Naretha

Rawlinna

Haig Private Track Nurina

Loongana No Access

Reid Private Road

Deakin ROAD

Coonana

TRANS ACCESS

'Rawlinna'

'Balgair'

'Kybo'

TRANS

ANKETELL ROAD

Deakin Obelisk

NULLARBOR REGIONAL RESERVE

Creek

CABLE HAUL ROAD

Private Track

COCKLEBIDDY RAWLINNA ROAD

Private Track

MADURA LOONGANA ROAD

MUNDRABILLA RD

EUCLA

REID ROAD

Border Quarantine Checkpoint

NULLARBOR NP

Pondana

'Moonera'

For more detail on this area, see HEMA's Great Desert Tracks Western sheet.

Border Village

To Adelaide

'Arubiddy'

EYRE

Madura

FORREST

Mundrabilla

HWY

Moopina

Eucla

To Norseman

Cocklebiddy Cave

'Madura'

Mundrabilla Motel

Eucla NP

Wilson Bluff

Cocklebiddy

351

HAMPTON TABLELAND

ROE PLAINS

EYRE

Longest straight stretch in Australia (146.6km)

Cocklebiddy Motel

Eyre Bird Observatory

Red Rocks Point

Quarantine
Do not take fruit, vegetables, plants or flowers across State and quarantine borders. Penalties Apply. Ph 1800 084 881 or email info@agric.wa.gov.au (WA Pest and Disease Information Service)

32°S

'Noondoonia'

'Woorlba'

Caiguna

HIGHWAY

Kanidal Beach

Scorpion Bight

Balladonia Roadhouse

HIGHWAY

371

Caiguna Blowhole

Twilight Cove

OLD COACH/TELEGRAPH RD

'Balladonia'

139

DUNDAS NATURE RESERVE

111

'Nanambinia'

Baxter Cliffs

Point Dover

GREAT AUSTRALIAN BIGHT

PARMANGO ROAD

BALLADONIA ROAD

NUYTSLAND

NATURE RESERVE

Toolinna Cove

Point Culver

Tower Peak
Mount Dean

CAPE ARID NP

Point Dempster

SOUTHERN

OCEAN

Boyatup
Mount Arid
Sandy Bight
Cape Arid
North East Point

Mount Baring

Point Malcolm

Israelite Bay

Cape Pasley

N

0 50 100 km

© Hema Maps Pty Ltd

124°E 126°E 128°E

1 2 3 4 5 6 7

NORTHERN TERRITORY

key map

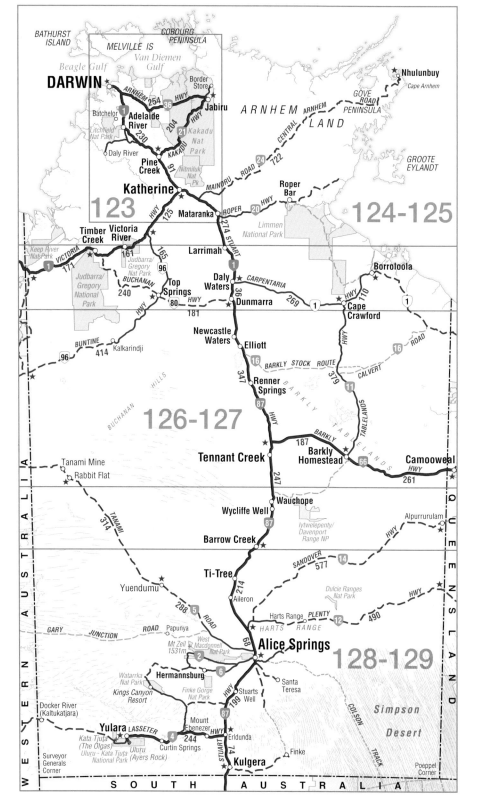

BATHURST
ISLAND

COBOURG
PENINSULA

MELVILLE IS
Van Diemen
Gulf

Beagle Gulf

DARWIN ★

★ **Nhulunbuy**
Cape Arnhem

Border
Store

Batchelor
Adelaide
River
254
36
Jabiru

GOVE
ROAD
GOVE
PENINSULA

ARNHEM

A R N H E M

L A N D

GROOTE
EYLANDT

Litchfield
Nat Park
204
230
21
Kakadu
Nat
Park

Daly River

Pine
Creek
91
Nitmiluk
Nat Pk

CENTRAL
ARNHEM

Katherine
MAINDRU
ROAD
24
722

123

Mataranka
125
ROPER
20 *HWY*
Roper
Bar
Limmen
National Park

124-125

Timber
Creek
Victoria
River
161
165
Larrimah
274 *STUART*
CARPENTARIA

★ **Borroloola**

Keep River
Nat Park
171 *VICTORIA*
96
Judbarra/
Gregory
Nat Park

Daly
Waters
1
36
HWY
110

Judbarra/
Gregory
National
Park

240
BUCHANAN
Top
Springs
80 *HWY*
Dunmarra
269
1
Cape
Crawford
1

181

BUNTINE
414 Kalkarindji
Newcastle
Waters
Elliott
319
ROAD
16

96
96
16
BARKLY STOCK ROUTE
CALVERT
11

HILLS
347
Renner
Springs
87
BARKLY

126-127

BUCHANAN
187
Barkly
Homestead
66
Camooweal
HWY

Tanami Mine
Rabbit Flat
Tennant Creek
247
261

TANAMI
314
Wauchope
Wycliffe Well
87
Iytwelepenty/
Davenport
Range NP

Alpurrurulam

Barrow Creek
SANDOVER
577
14

Ti-Tree
214
HWY

Yuendumu
Aileron
288
5
ROAD
Dulcie Ranges
Nat Park
HWY

GARY
JUNCTION
ROAD
Papunya
Harts Range *PLENTY*
12
490

Mt Zeil
1531m
West
Macdonnell
Nat Park
68
HARTS
RANGE

2
Alice Springs

128-129

Watarka
Nat Park
6
Hermannsburg
Santa
Teresa

Docker River
(Kaltukatjara)
Kings Canyon
Resort
Finke Gorge
Nat Park
199 *HWY*
Stuarts
Well

Simpson

Desert

COLSON

Mount
Ebenezer
87 *HWY*

Yulara LASSETER
4
244
Erldunda

Kata Tjuta
(The Olgas)
Uluru – Kata Tjuta
National Park
Curtin Springs
74
Finke
TRACK

Surveyor
Generals
Corner

Uluru
(Ayers Rock)
STUART
Kulgera
Poeppel
Corner

S O U T H   A U S T R A L I A

MINDIL BEACH (122 G1)

WANGI FALLS, LITCHFIELD NP (124 E3)

	Alice Springs									
Barrow Creek	284									
Borroloola	893	1177								
Camooweal	721	694	978							
Darwin	1412	940	1210	1494						
Halls Creek	1187	543	1143	1310	1046					
Jabiru	1169	251	1394	922	1192	1476				
Katherine	299	865	317	1095	623	893	1177			
Kulgera	1451	1750	1320	1768	1252	1451	558	274		
Kununurra	1678	512	811	358	829	1449	1049	1247	1404	
Mataranka	624	1339	112	411	977	429	983	511	781	1065
Nhulunbuy	739	1241	2078	729	1028	1594	1046	1722	1250	1520	1804
Uluru (Ayers Rock)	2267	1528	1867	337	1640	1939	1509	1957	1441	1640	747	463
Tennant Creek	970	1297	558	1024	781	670	969	1118	987	471	747	223	507

Distances are shown in kilometres and follow the most direct major sealed route where possible.

Darwin CBD

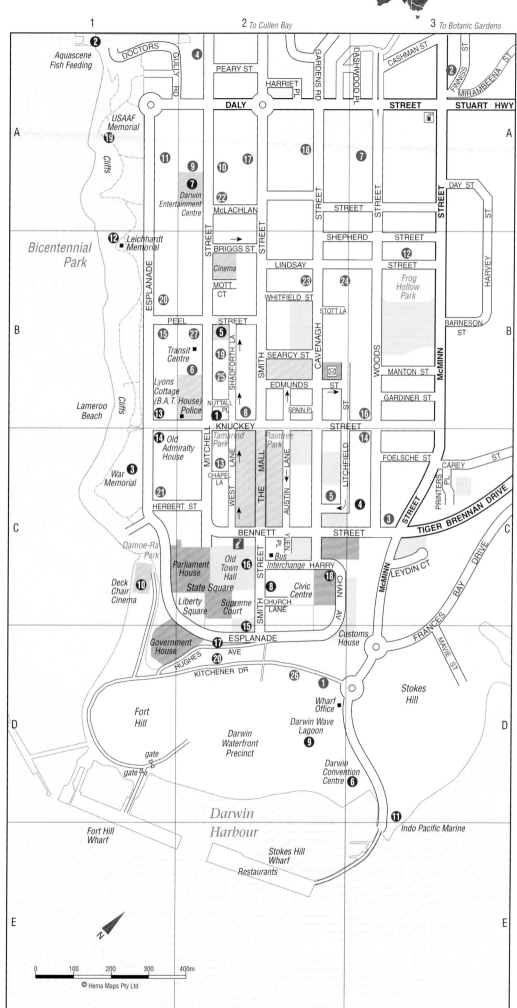

Major Road
Minor Road
One Way Road
Major Building
Govt Building
Theatre/Cinema
Shopping
Information
Post Office
24hr Fuel

Points of Interest
1. Aboriginal Fine Arts Gallery B2
2. Aquascene Fish Feeding A1
3. Cenotaph / War Memorial, The C1
4. Chung Wah Temple and Museum C3
5. Crocosaurus Cove B2
6. Darwin Convention Centre D3
7. Darwin Entertainment Centre A2
8. Darwin Theatre Company C2
9. Darwin Wave Lagoon D2
10. Deckchair Cinema, The C1
11. Indo Pacific Marine D3
12. Leichhardt Memorial B1
13. Lyons Cottage (B.A.T. House) B1
14. Old Admiralty House C1
15. Old Court House, The C2
16. Old Town Hall, The C2
17. Survivors Lookout D2
18. Tree of Knowledge, The C2
19. USS Peary Memorial / USAAF Memorial A1
20. WWII Oil Storage Tunnels D2

Accommodation
1. Adina Apartment Hotel Darwin D2
2. Alatai Holiday Apartments A3
3. Argus Apartments C3
4. Banyan View Lodge A2
5. Cavenagh Hotel Motel, The C2
6. Chilli's Backpackers B2
7. City Gardens Apartments A3
8. Darwin Central Hotel B2
9. Darwin City YHA A2
10. Dingo Moon Lodge A2
11. DoubleTree by Hilton Hotel Darwin A1
12. Frogshollow Backpackers B3
13. Hilton Darwin C2
14. Luma Luma Holiday Apartments C3
15. Mantra on the Esplanade B1
16. Mantra Pandanas B3
17. Marrakai Apartments A2
18. Mediterranean All Suite Hotel A2
19. Melaleuca On Mitchell Backpackers B2
20. Novotel Atrium Darwin B1
21. Palms City Resort C1
22. Poinciana Inn A2
23. Quest Serviced Apartments B2
24. Travelodge Mirambeena Resort B2
25. Value Inn B2
26. Vibe Hotel Darwin Waterfront D2
27. Youth Shack, The B2

TIMOR SEA

Beagle Gulf

Casuarina Coastal Reserve

Casuarina Coastal Reserve

Beagle Gulf

Lee Point Village Resort and Caravan Park

Royal Darwin Hospital
Darwin Private Hospital

Muirhead

Tiwi

Dripstone Park
Tiwi Park

Lyons
Dorisvale Park
Tracy Village Sports Club

Trower Road

Brinkin

Dripstone Middle School
Wanguri Oval

Nakara
Nakara Oval

Casuarina

Wanguri

Peace Park

Leanyer

Leanyer Swamp

Nightcliff Middle School
Ternau Park

Charles Darwin University Casuarina Campus

Casuarina Shopping Square

Hibiscus Shopping Town

Casuarina Coastal Reserve

Casuarina Beach

Rapid Creek

Alawa

Nightcliff
Sports ground
Chrisp Street Oval

Wagaman Oval

Wulagi

Wulagi Oval

Leanyer Recreation Park

Nightcliff Markets
Nightcliff Shopping Centre

Progress Dr

Trower Road

Wagaman

Casuarina Senior College

Water Gardens

Sanderson Middle School

Sunset Cove Estate

Millner

Jingili

Jingili Oval

Moil

Moil Oval

Anula

Yanyula Park

Malak

Coconut Grove

Ward Drive

Bagot Road

Bagot Oval

McMillans Road

Darwin General Cemetery

Rapid Creek

McMillans Road

Northlakes Shopping Ctr

Northlakes

Darwin Golf Club

Malak Park

Karama

HOLMES JUNGLE NATURE PARK

Dick Ward Dr

Kara Park

Marrara

Marrara Sporting Complex

Malak Caravan Park
KOA Caravan Park

Karama Shopping Centre

East Point

Military Museum

East Point Recreation Reserve

East Point

Marina

DARWIN INTERNATIONAL AIRPORT

Domestic and International Terminal

C.S.I.R.O. Research Centre

Emergency Services HQ

Fannie Bay

RAAF Golf Course

Johnson Av

Vanderlin Drive

Dudley Point

Lake Alexander

Bagot Road

Royal Australian Air Force Base

Amy Av

Waratah Oval

Ludmilla

The Narrows

HIGHWAY

Australian Aviation Heritage Centre

STUART

Showgrounds

Discovery Holiday Parks

Fannie Bay Shopping Centre

Fannie Bay Racecourse

Winnellie

Hook Road

Fannie Bay

Fannie Bay

Parap

Stuart

TIGER BRENNAN DRIVE

Amy Av

Johnson Av

Coonawarra

HMAS Coonawarra

HIGHWAY

To Palmerston

Museum and Art Gallery

Woolner

Woolner Dr

CHARLES DARWIN NATIONAL PARK

Brennan Drive

Hidden Valley Tourist Park

Berrimah

Bullocky Point

Darwin High School

Stuart Park

Bayview Haven

Tiger

Kormilda College

The Gardens

George Brown Darwin Botanic Gardens

Mindil Beach Sunset Markets

SKYCITY Casino

Brennan

Sailgroves

Charles Darwin

Richland Cr

Hidden Valley Motor Sports Complex

Berrimah Road

Myilly Point
Gullen Beach

Gardens Park Golf Course

Dinah Beach

Cullen Bay

Emery Point

Marina

Smith St

Daly St

McMinn St

Tiger

Marina

Fishermans Wharf

Frances Bay

Wishart Road

Larrakeyah Army Base

Elliot Point

Navy Patrol Boat Base

DARWIN

Doctors Gully

Bicentennial Park

Larrakeyah

Cameron Beach

Liberty Square

Stokes Hill

Stokes Hill Wharf

Darwin Harbour

Fort Hill Wharf
Boom Wharf

Bleesers

PORT DARWIN

ALICE SPRINGS – DARWIN RAILWAY

Railway Station

BERRIMAH

DARWIN BUSINESS PARK

East Arm Wharf

gate

Catalina Island

N

0   1   2km

© Hema Maps Pty Ltd

SEE PAGE 122

DARWIN

Melville Island

Pickertaramoor
Takamprimili Outstation
Tiwi
Muranapi Point
Irrititu Island
Cape Gambier
Moresby Shoals
Hancox Reef
Harris Reef

Beagle Shoals
Nihill Patch
Craven Patches
Taiyuan Shoal
Abbott Shoal
Wells Shoal
Bill Shoal
Barbara Shoal
Taylor Patches
Giles Shoal

Clarence Strait
Van Diemen

Margaret Shoal
Beatrice Reef

Arnhem Land
Waidaboonar

Beagle Gulf
Gunn Point
Foelsche Bank
Shoal Bay
Knight Reef
Fast Vernon Island
Vernon Islands Conservation Reserve
Gunn Reef
Stephens Bank

Cape Hotham
Draytons Reef
Elizabeth Reef
Ruby Island
Adam Bay

Chambers Bay
Point Stuart
Swim Creek

Gulf

Gardangarl (Field Island)
Djidbordu (Barron Island)
Gulárri (Point Farewell)
Pococks Beach
Point Stuart Wilderness Lodge
Finke Bay

Cannon Hill
Awunturna (Mount Borradaile)
Ubirr

ARNHEM LAND

Lee Point
Tree Point (Durdugu)
Casuarina Coastal Reserve
Charles Darwin
Mandorah
Belyuen (permit required)

'Howard Springs'
Palmerston
Howard Springs
Virginia
Mcminns Lagoon
Noonamah
Berry Springs
Humpty Doo
'Humpty Doo (Koolpinyah)'
'Acacia Larrakia (Acacia Gap)'

Woolner
'Lake Finniss Farm'
'Lake Finniss'
Melacca Swamp Conservation Area
Shoal Bay Coastal Reserve

'Melaleuca'
Shady Camp
Shady Camp Butcher

Mayambanjdju (Mount Hooper)
Carmor Plains Wildlife Reserve

KAKADU NATIONAL PARK

Four Mile Hole
Kapalga
Mudginberri
Hunters Camp
Mumakala
Mamukala Wetlands
Kakadu Resort
Chirreecarwoo Lagoon
Kakadu Visitor Centre
Bowali
Jabiru
Ranger Mineral Lease
Djirrbiyak
'Baroalba'
Koongarra
Nourlangie (Anlarrh)
Mirella Park
Sandy Billabong

DJUKBINJ NATIONAL PARK
MARY RIVER NATIONAL PARK

Limilngan-Wulna
Middle Point Village
'Window on the Wetlands'
Corroboree Park Tavern
Mary River Billabong
Bark Hut Inn
'Annaburroo'

ARNHEM HWY / HIGHWAY

Stuart Tree Fishing Camp
Palm Lagoon
MARY RIVER NP
Warradjan Cultural Centre
Cooinda
Yellow Water
Gagudju Lodge Cooinda
Jim Jim Ranger Station
Balma
Patonga (closed community)
Galurruyu
Marndoki
Deaf Adder (Golondjorr)
Djuwart
Kakadu

NATIONAL PARK

Mount Bundey Training Area
Mount Ringwood
Ringwood Range
Mount Ringwood
Mount Margaret
Mount Douglas

OLD JIM JIM ROAD

Goodparla 'Goodparla'
Djenjdjedmi
Maguk (Barramundi Gorge)
Gungkurdul (Twin Falls)
Barrkmalam (Jim Jim Falls)
Ankarrkarrkarrmi

Inbarin Hills
'Mary River Station'
Mount George
Gunlom Waterfall

Adelaide River
Batchelor
The Lost City Mount Tolmer
'Mount Mount Tolmer'

LITCHFIELD NATIONAL PARK

Prospect Hill
'Litchfield Outstation'
PORT KEATS ROAD

Brocks Creek
Grove Hill Hotel
'Burnside (abandoned)'
Burrundie
Mount Wells
Koolpin Gorge
Coronation Hill (Guratba)
Gimbat
Mount Evelyn (Garadbaluk)
Gunlom

Honeymoon House
Hayes Creek
The Shackle
Daly River
Daly River (Mt Nancar) Conservation Area
Hillcrest
Malak Malak
'Douglas'
Tipperary
Emerald Springs Roadhouse
Butterfly Gorge
Anwollolla Lagoon Douglas
Tjuwallyn (Douglas) Hot Springs Park
Douglas Crossing
'Setay Valley'

Bokan
Bokanj
Goymarr Tourist Park (Mary River Roadhouse)

KAKADU

Mount Gardiner
Mount Davis
Ngartluk

Pine Creek
Kybrook Farm
Kybrook (ruins)

Rock Candy Range
Mount Boulder
Beeboom Crossing
'Oolloo'

Umbrawarra Gorge Nature Park
Umbrawarra Gorge
Wagiman (No 2)
Foelsche Headland
Mount Giles
Fergusson River
Edith River
Leliyn (Edith Falls)

NITMILUK
Bambalmok
Mount Ebsworth
Mount David
Manyallaluk

(KATHERINE GORGE)

Phors Knob
'Fish River'
Douglas River / Daly River Esplanade Conservation Area
Fish River Gorge Block
Stray Creek Conservation Area
'Marilliyum'
'Claravale'
Wagiman (No 2)
Florina
Dorisvale
Wagiman (No 2)
Mount Mistake
Yubulyawun
Mount Pearce

Jawoyn
Northern Territory Rural College
Katherine
Manbulloo
Binjari (Wylunba)
Tindal
Nitmiluk Visitor Centre
Nitmiluk (Katherine Gorge) National Park
Katherine Gorge
Banatjarl

NITMILUK NATIONAL PARK
Manyallaluk (Eva Valley)

Upper Daly
Wombungi
'Carbeen Park'
Gwinning / Flora River Nature Park
Manbulloo Research Station
Cutta Cutta Caves
Cutta Cutta Caves Nature Park
Maranboy
Barunga (Bamyili)
Maranboy
Beswick

VICTORIA HWY
STUART HIGHWAY
CENTRAL ARNHEM RD / HIGHWAY

N
0 5 10 20km
© Hema Maps Pty Ltd

To Victoria River & Kununurra
To Tennant Creek

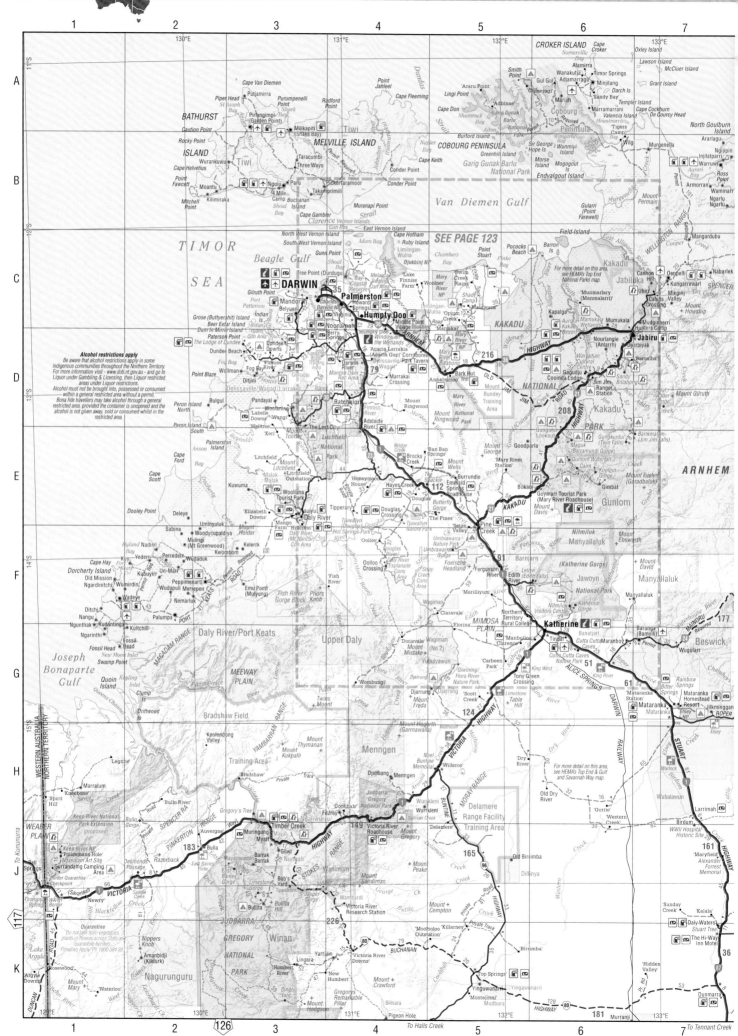

SEE PAGE 123

Alcohol restrictions apply
Be aware that alcohol restrictions apply in some
indigenous communities throughout the Northern Territory.
For more information visit - www.dob.nt.gov.au - and go to
Liquor under Gambling & Licensing, then Liquor restricted
areas under Liquor restrictions.
Alcohol must not be brought into, possessed or consumed
within a general restricted area without a permit.
Bona fide travellers may take alcohol through a general
restricted area, provided the container is unopened and the
alcohol is not given away, sold or consumed whilst in the
restricted area.

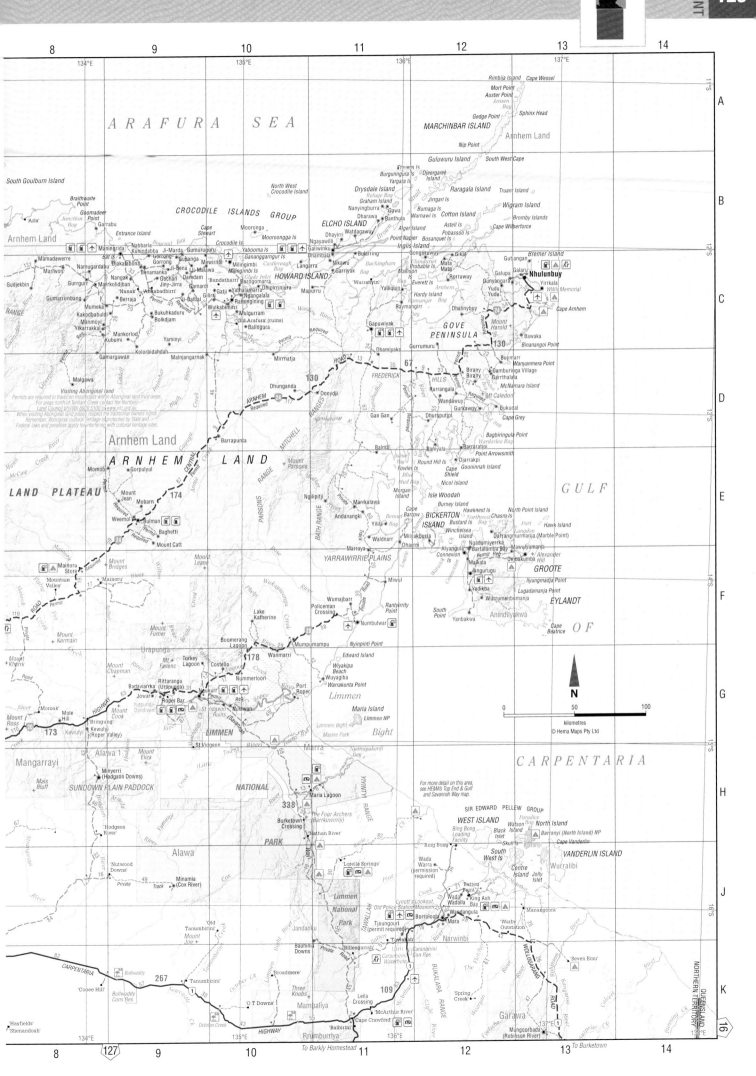

A R A F U R A   S E A

134°E

135°E

136°E

137°E

11°S

Rimbija Island • Cape Wessel
Mort Point
Auster Point
Jensen
Bay
Gedge Point   • Sphinx Head

MARCHINBAR ISLAND

Arnhem Land

Nip Point

A

Guluwuru Island   South West Cape

South Goulburn Island

Stevens Is
Burgunngura Is • Djeergaree
Yargara Is   Island
Drysdale Island   Raragala Island   Truant Island
Refuge Bay
Graham Island   Jirrgari Is   Wigram Island
Nanyingburra • Gawa   Bumaga Is   Cotton Island
Dharawa   Warnawi Is   Bromby Islands
Point Napier   Alger Island   Astell Is   Cape Wilberforce
Pobassoo Is
Inglis Island   Bosanquet Is

B

Braithwaite
Point
Goomadeer
Point   Garrabu

CROCODILE ISLANDS GROUP

Cape
Stewart

North West
Crocodile Island

'Arla'
Junction
Bay

Mooronga

ELCHO ISLAND
Watdagawuy

12°S

Entrance Island

Mooroongga Is
Crocodile Is

Ngayawilli

Galupa • Galan
Gutiangan,
Bremer Island

Arnhem Land

Mamadawerre
Marlwon

Nabbarla   Kunindabba   Yabooma Is
Ji-Marda   Gumuruguru

Dhambala   Bularring

Gonguruwuy   Gikal   Gunyangara   Nhulunbuy
Mata   Yirrkala
Ulunburrugu   Mata   Galupa
Probable Is

Namugardabu
Djakabona   Gorrong • Gupanga
Gorrong • Ji-Bena
Milingimbi   Langarra   Nikawu
Milingimbi Is

Mewirnbi   Ji-Malawa

Gurrgurr
Marrkolidjban   Nangak • Gochan   Garriyak   Mapurru
Jiny-Jirra   Ganambarr
Benamanka   Damdam   Yathalamarra

Everett Is   Arnhem   Rorruwuy   Gunyangara
Mallison   Bay   Yudu
Hardy Island   Ramungir   Dhalinybuy   Yudu   WWII Memorial
Raymangirr   Bay   Cape Arnham

Gumariirnbang
'Nanak'
Berraia
Ji-Balbal   Giliri   Ngangalala
Atkabadbirri   Ramingining

Gapuwiyak

GOVE
PENINSULA   130

Mount
Harold

C

Mumeka
Kakodbabuldi
Manmoyi   Mulgurram
Bukuhkaduru   'Old Arafura' (ruins)
Yikarrakkal   Bolkdjam   Balingura
Kubumi

Dhamiyaka
Gurrumuru

Buymarr   Wanyanmera Point
Camburinga Village
Birany   Garrthalala
Birany   McNamara Island

Bawaka

Binanangoi Point

Kolorbidahdah   Gamargawan

Malnjangarnak   Mirrnatja

ROAD   13   35   67
FREDERICK   9

Rurrangala   Mt Caledon

Dhuruputjpi   Bukudal

130

Dhunganda   Donydji   24   17
RANGES
Required

Gan Gan   Cape Grey

D

13°S

LAND PLATEAU

Malgawa

ARNHEM

CENTRAL

Barrapunta

Momob
Gorpulyul

ARNHEM   LAND   174

Mount   Mobarn
Jean

Weemol
Bulman
Baghetti
Mount Catt

Mainoru
Store

'Mountain
Valley'   Mainoru'

Mount
Bridges

ROAD

119

Mount
Karmain

Mount
Fumer

MITCHELL   Mount
Parsons

Balma

Round Hill Is
Fowler Is
Cape
Shield   Gooninnah Island
Nicol Island
Morgan   Isle Woodah
Island
Burney Island   Hawk Island
Cape   North Point Island
Barlow   Northwest   Chasm Is
Bickerton   Is   Port   Hawk Island
ISLAND   Winchelsea   Langdon
Is   Darrangmurmanja (Marble Point)
Milyakburra   Ngadumiyerrka
Dhagni   Alyangula   Bartalumba Bay   Mawulyumanja
Connexion   Permit   Req   Alexander
Is   Malkala   Omakumba   Hill
Angurugu   GROOTE

Ngilipitji
Marrkalawa
Andanangki
Yilila   Waldarr

Marraya
Waldnar

YARRAWIRRIE PLAINS

E

14°S

BATH RANGE

PARSONS   RANGE

Wardarlea Bay
Bagbiringula Point
Baniyala   Barratipi
Point Arrowsmith
Djarrakpi

G U L F

Miwul   Yedikba   EYLANDT
Wurrumenbumanja

O F

Wumajbarr
Policeman
Crossing   Rantyirrity
Point
Numbulwar
South
Point   Yanbakwa   Anindilyakwa   Cape
Beatrice

F

Boomerang
Lagoon
Mumpumampu
Nyinpinti Point

N

Urapunga
Mt
Favenc   Turkey
Lagoon   Costello   178   Wanmarri

Edward Island

Wiyakipa
Beach   0   50   100
Wuyagiba
Warrakunta Point   kilometres

© Hema Maps Pty Ltd

G

Rittarangu
Badawarrka (Urapunga)   Nummerloori
Jowar   Ngukurr
Roper Bar   St Vidgeon
Yutpundji-   Ruins
Djindiwirritj   Nulawan

Port
Roper

Limmen

Maria Island
Limmen NP

15°S

Mount
Ross
173   Kewulyi
Mole
Hill   'Bringung'
Kewulyi
(Roper Valley)

HIGHWAY   63

Mount
Cook

St Vidgeon

LIMMEN

Limmen Bight
Marine Park

Limmen
Bight

C A R P E N T A R I A

Mangarrayi   Alawa 1

Mais
Bluff

Mount
Eliza

Minyerri
(Hodgson Downs)

SUNDOWN PLAIN PADDOCK

NATIONAL

Marra
Nyamiyukunjmi
Bay

For more detail on this area,
see HEMA's Top End & Gulf
and Savannah Way map.

H

'Hodgson
River'

338   Maria Lagoon

13

The Four Archers
(Barrkuwirriji)
Burketown
Crossing
'Nathan River'

SIR EDWARD PELLEW GROUP

WEST ISLAND   Watson   North Island
Paradise
Bay
Bing Bong   Black   Skull Is
Loading   Islet   Barranyi (North Island) NP
Facility   Cape Vanderlin

'Nutwood
Downs'   Minamia
(Cox River)

PARK

Alawa

Bing Bong

Lorella Springs'

Wada   South
Warra   West Is   VANDERLIN ISLAND
(permission
required)   Centre   Wutralibi
Island   Jolly
Islet

J

Limmen
National   Batten
Point   Wada
Wadalla   King Ash
Bay
Old Police Station   Wadangula
'Old   Museum   Manangoora
Tanumbirini'
Mount   Jandanku   Tjoungouri   Borroloola   'Warby
Joe   (permit required)   Mara   Outstation'
Narwinbi

16°S

CARPENTARIA

'Cooee Hill'   Bulwaddy   267   Tanumbirini
Bulwaddy
Cons Res

'Broadmere'

Park   Billengarrah
Bauhinia
Downs   Caranbirini Con Res
Caranbirini
Waterhole

'Seven Emu'

WOOLOGORANG   ROAD

K

'Hayfields'
'Shenandoah'

134°E   'O T Downs'   Three
Knobs

Mampaiya

October Creek   43

HIGHWAY

135°E

'Balbirini'

Leila
Crossing

109   McArthur River
Cape Crawford

'Spring
Creek'   'Mungoorbada
(Robinson River)'

Garawa

Mungoorbada

137°E

136°E

Rrumburriya   To Barkly Homestead   To Burketown

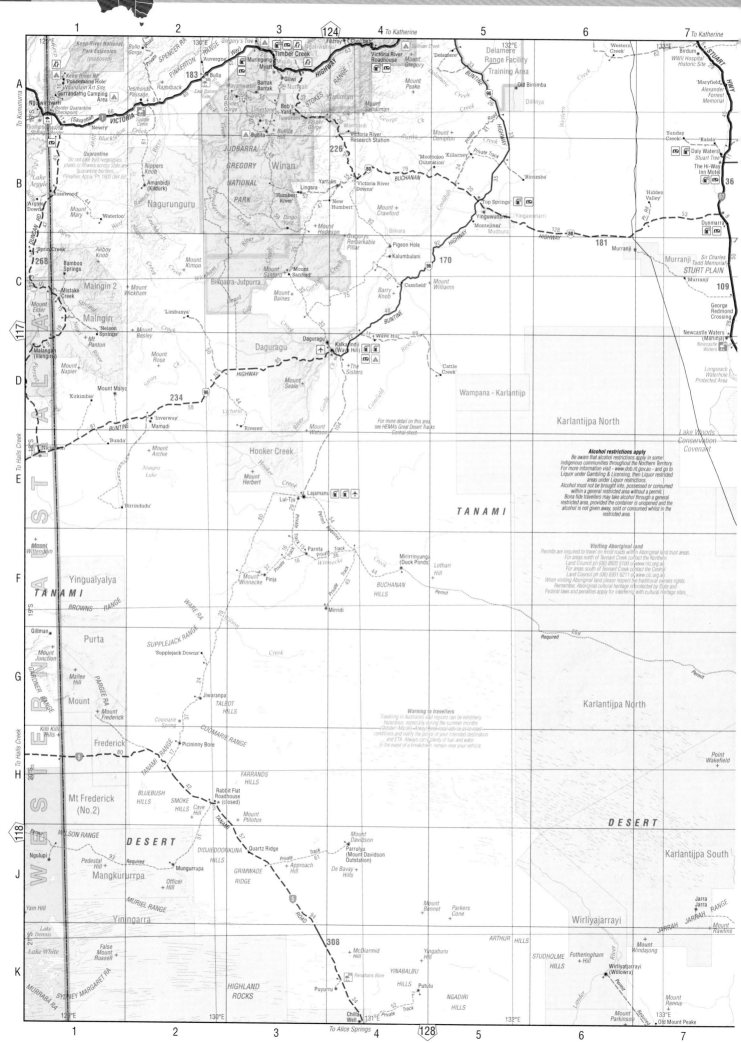

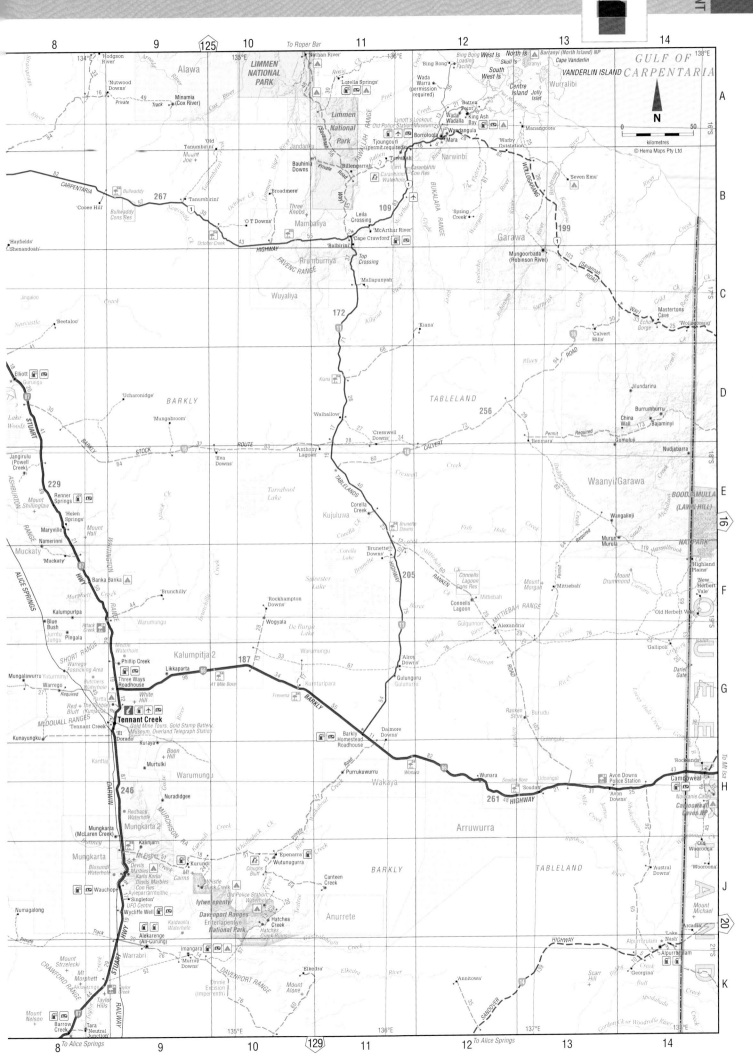

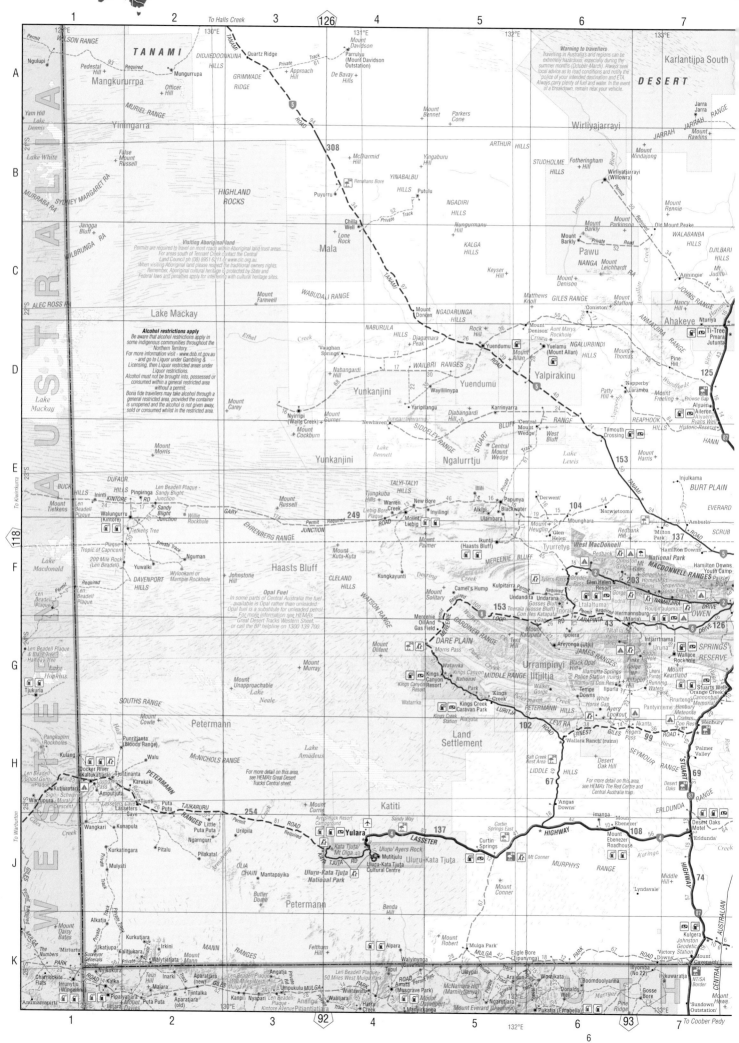

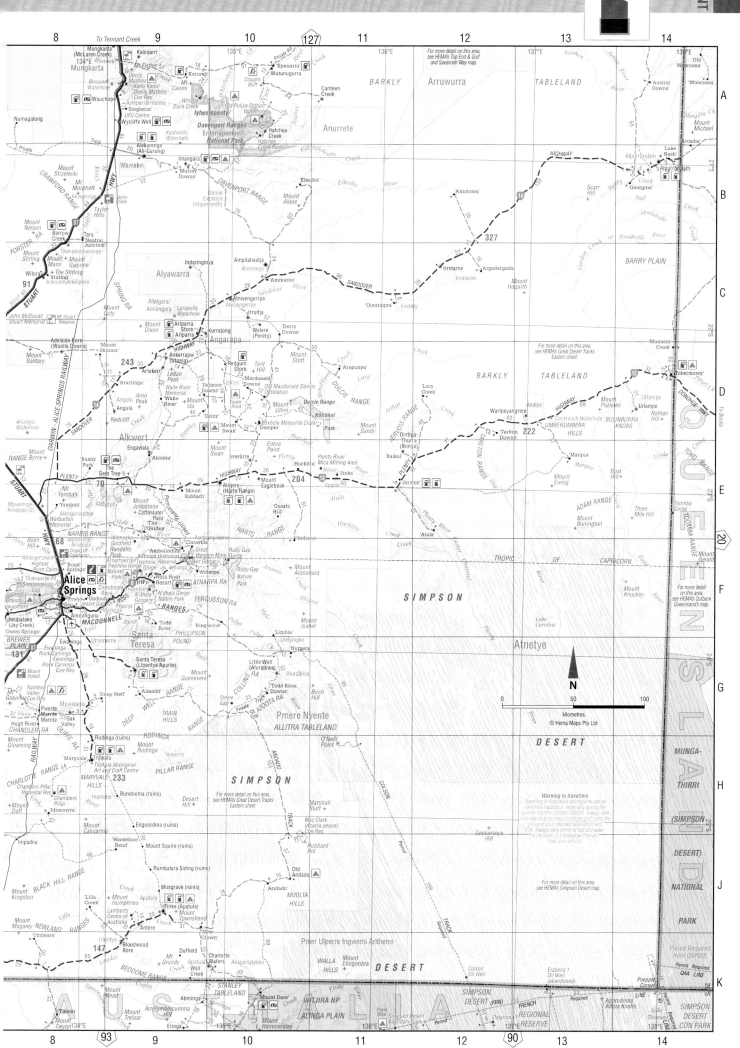

A

207 Mile Camp 115 E9
4 Mile Camp NT 124 B3
913 Mine WA 119 F2
A1 Mine Settlement VIC 64 G4 66 C5
Abbeyard VIC 64 E5 66 A6
Abbotsbury VIC 28 K2 30 B2 35 E9
Abbotsford NSW 27 E4 29 K9 31 A9
Abbotsham TAS 74 D3 77 H11
Aberbaldie NSW 39 J8
Aberbaldie Nature Res NSW 39 J8
Abercorn QLD 13 A10
Abercrombie NSW 36 H6
Abercrombie River Nat Park NSW 34 K1
    36 H6 44 A4
Aberdeen NSW 37 C9
Aberfeldy VIC 64 H4 66 D5
Aberfoyle Park SA 84 J5 86 K2 87 A6
Aberglasslyn NSW 33 A11
Abergowrie QLD 17 G11
Abermain NSW 33 B11
Abernethy NSW 33 C11 45 J4
Abington NSW 39 F8
Abminga SA 90 A1 93 A13 129 K9
Acacia Ridge QLD 3 H4 7 G10 11 C10
Acheron VIC 64 F2 66 B3
Acland QLD 13 F11
Acraman Creek Con Park SA 97 H12
Acton ACT 46 A1 47 D4
Adaminaby NSW 43 J14 44 F2 65 A11
Adams Estate VIC 57 K11
Adamsfield TAS 71 C8
Adamsfield Con Area TAS 71 C8
Adamstown NSW 33 C14
Adavale QLD 21 J9 23 A11
Addington VIC 59 D10
Adelaide SA 80 C2 81 G4 84 C5 86 H2
    89 H8 98 C3
Adelaide Bore (Woolla Downs) NT 129 D8
Adelaide River NT 123 E2 124 E4
Adelong NSW 43 H13 44 D1
Adjamarragu NT 124 A6
Adjungbilly NSW 43 G14
Advancetown QLD 11 G11 24 F1
Advancetown Lake QLD 11 G11 24 G1
Adventure Bay TAS 71 H13
Afterlee NSW 39 B12
Agery SA 88 F7 98 B1
Agnes Banks NSW 34 C7
Agnes Banks Nature Res NSW 34 C7
Agnes Water QLD 15 J12
Agnew WA 113 D10
Ailsa VIC 62 J5
Ainslie ACT 47 D5
Airds NSW 30 K1
Aireys Inlet-Fairhaven VIC 56 K1
    59 H11 61 G12
Airlie Beach QLD 15 B8 17 J14 21 A14
Airly VIC 64 J6
Airport West VIC 52 D6
Akaroa TAS 75 E14
Akuna Bay NSW 27 A6 29 B12
Alagala NSW 36 C2 41 J13 43 A13
Alamirra NT 124 A6
Alawa NT 122 C5
Alawoona SA 89 G12 98 C6
Albacutya VIC 42 J3 62 G4
Albanvale VIC 52 E4
Albany WA 109 K13 110 K6
Albany Creek QLD 3 B2 5 G8 9 K9
Albatross Bay QLD 19 E1
Alberrie Creek SA 90 K7 94 A7
Albert NSW 36 C2 41 J12 43 A12
Albert Park SA 82 J2 84 A2
Albert Park VIC 53 H8 56 D7
Alberton QLD 11 D11
Alberton SA 81 E2 82 H2 86 G1
Alberton TAS 75 E11
Alberton VIC 66 H6
Albinia Nat Park QLD 14 J7 21 G14
Albion QLD 3 D4 5 J10 7 A10
Albion VIC 52 F5 56 C6
Albury NSW 43 J11 64 B6
Alcomie TAS 76 F5
Alderley QLD 3 D3 5 J9 7 A9
Aldersyde WA 107 F9
Aldgate SA 81 K7 85 G10 86 K4 87 A7
Aldinga SA 87 D5
Aldinga Bay SA 87 E4
Aldinga Beach SA 87 D4 89 H8 98 D2
Aldinga Scrub Con Park SA 87 D4
Alectown NSW 36 E3 41 K14 43 C14
Alekarenge (Ali-Curung) NT 127 K9 129 B9
Alexander Heights WA 101 C4
Alexander Morrison Nat Park WA 112 G5
Alexandra VIC 64 F2 66 B3
Alexandra Bridge WA 108 F2
Alexandra Headland QLD 9 C10
Alexandra Hills QLD 11 B11
Alexandria NSW 31 C11
Alexandria Bay QLD 9 A10
Alford SA 88 E7 98 A1
Alfords Point NSW 27 J3 30 F6
Alfred Cove WA 101 H3 102 K4 104 A4
Alfred Nat Park VIC 65 G12
Algebuckina SA 90 F3
Algester QLD 3 J4 7 H10
Alice NSW 13 K12 39 C11
Alice QLD 14 H3 21 F11
Alice River QLD 14 A4 17 H12
Alice Springs NT 129 F8
Alkatja NT 92 A1 128 K1
Alkipi NT 128 E5
Allambie NSW 27 D6 29 G13
Allambie Heights NSW 29 G12
Allan QLD 10 H1 13 H11 39 A10

Allans Flat VIC 64 B6
Allansford VIC 58 H6 60 F3
Allanson WA 108 B6
Allawah NSW 31 F9
Alleena NSW 36 H1 43 E12
Allenby Gardens SA 81 F3 82 K3 84 B3
Allendale NSW 33 B11
Allendale East SA 98 J6
Allens Rivulet TAS 71 F12
Allestree VIC 58 H3
Allies Creek QLD 13 D10
Alligator Creek QLD 14 A5 17 H12
Allingham QLD 17 G11
Allora QLD 10 G1 13 H11
Allynbrook NSW 45 B6
Alma SA 89 F8 98 B3
Almaden QLD 17 E9
Almonds VIC 64 B3
Almoola QLD 14 C6 17 K13 21 A13
Almurta VIC 57 K12
Alnwick NSW 33 A13
Alonnah TAS 71 H13
Aloomba QLD 17 E11 18 E5
Alpara NT 92 A5 128 K4
Alpha QLD 14 H4 21 F12
Alpine Nat Park VIC 64 F5 66 B6
Alpurrurulam NT 20 B1 127 K14 129 B14
Alstonville NSW 39 C13
Althorpe Islands SA 88 J5
Alton QLD 12 H6
Alton Nat Park QLD 12 H6
Altona VIC 51 E1 52 H5 56 D6
Altona East VIC 52 G6
Altona Meadows VIC 51 E1 52 J4
Altona North VIC 52 G5
Alva Beach QLD 14 A6 17 H13
Alvie VIC 59 G9 61 F9
Alwal Nat Park (CYPAL) QLD 17 B8 19 J4
Alyangula NT 125 F12
Alyuen NT 128 D7
Amamoor QLD 13 D13
Amanbidji (Kildurk) NT 124 K2 126 B2
Amaroo ACT 47 A5
Amata (Musgrave Park) SA 92 A5 128 K4
Ambarvale NSW 35 G9
Amberley QLD 10 C7
Ambleside SA 86 J4
Amboola QLD 12 D3 21 K13
Amboyne Crossing VIC 44 J2 65 E10
Ambrose QLD 15 H11
Amby QLD 12 D4 21 K14
Amen Corner SA 88 J6
American River SA 88 K7 98 E1
Amery WA 107 A8
Amherst VIC 59 C10
Amity QLD 9 K13 11 A13 13 G14
Amoonguna NT 129 F8
Amosfield NSW 13 J11 39 B10
Amphitheatre VIC 59 C9
Ampilatwatja NT 129 C10
Amputjuta NT 128 H1
Amyton SA 89 B8 95 H8
Anabranch Hall NSW 42 E2
Anakie QLD 14 H6 21 F13
Anakie VIC 56 E2 59 F12 61 B13
Anakie East VIC 56 E2
Anakie Junction VIC 56 D2 59 F12 61 B13
Ancona VIC 64 E2 66 A3
Andamooka SA 94 C6
Andanangki NT 125 E11
Anderson VIC 66 H2
Anderson Islands TAS 78 E5
Andersons Flat NSW 37 A10 39 J8
Andersons Nature Res TAS 71 C12 73 K14
Ando NSW 44 H3 65 D12
Andover TAS 69 D2
Andrews QLD 11 H12
Andrews SA 89 D9
Anduramba QLD 8 H2 62 H6
Anembo NSW 44 F4 48 J7 65 A13
Angahook-Lorne State Park VIC 61 H11
Angas Place NSW 34 A1
Angaston SA 86 C7 89 G9 98 B3
Angatja SA 92 A4 128 K3
Angellala QLD 12 D2 21 K12
Angip VIC 42 K4 62 H5
Angle Park SA 82 H4
Angle Vale SA 86 E2 89 G8 98 C3
Anglers Rest VIC 64 E7
Anglesea VIC 56 K2 59 H11 61 F13
Angorichina Village SA 95 E9
Angourie NSW 39 D13
Angove Con Park SA 86 G3
Angula NT 129 D9
Angurugu NT 125 F12
Ankerrapw (Utopia) NT 129 D9
Anketell WA 104 J6
Anna Bay NSW 37 E12
Annan River (Yuku Baja-Muliku) Nat Park QLD
    17 C10 19 K7
Annandale NSW 31 B10
Annangrove NSW 28 C4
Anne Range NT 128 H1
Annerley QLD 3 H4 7 D10 11 B9
Annuello VIC 42 G4 62 C6
Ansons Bay TAS 75 C14 78 K6
Anstey Hill Rec Park SA 86 G4
Antere NT 129 J9
Antill Ponds TAS 69 C2
Antwerp VIC 42 K3 62 J4
Anula NT 122 D5
Anxious Bay SA 88 D1 94 K1 97 K13
Aparatjara (New) SA 92 A2 128 K2
Aparatjara (Old) SA 92 A2 118 J7 128 K2
Apollo Bay VIC 59 K10 61 J10
Appila SA 89 C8 95 J8
Appin NSW 35 H9 37 J9 44 A7
Appin VIC 42 J6 63 G9

Appin South VIC 63 G9
Apple Tree Flat NSW 36 D6
Applecross WA 101 H3 102 J4
Appleton Flat NSW 32 A6
Apslawn TAS 69 A6 75 K13
Apsley TAS 71 A12 73 J14
Apsley VIC 58 B1 98 G5
Apsley Con Area TAS 75 J14
Arabella QLD 12 D1 21 K12 23 B14
Arafura Sea QLD 19 C1
Arakoola Nature Res NSW 38 D7
Arakoon NSW 39 H12
Araleun SA 92 A7 128 K5
Araluen NSW 44 E4
Aralya SA 92 C1
Aramac QLD 14 G2 21 E10
Aramara QLD 13 C12
Arana Hills QLD 3 C2
Aranda ACT 47 D3
Ararat VIC 58 C7
Arariagu NT 124 B7
Aratula QLD 10 F6 13 H12
Arawata VIC 57 J14
Arcadia NSW 27 A3 28 A7 35 B10
Arcadia VIC 63 J13 64 C1
Arcadia Vale NSW 33 D13
Archdale VIC 59 A9 63 K8
Archer River Roadhouse QLD 19 F3
Archerfield QLD 3 H3 7 F9 11 C9
Archies Creek VIC 66 H3
Ardath WA 107 E13
Ardeer VIC 51 D1 52 F4
Ardlethan NSW 43 F11
Ardross WA 102 J4
Ardrossan SA 88 F7 98 B2
Areyonga NT 128 G6
Argyle VIC 59 B13
Argyle WA 108 C4 110 G3
Ariah Park NSW 36 J1 43 F12
Arkaroola Village SA 95 C10
Arkona VIC 42 K3 62 J4
Arlparra NT 129 C9
Arlparra Store NT 129 C9
Armadale VIC 51 E4 53 H9
Armadale WA 105 F11 106 E3 110 D3 112 K5
Armatree NSW 36 A4 38 K2 41 G14
Armidale NSW 39 G9
Armorran NT 124 B7
Armstrong VIC 58 C7
Armuna QLD 14 B7 17 J14 21 A14
Armytage VIC 59 H10
Arncliffe NSW 27 G4 31 E10
Arndell Park NSW 28 G2
Arnhem Land NT 124 H7
Arno Bay SA 88 E4
Arnold VIC 59 A10 63 K9
Arrawarra NSW 39 F13
Arrino WA 112 F5
Artarmon NSW 29 H11 35 C11
Artekerr NT 129 D9
Arthur River TAS 76 G3
Arthur River WA 109 B10 110 F5
Arthur-Pieman Con Area TAS 72 A2 76 J4
Arthurs Creek VIC 57 A9
Arthurs Lake TAS 73 E12 74 K7
Arthurton SA 88 F7 98 B1
Arthurville NSW 36 D4
Arundel QLD 11 F12 24 C3
Ascot QLD 3 D4 5 K11 7 A11 11 A9
Ascot VIC 59 D10
Ascot WA 101 F5 103 E8
Ascot Park SA 84 F4
Ascot Vale VIC 52 F7
Ashbourne SA 87 D7
Ashburton VIC 53 H11
Ashbury NSW 31 C9 35 D11
Ashcroft NSW 30 D3
Ashfield NSW 31 C9 35 D11
Ashfield WA 101 E5 103 D8
Ashford NSW 39 D8
Ashford SA 84 D4
Ashgrove QLD 3 D3 5 K8 7 B8
Ashley NSW 38 D5
Ashmore QLD 11 G12 24 E4
Ashton SA 81 G7 85 D10 86 H3
Ashville SA 89 J10 98 D4
Ashwood VIC 53 H11
Aspen Island ACT 46 C4
Aspendale VIC 54 E5 57 F8
Aspley QLD 3 B4 5 G10 9 K9 11 A9
Asquith NSW 29 D5 35 B10
Astrebla Downs Nat Park QLD 20 G4
Athelstone SA 81 E7 83 J9 85 A9 86 H3
Atherton QLD 17 E10 18 F3
Athlone VIC 57 H13 64 K2 66 F3
Athol Park SA 81 E3 82 H3
Atholwood NSW 13 K9 39 C8
Atitjere (Harts Range) NT 129 E10
Atnwengerrpe NT 129 C10
Attadale WA 101 H2 102 J3
Attunga NSW 38 H7
Attwood VIC 52 B6
Atwell WA 110 A4 112 H6
Aubrey VIC 62 H5
Auburn NSW 27 F5 29 K11 31 B11 35 D11
Auburn SA 89 E9 98 A3
Auburn VIC 53 G10
Auburn River Nat Park QLD 13 C10
Audley NSW 27 K3 35 F11
Augathella QLD 12 C1 21 J12 23 A14
Augusta WA 108 F2 110 J2
Augustine Heights QLD 6 J5
Auldana SA 81 G6 85 C8
Aurukun QLD 19 F1
Austinmer NSW 35 J10
Austinville QLD 11 H12 24 J2

Austral NSW 30 D1 35 E8
Austral TAS 72 E4
Australind WA 108 B4
Avalon NSW 35 A12
Avalon Beach NSW 35 A12
Avenel VIC 64 E1 66 A2
Avenue Range SA 98 G5
Avisford Nature Res NSW 36 D6
Avoca TAS 75 H11
Avoca VIC 59 C9
Avoca Beach NSW 33 J13 37 G10
Avoca Reg Res TAS 75 J12
Avoca Vale QLD 8 D3
Avon SA 89 F8 98 B2
Avon Valley Nat Park WA 106 D4 110 C3 112 J6
Avondale NSW 33 E12
Avondale QLD 13 A12 15 K12
Avondale Heights VIC 52 E6
Avonsleigh VIC 55 A13 57 E11
Awaba NSW 33 D13
Axedale VIC 59 A12 63 K11
Ayr QLD 14 A6 17 H13
Ayrford VIC 58 H7 60 F5
Ayton QLD 17 C10 19 K7

B

Baan Baa NSW 38 G5
Baandee WA 107 C12
Baandee North WA 107 B12
Babakin WA 107 E12
Babel Island TAS 78 B7
Babinda QLD 17 E11 18 G5
Bacala TAS 75 D8
Bacchus Marsh VIC 56 B3 59 E12
Badawarrka NT 125 G9
Baddaginnie VIC 63 K14 64 C3
Baden TAS 69 D2 71 A14
Badgebup WA 109 C14
Badgerys Creek NSW 35 E8
Badgingarra WA 110 A2 112 H5
Badgingarra Nat Park WA 110 A2 112 H5
Badjaling WA 107 E10
Badu (Mulgrave) Island QLD 19 A2
Baerami Creek NSW 32 B3 37 D8
Bagdad TAS 69 F1 71 C12 73 K14
Baghetti NT 125 E9
Bago Bluff Nat Park NSW 37 A13 39 K11
Bailieston VIC 59 A14 63 K12
Bailup WA 106 C5
Baird Bay SA 97 K12
Bairnsdale VIC 64 H7
Bajaminyi NT 127 D14
Bajool QLD 15 H10
Bakara SA 89 G11
Bakara Con Park SA 89 G11 98 B5
Baker VIC 62 H3
Baker Gully SA 87 B6
Bakers Creek QLD 15 D8
Bakers Hill WA 106 D5
Baking Board QLD 13 E9
Baladjie Lake Nature Res WA 110 B7 113 H9
Balaklava SA 89 F8 98 B2
Balbarrup WA 108 F6
Balcatta WA 101 D3 102 B4 106 D3
Balcolyn NSW 33 E13
Bald Hills QLD 3 A3 5 F9
Bald Knob NSW 39 E10
Bald Knob QLD 9 D9
Bald Rock VIC 42 J7 63 H10
Bald Rock Nat Park NSW 13 K11 39 B10
Baldry NSW 36 E4 41 K14 43 B14
Balfes Creek QLD 14 B3 17 J11 21 A11
Balfour TAS 76 H4
Balga WA 101 D3 102 B4
Balgal Beach QLD 17 H12
Balgo (Wirrimanu) WA 117 K13 118 A6
Balgowan SA 88 F6 98 B1
Balgowlah NSW 27 D6 29 H13 35 C12
Balgowlah Heights NSW 29 H13
Balgownie NSW 35 K10
Balhannah SA 85 F13 86 J4
Balingup WA 108 D5 110 G3
Balkuling WA 107 E8
Balladonia Roadhouse WA 113 K14 119 H1
Balladoran NSW 36 B4 41 H14
Ballajura WA 101 C5 102 A7
Ballalaba NSW 44 E4
Ballan VIC 56 B2 59 E12
Ballan North VIC 56 A2
Ballandean QLD 13 K11 39 B9
Ballangeich VIC 58 G7 60 E3
Ballarat VIC 59 E10
Ballark VIC 56 C1
Ballaying WA 109 B12
Ballbank NSW 42 H6 63 F9
Balldale NSW 43 J11 64 A5
Ballendella VIC 63 J11
Ballera Gas Plant QLD 22 D5
Balliang VIC 56 D3 59 F12 61 A14
Balliang East VIC 56 D3 59 F12 61 A14
Ballidu WA 110 A4 112 H6
Ballimore NSW 36 C5
Ballina NSW 13 K14 39 C14
Bally Bally WA 107 F8
Balma NT 125 E11
Balmain NSW 27 F5 29 K11 31 B11 35 D11
Balmoral NSW 27 E6 29 J12 31 A12 33 D13
    34 K7 35 C12
Balmoral QLD 3 E5 5 K11 7 B11
Balmoral VIC 58 C4 98 H7
Balnarring VIC 57 J8 59 H14 64 K1 66 G1
Balnarring Beach VIC 57 J8
Balook VIC 64 K5 66 G6
Balranald NSW 42 F6 63 C8
Balwyn VIC 51 D5 53 F10 57 D8

Bamaga QLD 19 B2
Bamawm VIC 63 H11
Bamawm Extension VIC 63 H11
Bambaroo QLD 17 G11
Bambill VIC 42 F2 62 B2
Bambra VIC 59 H11 61 F11
Ban Ban Nat Park QLD 13 C11
Ban Ban Springs QLD 13 C11
Banana QLD 15 J9
Banca TAS 75 C11 78 K4
Bancroft QLD 13 A10 15 K11
Bandiana VIC 64 B6
Bandon NSW 36 F3 43 D14
Bangalow NSW 13 J14 39 B13
Bangerang VIC 62 H5
Bangham SA 58 A1 62 K1 98 G6
Bangham Con Park SA 98 G6
Bangholme VIC 51 H6 54 E6
Bangor NSW 30 G7 35 F10
Bangor TAS 75 D8
Bania Nat Park QLD 13 A11 15 K11
Banjup WA 104 E6
Banks ACT 47 K4
Banks Strait TAS 78 H5
Banksia NSW 31 E10
Banksia Beach QLD 9 G10
Banksia Park SA 81 C7 83 F9
Banksmeadow NSW 27 H6 31 E12
Bankstown NSW 27 G2 30 D6 35 E10
Bannaby NSW 36 J7 44 B5
Bannerton VIC 42 G4 62 C6
Bannister NSW 36 K6 44 B4
Bannister WA 106 H6
Bannockburn VIC 56 F1 59 G11 61 C13
Banora Point NSW 11 J13
Banthula NT 125 B11
Banyabba Nature Res NSW 39 D12
Banyena VIC 62 K6
Banyo QLD 3 C5 5 H11
Barabba SA 86 A2
Barabon QLD 17 K8 21 B8
Baradine NSW 38 H3
Barakee Nat Park NSW 37 A11 39 K9
Barakula QLD 13 D9
Baralaba QLD 15 J9
Baranduda VIC 64 B6
Barcaldine QLD 14 H2 21 F10
Barden Ridge NSW 30 H6
Bardi (One Arm Point) WA 116 E6
Bardoc WA 111 A11 113 G11
Bardon QLD 3 E3 7 C8
Barduthulla QLD 12 C1 21 J12 23 A14
Bardwell Park NSW 31 E9
Bare Hill Con Park QLD 18 E3
Barellan NSW 43 F11
Barellan Point QLD 6 F4
Bargara QLD 13 A12 15 K13
Bargo NSW 35 J8 37 J8 44 A6
Bargo State Rec Area NSW 34 K7
Barham NSW 42 J7 63 F10
Baring VIC 42 H3 62 E4
Baringhup VIC 59 B11
Barjarg VIC 64 E3 66 A4
Bark Hut Inn NT 123 D4 124 D5
Barkly Homestead NT 127 G11
Barkstead VIC 59 D11
Barlee Range Nature Res WA 114 F5
Barmah VIC 43 J8 63 H12
Barmedman NSW 36 H1 43 E12
Barmera SA 89 F12 98 B6
Barmundu QLD 15 J11
Barna SA 88 C5 94 K5
Barnard Island Group Nat Park QLD 18 J7
Barnawartha VIC 64 B5
Barnes Bay TAS 69 J1 71 F13
Barney View QLD 11 J8
Barnie Bolac VIC 60 B6
Barnsley NSW 33 C12
Barongarook VIC 59 H10 61 F9
Barooga NSW 43 J9 63 G14 64 A2
Barool Nat Park NSW 39 E10
Barossa Valley SA 86 C6
Barpinba VIC 59 G10 61 D9
Barraba NSW 38 G6
Barrabool VIC 56 G2
Barradale WA 114 E4
Barragan NSW 36 F4 43 D14
Barrak Barrak NT 124 J3 126 A3
Barramunga VIC 59 J10 61 G10
Barranyi (North Island) Nat Park NT
    125 H13 127 A13
Barraport VIC 63 H8
Barrapunta NT 125 D10
Barraratjpi NT 125 D12
Barratta QLD 14 A5 17 H13
Barretta TAS 69 J1 71 F12
Barretts Creek NSW 39 D11
Barrington NSW 37 B12
Barrington TAS 74 E3 77 J11
Barrington Tops Nat Park NSW 37 C10
Barringun NSW 23 H13 41 A8
Barron Gorge Nat Park QLD 18 D4
Barrow Creek NT 127 K8 129 C8
Barrow Island WA 114 B4
Barrow Island Nature Res WA 114 B4
Barry NSW 36 G5 37 A10 39 K8
Barry Beach VIC 66 H5
Barry Mountains VIC 66 B7
Barryrenie NSW 36 G4 43 D14
Barrys Reef VIC 59 D12
Bartalumba Bay NT 125 F12
Bartle Frere QLD 18 G5
Barton ACT 46 D3 47 E5
Barton VIC 58 D7
Barton Siding SA 97 C9

Barunga (Bamyili) – Boronia Heights INDEX 131

Barunga (Bamyili) NT 123 J7 124 G7
Barwell Con Park SA 88 D2 94 K2
Barwon Heads VIC 56 H4 59 H12
Baryulgil NSW 39 D11
Bascombe Well Con Park SA 88 D2
Basin Pocket QLD 6 G2
Basin View NSW 44 D6
Basket Range SA 86 H4
Basket Swamp Nat Park NSW 39 C10
Bass VIC 57 K11 64 K2 66 G2
Bass Hill NSW 30 C6 35 E10
Bass Strait TAS 74 A4 77 B9 78 G1
Bassendean WA 101 E6 103 D8
Batchelor NT 123 E2 124 D4
Batchica VIC 42 K4 62 H5
Bateau Bay NSW 33 H13
Batehaven NSW 44 E5
Bateman WA 104 B5
Batemans Bay NSW 44 E5
Batemans Marine Park NSW 44 F6
Batesford VIC 59 G12 61 C13
Bathumi VIC 64 A3
Bathurst NSW 36 F6
Bathurst Bay QLD 17 A9 19 H5
Bathurst Island NT 124 A2
Batlow NSW 43 H13 44 E1
Battery Point TAS 68 C2
Bauhinia QLD 15 K8
Bauhinia Downs NT 125 J11 127 B10
Baulkham Hills NSW 27 D2 28 F5 35 C9
Bauple QLD 13 C13
Baw Baw Alpine Village VIC 64 H4
Baw Baw Nat Park VIC 64 H4 66 E5
Bawaka NT 125 C13
Bawley Point NSW 44 E6
Baxter VIC 54 K6 57 G9
Bay of Fires TAS 75 C14
Bay of Fires Con Area TAS 75 D14
Bayles VIC 57 G12 64 J2 66 F3
Baynton VIC 59 C13
Bayswater VIC 51 E7 57 D9
Bayswater WA 101 E5 102 D7
Bayulu WA 117 H10
Bayview NSW 27 B7 29 C14 35 B11
Bayview TAS 75 E14
Bayview Haven NT 122 G3
Beachmere QLD 9 H10 13 F13
Beachport SA 98 H5
Beachport Con Park SA 98 H5
Beacon WA 110 A6 112 H7
Beacon Hill NSW 29 F13
Beaconsfield NSW 27 G5 31 D11
Beaconsfield TAS 74 D6 77 H14
Beaconsfield VIC 55 E11 57 F10 64 J1 66 F2
Beaconsfield WA 104 B2
Beaconsfield Upper VIC
55 D11 57 F11 64 J1 66 E2
Beagle Bay WA 116 E6
Beagle Gulf NT 122 B2 123 B1 124 C3
Bealiba VIC 59 A9 63 K8
Beardmore VIC 64 H4 66 E5
Beargamil NSW 36 E3 41 K14 43 C14
Bears Lagoon VIC 42 K6 63 J9
Beauchamp VIC 63 F8
Beaudesert QLD 11 G9 13 H13
Beaufort VIC 59 D9
Beaufort River WA 109 C10
Beaumaris TAS 75 F14
Beaumaris VIC 54 C3
Beaumont SA 81 H5 84 D7
Beauty Point NSW 29 H12 65 C14
Beauty Point TAS 74 D6 77 G14
Beazleys Bridge VIC 59 A8 62 K7
Bebeah NSW 33 F10
Beckenham WA 101 H6 103 J9
Beckom NSW 43 F11
Bedford WA 101 E4 102 D6
Bedford Park SA 81 K3 84 G4
Bedfordale WA 105 F12
Bedourie QLD 20 G3
Bedunburra WA 116 F7
Beeac VIC 59 G10 61 D10
Beebo QLD 13 J9 38 B7
Beech Forest VIC 59 J9 61 H9
Beechboro WA 101 D5 103 B8
Beechford TAS 74 C7
Beechmont QLD 11 H11
Beechwood NSW 37 A13 39 K11
Beechworth VIC 43 K11 64 C5
Beecroft NSW 28 F7 35 C10
Beekeepers Nature Res WA 112 G4
Beela WA 108 A5
Beelbangera NSW 43 E10
Beeliar WA 104 E4
Beelu Nat Park WA 106 E4
Beenak VIC 57 D12
Beenleigh QLD 11 D11 13 G13
Beerburrum QLD 9 F9
Beermullah WA 106 A4
Beerwah QLD 9 E9 13 E13
Bega NSW 44 H4 65 D14
Beggan Beggan NSW 36 K3 43 F14 44 B1
Bejoording WA 106 B6
Belair SA 81 J5 84 F6 86 J2 87 A6
Belair Nat Park SA 81 J5 84 G7 86 J3 87 A6
Belbora NSW 37 B12
Belconnen ACT 47 C3 48 B4
Belconnen Town Centre ACT 47 C3
Beldon WA 101 A1
Belfield NSW 31 C8
Belford NSW 33 A9 45 F3
Belford Nat Park NSW 45 F3
Belgrave VIC 55 A10 57 E10 64 H1 66 E2
Belgrave South VIC 55 B10
Belka WA 107 D13
Bell NSW 34 C3
Bell QLD 13 E10
Bell Bay TAS 74 D6 77 G14
Bella Vista NSW 28 F4
Bellambi NSW 35 J10
Bellangry NSW 37 A13 39 J11
Bellara QLD 9 G11
Bellarine VIC 56 G5
Bellarine Peninsula VIC 56 G5
Bellarwi NSW 36 H1 43 E12
Bellata NSW 38 E5
Bellbird NSW 33 C10
Bellbird Creek VIC 65 H11
Bellbird Park QLD 6 J5 11 C8
Bellbowrie QLD 6 F5
Bellbrae VIC 56 J2 59 H12 61 E13
Bellbridge VIC 43 J12 64 B6
Bellbrook NSW 39 H11
Bellenden Ker QLD 17 E11 18 F5
Bellevue WA 101 E7 103 D11
Bellevue Heights SA 81 K4 84 H4 86 K2 87 A5
Bellevue Hill NSW 29 K13 31 B13
Belli Park QLD 9 B8
Bellingen NSW 39 G12
Bellinger River Nat Park NSW 39 G11
Bellingham TAS 75 C8
Bellmere QLD 9 G8
Bellmount Forest NSW 36 K5 44 C3
Bells Marsh Forest Reserve TAS 75 E13
Bellthorpe Nat Park QLD 8 E7
Belltrees NSW 37 B10
Belmont NSW 33 D13 37 E11 40 H1 42 A1
Belmont QLD 3 F6 7 D13
Belmont VIC 56 G2
Belmont WA 101 F5 103 F8
Belmore NSW 27 G4 31 D8 35 E11
Belmunging WA 107 D8
Beloka NSW 43 K14 44 H2 65 C11
Belowra NSW 44 F4 65 B13
Belrose NSW 29 E12 35 B11
Beltana Roadhouse SA 95 D8
Belton SA 89 A9 95 G9
Belyando Crossing QLD 14 D5
Belyuen NT 123 C1
Bemboka NSW 44 H4 65 D13
Bemboka Walls NSW 44 H4 65 D13
Bemm River VIC 65 H11
Ben Boyd Nat Park NSW 44 J5 65 F14
Ben Buckler NSW 31 C14
Ben Bullen NSW 32 K1 36 F7
Ben Halls Gap Nat Park NSW 37 A10 39 K8
Ben Lomond NSW 39 F9
Ben Lomond Nat Park TAS 75 G11
Bena NSW 36 F1 43 D12
Bena VIC 57 K13
Benalla VIC 43 K10 64 C3
Benamanka NT 125 C9
Benambra VIC 65 E8
Benambra Nat Park NSW 64 A6
Benandarah NSW 44 E5
Benaraby QLD 15 J11
Benarkin QLD 8 F2
Benarkin Nat Park QLD 8 D3
Benayeo VIC 58 B1
Bencubbin WA 110 B6 112 H7
Bendalong NSW 44 D6
Bendeela NSW 37 K8 44 C6
Bendemeer NSW 39 H8
Bendering WA 107 G13
Bendering Nature Res WA 107 F14
Bendick Murrell NSW 36 H4 43 E14 44 A2
Bendidee Nat Park QLD 13 H8 38 A6
Bendigo VIC 59 A12 63 K10
Bendoc VIC 44 J2 65 F11
Bendoc North VIC 65 F11
Bendolba NSW 37 C11
Beneree NSW 36 F5
Bengeo TAS 73 B11 74 F5 77 K13
Benger WA 106 K3 108 A5
Bengerang NSW 12 K6
Bengworden VIC 64 J7
Beni NSW 36 C4
Beninbi Nat Park QLD 13 C11
Benjaberring WA 107 A9
Benjeroop VIC 63 F9
Benjinup WA 108 D7
Benowa QLD 11 G12 24 E4
Bensville NSW 33 J12
Bentinck Island QLD 16 E3
Bentleigh VIC 53 K10 54 A3
Bentley NSW 39 B12
Bentley WA 101 H5 102 H7
Benwerrin VIC 59 H11 61 G11
Berajondo QLD 15 K12
Berala NSW 30 B7 35 D10
Berambing NSW 34 B5 37 G8
Berat QLD 10 G2
Beremboke VIC 56 C2
Beresfield NSW 33 B13 45 H7
Beresford SA 90 J5
Bergalia NSW 44 F5
Bergen QLD 8 J1
Bergins Hill QLD 6 H3
Bergins Pocket QLD 8 A7
Berkeley Vale NSW 33 H12
Berkshire Park NSW 35 C8
Bermagui NSW 44 G5 65 C14
Bermagui South NSW 44 G5 65 C14
Bernacchi TAS 73 D11 74 J5
Bernafai Ridge Con Area TAS 72 C3
Bernes Paddocks TAS 73 C11 74 H6
Bernier and Dorre Islands Nature Res WA
114 H1
Berowra NSW 27 A4 29 B9 35 B10
Berowra Heights NSW 27 A5 29 A10
Berowra Valley Regional Park NSW 27 A4
35 B10
Berowra Waters NSW 29 A9 35 A10
Berrara NSW 44 D6
Berri SA 42 F1 89 F12 98 B6
Berrico NSW 37 C11
Berridale NSW 44 G2 65 C11
Berriedale TAS 69 G1 71 D12
Berrigan NSW 43 J9 63 F14
Berrilee NSW 29 A8 35 B10
Berrima NSW 37 J8 44 B6
Berrimah NT 122 G7
Berrinba QLD 7 J12
Berring WA 106 A7
Berringa VIC 59 E10 61 A10
Berringama VIC 43 K13 65 B8
Berriwillock VIC 42 J5 62 F7
Berry NSW 37 K9 44 C7
Berry Springs NT 123 D1
Berrybank VIC 59 F9 61 C8
Bertram WA 104 K5
Berwick VIC 55 E11 57 F10 64 J1 66 F2
Bessiebelle VIC 58 G4
Bet Bet VIC 59 B10
Beta QLD 14 H4 21 F11
Bete Bolong VIC 65 H10
Bethanga VIC 64 B6
Bethania QLD 3 K6 7 K14
Bethany SA 86 C6
Bethungra NSW 36 K2 43 G13
Betoota QLD 20 J5 22 A3
Beulah TAS 73 A10 74 F4 77 J12
Beulah VIC 42 J4 62 G5
Beulah East VIC 42 J4 62 G5
Beulah Park SA 81 G5 84 C7
Beulah West VIC 42 J4 62 G5
Bevendale NSW 36 J5 44 B3
Beveridge VIC 59 D14 66 C1
Beveridges Station VIC 64 E6 66 A7
Beverley SA 82 K3 84 A3
Beverley WA 107 E8 110 D4 112 K6
Beverley Park NSW 31 F9
Beverly Hills NSW 27 G4 31 E8 35 E11
Bexley NSW 35 E11
Bexley North NSW 31 E9
Biala NSW 36 K5 44 B3
Biamanga Nat Park NSW 44 H5 65 D14
Biarra QLD 8 H4
Bibbenluke NSW 44 H3 65 E12
Biboohra QLD 18 D2
Bibra Lake WA 101 K3 104 C5
Bicheno TAS 75 J14
Bickley WA 103 H13
Bicton WA 101 H2 102 J3
Biddaddaba QLD 11 G10
Biddon NSW 36 A5 38 K2
Bidgeemia NSW 43 H11
Bidijul WA 117 H9
Bidwill NSW 28 F1
Bidyadanga (Lagrange) WA 116 H5
Big Bush Nature Res NSW 36 J1 43 F12
Big Desert Wilderness Park VIC
42 J2 62 F1 89 K13 98 E7
Big Heath Con Park SA 98 H6
Big Pats Creek VIC 57 C13
Bigga NSW 36 H5 44 A3
Biggara VIC 65 B9
Biggenden QLD 13 B12
Biggera Waters QLD 24 C4
Biggs Flat SA 85 J11 86 K4 87 A7
Bilambil NSW 11 J13
Bilbarin WA 107 F12
Bilbaringa SA 86 E4
Bilbul NSW 43 E10
Bilgola NSW 35 A12
Bilgola Plateau NSW 29 B14
Bilinga QLD 24 J7
Billabong Roadhouse WA 112 B3
Billericay WA 107 F14
Billiatt Con Park SA 89 H12 98 C5
Billiluna WA 117 J12
Billimari NSW 36 G4 43 D14
Billinga QLD 11 H13
Billinudgel NSW 39 B13
Billyrimba NSW 13 K12 39 C10
Billys Creek NSW 39 F11
Billys Lagoon QLD 19 E2
Biloela QLD 15 J10
Bilpa Morea Claypan QLD 20 H4
Bilpin NSW 34 B5 37 G8
Bilwon QLD 18 D3
Bilyana QLD 17 F11
Bimberamala Nat Park NSW 44 E5
Bimberi Nature Res NSW 43 H14 44 E2 48 D1
Bimbi NSW 36 H2 43 E13
Binalong NSW 36 K4 43 F14 44 B2
Binalong Bay TAS 75 D14
Binbee QLD 14 B6 17 J13 21 A13
Binda NSW 36 J6 44 A4
Bindango QLD 12 D5 21 K14
Bindarri Nat Park NSW 39 G12
Bindi VIC 65 F8
Bindi Bindi WA 110 A3 112 H6
Bindoon WA 106 B4 110 C3 112 J5
Bingara NSW 38 E6
Bingera Nat Park QLD 13 A12
Bingil Bay QLD 17 F11 18 K6
Binginwarri VIC 66 H5
Biniguy NSW 38 D6
Binjour QLD 13 B10
Binna Burra QLD 11 J11
Binnaway NSW 36 A6 38 K4
Binnaway Nature Res NSW 36 A6 38 K4
Binningup WA 106 K2 108 A4 110 F3
Binnu WA 112 D4
Binnum SA 58 B1
Binya NSW 43 E10
Binya Nat Park QLD 23 G13 41 A9
Birany Birany NT 125 D12
Birchip VIC 42 J5 62 G6
Birchs Bay TAS 69 K1 71 G12
Bird Island SA 88 E6
Birdsville QLD 20 J3 22 A1 91 A11
Birdum NT 124 J7 126 A7
Birdwood NSW 37 A13 39 K10
Birdwood SA 86 G6 89 G9 98 C3
Birdwoodton VIC 42 F3 62 A4
Biriwal Bulga Nat Park NSW 37 A12 39 K10
Birkdale QLD 3 F7 11 B11
Birkenhead SA 81 D1 82 G2
Birnam Range QLD 11 F10
Birralee TAS 73 A12 74 F6 77 J14
Birrego NSW 43 G11
Birregurra VIC 59 H10 61 F10
Birriwa NSW 36 C6
Birrong NSW 27 F2 30 C6
Birru QLD 10 C6
Bishopsbourne TAS 73 B13 74 G7
Bittern VIC 57 J9
Black Bobs TAS 71 A9 73 H11
Black Brush TAS 69 F1 71 C12 73 K14
Black Forest SA 81 H3 84 D4
Black Hill SA 89 G10 98 C4
Black Hill Con Park SA
81 E7 83 J9 85 A9 86 H3
Black Hills TAS 71 C11
Black Mountain NSW 39 F9
Black Range State Park VIC 58 C5
Black River TAS 76 E6
Black Rock SA 89 B9 95 J9
Black Rock VIC 51 G4 54 C3 56 E7
Black Rock Con Park SA 89 B9 95 J9
Black Springs NSW 36 G7
Black Springs SA 89 E9 98 A3
Blackall QLD 14 J3 21 G10
Blackalls Park NSW 33 D13
Blackbraes Nat Park QLD 14 A1 17 H9
Blackbull QLD 16 F6
Blackburn VIC 51 D6 53 G12
Blackburn North VIC 53 F13
Blackburn South VIC 53 G12
Blackbutt QLD 8 E2 13 E12
Blackdown Tableland Nat Park QLD 15 H8
Blackheath NSW 34 D3 37 G8
Blackmans Bay TAS 69 J1 71 F13
Blacksmiths NSW 33 D14
Blackstone QLD 6 H3
Blackstone (Papulankutja) WA 118 J6
Blacktown NSW 27 D1 28 G3 35 D9
Blackville NSW 37 A8
Blackwater NSW 39 F9
Blackwater NT 128 E5
Blackwater QLD 15 H8
Blackwood SA 81 K4 84 G6 86 K3 87 A6
Blackwood VIC 59 D12
Blackwood Creek TAS 73 C12 74 H7
Blackwood Nat Park QLD 14 D5 21 C12
Blackwood River Nat Park WA 108 E2 110 H2
Bladensburg Nat Park QLD 20 E7
Blair Athol QLD 14 F6 21 E13
Blair Athol SA 81 E4 82 H5
Blairgowrie VIC 56 J6
Blakehurst NSW 27 H4 31 G9 35 E11
Blakeview SA 86 E3
Blakeville VIC 56 A2 59 D11
Blakney Creek NSW 36 K5 44 B3
Blanchetown SA 89 F10 98 B4
Blanchewater SA 22 J1 91 K11 95 A11
Bland NSW 36 H2 43 E13
Blandford NSW 37 B9
Blanket Flat NSW 36 H5 44 A3
Blaxland NSW 34 D6 37 G8
Blaxlands Ridge NSW 34 A7
Blayney NSW 36 G5
Blenheim QLD 10 C4
Blessington TAS 75 G10
Blewitt Springs SA 87 C6
Bli Bli QLD 9 C10 13 E13
Bligh Park NSW 35 C8
Blighty NSW 43 H9 63 F13
Blind Bight VIC 55 K10
Blinman SA 95 E9
Bloods Creek SA 90 A1 93 A13
Bloodwood Bore NT 129 K9
Bloomsbury QLD 14 C7 17 K14 21 B14
Blow Clear NSW 36 G1 43 D12
Blue Bay NSW 33 G13
Blue Bush NT 127 F8
Blue Hill SA 93 D9
Blue Mountains Nat Park NSW 34 C5 37 G8
Blue Range VIC 66 C3
Blue Rocks TAS 78 C4
Bluewater Springs Roadhouse QLD
14 A3 17 H11
Bluff QLD 15 H8
Bluff Hill Nat Park QLD 14 C7
Bluff River Nature Res NSW 39 C10
Blumont TAS 75 D9
Blyth SA 89 E8 98 A2
Blythdale QLD 12 D6
Blythe River Con Area TAS 74 C2 77 G10
Boambee NSW 39 G12
Boat Harbour TAS 77 F8
Bob's Yard NT 124 J3 126 A3
Bobadah NSW 41 H11 43 A11
Bobbin Head NSW 27 A5 29 C10 35 B10
Boco TAS 72 C5
Bodalla NSW 44 F5 65 B14
Bodallin WA 110 C7 113 J9
Bodangora NSW 36 D5
Boddington WA 106 H6 110 F3
Bogan Gate NSW 36 E2 41 K13 43 C13
Bogangar NSW 13 J14 39 A14
Bogantungan QLD 14 H5 21 F13
Bogee NSW 32 G1 36 E7
Boggabilla NSW 13 J8 38 B6
Boggabri NSW 38 H5
Boginderra Hills NSW 36 J2 43 F13
Bogong VIC 64 D6
Boho VIC 63 K14 64 D2
Boho South VIC 63 K14 64 D2
Boigbeat VIC 42 H5 62 F6
Boinka VIC 42 H2 62 E3
Boisdale VIC 64 H6 66 E7
Bokal WA 109 B9
Bokanj NT 123 G5 124 E6
Bokarina QLD 9 D10
Bolgart WA 106 A6 110 C4 112 J6
Bolinda VIC 59 D13
Bolivar SA 81 B4 82 D5 86 E2 86 F2
Bolivia NSW 39 D10
Bolkadjam NT 125 C9
Bollon QLD 12 H3
Bolton VIC 42 G5 62 D6
Bolton Point NSW 33 D13
Bolwarra NSW 33 A12
Bolwarra VIC 58 H3
Bolwarra Heights NSW 45 G6
Bolwarrah VIC 56 A1 59 D11
Bomaderry NSW 37 K8 44 C6
Bombala NSW 44 J3 65 E12
Bombo NSW 37 K9 44 B7
Bomera NSW 36 A7 38 K4
Bonalbo NSW 13 K12 39 B11
Bonang VIC 44 J2 65 F11
Bonbeach VIC 54 F5 57 F8
Bondi NSW 27 F7 31 C13 35 D12
Bondi Beach NSW 31 C13
Bondi Gulf Nature Res NSW 44 J3 65 F12
Bondi Junction NSW 27 F6 31 C12
Bonegilla VIC 43 K11 64 B6
Boneo VIC 56 K7
Bongaree QLD 9 G11 13 F13
Bongil Bongil Nat Park NSW 39 G12
Bonnells Bay NSW 33 E13
Bonnet Bay NSW 27 J3 30 G7
Bonnie Doon VIC 64 E3 66 A4
Bonnie Rock WA 110 A7 113 H8
Bonnie Vale WA 111 B11 113 H11
Bonnington Park NSW 45 A5
Bonny Hills NSW 37 A14 39 K12
Bonnyrigg NSW 30 C2 35 E9
Bonnyrigg Heights NSW 30 C2
Bonogin QLD 11 H12 24 J3
Bonshaw NSW 13 K10 39 C8
Bonville NSW 39 G12
Bonython ACT 47 J3
Boobyalla TAS 75 B12 78 J4
Booderee Nat Park NSW 44 D6
Boodjamulla (Lawn Hill) Nat Park QLD
16 G1 127 E14
Booie QLD 8 B1
Bookaar VIC 59 G8 60 D6
Bookabie SA 97 F9
Bookaloo SA 94 F6
Booker Bay NSW 33 J12
Bookham NSW 36 K4 43 G14 44 C2
Bookin QLD 16 K5 20 B5
Boolading WA 109 B8
Boolaroo NSW 33 C13
Boolarra VIC 64 K4 66 G5
Boolba QLD 12 H4
Boolburra QLD 15 H9
Booleroo Centre SA 89 B8 95 J8
Booligal NSW 43 E8
Boolite VIC 62 J6
Boomdoolyanna SA 93 A8 128 K6
Boomerang Lagoon NT 125 G10
Boomi NSW 12 J7 38 B4
Boonah QLD 10 G7 13 H12
Boonal NSW 38 B4
Boonanarring Nature Res WA
106 A3 110 B3 112 J5
Boonarga QLD 13 E9
Boondall QLD 3 B5 5 F11 9 K10 11 A10
Boondina Con Park SA 97 F9
Boondooma QLD 13 D10
Boonmoo QLD 17 E10
Boonoo Boonoo NSW 39 C10
Boonoo Boonoo Nat Park NSW 13 K12 39 B10
Boonooroo QLD 13 C13
Booraan WA 107 B14
Boorabbin WA 111 B10 113 J10
Boorabbin Nat Park WA 111 B9 113 H10
Booragoon WA 101 J3 102 K4 104 A4
Booragul NSW 33 D13
Booral NSW 37 D12
Boorara Gardner Nat Park WA 108 H6
Boorcan VIC 59 G8 60 E6
Boorhaman VIC 64 B4
Boorindal NSW 41 D10
Boorongie North VIC 42 G4 62 D5
Booroopki VIC 58 A2 62 K2
Booroorban NSW 43 G8 63 D11
Boorowa NSW 36 J4 43 F14 44 B2
Boort VIC 42 K6 63 H9
Boosey VIC 63 H14 64 B2
Booti Booti Nat Park NSW 37 C13
Booval QLD 6 H3
Booyal QLD 13 B12
Bopeechee SA 90 K6 94 A6
Boppy Mountain NSW 41 G10
Borallon QLD 10 B7
Borambil NSW 36 B7
Borden WA 110 H7
Border Ranges Nat Park NSW
11 K8 13 J13 39 A12
Border Village SA 96 F1 119 G7
Borderdale WA 109 E11
Bordertown SA 42 K1 62 J1 98 F6
Boree NSW 36 F4
Boree QLD 17 K8 21 B8
Boree Creek NSW 43 G11
Boreen Point QLD 13 D13
Bornholm WA 109 K12
Boro NSW 44 D4
Borogomarra NT 125 C10
Boronga Nature Res NSW 38 B4
Boronia VIC 57 D9
Boronia Heights QLD 3 K4 7 K10

Boroobin QLD 9 E8
Bororen QLD 15 J11
Borrika SA 89 H11 98 C5
Borroloola NT 125 J12 127 A12
Borung VIC 42 K6 63 J9
Boscabel WA 109 C10
Bossley Park NSW 28 K2 30 B2 35 E9
Bostobrick NSW 39 G11
Bostocks Creek VIC 60 E6
Botany NSW 27 H6 31 E11 35 E11
Botany Bay NSW 27 H5 35 E12 37 H10
Botany Bay Nat Park NSW
    27 J6 31 F12 35 E12 37 H10
Botherling WA 106 A7
Bothwell TAS 71 A11 73 H13
Bottle Creek NSW 39 B11
Bouddi Nat Park NSW 33 J13 37 G10
Boulder WA 111 A11 113 H12
Bouldercombe QLD 15 H10
Boulia QLD 20 E3
Boundain WA 107 J9
Boundary Bend VIC 42 G5 62 C7
Bourke NSW 23 K13 41 D10
Bournda Nat Park NSW 44 H5 65 E14
Bow NSW 37 C8
Bow Bowing NSW 30 G1
Bow Bridge WA 109 J10
Bowan Park NSW 36 F4
Bowden WA 80 A1 82 K4 84 B4
Bowelling WA 109 B8 110 G4
Bowen QLD 14 B7 17 J14 21 A14
Bowen Hills QLD 5 K10 7 B10
Bowen Mountain NSW 34 B6
Bowenfels NSW 34 C2
Bowenville QLD 13 F10
Bower SA 89 F10 98 B4
Boweya VIC 64 B3
Bowhill SA 89 H10 98 C4
Bowillia SA 89 E8 98 A2
Bowling Green Bay Nat Park QLD 14 A5 17 H13
Bowman QLD 15 F9
Bowmans SA 89 F8 98 B2
Bowmans Creek NSW 37 C10 45 A1
Bowna NSW 43 J12 64 H4
Bowning NSW 36 K4 44 C2
Bowraville NSW 39 H12
Box Hill NSW 28 C2 35 C8
Box Hill VIC 51 D6 53 G12 57 D9
Box Hill North VIC 53 F12
Boxwood Hill WA 110 H7
Boya WA 103 D12
Boyagarring Con Park WA 106 G6
Boyagin Nature Res WA 106 G7 110 E4 112 K6
Boyanup WA 108 B4 110 G3
Boyatup WA 111 G14 119 K1
Boydtown NSW 44 J5 65 F14
Boyeo VIC 42 K2 62 J3
Boyer TAS 71 D12
Boyerine WA 109 C12
Boykambil QLD 24 A3
Boyland QLD 11 F10
Boyndaminup Nat Park WA 109 G8
Boyne Island QLD 15 J11
Boyup Brook WA 108 D7 110 G4
Bracalba QLD 9 G8
Brachina SA 95 E8
Bracken Ridge QLD 3 A4 5 F10 9 J9
Brackendale NSW 39 J9
Bracknell TAS 73 C13 74 G7
Bradbury NSW 30 K1 35 G9
Bradbury SA 81 F3 82 K4 84 B4
Braddon ACT 47 D5
Bradvale VIC 59 F9 61 A8
Braefield NSW 37 A9 38 K6
Braeside QLD 10 K1 13 J11 39 A10
Braeside VIC 51 H5 54 D5 57 F8
Brahma Lodge SA 81 B5 82 D7
Braidwood NSW 44 E5
Bramble Bay QLD 3 A5 9 J10
Bramfield SA 88 D1
Bramley Nat Park WA 108 E2 110 H2
Brampton Island QLD 15 C8
Bramston Beach QLD 17 E11 18 G6
Bramwell Roadhouse QLD 19 D2
Brandon QLD 14 A6 17 H13
Brandum TAS 73 D11 74 J5
Brandy Bottom TAS 69 E2 71 B13
Brandy Creek VIC 57 G14
Branxholm TAS 75 D11
Branxholme VIC 58 F4
Branxton NSW 33 A10 37 D10 45 F4
Brassall QLD 6 G1
Braunstone NSW 39 E12
Brawlin NSW 36 K3 43 G13 44 B1
Bray Junction SA 98 H5
Bray Park NSW 11 K12
Bray Park QLD 5 D8
Braybrook VIC 51 C1 52 F5
Brays Creek NSW 11 K11
Brayton NSW 36 K7 44 B5
Breadalbane NSW 36 K6 44 C4
Breadalbane TAS 73 B14 75 G8
Break O Day NSW 64 C2
Breakfast Creek NSW 36 H4 43 E14 44 A2
Breakfast Creek TAS 5 K10 7 A10
Bream Creek TAS 69 G4
Breamlea VIC 56 H3 61 E14
Bredbo NSW 44 F3 65 A12
Breelong NSW 36 B4
Breeza NSW 38 J6
Bremer Bay WA 111 H8
Brendale QLD 3 A3 5 F8
Brentwood SA 88 G6
Brentwood VIC 42 J3 62 G4
Brentwood WA 102 K5 104 A5
Breona TAS 73 D11 74 H6
Bretti NSW 37 B12

Brewarrina NSW 41 C11
Brewer Hall NSW 43 D10
Brewster VIC 59 D9
Briaba QLD 14 C6 17 K13 21 A13
Briagolong VIC 64 H6 66 E7
Bribbaree NSW 36 H2 43 E13
Bribie Island QLD 9 F10 13 E14
Bribie Island Nat Park QLD 9 F10 13 F14
Bridge Creek VIC 64 E3 66 A4
Bridgeman Downs QLD 3 B3 5 G8
Bridgenorth TAS 73 A13 74 E7
Bridgetown WA 108 E6 110 H3
Bridgewater SA
    85 G11 86 J4 87 A7 89 H9 98 C3
Bridgewater TAS 69 G1 71 C12
Bridgewater VIC 63 K9
Bridport TAS 75 C9 78 K1
Brigalow QLD 13 E9
Briggs Reg Res TAS 74 D5 77 G14
Bright VIC 64 D6
Brighton QLD 3 A4 5 E10 9 J10
Brighton SA
    81 K2 84 G2 86 K1 87 A4 89 H8 98 C2
Brighton TAS 69 F1 71 C12
Brighton VIC 51 F3 53 K8 54 A2 56 E7
Brighton-Le-Sands NSW 27 H5 31 E10 35 E11
Brightview QLD 10 B5
Brightwaters NSW 33 E13
Brim VIC 42 K4 62 H5
Brimbago SA 42 K1 98 F5
Brimboal VIC 58 D2
Brimpaen VIC 58 B5
Brindabella NSW 48 D1
Brindabella Nat Park NSW 43 H14 44 D2 48 B1
Bringalbert VIC 58 B2 98 G6
Bringelly NSW 35 F8
Brinkin NT 122 B4
Brinkworth SA 89 D8 98 A2
Brisbane QLD 2 B2 3 E4 7 C10 11 B9 13 G13
Brisbane Forest Park QLD 3 D1
Brisbane Ranges Nat Park VIC
    56 2D 59 E12 61 A14
Brisbane Water Nat Park NSW 33 J11 37 G10
Brit Brit VIC 58 D4 98 H7
Britannia Creek VIC 57 C12
Brittons Swamp TAS 76 F4
Brixton QLD 14 H2 21 F10
Broad Arrow WA 111 A11 113 G11
Broadbeach QLD 11 G13 24 F5
Broadbeach Waters QLD 24 E5
Broadford VIC 59 C14 66 B1
Broadmarsh TAS 71 C12 73 K14
Broadmeadows SA 86 E3
Broadmeadows TAS 67 E5
Broadmeadows VIC 51 B3 52 C7 56 B7
Broadview SA 82 J6 84 A6
Broadwater NSW 13 K14 39 C13
Broadwater QLD 8 B2
Broadwater VIC 58 F5
Broadwater Nat Park NSW 13 K14 39 C13
Brocklehurst NSW 36 C4 41 H14
Brocklesby NSW 43 J14 64 A5
Brockman WA 114 D6
Brockman Nat Park WA 108 G5
Brocks Creek NT 123 F3 124 E4
Brodribb River VIC 65 H10
Brogo NSW 44 H4 65 D14
Broke NSW 33 C8 37 D10 45 H1
Broken Bay NSW 33 K12 35 A12
Broken Hill NSW 40 H2 42 A2 95 G14
Bromelton QLD 11 F9
Brompton SA 81 F3 82 K4 84 B4
Bromus WA 111 E12 113 K12
Bronte NSW 31 C13 35 D12
Bronte TAS 73 G10
Bronte Park TAS 73 F10
Bronzewing VIC 42 H4 62 E5
Brookdale NSW 43 G11
Brooker SA 88 E3
Brookfield NSW 37 D11
Brookfield QLD 3 E1 6 C6 11 B8
Brookfield Con Park SA 89 F10 98 B4
Brookhampton WA 108 C5
Brooking Gorge Con Park WA 117 G10
Brooklands QLD 11 E9
Brooklyn NSW 33 K11 35 A11 37 G10
Brooklyn VIC 51 D1 52 G5
Brooklyn Park SA 81 G3 84 C3
Brooksby VIC 58 B4
Brookside TAS 71 D11
Brookstead QLD 13 G10
Brookton WA 107 F8 110 E5 112 K6
Brookvale NSW 27 D6 29 G13 35 C12
Brookville VIC 65 F8
Brookwater QLD 6 K6
Brooloo QLD 8 B7 13 E13
Broome WA 116 G5
Broomehill WA 109 D13 110 G6
Brooms Head NSW 39 E13
Brooweena QLD 13 C12
Brougham Sugarloaf Con Area TAS 78 C5
Broughton VIC 62 H2
Brovinia QLD 13 C10
Brown Hill Creek SA 84 E7
Brown Hill Creek Rec Park SA 86 J3
Brownlow SA 89 F10 98 B4
Brownlow Hill NSW 34 G7
Brownmore NSW 45 A7
Browns Creek NSW 36 F4
Browns Plains QLD 3 K4 7 K10 11 D10
Brownville QLD 18 H2
Bruarong VIC 43 K11 64 C5
Bruce ACT 47 C4
Bruce SA 89 A8 95 H8
Bruce Rock WA 107 D13 110 D6 113 K8
Brucknell VIC 58 H7 60 G5
Bruinbun NSW 36 E6
Brukunga SA 86 J6

Brungle NSW 43 G14
Brunkerville NSW 33 D12 45 K5
Brunswick VIC 51 C3 53 E8 56 C7
Brunswick Heads NSW 13 J14 39 B14
Brunswick Junction WA 108 A5 110 F3
Bruthen VIC 65 H8
Bryden QLD 8 J6
Buangor VIC 59 D8
Buaraba QLD 8 K4 10 A4
Bucasia QLD 15 D8
Buccleuch SA 89 J11 98 D5
Buchan VIC 44 K1 65 G9
Buchan South VIC 65 G9
Buchanan NSW 33 B12 45 H6
Buchanans Valley NSW 37 B9
Bucheen Creek VIC 43 K12 64 C7
Buchfelde SA 86 D3
Buckaroo NSW 36 D6
Bucketty NSW 33 F9 37 E10
Buckingham WA 108 B7
Buckland QLD 8 D1
Buckland TAS 69 F3
Buckleboo SA 88 B4 94 J4
Buckley VIC 56 H1 59 G11 61 E13
Buckley Swamp VIC 58 F5
Buckrabanyule VIC 63 H8
Budawang Nat Park NSW 44 D5
Buddabaddah NSW 36 B1 41 H12
Budderoo Nat Park NSW 37 K8 44 B6
Buddigower NSW 43 E12
Buddina QLD 9 D10
Budelah Nature Res QLD 12 J6
Buderim QLD 9 C10 13 E13
Budgee QLD 10 E1
Budgee Budgee NSW 36 D6
Budgeree VIC 64 K4 66 G5
Budgerum VIC 63 G8
Budgewoi NSW 33 F13
Buff Point NSW 33 F13
Buffalo VIC 66 H4
Buffalo River VIC 64 D5
Bugaldie NSW 38 J3
Bugilbone NSW 38 F2
Bugtown NSW 48 K1
Builyan QLD 15 K11
Bukalong NSW 44 H3 65 D12
Bukkulla NSW 39 D8
Bukudal NT 125 D12
Bukunkaduru NT 125 C9
Bulahdelah NSW 37 D12
Bularring NT 125 B11
Bulart VIC 58 E4
Bulburin Nat Park QLD 15 J11 15 K12
Buldah VIC 44 K3 65 F12
Bulga NSW 32 B7 37 D9
Bulgandra NSW 43 H11
Bulgobac TAS 72 C5
Bulgul NT 124 D2
Bulimba QLD 3 D4 5 K11 7 B11 11 A9
Bull Creek WA 101 J4 102 K5 104 A5
Bull Swamp VIC 57 H14
Bulla NT 124 J2 126 A2
Bulla VIC 51 A1 52 A5 56 B6 59 E13
Bullabulling WA 111 B10 113 H11
Bullaburra NSW 34 D5
Bullagreen NSW 36 A3 38 J1 41 G13
Bullarah NSW 38 D3
Bullaring WA 107 G11
Bullarook VIC 59 D11
Bulleen VIC 53 E11 57 C8
Bullen Range Nature Res ACT 47 H1 48 D3
Bullenbong NSW 43 G11
Bullengarook VIC 56 A4
Bulleringa Nat Park QLD 17 F8
Bullfinch WA 111 B8 113 H9
Bullhead Creek VIC 43 K12 64 C7
Bulli NSW 35 J10 37 J9 44 A7
Bullioh VIC 43 K12 64 B7
Bullita Outstation NT 124 J3 126 B3
Bullock Creek QLD 17 F9
Bullocks Bow NSW 37 B12
Bulls Creek SA 87 C7
Bullsbrook WA 106 C3
Bullumwaal VIC 64 G7
Bullyard QLD 13 A12 15 K12
Bulyee WA 107 F10
Bumberry NSW 36 E4 41 K14 43 C14
Bumbunga SA 89 E8 98 A2
Bunbartha VIC 63 H13 64 B1
Bunburra QLD 10 G7
Bunbury WA 108 B4 110 G3
Bundaberg QLD 13 A12 15 K13
Bundaburrah NSW 36 F2 43 D13
Bundalaguah VIC 64 J6 66 F7
Bundall QLD 11 G12 24 E4
Bundalong VIC 43 J10 64 A4
Bundamba QLD 6 G3
Bundanoon NSW 37 K8 44 B6
Bundarra NSW 39 F8
Bundeena NSW 27 K5 31 K10 35 F12 37 H10
Bundook NSW 37 B12
Bundoora VIC 51 B5 53 C10 57 B8
Bundure NSW 43 G10
Bung Bong VIC 59 C9
Bunga NSW 44 H5 65 D14
Bungador VIC 59 H9 61 F8
Bungal VIC 56 C1 59 E11
Bungalien QLD 20 C3
Bungarby NSW 44 H3 65 D11
Bungaree VIC 59 E11

Bungawalbin Nat Park NSW 39 C12
Bungeet VIC 64 B3
Bungendore NSW 44 D4
Bungil VIC 43 J12 64 B7
Bungonia NSW 36 K7 44 C5
Bungonia Nat Park NSW 36 K7 44 C5
Bungowannah NSW 43 J11 64 A5
Bungulla NSW 39 C10
Bungulla WA 107 C10
Bunguluke VIC 63 H8
Bungunya QLD 12 J7 38 A4
Bungwahl NSW 37 D13
Buninyong VIC 59 E10
Bunjurgen QLD 10 G6
Bunna Bunna NSW 38 E4
Bunnaloo NSW 42 J7 63 G11
Bunnan NSW 37 B9
Buntine WA 112 G6
Buntine Nature Res WA 112 G6
Bunurong Marine Park VIC 66 H3
Bunya QLD 3 C2 4 G7
Bunya Mountains Nat Park QLD 13 E11
Bunyah NSW 37 C12
Bunyan NSW 44 G3 65 B12
Bunyaville State Forest Park QLD 3 C2
Bunyip VIC 57 F13 64 J2 66 F3
Bunyip State Park VIC 57 E13 64 J2 66 E3
Burabadji WA 106 A7
Buraja NSW 43 J10 64 A4
Burakin WA 110 A5 112 H7
Buranda QLD 7 D10
Burbank QLD 3 G6 7 F13 11 B11
Burbong NSW 48 C6
Burcher NSW 36 F1 43 D12
Burekup WA 108 B5
Burges WA 106 D7
Burgooney NSW 43 D11
Burke & Wills Roadhouse QLD 16 H4
Burketown QLD 16 F3
Burketown Crossing NT 125 H10
Burleigh VIC 57 D11
Burleigh Head Nat Park QLD 11 G13
Burleigh Heads QLD 11 G13 13 H14 24 G5
Burleigh Waters QLD 24 G5
Burma Road Nature Res WA 112 F4
Burnbank VIC 59 C10
Burnett Heads QLD 13 A12 15 K13
Burnie TAS 74 C1 77 G9
Burning Mountain Nature Res NSW 37 B9
Burnley VIC 53 G9
Burns Beach WA 106 C2
Burns Creek TAS 75 F10
Burnside SA 81 G6 84 C7 86 H3
Burnside VIC 52 E3
Burnside Heights VIC 52 D3
Burnt School Nature Res NSW 48 J7
Buronga NSW 42 E3 62 A4
Burpengary QLD 9 H9 13 F13
Burra NSW 44 E3 48 F6
Burra QLD 14 C2 17 K10 21 B10
Burra SA 89 D9 98 A3
Burra Creek Nature Res NSW 48 F6
Burraboi NSW 42 H7 63 E10
Burracoppin WA 107 B14 110 C7 113 J8
Burraga NSW 36 H6
Burragate NSW 44 J4 65 E13
Burragorang Rec Park NSW 34 G6
Burramboot VIC 63 J12
Burramine North VIC 63 G14 64 A3
Burramine South VIC 63 H14 64 A3
Burraneer NSW 27 K4 31 J9
Burrell Creek NSW 37 B12
Burren Junction NSW 38 F3
Burrill Lake NSW 44 D6
Burringbar NSW 13 J14 39 A13
Burringurrah WA 114 H6
Burrinjuck NSW 43 G14 44 C2
Burrinjuck Nature Res NSW 43 G14 44 C2
Burroin VIC 62 F5
Burrowa-Pine Mountain Nat Park VIC 65 B8
Burroway NSW 36 B3 41 H14 43 A14
Burrowye VIC 43 J14 64 A7
Burrum VIC 58 A7 62 K6
Burrum Coast Nat Park QLD 13 A12
Burrum Heads QLD 13 B13
Burrumbeet VIC 59 D10
Burrumburru NT 127 D14
Burrumbuttock NSW 43 J11 64 A5
Burrundie NT 123 F4 124 E5
Burswood WA 101 F4 102 F6
Burton SA 81 A4 82 C5 86 F2
Burtville WA 113 E13
Burwood NSW 27 F4 29 K9 31 B9 35 D11
Burwood VIC 51 E5 53 H11 57 D8
Burwood East VIC 51 E6 53 H12
Busby NSW 30 D2
Busbys Flat NSW 39 C12
Bushfield VIC 58 H6 60 F2
Bushy Park NSW 37 B14 39 K11
Bushy Park TAS 71 C11
Bushy Park VIC 64 H6 66 E7
Busselton WA 108 C3 110 G2
Butchers Ridge VIC 44 K1 65 F9
Bute SA 88 E7 98 A2
Butler Tanks SA 88 C4
Butlers Ridge Nature Res TAS 69 C4
Butterleaf Nat Park NSW 39 D10
Buxton NSW 37 A13 39 K11
Buxton QLD 13 B12
Buxton VIC 64 G2 66 C3
Buymarr NT 125 D12
Byabarra NSW 37 A13 39 K11
Byaduk VIC 58 F4
Byaduk North VIC 58 F4
Byangum NSW 11 K12
Byawatha VIC 64 B4
Byee QLD 13 D11
Byfield QLD 15 G10
Byfield Nat Park QLD 15 G10

Byford WA 105 J10 106 F4 110 D3 112 K5
Bygnunn WA 116 E6
Bylong NSW 36 C7
Byrneside VIC 63 J13 64 C1
Byrnestown QLD 13 B11
Byrock NSW 41 E10
Byron Bay NSW 13 J14 39 B14

C

Cabanda QLD 10 C6
Cabarita NSW 29 J9 31 A9
Cabarita Beach NSW 11 K14
Cabarlah QLD 8 K1 10 A1
Cabawin QLD 13 F8
Cabbage Tree Creek VIC 65 H10
Caboolture QLD 9 G9 13 F13
Caboonbah QLD 8 H5
Cabramatta NSW 27 F1 30 C4 35 E9
Cabramatta West NSW 30 C3
Cabramurra NSW 43 J14 44 F1 65 A10
Cacoory QLD 20 H3
Cadelga Outstation SA 20 K4 22 B3 91 A13
Cadell SA 89 E11 98 A5
Cadney Park SA 93 F12
Cadoux WA 110 B5 112 H7
Caffey QLD 10 D3
Cahills Crossing NT 124 C7
Caiguna WA 119 H3
Cairns QLD 17 E11 18 D5
Cairns Bay TAS 71 G11
Cal Lal NSW 42 E1 62 A1 89 F13 98 B7
Calamvale QLD 3 J4 7 H10 11 C10
Calca SA 97 J12
Calcarra WA 106 A6
Calcium QLD 14 A5 17 J12
Calder TAS 77 G8
Caldermeade VIC 57 H12
Caldwell NSW 42 J7 63 F11
Calen QLD 15 C8
Calga NSW 33 J11
Calingiri WA 106 A5 110 B4 112 J6
Calista WA 104 K3
Calivil VIC 63 J10
Callana SA 90 K7 94 A7
Callaroy Plateau NSW 29 E13
Callawadda VIC 58 A7 62 K6
Calleen NSW 36 G1 43 D12
Callide QLD 15 J10
Callide Coalfield QLD 15 J10
Callington SA 89 H9 98 D3
Callion WA 113 G11
Calliope QLD 15 J11
Caloona NSW 12 K6 38 B3
Caloundra QLD 9 E10 13 E13
Calpatanna Waterhole Con Park SA 97 J12
Caltowie SA 89 C8 95 K8
Calulu VIC 64 H7
Calvert QLD 10 D5
Calvert VIC 58 D7
Calwell ACT 47 J4
Camballin WA 117 G8
Cambalong NSW 44 J3 65 E12
Cambarville VIC 57 A14 64 G3 66 D4
Camberwell NSW 37 D10
Camberwell VIC 51 D5 53 G10 57 D8
Cambewarra NSW 37 K8 44 C6
Cambooya QLD 13 G11
Cambrai SA 89 G10 98 C4
Cambray WA 108 D4
Cambridge NSW 34 D7
Cambridge TAS 69 G2 71 D13
Cambridge Gulf WA 117 C13
Cambroon Bridge QLD 8 C7
Camburinga Village NT 125 D12
Camdale TAS 74 C1 77 F9
Camden NSW 35 G8 37 H9
Camden Haven NSW 37 B14 39 K11
Camden Park SA 84 E3
Camden South NSW 35 G8
Camel Lake Nature Res WA 109 F13
Camel's Hump NT 128 F5
Camellia NSW 28 J6
Camena TAS 74 D2 77 G10
Cameron Corner NSW QLD SA
    22 H4 40 B1 91 J14
Cameron Reg Res TAS 75 C12 78 K4
Camira QLD 3 J1 6 J7 11 C9
Camira Creek NSW 39 D12
Cammeray NSW 29 J12
Camooweal QLD 16 J1 20 A1 127 H14
Camooweal Caves Nat Park QLD 16 J1 20 A1
Camp Hill QLD 3 F5 7 D11 11 B10
Camp Mountain QLD 3 C1 4 H5 9 K8 11 A8
Camp Spur TAS 72 G5
Campania TAS 69 F2 71 C13
Campbell ACT 46 B4 47 E5
Campbell Town TAS 75 K10
Campbellfield VIC 51 B3 53 C8 56 B7
Campbells Bridge VIC 58 B7
Campbells Creek VIC 59 C11
Campbells Forest VIC 59 A11 63 K10
Campbelltown NSW 30 J1 35 G9 37 H9 44 A7
Campbelltown SA 81 F6 82 J7 84 A7 86 H3
Campbelltown VIC 59 C11
Campbellville QLD 9 E10
Camperdown NSW 27 F5 31 C10 35 D11
Camperdown VIC 59 G8 60 E7
Campsie NSW 31 D9
Campwin Beach QLD 15 D8
Camurra NSW 38 D5
Canada Bay NSW 29 K9 31 B9
Canaga QLD 13 E9
Canbelego NSW 41 G10
Canberra City ACT 44 D3 46 A3 47 D5 48 B5
Candelo NSW 44 H4 65 D13

Candlelight WA 107 K12 109 A14
Cane River Con Park WA 114 D4
Canegrass WA 113 G11
Cangai NSW 39 D11
Cania Gorge Nat Park QLD 15 K11
Caniambo VIC 63 J14 64 C2
Canley Heights NSW 30 C4
Canley Vale NSW 30 C4
Cann River VIC 65 G12
Canna WA 112 E5
Cannie VIC 63 G8
Canning Mills WA 105 A13
Canning Vale WA 101 J5 104 B7
Canningdale WA 105 J13
Cannington WA 101 I10 103 I10
Cannington Mine Village WA 20 C5
Cannon Creek QLD 10 G7
Cannon Hill NT 123 C7
Cannon Hill QLD 3 E5 7 B12 11 B10
Cannons Creek VIC 55 K10 57 H10
Cannonvale QLD 15 B8
Cannum VIC 62 J5
Canonba NSW 41 F12
Canowie SA 89 D9 95 K9
Canowindra NSW 36 G4 43 D14
Canteen Creek NT 127 J11 129 A11
Canterbury NSW 27 G4 31 D9 35 E11
Canterbury VIC 53 G11
Canunda Nat Park SA 98 J5
Canungra QLD 11 G10 13 H13
Canyonleigh NSW 36 K7 44 B5
Capalaba QLD 3 G7 11 B11 13 G13
Capalaba West QLD 3 F7 7 D14
Cape Arnhem NT 125 C13
Cape Arid Nat Park WA 111 G14 119 K1
Cape Barren Island TAS 78 F5
Cape Bauer SA 97 H12
Cape Beatrice NT 125 F13
Cape Bedford QLD 17 B10 19 J7
Cape Bernier WA 117 A12
Cape Bernier Nature Res TAS 69 F5
Cape Bougainville WA 117 A10
Cape Bouvard WA 106 H2
Cape Bowen QLD 19 H6
Cape Bridgewater VIC 58 H3 98 K7
Cape Bruny TAS 71 J12
Cape Byron Marine Park NSW 39 B14
Cape Clear VIC 59 F10 61 A9
Cape Direction QLD 19 F4
Cape Flattery QLD 17 B10 19 J7
Cape Freycinet WA 108 E1 110 H2
Cape Gambier NT 123 A1 124 B3
Cape Gantheaume SA 88 K6 98 E1
Cape Gantheaume Con Park SA 88 K6 98 E1
Cape Grafton QLD 18 D5
Cape Grenville QLD 19 D3
Cape Hamelin WA 108 F1
Cape Hillsborough Nat Park QLD 15 C8
Cape Hotham NT 123 B3 124 A6
Cape Howe Marine Nat Park VIC 65 G14
Cape Jervis SA 87 H1 88 J7 98 D2
Cape Keerweer QLD 19 G1
Cape Keith NT 124 B4
Cape Le Grand Nat Park WA 111 H13
Cape Leeuwin WA 108 G2
Cape Londonderry WA 117 A12
Cape Melville QLD 17 A9 19 H5
Cape Melville Nat Park QLD 17 A9 19 H6
Cape Moreton QLD 9 G13
Cape Naturaliste WA 108 C1
Cape Nelson VIC 98 K7
Cape Otway VIC 61 K9
Cape Palmerston Nat Park QLD 15 E9
Cape Paterson VIC 66 H3
Cape Range Nat Park WA 114 D2
Cape River QLD 14 C3 17 K10 21 A10
Cape Schanck VIC 56 K7
Cape Sidmouth QLD 19 F4
Cape St Lambert WA 117 B13
Cape Talbot WA 117 A12
Cape Tribulation QLD 17 C10
Cape Upstart Nat Park QLD 14 A6 17 J13
Cape Vanderlin NT 125 H13
Cape Voltaire WA 117 B10
Cape Wessel NT 125 A13
Cape Weymouth QLD 19 E4
Cape Wilberforce NT 125 B12
Cape Willoughby SA 98 E2
Cape York QLD 19 B2
Cape York Peninsula QLD 19 F2
Capeen NSW 39 B11
Capel WA 108 C4 110 G2
Capella QLD 14 G6 21 E14
Capels Crossing VIC 63 F9
Capertee NSW 32 J1 36 F7
Capital Hill ACT 46 D2 47 E5 48 C5
Capoompeta Nat Park NSW 39 D10
Capricorn Roadhouse WA 115 F10
Capricornia Cays Nat Park (Scientific) QLD 15 J13
Captain Billy Landing QLD 19 C3
Captains Flat NSW 44 E4
Carabost NSW 43 H13
Caragabal NSW 36 G2 43 E13
Caralue SA 88 D4 94 K4
Caramut VIC 58 F6 60 C3
Carapooee VIC 59 A9 63 K8
Carapook VIC 58 E3
Carappee Hill Con Park SA 88 D4 94 K4
Caravan Head NSW 27 J4 31 G8
Caravonica QLD 17 E11
Carawa SA 97 H12
Carbarup WA 109 G13
Carboor VIC 64 D4
Carbrook QLD 11 C11
Carbunup River WA 108 D2
Carcoar NSW 36 G5
Carcuma Con Park SA 89 J11 98 E5

Cardiff NSW 33 C13 45 K7
Cardigan Village VIC 59 D10
Cardinia VIC 55 H12 57 G11
Cardross VIC 62 B4
Cardup WA 105 K9
Cardup Nature Res WA 105 K10
Cardwell QLD 17 G11
Careunga Nature Res NSW 38 C5
Carew VIC 42 K1
Carey Bay NSW 33 D13
Carey Gully SA 85 D11 86 J4
Cargerie VIC 59 F11 61 A11
Cargo NSW 36 F4
Carina QLD 3 F5 7 C12
Carina VIC 42 H2 62 F1
Carina Heights QLD 3 F5 7 D12
Carinda NSW 41 D13
Carindale QLD 3 F6 7 D12 11 B10
Carine WA 101 D2 102 B2
Caringbah NSW 27 J4 31 H9 35 F11
Caringbah South NSW 31 J9
Carisbrook VIC 59 B10
Carlecatup WA 109 D11
Carlingford NSW 27 D3 28 G7 35 C10
Carlisle WA 101 G5 102 G7
Carlisle River VIC 59 J9 61 G8
Carlisle State Park VIC 61 G8
Carlotta WA 108 E5
Carlton NSW 31 F9
Carlton TAS 69 H3 71 D14
Carlton VIC 50 A3 51 D3 53 F8
Carmel WA 103 J13
Carmila QLD 15 E9
Carmila Beach QLD 15 E9
Carmila West QLD 15 E8
Carnamah WA 112 G5
Carnarvon WA 114 H2
Carnarvon Nat Park QLD 12 A3 14 K6 21 H13
Carnegie VIC 53 J10 54 A4
Carnes SA 97 B13
Carnes Hill NSW 35 E9
Carngham VIC 59 D9
Caroda NSW 38 F6
Carole Park QLD 6 H7
Caroline Springs VIC 52 D3
Carool NSW 11 J13
Caroona NSW 37 A8 38 J6
Carpa SA 88 E5
Carpendeit VIC 59 H8 60 F7
Carpolac VIC 58 A2 62 K2
Carrabin WA 110 C7 113 J8
Carrai Nat Park NSW 39 H10
Carrajung VIC 64 K5 66 G6
Carramar NSW 30 C4 35 E9
Carranballac VIC 59 E8
Carrara QLD 11 G12 24 E3
Carrathool NSW 43 F9 63 B13
Carrick TAS 73 B13 74 G7
Carrickalinga SA 87 K2 98 J8 98 D2
Carrieton SA 89 A8 95 H8
Carrington NSW 33 C14
Carroll NSW 38 H6
Carrolup WA 109 C11
Carrum VIC 51 J5 54 F5 57 F8 59 G14 64 J1 66 F1
Carrum Downs VIC 51 J6 54 G6 57 F9 64 J1 66 F1
Carseldine QLD 3 B4 5 F9 9 K9
Carss Park NSW 31 F9
Carters Ridge QLD 8 A7
Cartwright NSW 30 D3 35 E9
Carwarp VIC 42 F3 62 B4
Cascade WA 111 G11
Cascade Nat Park NSW 39 F11
Casey ACT 47 A4
Cashmere QLD 3 A1 4 E6 9 J9
Cashmore VIC 58 H3
Casino NSW 13 K13 39 C12
Cassilis NSW 36 B7
Cassilis VIC 64 F7
Castambul SA 83 J11 85 A11 86 H4
Castaways Beach QLD 9 A10
Castella VIC 57 A11
Casterton VIC 58 E3 98 H7
Castle Cary Reg Res TAS 75 H11
Castle Cove NSW 29 G11
Castle Forbes Bay TAS 71 F11
Castle Hill NSW 27 C2 28 F5 35 C10
Castle Rock NSW 37 C9
Castle Tower Nat Park QLD 15 J11
Castleburn VIC 64 G6
Castlecrag NSW 27 D6 29 H12
Castlemaine VIC 59 B11
Castlereagh NSW 34 C7
Castlereagh Nature Res NSW 34 C7
Casuarina NT 122 C5
Casuarina WA 104 K5
Casuarina Coastal Reserve NT 122 A4
Casula NSW 30 E3 35 E9
Cataby WA 110 B2 112 H5
Catalina Island NT 122 K6
Catamaran TAS 71 K11
Catani VIC 57 G12 64 J2 66 F3
Cataract Nat Park NSW 39 B11
Cathcart NSW 44 H3 65 E12
Cathcart VIC 58 C7
Cathedral Beach QLD 13 B14
Cathedral Range VIC 66 C3
Cathedral Range State Park VIC 64 F2 66 C3
Cathedral Rock Nat Park NSW 39 G10
Catherine Field NSW 35 F8
Catherine Hill Bay NSW 33 E14
Cathkin VIC 64 F2 66 B3
Cathundral NSW 36 B2 41 H13
Cattai NSW 35 A8
Cattai Nat Park NSW 35 A8
Catumnal VIC 42 K6 63 H8
Caulfield VIC 51 E5 53 J10 57 D8

Caulfield North VIC 53 H9
Cavan NSW 44 C2
Cavan SA 81 D4 82 G5 86 G2
Caveat VIC 64 F2 66 B2
Cavendish VIC 58 E5
Caversham WA 101 D6 103 C9
Caves Beach NSW 33 E14
Caveside TAS 73 B10 74 G4
Caveton SA 98 J6
Cawarral QLD 15 G10
Cawdor NSW 35 G8
Cawongla NSW 39 B12
Cecil Park NSW 28 K1 30 B1 35 E9
Cecil Plains NSW 30 C1
Cecil Plains QLD 13 G10
Cedar Bay Nat Park QLD 17 C10 19 K7
Cedar Brush NSW 31 C11
Cedar Creek QLD 4 F3 9 J8 11 E11
Cedar Grove QLD 11 F9
Cedar Point NSW 39 B12
Cedarton QLD 9 E8
Ceduna SA 97 G11
Cement Creek VIC 57 C13
Centennial Park NSW 31 C12
Central Castra TAS 74 E2
Central Mangrove NSW 33 G11
Central McDonald NSW 33 H11
Central Plateau Con Area TAS 73 D10 74 J5
Central Tilba NSW 44 G5
Centre Bore SA 93 B8
Ceratodus QLD 13 B10
Ceres VIC 56 G2 59 G12 61 D13
Cervantes WA 110 A1 112 H4
Cessnock NSW 33 C10 37 E10 45 J4
Cethana TAS 73 A8 74 F3 77 K11
Chadstone VIC 51 E5 53 J11 54 A5
Chaelundi Nat Park NSW 39 F11
Chaffey Irrigation Area SA 42 E1
Chain of Lagoons TAS 75 H14
Chain of Ponds SA 83 G13 86 G5
Chain Valley Bay NSW 33 E13
Chakola NSW 44 F3 65 B12
Chambers Bay NT 123 B3 124 C4
Chambers Flat QLD 11 D9
Chandada SA 88 B1 94 J1 97 J13
Chandler QLD 3 F7 7 D14 11 B10
Chandler SA 93 C10
Chandler WA 107 A14
Chandlers Creek VIC 44 K3 65 F12
Chandlers Hill SA 84 J6
Channing QLD 12 E7
Chapel Hill QLD 3 F2 6 D7 11 B9
Chapman ACT 47 G2
Chappell Islands TAS 78 E4
Chappell Islands Nature Res TAS 78 E4
Chapple Vale VIC 59 J9 61 H8
Charam VIC 58 B3
Charbon NSW 36 E7
Charles Darwin NT 122 G4
Charles Darwin Nat Park NT 122 G4
Charleston SA 86 H5
Charleston Con Park SA 86 H6
Charlestown NSW 33 C14 37 E11
Charleville QLD 12 D1 21 A13 23 B14
Charleys Creek VIC 59 J9 61 H9
Charlotte Waters NT 90 A1 93 A13 129 K10
Charlottes Pass NSW 43 K14 44 G1 65 C10
Charlton VIC 42 K5 63 H8
Charlwood QLD 10 G6
Charmhaven NSW 33 F12
Charnockite Flats WA 128 K1
Charnwood ACT 47 B2
Charra SA 97 G10
Charters Towers QLD 14 B4 17 J11 21 A11
Chatham Village NSW 30 E3
Chatsbury NSW 36 J7 44 B5
Chatswood NSW 27 D5 29 H11 35 C11
Chatswood West NSW 27 D5 29 G10
Chatsworth NSW 39 D13
Chatsworth VIC 58 F7 60 B3
Cheadanup Nature Res WA 111 G10
Cheepie QLD 21 K10 23 C11
Cheetams Flats NSW 34 D2
Chelmer QLD 3 F3 7 D8
Chelsea VIC 51 H5 54 E5 57 F8
Chelsea Heights VIC 54 E5
Cheltenham NSW 27 C3 29 F8 35 C10
Cheltenham SA 81 E2 82 H2
Cheltenham VIC 51 G4 54 C3 57 E8
Cheltenham North VIC 54 C4
Cherbourg QLD 13 D11
Cherbourg Nat Park QLD 8 A1
Chermside QLD 3 C4 5 H10 9 K9 11 A9
Chermside West QLD 3 C3 5 H9
Cherry Gardens SA 84 J7 86 K3 87 A6
Cherry Tree Pool WA 109 D11
Cherrybrook NSW 27 C3 28 E6 35 C10
Cherrypool VIC 58 C5
Cherryville SA 83 K10 85 B10 86 H4
Cheshunt VIC 64 D4
Chester Hill NSW 30 B6 35 D10
Chester Nature Res WA 108 F3
Chesterton Range Nat Park QLD 12 D3 21 K13
Chetwynd VIC 58 D3 98 H7
Cheviot VIC 64 F2 66 B2
Chevron Island QLD 24 E5
Chewko QLD 18 E2
Chewton VIC 59 B12
Cheyne Beach WA 109 J14 110 J7
Chichester NSW 37 C11
Chiddarcooping Nature Res WA 110 B7 113 H8
Chidlow WA 106 D5 110 D3 112 K6
Chifley ACT 47 F3
Chifley NSW 31 C13 35 D12
Chifley WA 111 B14 113 H13
Childers QLD 13 B12
Chilla Well NT 126 K4 128 C4
Chillagoe QLD 17 E9

Chillagoe-Mungana Caves Nat Park QLD 17 E9
Chillingham NSW 11 K11 39 A13
Chillingollah VIC 42 H5 62 E7
Chiltern VIC 43 K11 64 B5
Chiltern Box-Ironbark Nat Park VIC 64 B5
China Wall NT 127 D14
Chinaman Creek SA 88 B7 94 J7
Chinaman Flat VIC 42 J3
Chinaman Island VIC 57 H10
Chinaman Wells SA 98 F4
Chinbi QLD 21 C8
Chinchilla QLD 13 E9
Chinderah NSW 11 J13 39 A14
Chinghee Creek QLD 11 J9
Chinkapook VIC 42 H5 62 E6
Chinocup Nature Res WA 110 F7
Chippenale NSW 31 C11
Chipping Norton NSW 30 D4 35 E10
Chisholm ACT 47 J4
Chiswick NSW 29 K10 31 B9
Chittaway Point NSW 33 G12
Chorkerup WA 109 J13
Chorregon QLD 21 E8
Chowerup WA 109 E8
Chowilla Reg Res SA 42 D1 89 E13 98 A6
Christies Beach SA 87 B4
Christmas Creek QLD 11 H9
Christmas Hills TAS 76 E4
Christmas Hills VIC 57 B12
Chudleigh TAS 73 B10 74 G4 77 K13
Chullora NSW 30 C7
Chum Creek VIC 57 B11
Church Point NSW 27 A7 29 B14 35 B11
Churchill QLD 6 J1
Churchill VIC 64 K4 66 G5
Churchill Island VIC 57 K10
Churchill Island Marine Nat Park VIC 57 K10 64 K1 66 G2
Churchill Nat Park VIC 55 B8 57 E9
Churchlands WA 102 E3
Chute VIC 59 D9
Chuwar QLD 6 H1
City Beach WA 101 F2 102 E2
Clackline WA 106 C6
Clairview QLD 15 E9
Clandulla NSW 36 E7
Clapham SA 81 J4 84 F5
Clare QLD 14 A5 17 J13
Clare SA 89 E8 98 A3
Claremont TAS 69 G1 71 D12
Claremont WA 101 G2 102 G2
Clarence NSW 34 B3
Clarence Gardens SA 81 H4 84 E4
Clarence Park SA 84 E4
Clarence Point TAS 74 D6 77 G14
Clarence Strait NT 123 A1 124 B3
Clarence Town NSW 37 D11
Clarendon NSW 34 B7
Clarendon SA 87 B6
Clarendon TAS 73 B14 75 G9
Clarendon VIC 59 E11
Clareville NSW 29 B14 35 A12
Clarinda VIC 53 K11 54 B5
Clarke Island TAS 78 G6
Clarke Island Nature Res TAS 78 G6
Clarkefield VIC 59 D13
Claude Road TAS 73 A9 74 F3 77 J11
Claverton QLD 23 D13
Clayfield QLD 3 D4 5 J10 7 A10
Claymore NSW 23 J14 41 C11
Clayton SA 89 J9 98 D3
Clayton VIC 51 F5 53 K11 54 B5 57 E8
Clayton North VIC 53 J12 54 A5
Clayton South VIC 54 B5
Clear Island Waters QLD 11 G12 24 F4
Clear Lake VIC 58 B4
Clear Mountain QLD 3 A1 4 E6
Clear Ridge NSW 36 G1 43 D12
Clearview SA 81 E4 82 H5
Cleland Con Park SA 81 H6 85 E8 86 J3
Clematis VIC 55 A12 57 E11
Clements Gap Con Park SA 88 D7
Clemton Park NSW 31 D8
Clermont QLD 14 G6 21 E13
Cleve SA 88 D4
Cleveland QLD 11 B11
Cleveland TAS 75 J9
Cliffordville WA 107 H10
Clifton NSW 35 H11
Clifton QLD 10 F1 13 H11
Clifton Beach QLD 17 D11 18 C4
Clifton Beach TAS 69 H2 71 E14
Clifton Creek VIC 65 H8
Clifton Gardens NSW 27 E6 29 J12 31 A12
Clifton Grove NSW 36 F5
Clifton Hill VIC 53 F9
Clifton Springs VIC 56 G4 59 G13
Clinton Centre SA 88 F7 98 B2
Clinton Con Park SA 88 F7 98 B2
Clintonvale QLD 10 G2
Cloncurry QLD 16 K4 20 B4
Clontarf NSW 27 E6 29 H13 35 C12
Clontarf QLD 5 C11 13 H10
Closeburn QLD 3 E4
Clothiers Creek NSW 11 K13
Clovelly NSW 31 C13 35 D12
Clovelly Park SA 81 J3 84 F4
Cloverdale WA 101 F6 103 F8
Cluan TAS 73 B12 74 G6
Club Terrace VIC 65 G11
Clump Mountain Nat Park QLD 18 K7
Clunes NSW 13 K14 39 B13
Clunes VIC 59 C10
Clybucca NSW 39 H12
Clyde NSW 28 J6 30 A6
Clyde VIC 55 H10 57 G10
Clydebank VIC 64 J6
Clydesdale VIC 59 B11
Coal Point NSW 33 D13

Coalcliff NSW 35 H11
Coaldale NSW 39 D12
Coalfalls QLD 6 H1
Coalseam Con Park WA 112 E5
Coalstoun Lakes QLD 13 C11
Cobains VIC 64 J6
Cobaki NSW 11 J13
Cobar NSW 41 G9
Cobargo NSW 44 G5 65 C14
Cobaw VIC 59 C13
Cobbadah NSW 38 F6
Cobba-Da-Mana QLD 13 J10 39 A8
Cobbannah VIC 64 G6
Cobbity NSW 35 F8
Cobbler Creek Rec Park SA 86 F3
Cobboboonee Nat Park VIC 58 G3
Cobbora NSW 36 B6
Cobby Cobby Island QLD 11 D12
Cobden VIC 59 H8 60 F6
Cobdogla SA 89 F12 98 B6
Cobera SA 89 G12 98 C5
Coblinnie Nature Res WA 109 C13
Cobourg Peninsula NT 124 A6
Cobram VIC 43 J9 63 G14 64 A2
Cobrico VIC 59 H8 60 E6
Cobungra VIC 64 E7
Coburg VIC 51 C3 53 E8 56 C7
Coburg North VIC 53 D8
Cocamba VIC 42 G5 62 D6
Cocata Con Park SA 88 C2 94 K2 97 K14
Cochranes Creek VIC 59 A9 63 K8
Cockaleechie SA 88 F3
Cockatoo QLD 11 D12
Cockatoo VIC 55 B13 57 E11 64 H2 66 E2
Cockatoo WA 116 D7
Cockatoo Valley SA 86 D5
Cockburn SA 40 H1 42 A1 89 A13 95 G13
Cockle Creek TAS 71 K10
Cocklebiddy Motel WA 119 H4
Coconut Grove NT 122 D3
Cocoparra Nat Park NSW 43 E10
Cocoparra Nature Res NSW 43 E10
Codrington SA 58 H4
Coen QLD 19 G3
Coffin Bay SA 88 G2
Coffin Bay Nat Park SA 88 F2
Coffs Harbour NSW 39 G12
Coghills Creek VIC 59 D10
Cohuna VIC 42 J7 63 G10
Cokum VIC 62 G7
Colac VIC 59 H10 61 F9
Colbinabbin VIC 63 K11
Coldstream VIC 57 C10 64 H1 66 D2
Coleambally NSW 43 G10 63 C14
Colebee NSW 28 E2 35 C8
Colebrook TAS 69 E2 71 B13
Coledale NSW 35 J11 37 J9
Coleraine VIC 58 E3 98 J7
Coles Bay TAS 69 B6
Coles Bay Con Area TAS 69 B7
Coleyville QLD 10 E6
Colignan VIC 42 F4 62 B5
Colinroobie NSW 43 F11
Colinton NSW 48 K5
Colinton QLD 8 F4
Collarenebri NSW 38 D2 41 B14
Collaroy NSW 27 C7 29 F14 35 B12 36 C7
Collector NSW 36 K6 44 C4
College Park SA 82 K6 84 D6
Collerina NSW 23 J14 41 C11
Colley SA 88 C1 94 J1 97 J13
Collgar WA 107 C14
Collie NSW 36 A3 38 K1 41 G14
Collie WA 108 B6 110 G3
Collie Cardiff WA 108 B6
Collier Range Nat Park WA 115 H9
Collingullie NSW 43 G12
Collingwood VIC 51 D4 53 F9 57 D8
Collingwood Park QLD 6 H5
Collins WA 108 G6
Collins Cap TAS 71 D12
Collinsvale TAS 69 G1 71 D12
Collinsville QLD 14 C6 17 K13 21 B13
Collinswood SA 82 J5 84 A5
Colly Blue NSW 37 A8 38 K5
Colmslie QLD 5 K11 7 B11
Colo NSW 33 K8 34 A7
Colo Heights NSW 32 J7 37 F9
Colo Vale NSW 37 J8 44 B6
Colonel Light Gardens SA 84 F5
Colton QLD 13 B13
Colton SA 88 D1 94 K1 97 K13
Columboola QLD 13 E8
Colyton NSW 35 D8
Comara NSW 39 H10
Comaum SA 58 C1
Combaning NSW 36 J2 43 F13
Combaning South NSW 36 J2 43 F13
Combara NSW 38 J1 41 F14
Combienbar VIC 44 K3 65 G11
Comboyne NSW 37 A13 39 K11
Come By Chance NSW 38 F1 41 D14
Comet QLD 14 H7 21 F14
Comleroy Road NSW 34 B6
Commodore Heights NSW 33 K12 35 A11
Como NSW 27 J3 30 G7 35 F10
Como NSW 101 H4 102 H6
Comstock TAS 72 E4
Conara TAS 75 J9
Conargo NSW 43 H8 63 E13
Concord NSW 27 E4 29 K8 31 A8 35 D11
Concord West NSW 29 K8 31 B8
Concordia SA 86 D4
Condah VIC 58 F4 98 J7
Condamine QLD 13 E8
Condell Park NSW 30 D6 35 E10
Conder ACT 47 K4
Conder Point NT 124 B4
Condingup WA 111 G13

Condobolin NSW 36 E1 41 K12 43 C12
Condong NSW 11 K13
Condowie SA 89 E8 98 A2
Congelin WA 106 J7
Congewai NSW 33 E10
Congo NSW 44 F5
Congupna VIC 43 K9 63 J13 64 B1
Conimbla Nat Park NSW 36 G4 43 D14
Coningham TAS 69 J1 71 F13
Coniston NSW 35 K10
Conjola Nat Park NSW 44 D6
Conmurra SA 98 H5
Connells Lagoon NT 127 F12
Connells Point NSW 27 H4 31 F8
Connellys Marsh TAS 69 H3
Connemarra NSW 36 A7 38 K4
Connewarre VIC 56 H3 61 E14
Conoble NSW 41 K8 43 C8
Conondale QLD 8 D7 13 E13
Conondale Nat Park QLD 8 D6 13 E12
Contine WA 107 J8
Conway Beach QLD 15 C8
Conway Nat Park QLD 15 C8
Coober Pedy SA 90 H1 93 H13
Coobowie SA 88 H7 98 C1
Coochiemudlo Island QLD 11 C12
Coochin Creek QLD 9 E10
Coodanup WA 106 J7
Cooee TAS 74 C1 77 F9
Coogee NSW 27 G6 31 D13 35 D12
Coogee WA 104 D2
Coojar VIC 58 D3 98 H7
Cook ACT 47 D3
Cook SA 96 C4
Cookardinia NSW 43 H12
Cooke Plains SA 89 J10 98 D4
Cookernup WA 106 J3
Cooktown QLD 17 C10 19 K7
Cookville TAS 71 H13
Coolabah NSW 41 F11
Coolabunia QLD 13 E11
Coolac NSW 36 K3 43 G13 44 C1
Cooladdi QLD 21 K10 23 C12
Coolah NSW 36 C7
Coolah Tops Nat Park NSW 36 A7 38 K5
Coolamon NSW 36 K1 43 G12
Coolana QLD 10 B6
Coolangatta QLD 11 H14 13 H14 24 K7 39 A14
Coolaroo VIC 51 A2 52 B7 56 B7
Coolatai NSW 38 C7
Coolatoo SA 98 F4
Coolbaggie Nature Res NSW 36 B4
Coolbellup WA 104 C3
Coolbinia WA 101 E4 102 D5
Coolgardie WA 111 B11 113 H11
Coolimba WA 112 G4
Coolongolook NSW 41 C12
Cooloola Cove QLD 13 C13
Cooloolabin QLD 9 B9
Cooltong SA 89 F12 98 B6
Cooltong Con Park SA 89 F12 98 B6
Coolum Beach QLD 9 B10 13 E13
Coolumbooka Nature Res NSW 44 J3 65 E12
Coolup WA 106 H3 110 E3
Cooma NSW 44 G3 65 B12
Cooma TAS 78 D6
Cooma VIC 63 J12
Coomandook SA 89 J10 98 D4
Coomba Park NSW 37 C13
Coombabah QLD 11 F12 24 B3
Coombabah Lake QLD 11 F12 24 B3
Coombah NSW 40 K2 42 C2
Coombe SA 89 K11 98 E5
Coomberdale WA 110 A3 112 H5
Coomealla NSW 42 E3 62 A4
Coomera QLD 11 E12 24 A2
Coomera Island QLD 11 E12 24 A4
Coominya QLD 8 K5 10 A5 13 G12
Coonabarabran NSW 38 J3
Coonalpyn SA 89 K11 98 E5
Coonamble NSW 38 H1 41 F14
Coonana NSW 111 B14 113 H14 119 F1
Coonawarra NT 122 G6
Coonawarra SA 58 D1 98 H6
Coondle WA 106 B5
Coongie SA 22 D2 91 D12
Coongoola QLD 23 E13
Coongulla VIC 64 H5 66 E7
Coonooer Bridge VIC 42 K5 63 J8
Coonoor NSW 37 B13
Coopers Creek VIC 64 J4 66 E5
Coopers Plains QLD 3 G4 7 F10
Cooplacurripa NSW 37 A12 39 K9
Coopracambra Nat Park VIC 65 F12
Coorabakh Nat Park NSW 37 B13
Coorabie SA 97 G8
Cooran QLD 13 D13
Cooranbong NSW 33 E12 37 E10
Cooranga North QLD 13 C10
Cooriemungle VIC 59 J8 60 G6
Coornartha Nature Res NSW 44 G3 65 B12
Coorong Nat Park SA 89 K10 98 E4
Coorow WA 112 G5
Cooroy QLD 9 A9 13 D13
Coorparoo QLD 3 F4 7 C10
Cootamundra NSW 36 K3 43 F13 44 B1
Coothalla QLD 21 K11 23 B13
Cooya QLD 18 A2
Cooyal NSW 36 D7
Cooyar QLD 13 F11
Copacabana NSW 33 J13
Cope Cope VIC 42 K5 62 J7
Copeland NSW 37 B11
Copeville SA 89 G11 98 C5
Copmanhurst NSW 39 E12
Coppabella QLD 14 E7 21 C14
Copperfield WA 113 F10
Copperhannia Nature Res NSW 36 G5

Copping TAS 69 G4
Cora Lynn VIC 57 G12 64 J2 66 F3
Corack East VIC 42 K5 62 H7
Corackerup Nature Res WA 110 H7
Coragulac VIC 59 H9 61 E9
Coraki NSW 13 K14 39 C13
Coral Sea QLD 17 B11
Coramba NSW 39 F12
Cordalba QLD 13 B12
Cordalba Nat Park QLD 13 A12
Cordelia QLD 17 G11
Coreen NSW 43 J10
Corella Creek NT 127 E11
Corfield QLD 21 C8
Corinda QLD 3 G3 7 E8
Corindhap VIC 59 F10 61 B10
Corindi Beach NSW 39 F12
Corinella NSW 36 F2 43 D12
Corinella VIC 57 K11 64 K1 66 G2
Corinna TAS 72 C3
Corio VIC 56 F3 61 C14
Corner Inlet Marine and Coastal Park VIC 66 J5
Corner Inlet Marine Nat Park VIC 66 J5
Cornucopia VIC 57 F12
Cornwall TAS 75 G13
Cornwallis NSW 34 B7
Corny Point SA 88 G5
Corobimilla NSW 43 G10
Coromandel East SA 81 K5 84 H7
Coromandel Valley SA 81 K4 84 H6 86 K3 87 A6
Coromby VIC 62 K5
Coronet Bay VIC 57 K11 64 K1 66 G2
Corop VIC 63 J12
Cororooke VIC 59 H9 61 E9
Corowa NSW 43 J10 64 A4
Corra Linn TAS 73 A14 75 F8
Corrigin WA 107 F12 110 D6 112 K7
Corrimal NSW 35 K10 37 J9 44 B7
Corroboree Park Tavern NT 123 D3 124 D4
Corrowong NSW 44 J2 65 E11
Corryong VIC 43 K13 65 B8
Cosgrove VIC 64 C2
Cosmo Newbery WA 113 D13 119 B1
Cossack WA 114 B6
Costello NT 125 G10
Costerfield VIC 59 B13
Cottage Point NSW 29 A11 35 B11
Cottan-Bimbang Nat Park NSW 37 A12 39 J9
Cottesloe WA 101 G1 102 G2
Cottles Bridge VIC 53 A14 57 B9
Cougal NSW 11 K9 39 A12
Coulomb Point Nature Res WA 116 F5
Coulson QLD 10 F7
Coulston NSW 45 B5
Coulta SA 88 F2
Countegany NSW 44 G4 65 B13
Couta Rocks TAS 76 H3
Coutts Crossing NSW 39 E12
Cowabbie NSW 43 F11
Cowan NSW 29 A10 35 A10
Cowan Cowan QLD 9 H12
Cowandilla SA 84 C4
Cowangie VIC 42 H2 62 E2 89 J14 98 D7
Cowaramup WA 108 D2 110 H2
Coward Springs SA 93 F11
Cowcowing Lakes WA 110 B5 112 H7
Cowell SA 88 D5
Cowes VIC 57 K9 64 K1 66 G1
Cowley Beach QLD 18 J7
Cowper NSW 39 E12
Cowley QLD 10 C2
Cowra NSW 36 G4 43 E14
Cowrie Point TAS 76 E6
Cowwarr VIC 64 J5 66 F6
Cox Scrub Con Park SA 87 E7
Coyrecup WA 109 C13
Crabtree TAS 71 E11
Crace ACT 47 B5
Cracow QLD 13 B8
Cradle Mountain-Lake St Clair Nat Park TAS 72 D7 74 J1
Cradle Valley TAS 72 C7 74 G2
Cradoc TAS 71 F11
Cradock SA 95 G8
Crafers SA 81 J6 85 F9 86 J3
Crafers West SA 81 J6 85 F8
Craigburn Farm SA 84 H5
Craigie NSW 44 J3 65 E11
Craigie VIC 59 C10
Craigie WA 101 B2
Craigieburn VIC 56 B7 59 E14 66 D1
Craiglie QLD 17 D10 18 B3
Craigmore SA 83 A9
Craigs Pocket QLD 17 G10
Cramenton VIC 42 G4 62 C5
Cramps TAS 73 D12 74 J6
Cranbourne VIC 51 J7 55 G8 57 G9 64 J1 66 F2
Cranbourne North VIC 55 F9
Cranbourne South VIC 55 H8 64 J1 66 F1
Cranbrook TAS 69 A5 75 K13
Cranbrook WA 109 F12 110 H5
Cranebrook NSW 34 C7
Craneford SA 86 B2
Cranley QLD 10 B1
Craven NSW 37 C12
Cravensville VIC 64 C7
Crawfordville NSW 33 C10
Crawley WA 101 G3 102 G4
Crayfish Creek TAS 76 E7
Creek Junction VIC 63 K14 64 D3
Cremorne NSW 27 E6 29 J12 31 A12 35 D11
Cremorne TAS 69 H2 71 E14
Cremorne Point NSW 29 K12 31 A12
Crescent Head NSW 39 J12
Cressy TAS 73 C13 75 H8
Cressy VIC 59 G10 61 C9
Crestmead QLD 3 K5 11 D10

Crestwood NSW 47 F7
Creswick VIC 59 D10
Crib Point VIC 57 J9 64 K1 66 G1
Croajingolong Nat Park VIC 65 H13
Crocodile Islands Group NT 125 B10
Croftby QLD 10 H6
Croker Island NT 124 A6
Cromer NSW 29 F13
Cromer Con Park SA 86 F6
Cromer Heights NSW 29 E13
Cronulla NSW 27 K5 31 J10 35 F12
Crooble NSW 38 C6
Crooked River VIC 64 F6
Crookwell NSW 36 J6 44 B4
Croppa Creek NSW 38 C6
Crossdale QLD 8 H6
Crossman WA 106 H6
Crotty Con Area TAS 72 F6
Crow Mountain NSW 38 G7
Crowdy Bay Nat Park NSW 37 B13
Crowes VIC 59 J9 61 J8
Crowlands VIC 59 C8
Crows Nest NSW 27 E5 29 J11 31 A11
Crows Nest QLD 8 J2 13 F11
Crows Nest Nat Park QLD 8 J2 13 F12
Croydon NSW 31 C9
Croydon QLD 16 F6
Croydon SA 81 F3 82 K4 84 A4 86 H2
Croydon VIC 57 C10
Croydon Park NSW 31 C9
Croydon Park SA 82 J4 84 A4
Crusoe Island QLD 11 D13
Crymelon VIC 42 K4 62 H5
Cryon NSW 38 E2 41 C14
Crystal Brook SA 89 D8 95 K8
Crystal Creek NSW 11 J12
Cuballing WA 107 J9 110 E5
Cudal NSW 36 F4 43 C14
Cudgee VIC 58 H7 60 F3
Cudgegong NSW 36 D7
Cudgen NSW 11 J14 39 A14
Cudgen Lake NSW 11 K14
Cudgera Creek NSW 11 K13
Cudgewa VIC 43 K13 65 B8
Cudgewa North VIC 43 J13 65 B8
Cudlee Creek SA 83 G13 86 G5
Cudlee Creek Con Park SA 83 G13 86 G5
Cudmirrah NSW 44 D6
Cudmore Nat Park QLD 14 G4 21 E11
Cue NSW 112 C7
Culbin NSW 106 K7 109 A9
Culburra NSW 44 C7
Culburra SA 89 K11 98 E5
Culcairn NSW 43 J12
Culgoa VIC 42 J5 62 G7
Culgoa Floodplain Nat Park QLD 12 K2 41 A11
Culgoa Nat Park NSW 12 K2 41 A11
Culgoora NSW 38 F4
Culham WA 106 B6
Cullacabardee WA 101 C4
Cullen Bay NT 122 H1
Cullen Bullen NSW 34 A1
Cullendulla NSW 44 E5
Cullerin NSW 36 K6 44 C4
Cullulleraine VIC 42 F2 62 B3 89 F14 98 B7
Cumberland Park SA 84 E5
Cumborah NSW 41 C13
Cummins SA 88 F3
Cumnock NSW 36 E4
Cundare North VIC 59 G9 61 D9
Cundeelee WA 111 A14 113 H14 119 F1
Cunderdin WA 107 C9 110 C5 112 J7
Cundinup WA 108 D5
Cundumbul NSW 36 E5
Cungena SA 88 B1 94 H1 97 H13
Cungulla QLD 14 A5 17 H12
Cunjurong NSW 44 D6
Cunliffe SA 88 E7 98 A1
Cunnamulla QLD 23 F13
Cunnawarra Nat Park NSW 39 H10
Cunningham SA 88 F7 98 B1
Cunninyeuk NSW 42 H6 63 E9
Cuprona SA 74 D2 77 G10
Curban NSW 36 A4 38 K2 41 G14
Curdie Vale VIC 58 J7 60 G4
Curdimurka SA 90 K6
Curl Curl NSW 27 D7 29 G14 35 C12
Curlewis NSW 38 J6
Curlewis VIC 56 G4
Curlwaa NSW 42 E3 62 A4
Currababula NSW 38 J7
Curracabundi Nat Park NSW 37 A11 39 K9
Curramulka SA 88 G7 98 C1
Currarong NSW 44 C7
Currawang NSW 44 C4
Currawarna SA 43 G12
Currawinya Nat Park QLD 23 G11 40 A7
Currawong Beach NSW 29 A14
Currency Creek SA 87 E7
Currie TAS 78 D1
Currimundi QLD 9 D10
Currumbin QLD 11 H13 24 J6 39 A13
Currumbin Valley QLD 11 H12 24 K5
Currumbin Waters QLD 11 H13 24 J6
Curtin ACT 47 F3
Curtin WA 111 B12 113 H12
Curtin Springs NT 128 J5
Curtis Island QLD 15 H11
Curtis Island Con Park QLD 15 H11
Curtis Island Nat Park QLD 15 H11
Curyo VIC 62 G6
Cuttabri NSW 38 F3
Cuumbeun Nature Res NSW 48 D6
Cygnet TAS 71 G12
Cygnet River SA 88 J6 98 E1
Cynthia QLD 13 B10
Cypress Gardens QLD 24 F4

D

D'Aguilar QLD 9 F8
D'Aguilar Nat Park QLD 4 D2 6 B3 8 G7 13 F13
D'Entrecasteaux Channel TAS 71 G12
D'Entrecasteaux Nat Park WA 108 H4 110 J3
Daandine QLD 13 F9
Daceyville NSW 31 D12
Dadswells Bridge VIC 58 B6
Daglish WA 102 F3
Daguragu NT 126 D3
Dahlen VIC 58 A5 62 K4
Dahwilly NSW 43 H8 63 E12
Daintree QLD 17 D10
Daintree Nat Park QLD 17 C10 18 A1
Dairy Flat NSW 10 K7
Daisy Dell TAS 73 B8 74 G2 77 K10
Daisy Hill QLD 3 J7 7 H14 11 C11
Daisy Hill State Forest QLD 3 J7
Dajarra QLD 20 C3
Dakabin QLD 5 B8 9 H9
Dalbeg QLD 14 B5 17 J13 21 A13
Dalby QLD 13 F10
Dales Creek VIC 56 A2
Dalgarup Nat Park WA 108 E5
Dalgety NSW 44 G2 65 C11
Dalhousie SA 90 B2
Dalkeith WA 101 H2 102 H3
Dallarnil QLD 13 B12
Dalman NSW 10 K5
Dalmeny NSW 44 G5
Dalmore VIC 55 J12 57 G11
Dalrymple Nat Park QLD 14 A4 17 J11
Dalton NSW 36 K5 44 B3
Dalwallinu WA 110 A4 112 G6
Daly River NT 123 G1 124 E3
Daly River (Mt Nancar) Con Area NT 123 G1 124 E3
Daly Waters NT 124 K7 126 B7
Dalyston VIC 66 H2
Damdam NT 125 C9
Dampier WA 114 B6
Dan Dan Nat Park QLD 15 J11
Dananbilla Nature Res NSW 36 H4 43 E14
Danbulla Nat Park QLD 17 E11 18 E3
Dandaloo NSW 36 A2 41 G14
Dandaragan WA 110 A2 112 H5
Dandenong VIC 51 G7 54 D7 57 G9 64 J1 66 E1
Dandenong North VIC 51 G7 54 C7
Dandenong Ranges Nat Park VIC 55 A11 57 D10 64 H2 66 E2
Dandenong South VIC 51 H7 54 D7
Danderoo QLD 10 J3
Dandongadale VIC 64 D5
Dangelong Nature Res NSW 44 G3 65 C12
Danggali Con Park SA 42 D1 89 D13 95 K13
Dangin WA 107 E9 110 D5 112 K7
Danyo VIC 42 H2 62 E2
Dapper Nature Res NSW 36 C5
Darbalara NSW 43 G14 44 C1
Darby Falls NSW 36 G5
Dardadine WA 109 A9
Dardanup WA 108 B4 110 G3
Dareton NSW 42 E3 62 A4
Dargo VIC 64 G6
Darimah Village QLD 16 G2
Dark Corner NSW 36 F7
Darkan NSW 109 B9 110 F4
Darke Peak SA 88 D4 94 K4
Darkes Forest NSW 35 H10
Darley VIC 56 B3
Darling Downs WA 105 H10
Darling Harbour NSW 26 C7
Darling Point NSW 27 F6 29 K12 31 B12
Darlinghurst NSW 26 D3 27 F6 31 C12
Darlington NSW 31 C11
Darlington QLD 11 H10
Darlington SA 81 K3 84 H3
Darlington TAS 69 E5
Darlington VIC 59 F8 60 C6
Darlington WA 103 D13
Darlington Point NSW 43 F10
Darnick NSW 40 K6 42 B6
Darnum VIC 64 J3 66 F4
Darr QLD 14 G1 21 E9
Darra QLD 3 G2 6 F7
Darradup WA 108 E3
Darrangmurmanja (Marble Point) NT 125 E12
Darraweit Guim VIC 59 D14
Darriman VIC 64 K6 66 G7
Dartmoor VIC 58 F2 98 J6
Dartmouth QLD 14 J7 21 F11
Dartmouth VIC 43 K12 64 C7
Darwin NT 121 B2 122 H2 123 C1 124 C3
Darwin River NT 123 D1 124 D4
Dattening WA 106 G7
Davenport Ranges Nat Park
    see lytewependy/Davenport Ranges Nat Park
Daveyston SA 86 B5
Davidson NSW 27 C5 29 E11 35 C11
Davies Creek Nat Park QLD 18 E3
Davis Creek NSW 37 C10
Davis Town NSW 33 J12
Davoren Park SA 83 A8
Davyhurst WA 113 G11
Dawes QLD 15 K10
Dawes Nat Park QLD 15 K11
Dawes Point NSW 26 A2
Dawesley SA 86 K6
Dawesville WA 106 H2
Dawson SA 89 B9 95 J9
Dawsons Hill NSW 37 C10
Dayboro QLD 4 A3 9 H8 13 F13
Daylesford VIC 59 D11
Daymar QLD 12 J6 38 A3
Daysdale NSW 43 J10

Daytrap Corner VIC 42 H4 62 E6
De La Poer Range Nature Res WA 113 C13 119 B1
De Salis NSW 47 G7
Deagon QLD 3 A5 5 F11
Deakin ACT 46 D1 47 F4
Deanmill WA 108 F6 110 H3
Deans Marsh VIC 59 H10 61 F11
Dears Ridge TAS 71 G12
Deception Bay QLD 5 A9 9 H10 13 F13
Deddington TAS 75 G9
Dederang VIC 43 K11 64 C6
Dee TAS 73 G11
Dee Why NSW 27 C7 29 F14 35 C12
Deebing Creek QLD 6 K2
Deeford QLD 15 J10
Deep Creek TAS 75 B14 78 K6
Deep Creek Con Park SA 87 H2 89 J8 98 E2
Deep Lead VIC 58 B7
Deepwater NSW 39 D9
Deepwater Nat Park QLD 15 J12
Deer Park VIC 52 F3 56 C6
Deer Reserve Nat Park QLD 8 G5
Deer Vale NSW 39 G11
Deeragun QLD 14 A4 17 H12
Deeral QLD 17 E11 18 F5
Delamere SA 87 H2 89 J8 98 D2
Delaneys Creek QLD 9 G8
Delatite VIC 64 E6 66 B5
Delatite Arm VIC 64 E3 66 B4
Delegate NSW 44 J3 65 E11
Deleye NT 124 E2
Delfin Island SA 81 E1
Della Satellite Gas Station SA 22 F3 91 F13
Dellhurst WA 45 A2
Dellicknora VIC 44 J2 65 F10
Dellyanine WA 109 B10
Deloraine TAS 73 B11 74 G5 77 K13
Delungra NSW 38 E7
Demon Nature Res NSW 39 C10
Denbarker WA 109 H11
Denham WA 112 A2 114 K2
Denham Court NSW 30 F1
Denham Island QLD 16 D2
Denial Bay SA 97 G11
Denicull Creek VIC 58 B7
Deniliquin NSW 43 H8 63 F12
Denistone NSW 29 H8
Denistone East NSW 29 G8
Denman NSW 37 C9
Denman SA 96 D3
Denmark WA 109 J11 110 K5
Dennes Point TAS 69 J1 71 F13
Dennington VIC 58 H6 60 F2
Deptford VIC 65 G8
Derby TAS 75 D11
Derby VIC 59 A11 63 K9
Derby WA 116 F7
Dereel VIC 59 F10 61 A10
Dergholm VIC 58 D2 98 H6
Dergholm State Park VIC 58 D2 98 H7
Dering VIC 42 H3 62 E4
Dernancourt SA 81 E6 83 H8
Deroora QLD 14 H2 21 F10
Derriers Flat QLD 8 B6
Derrimut VIC 52 G4
Derrinallum VIC 59 F8 60 B7
Derrymore QLD 10 C2
Derwent Bridge TAS 73 F9
Desdemona WA 113 F11
Desert Oaks Motel NT 128 J7
Detention Falls Con Area TAS 77 F8
Detpa VIC 62 H4
Deua Nat Park NSW 44 E5 65 A14
Devenish VIC 63 J14 64 C3
Deviot TAS 74 D7
Devon VIC 66 H6
Devon Meadows VIC 55 J9 57 G10
Devon Park SA 82 J4 84 A4
Devoncourt QLD 20 C4
Devonian Reef Con Park WA 117 G9
Devonport TAS 74 D4 77 G12
Dewars Pool WA 106 B5
Dhalinybuy NT 125 C12
Dhambala NT 125 C11
Dhampiyaka NT 125 D11
Dharawa NT 125 B11
Dharawal Nature Res NSW 35 H10
Dharawal State Rec Area NSW 35 H10
Dharrni NT 125 E11
Dharug Nat Park NSW 33 J10 37 G10
Dhayirri NT 125 B11
Dhipirrinjura NT 125 C10
Dhunganda NT 125 D11
Dhuruputjni NT 125 D12
Diamantina Nat Park QLD 20 F5
Diamond Bay NSW 29 K14 31 B14
Diamond Creek VIC 51 A6 53 C12 57 B9
Dianas Beach TAS 75 F14
Dianella WA 101 D4 102 C5
Diapur VIC 62 J3
Dickson ACT 47 C5
Dicky Beach QLD 9 D10
Dickygundi NSW 36 C4 41 H14 43 A14
Diddleum Plains TAS 75 E10
Digby SA 98 J7
Digby VIC 58 F3
Diggers Rest VIC 52 A2 56 B5 59 E13
Dillalah QLD 23 C13
Dillcar QLD 21 D8
Dilling WA 107 G11
Dilpurra NSW 42 H6 63 E8
Dilston TAS 75 E8
Dimboola VIC 42 K3 62 J4
Dimbulah QLD 17 E10 18 F1

Dinden Nat Park QLD 17 E11 18 E4
Dingee VIC 42 K7 63 J10
Dingley Village VIC 51 G5 54 C5 57 E8
Dingo QLD 15 H8
Dingup WA 108 F7
Dingwall VIC 42 J6 63 G9
Dinmore QLD 6 G4 11 C8
Dinner Plain VIC 64 E7
Dinninup WA 109 D8 110 G4
Dinoga NSW 38 F6
Dinyarrak VIC 62 J1
Dip Range Reg Res TAS 76 F7
Dipperu Nat Park (Scientific) QLD 15 E8 21 D14
Direk SA 81 A4 82 B5 86 F2
Dirnaseer NSW 36 K2 43 F13
Dirranbandi QLD 12 J4 38 A1
Discovery Bay VIC 98 K6
Discovery Bay Coastal Park VIC 98 K6
Discovery Bay Marine Nat Park VIC 58 H2
Ditchi NT 124 F1
Ditjini NT 124 D3
Dittmer QLD 14 C7 17 K14 21 A14
Dixie VIC 58 H7 60 E5
Dixons Creek VIC 57 B11 64 G1 66 D2
Djakalabona NT 125 C9
Djalibang NT 124 H4
Djarawong QLD 18 K6
Djarrakpi NT 125 E12
Djarrung NT 124 G5
Djirrbiyak NT 123 D7 124 D6
Djiru Nat Park QLD 18 K6
Djuan QLD 8 G1
Djugerari WA 117 H10
Djukbinj Nat Park NT 123 B3 124 C4
Dobroyd Point NSW 29 K10 31 B9
Docker VIC 64 C4
Docker River (Kaltukatjara) NT 118 G7 128 H1
Doctors Flat VIC 65 F8
Doctors Point TAS 73 D11 74 J6
Doctors Rocks TAS 74 C1 77 F9
Dodges Ferry TAS 69 G3 71 D14
Dodnun WA 117 E11
Dog Kennels Reg Res TAS 75 H12
Dolans Bay NSW 31 J9
Dolls Point NSW 31 G10
Dombakup WA 108 H6
Dombarton NSW 37 J9 44 B7
Dominicks Bight NSW 37 F9
Don TAS 74 D4 77 G12
Don Valley VIC 57 C12
Donald VIC 42 K5 62 J7
Donalds Well SA 93 A8 128 K6
Doncaster VIC 51 C6 53 F12 57 C9
Doncaster East VIC 53 F13
Dongara WA 112 F4
Donnelly River WA 108 E5
Donnybrook QLD 9 F10
Donnybrook VIC 56 A7
Donnybrook WA 108 C5 110 G3
Donnybrook-Boyup Brook Road Nature Res WA 108 D6
Donvale VIC 53 F13
Donydji NT 125 D11
Doo Town TAS 69 J5
Dooboobetic VIC 62 J7
Doodenanning WA 107 D9
Doodlakine WA 107 C12 110 C6 112 J7
Dooen VIC 58 A5 62 K5
Dookie VIC 43 K9 63 J14 64 B2
Doolandella QLD 3 J3 7 H8
Doomadgee QLD 16 F2
Doomben QLD 3 D5 5 J11 7 A11 9 K10 11 A9
Doon Doon Roadhouse WA 117 E13
Doonan QLD 9 A9
Doonside NSW 28 G2 35 D9
Dooragan Nat Park NSW 37 B14
Dooralong NSW 33 F11 37 F10
Dora Creek NSW 33 E12
Doreen VIC 57 B9 59 E14 64 G1 66 D1
Dorodong VIC 58 D1
Dorrigo NSW 39 G11
Dorrigo Nat Park NSW 39 G11
Dorrington VIC 5 K9 7 B9
Dorset Vale SA 85 K8 86 K3 87 B6
Double Bay NSW 31 C12
Double Bridges VIC 65 G8
Double Creek TAS 69 E4
Double Island QLD 18 C4
Double Sandy Point Con Area TAS 75 B9 78 K1
Doubleview WA 102 D2
Douglas QLD 8 K1
Douglas NSW 58 B3
Douglas Crossing NT 123 G3 124 E4
Douglas Park NSW 35 H8 37 J9 44 A7
Douglas River TAS 75 J14
Douglas-Apsley Nat Park TAS 75 H14
Dove River Con Area TAS 73 B8 74 G2
Dover TAS 71 H11
Dover Gardens SA 84 G3
Dover Heights NSW 27 F7 29 K14 31 B13 35 D12
Doveton VIC 51 G7 55 D8
Dowerin WA 107 A8 110 B5 112 J6
Downer ACT 47 C5
Downside NSW 43 G12
Doyalson NSW 33 F13
Doyles Creek NSW 32 A5
Dragon Rocks Nature Res WA 111 E8
Dragon Tree Soak Nature Res WA 115 A14 116 J7
Drake NSW 13 K12 39 C11
Draper QLD 4 F6
Drayton QLD 10 C1
Dreeite VIC 59 G9 61 D9
Drewvale QLD 3 J4 7 J10
Driffield VIC 64 K4 66 G5

Driftway NSW 36 G3 43 D13
Drik Drik VIC 58 G2
Drillham QLD 13 E8
Drinane NSW 36 B4 41 H14
Dripstone NSW 36 D5
Dromana VIC 56 J7 59 H14 66 G1
Dromedary TAS 71 C12
Dronfield QLD 20 C4
Drouin VIC 57 G14 64 J3 66 F3
Drouin South VIC 57 G14 64 J4 66 F3
Drouin West VIC 57 F14
Drovers Cave Nat Park WA 110 A1 112 G4
Drumborg VIC 58 G3
Drummond QLD 14 H5 21 F12
Drummond Cove WA 112 E3
Drummoyne NSW 27 E5 29 K10 31 B10 35 D11
Drung Drung VIC 58 A5 62 K5
Dry Creek SA 81 D4 82 G5
Dry Creek VIC 64 E3 66 A4
Dryander Nat Park QLD 14 B7 17 J14 21 A14
Drysdale VIC 56 G4 59 G13
Drysdale River Nat Park WA 117 C12
Duaringa QLD 15 H9
Dubbil Barril TAS 72 G5
Dubbo NSW 36 C4 41 H14 43 A14
Dubelling WA 107 E9
Dublin SA 89 F8 98 B2
Dublin Town TAS 75 G13
Duchess QLD 20 C3
Duck Island VIC 56 H5
Duckenfield NSW 33 A13
Dudauman NSW 36 J2 43 F13
Duddo VIC 62 E2
Dudinin WA 107 J12 110 F6
Dudley NSW 33 C14
Dudley Con Park SA 88 K7 98 E1
Dudley Park SA 81 E4 82 J4 84 A4
Duffholme VIC 58 A3 62 K3
Duffield VIC 129 K9
Duffy ACT 47 F2
Duffys Forest NSW 27 B5 29 C11 35 B11
Duggan WA 107 K13
Dularcha Nat Park QLD 9 D9
Dulbolla QLD 11 J8
Dulbydilla QLD 12 D3 21 K13
Dulcie Range Nat Park NT 129 D11
Dulcot TAS 69 G2 71 D13
Dululu QLD 15 H10
Dulwich SA 81 G5 84 C6
Dulwich Hill NSW 31 C9
Dum Dum NSW 11 K12
Dumaresq NSW 39 G9
Dumbalk VIC 66 H4
Dumbalk North VIC 66 H4
Dumberning WA 107 J8
Dumbleyung WA 109 B13 110 F6
Dumosa VIC 42 J5 62 G7
Dunalley TAS 69 H4
Dunbible NSW 11 K12
Duncan TAS 75 G12
Duncraig WA 101 C2 102 A2
Dundas NSW 35 D10
Dundas QLD 8 J3
Dundas TAS 72 D5
Dundas Nature Res WA 111 E13 113 K13 119 H1
Dundas Valley NSW 27 D3 28 H7
Dundee NSW 39 D9
Dundee Beach NT 124 D3
Dundee Downs NT 124 D3
Dundonnell VIC 59 F8 60 B5
Dundowran QLD 13 B13
Dundurrabin NSW 39 F11
Dunedoo NSW 36 B6
Dungay NSW 11 J12
Dunggir Nat Park NSW 39 H11
Dungog NSW 37 D11
Dungowan NSW 39 D9
Dunk Island QLD 18 K7
Dunkeld NSW 36 F6
Dunkeld QLD 12 E4
Dunkeld VIC 58 E6
Dunlop ACT 47 A2
Dunluce QLD 17 K8 21 B8
Dunmarra NT 124 K7 126 B7
Dunn Rock Nature Res WA 111 F8
Dunnstown VIC 59 E11
Dunolly VIC 59 B10
Dunoon NSW 39 B13
Dunorlan TAS 73 A10 74 F5 77 K13
Dunrobin VIC 58 E2
Dunsborough WA 108 C2 110 G2
Dunwich QLD 11 B13 13 G14
Durack QLD 3 H3 7 G9
Dural NSW 27 B3 28 D7 35 C10
Duramana NSW 36 F6
Duranbah NSW 11 J13
Duranillin WA 109 C9 110 G4
Durdidwarrah VIC 56 D1 59 F11 61 A13
Durham QLD 17 G8
Durham Lead VIC 59 E10
Durham Ox VIC 42 K6 63 H9
Durong South QLD 13 D10
Durras NSW 44 E6
Durundur QLD 8 F7
Dutton Park QLD 3 F4 7 D10
Duvernay VIC 64 J8
Dwarda WA 107 H6 110 E4
Dwellingup WA 106 H4 110 E3
Dyliabing WA 109 C14
Dynnyrne TAS 68 D1
Dyraaba Arm NSW 39 B12
Dysart QLD 14 F7 21 D14
Dysart TAS 69 E1 71 B12 73 K14

E

E'ville NSW 35 D11
Eagle Bay WA 108 C1 110 G2
Eagle Bore (Tipunynga) SA 92 A7 128 K6
Eagle Farm QLD 3 D5 5 K11 7 B11
Eagle Heights QLD 11 F11
Eagle Junction QLD 5 J11 7 A11
Eagle On The Hill SA 81 J6 85 E8
Eagle Point VIC 65 H8
Eagle Vale NSW 30 H1 35 F9
Eagleby QLD 11 D11
Eaglehawk VIC 59 A12 63 K10
Eaglehawk Bay-Flinders Bay Con Area TAS 69 J4
Eaglehawk Neck TAS 69 J4
Earles Court QLD 18 K5
Earlston VIC 63 J14 64 C2
Earlwood NSW 31 D9 35 E11
East Arthur WA 109 B10
East Bentleigh VIC 53 K10 54 A4
East Botany NSW 31 E12
East Brisbane QLD 3 E4 7 C10
East Bullsbrook WA 100 C3 112 J5
East Cannington WA 103 H9
East Fremantle WA 101 H2 102 K2 104 A2
East Gosford NSW 33 J12
East Gresford NSW 45 C6
East Hills NSW 27 H2 30 E5 35 E10
East Ipswich QLD 6 H2
East Jindabyne NSW 43 K14 44 G2 65 C10
East Kangaroo Island TAS 78 D4
East Kew VIC 53 F10
East Killara NSW 27 D5 29 F11
East Kurrajong NSW 34 A7
East Lindfield NSW 29 G11
East Lynne NSW 44 E5
East Maitland NSW 45 G6
East Melbourne VIC 50 C4
East Palmerston VIC 17 F11 18 H5
East Perth WA 100 B4 101 F4 102 F6
East Point NT 122 E1
East Rockingham WA 104 K2
East Ryde NSW 27 E4 29 H9
East Sassafras TAS 74 E5 77 H13
East Tamar Junction TAS 73 A14 75 F8
East Vernon Island NT 123 B2 124 B4
East Victoria Park WA 101 G5 102 G7
East Yolla TAS 77 G8
East Yuna Nature Res WA 112 E4
Eastbrook WA 108 G6
Easter Nat Park WA 108 F5
Eastern Creek NSW 28 H2 35 D8
Eastern Heights QLD 6 H2
Eastern Spencer Gulf Marine Park SA 88 F6 98 B1
Eastlakes NSW 31 D12
Eastwood NSW 27 D3 29 H8 35 C10
Eastwood SA 80 D4 84 D6
Eaton WA 108 B4
Eatons Hill QLD 3 B2 4 F7
Ebbw Vale QLD 6 H3
Ebenezer NSW 35 B8
Ebor NSW 39 G10
Echo Hill SA 93 B9
Echuca VIC 43 K8 63 H11
Echunga SA 85 K12 89 H9 98 C3
Ecklin South VIC 58 H7 60 F5
Eddington VIC 59 B10
Eden NSW 44 J5 65 F14
Eden SA 87 A5
Eden Hill WA 101 E5 103 C8
Eden Hills SA 81 K4 84 G5 86 K2
Eden Island QLD 11 D12
Eden Valley SA 86 E7
Edenhope VIC 58 C2 98 H7
Edensor Park NSW 30 C2 35 E9
Edgcumbe Beach TAS 55 C9
Edgecliff NSW 31 C12 35 D12
Edgeroi NSW 38 F5
Edgewater WA 101 A2
Edgeworth NSW 33 C13 45 K7
Edi VIC 64 D4
Ediacara Con Park SA 95 D8
Edillilie SA 88 F3
Edinburgh SA 82 B6
Edith NSW 34 F1 36 G7
Edith Creek TAS 76 F5
Edith River NT 123 H5 124 F5
Edithburgh SA 88 H7 98 C1
Edithvale VIC 51 H5 54 E5 57 F8 59 G14 64 J1 66 F1
Edmondson Park NSW 30 E2 35 F9
Edmonton QLD 18 E4
Edrom NSW 44 J5 65 F14
Edungalba QLD 15 H9
Edwards Creek SA 90 G3
Edwardstown SA 81 J3 84 F4
Eerwah Vale QLD 9 A8
Egg Lagoon TAS 78 A1
Eidsvold QLD 13 B10
Eight Mile Plains QLD 3 H5 7 G11 11 C10
Eildon VIC 64 F3 66 B4
Eimeo QLD 15 D8
Einasleigh QLD 17 G9
Ekibin QLD 7 D10
El Arish QLD 17 F11 18 K6
Elabbin WA 107 A13
Elaine VIC 59 E11 61 A12
Elalie QLD 15 E9
Elands NSW 37 A12 39 K10
Elanora QLD 24 J5
Elanora Heights NSW 27 B7 29 D13 35 B11
Elba NSW 33 J12
Elbow Hill SA 88 D5
Elbow Valley QLD 10 K3
Elcho Island NT 125 B11
Elcombe NSW 38 E6

Elderslie NSW 33 A10
Elderslie TAS 71 B12 73 K13
Eldon TAS 69 E2 71 B13
Eldorado VIC 64 B5
Electrona TAS 69 J1 71 F12
Eleebana NSW 33 D13
Elgin WA 108 C4
Elgin Vale QLD 8 A3 13 D12
Elimbah QLD 9 G9
Elizabeth SA 81 A5 82 B7 86 F3 89 G9 98 C3
Elizabeth Bay NSW 29 K12 31 B12
Elizabeth Downs SA 83 A8
Elizabeth East SA 81 A6 83 B8
Elizabeth Grove SA 81 A6 83 C8
Elizabeth Island VIC 57 K10
Elizabeth North SA 83 A8
Elizabeth Park SA 83 B8
Elizabeth South SA 82 B7
Elizabeth Town TAS 71 A11 74 F5 77 K13
Elizabeth Vale SA 83 C8
Elizabeth West SA 82 A7
Ella Bay Nat Park QLD 17 E11 18 G6
Ellalong NSW 33 D10 45 K3
Ellam VIC 42 K3 62 H4
Elleker WA 109 K13
Ellen Grove QLD 6 H7
Ellenborough NSW 37 A13 39 K11
Ellenbrook WA 101 B6
Ellendale TAS 71 C10 73 K11
Ellerslie VIC 58 G7 60 C4
Ellerston NSW 37 B10
Elliminyt VIC 59 H10 61 F9
Ellinbank VIC 57 H14 64 K3 66 F4
Elliot Price Con Park SA 90 H6
Elliott NT 127 D8
Elliott QLD 13 A12 15 K13
Elliott TAS 74 C1 77 G9
Elliott Heads QLD 13 A12 15 K13
Ellis Beach QLD 18 C4
Elliston SA 88 D1
Elmhurst VIC 59 C8
Elmore VIC 43 K8 63 J11
Elong Elong NSW 36 C5
Elphinstone QLD 10 F1 14 D7
Elphinstone VIC 59 C12
Elsey NT 124 G7
Elsey Nat Park NT 124 G7
Elsmore NSW 39 E8
Elsternwick VIC 53 J9
Eltham VIC 51 B6 53 D12 57 C9
Elura Mine NSW 41 F9
Elvina Bay NSW 29 B13
Elwood VIC 51 E3 53 J8
Embleton WA 102 D7
Emerald QLD 14 H7 21 F14
Emerald VIC 55 B12 57 E11 64 H1 66 E2
Emerald Beach NSW 39 F13
Emerald Hill NSW 38 H5
Emerald Springs Roadhouse NT 123 G3 124 E5
Emita TAS 78 C4
Emmaville NSW 39 D9
Emmet QLD 14 K1 21 G9
Empire Bay NSW 33 J12
Empire Vale NSW 39 C13
Emu VIC 59 A9 63 K8
Emu Bay SA 88 J6 98 D1
Emu Creek QLD 10 E1
Emu Downs SA 89 E9 98 A3
Emu Flat VIC 59 C13
Emu Hill WA 107 E14
Emu Junction SA 93 H8
Emu Park QLD 15 G11
Emu Plains NSW 34 D7
Emu Point (Mulyung) NT 124 F3
Emu Vale QLD 10 J3
Emuford QLD 17 H9
Encounter Bay SA 87 H7
Encounter Bay Marine Park SA 98 E2
Endeavour Hills VIC 55 C9
Endeavour River Nat Park QLD 17 C10 19 K7
Endeavour Strait QLD 19 B1
Eneabba WA 112 G4
Enfield NSW 27 F4 31 C8 35 D11
Enfield SA 81 E4 82 H5 86 G2
Enfield TAS 69 F2 71 C13
Enfield VIC 59 E10
Enfield State Park VIC 61 A11
Engadine NSW 27 K2 30 J6 35 F10
Engawala NT 129 E9
Englefield VIC 58 D4
English Town TAS 75 G10
Engoordina NT 129 H9
Enmore NSW 31 C10 35 D11
Enngonia NSW 23 J13 41 B9
Enoggera QLD 3 D3 5 J8 7 A8
Enoggera Reservoir QLD 4 K6 6 B6
Ensay VIC 65 F8
Ensay North VIC 65 F8
Ensay South VIC 65 E8
Eppalock VIC 59 A12 63 K10
Epping NSW 27 D3 29 G8 35 C10
Epping VIC 51 A4 53 B10 57 B8
Epping Forest TAS 75 H9
Epping Forest Nat Park (Scientific) QLD 14 F5 21 D12
Epsom QLD 15 D8
Epsom VIC 59 A12 63 K10
Eraring NSW 33 E13
Ercildoun VIC 59 D10
Eric Bonython Con Park SA 87 H3
Erica VIC 64 J4 66 E5
Erigolia NSW 43 E10
Erikin WA 107 D12 110 D6 112 K7
Erina NSW 33 J12
Erindale SA 81 G6 84 C7
Eringa SA 90 B1 93 B13 129 K9
Ermington NSW 27 E3 28 H7 35 D10
Ernest QLD 11 F12

Eromanga QLD 21 K8 23 C8
Erriba TAS 73 A8 74 F3 77 K11
Errinundra VIC 44 K2 65 G11
Errinundra Nat Park VIC 44 K2 65 F11
Erskine Park NSW 35 D8
Erskineville NSW 31 C11
Esk QLD 8 J5 13 F12
Esk Nat Park QLD 8 J4
Eskdale VIC 64 C6
Esmond VIC 64 B4
Esperance WA 111 G12
Essendon VIC 51 C2 52 E7 56 C7
Estcourt VIC 57 E12
Estella NSW 43 G12
Estelville WA 45 K7
Ethelton SA 82 H1
Eton QLD 15 D8
Ettalong Beach NSW 33 J12 37 G10
Etty Bay QLD 18 H6
Euabalong NSW 41 K11 43 C11
Euabalong West NSW 41 K10 43 C10
Eubenangee Swamp Nat Park QLD 18 G6
Euchareena NSW 36 E5
Eucla WA 96 F1 119 G7
Eucumbene NSW 43 K14 44 F2 65 B10
Eudlo QLD 9 D9
Eudlo Creek Nat Park QLD 9 D9
Eudunda SA 89 F9 98 B3
Eugenana TAS 74 D4 77 H11
Eugowra NSW 36 F3 43 D14
Eujinyn WA 107 D12
Eulo QLD 23 F12
Eumundi QLD 9 B9 13 E13
Eumungerie NSW 36 B4 41 H14
Eungai NSW 39 H12
Eungella NSW 11 K12
Eungella QLD 14 D7 21 B14
Eungella Nat Park QLD 14 D7 17 K14 21 B14
Eurack VIC 59 G10 61 D10
Euramo QLD 17 F11
Eurebia TAS 76 F5
Eurelia SA 89 B8 95 H8
Eurilla Con Park SA 86 J3
Eurimbula Nat Park QLD 15 J12
Euroa VIC 63 K14 64 D2
Eurobin VIC 64 D5
Eurobodalla NSW 44 F5 65 B14
Eurobodalla Nat Park NSW 44 F5
Euroka NSW 34 E3
Eurong QLD 13 B14
Eurongilly NSW 36 K2 43 G13
Euston NSW 42 F4 62 C6
Eva Valley NT 123 J7 124 F7
Evandale SA 82 K6 84 B6
Evandale TAS 73 B14 75 G9
Evans Crown Nature Res NSW 34 D1
Evans Head NSW 13 K14 39 C13
Evans Landing QLD 19 E1
Evansford VIC 59 C10
Evanston SA 86 D4
Evatt ACT 47 B3
Everard Park SA 84 D4
Eversley VIC 59 C8
Everton VIC 43 K11 64 C5
Everton Hills QLD 3 C2 5 H8
Everton Park QLD 3 C3 5 J9 9 K9 11 A9
Ewaninga NT 129 G8
Ewlyamartup WA 109 C13
Exeter NSW 37 K8 44 B6
Exeter SA 82 G1
Exeter TAS 74 E7
Exford VIC 56 C4
Exmouth WA 114 D2
Expedition (Limited Depth) Nat Park QLD 12 B6
Exton TAS 73 B11 74 F6 77 K14

F

Fadden ACT 47 H4
Fairbank VIC 57 K14
Fairfield NSW 27 F1 28 K4 30 B4 35 E9
Fairfield QLD 7 D9
Fairfield VIC 53 F9
Fairfield East NSW 28 K5 30 B5
Fairfield Heights NSW 28 K4 30 B4
Fairfield West NSW 27 F1 28 K3 30 B3
Fairhaven VIC 56 K1 57 J9
Fairholme NSW 36 F1 43 C12
Fairlea TAS 75 E14
Fairlight NSW 29 H13
Fairneyview QLD 10 B6
Fairview Con Park SA 98 G5
Fairview Park SA 81 C7 83 F9
Fairy Glen TAS 71 D12
Fairy Hill NSW 39 B12
Fairy Meadow NSW 35 K10
Falbrook NSW 45 C1
Falcon WA 106 G2 110 E2
Falls Creek NSW 44 C5
Falmouth TAS 75 F14
Fannie Bay NT 122 F2
Far West Coast Marine Park SA 97 G8
Faraday VIC 59 B12
Farina SA 95 B8
Farleigh QLD 15 D8
Farnham NSW 36 E5
Farrar WA 109 D10
Farrell Flat SA 89 E9
Farrendale NSW 36 C2 41 J13 43 A13
Farrer ACT 47 G4
Fassifern NSW 33 D13
Fassifern QLD 10 F6
Father Woods Broom SA 98 H6

Faulconbridge NSW 34 D6
Faulkland NSW 37 C11
Fawcett VIC 64 E2 66 B3
Fawkner VIC 51 B3 53 D8
Feilton TAS 71 D11
Felixstow SA 81 F5 82 J7 84 A7
Feluga QLD 17 F11 18 K6
Fentonbury TAS 71 C10 73 K12
Fentons Creek VIC 63 K8
Ferguson VIC 59 J9 61 H9
Fergusson River NT 123 H4 124 F5
Fern Tree TAS 69 H1 71 E12
Fernances NSW 33 G9
Fernbank VIC 64 H7
Fernbrook WA 108 B5
Ferndale NSW 43 H11
Ferndale VIC 57 J14
Ferndale WA 101 H5 102 J7
Ferndene TAS 74 D2 77 G10
Fernihurst VIC 63 H9
Fernlees QLD 14 H7 21 F14
Fernshaw VIC 57 B12
Ferntree Creek Nat Park QLD 9 C9
Ferntree Gully VIC 57 D10
Fernvale NSW 11 K13
Fernvale QLD 10 A7 13 G12
Ferny Glen QLD 11 G11
Ferny Grove QLD 3 C1 4 H6 9 K9 11 A9
Ferny Hills QLD 3 C2 4 H7
Ferryden Park SA 81 E3 82 J4 84 A4
Fiddletown NSW 28 A7 35 B9
Field Island NT 123 B5 124 C6
Fiery Flat VIC 63 J9
Fifield NSW 36 D1 41 K12 43 B12
Fig Tree NSW 35 K10
Fig Tree Pocket QLD 3 F2 7 E8
Finch Hatton QLD 14 D7 21 B14
Findon SA 81 F2 82 K3 84 B3 86 H1
Fine Flower NSW 39 D11
Fingal NSW 11 J14
Fingal TAS 75 G12
Fingal Head NSW 39 A14
Finger Post NSW 36 D5
Fingerpost TAS 72 A6 77 J8
Finke (Apatula) NT 129 J9
Finke Bay NT 123 B5 124 C5
Finke Gorge Nat Park NT 128 G7
Finley NSW 43 H9 63 F14
Finniss SA 89 J9 98 D3
Finniss Con Park SA 87 D7
Finucane Island Nat Park QLD 16 F3
Firle SA 82 K7 84 B7
Fish Creek VIC 66 H4
Fish Point VIC 63 F9
Fish River Dam NSW 34 F1
Fisher ACT 47 G3
Fisher SA 96 C5
Fisherman Islands QLD
 3 C7 5 G14 9 K11 11 A11
Fishermens Bend VIC 51 D2 52 G7
Fishing Point NSW 33 D13
Fiskville VIC 56 B2
Fitzgerald TAS 71 D9
Fitzgerald WA 111 G8
Fitzgerald River Nat Park WA 111 H8
Fitzgibbon QLD 3 B4 5 F10
Fitzroy NT 124 H4 126 A4
Fitzroy SA 80 A2 81 F4 82 K5 84 B5
Fitzroy VIC 50 A4 51 D3 53 F8
Fitzroy Crossing WA 117 G10
Fitzroy Falls NSW 37 K8 44 B6
Fitzroy Island Nat Park QLD 18 D6
Five Dock NSW 29 K9 31 B9
Five Mile Pinnacles Con Area TAS
 73 E12 74 K6
Five Ways NSW 36 B1 41 H12 43 A12
Fiveways VIC 55 J10 57 G10
Flaggy Rock QLD 15 E9
Flagstaff Hill SA 84 H4 86 K2 87 A5
Flagstone Creek QLD 10 C2
Flaxton QLD 9 C8
Fleurieu Peninsula SA 87 G3 89 J8 98 D2
Flicks Hole NT 125 H8 127 A8
Flinders QLD 10 E7
Flinders VIC 57 K8 59 H14 66 G1
Flinders Bay WA 108 G2
Flinders Chase Nat Park SA 88 K4
Flinders Group Nat Park QLD 17 A9 19 H5
Flinders Island QLD 17 A9 19 H5
Flinders Island TAS 78 B5
Flinders Park SA 81 F3 82 K3 84 B3
Flinders Peak Con Park QLD 11 E8
Flinders Ranges Nat Park SA 95 E9
Flinders View QLD 6 J2
Flintstone TAS 73 E12 74 K6
Flora River Nature Park NT 123 K4 124 G5
Floreat WA 101 F2 102 E3
Florentine TAS 71 D9
Florey ACT 47 B3
Florida WA 106 H2
Florieton SA 89 E10 98 A4
Flowerdale TAS 77 F8
Flowerdale VIC 64 F1 66 C2
Flowerpot TAS 69 K1 71 G12
Flowery Gully TAS 74 D6 77 H14
Fluorspar QLD 17 E9
Flyers Creek NSW 36 G5
Flying Fish Point QLD 17 E11 18 H6
Flynn ACT 47 B3
Fog Bay NT 124 D3
Footscray VIC 51 D2 52 F7 56 C6
Forbes NSW 36 F3 43 D13
Forcett TAS 69 G3 71 D14
Forde ACT 47 A5
Fords SA 86 A5
Fords Bridge NSW 23 K12 41 C9
Fordsdale QLD 10 D2
Forest TAS 76 E6

Forest Den Nat Park QLD 14 E2 21 D10
Forest Glen NSW 37 C11
Forest Grove Nat Park WA 108 F2
Forest Hill NSW 43 G12
Forest Hill QLD 10 C4
Forest Hill VIC 53 G13
Forest Lake QLD 3 J2 7 H8 11 C9
Forest Range SA 85 C11 86 H4
Forest Reefs NSW 36 F5
Forestdale QLD 3 K3 7 J9 11 C9
Forester TAS 75 C11
Foresters Beach NSW 33 H13
Forestier Peninsula TAS 69 H5
Forestville NSW 27 D6 29 G12 35 C11
Forestville SA 84 D4
Forge Creek VIC 64 H7
Forrest ACT 46 D2 47 E4
Forrest VIC 59 J10 61 G10
Forrest WA 119 F6
Forrestdale WA 105 E8
Forrestdale Lake Nature Res WA 105 F8
Forrestfield WA 101 G7 103 G10
Forreston SA 86 G5
Forsayth QLD 17 G8
Forster NSW 37 C13
Forsyth Islands QLD 16 E2
Fort Glanville Con Park SA 82 H1 86 G1
Fort Lytton Nat Park QLD 3 D6 9 K10 11 A10
Fortescue River Roadhouse WA 114 C5
Forth TAS 74 D3 77 H11
Fortis Creek Nat Park NSW 39 D12
Fortitude Valley QLD 2 A3 3 E4 5 K10 7 B10
Forty Mile Scrub Nat Park QLD 17 F10
Fossil Head NT 124 G1
Foster VIC 66 H5
Fosterville VIC 59 A12 63 K11
Fountain Gate VIC 55 D9
Four Corners NSW 43 H10 63 E14
Four Mile Creek TAS 75 G14
Fourways TAS 72 B7 74 G1
Fowlers Bay SA 97 G8
Fowlers Bay Con Park SA 97 G9
Fox Valley NSW 29 F8
Foxdale QLD 14 B7 17 K14 21 A14
Foxhow VIC 59 G9 61 C8
Framlingham VIC 58 H7 60 E4
Frampton NSW 36 K2 43 F13
Frances SA 58 A1 62 K1 98 G6
Frances Bay NT 122 H3
Francistown TAS 71 H11
Francois Peron Nat Park WA 112 A2 114 J2
Frank Hann Nat Park WA 111 F10
Frankford TAS 74 E6 77 J14
Frankland WA 110 H5
Frankland Group Nat Park QLD 18 F7
Frankland River WA 109 G10
Franklin ACT 47 B5
Franklin TAS 71 F11
Franklin Harbor Con Park SA 88 E5
Franklin Harbor Marine Park SA 88 D6
Franklin Islands SA 97 H11
Franklin Sound TAS 78 E5
Franklin Vale QLD 10 D5
Franklinford VIC 59 C11
Franklin-Gordon Wild Rivers Nat Park TAS
 70 A5 72 H7
Frankston VIC 54 H5 57 G8 59 G14 64 J1 66 F1
Frankston North VIC 54 G6
Frankton SA 89 F10 98 B4
Fraser ACT 47 A3
Fraser Bluff TAS 78 C3
Fraser Island QLD 13 B14 15 K14
Frederickton NSW 39 J12
Freeling SA 86 B4 89 F9 98 B3
Freemans Reach NSW 35 B8
Freemans Waterhole NSW 33 D12
Freestone QLD 10 H3
Fregon (Kaltjiti) SA 92 C7
Fremantle WA 101 J1 102 K1 104 A1 106 E2
 110 D3 112 K5
French Island VIC 57 J10
French Island Marine Nat Park VIC
 57 H10 64 K1 66 G2
French Island Nat Park VIC 57 J10 64 K1 66 G2
French Park NSW 43 H11
Freshwater Creek VIC 56 H2 59 G12 61 E13
Freshwater Nat Park QLD 9 H9
Frewhurst QLD 17 F9
Frewville SA 84 D6
Freycinet Nat Park TAS 69 B6 75 K14
Freycinet Peninsula TAS 69 C7
Frogmore NSW 36 J4 44 A2
Fulham SA 81 G2 84 C2 86 H1
Fulham Gardens SA 81 F2 82 K2 84 B2
Fulham Vale QLD 8 G5
Fullarton SA 81 H5 84 D6 86 J2
Fullerton NSW 36 H6 44 A4
Fumina VIC 64 H3 66 E4
Furneaux Group TAS 78 C3
Furner SA 98 H5
Fyans Creek VIC 58 C6
Fyansford VIC 56 G2
Fyshwick ACT 47 F6 48 C5

G

Gadgarra Nat Park QLD 18 F4
Gaffneys Creek VIC 64 G4 66 C5
Gagebrook TAS 69 G1 71 D12
Gagudju Cooinda Lodge NT 123 D6 124 D6
Gailes QLD 3 J1 6 H6 11 C8
Gairdner WA 111 H8
Galah VIC 42 G3 62 D4
Galaquil VIC 42 J4 62 H5
Galaquil East VIC 62 H5

Galaru NT 125 C13
Gale NSW 47 H7
Galga SA 89 G11 98 C5
Galiwinku NT 125 B11
Gallanani QLD 8 H4
Gallangowan QLD 8 A4
Galong NSW 36 K4 43 F14 44 B2
Galore NSW 43 G11
Galston NSW 27 A3 28 C7 35 B10
Galupa NT 125 C13
Gama VIC 42 H4 62 F5
Gamardi NT 125 C9
Gamargawan NT 125 D8
Gambier Islands Group Marine Park SA 88 H4
Gan Gan NT 125 D11
Ganmain NSW 36 K1 43 G12
Gannawarra VIC 63 G10
Gapsted VIC 64 C5
Gapuwiyak NT 125 C11
Garah NSW 12 K7 38 C4
Garden City VIC 52 H7
Garden Island SA 81 C2 82 F3 86 G1
Garden Island WA 106 F2
Garden Island Creek TAS 71 G12
Garden Island Sands TAS 71 G12
Gardens of Stone Nat Park NSW 34 A2 36 F7
Gardners Bay TAS 71 G12
Garema NSW 36 G3 43 D13
Garfield VIC 57 F13 64 J2 66 F3
Garfield North VIC 57 F12
Garie NSW 35 G11
Garig Gunak Barlu Nat Park NT 124 A5
Garigal Nat Park NSW 27 C5 29 D12
Garrabu NT 125 B8
Garradunga QLD 18 H6
Garran ACT 47 F4
Garriyak NT 125 C11
Garrthalala NT 125 D12
Garvoc VIC 58 H7
Gascoyne Junction WA 114 H4
Gateshead NSW 33 C14
Gatji NT 125 C9
Gatton QLD 10 C4 13 G12
Gatum VIC 58 D4
Gaven QLD 11 F12 24 C2
Gawa NT 125 B11
Gawler NSW 86 D4 89 G9 98 B3
Gawler TAS 74 D3 77 G11
Gawler Ranges Nat Park SA
 88 A2 94 H2 97 H14
Gayndah QLD 13 C11
Gaythorne QLD 3 D3 5 J8 7 A8
Gazette VIC 58 F5
Geebung QLD 3 C4 5 G10
Geegeela Con Park SA 98 G6
Geehi NSW 43 K13 44 G1 65 C9
Geelong VIC 56 G3 59 G12 61 D14
Geera QLD 14 H3 21 F10
Geeralying WA 107 J8
Geeveston TAS 71 G11
Geham QLD 8 K1 10 A1
Geham Nat Park QLD 8 K2
Geikie Gorge Nat Park WA 117 G10
Gelantipy VIC 44 J1 65 F9
Gellibrand VIC 59 J9 61 G9
Gelorup WA 110 G3
Gem Tree Caravan Park NT 129 E9
Gembrook VIC 55 B14 57 E12 64 H2 66 E3
Gemoka QLD 16 K7 20 B7
Genoa VIC 44 K4 65 G13
Geographe Bay WA 108 B2
George Redmond Crossing NT 126 C7
George Town TAS 74 C6 77 G14
Georges Creek NSW 39 H10
Georges Hall NSW 30 D6 35 E10
Georges Heights NSW 29 J13 31 A13
Georges Plains NSW 36 G6
Georges River Nat Park NSW 27 H2
Georgetown QLD 17 G8
Georgetown SA 89 D8 95 K8
Gepps Cross SA 81 D4 82 H5 86 G2
Geraldton WA 112 E3
Gerang Gerung VIC 62 J4
Geranium SA 89 J11 98 D5
German Creek QLD 14 G7 21 E14
German Town TAS 75 G14
Gerringong NSW 37 K9 44 C7
Gerroa NSW 37 K9 44 C7
Geurie NSW 36 C5
Gheerulla QLD 8 B7
Gherang VIC 56 J1
Gheringhap VIC 56 F2 61 C13
Ghin-Doo-Ee Nat Park NSW 37 C12
Gibberagee NSW 39 D12
Gibinbell QLD 13 J9
Gibraltar Range Nat Park NSW 39 D10
Gibson WA 111 G12
Gibson Desert Nature Reserve WA 118 G3
Gibson Island QLD 3 D6 5 K12
Gibsonvale NSW 43 D11
Gidgegannup WA 106 D4
Gidginbung NSW 36 J1 43 F12
Giffard VIC 64 K6 66 G7
Gikal NT 125 C12
Gilbert River QLD 16 F7
Gilberton SA 80 A3 82 K5 84 B5
Gilderoy VIC 57 D13
Gilead NSW 35 G9
Giles Meteorological Station WA 118 G6
Gilgai NSW 39 E8
Gilgandra NSW 36 A4 38 K2 41 G14
Gilgooma NSW 38 H2 41 E14
Gilgunnia NSW 41 J10 43 A10
Gilirri NT 125 C10
Gilles Plains SA 81 E5 82 H7 86 G3
Gilliat QLD 16 K5 20 B5
Gillieston Heights NSW 33 B12 45 H6
Gillman SA 82 G3

Gillman WA 126 G1
Gilmore ACT 47 H5
Gilston QLD 11 G12 24 F2
Gilwi NT 124 J3 126 A3
Gimbat NT 123 G6 124 E6
Gin Gin NSW 36 B3 41 H13
Gin Gin QLD 13 A11 15 K12
Gina SA 97 A13
Gindalbie WA 111 A12 113 G12
Gindie QLD 14 H7 21 F14
Gingilup Swamps Nature Res WA 108 F3
Gingin WA 106 B3 110 C3 112 J5
Gingkin NSW 34 G2
Gipsy Point VIC 65 G13
Giralang ACT 47 B4
Girgarre VIC 43 K8 63 J12
Girilambone NSW 41 F11
Giro NSW 37 B11
Girral NSW 36 G1 43 D12
Girramay Nat Park QLD 17 F11
Girraween NSW 28 H4 35 D9
Girraween Nat Park QLD 13 K11 39 B10
Girrawheen WA 101 C3 102 A4
Girringun Nat Park QLD 17 G11
Giru QLD 14 A5 17 H12
Girvan NSW 37 D12
Gisborne VIC 59 D13
Gladesville NSW 27 E4 29 J9 31 A9
Gladfield QLD 10 G3
Gladfield VIC 42 J6 63 H9
Gladstone NSW 39 J12
Gladstone QLD 15 H11
Gladstone SA 89 C8 95 K8
Gladstone TAS 75 B13 78 K5
Gladstone Park VIC 52 C6
Gladysdale VIC 57 D12 64 H2 66 E3
Glamorgan Vale QLD 10 B6
Glan Devon QLD 8 C1
Glance Creek TAS 74 D1 77 G9
Glandore SA 81 H3 84 E3
Glanville SA 82 G1
Glass House Mountains QLD 9 E9 13 E13
Glass House Mountains Nat Park QLD 9 E8
Glastonbury QLD 13 D12
Glastonbury Nat Park QLD 13 D12
Glaziers Bay TAS 71 G11
Glebe NSW 27 F5 29 K11 31 B11 35 D11
Glebe TAS 68 B2
Glen Alice NSW 32 G2 37 E8
Glen Alvie VIC 57 K12 66 H3
Glen Davis NSW 32 H3 37 E8
Glen Dhu TAS 71 D12
Glen Eagle WA 106 F4
Glen Elgin NSW 39 D9
Glen Forbes VIC 57 K12
Glen Forrest WA 103 D13
Glen Gallic NSW 32 A5 37 D9
Glen Helen Resort NT 128 F6
Glen Hill WA 117 E13
Glen Huon TAS 71 F11
Glen Innes NSW 39 E9
Glen Iris VIC 53 H10
Glen Lomond QLD 10 C1
Glen Osmond SA 81 H5 84 D7 86 J3
Glen Valley VIC 64 E7
Glen Waverley VIC 51 E6 53 J13 57 D9
Glenaire VIC 59 K9 61 J8
Glenaladale VIC 64 H7
Glenalbyn VIC 42 K6 63 J9
Glenalta SA 81 K5 84 G6
Glenapp QLD 11 J8 39 A12
Glenaroua VIC 59 C14 66 B1
Glenbar Nat Park QLD 13 C12
Glenbrae VIC 59 D9
Glenbrook NSW 34 D6 37 G8
Glenburn VIC 64 G1 66 C2
Glenburnie SA 58 F1 98 J6
Glencairn QLD 10 H2
Glencairn VIC 64 G5 66 C6
Glencoe NSW 39 E9
Glendale Crossing ACT 48 G4
Glendalough WA 102 A4
Glendambo SA 94 D3
Glenden QLD 14 D7 21 C14
Glendenning NSW 28 F1
Glendevie TAS 71 G11
Glendon Brook NSW 37 D10 45 D3
Gleneagle QLD 11 F9
Glenelg SA 81 J2 84 E2 86 J1 89 H8 98 C2
Glenelg East SA 84 E3
Glenelg North SA 81 H2 84 E2
Glenelg South SA 84 F2
Glenfern QLD 8 F6
Glenfern TAS 71 D11
Glenferrie VIC 53 G10
Glenfield NSW 30 F3 35 F9
Glenfyne VIC 58 H6 60 F5
Glengarrie NSW 11 J12
Glengarry TAS 74 E6
Glengarry VIC 64 J5 66 F6
Glengower VIC 59 C10
Glengowrie SA 81 J2 84 F3
Glenhaven NSW 28 E6 35 C9
Glenhuntly VIC 53 J10 54 A3
Glenisla VIC 58 C5
Glenlee VIC 42 K3 62 J4
Glenlofty VIC 59 C8
Glenlusk TAS 69 G1 71 D12
Glenlyon VIC 59 C11
Glenlyon Lake QLD 39 C8
Glenmaggie VIC 64 H5 66 E6
Glenmore NSW 34 G7
Glenmore VIC 56 C2
Glenmore Park NSW 34 D7
Glenmorgan QLD 12 F7
Glenora TAS 71 C11
Glenoran WA 108 F5
Glenorchy TAS 69 G1 71 D12

Glenorchy VIC 58 B6
Glenore TAS 73 B12 74 G7
Glenore Grove QLD 10 B4
Glenorie NSW 27 A2 28 A6 35 B9 37 G9
Glenormiston VIC 59 G8 60 D5
Glenpatrick VIC 59 C9
Glenreagh NSW 39 F12
Glenrock NSW 37 A10 39 K8
Glenrowan VIC 43 K10 64 C4
Glenroy NSW 34 C2
Glenroy SA 58 C1
Glenroy VIC 52 C7
Glenside SA 81 G5 84 D6
Glenthompson VIC 58 E6
Glenunga SA 81 H5 84 D6
Glenusk QLD 14 J3 21 G11
Glenwood NSW 28 F4 35 C9
Glenwood QLD 13 C13
Globe Derby Park SA 82 E5
Glossodia NSW 34 B7 37 G9
Gloucester NSW 37 B12
Gloucester Island QLD 17 J14 21 A14
Gloucester Island Nat Park QLD
 14 B7 17 J14 21 A14
Gloucester Nat Park WA 108 G6
Glynde SA 82 K7 84 B7
Gnangara WA 101 B4
Gnarming WA 107 H13
Gnarwarre VIC 56 G1 61 D13
Gnotuk VIC 59 G8 60 D6
Gnowangerup WA 109 E14 110 H6
Goangra Head NSW 38 F1 41 D14
Gobur VIC 64 E2 66 A3
Gochan Jiny-Jirra NT 125 C9
Gocup WA 43 H13 44 F1
Godfreys Creek NSW 36 H4 43 E14 44 A2
Godwin Beach QLD 9 G3
Gog Range Reg Res TAS 73 B10 74 F4 77 K12
Gogango QLD 15 H9
Gogeldrie NSW 43 F10
Gol Gol NSW 42 E3 62 A4
Golconda TAS 75 D9
Gold Coast QLD 11 G13 13 H14
Golden Bay WA 106 G2
Golden Beach QLD 9 E10
Golden Grove SA 81 C7 83 E9 86 G3
Golden Hill WA 109 J11
Golden Ridge WA 111 B12 113 H12
Golden Valley TAS 73 B11 74 G6
Goldfields Woodlands Con Park WA
 111 B10 113 J11
Goldfields Woodlands Nat Park WA
 111 B13 J10
Goldsborough VIC 59 A10 63 K9
Goldsmith TAS 69 A1 75 K9
Goldsmiths QLD 17 G8
Gollan NSW 36 C5
Golspie NSW 36 J6 44 A4
Gomersal SA 86 C5
Goneaway Nat Park QLD 20 F6
Gongolgon NSW 41 D11
Gonguruwuy NT 125 C12
Goobang Nat Park NSW 36 D3 41 J14 43 B14
Good Hope NSW 36 K4 44 C2
Good Night Scrub Nat Park QLD 13 B11
Goodedulla Nat Park QLD 15 G9
Goodger QLD 13 E11
Goodna QLD 3 J1 6 H6 11 C8
Goodnight NSW 42 G3 62 B5
Goodooga NSW 12 K3 41 A12
Goodparla NT 123 F5 124 E5
Goodwood QLD 13 B12
Goodwood SA 81 H4 84 D5
Goolgowi NSW 43 E9
Goolhi NSW 38 H4
Goolma NSW 36 C6
Goolmangar NSW 39 B13
Gooloogong NSW 36 G4 43 D14
Goolwa SA 87 G7 89 J9 98 D3
Goomalibee VIC 63 J14 64 C3
Goomalling WA 106 B7 110 C4 112 J6
Goomarin WA 107 A14
Goombi QLD 13 E8
Goomboorian Nat Park QLD 13 D13
Goombungee QLD 13 F11
Goomburra QLD 10 G2
Goomeri QLD 13 D12
Goon Nure VIC 64 J7
Goondah NSW 36 K4 43 G14 44 B2
Goondiwindi QLD 13 J8 38 A6
Goongarrie WA 113 G11
Goongarrie Nat Park WA 113 G12
Goongee VIC 62 D2
Goongerah VIC 44 K2 65 F10
Goonoo Goonoo NSW 38 J7
Goonumbla NSW 36 E3 41 K13 43 C13
Goonyella QLD 14 E6 21 C14
Gooram VIC 64 E2 66 A3
Goorambat VIC 63 J14
Gooramgoola NSW 45 A1
Goornong VIC 59 A12 63 K11
Gooroc VIC 42 K5 62 J7
Goorooyarroo Nature Res NSW 48 B6
Gooseberry Hill WA 103 F12
Goovigen QLD 15 J10
Goowarra QLD 15 H8
Gorae VIC 58 H3
Gorae West VIC 58 H3
Goranba QLD 12 F7
Gordon ACT 47 K4
Gordon NSW 27 D5 29 F10 35 C11
Gordon SA 95 G8
Gordon TAS 69 K1 71 G12
Gordon VIC 56 A1 59 E11
Gordon Downs WA 117 H14
Gordon Park QLD 3 D4 5 J10 7 A10
Gordonvale QLD 17 E11 18 E4
Gordonvale TAS 71 B8 73 K9

Gore QLD 13 H10 39 A9
Gore Hill NSW 29 J11
Gorge Rock WA 107 G12
Gormandale VIC 64 K5 66 G6
Gormanston TAS 72 F5
Gorokan NSW 33 G13
Goroke VIC 58 A3 62 K3 98 G7
Gorpulyu NT 125 E9
Gorrong NT 125 C9
Gosford NSW 33 H12 37 F10
Gosforth NSW 33 A11
Goshen TAS 75 E13
Gosnells WA 101 K6 105 C10
Gosse Bore SA 93 A9 128 K7
Gostwyck NSW 39 H9
Goughs Bay VIC 64 F3 66 B4
Goulburn NSW 36 K6 44 C4
Goulburn River Nat Park NSW 32 A1 36 C7
Gould Creek SA 83 C9
Goulds Country TAS 75 D13
Goulds Landing TAS 70 B4 72 K6
Gourock Nat Park NSW 44 F4 65 A13
Gove Peninsula NT 125 C13
Gowanford VIC 42 H5 62 E7
Gowar East VIC 63 J8
Gowrie ACT 47 H4
Gowrie Park TAS 73 A9 74 F3 77 K11
Goymarr Tourist Park (Mary River Roadhouse)
    NT 123 G5 124 E6
Goyura VIC 62 G5
Grabben Gullen NSW 36 J6 44 B4
Gracefield WA 109 E11
Gracemere QLD 15 H10
Gracetown WA 108 D1 110 H2
Graceville QLD 3 F3 7 D8
Gradgery NSW 41 F13
Gradule QLD 12 J6 38 A3
Grafton NSW 39 E12
Grahamstown NSW 43 H13 44 D1
Graman NSW 38 D7
Grampians Nat Park VIC 58 C6
Grandchester QLD 10 C5
Grange QLD 3 D3 5 J9 7 A9
Grange SA 81 F2 82 K2 84 B2 86 H1
Granite Island SA 87 H6
Granite Tor Con Area TAS 72 C6 74 H1
Grant VIC 64 F6
Grantham QLD 10 C3
Granton TAS 69 G1 71 D12
Granton VIC 57 A13
Grantville VIC 57 K11 64 K2 66 G2
Granville NSW 27 E2 28 J6 30 A6 35 D10
Granville Harbour TAS 72 D3
Granya VIC 43 K12 64 B7
Grass Flat VIC 58 A4 62 K4
Grass Patch WA 111 F12
Grass Valley WA 106 C7
Grassdale VIC 58 H6 60 E3
Grassmere VIC 58 H6 60 E3
Grasstree Beach QLD 15 D8
Grasstree Hill TAS 69 G1 71 D13
Grassy TAS 78 D2
Grattai NSW 36 D6
Gravelly Beach TAS 74 E7
Gravelly Ridge Con Area TAS 69 E2 71 B14
Gravesend NSW 38 D6
Grawin NSW 41 C13
Gray TAS 75 G14
Grays Point NSW 27 K3 31 J8
Grayson QLD 10 J3
Graytown VIC 59 A14 63 K12
Great Australian Bight Marine Park SA 96 F4
Great Barrier Reef QLD 18 B5
Great Barrier Reef Coast Marine Park QLD
    15 A8 17 H14 18 F6 19 D5
Great Basalt Wall Nat Park QLD 14 B2
    17 J10 21 A10
Great Keppel Island QLD 15 G11
Great Lake TAS 73 D12 74 J6
Great Lake Con Area TAS 73 E12 74 J7
Great Otway Nat Park VIC
    56 K1 59 J9 60 J7 61 J10
Great Oyster Bay TAS 69 C6
Great Sandy Island Nature Res WA 114 C4
Great Sandy Nat Park QLD
    9 A10 13 A13 15 K14
Great Victoria Desert Nature Res WA
    92 J1 96 A1 119 F6
Great Western VIC 58 C7
Great Western Tiers Con Area TAS
    69 A1 73 E14 75 K8
Greater Beedelup Nat Park WA 108 F5 110 H3
Greater Bendigo Nat Park VIC 59 A12 63 K10
Greater Dordagup Nat Park WA 108 G7
Greater Hawke Nat Park WA 108 G5
Greater Kingston Nat Park WA 110 E7
Greater Preston Nat Park WA 108 C6
Gredgwin VIC 42 J6 63 G8
Green Fields SA 81 C4 82 E5
Green Head WA 112 G4
Green Hill NSW 39 J11
Green Island QLD 9 K11 11 A11
Green Island Nat Park QLD 11 C6
Green Mountains QLD 11 J10
Green Pigeon NSW 39 B12
Green Point NSW 33 J12
Green Valley NSW 35 E9
Green Valley NSW 109 J13
Greenacre NSW 27 G3 30 C7 35 E10
Greenacres SA 81 E5 82 H6
Greenbank QLD 11 D9
Greenbushes WA 108 D6 110 G3
Greendale NSW 34 F7
Greendale VIC 56 A2 59 E12
Greenethorpe NSW 36 H4 43 E14
Greenfield Park NSW 30 C2
Greengrove NSW 33 J11

Greenhill QLD 15 E9
Greenhill SA 81 G6 85 D8
Greenhills WA 107 D8 110 D4 112 K6
Greenland NSW 45 B1
Greenmount QLD 13 G11
Greenmount VIC 66 H6
Greenmount WA 103 D12
Greenmount East QLD 10 D1
Greenmount Nat Park QLD 103 D12 106 D4
Greenock SA 86 B6 89 F9 98 B3
Greenough WA 112 F4
Greens Beach TAS 74 C6 77 G14
Greens Creek VIC 58 B7
Greensborough VIC 51 B5 53 C11 57 C8
Greenslopes QLD 3 F4 7 D10
Greenvale NSW 43 G11
Greenvale QLD 17 H10
Greenvale VIC 51 A2 52 A6 56 B6
Greenwald VIC 58 G3
Greenway ACT 47 J3
Greenways SA 98 H5
Greenwell Point NSW 44 C7
Greenwich NSW 29 J11 31 A11 35 D11
Greenwich Park NSW 36 K7 44 B5
Greenwith SA 81 B7 83 D9
Greenwood WA 101 C2 102 A3
Greeta TAS 75 D9
Gregors Creek QLD 8 F5
Gregory QLD 14 G7 21 E14
Gregory Downs QLD 16 G2
Gregory Nat Park see Judbarra Nat Park
Greigs Flat NSW 44 J5 65 E14
Grenfell NSW 36 H3 43 E13
Grenville VIC 59 E10 61 A11
Gresford NSW 37 D11 45 C6
Greta NSW 33 A10 37 D10 45 F4
Greta VIC 64 C4
Greta West VIC 64 C4
Gretna TAS 71 C11 73 K13
Grey Peaks Nat Park QLD 18 E5
Greystanes NSW 27 E1 28 H4 35 D9
Greythorn VIC 53 F11
Griffin QLD 5 D10 9 J10
Griffith ACT 47 F5
Griffith NSW 43 F10
Griffiths Island VIC 60 F1
Grimwade WA 108 D6 110 G3
Grindelwald TAS 74 E7
Gringegalgona VIC 58 D4
Grinings Landing TAS 70 C5 72 K6
Grogan NSW 36 J2 43 F13
Grong Grong NSW 43 G11
Grongah Nat Park QLD 13 C12
Gronos Point NSW 35 B8
Groote Eylandt NT 125 F13
Grose Vale NSW 34 B6
Grose Wold NSW 34 B7
Grove TAS 71 E12
Grovedale VIC 56 H2 61 D14
Grovely QLD 3 C2 5 J8 7 A8
Gruyere VIC 57 C11
Guanaba QLD 11 F11
Gubbata NSW 43 D11
Gudjekbin NT 125 C8
Guilderton WA 106 B1 110 C2 112 J5
Guildford NSW 27 F2 28 K5 30 B5 35 D10
Guildford TAS 72 A6 77 J8
Guildford VIC 59 C11
Guildford WA 101 E6 103 D9
Guildford West NSW 28 K5 30 B5
Gul Gul NT 124 A6
Gulaga Nat Park NSW 44 G5 65 C14
Gular NSW 38 J1 41 F14
Gulargambone NSW 38 J1 41 F14
Gulera QLD 13 F9
Gulf Creek NSW 38 F5
Gulf of Carpentaria NT 125 E14 127 A14
Gulf of Carpentaria QLD 16 A2
Gulf St Vincent SA
    81 G1 82 B1 86 G1 88 G7 98 C2
Gulgong NSW 36 C6
Gulguer Nature Res NSW 34 F7
Gulmarrad NSW 39 D13
Gulnare SA 89 C8
Guluguba QLD 13 D8
Gulunguru NT 127 C11
Gum Creek NSW 43 F9 63 C13
Gum Flat NSW 36 E5
Gum Lagoon Con Park SA 98 F5
Gumarrirnbang NT 125 C8
Gumble NSW 36 E4 41 K14 43 C14
Gumdale QLD 3 F6 7 D13
Gumeracha SA 86 G5 89 F9 98 C3
Gumlu QLD 14 B6 17 J13 21 A13
Gumly Gumly NSW 43 G12
Gumtop TAS 71 D12
Gumuluji NT 127 E13
Gumuruguru NT 125 C9
Gunalda QLD 13 C12
Gunbar NSW 43 E9 63 A13
Gunbower VIC 42 J7 63 G10
Gundabloui NSW 12 K5 38 C2 41 B14
Gundabooka Nat Park NSW 41 E9
Gundabooka State Con Area NSW 41 D9
Gundagai NSW 43 G13 44 C1
Gundamaian NSW 31 J8
Gundaring WA 109 B12
Gundaroo WA 44 C3
Gunderman NSW 33 J10
Gundowring VIC 64 C6
Gundy NSW 37 B9
Gunebang NSW 41 K11 43 C11
Gungahlin ACT 44 A5 48 A5
Gungal NSW 37 C8
Gunnary NSW 36 J4 44 A2
Gunnedah NSW 38 H6
Gunnewin QLD 12 C5 21 J14

Gunning NSW 36 K5 44 C3
Gunningbland NSW 36 E3 41 K13 43 C13
Gunningrah NSW 44 H3 65 D12
Gunns Plains TAS 74 E2
Gunns Plains Cave TAS 77 H10
Gunpowder QLD 16 J3 20 A3
Gunyangara NT 125 C12
Gunyarra QLD 14 C7 17 K14 21 A14
Gupanga NT 125 C9
Gurkawuy NT 125 D12
Gurley NSW 38 E5
Gurrai SA 89 H12 98 D6
Gurrandalng Camping Area NT 124 J1 126 A1
Gurrgurr NT 125 C8
Gurrumuru NT 125 D12
Gurulmundi QLD 13 D8
Gutha WA 112 F5
Guthalungra QLD 14 B6 17 J13 21 A13
Guthega NSW 43 K14 44 G1 65 C10
Gutjangan NT 125 C13
Guy Fawkes River Nat Park NSW 39 E10
Guyong NSW 36 F5
Guyra NSW 39 F9
Guys Forest VIC 43 J13 65 B8
Gwabegar NSW 38 G3
Gwambygine WA 106 E7
Gwandalah NSW 33 E13
Gwandalan TAS 69 J3
Gwelup WA 102 B3
Gwindinup WA 108 C4
Gymbowen VIC 58 A3 62 K3
Gymea NSW 31 H8 35 F11
Gymea Bay NSW 31 H8
Gympie QLD 13 D13
Gympie Nat Park QLD 13 D13
Gypsum VIC 42 H4 62 E5
Gypsum Cliff SA 91 E9

H

Haberfield NSW 31 C9
Hackett ACT 47 C5
Hacketts Gully WA 103 G14
Hackham SA 87 B5
Hackney SA 80 B4 81 F5 84 B6
Haddon VIC 59 E10
Haddon Corner QLD SA 20 J5 22 A4 91 A14
Haden QLD 13 F11
Hadfield VIC 53 D8
Hadleigh NSW 38 D6
Hadspen TAS 73 B13 75 F8
Hagley TAS 73 B12 74 G7
Hahndorf SA 85 G13 86 K4 89 H9 98 C3
Haig WA 119 F4
Haigslea QLD 10 C6
Haines Junction VIC 59 J10 61 H10
Halbury SA 89 E8
Hale Con Park SA 86 E5
Halekulani NSW 33 F13
Hales Siding QLD 18 G1
Halfway Creek NSW 39 F12
Halidon SA 89 H11 98 C5
Halifax QLD 17 G11
Hall ACT 47 A3 48 A4
Hall NSW 27 G2 44 D3
Hallam VIC 55 D8
Hallet Cove SA 87 A4
Hallett SA 89 D9 95 K9
Hallett Cove SA 84 J2 86 K1
Hallett Cove Con Park SA 86 K1
Hallidays Point NSW 37 C13
Hallora VIC 57 H14
Halls Creek TAS 72 F5
Halls Creek WA 117 H12
Halls Gap VIC 58 C6
Hallston VIC 64 K3 66 G4
Halton NSW 45 A5
Hamel WA 106 J3
Hamelin Bay WA 108 F1
Hamelin Pool Marine Nature Res WA 112 B3
Hamersley WA 101 D3 102 B4 106 D7
Hamilton NSW 33 C14
Hamilton QLD 3 D4 5 K11 7 B11
Hamilton SA 89 F9 98 B3
Hamilton TAS 71 B10 73 J12
Hamilton VIC 58 E4
Hamilton Hill WA 101 K2 104 C2
Hamilton Hotel QLD 20 E4
Hamilton Island QLD 15 B8
Hamley Bridge SA 86 A3 89 F9 98 B3
Hammond SA 89 B9 95 H8
Hammond Island QLD 19 B2
Hammondville NSW 30 E11
Hampshire TAS 74 E1 77 H9
Hampstead Gardens SA 82 J6 84 A6
Hampton NSW 34 C2 36 G7
Hampton QLD 8 K2 10 A2 13 F11
Hampton VIC 54 B3
Hampton Park VIC 55 E9
Hanging Rock NSW 37 A10 39 K8
Hann River Roadhouse QLD 18 B8 19 J5
Hann Tableland Nat Park QLD 17 D10 18 D1
Hannahs Bridge NSW 36 B6
Hannan NSW 43 D10
Hansborough SA 89 F9 98 B3
Hanson SA 82 J2 98 A3
Hansonville VIC 64 C4
Hanwood NSW 43 F10
Happy Valley QLD 13 B14
Happy Valley SA 84 K4 87 B5
Happy Valley VIC 42 G4 62 C6 64 C5
Harbord NSW 29 G14
Harcourt VIC 59 B12
Harden NSW 36 J3 43 F14 44 B1
Hardwicke Bay SA 88 G6 98 C1

Harefield NSW 43 G12
Harford TAS 74 D5 77 H13
Hargraves NSW 36 D6
Harkaway VIC 55 D10
Harlin QLD 8 F4 13 F12
Harman ACT 47 F6
Harmers Haven VIC 66 H3
Harrington NSW 37 B13
Harris Nature Res WA 110 F7
Harris Park NSW 28 J6 30 A6
Harrismith WA 107 J12 110 F6
Harrison ACT 47 A5
Harrisville QLD 10 E7
Harrogate SA 86 J7
Harrow VIC 58 C3 64 H7 98 H7
Harry Creek SA 92 B5 128 K4
Harry Walker Tier Con Area TAS 71 B12 73 K13
Hart SA 89 E8 98 A2
Hartley NSW 34 C3
Hartley Vale NSW 34 C3
Hartwell VIC 53 H11
Hartz Mountains Nat Park TAS 71 G10
Harvey WA 106 K3 108 A5 110 F3
Harveytown TAS 71 H11
Harwood NSW 39 D13
Haslam SA 97 H12
Hassall Grove NSW 28 F1
Hassell Nat Park WA 110 J7
Hastings TAS 71 J11
Hastings VIC 57 J9 64 K1 66 G1
Hastings Point NSW 11 K14 39 A14
Hat Head NSW 39 J12
Hat Head Nat Park NSW 39 J12
Hatches Creek NT 127 J10 129 A10
Hatfield NSW 72 B6 77 K8
Hatherleigh SA 98 H5
Hattah VIC 42 G3 62 C5
Hattah-Kulkyne Nat Park VIC 42 G4 62 C5
Hatton Vale QLD 10 C5
Havelock SA 59 B10
Haven SA 58 A5 62 K5
Hawker ACT 47 C2
Hawker SA 95 G8
Hawkesdale VIC 58 G6 60 D1
Hawkesdale West VIC 58 G5 60 D1
Hawks Nest NSW 37 D12
Hawley Beach TAS 74 D5 77 G13
Hawthorn SA 84 E5
Hawthorn VIC 51 D4 53 G9
Hawthorn East VIC 53 G10
Hawthorndene SA 81 K5 84 G6
Hawthorne QLD 3 E4 7 B11
Hay NSW 43 F6 63 B12
Haydon QLD 16 F5
Hayes TAS 71 D11
Hayes Creek NT 123 G3 124 E4
Hayman Island QLD 15 B8
Haysdale VIC 42 G5 62 D7
Hazelbrook NSW 34 D5
Hazeldean QLD 8 G5
Hazelgrove NSW 34 E1
Hazelmere WA 101 E7 103 D10
Hazelvale WA 109 J9
Hazelwood VIC 64 K4 66 G5
Hazelwood Park SA 81 G5 84 D7
Headinton Hill QLD 10 F1
Healesville VIC 57 B11 64 G2
Hearson WA 114 B6
Heartlea WA 109 E8
Heath Hill VIC 57 H13
Heathcote NSW
    27 K2 30 K6 35 F10 37 H9 44 A7
Heathcote VIC 59 B13
Heathcote Nat Park NSW 27 K2 30 K5 35 G10
Heathcote-Graytown Nat Park VIC
    59 A14 63 K12
Heatherton VIC 54 B4
Heathfield SA 81 K7 85 G9 86 K3 87 A7
Heathmere VIC 58 H3
Heathpool SA 84 C7
Heathwood QLD 3 J3 7 J8
Hebden NSW 37 C10
Hebel QLD 12 K3 41 A13
Hebersham NSW 28 F1
Heckenberg NSW 30 D3
Hectorville SA 81 F6 82 K7 84 A7
Heddon Greta NSW 33 B12 45 H6
Hedges WA 107 F14
Heidelberg VIC 51 C4 53 E10 57 C8
Heidelberg West VIC 53 D10
Heigh Ridge QLD 8 A7
Heirisson Island WA 100 D4
Heka TAS 74 E2 77 H10
Helena Nat Park WA 106 E5
Helena Valley WA 103 E11
Helensburgh NSW 35 G10 37 J9 44 A7
Helensvale QLD 11 F12 13 H14 24 B2
Helenvale QLD 11 C10 19 K7
Helidon QLD 10 B2 13 G12
Hell Hole Gorge Nat Park QLD 21 J9
Hells Gate Roadhouse QLD 16 F1
Hellyer TAS 76 E7
Hemmant QLD 3 E6 5 K13 7 B13
Henbury Meteorite Craters NT 128 H7
Henbury Meteorite Craters Con Res NT 128 H7
Henderson WA 104 F2
Hendon QLD 10 G1 13 H11
Hendon SA 82 J2 98 A3
Hendra QLD 5 J11 7 A11
Henley NSW 29 J9 31 A9
Henley Beach SA 81 F2 82 K1 84 B1 86 H1
Henley Beach South SA 84 C2
Henley Brook WA 101 B6
Henrietta TAS 77 G8
Hensley Park VIC 58 E5
Henty NSW 43 H12
Henty VIC 58 E3

Hepburn Springs VIC 59 C11
Herberton QLD 17 E10 18 G2
Herdsman WA 102 D3
Heritage Park QLD 3 K5 7 K11
Hermannsburg (Ntaria) NT 128 G6
Hermidale NSW 41 G11
Hermitage QLD 10 J2
Hermitage TAS 73 G12
Hernani NSW 39 G11
Herne Hill WA 101 C7 103 A12
Heron Island QLD 15 H12
Herrick TAS 75 C12
Herston QLD 5 K9 7 B9
Hervey Bay QLD 13 B13
Hervey Bay Marine Park QLD 13 A13 15 K14
Hervey Range QLD 17 H12
Hesso SA 88 A6 94 G6
Hester WA 108 D6
Hewitt NSW 35 D8
Hexham NSW 33 B13
Hexham VIC 58 F7 60 C4
Heybridge TAS 74 C2 77 G10
Heyfield VIC 64 J5 66 E6
Heywood VIC 58 G3 98 K7
Heywood Islands WA 117 C8
Hidden Vale QLD 10 D5
Hidden Valley QLD 17 H11
Higgins ACT 47 C2
Higginsville WA 111 C12 113 J12
High Island QLD 18 F6
High Wycombe WA 101 F7 103 F10
Highbury SA 81 E6 83 H9 86 G3
Highbury WA 107 K9 110 F5
Highclere TAS 74 D1 77 H9
Highcroft TAS 69 K4
Higher McDonald NSW 33 G8
Highgate SA 84 E6
Highgate WA 101 F4 102 E6
Highgate Hill QLD 7 C9
Highland Park QLD 24 E2
Highlands VIC 64 E1 66 B2
Highton VIC 56 G2
Highvale QLD 4 G4
Hilgay VIC 58 E3
Hill End NSW 36 E6
Hill End QLD 7 C9
Hill End VIC 64 J3 66 E4
Hillarys WA 101 B1
Hillbank SA 81 A6 83 C8
Hillcrest QLD 3 K4 7 K10
Hillcrest SA 81 E5
Hilldale NSW 45 B5
Hillgrove NSW 39 G9
Hillier SA 86 D3
Hilliger Nat Park WA 108 F4 110 H3
Hillman WA 109 B9
Hillsdale NSW 31 E12
Hillsdale QLD 8 B1
Hillside NSW 28 A5 36 A4 38 K2 41 G14
Hillside VIC 52 C3 64 H7
Hillston NSW 43 D9
Hilltop NSW 44 A7
Hilltown SA 89 D9 98 A3
Hillview QLD 11 J9
Hilltaba SA 94 G2 97 G14
Hilton SA 84 C4
Hilton WA 101 J2 104 B3
Hinchinbrook NSW 30 D2
Hinchinbrook Island QLD 17 G12
Hinchinbrook Island Nat Park QLD 17 G11
Hincks Con Park SA 88 E3
Hindmarsh SA 81 F3 82 K4 84 B4 86 H2
Hindmarsh Valley SA 87 F6
Hines Hill WA 107 C12
Hinnomunjie VIC 65 E8
Hinton NSW 33 A13 45 G7
Hinze Dam QLD 24 E1
Hirstglen QLD 10 E2
Hivesville QLD 13 D11
HMAS Cerberus VIC 57 J9
Hobart TAS 62 C6 69 H1 71 E13
Hocking WA 101 A3
Hoddles Creek VIC 57 D12
Hodgeleigh QLD 8 C1
Hodgson QLD 12 D5 21 K14
Hoffmans Mill WA 106 J4
Holbrook NSW 43 J12
Holden Hill SA 81 E6 83 H8
Holder ACT 47 F3
Holder SA 89 F11 98 B5
Holdfast Bay SA 86 J1
Holey Plains State Park VIC 64 J5 66 F7
Holgate NSW 33 H13
Holland Park QLD 3 F4 7 D11
Holland Park West QLD 7 E11
Hollands Landing VIC 64 J7
Hollow Tree TAS 71 B11 73 J13
Holloways Beach QLD 18 D4
Holly WA 109 D12
Hollywell QLD 24 B4
Holmes Jungle Nature Park NT 122 D7
Holmeville NSW 33 C12
Holmwood NSW 36 G4
Holroyd NSW 28 J6 30 A6
Holsworthy NSW 27 H1 30 F5 35 E10
Holsworthy Barracks NSW 30 F4
Holt ACT 47 B2
Holt Rock WA 111 H8
Holts Flat NSW 44 H3 65 D12
Holwell TAS 74 E6 77 H14
Home Hill QLD 14 A6 17 J13
Homebush NSW 29 K8 31 B8 35 D10
Homebush QLD 15 D8
Homebush Bay NSW 27 E3 29 J8 31 A8 35 D10
Homebush West NSW 31 B8

Homecroft VIC 42 K4 62 H6
Homerton VIC 58 G4
Homestead QLD 14 B3 17 K11 21 A11
Homevale Nat Park QLD 14 D7 21 C14
Homewood VIC 64 F1 66 B2
Honeybugle NSW 41 G11
Honeymoon Beach WA 117 A11
Hookina SA 95 F8
Hope Channel TAS 76 B3
Hope Island QLD 24 A3
Hope Vale QLD 17 B10 19 J6
Hope Valley SA 81 D6 83 G8 86 G3
Hope Valley WA 104 H3
Hopefield NSW 43 J11 64 A4
Hopetoun VIC 42 J4 62 G5
Hopetoun WA 111 H9
Hopetoun West VIC 42 J3 62 G4
Hopevale VIC 42 J4 62 G5
Hopkins Nature Res WA 107 H13
Hoppers Crossing VIC 52 J2 56 D5
Horfield VIC 42 J7 63 G10
Hornsby NSW 27 B3 29 D8 35 C10 37 G10
Hornsby Heights NSW 27 B4 29 C8
Horrocks WA 112 E3
Horsham VIC 58 A5 62 K5
Horsley Park NSW 28 K1 30 B1 35 E8
Horsnell Gully Con Park SA 81 G7 85 C9 86 H3
Hoskinstown NSW 44 D4
Hotham Heights VIC 64 E6
Hotspur VIC 58 F3
Houghton SA 83 G10 89 G9 98 C3
Hove SA 84 G3
Hovea WA 103 C14
Howard QLD 13 B12
Howard Springs NT 123 C2 124 C4
Howden TAS 69 J1 71 F13
Howes Valley NSW 37 E9
Howick Island QLD 17 A10 19 H6
Howitt Plains VIC 64 B6
Howlong NSW 43 J11 64 A5
Howqua VIC 64 F3 66 B4
Howqua Hills VIC 64 F4 66 B5
Howrah TAS 69 H2 71 E13
Howth TAS 74 C2 77 G10
Hoxton Park NSW 30 E1 35 E9
Hoyleton SA 89 E8 98 A3
Hugh River NT 129 G8
Hughenden QLD 14 C1 17 K9 21 B9
Hughes ACT 47 F4
Hughes SA 96 D2
Humbug Point Con Area TAS 75 E14
Humbug Scrub SA 83 B12
Hume ACT 47 H5
Hume NSW 48 D5
Humpty Doo NT 123 C2 124 C4
Humula NSW 43 H13
Hungerford QLD 23 H10 40 A7
Hunter VIC 42 K7 63 J11
Hunter Island TAS 76 C3
Hunter Island Con Area TAS 76 C3
Hunter Wetlands Nat Park NSW 45 J7
Hunters Camp NT 123 C7 124 C7
Hunters Hill NSW 27 E5 29 J10 31 A10 35 D11
Hunting Ground TAS 71 B12
Huntingdale VIC 53 K11 54 A5
Huntingdale WA 101 K6 105 B9
Huntingwood NSW 28 H2
Huntleys Point NSW 29 J10 31 A10
Huntly VIC 59 A12 63 K10
Huonville TAS 71 F11
Hurlstone Park NSW 31 D9
Hurstbridge VIC
    51 A6 53 A13 57 B9 64 G1 66 D1
Hurstville NSW 27 H4 31 F8 35 E11
Hurstville Grove NSW 31 F8
Huskinsson NSW 44 C6
Hyde Park SA 84 D5
Hyden WA 110 E7 113 K9
Hyland Park NSW 39 H12
Hynam SA 58 B1 98 G6

I

Ida Bay TAS 71 J11
Idalia Nat Park QLD 14 K2 21 H9
Iga Warta SA 95 C9
Ikuntji (Haasts Bluff) NT 128 F5
Ilbilbie QLD 15 E8
Ilford NSW 36 E7
Ilfracombe QLD 14 H1 21 F9
Ilfraville TAS 74 D6 77 G14
Illabarook VIC 59 F10 61 A10
Illabo NSW 36 K2 43 G13
Illalong Creek NSW 36 K4 43 G14 44 B2
Illawong NSW 30 G7
Illawong WA 112 G4
Ililii NT 128 E5
Illilliwa NSW 43 F8 63 B12
Illowa VIC 58 H6 60 F2
Illyomba (No 22) SA 93 A9 128 K7
Ilpurla NT 128 G6
Iltur SA 92 E4
Iluka NSW 39 D13
Ilykuwaratja SA 93 A9 128 K7
Imangara NT 127 K9 129 B9
Imanpa NT 128 J6
Imbil QLD 8 A7 13 D13
Imintji WA 117 F10
Impadna NT 129 J8
Inala QLD 3 H2 7 B8 11 C9
Inarki SA 92 A2 128 K2
Indaringinya NT 129 C9
Indented Head VIC 56 G5 59 G13
Indooroopilly QLD 3 F3 7 D8
Indulkana (Iwantja) SA 93 C10
Indwarra Nat Park NSW 39 F8

Ingalba Nature Res NSW 36 J1 43 F12
Ingar NSW 45 C3
Ingebirah NSW 44 H2 65 D10
Ingham QLD 17 G11
Ingle Farm SA 81 D5 82 G7 86 G3
Ingleburn NSW 30 G2 35 F9
Ingleside NSW 27 B6 29 C13 35 B11
Inglewood QLD 13 J9 39 A8
Inglewood SA 83 F11 86 G4
Inglewood VIC 63 K9
Inglewood WA 101 E4 102 D6
Ingliston VIC 56 B2
Ingoldsby QLD 10 D3
Ininti NT 118 E7 128 E1
Injilatparri NT 124 B7
Injinoo QLD 19 B2
Injulkama NT 128 E7
Injune QLD 12 C5 21 J14
Inkerman QLD 14 A6 17 J13
Inkerman SA 89 F8 98 B2
Inman Valley SA 87 G4
Innaloo WA 101 J2 102 C3
Innamincka SA 22 E4 91 F13
Innamincka Reg Res SA 22 D3 91 D13
Innes Nat Park SA 88 H5
Innisfail QLD 17 E11 18 H6
Innisplain QLD 11 H9
Innot Hot Springs QLD 17 F10 18 J1
Interlaken TAS 69 D1 71 A13 73 H14
Intjarrtnama NT 128 G7
Inveralochy NSW 44 C4
Inverell NSW 39 E8
Inverleigh VIC 56 G1 59 G11 61 D12
Inverloch VIC 66 H3
Inverramsay QLD 10 G3
Investigator Group Con Park SA 88 E1
Investigator Marine Park SA 88 E1
Investigator Strait SA 88 J5 98 D1
Inyilingi NT 128 E5
Iona VIC 57 G13 64 J2 66 F3
Ipolera NT 128 G6
Ipswich QLD 6 H2 10 C7 13 G13
Irintata (Erindata) SA 92 C7
Irish Town TAS 75 G14
Irishtown TAS 76 F5
Irishtown WA 106 C6
Irkini NT 92 A2 118 J7 128 K2
Iron Baron SA 88 C6 94 J6
Iron Knob SA 88 B6 94 J6
Iron Range Nat Park
    see Kutini Payamu Nat Park
Ironbank SA 81 K6 85 H8 86 K3 87 A6
Ironbark Dam Camp NSW 38 D7
Ironbark Nature Res NSW 38 F7
Irondale NSW 34 B1
Ironhouse Point TAS 75 G14
Ironmungy Nature Res NSW 44 H3 65 D11
Ironside QLD 7 D9
Ironwood Bore SA 93 C8
Irrapatana Siding SA 90 H4
Irrerlirre NT 129 E10
Irrewarra VIC 59 H10 61 E9
Irrewillipe VIC 59 H9 61 F8
Irrmarne NT 129 C12
Irrultja NT 129 C10
Irrunytju (Wingellina) WA 118 J6 128 K1
Irvinebank QLD 17 E10 18 G1
Irymple VIC 42 F3 62 A4
Isaacs ACT 47 G4
Isabella NSW 36 H6
Isabella Plains ACT 47 J4
Isis TAS 73 D14 75 J8
Isisford QLD 14 J1 21 G9
Isla Gorge Nat Park QLD 12 A7
Island Lagoon SA 94 E5
Isle of Capri QLD 24 E5
Isles of St Francis Con Park SA 97 H10
Ithaca QLD 5 K9 7 B9
Ivanhoe NSW 40 K7 42 C7
Ivanhoe VIC 53 E10
Iveragh QLD 15 J11
Ivory Creek QLD 8 G4
Iwupataka (Jay Creek) NT 129 F8
Iytwelepenty/Davenport Ranges Nat Park NT
    127 J10 129 A10

J

Jabiru NT 123 D7 124 D7
Jabuk SA 89 J11 98 D5
Jack River VIC 66 H6
Jack River Nat Park QLD 17 B9 19 J6
Jackadgery NSW 39 E11
Jackeys Marsh TAS 73 C11 74 H6
Jacks Creek NSW 37 B9 38 K6
Jackson QLD 12 E7
Jackson Oil Plant QLD 22 E7
Jacobs Well QLD 11 E12 13 G14
Jacobs Well WA 107 E9
Jalbarragup WA 108 E4
Jalloonda QLD 17 H12
Jallukar VIC 58 C7
Jallumba VIC 58 B4
Jaloran WA 107 K10 109 A12
Jam Jerrup VIC 57 J11
Jamberoo NSW 37 K9 44 B7
Jambin QLD 15 J10
Jamboree Heights QLD 3 G2 6 F7
Jamestown SA 89 C9 95 K9
Jamieson VIC 64 F3 66 B4
Jamisontown NSW 34 D7
Jan Juc VIC 56 J2 61 F14
Jancourt VIC 59 H8 60 F6
Jancourt East VIC 59 H8 60 F7
Jandabup WA 101 A3
Jandakot WA 101 K4 104 C5 106 E3

Jandowae QLD 13 E10
Jane Brook WA 103 B12
Jane Nat Park WA 108 H7
Jannali NSW 27 J3 31 G8
Japoon QLD 18 J5
Japoon Nat Park QLD 18 J5
Japoonvale QLD 17 F11 18 J5
Jaraga QLD 14 B6 17 J14 21 A14
Jardee WA 108 F6
Jardine River Nat Park QLD 19 C2
Jardine Valley QLD 14 C1 17 K9 21 B9
Jarklin VIC 42 K6 63 H9
Jarlmadangah-Burr WA 117 G8
Jarra Jarra NT 126 J7 128 A7
Jarrahdale WA 106 F4
Jarrahwood WA 108 D4 110 G3
Jaurdi Con Park WA 111 A9
Jay Park WA 7 D8
Jeetho VIC 57 J13
Jeffcott VIC 42 K5 62 J7
Jennaberring WA 107 D10
Jennacubbine WA 106 B7
Jennapullin WA 106 B7
Jenolan Caves NSW 34 F2 36 G7
Jeparit VIC 42 K3 62 H4
Jerangle NSW 44 F3 48 K7 65 A13
Jerdacuttup Lakes Nature Res WA 111 H10
Jericho QLD 14 H4 21 F11
Jericho TAS 69 D1 71 A13 73 H14
Jericho VIC 64 G4 66 D5
Jerilderie NSW 43 H9 63 E14
Jerona QLD 14 A5 17 H13
Jerrabomberra NSW 47 H6
Jerramungup WA 111 H8
Jerrawa NSW 36 K5 44 C3
Jerrawangala Nat Park NSW 44 C6
Jerrys Plains NSW 37 D9
Jervis Bay Marine Park NSW 44 C7
Jervis Bay Nat Park NSW 44 C7
Jervois SA 89 H10 98 D4
Jetsonville TAS 75 D10
Ji-Balbal NT 125 C9
Ji-Bena NT 125 C9
Jigalong WA 115 F11
Jil Jil VIC 42 J5 62 G7
Jilbadji Nature Res WA 111 C9 113 J10
Jilliby NSW 33 G12
Jilliby State Con Area NSW 37 F10
Jilundarina NT 127 D14
Jim Jim Ranger Station NT 123 D6 124 D6
Ji-Malawa NT 125 C9
Ji-Marda NT 125 C9
Jimaringle NSW 42 H7 63 E10
Jimboomba QLD 11 E10 13 H13
Jimbour QLD 13 E10
Jimna QLD 8 C5 13 E12
Jincumbilly NSW 44 H3 65 D12
Jindabyne NSW 43 K14 44 G2 65 C10
Jindalee QLD 3 G2 6 E7 11 B9
Jindera NSW 43 J11 64 A6
Jindivick VIC 57 F14 64 J3 66 F4
Jindivick North VIC 57 F14
Jindivick West VIC 57 F14
Jindong WA 108 D2
Jingalup WA 109 E10
Jingellic NSW 43 J13 65 A8
Jingellic Nature Res NSW 65 A8
Jingera NSW 44 E4 48 J7 65 A13
Jingili NT 122 D4
Jitarning NSW 107 H12 110 E6
Jiwaranpa NT 126 G2
Joadja NSW 37 J8 44 B6
Joanna SA 58 C1
Joel VIC 59 B8
Jogo QLD 18 G6
Johanna NSW 59 K9 61 J8
John Forrest Nat Park WA 103 B13 106 D4
    110 D3 112 K5
Johnburgh SA 89 A9 95 H9
Johnstown QLD 8 A2
Jolimont WA 101 F3 102 F3
Jollys Lookout QLD 4 J4 6 A4
Jondaryan QLD 13 F11
Jones Gully QLD 8 H1
Joondalup WA 101 A2
Joondanna NSW 31 E8 102 D4
Josbury WA 106 K7 109 A9
Joseph Bonaparte Gulf NT 124 G1
Joseph Bonaparte Gulf WA 117 B14
Josephville QLD 11 G9
Joslin SA 82 K6 84 B6
Jowar NT 125 G9
Joycedale QLD 14 H3 21 F11
Joyces Creek VIC 59 C11
Joyner QLD 4 D7
Jubilee QLD 5 K8 7 B8
Jubilee Vale QLD 8 G1
Jubuk WA 107 F11
Judbarra (Gregory) Nat Park NT 124 K3 126 B3
Judbury TAS 71 E11
Juenburra QLD 20 C3
Jugiong NSW 36 K3 43 G14 44 C1
Julatten QLD 17 D10 18 D2
Julia Creek QLD 16 K6 20 B6
Jumbunna VIC 57 K13 64 K2 66 G3
Jump Spur NSW 37 C10
Junabee QLD 10 J2
Junee NSW 36 K2 43 G12
Junee Nat Park QLD 15 G8
Junee Reefs NSW 36 K2 43 F13
Jung VIC 58 A5 62 K5
Junjuwa WA 117 G10
Junortoun VIC 59 A12 63 K10
Junuy Juluum Nat Park NSW 39 G11
Jura WA 107 D13

Jurema QLD 14 G7 21 E14
Jurien Bay WA 110 A1 112 G4

K

Kaarimba VIC 43 K9 63 H13 64 B1
Kaban QLD 17 E10 18 H2
Kabelbara QLD 14 G7 21 F14
Kabra QLD 15 H10
Kadina SA 88 E7 98 A1
Kadjina WA 117 H9
Kadnook VIC 58 C2
Kadungle NSW 36 D2 41 J13 43 B13
Kagaru QLD 11 E9
Kaimkillenbun QLD 13 F10
Kainton SA 88 F7 98 A2
Kairi QLD 17 E10 18 F3
Kaiserstuhl Con Park SA 86 D6
Kajabbi QLD 16 J3 20 A3
Kajuligah Nature Res NSW 40 J7 42 B7
Kakadu Nat Park NT 123 C5 124 C5
Kakodbabuldi NT 125 C8
Kalamia Estate QLD 14 A6 17 H13
Kalangadoo SA 98 J6
Kalannie NSW 110 A5 112 G7
Kalarka QLD 15 F9
Kalaru NSW 44 H5 65 D14
Kalayapiti SA 92 D3
Kalbar QLD 10 F6 13 H12
Kalbarri WA 112 D3
Kalbarri Nat Park WA 112 D3
Kaleen ACT 47 C4
Kalgan WA 109 J14
Kalgoorlie WA 111 A11 113 H12
Kalimna West VIC 65 H8
Kalinga QLD 5 J10 7 A10
Kalinjarri NT 127 J9 129 A9
Kalitjukara NT 92 A2 128 K2
Kalka SA 92 A1 118 J7 128 K1
Kalkallo VIC 56 A7 59 D14 66 C1
Kalkarindji (Wave Hill) NT 126 D4
Kalkee VIC 62 K5
Kallangur QLD 5 C9 9 J9
Kallaroo WA 101 B1
Kallista VIC 57 D10
Kalorama VIC 57 D10
Kalpowar QLD 15 K11
Kalumbulani NT 126 C4
Kalumburu WA 117 B11
Kalumpurlpa NT 127 F8
Kalyan SA 89 H11 98 C5
Kalyarr Nat Park NSW 42 F7
Kamarah NSW 43 F11
Kamarooka VIC 63 J10
Kambah ACT 47 H3
Kambalda WA 111 B12 113 J12
Kambalda West WA 111 B12
Kamballup WA 109 H14
Kamma QLD 18 E4
Kamona TAS 75 D11
Kampurarr Pirti WA 118 J5
Kanagulk VIC 58 C4
Kanangra-Boyd Nat Park NSW
    34 G3 36 H7 44 A5
Kandanga QLD 8 A7 13 D13
Kandiwal WA 117 B10
Kandos NSW 36 E7
Kangarilla SA 87 B6 98 D3
Kangaroo Flat SA 83 B13
Kangaroo Flat VIC 59 A12 63 K10
Kangaroo Ground VIC 51 B7 53 C13 57 B9
Kangaroo Hills TAS 75 F10
Kangaroo Island QLD 11 D12
Kangaroo Island SA 88 K5 98 E1
Kangaroo Point NSW 31 G8
Kangaroo Point QLD 2 C4 7 C10
Kangaroo Valley NSW 37 K8 44 C6
Kangawall VIC 58 B3
Kangy Angy NSW 33 G13
Kaniva VIC 42 K2 62 J2 98 F7
Kanmantoo SA 86 K6
Kanni SA 89 F11 98 B5
Kanowna WA 111 A12 113 H12
Kanpi SA 92 B3 128 K3
Kanumbra VIC 64 E2 66 A3
Kanunnah Bridge TAS 76 G4
Kanwal NSW 33 G13
Kanya VIC 59 A8 62 K7
Kanyaka SA 95 G8
Kaoota TAS 71 F12
Kapalga NT 123 C5 124 C6
Kapinnie SA 88 E2
Kapunda SA 86 A6 89 F9 98 B3
Kara Kara Nat Park VIC 59 B8
Karabar NSW 47 G7
Karabeal VIC 58 E5
Karadoc VIC 62 B5
Karalee QLD 6 F3
Karama NT 122 C4
Karana Downs QLD 6 E3 11 B8
Karanja SA 71 C10 73 F13
Karara QLD 13 H10 39 A9
Karatta SA 88 K5
Karawara WA 102 H6
Karawatha QLD 3 J5 7 H11
Kardella VIC 57 K14
Kardella South VIC 57 K14
Kardinya WA 101 J3 104 B4
Kareela NSW 27 J3 31 G8 35 F11
Kariah VIC 59 G8 60 D7
Karijini Nat Park WA 115 E1
Kariong NSW 33 J12
Karkoo SA 88 E3

Karlgarin WA 110 E7 113 K8
Karnak VIC 98 G7
Karonie WA 111 B13 113 H13
Karook VIC 43 K8 63 J12
Karoola TAS 75 E8
Karoon QLD 14 C2 17 K9 21 B9
Karoonda SA 89 H11 98 D5
Karragarra Island QLD 11 C12
Karragullen WA 105 D14
Karragarra Island QLD 11 C12
Karramomus North VIC 63 J13 64 C2
Karrandgin WA 106 A7
Karratha WA 114 B6
Karridale WA 108 F2 110 H2
Karrinyarra NT 128 D5
Karrinyup WA 101 D2 102 B2
Karrku WA 118 G5
Karroun Hill Nature Res WA 113 G8
Kars Springs NSW 37 B9
Karte VIC 42 H1 89 H12 98 D6
Karte Con Park SA 42 H1 89 H12 98 D6
Karuah NSW 37 D11
Karuah Nat Park NSW 37 D11
Karukaki NT 118 G7 128 H2
Karumba QLD 16 F4
Karween VIC 62 B2
Katamatite VIC 43 J9 63 H14 64 B2
Katandra VIC 63 H14 64 B2
Katanning WA 109 C12
Katherine NT 123 J5 124 G6
Kati Thanda-Lake Eyre Nat Park SA 90 G7
Katoomba NSW 34 E4 37 G8
Katrine WA 106 C6
Kattanning WA 110 G5
Kattyoong VIC 62 D4
Katunga VIC 43 J9 63 G13 64 A2
Katyil VIC 62 J4
Kau Rock Nature Res WA 111 G13
Kawarren VIC 59 H10 61 G9
Kayena TAS 74 D7
Kealba VIC 52 D5
Kearsley NSW 33 C11
Kedron QLD 5 C4 5 J10 9 K10 11 A9
Keep River Nat Park NT
    117 D14 124 J1 126 A1
Keera NSW 38 F7
Keilor VIC 51 B1 52 D5 56 C6
Keilor East VIC 52 E6
Keilor North VIC 51 B1 52 C4
Keinbah NSW 45 G4
Keirbar NSW 33 B11
Keith SA 98 F5
Kelerrk NT 124 F3
Kellalac VIC 42 K4 62 J5
Kellatier TAS 77 G8
Kellerberrin WA 107 C11 110 C6 112 J7
Kellervie TAS 69 G4
Kellidie Bay Con Park SA 88 G2
Kelly Hill Con Park SA 88 K5
Kellyville NSW 27 B1 28 D4 35 C9
Kelmscott WA 105 D11 106 E4 110 D3 112 K5
Kelso TAS 74 C6 77 G14
Kelvin NSW 38 H6
Kelvin Grove QLD 2 A2 3 E3 5 K9 7 B9
Kembla Heights NSW 35 K10
Kemps Creek NSW 35 E8
Kempsey NSW 39 J11
Kempton TAS 69 E1 71 B12 73 J14
Kendall NSW 37 A13 39 K11
Kendenup WA 109 G12 110 J6
Kenebri NSW 38 H3
Kenilworth QLD 8 C7 13 E13
Kenley VIC 62 D7
Kenmare VIC 42 J3 62 G4
Kenmore QLD 3 F2 6 D7 11 B9
Kenmore Hills QLD 3 F2 6 C7
Kennedy QLD 17 F11
Kennedy Range Nat Park WA 114 H4
Kennedys Creek VIC 59 J8 60 H7
Kenneth Stirling Con Park SA 85 D12 86 J4
Kennett River VIC 59 J10 61 H11
Kenny ACT 47 B5
Kensington NSW 31 D12 35 D12
Kensington SA 81 G5 84 C7 86 H3
Kensington VIC 51 D3 52 F7
Kensington WA 101 G4 102 H6
Kensington Gardens SA 81 G6 84 C7
Kensington Park SA 84 C7
Kent Island QLD 18 J7
Kent Town SA 80 C4 84 C6
Kentbruck VIC 58 G2 98 K7
Kentdale WA 109 J10
Kenthurst NSW 27 B2 28 C5
Kentlyn NSW 30 K2 35 G9
Kenton WA 109 J10
Kenton Valley SA 86 G5
Kentucky NSW 39 H8
Kentville QLD 10 B5
Kenwick WA 101 J6 103 K9 105 A9
Keperra QLD 3 D2 5 J8 7 A8 9 K9 11 A9
Keppel Bay Islands Nat Park (Scientific) QLD
    15 G11
Keppel Sands QLD 15 H11
Keppoch SA 98 G6
Kerang VIC 42 J6 63 G9
Kerang East VIC 42 J6 63 G9
Kerang South VIC 42 J6 63 G9
Kergunyah VIC 43 K12 64 C6
Kernot VIC 57 K12 64 K2 66 G3
Kerrabee NSW 37 C8
Kerrisdale VIC 64 E1 66 B2
Kerriwah NSW 36 C1 41 J12 43 A12
Kerrs Creek NSW 36 E5
Kerry QLD 11 H9
Kersbrook SA 83 E14 86 G5 89 G9 98 C3
Keswick SA 80 D1 84 D4
Kettering TAS 69 K1 71 F12

Keverstone Nat Park NSW 36 H5 44 A3
Kevin SA 97 G10
Kevington VIC 64 F3 66 C5
Kew NSW 37 A13 39 K11
Kew VIC 51 D4 53 F9
Kewdale WA 101 G6 103 G8
Kewell VIC 62 J5
Kewulyi (Roper Valley) NT 125 G8
Keysborough VIC 51 H6 54 D6 57 F9
Keysbrook WA 106 G3
Khancoban NSW 43 K13 44 G1 65 B9
Khappinghat Nature Res NSW 37 C13
Kholo QLD 6 E1 10 B7
Ki Ki SA 89 J11 98 D4
Kia Ora VIC 58 D7
Kiah NSW 44 J4 65 F14
Kialla NSW 36 J6 44 B4
Kiama NSW 37 K9 44 B7
Kiamal VIC 42 G4 62 D5
Kiandra NSW 44 F2
Kianga NSW 44 G5
Kianga QLD 15 K9
Kiara WA 103 C8
Kiata VIC 42 K3 62 J3 98 F7
Kibbleup WA 109 D13
Kidaman Creek QLD 8 C7
Kidman Park SA 81 F2 82 K3 84 B3
Kidston QLD 17 G9
Kielpa SA 88 D4
Kiewa VIC 64 B6
Kikoira NSW 43 D11
Kilburn SA 81 E4 82 H5 86 G2
Kilcoy QLD 8 F6 13 F12
Kilcunda VIC 66 H2
Kilgra NSW 39 B12
Kilimiraka NT 124 B2
Kilkenny SA 81 F3 82 J3 84 A3
Kilkivan QLD 13 D12
Killabakh NSW 37 B13
Killara NSW 27 D5 29 G10 35 C11
Killara VIC 57 C11
Killarney QLD 10 K4 13 J12 39 A11
Killarney VIC 58 H6 60 F1
Killarney Heights NSW 27 D6 29 G12 35 C11
Killarney Vale NSW 33 H13
Killcare NSW 33 J13
Killiecrankie TAS 78 A4
Killingworth NSW 33 C12 37 E11 45 K6
Killora TAS 69 J1 71 F13
Kilmany VIC 64 J5 66 F7
Kilmore VIC 59 C14 66 B1
Kimba SA 88 C4 94 K4
Kimberley TAS 73 A10 74 F4 77 J13
Kimburra QLD 14 C3 17 K10 21 A10
Kin Kin QLD 13 E11
Kinchega Nat Park NSW 40 J3 42 B3
Kinchela NSW 39 J12
Kincumber NSW 33 J13
Kindred TAS 74 D3 77 H11
King Ash Bay NT 125 J12 127 A12
King Island QLD 17 A9 19 H5
King Island TAS 78 C1
King Leopold Ranges Con Park WA 117 F10
King River WA 109 J13
King Valley VIC 64 D4
Kingaroy QLD 13 E11
Kingfisher Bay QLD 13 B13
Kinglake VIC 57 A10 64 G1 66 C2
Kinglake Central VIC 57 A10 64 G1 66 C2
Kinglake East VIC 57 A10
Kinglake Nat Park VIC 57 A10 64 G1 66 C1
Kinglake West VIC 64 G1 66 C1
Kingoonya SA 94 D2 97 D14
Kingower VIC 59 A10 63 K9
Kings Canyon Resort NT 128 G5
Kings Creek Caravan Park NT 128 G5
Kings Cross NSW 26 C4 29 K12 31 B12 35 D11
Kings Langley NSW 27 C1 28 F4
Kings Meadows TAS 73 A14 75 F8
Kings Park NSW 28 F3
Kings Park SA 84 E5
Kings Park VIC 52 D4
Kings Park WA 100 B1
Kings Plains Nat Park NSW 39 D8
Kings Point NSW 44 D6
Kingsborough QLD 17 E10
Kingsbury VIC 51 B4 53 D10 57 C8
Kingscliff NSW 11 J14 13 J14 39 A14
Kingscote SA 88 J6 98 E1
Kingsdale NSW 36 K6 44 B4
Kingsford NSW 27 G6 31 D12 35 D12
Kingsgrove NSW 31 E8
Kingsholme QLD 11 E11
Kingsley WA 101 B2
Kingsthorpe QLD 13 G11
Kingston ACT 46 D4 47 E5
Kingston QLD 3 K5 7 J12 11 C10
Kingston TAS 69 H1 71 E13
Kingston VIC 59 D11
Kingston Park SA 84 H2
Kingston SE SA 98 G4
Kingston-on-Murray SA 89 F12 98 B5
Kingstown NSW 39 G8
Kingsvale NSW 36 J3 43 F14 44 B1
Kingswood NSW 34 D7
Kingswood SA 81 H4 84 E6
Kinimakatka VIC 62 J3
Kinlyside ACT 47 A3
Kinnabulla VIC 62 G6
Kinrara Nat Park QLD 17 G10
Kippa-Ring QLD 5 B11
Kipper QLD 8 J4
Kirkstall VIC 58 H5 60 E1
Kirrama Nat Park QLD 17 F11
Kirrawee NSW 27 J3 31 H8
Kirribilli NSW 27 H12 31 B12
Kirup WA 108 D5
Kital QLD 10 G2

Kitchener NSW 33 C11 45 J4
Kithbrook VIC 63 K14 64 D2
Kittens SA 96 B7
Kiwirrkurra WA 118 D5
Kleinton QLD 8 K1 10 A1
Klemzig SA 81 E5 82 J6 84 A6
Knapp Creek Con Park QLD 10 H7
Knowsley VIC 59 A13 63 K11
Knoxfield VIC 53 J14 57 D9
Koah QLD 18 D4
Koala Park QLD 24 G5
Kodj Kodjin WA 107 B11
Koetong VIC 43 K12 64 B7
Kogan QLD 13 F9
Kogarah NSW 27 H4 31 E9
Kogarah Bay NSW 31 F9
Koimbo VIC 42 G4 62 D6
Kojonup WA 109 D10 110 G5
Kokotungo QLD 13 F9
Kolan QLD 13 A12 15 K12
Kolan South QLD 13 A12 15 K12
Koloona NSW 38 D7
Kolorbidahdah NT 125 C9
Komungla NSW 36 K6 44 C4
Kondalilla Nat Park QLD 9 C8
Kondinin WA 107 G13 110 E6 113 K8
Kongorong SA 98 J5
Kongwak VIC 66 H3
Konong Wootong VIC 58 E3
Konupa QLD 14 K1 21 H9
Kookynie WA 113 F12
Koolamarra QLD 16 J4 20 A4
Koolan WA 116 D7
Koolendong Valley NT 124 H2
Koolewong NSW 33 J12
Kooloonong VIC 62 D7
Kooltandra QLD 15 F9
Koolunga SA 89 D8
Koolyanobbing WA 111 B8 113 H9
Koombooloomba QLD 17 F11 18 K4
Koombooloomba Dam QLD 18 K4
Koombooloomba Nat Park QLD 17 F11 18 K3
Koonadgin WA 107 C14
Koonda VIC 63 J14 64 C2
Koondoola WA 101 C4 102 A5
Koondrook VIC 42 J7 63 F10
Koongamia WA 103 D11
Koongawa SA 88 C3 94 K3
Koonoomoo VIC 63 G14 64 A2
Koonunga SA 86 A6
Koonwarra VIC 66 H4
Koonya TAS 69 J4
Kooraban Nat Park NSW 44 G5 65 C14
Koorabye WA 117 H9
Kooragang NSW 33 B14
Kooralbyn QLD 11 G8 13 H13
Koorarawalyee WA 111 B9 113 J10
Koorawatha NSW 36 H4 43 E14
Koorawatha Nature Res NSW 36 H4 43 E14 44 A2
Koorboora QLD 17 E9
Koorda WA 110 B5 112 H7
Kooreh VIC 59 A9 63 K8
Kooringal QLD 9 K13 11 A13
Koorkab VIC 42 G5 62 C7
Koorlong VIC 62 B4
Kooroocheang VIC 59 C11
Kootingal NSW 38 J7
Koo-Wee-Rup VIC 55 K13 57 H11 64 J2 66 F2
Koo-Wee-Rup North VIC 57 G11
Kooyong VIC 53 H10
Kooyoora State Park VIC 63 K9
Kopi SA 88 D3 94 K3
Koppio SA 88 F3
Korbel WA 107 C13 110 C6 113 J8
Koreelah Nat Park NSW 10 J5 13 J12 39 A11
Koriella VIC 64 F2 66 B3
Korobeit VIC 56 A3
Koroit VIC 58 H6 60 E2
Korong Vale VIC 42 K6 63 J9
Koroop VIC 42 J7 63 G10
Korora Bay NSW 39 G12
Korrak Korrak VIC 63 G8
Korrelocking WA 107 A10
Korumburra VIC 57 K13 64 K2 66 G3
Korumburra South VIC 57 K14
Korunye SA 86 C1
Kosciuszko Nat Park NSW 43 H14 44 E1 48 G1 65 B10
Kotta VIC 42 K7 63 H11
Kotupna VIC 43 K8 63 H12 64 B1
Koumala QLD 15 E8
Koumala South QLD 15 E8
Kowanyama QLD 16 C5 19 K1
Kowguran QLD 13 D8
Kowrowa QLD 18 D4
Kowtah WA 113 E12
Koyuga VIC 63 H12
Krambach NSW 37 C12
Kringin SA 89 H13 98 C6
Kroombit Tops Nat Park QLD 15 J11
Krowera VIC 57 K12 64 K2 66 G3
Kubumi NT 125 C8
Kubuyirr NT 124 F2
Kudantinga NT 124 G1
Kudardup WA 108 F2 110 H2
Kudla SA 86 E3
Kuender WA 107 J14
Kukerin WA 107 K13 109 A14 110 F6
Kulang NT 128 H1
Kulde SA 89 H10 98 D4
Kulgera NT 128 K7
Kulgera Rail Head NT 93 A10
Kulgera Roadhouse NT 128 K7
Kulikup WA 109 D8
Kulin WA 107 H13 110 E6
Kulinchin QLD 16 A5 19 H1
Kulitjara SA 93 C8

Kulja WA 110 A5 112 H7
Kulkami SA 89 H12 98 D5
Kulkyne VIC 42 F4 62 C5
Kulla (McIlwraith Range) Nat Park (CYPAL) QLD 19 G4
Kulliparu SA 88 C1 97 K13
Kulliparu Con Park SA 88 C1 94 J1 97 J13
Kulnine VIC 42 F2 62 A2 89 F14 98 B7
Kulnine East VIC 42 F2 62 A3
Kulnura NSW 33 G11 37 F10
Kulpara SA 88 E7 98 A2
Kulpi QLD 13 F11
Kulpitarra NT 128 F5
Kultanaby SA 94 D3
Kultchill NT 124 G2
Kulwin VIC 42 G4 62 D6
Kulyalling WA 107 G8
Kumarina Roadhouse WA 115 H9
Kumbarilla QLD 13 F9
Kumbatine Nat Park NSW 39 J11
Kumbia QLD 13 E11
Kunamata SA 92 B4
Kunapula NT 128 J1
Kunat QLD 63 F8
Kunatjara SA 92 B1 118 J7
Kunda QLD 10 G2
Kundabung NSW 39 J11
Kundana WA 113 H11
Kundat Djaru WA 117 H14
Kundora QLD 20 B4
Kungala NSW 39 F12
Kungarrewari NT 124 C7
Kunghur NSW 39 B13
Kungkayunti NT 128 F4
Kunjin WA 107 F11
Kunlara SA 89 G11 98 C5
Kunmarnara Bore WA 118 J6
Kununoppin WA 107 A12
Kununurra WA 117 D14
Kunwarara QLD 15 G10
Kunytjanu SA 92 C2 118 K7
Kupungarri WA 117 E10
Kupuru SA 118 J7
Kuraby QLD 3 J5 7 H11 11 C10
Kuranda QLD 17 D11 18 D4
Kuranda Nat Park QLD 17 D10
Kuraya NT 127 H9
Kurbayia QLD 20 B3
Ku-ring-gai Chase Nat Park NSW 27 A6 29 A11 33 K11 35 A11 37 G10
Kurkatingara NT 128 J1
Kurkutjara NT 92 A2 128 K2
Kurmond NSW 34 B7
Kurnell NSW 27 J6 31 G11 35 E12
Kurow QLD 17 F11
Kurracca VIC 63 J8
Kurracca West VIC 42 K6 63 J8
Kurrajong NSW 34 B6 37 G9
Kurrajong NT 129 C9
Kurrajong WA 113 E11
Kurrajong Heights NSW 34 B6
Kurralta Park SA 81 H3 84 D4
Kurrawang WA 111 B11 113 H11
Kurri Kurri NSW 33 B12 37 E10 45 H5
Kurrimine QLD 17 F11 18 J6
Kurrimine Beach Nat Park QLD 18 J6
Kurumbul QLD 13 J9
Kurwongbah QLD 9 J8 4 B6
Kutini Payamu (Iron Range) Nat Park (CYPAL) QLD 19 E4
Kutjurntari WA 118 G6 128 H1
Kutkububba WA 113 B10
Kuttabul QLD 15 D8
Kuwuma NT 124 E3
Kuy NT 124 F2
Kweda WA 107 F10
Kwelkan WA 107 A12
Kwiambal Nat Park NSW 13 K9 38 C7
Kwinana WA 106 F3 110 D3 112 K5
Kwinana Beach WA 104 J2
Kwinana Town Centre WA 104 K4
Kwobrup WA 109 C14
Kwolyin WA 107 D11
Kwombom NT 124 F3
Kyabram VIC 43 K8 63 J12
Kyalite NSW 42 G6 63 D8
Kyancutta SA 88 C2 94 K2
Kybeyan NSW 44 G4 65 C13
Kybunga SA 89 E8 98 A3
Kybybolite SA 58 B1 98 G6
Kydra NSW 44 G3 65 C12
Kyeema Con Park SA 87 D6
Kyle Bay NSW 31 F8
Kylie WA 109 B10
Kyneton VIC 59 C12
Kynuna QLD 20 C6
Kyogle NSW 13 J13 39 B12
Kyvalley VIC 63 H12
Kywong NSW 43 G11

L

La Perouse NSW 27 H6 31 F12 35 E12
Laanecoorie VIC 59 A10 63 K9
Laang VIC 58 H7 60 F4
Labertouche VIC 57 F13 64 J2 66 F3
Labillardiere Penninsula TAS 71 J12
Labrador QLD 11 F13 24 C4
Lacepede Bay SA 98 G4
Lacepede Islands WA 116 E5
Laceys Creek QLD 4 A2
Lachlan TAS 71 D11
Lackrana TAS 78 C6
Lackrana Con Area TAS 78 C6
La-Djadarr Bay WA 116 E7
Lady Barron TAS 78 D6

Lady Bay SA 87 F2
Lady Elliott Island QLD 15 J13
Lady Musgrave Island QLD 15 J13
Ladys Pass VIC 59 A13
Ladysmith NSW 43 H12
Laen VIC 42 K4 62 J6
Laggan NSW 36 J6 44 B4
Lagoon Flat QLD 39 C8
Lagoon Island QLD 11 D12
Laguna NSW 33 E9 37 E10
Laguna Bay QLD 9 A10
Laguna Quays QLD 14 C7 17 K14 21 B14
Lah VIC 42 K4 62 H5
Laharum VIC 58 B5
Laheys Creek NSW 36 C6
Laidley QLD 10 C5 13 G12
Lajamanu NT 126 E3
Lake Acraman SA 94 G2 97 G14
Lake Albacutya VIC 42 J3 62 G4
Lake Amadeus NT 128 H4
Lake Argyle WA 117 E14
Lake Argyle Resort WA 117 E14
Lake Atkinsons QLD 8 K4 10 A4
Lake Austin WA 113 D8
Lake Ballard WA 113 F11
Lake Barambah QLD 8 A1
Lake Barlee WA 113 F10
Lake Baroon QLD 9 D8
Lake Barrine QLD 18 F6
Lake Bathurst NSW 44 C4
Lake Beatrice Con Area SA 72 E6
Lake Biddy WA 111 F8
Lake Bindegolly Nat Park QLD 23 F10
Lake Blanche SA 22 J2 91 J11
Lake Boga VIC 42 H6 63 F8
Lake Bolac VIC 58 E7 60 A5
Lake Borumba QLD 8 B6
Lake Broadwater Con Park QLD 13 F10
Lake Buchanan QLD 14 E3 21 C11
Lake Buloke VIC 42 K5 62 J6
Lake Burley Griffin ACT 48 C4
Lake Burragorang NSW 34 F5
Lake Burrendong NSW 36 D5
Lake Burrinjuck NSW 44 C2
Lake Cadibarrawirracanna SA 90 H3
Lake Callabonna SA 22 K2 91 K12 95 A12
Lake Campion WA 107 A14
Lake Campion Nature Res WA 107 A14 110 B7 113 H9
Lake Carey WA 113 F13
Lake Cargelligo NSW 43 C10
Lake Carnegie WA 113 A13 115 K13
Lake Cathie NSW 37 A14 39 K12
Lake Cawndilla NSW 40 J3 42 B3
Lake Charm VIC 42 J6 63 F9
Lake Clarendon QLD 10 B4
Lake Clifton WA 106 J2
Lake Colac VIC 59 H10 61 E9
Lake Colongulac VIC 60 D7
Lake Conjola NSW 44 D6
Lake Conjola West NSW 44 D5
Lake Coolmunda QLD 39 A8
Lake Cootharaba QLD 13 D14
Lake Copeton NSW 38 E7
Lake Corangamite VIC 59 G9 61 D8
Lake Cowal NSW 36 G1 43 D12
Lake Cowan WA 111 C12 113 J12
Lake Crescent TAS 73 G14
Lake Cressbrook QLD 8 J3
Lake Dartmouth QLD 21 J10 23 A12
Lake Dartmouth VIC 64 D7
Lake Dennis WA 118 B7 126 K1 128 B1
Lake Disappointment WA 115 F13
Lake Dundas WA 111 E12
Lake Dutton SA 94 F6
Lake Dyer QLD 10 C4
Lake Eacham QLD 18 F4
Lake Echo TAS 73 F11
Lake Eildon VIC 64 E3 66 A4
Lake Eildon Nat Park VIC 64 F3 66 B4
Lake Etamunbanie SA 22 B2 91 B11
Lake Eucumbene NSW 43 K14 44 F2 65 B11
Lake Everard SA 94 E2 97 F14
Lake Eyre North SA 90 G6
Lake Eyre South SA 90 J6
Lake Finnis NT 123 C3
Lake Finniss SA 94 F5
Lake Frome SA 95 C11
Lake Frome Con Park SA 98 J5
Lake Frome Reg Res SA 95 D11
Lake Gairdner SA 97 E14 94 E3
Lake Gairdner Nat Park SA 94 E2 97 E14
Lake Galilee QLD 14 F3 21 D11
Lake George NSW 44 C4 48 A7
Lake Gilles SA 88 B5 94 J5
Lake Gilles Con Park SA 88 C5 94 J5
Lake Ginninderra ACT 48 B4
Lake Glenbawn NSW 37 C10
Lake Goldsmith VIC 59 E9
Lake Goran NSW 38 J5
Lake Gordon TAS 70 C7
Lake Goyder (Coolangirie) SA 22 D2
Lake Grace WA 107 K14 110 F7
Lake Grahamstown NSW 33 A14
Lake Gregory SA 22 H1 91 H10
Lake Gregory WA 117 K12
Lake Harris SA 94 D2 97 D14
Lake Harry SA 91 K8
Lake Hart SA 94 D4
Lake Hindmarsh VIC 42 K3 62 H4
Lake Hope WA 111 E10 113 K10
Lake Hume NSW 64 B6
Lake Jindabyne NSW 44 G2 65 C10
Lake Johnston WA 111 D10 113 K11
Lake Katherine NT 125 F10
Lake Keepit NSW 38 H6
Lake King WA 111 F9
Lake King Nature Res WA 111 F8

Lake King William TAS 73 G9
Lake Kurwongbah QLD 9 J9
Lake Leaghur NSW 42 D5
Lake Leake TAS 69 A4 75 K11
Lake Lefroy WA 111 B12 113 J12
Lake Leslie QLD 10 J1 39 A10
Lake Lewis NT 128 E6
Lake Liddell NSW 37 C9
Lake Linlithgow VIC 60 A1
Lake Lonsdale VIC 58 B6
Lake Lyall NSW 34 C2
Lake Macdonald WA 118 F6 128 F1
Lake MacFarlane SA 94 F5
Lake Machattie QLD 20 H3
Lake Mackay WA 118 D6 128 D1
Lake Macleod WA 114 G2
Lake Macquarie NSW 33 E13
Lake Magenta Nature Res WA 111 G8
Lake Manchester QLD 6 C2 10 B7
Lake Maraboon QLD 14 H6 21 F14
Lake Margaret TAS 72 E5
Lake Marmal VIC 42 K6 63 H8
Lake Maroon QLD 10 H6
Lake Marrakoonamooka SA 22 E2
Lake Mason WA 113 D9
Lake Maurice SA 92 K5 96 A5
Lake Mcdonald QLD 9 A9
Lake Menindee NSW 40 J3 42 A3
Lake Meran VIC 42 J6 63 G9
Lake Mitchell QLD 18 D2
Lake Mokoan VIC 64 C3
Lake Moogerah QLD 10 G5
Lake Moore WA 112 F7
Lake Muir WA 109 G8
Lake Muir Nat Park WA 109 G8 110 J4
Lake Muir Nature Res WA 109 G9
Lake Mundi VIC 58 E1 98 J6
Lake Munmorah NSW 33 F13 37 F11
Lake Murphy Con Park QLD 12 B7
Lake Neale NT 128 G3
Lake Newland Con Park SA 88 D1 94 K1 97 K13
Lake Noondie WA 113 E9
Lake Pedder TAS 70 E7
Lake Raeside WA 113 E11
Lake Rowallan TAS 73 D9 74 J3
Lake Rowan VIC 43 K10 64 B3
Lake Saint Clair NSW 45 B3
Lake Samsonvale QLD 9 J9
Lake Seabrook WA 111 B9 113 H10
Lake Shaster Nature Res WA 111 G10
Lake Somerset QLD 8 G6
Lake Sorell TAS 69 B1 73 F14
Lake St Clair NSW 37 C10
Lake St Clair TAS 73 F4 74 K3
Lake Tabourie NSW 44 E6
Lake Thomas SA 20 K1
Lake Throssell WA 119 B2
Lake Tinaroo QLD 18 F3
Lake Torrens SA 94 D7
Lake Torrens Nat Park SA 94 C7
Lake Tuggeranong ACT 48 D4
Lake Tyers VIC 65 H9
Lake Tyers State Park VIC 65 H9
Lake Tyrell VIC 42 H4 62 E6
Lake Uloowaranie SA 20 K3 22 B1 91 B11
Lake Victoria NSW 42 E2 62 A2 89 E14 98 A7
Lake View SA 89 D8 98 A2
Lake Wellington VIC 64 J7
Lake Wells WA 113 B14 119 A1
Lake Weyba QLD 9 A10
Lake White WA 118 C7 126 K1 128 B1
Lake Wills WA 118 C6
Lake Windemere NSW 36 D7
Lake Wivenhoe QLD 8 J6 10 A6 13 F12
Lake Woods NT 127 D8
Lake Wyangala NSW 36 H5
Lake Wyangan NSW 43 E10
Lake Wyara QLD 23 G10
Lake Yamma Yamma (Mackillop) QLD 20 K5 22 B5
Lake Yindinlgooda WA 111 A12 113 H12
Lake Younghusband SA 94 D4
Lakefield Nat Park see Rinyirru Nat Park QLD
Lakeland QLD 17 C10 19 K6
Lakemba NSW 31 D8 35 E11
Lakes Entrance VIC 65 H8
Lakeside VIC 57 E11
Lakeview NSW 33 E13
Lakewood Estate NSW 43 K14 44 G2 65 C10
Lal Lal VIC 59 E11
Lalbert VIC 42 J5 63 F8
Lalbert Road VIC 42 H5
Lalla TAS 75 E8
Lalor VIC 53 B9
Lalor Park NSW 28 F4 35 D9
Lama Lama Nat Park (CYPAL) QLD 17 A8 19 H4
Lamb Island QLD 11 C12
Lameroo SA 42 H1 89 J12 98 D6
Lamington QLD 11 J9 39 A12
Lamington Nat Park QLD 11 J11 13 J13 39 A12
Lamplough VIC 59 C9
Lana QLD 21 D8
Lancaster VIC 63 J12 64 B1
Lancefield VIC 59 C13
Lancelin WA 110 B2 112 H4
Lancevale QLD 14 H3 21 F11
Landsborough QLD 8 E9 13 E13
Landsborough VIC 59 B8
Landsdale WA 101 B4
Lane Cove NSW 27 E5 29 H10 35 C11
Lane Cove Nat Park NSW 27 D4
Lane Cove West NSW 29 H10
Lane Poole Res WA 106 J4
Lane Poole Reserve WA 110 F4
Lanena-Blackwall TAS 74 F7
Lang Lang VIC 57 H12 64 K2 66 G2
Langarra NT 125 C10

Langford WA 101 J5 103 K8 105 A8
Langhorne Creek SA 89 J9 98 D3
Langkoop VIC 58 C1
Langlo Crossing QLD 21 K11 23 A13
Langloh TAS 71 B10 73 J12
Langwarrin VIC 54 J6 57 G9
Lankeys Creek NSW 43 J13 65 A8
Lansdowne NSW 27 F2 30 C5 37 B13
Lansvale NSW 30 C5 35 E10
Lapaku WA 118 G6
Lapoinya TAS 77 F8
Lappa QLD 17 E10
Lapstone NSW 34 D6
Lara VIC 56 F3 59 G12 61 C14
Laramba NT 128 D6
Larapinta QLD 7 H9
Laravale QLD 11 G9
Lardner VIC 57 H14
Largs NSW 33 A12
Largs Bay SA 81 D1 82 G1 86 G1
Largs North SA 82 F2
Larke Quarry Con Park QLD 20 E7
Larpent VIC 59 H9 61 F9
Larrakeyah NT 122 H1
Larras Lee NSW 36 E5
Larrimah NT 124 H7 126 A7
Lascelles VIC 42 J4 62 F6
Lasseters Cave NT 128 H2
Laterite Con Park WA 117 C10
Latham ACT 47 B2
Latham WA 112 G6
Lathami Con Park SA 88 J6
Lathlain WA 102 G7
Latrobe TAS 74 D4 77 H12
Lauderdale TAS 69 H2 71 E14
Launceston TAS 73 A14 75 F8
Launching Place VIC 57 C12 64 H2 66 D3
Laura QLD 17 C9 19 K5
Laura SA 89 C8 95 K8
Laura Bay SA 97 C11
Laurieton NSW 37 B14 39 K11
Lauriston VIC 59 C12
Lavers Hill VIC 59 J9 61 J8
Laverton VIC 52 H3 56 D6
Laverton WA 113 E13
Laverton North VIC 52 H3
Lavington NSW 64 A6
Lawitta TAS 71 D11
Lawler VIC 42 K4 62 J6
Lawlers WA 113 D10
Lawley River Nat Park WA 117 B10
Lawloit VIC 42 K2 62 J3
Lawnton QLD 5 D8 9 J9
Lawrence NSW 39 D12
Lawrenny TAS 71 B10 73 J12
Lawson ACT 47 C4
Lawson NSW 34 D5 37 G8
Leabrook SA 84 C7
Leadville NSW 36 B6
Leaghur VIC 63 G9
Leaghur State Park VIC 63 G9
Leanyer NT 122 C6
Learmonth VIC 59 D10
Learmonth WA 114 D2
Leawood Gardens SA 84 E7
Lebrina TAS 75 D8
Leda WA 104 K3
Ledge Point WA 106 A1 110 B2 112 J5
Ledknapper Crossing NSW 23 J13 41 B10
Ledknapper Nature Res NSW
   12 K1 23 H14 41 B10
Leedawooloo WA 117 H13
Leederville WA 102 E4
Leeka TAS 78 B4
Leeman WA 112 G4
Leeming WA 101 J4 104 B5
Leeor VIC 62 J1
Leeton NSW 43 F10
Leeuwin-Naturaliste Nat Park WA
   108 C1 110 H2
Lefevre Peninsula SA 81 B2 82 D2
Lefroy TAS 74 C7
Legana TAS 73 A13 74 E7
Legerwood TAS 75 D11
Legume NSW 64 K4 13 J12 39 A11
Legunia TAS 75 E12
Leichhardt NSW 27 F5 31 C10 35 D11
Leichhardt QLD 6 H1
Leigh Creek SA 95 C8
Leighton SA 89 D9
Leila Crossing NT 125 K11 127 B11
Leinster WA 113 D11
Leitchville VIC 42 J7 63 G10
Leith TAS 74 D3 77 G11
Leitpar VIC 42 G4 62 D6
Lemana TAS 73 B11 74 F5 77 K13
Lemon Tree Passage NSW 37 E12
Lemont TAS 69 C3
Leneva VIC 64 B6
Lennox Head NSW 13 K14 39 B14
Lenswood SA 85 C14 86 H4
Leonards Hill VIC 59 D11
Leonay NSW 34 D7
Leongatha VIC 57 K14 64 K3 66 G4
Leongatha South VIC 66 H4
Leonora WA 113 E11
Leopold VIC 56 G4 59 G12
Leppington NSW 35 F8
Leprena TAS 71 J11
Lerderderg State Park VIC 56 A3 59 D12
Leslie Manor VIC 59 G9 61 D8
Leslie Vale TAS 69 H1 71 E12
Lesmurdie WA 103 H12
Lesmurdie Nat Park WA 101 G7 103 H11
Lesueur Con Park SA 88 K7 98 E2
Lesueur Nat Park WA 112 G4
Letchworth NSW 47 G7
Lethbridge VIC 56 E1 59 F11 61 B13

Leumeah NSW 30 J1 35 F9
Leura NSW 34 D4 37 G8
Leven Canyon Reg Res TAS 72 A7 74 E2 77 J10
Levendale TAS 69 E3 71 B14
Lewana WA 108 D5
Lewinsbrook NSW 45 C6
Lewisham NSW 31 C10
Lewisham TAS 69 G3 71 D14
Lewiston SA 86 D2
Lexia WA 101 B5
Lexton VIC 59 C9
Leyburn QLD 13 H10
Liawenee TAS 73 E11 74 J5
Licola VIC 64 G5 66 D6
Lidcombe NSW 27 F3 28 K7 30 B7 35 D10
Lidsdale NSW 34 B1
Liena TAS 73 B9 74 G3 77 K11
Lietinna TAS 75 D10
Liffey TAS 73 C12 74 H6
Light Pass SA 86 B7
Lightning Ridge NSW 41 B13
Likkaparta NT 127 G9
Lileah TAS 76 F5
Lilli Pilli NSW 31 J9 35 F11
Lillico TAS 74 D3 77 G11
Lillimur VIC 42 K2 62 J2
Lillimur South VIC 62 J2
Lilydale QLD 10 C2
Lilydale TAS 75 E9
Lilydale VIC 57 C10
Lilyfield NSW 29 K10 31 B10
Lilyvale NSW 35 G10
Lima VIC 64 D3
Lima South VIC 64 D3
Limbri NSW 39 J8
Lime Lake WA 109 B11
Limeburners Creek Nat Park NSW
   37 A14 39 K12
Limekilns NSW 36 F7
Limerick NSW 36 H6 44 A4
Limestone NSW 64 F2 66 B2
Limevale QLD 13 J10 39 B8
Limmen Bight NT 125 G11
Limmen Nat Park NT 125 G10 127 A10
Limpinwood NSW 11 J11
Lincoln Con Park SA 88 G3
Lincoln Nat Park SA 88 G3
Lind Nat Park VIC 65 G11
Linda TAS 72 F6
Lindeman Island QLD 15 C8
Lindeman Islands Nat Park QLD 15 C8
Linden NSW 34 D5
Linden Park SA 84 D7
Lindenow VIC 64 H7
Lindesay Creek NSW 10 K6
Lindesay View NSW 11 K8 39 A12
Lindfield NSW 27 D5 29 G10 35 C11
Lindisfarne TAS 69 G1 71 D13
Lindum QLD 5 K13 7 B13
Line Creek NT 124 J3 126 A3
Linga VIC 42 H3 62 E3
Lingara NT 124 K3 126 B3
Linley Point NSW 29 J10 31 A10
Linton VIC 59 E9
Linton Nature Res NSW 38 G7
Linville QLD 8 E4 13 E12
Lipson SA 88 F4
Liptrap VIC 66 J4
Lisarow NSW 45 G4
Lisle TAS 75 D9
Lismore NSW 13 K14 39 F13
Lismore VIC 59 F9 61 B8
Liston QLD 13 J11 39 B10
Litchfield VIC 42 K5 62 J6
Litchfield Nat Park NT 123 F1 124 E3
Lithgow NSW 34 C2 36 F7
Littabella Nat Park QLD 15 K12
Little Ballroom TAS 75 C9
Little Bay NSW 31 F12
Little Billabong NSW 43 H12
Little Boobyalla River Con Area TAS
   75 B12 78 K4
Little Desert Nat Park VIC 58 A1 62 K1 98 G7
Little Dip Con Park SA 98 H4
Little Grove WA 110 K6
Little Hartley NSW 33 J11
Little Mulgrave QLD 17 E11 18 F4
Little Puta Puta NT 128 J2
Little River VIC 56 E4 59 F12
Little Swanport TAS 69 D5
Little Topar NSW 40 H3
Little Well (Aluralkwa) NT 129 G10
Littlehampton SA 85 H14 86 K5
Littlemore QLD 15 J12
Liverpool NSW 27 G1 30 D3 35 E9
Livesey Crossing WA 107 C10
Livingstone Nat Park NSW 43 H12
Lizard Island QLD 17 A10 19 H7
Llandaff TAS 69 A6 75 K14
Llandilo NSW 34 C7
Llangothlin NSW 39 F9
Llewellyn TAS 75 J10
Loadstone NSW 11 K9
Loamside QLD 10 L D7
Lobethal SA 86 H5 89 H9 98 C3
Loccota TAS 78 D5
Loch VIC 57 J13 64 K2 66 G3
Loch Lea TAS 74 E7
Loch Lomond QLD 10 K3 13 J12
Loch Sport VIC 64 J7
Lochern Nat Park QLD 21 G8
Lochiel NSW 44 J4 65 E14
Lochiel SA 89 E8 98 A2
Lochinvar NSW 33 A11 37 D11 45 G5
Lochnagar QLD 14 H3 21 F11
Lock SA 88 D3
Lockhart NSW 43 H11
Lockhart River QLD 19 E4

Lockington VIC 42 K7 63 H11
Lockleys SA 81 G2 84 C3 86 H1
Lockridge WA 101 D6 103 C8
Lockrose QLD 10 B5
Locksley VIC 63 K13 64 D1
Lockwood NSW 59 A11 63 K10
Lockwood South VIC 59 A11
Lockyer QLD 10 B2
Lockyer Waters QLD 10 A4
Loddon QLD 21 K11 23 B13
Loddon Vale VIC 42 J6 63 H9
Loftus NSW 27 K3 30 J7 35 F10
Logan QLD 13 G13
Logan VIC 59 A9 63 K8
Logan Central QLD 3 J5 7 J12
Logan Lagoon Con Area TAS 78 D7
Logan Village QLD 11 E11
Loganholme QLD 3 K7 11 D11
Loganlea QLD 3 K6 7 K13 11 D10
Logie Brae NSW 43 H9 63 F13
Loira TAS 74 E7
Lombadina WA 116 E6
Lomos WA 107 F10
London Lakes TAS 73 F10
Londonderry NSW 34 C7
Long Beach NSW 44 E5
Long Flat NSW 37 A13 39 K11
Long Gully VIC 57 B11
Long Island QLD 9 F10 11 D12
Long Plains SA 89 F8 98 B2
Long Pocket QLD 3 E3 7 D9
Long Point NSW 30 G3
Long Reach TAS 74 D7
Longford NSW 39 H8
Longford TAS 73 B14 75 G8
Longford VIC 64 J6 66 F7
Longlea VIC 59 A12 63 K10
Longley TAS 69 H1 71 E12
Longreach QLD 14 H1 21 F9
Longueville NSW 29 J10 31 A10
Longwarry VIC 57 G13 64 J2 66 F3
Longwarry North VIC 57 F13
Longwood SA 81 K7 85 H10 86 K3 87 A7
Longwood VIC 63 K13 64 D1
Lonnavale TAS 71 E10
Lonsdale SA 84 K1 87 B4
Looma WA 117 G8
Loomberah NSW 38 J7
Loongana QLD 72 A7 74 F2 77 J10
Loongana WA 119 F5
Loorana TAS 78 C1
Lorinna TAS 73 B8 74 G3 77 K11
Lorna Glen Con Park WA 113 A11
Lorne SA 89 F8 98 B2
Lorne VIC 59 J11 61 G12
Lorquon VIC 62 H3
Lostock NSW 37 C10 45 A5
Lota QLD 3 E7 7 C14 11 B11
Lottah TAS 75 D13
Loughnan Nature Res NSW 43 D9
Louisville TAS 69 E4
Louth NSW 41 E8
Louth Bay SA 88 F3
Loveday SA 89 F12 98 B6
Lovett Bay NSW 27 A7 29 B13
Low Head TAS 74 C6 77 G14
Low Isles QLD 18 A3
Lowan Vale SA 42 K1
Lowana TAS 72 G4
Lowden WA 108 C5 110 G3
Lowdina TAS 69 F2 71 C13
Lower Barrington TAS 74 E3 77 H11
Lower Beechmont QLD 11 G11
Lower Belford NSW 33 A10
Lower Bendoc VIC 65 F11
Lower Beulah TAS 73 A10 74 F4 77 K12
Lower Bucca NSW 39 F12
Lower Cresswell QLD 8 G5
Lower Gellibrand VIC 59 K8 60 J7
Lower Glenelg Nat Park VIC 58 G2 98 K6
Lower Hawkesbury NSW 45 J9
Lower Hermitage SA 83 E12 86 G4
Lower Heytesbury VIC 58 J7 60 H5
Lower Hunter Valley Vineyards NSW 33 B10
Lower Longley TAS 71 E12
Lower Mangrove NSW 33 J11
Lower Marshes TAS 69 D1 71 A12 73 H14
Lower Mitcham SA 84 E5
Lower Molonglo Nature Res ACT 47 D2 48 B4
Lower Mookerawa NSW 36 D5
Lower Mount Hicks TAS 64 E3 66 A4
Lower Mount Walker QLD 10 D5
Lower Norton SA 58 A5 62 K4
Lower Plenty VIC 53 E11
Lower Portland NSW 33 K9 35 A8
Lower South East Marine Park SA 98 J5
Lower Templestowe VIC 53 E12
Lower Turners Marsh TAS 75 D8
Lower Wilmot TAS 74 E3 77 J11
Lower Yorke Peninsula Marine Park SA
   88 H6 98 D1
Lowesdale NSW 43 J10 64 A4
Lowlands NSW 34 B7 41 K9 43 C9
Lowmead QLD 15 K12
Lowood QLD 10 B6
Lowther NSW 34 D2
Loxford NSW 45 H5
Loxton SA 42 F1 89 G12 98 B6
Loyetea TAS 74 E2 77 H10
Lubeck VIC 58 A6 62 K5
Lucas Heights NSW 27 J2 30 H5 35 F10
Lucaston TAS 71 E11
Lucinda QLD 17 G11
Lucindale SA 98 G5
Lucknow NSW 36 F5
Lucknow VIC 65 H8
Lucky Bay SA 88 D5
Lucyvale VIC 43 K13 65 B8

Luddenham NSW 34 E7 37 H9
Ludlow WA 108 C3 110 G2
Ludmilla NT 122 F3
Lue NSW 36 D7
Lugarno NSW 30 F7 35 E10
Lughrata TAS 78 B4
Luina TAS 72 A4 76 K7
Lul-Tju NT 126 E3
Lulworth TAS 75 C8
Lumeah WA 109 E11
Lumuku (Osmond Valley) WA 117 F13
Lunawanna TAS 71 H12
Lune River TAS 71 J11
Lupton Con Park WA 107 G6 110 E4 112 K6
Lurg VIC 64 C3
Lurnea NSW 30 E3 35 E9
Luscombe QLD 11 E11
Lutwyche QLD 3 D4 5 J10 7 A10
Lyme Regis TAS 75 A13 78 H5
Lymington TAS 71 G12
Lymwood TAS 78 D2
Lynchford TAS 72 F5
Lyndbrook QLD 17 F9
Lyndhurst NSW 36 G5
Lyndhurst SA 95 C8
Lyndhurst VIC 51 H7 55 E8 57 F9 64 J1 66 F2
Lyndoch SA 86 D5 89 G9 98 B3
Lyneham ACT 47 C5
Lynton SA 84 F5
Lynwood WA 103 K8 105 A8
Lyons ACT 47 F3
Lyons SA 97 C11
Lyons VIC 58 G3
Lyrup SA 89 F12 98 B6
Lysterfield VIC 55 B9
Lysterfield Lake Park VIC 57 E10
Lytton QLD 3 D6 5 J14 7 A14 9 K10 11 A10

Luddenham NSW 34 E7 37 H9

M

Ma Ma Creek QLD 10 C3
Maaroom QLD 13 C13
Macalister QLD 13 F10
Macarthur ACT 47 H5
Macarthur VIC 58 G4
Macclesfield SA 89 H9 98 D3
Macclesfield VIC 55 A13 57 D11
Macedon VIC 59 D13
Macgregor ACT 47 B2
Macgregor QLD 3 G5 7 F11 11 C10
Machans Beach QLD 18 D4
Mackay QLD 15 D8
Mackenzie QLD 3 G6 7 E13
Macksville NSW 39 H12
Maclean NSW 39 D13
Macleay Island QLD 11 C12
Macleod VIC 51 B5 53 D10 57 C8
Macorna VIC 42 J7 63 G9
Macquarie ACT 47 C3
Macquarie Fields NSW 30 F3 35 F9
Macquarie Harbour TAS 72 H4
Macquarie Harbour Historical Site TAS
   70 A3 72 H5
Macquarie Links NSW 30 F2
Macquarie Marshes Nature Res NSW 41 E12
Macquarie Park NSW 29 G9
Macquarie Plains TAS 71 C11
Macrossan QLD 14 B4 17 J12 21 A12
Maddarr WA 116 F7
Maddington WA 101 J7 103 K10 105 A10
Madora WA 106 G2
Madura WA 119 H5
Mafeking VIC 58 D6
Maffra VIC 64 J6 66 E7
Maggea SA 89 G11 98 B5
Magill SA 81 F6 83 K8 85 B8 86 H3
Magnet TAS 72 A5 76 J7
Magnetic Island Nat Park QLD 17 H12
Magra TAS 71 D11
Maianbar NSW 31 K9 35 F11
Maida Vale WA 101 F7 103 F11
Maidenwell QLD 13 E11
Maids Valley NSW 39 C9
Maidstone VIC 52 F6
Mailors Flat VIC 58 H6 60 E2
Maimuru NSW 36 J3 43 E14 44 A1
Main Beach QLD 11 F13 24 D5
Main Range Nat Park QLD 10 F4 13 H12 39 A11
Maindample VIC 64 E3 66 A4
Maitland NSW 33 A12 37 D11 45 G6
Maitland SA 88 F7 98 B1
Maitland Vale NSW 33 A12
Majorca VIC 59 C10
Majors Creek NSW 44 E4
Majura ACT 47 C6
Makiri SA 92 D6
Makowada QLD 15 J12
Malaan Nat Park QLD 18 H3
Malabar NSW 27 H6 31 F12
Malaburra WA 116 F7
Malaga WA 101 D5 102 B7
Malak NT 122 D6
Malanda QLD 17 E11 18 G3
Malangan (Illengirri) WA 117 F14 126 D1
Malar QLD 8 B1
Malara SA 92 B2 128 K2
Malbina NSW 71 D11
Malbon QLD 20 B4
Malbooma SA 97 C12
Malcolm WA 113 E12
Maldon NSW 35 H8
Maldon VIC 59 B11
Malebelling WA 106 D7
Maleny QLD 9 D8 13 E13
Maleny Nat Park QLD 8 C7
Malgawa NT 125 D8

Malinong SA 89 J10 98 D4
Malkala NT 125 F12
Malkumba-Coongie Lakes Nat Park SA
   22 D2 91 D12
Mallacoota VIC 65 G13
Mallala SA 86 B1 89 F8 98 B2
Mallanganee NSW 39 C12
Mallanganee Nat Park NSW 39 C12
Mallee Cliffs Nat Park NSW 42 F4 62 A5
Malmsbury VIC 59 C12
Malnjangarnak NT 125 D9
Malua Bay NSW 44 F5
Malvern SA 81 H4 84 D5
Malvern VIC 53 H10
Malvern East VIC 53 J11
Malyalling WA 107 H10
Mamadawerre NT 125 C9
Mamadi NT 126 D2
Mamboo QLD 14 H5 21 F12
Mambray Creek SA 88 B7 94 J7
Mamungari Con Park SA 92 G3
Manangatang VIC 42 G5 62 D6
Mandalong NSW 33 E12
Mandogalup WA 104 G5
Mandorah NT 124 C3
Mandurah WA 106 G2 110 E3
Mandurama NSW 36 G5
Mangalo SA 88 D5
Mangalore QLD 23 C13
Mangalore TAS 69 F1 71 C12 73 K14
Mangalore VIC 64 E1 66 A1
Mangana TAS 75 G12
Mangardubu NT 124 C7
Mango Hill QLD 5 B10
Mangoplah NSW 43 H12
Mangrove Creek NSW 33 H10
Mangrove Creek Dam NSW 33 G10
Mangrove Islands WA 114 C4
Mangrove Mountain NSW 33 H10 37 F10
Manguri SA 93 H12
Manildra NSW 36 F4 41 K14 43 C14
Manilla NSW 38 H7
Maningrida NT 125 B9
Manjimup WA 108 F6 110 H3
Mankorlod NT 125 C9
Manly NSW 27 D7 29 H14 35 C12 37 G10
Manly QLD 3 D7 5 K14 7 B14 11 B11
Manly Vale NSW 27 D6 29 G13 35 C11
Manly West QLD 3 E7 7 C14
Manmoyi NT 125 C8
Mann River Nature Res NSW 39 E10
Manna Hill SA 95 H11
Mannanarie SA 89 C9 95 J9
Mannerim VIC 56 H4
Mannering Park NSW 33 E13
Mannibadar VIC 61 A9
Manning WA 101 H4 102 J5
Manningham VIC 82 J6 84 A6
Manns Beach VIC 66 H6
Mannum SA 43 J13 65 A9
Manobalai Nature Res NSW 37 C9
Manoora SA 89 E9 98 A3
Manor VIC 56 E4
Mansfield QLD 3 G5 7 E12
Mansfield VIC 64 E3 66 A4
Mansfield Park SA 82 H3
Mantamaru (Jameison) WA 118 H5
Mantapayika NT 128 J3
Manton Dam Rec Area NT 123 D2 124 D4
Mantung SA 89 G11 98 C5
Manuka ACT 47 F5
Manumbah Mill QLD 8 A4
Manumbar QLD 8 A3
Many Peaks QLD 15 K11
Manyirkanga SA 92 B6 128 K4
Manypeaks WA 110 J6
Mapleton QLD 9 C8 13 E13
Mapleton Falls Nat Park QLD 9 C8
Mapoon QLD 19 D1
Mapurru NT 125 J12
Mara NT 125 J12 127 A12
Maralinga SA 96 B7
Marama SA 89 H11 98 D5
Marananga SA 86 C6
Maranboy NT 123 K7 124 G6
Marandoo WA 114 E7
Marangaroo WA 101 C3
Marathon QLD 17 K8 21 B8
Maraylya NSW 35 B8
Marayong NSW 28 F2 35 C9
Marbelup WA 109 J13
Marble Bar WA 115 C9
Marble Hill SA 85 C11 86 H4
Marburg QLD 10 B6 13 G12
Marchagee WA 112 G5
Marchinbar Island NT 125 A12
Marcoo SA 96 A7
Marcoola QLD 9 C10
Marcus Beach QLD 9 A10
Marcus Hill VIC 56 H4 59 G13
Mardan VIC 64 K3 66 G4
Mardella WA 106 F3
Marden SA 82 K6 84 A6
Mareeba QLD 17 E10 18 E2
Marengo VIC 59 K10 61 J10
Margaret River WA 108 E1 110 H2
Margate QLD 5 C12 9 J10
Margate TAS 69 J1 71 F12
Margooya VIC 62 C6
Maria Creek Nat Park QLD 18 K6
Maria Island TAS 69 F5
Maria Island Nat Park TAS 69 F6
Maria Lagoon NT 125 H10
Mariah NT 124 A6
Mariala Nat Park QLD 21 J10 23 A11
Marian QLD 15 D8

Maribyrnong VIC 52 E6
Marimo QLD 16 K4 20 B4
Marino SA 81 K2 84 H2 86 K1 87 A4
Marino Con Park SA 86 K1 87 A5
Marion SA 81 K3 84 F3 86 J2 87 A5
Marion Bay SA 88 H5
Marion Bay TAS 69 G4
Marion Con Park SA 84 H2
Mark Oliphant Con Park SA 85 G9 86 K3 87 A7
Marks Point NSW 33 D13
Markwood VIC 43 K11 64 C4
Marla SA 93 D11
Marlborough QLD 15 G9
Marleston SA 81 G3 84 D4
Marley Pool WA 100 D7
Marlo VIC 65 H10
Marlwon NT 125 C8
Marma VIC 58 A6 62 K5
Marmion WA 101 C1 102 A1
Marmor QLD 15 H10
Marnoo VIC 58 A7 62 K6
Marnoo East VIC 58 A7 62 K7
Marong VIC 59 A11 63 K10
Maroochy River QLD 9 C9
Maroochydore QLD 9 C10 13 E13
Maroon QLD 10 H7 13 H13 39 A12
Maroona VIC 58 D7
Maroota NSW 33 K9
Maroota South NSW 33 K9 35 A8
Maroubra NSW 27 G6 31 E12 35 E12
Maroubra Junction NSW 31 E12
Marp VIC 58 F2
Marraba QLD 20 B4
Marrabel SA 89 F9 98 B3
Marracoonda WA 109 C12
Marradong WA 106 J5 110 F4
Marrakai Crossing NT 124 D4
Marralum NT 124 H1
Marramarra Nat Park NSW 33 K10 35 A9
Marramarrani NT 124 A6
Marrangaroo NSW 34 B2
Marrar NSW 36 K1 43 G12
Marrara NT 122 D6
Marrawah TAS 76 F3
Marraweeny VIC 63 K14 64 D2
Marraya NT 125 F11
Marree SA 91 K8 95 A8
Marrickville NSW 31 D10 35 D11
Marrkalawa NT 125 E11
Marrkolidjban NT 125 C9
Marryat SA 93 B10
Marryatville SA 84 D2
Marsden NSW 36 G2 43 D12
Marsden QLD 3 K5 7 K12 11 D10
Marsden Park NSW 28 D1 35 C8
Marsfield NSW 27 D4 29 G9 35 C10
Marshall VIC 56 H3
Marshall Bay TAS 78 B4
Marshdale NSW 37 D11
Martin WA 105 B11
Martin Washpool Con Park SA 98 F4
Martins Creek NSW 45 E7
Martinsville NSW 33 E11
Marton QLD 17 B10 19 K6
Marulan NSW 36 K7 44 B5
Marunbabidi WA 117 C11
Marvel Loch WA 111 C8 113 J9
Mary River Nat Park NT 123 B3 124 D5
Maryborough QLD 13 B13
Maryborough VIC 59 B10
Maryknoll VIC 57 F12
Maryland NSW 33 C13
Maryland Nat Park NSW 39 A10
Marysville VIC 57 A13 64 G2 66 C3
Maryvale NSW 36 D5
Maryvale QLD 10 G3
Maryville NT 127 E8
Mascot NSW 27 G5 31 D11 35 D11
Maslin Beach SA 87 C4 89 H8 98 D2
Massey VIC 42 K5 62 H6
Mastertons Cave NT 127 C14
Mata Mata NT 125 C12
Mataranka NT 124 G7
Mataranka Homestead Resort NT 124 G7
Matcham NSW 33 H13
Mathinna TAS 75 F12
Mathoura NSW 43 J8 63 G12
Merewether NSW 33 C14
Matlock VIC 64 G4 66 D5
Matong NSW 43 G10
Matraville NSW 27 H6 31 E12 35 E12
Maude NSW 42 F7
Maude VIC 56 E1 59 F11 61 B13
Maudsland QLD 11 F11 24 C1
Mawbanna TAS 76 F7
Mawson ACT 47 G4
Mawson WA 107 E9
Mawson Lakes SA 81 C4 82 F5
Mawulyumanja NT 125 F12
Maxwelton QLD 16 K7 20 B7
Maya WA 112 G6
Mayanup WA 108 E7 110 H4
Mayberry TAS 73 B9 74 G4 77 K12
Maybole NSW 39 E9
Maydena TAS 71 D9
Mayfield NSW 33 B14
Maylands SA 82 K6 84 B6
Maylands WA 101 F5 102 E7
Maynard Bore SA 93 D8
Mayrung NSW 43 H9 63 F13
Mays Hill NSW 28 H5
Mazeppa Nat Park QLD 14 F5 21 D13
Mbunghara NT 128 E6
McAlinden WA 108 C7
McCaul Bore SA 92 B7
McCrae VIC 56 J7
Mcdowall QLD 3 C3 5 G8
McGraths Hill NSW 28 A1 35 B8
McIntyre VIC 59 A10 63 K9

Mckellar ACT 47 B3
McKenzie Creek VIC 58 A5 62 K4
McKinley QLD 20 C5
McKinnon VIC 51 F4 53 K10 54 A3
McLaren Flat SA 87 C5
McLaren Vale SA 87 C5 89 H8 98 D2
McLoughlins Beach VIC 66 H7
McMahons Creek VIC 57 C14 64 H3 66 D3
McMahons Point NSW 29 K11 31 B11
McMahons Reef NSW 36 K4 43 F14 44 B1
Mcmasters Beach NSW 33 J13
Meadowbank NSW 29 H8
Meadowbrook QLD 7 J13
Meadows SA 87 C7 89 H9 98 D3
Moondarra QLD 12 F7
Meander TAS 73 C11 74 G5
Meandu Creek QLD 8 D1
Mears WA 107 F9
Meatian VIC 42 H5 63 F8
Mebbin Nat Park NSW 11 K10 39 A13
Meckering WA 107 C8 110 C5 112 J6
Medina WA 104 K3 106 F3
Medindie SA 80 A3 82 K5 84 B5
Medindie Gardens SA 82 J5 84 A5
Medlow Bath NSW 34 C7 37 G8
Medowie NSW 33 A14
Meeandah QLD 3 D5 5 J12 7 A12
Meekatharra WA 113 B8 115 K8
Meenaar WA 106 C7
Meeniyan VIC 66 H4
Meerawa QLD 18 F5
Meerlieu VIC 64 J7
Megalong NSW 34 E3
Megan NSW 39 G11
Melaleuca TAS 70 J7
Melawondi QLD 8 A6
Melba ACT 47 B3
Melba TAS 72 D4
Melbourne VIC
  50 B2 51 D3 53 G8 56 C7 59 F14 66 E1
Meldale QLD 9 G10
Mella TAS 76 E5
Melros WA 106 H2
Melrose NSW 41 J11
Melrose SA 89 B8
Melrose TAS 74 D3 77 H11
Melrose Park NSW 29 H8
Melrose Park SA 81 J4 84 E4
Melsonby (Gaarraay) Nat Park QLD
  17 B10 19 J6
Melton SA 88 E7 98 A2
Melton VIC 56 B4 59 E13
Melton Mowbray TAS 71 B12 73 J14
Melton South VIC 56 C4
Melville WA 101 J2 102 K3 104 A3
Melville Forest VIC 58 D4
Melville Island NT 123 A1 124 A4
Melville Range Nature Res NSW 38 J6
Melwood VIC 64 H7
Memana TAS 78 C5
Memerambi QLD 13 D11
Mena Creek QLD 18 J6
Mena Flat SA 88 F2
Mena Park VIC 59 D9
Menai NSW 27 J2 30 G6 35 F10
Menangle NSW 35 G8
Menangle Park NSW 35 G8
Mendooran NSW 36 B5
Mengha TAS 76 E6
Menindee NSW 40 J4 42 B3
Meningie SA 89 K10 98 E4
Menngen NT 124 H4
Menora WA 102 D5
Mentone VIC 51 G5 54 C4 57 E8
Menzies WA 113 F11
Menzies Creek VIC 55 A12 57 E11
Mepunga East VIC 58 H7 60 G4
Mepunga West VIC 58 H7 60 F3
Merah North NSW 38 F3
Merbein VIC 42 E3 62 A4
Merbein West VIC 62 A4
Mercunda SA 89 G11
Mercury Passage TAS 69 F5
Merebene NSW 38 G3
Meredith VIC 56 D1 59 F11 61 A12
Meredith Range Reg Res TAS 72 B4 76 K6
Merewether NSW 33 C14
Meribah SA 42 G1 62 C1 89 G13 98 C6
Merimbula NSW 44 J5 65 E14
Merinda QLD 14 B7 17 J14 21 A14
Meringandan QLD 13 G11
Meringur VIC 62 A2 89 F14 98 B7
Merino SA 47 E3
Merino VIC 58 E3
Merivale QLD 18 G3
Mermaid Beach QLD 11 G13 24 F5
Mermaid Waters QLD 24 F5
Mernda VIC 57 B8 59 E14 64 G1 66 D1
Meroo Nat Park NSW 44 E6
Merredin WA 107 B13 110 C6 113 J8
Merrepen NT 124 F2
Merriang NT 124 C5
Merriangaah Nature Res NSW 44 H3 65 D11
Merricks VIC 57 J8
Merricks Beach VIC 57 K8
Merricks North VIC 57 J8
Merrigum QLD 43 K8 63 J12 64 C1
Merrijig VIC 64 E4 66 B5
Merrimac QLD 11 G12 24 F4
Merrinee VIC 42 F3 62 B3
Merriton SA 89 D8 95 K8
Merriwa NSW 37 J8
Merriwagga NSW 43 E9
Merrylands NSW 27 E2 28 J5 30 A5 35 D10
Merrylands West NSW 28 J5 30 A5
Merryvale QLD 10 E6
Merrywinebone NSW 38 E2
Merseylea TAS 73 A10 74 E4 77 J12

Merthyr QLD 7 C10
Merton VIC 64 E2 66 A3
Meryula NSW 36 C1 41 G10 41 J12 43 A12
Messent Con Park SA 89 K11 98 E4
Messines QLD 39 B9
Metcalfe VIC 59 C12
Metricup WA 108 D2
Metung VIC 65 H8
Metz NSW 39 G9
Meunna TAS 76 G7
Meunna Hills TAS 76 G7
Mewirnbi NT 125 C9
Mia Mia VIC 59 B13
Miallo QLD 17 D10 18 A2
Miami QLD 11 G13 24 G5
Miami Keys QLD 24 F5
Miandetta NSW 41 G11
Miara QLD 15 K12
Michaelmas Cay Nat Park QLD 18 B6
Michelago NSW 44 E3 48 H5
Mickleham VIC 56 A7
Middle Brother Nat Park NSW 37 B13
Middle Camp NSW 33 E14
Middle Cove NSW 29 H12
Middle Dural NSW 27 A2 28 B6
Middle Lagoon WA 116 E6
Middle Park QLD 6 F6 11 B9
Middle Park VIC 53 H8
Middle Point Village NT 123 C2 124 C4
Middle Swan WA 101 D7 103 B11
Middlemount QLD 14 G7 21 E14
Middleton SA 87 G7 89 J9 98 D3
Middleton TAS 69 K1 71 G12
Middlingbank NSW 43 K14 44 G2 65 B11
Midland WA
  101 D7 103 C10 106 D4 110 D3 112 K5
Midvale WA 103 C11
Midway Point TAS 69 G2 71 D14
Mielings Timber Mill QLD 17 G10
Miena TAS 73 E11 74 K6
Miepoll VIC 63 K13 64 C2
Miga Lake VIC 58 B3
Mila NSW 44 J3 65 E12
Milabena TAS 76 F7
Milang SA 89 J9 98 D3
Milawa VIC 43 K11 64 C4
Milbrodale NSW 32 B7
Milbrulong NSW 43 H11
Mildura VIC 42 E3 62 A4
Mile End SA 80 C1 81 G3 84 C4
Mile End South SA 84 C4
Miles QLD 13 E8
Milford QLD 10 G7
Milguy NSW 38 D6
Milikapiti (Snake Bay) NT 124 A3
Miling WA 110 A3 112 H6
Milingimbi NT 123 A1 124 A4
Mill Park VIC 51 A4 53 B10
Millaa Millaa QLD 17 E11 18 H4
Millargoon WA 116 E6
Millaroo QLD 14 B5 17 J13 21 A13
Millbank NSW 39 H11
Mil-Lel SA 58 F1
Miller NSW 30 D2 35 E9
Millers Forest NSW 33 A13
Millers Point NSW 26 A1 29 K11 31 B11
Millfield NSW 33 D10 37 E10 45 J3
Millgrove VIC 57 C12 64 H2 66 D3
Millicent SA 98 J5
Millie NSW 38 E4
Millmerran QLD 13 H10
Millner NT 122 D4
Milloo VIC 42 K7 63 J10
Millstream Chichester Nat Park WA 114 C6
Millswood SA 81 H4 84 D5
Millthorpe NSW 36 F5
Milltown VIC 58 G4
Millvale TAS 71 C12
Milparinka NSW 22 K6 40 C2
Milperra NSW 27 G2 30 E5 35 E10
Milsons Point NSW 29 J11 31 A11
Miltale SA 88 D5
Milton NSW 44 D6
Milton QLD 7 C9 11 B9
Milvale NSW 36 J2 43 F13
Milyakburra NT 125 E12
Milyeannup Nat Park WA 108 F4
Milyu Nature Res WA 100 D1
Mimili (Everard Park) SA 93 C9
Mimosa Rocks Nat Park NSW 44 H5 65 D14
Minamia (Cox River) NT 125 J9 127 A9
Mincha VIC 42 K7 63 H10
Minchinbury NSW 28 H1
Mindaribba NSW 45 F6
Mindarie SA 89 G12 98 C5
Minden QLD 10 B6
Mindijup WA 109 H14
Miners Rest VIC 59 D10
Minerva VIC 14 J7 21 F14
Minerva Hills Nat Park QLD 14 J6 21 G14
Mingary SA 40 H1 42 A1 89 A13 95 G13
Mingay VIC 59 F9 60 A7
Mingela QLD 14 B4 17 J12 21 A12
Mingenew WA 112 F4
Minhamite VIC 58 F6
Mini Moxham QLD 18 E1
Minilya Roadhouse WA 114 G2
Minimay VIC 58 A2 62 K2
Mininera VIC 58 E7
Minjah VIC 58 G6 60 C2
Minjary Nat Park NSW 43 H13 44 D1
Minjilang NT 124 A6
Minlaton SA 88 G6 98 C1
Minmi NSW 33 C13 45 J7
Minnamite VIC 60 C1
Minnamurra NSW 37 K9 44 B7
Minnie Water NSW 39 E13
Minnipa SA 88 B2 94 J2 97 J14

Minnivale WA 107 A9
Minore NSW 36 C4 41 H14 43 A14
Mintabie SA 93 D10
Mintaro SA 89 E9 98 A3
Minto NSW 30 H1 35 F9
Minto Heights NSW 30 H2
Minyerri (Hodgson Downs) NT 125 H8
Minyip VIC 42 K4 62 J6
Miralie VIC 42 G5 62 D7
Miram VIC 42 K2 62 J2
Miram South VIC 62 J2
Miranda NSW 27 J4 31 H9 35 F11
Mirani QLD 15 D8
Mirannie NSW 37 C10 45 B4
Mirboo VIC 64 K4 66 G5
Mirboo North VIC 64 K3 66 G4
Miriam Vale QLD 15 J12
Mirimbah VIC 64 E4 66 B5
Mirirrinyunga (Duck Ponds Outstation) NT
  126 F4
Miriwinni QLD 17 E11 18 G5
Mirrabooka QLD 23 D13
Mirrabooka WA 101 D4 102 B6
Mirranatwa VIC 58 D6
Mirridi NT 126 F3
Mirrnatja NT 125 D10
Mirrool NSW 36 J1 43 F12
Mission Beach QLD 17 F11 18 K7
Mistake Creek NT 126 C1
Mitakoodi QLD 20 B4
Mitcham SA 81 J4 84 F6 86 J2
Mitcham VIC 51 D7 53 G13
Mitchell ACT 47 B5
Mitchell QLD 12 D4 21 K13
Mitchell Park SA 84 F4
Mitchell River Nat Park VIC 64 G7
Mitchell River Nat Park WA 117 C10
Mitchell-Alice Rivers Nat Park
  see Errk Oykangand Nat Park
Mitchellville SA 88 D6
Mitchelton QLD 3 D2 5 J8 7 A8
Mitiamo VIC 42 K7 63 H10
Mitre VIC 58 A4 62 K3
Mitta Mitta VIC 64 C7
Mittagong NSW 37 J8 44 B6
Mittyack VIC 42 H4 62 E6
Miwul NT 125 F11
Moa Island QLD 19 A2
Moama NSW 43 K8
Moama VIC 63 H11
Moana SA 87 C4
Moana Sands Con Park SA 87 C4
Moantu NT 124 B2
Mobarn NT 125 C8
Mobrup WA 109 E9
Mockinya VIC 58 B5
Modanville NSW 13 K14 39 B13
Modbury SA 81 D6 83 G8 86 G3
Modbury Heights SA 81 C6 83 F8
Modbury North SA 81 D6 83 G8
Modella VIC 57 G13 64 J2 66 F3
Modewarre VIC 56 H1
Modong Nature Res WA 104 J7
Moe VIC 64 J4 66 F5
Moffat VIC 60 B3
Moggill QLD 3 H1 6 F5 11 C8
Moglonemby VIC 64 D2
Mogo NSW 44 E5
Mogriguy NSW 36 B4 41 H14 43 A14
Moil NT 122 D5
Moina TAS 73 A8 74 F2 77 K10
Mokepilly VIC 58 C6
Mole Creek TAS 73 B10 74 G4 77 K12
Mole Creek Karst Nat Park TAS 73 B9 74 G3
Mole Hill NT 125 C8
Mole River NSW 13 K10 39 C9
Molendinar QLD 24 E5
Molesworth NSW 37 C11
Molesworth TAS 71 D12
Molesworth VIC 64 E2 66 B2
Moliagul VIC 59 A10 63 K9
Mollymook NSW 44 D6
Molong NSW 36 E5
Molonglo Gorge Nature Res ACT 48 C6
Moltema TAS 74 D3 74 F5 77 K13
Molyullah VIC 64 D3
Momob NT 125 E9
Mona NSW 27 B7 29 C14 35 B12 37 G10
Mona Vale NSW 27 C14 29 D14
Mona Vale TAS 69 B2
Monadnocks Con Park WA 110 E4 112 K6
Monash ACT 47 H4
Monash SA 89 F12 98 B6
Monbulk VIC 57 D11 64 H1 66 E2
Monea VIC 64 D1 66 A2
Monegeetta VIC 59 D13
Monga NSW 44 E5
Monga Nat Park NSW 44 E5 65 A14
Mongarlowe NSW 44 D5
Monkerai NSW 37 C11
Monkey Mia WA 112 A2 114 K2
Monogorilby QLD 13 C10
Monomeith VIC 55 K14 57 H11
Monsildale QLD 8 D5
Mont Albert VIC 53 G11
Montacute SA 81 F7 83 K10 85 B10 86 H4
Montacute Con Park SA 83 J11 85 A11 86 H4
Montagu TAS 76 E4
Montagu Bay TAS 68 B4
Montague Island NSW 44 G5
Montague Island Nature Res NSW 44 G5
Montana TAS 73 B11 74 G5
Monteagle NSW 36 H3 43 E14 44 A1
Montebello Islands Marine Park WA 114 B4
Montefiores NSW 36 D5
Monterey NSW 27 H5 31 F10 35 E11
Montgomery Islands WA 117 D8
Montmorency VIC 53 D12
Monto QLD 13 A10 15 K11
Montumana TAS 76 F7

Montville QLD 9 D8
Mooball Nat Park NSW 11 K13 39 A13
Moockra SA 89 A8 95 H8
Moodiarrup WA 109 C9
Moodini Bluff WA 119 H5
Moodlu QLD 9 G8
Moogara TAS 71 D11
Moogerah QLD 10 G6
Moogerah Peaks Nat Park QLD 10 G6
Moojebing WA 109 C12
Moolap VIC 56 G3
Mooliabeenie WA 106 B4
Mooloolaba QLD 9 K9
Mooloolah QLD 9 D9
Mooloolah River Nat Park QLD 9 D10
Moolort VIC 59 B10
Moolpa NSW 42 G6 63 D9
Moomba SA 22 F3 91 F12
Moombra QLD 8 J5
Moona Plains NSW 39 J9
Moonabie SA 88 C6 94 K6
Moonah TAS 69 G1 71 D13
Moonambel VIC 59 B9
Moonameeta TAS 75 G12
Moonan Flat NSW 37 B10
Moonaran NSW 38 H7
Moonbah NSW 43 K14 44 G2
Moonbi NSW 38 H7
Moonda Lake QLD 20 J4 22 A3
Moondarra VIC 64 J4 66 F5
Moondarra State Park VIC 64 J4 66 F5
Moondyne Nature Res WA
  106 C5 110 C3 112 J5
Moonee Beach NSW 39 F12
Moonee Ponds VIC 52 E7
Mooney Mooney NSW 33 K11 35 A11
Moonford QLD 13 A10 15 K11
Moongardie WA 117 H11
Moongobulla QLD 17 H11
Moonie QLD 13 G8
Moonta SA 88 E6 98 A1
Moonta Bay SA 88 E6 98 A1
Moora WA 110 A3 112 H5
Moora (Mathiesons) VIC 63 K12
Moorabbin VIC 51 F5 53 K10 54 B4 57 E8
Moorabool VIC 56 F2
Mooradung Nature Res WA 106 J6
Mooralla VIC 58 D5
Moore QLD 8 E4 13 E12
Moore Creek NSW 38 H7
Moore Park NSW 31 C12
Moore Park QLD 13 A12 15 K13
Moore River Nat Park WA
  106 A2 110 B2 112 J5
Moore River Nature Res WA 106 A2
Moorebank NSW 27 G1 30 E4 35 E10
Moores Landing TAS 70 C5 72 K6
Moores Pocket QLD 6 G2
Mooreville TAS 74 C1 77 G9
Moorilim VIC 63 K13 64 D1
Moorina TAS 75 D12
Moorine Rock WA 111 B8 113 J9
Moorlands SA 89 J10 98 D4
Moorleah TAS 77 F8
Moornaming WA 109 C14
Mooronga NT 125 B10
Moorooduc VIC 57 H8
Moorook SA 89 F12 98 B5
Moorooka QLD 3 G4 7 F10
Mooroopna VIC 63 J13 64 C1
Moorrinya Nat Park QLD 14 D2 21 C10
Moorumbine WA 107 G9
Mootai NSW 33 D10
Moranbah QLD 14 E6 21 D14
Morangarell NSW 36 H2 43 E13
Morans Crossing NSW 44 H4 65 D13
Morawa WA 112 F5
Morayfield QLD 9 G9
Morchard SA 89 B8 95 J8
Mordalup WA 109 F8
Mordialloc VIC 51 H5 54 D4 57 F8
Morea VIC 58 A2 62 K2
Moree NSW 38 D5
Morella QLD 21 E8
Moresby QLD 18 J6
Moreton TAS 74 E3 77 H14
Moreton Bay QLD 3 A6 5 E12 9 J11
Moreton Bay Marine Park QLD
  9 K12 11 A13 13 F14
Moreton Island (Gnoorganbin) QLD
  9 H12 13 F14
Moreton Island Nat Park QLD 9 H12 13 F14
Moreton Telegraph Station QLD 19 E3
Morgan SA 89 E11 98 A4
Moriac VIC 56 H1 59 G11 61 B13
Morialta Con Park SA 81 F7 83 K9 85 B9 86 H3
Moriarty TAS 74 D4 77 H12
Morisset NSW 33 E12 37 F10
Morisset Park NSW 33 E13
Morkalla VIC 42 F2 62 B1
Morley WA 101 D5 102 C7
Morning Bay NSW 29 B13
Morningside QLD 3 E5 7 C11
Mornington NSW 54 K3 56 H7 59 G14 66 F1
Mornington (Gununa) QLD 16 D2
Mornington Island QLD 16 D2
Mornington Peninsula VIC 57 J8
Mornington Peninsula Nat Park VIC
  56 J6 57 K6
Morongla Creek NSW 36 H4 43 E14
Morpeth NSW 33 A12 45 G7
Morphett Vale SA 87 B5 89 H8 98 D2
Morphettville SA 81 J3 84 F3
Morrisons VIC 56 J2 59 F11 61 A12
Morri Morri VIC 58 B7
Mortchup VIC 59 E9
Mortdale NSW 31 F8 35 E11
Mortlake NSW 29 J9 31 A9

Mortlake **VIC** 58 G7
Morton Nat Park **NSW** 37 K8 44 C6
Morton Plains **VIC** 62 H6
Morundah **NSW** 43 G10
Moruya **NSW** 44 F5
Moruya Heads **NSW** 44 F5
Morven **NSW** 43 J12
Morven **QLD** 12 D2 21 K12
Morwell **VIC** 64 K4 66 G5
Morwell Nat Park **VIC** 64 K4 66 G5
Moselle **QLD** 17 K8 21 B8
Mosman **NSW** 27 E6 29 J12 31 A12 35 C12
Mosman Park **WA** 101 H1 102 J2
Moss Glen **TAS** 71 K10
Moss Gully Con Area **TAS** 75 H10
Moss Vale **NSW** 37 K8 44 B6
Mossgiel **NSW** 42 C7
Mossiface **VIC** 65 H8
Mossman **QLD** 17 D10 18 A2
Moulamein **NSW** 42 G7 63 D9
Moule **SA** 97 G11
Moulyinning **WA** 107 K12 109 A14
Mount Aberdeen Nat Park **QLD** 14 B6 17 J13 21 A13
Mount Alford **QLD** 10 G6
Mount Annan **NSW** 35 G8
Mount Arapiles-Tooan State Park **VIC** 58 A3 62 K3
Mount Archer Nat Park **QLD** 15 H10
Mount Augustus (Burringurrah) Nat Park **WA** 114 G6
Mount Barker **SA** 85 J14 86 K5 89 H9 98 C3
Mount Barker **WA** 109 H13 110 J6
Mount Barker Junction **SA** 86 K5
Mount Barkly **NT** 128 C6
Mount Barnett Roadhouse **WA** 117 E10
Mount Barney Nat Park **QLD** 10 J7 13 J12 39 A11
Mount Bauple Nat Park (Scientific) **QLD** 13 C12
Mount Beau Brummell Con Park **QLD** 10 E4
Mount Beauty **VIC** 64 D6
Mount Beppo **QLD** 8 H5
Mount Berryman **QLD** 10 D4
Mount Bethune Con Area **TAS** 71 C10 73 K12
Mount Boothby Con Park **SA** 89 K11 98 E4
Mount Brown Con Park **SA** 88 A7
Mount Bryan **SA** 89 D9
Mount Buffalo Chalet **VIC** 64 D5
Mount Buffalo Nat Park **VIC** 64 D5
Mount Buller Alpine Village **VIC** 64 F4 66 B5
Mount Burnett **VIC** 55 C14 57 E11
Mount Burr **SA** 98 J5
Mount Bute **VIC** 59 F9 61 B8
Mount Carbine **QLD** 17 D10 18 B1
Mount Catt **NT** 125 E9
Mount Chinghee Nat Park **QLD** 11 J9 39 A12
Mount Christie Siding **SA** 97 C10
Mount Claremont **WA** 101 F2 102 F2
Mount Clunie Nat Park **NSW** 10 J5 39 A11
Mount Colah **NSW** 27 B4 29 C9 35 B10
Mount Colliery **QLD** 10 J4
Mount Compass **SA** 87 E6 89 J8 98 D3
Mount Coolon **QLD** 14 D5 21 C13
Mount Coolum **QLD** 9 C10
Mount Coolum Nat Park **QLD** 9 B10
Mount Coot-tha **QLD** 3 E2 7 C8 11 B9
Mount Cotton **QLD** 11 C11
Mount Cottrell **VIC** 52 F1 56 C5 59 E13
Mount Crawford Forest **SA** 86 F6
Mount Crosby **QLD** 6 D3 11 B8
Mount Damper **SA** 88 C2 94 K2 97 K14
Mount Dandenong **VIC** 57 D10
Mount David **NSW** 36 G6
Mount Direction **TAS** 74 D7
Mount Doreen **NT** 128 C4
Mount Dowling Nature Res **NSW** 44 F3 65 A12
Mount Druitt **NSW** 28 G1 35 D8
Mount Dundas Reg Res **TAS** 72 F4
Mount Duneed **VIC** 56 H3
Mount Dutton **SA** 90 E3
Mount Eaglebeak **NT** 129 E10
Mount Ebenezer Roadhouse **NT** 128 J6
Mount Eccles Nat Park **VIC** 58 G4 98 K7
Mount Eckersley **VIC** 58 G3
Mount Egerton **VIC** 56 B1 59 E11
Mount Eliza **VIC** 54 J4 57 G8 59 G14 66 F1
Mount Elvire Con Park **WA** 113 F10
Mount Emu **VIC** 59 E9
Mount Farrell Reg Res **TAS** 72 C6
Mount Field Nat Park **TAS** 71 C9 73 K11
Mount Frankland Nat Park **WA** 109 H8 110 J4
Mount Gambier **SA** 58 F1 98 J6
Mount George **NSW** 37 B12
Mount George **SA** 85 F11
Mount Glorious **QLD** 4 F2 8 J7
Mount Gravatt **QLD** 3 G5 7 E11 11 B10
Mount Gravatt East **QLD** 7 E11
Mount Hawthorn **WA** 101 E3 102 E4
Mount Heemskirk Reg Res **TAS** 72 D3
Mount Helen **VIC** 59 E10
Mount Hope **NSW** 41 K10 43 B10
Mount Hope **SA** 88 E2
Mount Hunter **NSW** 35 G8
Mount Hypipamee Nat Park **QLD** 18 G3
Mount Ida **WA** 113 E10
Mount Imlay Nat Park **NSW** 44 J4 65 F13
Mount Irvine **NSW** 34 B5
Mount Isa **QLD** 16 K12 118 A5
Mount Jean **NT** 125 E9
Mount Jerusalem Nat Park **NSW** 39 B13
Mount Kaputar Nat Park **NSW** 38 F5
Mount Keith Mine Village **WA** 113 C11
Mount Kokeby **WA** 107 F8
Mount Kororoit **VIC** 56 B5
Mount Kuring-gai **NSW** 27 A5 29 B9 35 B10
Mount Larcom **QLD** 15 H11
Mount Lawley **WA** 101 F4 102 E6

Mount Lewis **NSW** 30 D7
Mount Liebig **NT** 128 E4
Mount Lloyd **TAS** 71 D11
Mount Lonarch **VIC** 59 C9
Mount Low **QLD** 17 H12
Mount Macedon **VIC** 59 D13
Mount Mackay Nat Park **QLD** 18 K5
Mount Magnet **WA** 112 D7
Mount Magnificent Con Park **SA** 87 D7
Mount Maiyo **NT** 126 D1
Mount Manning Range Nature Res **WA** 113 G10
Mount Margaret **WA** 113 E12
Mount Martha **VIC** 57 H7
Mount Martin Nat Park **QLD** 14 C7
Mount Mary **SA** 89 F10 98 B4
Mount Mee **QLD** 8 G7
Mount Mercer **VIC** 59 F10 61 A11
Mount Molloy **QLD** 17 D10 18 C2
Mount Morgan **QLD** 15 H10
Mount Morgans **WA** 113 E12
Mount Moriac **VIC** 56 H1
Mount Mort **QLD** 10 E5
Mount Murchison Reg Res **TAS** 72 D6
Mount Nasura **WA** 105 E11
Mount Nathan **QLD** 11 F11 24 D1
Mount Nebo **QLD** 4 G2 8 K7 13 G13
Mount Neville Nature Res **NSW** 13 K13 39 D12
Mount Nothofagus Nat Park **NSW** 10 K6
Mount Olive **NSW** 45 B2
Mount Ommaney **QLD** 3 G2 6 E7
Mount Osmond **SA** 84 D7
Mount Perry **QLD** 13 B11
Mount Perry Con Park **QLD** 11 D8
Mount Pikapene Nat Park **NSW** 39 C11
Mount Pleasant **NSW** 37 D10 45 C2
Mount Pleasant **QLD** 8 H7
Mount Pleasant **SA** 86 F7 89 G9 98 C3
Mount Pleasant **WA** 101 H3 102 J5
Mount Pritchard **NSW** 27 G1 30 C3 35 E9
Mount Remarkable Nat Park **SA** 88 B7 94 J7
Mount Richmond Nat Park **VIC** 58 H3
Mount Rivers **NSW** 45 B5
Mount Roe Nat Park **WA** 109 H10 110 J5
Mount Roland Reg Res **TAS** 73 A9 74 F3 77 K11
Mount Russell **NSW** 38 E7
Mount Samson **QLD** 4 E5 9 J8
Mount Scott Con Park **SA** 98 G5
Mount Seaview **NSW** 37 A12 39 K10
Mount Selwyn **NSW** 43 J14 44 F1 65 A10
Mount Seymour **TAS** 69 D2 71 A13
Mount Spurgeon Nat Park **QLD** 17 D10
Mount Squire **NT** 129 J9
Mount Stanley **QLD** 8 C3
Mount Sturt **QLD** 10 J3
Mount Surprise **QLD** 17 F9
Mount Sylvia **QLD** 10 D3
Mount Tamborine **QLD** 11 F11
Mount Tarampa **QLD** 10 A5
Mount Taylor **VIC** 64 H7
Mount Thorley **NSW** 37 A8 45 E1
Mount Torrens **SA** 86 H6 89 G9 98 C3
Mount Vernon **WA** 28 K1 30 B1 35 E8
Mount Victoria **NSW** 34 C3 37 G8
Mount View **NSW** 33 C10
Mount Vincent **NSW** 33 C12 45 K5
Mount Walker **QLD** 10 E5
Mount Wallace **VIC** 56 C2 59 E11
Mount Walsh Nat Park **QLD** 13 C11
Mount Warning Nat Park **NSW** 11 K11
Mount Waverley **VIC** 51 E6 53 J12
Mount Wedge **SA** 88 D2 94 K2 97 K14
Mount Wells **NT** 124 E5
Mount White **NSW** 33 J11
Mount Whitestone **QLD** 10 C3
Mount William Nat Park **TAS** 75 B14 78 K6
Mount Wilson **NSW** 34 B4 37 G8
Mount Windsor Nat Park **QLD** 17 D10 18 A1
Mountain Creek **NSW** 43 J12 64 A6
Mountain Creek **QLD** 9 D10
Mountain River **TAS** 71 E12
Mountain View **VIC** 57 H14
Moura **QLD** 15 K9
Mourilyan **QLD** 17 F11 18 H6
Moutajup **VIC** 58 E5
Mowbray Heights **TAS** 73 A14 75 F8
Mowbray Nat Park **QLD** 17 D10 18 B3
Mowbray Park **NSW** 34 H7
Mowla Bluff **WA** 116 H7
Moyarra **VIC** 57 K13
Moyhu **VIC** 64 C4
Moyston **VIC** 58 D7
Muchea **WA** 106 C3 110 C3 112 J5
Muckadilla **QLD** 12 D5 21 K14
Muckatah **VIC** 63 H14 64 A2
Mud Island **QLD** 9 K11
Mud Islands **VIC** 56 H6
Mudamuckla **SA** 97 G12
Mudgee **NSW** 36 D6
Mudgeeraba **QLD** 11 G12 13 H14 24 G3
Mudgegonga **VIC** 43 K11 64 C5
Mudginberri **NT** 123 C7 124 C7
Mudjimba **QLD** 9 C10 13 E13
Mudlo Nat Park **QLD** 13 C12
Muiron Islands Nature Res **WA** 114 D3
Muja Con Park **WA** 108 C7
Mukinbudin **WA** 110 B6 113 H8
Mulan **NT** 124 A5 118 A5
Mulanggari **ACT** 47 B5
Mulbring **NSW** 33 C12 37 E10 45 K5
Mulcra **VIC** 62 E1
Mulga Bore **SA** 92 C7
Mulgildie **QLD** 13 A10 15 K11
Mulgoa **NSW** 34 E7
Mulgowie **QLD** 10 D4
Mulgrave **NSW** 28 B1 35 B8
Mulgrave **VIC** 53 K13 54 B6 57 E9

Mulgurram **NT** 125 C10
Mulingi (Mt Greenwood) **NT** 124 F2
Mullaley **NSW** 38 J5
Mullaloo **WA** 101 A1 106 D2
Mullalyup **WA** 108 D5
Mullengandra **NSW** 43 J12 64 A6
Mullengudgery **NSW** 36 A1 41 G12
Mullewa **WA** 112 E5
Mullion Creek **NSW** 36 E5
Mullumbimby **NSW** 13 J14 39 B13
Mulpata **SA** 89 H12 98 D5
Muludja **WA** 117 G10
Mulwala **NSW** 43 J10 64 A3
Mulyandry **NSW** 36 G3 43 D13
Mulyati **NT** 128 J1
Mumballup **WA** 108 C6 110 G3
Mumbannar **VIC** 58 F2
Mumberkine **WA** 106 B6
Mumbil **NSW** 36 D5
Mumeka **NT** 125 C8
Mummel Gulf Nat Park **NSW** 37 A11 39 J9
Mummulgum **NSW** 13 K13 39 C12
Mumpumpampu **NT** 125 F10
Mumu **QLD** 17 K8 21 B8
Mumukala **NT** 123 C7 124 C6
Mundaring **WA** 106 D4 110 D3 112 K6
Mundaring Weir **WA** 106 E4
Mundarlo **NSW** 43 G13
Munderoo **NSW** 43 J13 64 B1
Mundijong **WA** 106 F3 110 E3 112 K5
Mundiwindi **WA** 115 F10
Mundoona **VIC** 63 H13 64 B1
Mundoonen Nature Res **NSW** 44 C3
Mundoora **SA** 88 D7
Mundrabilla Motel **WA** 119 H6
Mundubbera **QLD** 13 B10
Mundulla **SA** 42 K1 98 F6
Mungalawurru **NT** 127 G8
Mungallala **QLD** 12 D3 21 K13
Mungana **QLD** 17 E9
Mungar **QLD** 13 C13
Mungaroona Range Nature Res **WA** 115 C1
Munga-Thirri (Simpson Desert) Nat Park **QLD** 20 H1 91 A8 129 H14
Mungeribar **NSW** 36 C3 41 H13 43 A13
Mungery **NSW** 36 D2 41 J13 43 B13
Munghorn Gap Nature Res **NSW** 36 C7
Mungilli **WA** 118 G1
Mungindi **NSW** 12 K6 38 C3
Mungkan Kandju Nat Park **QLD** 19 F2
Mungkarta (Mclaren Creek) **NT** 127 H9
Munglinup **WA** 111 G10
Mungo Brush **NSW** 37 D12
Mungo Nat Park **NSW** 42 D5
Mungoorbada (Robinson River) **NT** 125 K13 127 B13
Mungullah **WA** 114 H2
Mungunburra **QLD** 14 B3 17 J11 21 A11
Mungungo **QLD** 13 A10 15 K11
Mungurrupa **NT** 126 J2 128 A2
Munjina (Auski) Roadhouse **WA** 115 D8
Munmorah State Rec Area **NSW** 33 F14
Munno Para **SA** 86 E3
Munro **VIC** 64 H6
Munster **WA** 104 E3
Muntadgin **WA** 110 C7 113 J8
Munyaroo Con Park **SA** 88 D6 94 K6
Muogamarra Nature Res **NSW** 35 A10
Muradup **WA** 109 D3
Muralug **QLD** 19 B2
Muralug **QLD** 19 B2
Murarrie **QLD** 3 E6 5 K12 7 B12
Murcheboluc **VIC** 56 G1
Murchison **VIC** 63 K13 64 D1
Murchison **WA** 112 C5
Murdinga **SA** 88 D3
Murdoch **WA** 101 J3 104 B4
Murdong **WA** 109 D2
Murdunna **TAS** 69 H4
Muresk **WA** 106 D6
Murga **NSW** 36 F4 43 D14
Murgenella **NT** 124 B7
Murgon **QLD** 13 D11
Muriel **NSW** 41 G11
Muringung **NT** 124 J3 126 A3
Muronbung **NSW** 36 C5
Murphys Creek **QLD** 10 B2 13 G11
Murra Warra **VIC** 42 K4 62 J5
Murrabit **VIC** 42 H6 63 F9
Murradoc **VIC** 56 G5
Murramarang Nat Park **NSW** 44 E6
Murranji **NT** 126 C6
Murrawal **NSW** 36 A6 38 K3
Murray Bridge **QLD** 10 J2
Murray Bridge **SA** 89 H10 98 D4
Murray River Nat Park **SA** 42 F1 89 F12 98 B6
Murray Town **SA** 89 C8 95 J8
Murray-Sunset Nat Park **VIC** 42 G2 62 C2 89 G14 98 C7
Murrayville **VIC** 42 H2 62 E3 89 J13 98 D7
Murrin Bridge **NSW** 41 K10 43 C10
Murrindal **VIC** 44 K1 65 G9
Murrindindi **VIC** 64 F2 66 C2
Murringo **NSW** 36 J4 43 F14 44 A2
Murroon **VIC** 59 H10 61 F11
Murrumba Downs **QLD** 5 C9
Murrumbah **NSW** 36 C2 41 H13 43 A13
Murrumbateman **NSW** 44 C3
Murrumbeena **VIC** 53 J10 54 A4
Murrumburrah **NSW** 36 J3 43 F14 44 B1
Murrungowar **VIC** 65 G11
Murrurundi **NSW** 37 B9
Murtoa **VIC** 58 A6 62 H5
Murtulki **NT** 127 H9
Murun Murula **NT** 127 E14
Murweh **QLD** 23 C13
Murwillumbah **NSW** 11 K13 13 J14 39 A13
Musgrave **NT** 129 J9
Musselboro **TAS** 75 F10

Musselroe Bay **TAS** 75 A14 78 J6
Musselroe Bay Con Area **TAS** 75 A13 78 J5
Muswellbrook **NSW** 37 C9
Mutarnee **QLD** 17 H11
Mutawintji Nat Park **NSW** 40 F3
Mutawintji Nature Res **NSW** 40 F4
Mutchilba **QLD** 17 E10 18 F1
Mutdapilly **QLD** 10 D7
Mutitjulu **NT** 128 J4
Muttaburra **QLD** 14 F1 21 D9
Muttama **NSW** 36 K3 43 G13 44 C1
Mutton Hole Wetlands Con Park **QLD** 16 F5
Myall **VIC** 63 F9
Myall Creek **NSW** 38 E7
Myall Lake **NSW** 37 D13
Myall Lakes Nat Park **NSW** 37 D12
Myalla **TAS** 77 F8
Myalup **WA** 106 K2 108 A4
Myamyn **VIC** 58 G4
Myaree **WA** 102 K3 104 A4
Myatt **NT** 124 J3 126 A3
Mylestom **NSW** 39 G12
Mylor **SA** 85 H11 86 K4 87 A7
Mylor Con Park **SA** 85 H11
Mylor Recreation Centre **SA** 86 K4
Myola **VIC** 59 A13 63 K11
Mypona **SA** 87 E3
Myponga Beach **SA** 87 E3 89 J8 98 D2
Myponga Con Park **SA** 87 F4
Myrla **SA** 89 F12
Myrniong **VIC** 56 B3 59 E12
Myrrhee **VIC** 64 D4
Myrtle Bank **SA** 81 H5 84 D6
Myrtle Bank **TAS** 75 E9
Myrtleford **VIC** 64 C5
Myrtletown **QLD** 3 C6 5 H13
Myrtleville **NSW** 36 J7 44 B5
Mysia **VIC** 42 K6 63 H9
Mystic Park **VIC** 42 H6 63 F9
Myubee **QLD** 20 C3

N

Naas **ACT** 48 F4
Nabageena **TAS** 76 F5
Nabarlek **NT** 124 C7
Nabawa **WA** 112 E4
Nabiac **NSW** 37 C13
Nabowla **TAS** 75 D9
Naccowlah Oil Plant **QLD** 22 E6
Nackara **SA** 89 B10 95 J10
Nadgee Nature Res **NSW** 44 K5 65 G14
Nadgigomar Nature Res **NSW** 44 D5
Nadirri **NT** 124 F2
Nagambie **VIC** 59 A14 63 K12 64 D1
Nagoorin **QLD** 15 J11
Nailsworth **SA** 81 E4 82 J5 84 A5
Nairana Nat Park **QLD** 14 E5 21 C12
Nairne **SA** 86 K6 89 H9
Nakara **NT** 122 C5
Nala **TAS** 69 C2
Nalangil **VIC** 59 H9 61 E8
Nalinga **VIC** 43 K9 63 J14 64 C2
Nalya **WA** 107 F9
Namadgi Nat Park **ACT** 44 E2 47 K1 48 F2
Nambling **WA** 107 A8
Nambour **QLD** 9 C13 13 E13
Nambrok **VIC** 64 J5 66 F7
Nambucca Heads **NSW** 39 H12
Nambung Nat Park **WA** 110 A2 112 H4
Namerinni **NT** 127 E8
Namming Nature Res **WA** 110 B2 112 H5
Namugardabu **NT** 125 C8
Nana Glen **NSW** 39 F12
Nanango **QLD** 8 C1 13 E11
Nanarup **WA** 109 J14 110 K6
Nandaly **VIC** 42 H4 62 E6
Nanga **WA** 106 J4
Nanga Station **WA** 112 B2 114 K2
Nangak **NT** 125 C9
Nangana **VIC** 57 D11
Nangar Nat Park **NSW** 36 F4 43 D14
Nangeenan **WA** 107 C13
Nangiloc **VIC** 42 F4 62 B5
Nangkita **SA** 87 E6
Nangu **NT** 124 F1
Nangur Nat Park **QLD** 13 D11
Nangus **NSW** 43 G13
Nangwarry **SA** 58 E1 98 J6
Nannine **WA** 113 B8
Nannup **WA** 108 E4 110 H3
Nantawarra **SA** 89 E8 98 A2
Nanutarra Roadhouse **WA** 114 E4
Nanyingburra **NT** 125 B11
Napier **WA** 109 J14
Napperby **SA** 89 C8 95 K8
Napranum **QLD** 19 E1
Nar Nar Goon **VIC** 57 F12 64 J2 66 F3
Nar Nar Goon North **VIC** 57 F12
Naracoopa **TAS** 78 C3
Naracoorte **SA** 98 G6
Naracoorte Caves Nat Park **SA** 98 H6
Naradhan **NSW** 43 D10
Narangba **QLD** 4 A7 9 H9 13 F13
Narara **NSW** 33 H12
Narawntapu Nat Park **TAS** 74 D5 77 G13
Narbethong **VIC** 57 A12 64 G2 66 D3
Nardoo **QLD** 23 E13
Naree Budjong Djara Nat Park **QLD** 11 B13
Nareen **VIC** 58 D3
Narellan **NSW** 35 G8
Narellan Vale **NSW** 35 G8
Naremben **WA** 107 E14 110 D7 113 K8
Naremburn **NSW** 29 J11
Naretha **WA** 119 F3
Nariel **VIC** 43 K13 65 C8

Nariel Creek **VIC** 43 K13 65 C8
Naringal **VIC** 58 H7 60 F4
Naroghid **VIC** 60 E6
Narooma **NSW** 44 G5
Narrabeen **NSW** 27 C7 29 E14 35 B12
Narrabri **NSW** 38 F5
Narrabri West **NSW** 38 F5
Narrabundah **ACT** 47 F5
Narraburra **NSW** 36 J2 43 F13
Narran Lake Nature Res **NSW** 41 C12
Narrandera **NSW** 43 G11
Narraport **VIC** 62 H7
Narrawa **TAS** 73 A8 74 F3 77 J11
Narrawah **NSW** 36 J5 44 B3
Narraweena **NSW** 27 C7 29 F13 35 C12
Narrawong **VIC** 58 H4
Narre Warren **VIC** 55 C11 57 E10
Narre Warren East **VIC** 55 C11 57 E10
Narre Warren North **VIC** 55 C9 57 E10
Narrewillock **VIC** 63 H8
Narridy **SA** 89 D8 95 K8
Narrien Range Nat Park **QLD** 14 G5 21 E12
Narrikup **WA** 109 H13 110 J6
Narromine **NSW** 36 C3 41 H14 43 A14
Narrung **SA** 89 J9
Narrung **VIC** 42 G5 62 C7
Narwee **NSW** 31 H8
Nashdale **NSW** 36 F5
Nat Park **TAS** 71 C10 73 K11
Nathalia **VIC** 43 J8 63 H13 64 B1
Nathan **QLD** 3 G4 7 E11
Nathan Heights **QLD** 7 E10
Natimuk **VIC** 58 A4 62 K4
Native Corners **TAS** 69 F1 71 B13
Natone **TAS** 74 D1 77 G9
Nattai **NSW** 34 H6 37 H8 44 A6
Nattai Nat Park **NSW** 34 J6 37 J8 44 A6
Nattai State Rec Park **NSW** 34 H6
Natte Yallock **VIC** 59 B9
Natural Bridge **QLD** 11 J11
Naturi **SA** 89 H10 98 D4
Natya **VIC** 62 D7
Nauiyu **NT** 124 E3
Naval Base **WA** 104 H2
Navarre **VIC** 59 B8
Nayook **VIC** 57 E14 64 H3 66 E4
Nea **NSW** 38 J6
Neale Junction Nature Res **WA** 119 C4
Nearie Lake Nature Res **NSW** 42 D3
Neath **NSW** 33 C11 45 H4
Nebo **QLD** 14 E7 21 C14
Nedlands **WA** 101 G2 102 G3
Needalling **WA** 107 K14
Needles **TAS** 73 B11 74 G5 77 K13
Neerabup Nat Park **WA** 106 C2 110 C3 112 J5
Neeralin Pool **WA** 107 K9 109 A11
Neerim **VIC** 64 J3 66 E4
Neerim South **VIC** 64 J3 66 F4
Neeworra **NSW** 38 C3
Neika **TAS** 69 H1 71 E12
Neilrex **NSW** 36 A6 38 K3
Nelia **QLD** 16 K6 20 B6
Nelligen **NSW** 44 E5
Nelly Bay **QLD** 17 H12
Nelshaby **SA** 89 C8 95 K8
Nelson **NSW** 28 C3 35 C9
Nelson **VIC** 58 G1 98 K6
Nelson Bay **NSW** 37 D12
Nelsons Plains **NSW** 33 A13
Nemarluk **NT** 124 F2
Nembudding **WA** 107 A10
Nemingha **NSW** 38 J7
Neptune Islands Con Park **SA** 88 H3
Neptune Islands Group Marine Park **SA** 88 H3
Nerang **QLD** 11 F12 13 H14 24 E2
Neranwood **QLD** 11 H12
Nerriga **NSW** 44 D5
Nerrigundah **NSW** 44 F5 65 B14
Nerrin Nerrin **VIC** 59 F8 60 A6
Nest Hill Nature Res **NSW** 43 H12
Netherby **SA** 84 E6
Netherby **VIC** 62 H3
Nethercote **NSW** 44 J4 65 E14
Netherdale **QLD** 14 D7 21 B14
Netherton **SA** 89 J11 98 D5
Netley **SA** 81 H3 84 D3
Neuarpurr **VIC** 58 A1 62 K2
Neumgna **QLD** 8 E1
Neurea **NSW** 36 D5
Neurum **QLD** 8 F7
Neutral Bay **NSW** 27 E6 29 J12 31 A12
Nevertire **NSW** 33 G10 36 B2 41 G13
Neville **NSW** 36 G5
Nevilton **QLD** 10 E1
New Beith **QLD** 11 D9
New Bore **NT** 128 E4
New Brighton **NSW** 39 B14
New Chum **QLD** 6 H4
New England **NSW** 39 G9
New England Nat Park **NSW** 39 G11
New Farm **QLD** 3 E4 7 C10 11 B10
New Gisborne **VIC** 59 D13
New Ground **TAS** 74 D5 77 H13
New Looma **WA** 117 G8
New Mapoon **QLD** 19 B2
New Mollyan **NSW** 36 B5
New Norcia **WA** 110 B3 112 H5
New Norfolk **TAS** 71 D11
New Town **TAS** 68 A1 69 F1 71 D13
Newbridge **NSW** 36 G6
Newbridge **VIC** 59 A10 63 K9
Newburn **WA** 101 G6 103 G9
Newbury **VIC** 59 D12
Newcastle **NSW** 33 C14 37 E11
Newcastle Waters (Marlinja) **NT** 126 D7

Newdegate WA 111 F8
Newell QLD 17 D10 18 A2
Newfield VIC 59 J8 60 H6
Newham VIC 59 C13
Newhaven VIC 66 H2
Newington NSW 28 J7 30 A7
Newland Head Con Park SA 87 H5 89 J8 98 E2
Newlands QLD 14 D6 21 C13
Newlands WA 108 C5
Newlyn VIC 59 D11
Newman WA 115 F9
Newmarket QLD 3 D3 5 J9 7 A9
Newmarket QLD 52 F7
Newmerella VIC 65 H10
Newnes NSW 32 J3 37 F8
Newnes Junction NSW 34 B3
Newnham TAS 73 A14 75 F8
Newport NSW 27 A7 29 C14 35 B12
Newport VIC 51 E2 52 H6 56 D6
Newry VIC 64 H5 66 E7
Newrybar NSW 39 B13
Newstead QLD 3 E4 5 K10 7 B10
Newstead VIC 59 C11
Newton SA 81 F6 83 J8 85 A8
Newton Boyd NSW 39 E10
Newtown NSW 27 F5 31 C10
Newtown QLD 6 H2
Newtown VIC 56 G3
Ngadumiyerrka NT 125 E12
Ngalingkadji WA 117 H10
Ngambaa Nature Res NSW 39 H11
Ngangalala NT 125 C10
Ngardinitchi NT 124 F1
Ngarinthi NT 124 G1
Ngarkat Con Park SA 42 J1 89 K12 98 E6
Ngarlu Ngarlu NT 124 B7
Ngarngurr NT 128 J2
Ngarutjara SA 92 B7 128 K5
Ngayawilli NT 125 B11
Ngijipin NT 124 B7
Ngilipitji NT 125 E11
Nguiu NT 124 B3
Ngukurr NT 125 G9
Ngulin Nature Res NSW 37 A11 39 J9
Ngulupi WA 118 B7 126 J1 128 A1
Ngulwirriwirri WA 124 J1 126 A1
Nguman NT 128 F2
Ngumpan WA 117 H10
Ngunjiwirri WA 117 H12
Ngunnawal ACT 47 A4
Ngunthak NT 124 G1
Ngurtuwarta WA 117 G10
Nhill VIC 42 K3 62 J3 98 F7
Nhulunbuy NT 125 C13
Niagara WA 113 F12
Niagara Park NSW 33 H12
Nicholls ACT 47 A4
Nicholls Rivulet TAS 71 G12
Nicholson VIC 65 H8
Nicholson Camp WA 117 H12
Nicolas Baudin Island Con Park SA 97 J12
Nicoll Scrub Nat Park QLD 11 H13 24 K5
Niddrie VIC 52 E6
Niemur NSW 42 H7 63 E10
Nierinna TAS 69 J1 71 F12
Nietta TAS 73 A8 74 E2 77 J10
Nightcap Nat Park NSW 13 J14 39 B13
Nightcliff NT 122 C3
Nildottie SA 89 G10 98 C4
Nile TAS 75 G9
Nilgen Nature Res WA 112 H4
Nimaru QLD 21 K11 23 B13
Nimbin NSW 13 J13 39 B13
Nimmitabel NSW 44 G3 65 C12
Ninda VIC 42 H4 62 F6
Nindigully QLD 12 H5 38 A2
Ninety Mile Beach Marine Nat Park VIC 64 K6
Ningaloo Marine Park WA 114 E2
Ningi QLD 9 G10
Ninnes SA 88 E7 98 A2
Nippering WA 109 B13
Nirranda VIC 58 J7 60 G4
Nirranda East VIC 58 J7 60 G5
Nirrippi NT 128 D3
Nitmiluk (Katherine Gorge) Nat Park NT 123 H6 124 F6
Nixon Skinner Con Park SA 87 F4
Noarlunga SA 89 H8 98 D2
Noarlunga Centre SA 87 B5
Nobby QLD 10 E1 13 G11
Nobby Beach QLD 24 F5
Nobbys Creek NSW 11 J12
Noble Park VIC 51 G6 54 C6 57 E9
Noccundra QLD 22 E7
Nocoleche Nature Res NSW 23 K10 40 C6
Noggerup WA 108 C6 110 G3
Nokarning WA 107 B13
Nollajup Nature Res WA 108 D7
Nollamara WA 101 D3 102 C4
Nomans Lake WA 107 J10
Nombinnie Nature Res NSW 41 K9 43 C9
Nombinnie State Con Area NSW 41 K9 43 C9
Nome QLD 14 A5 17 H12
Nonda QLD 16 K7 20 B7
Nongra Lake NT 126 E2
Noogoora QLD 10 B7
Noojee VIC 64 H3 66 E4
Nook TAS 74 E4 77 J12
Noonamah NT 124 C4
Noonbinna NSW 36 H4 43 E14
Noondoo QLD 12 J5 38 A1
Noorat VIC 58 G7 60 C5
Noorinbee VIC 65 G12
Noorinbee North VIC 44 K3 65 G12
Noosa Heads QLD 9 A10 13 D13
Noosa Nat Park QLD 9 A10 13 D14
Noosaville QLD 9 A10
Nora Creina SA 98 H4

Noradjuha VIC 58 B4
Norah Head NSW 33 G13
Norahville NSW 37 F11
Noranda WA 101 D5 102 B7
Noraville NSW 33 G13
Nords Wharf NSW 33 E13
Norfolk Bay TAS 69 H4
Norlane VIC 56 F3
Norman Park QLD 7 C11
Normanhurst NSW 29 E8 35 C10
Normanton QLD 16 F5
Normanville SA 87 F3 98 D2
Nornakin WA 107 F12
Nornalup WA 109 K9 110 K4
Norpa WA 107 C14
Norseman WA 111 D12 113 K12
North Adelaide SA 80 A2 81 F4 82 K5 84 B5
North Arm QLD 9 B9
North Balgowah NSW 29 G12
North Balwyn VIC 53 F11
North Bannister WA 106 G5
North Beach WA 101 D1 102 B2
North Bondi NSW 31 B13 35 D12
North Booval QLD 6 G3
North Brighton SA 84 F2
North Bruny Island TAS 69 J2 71 F13
North Curl Curl NSW 29 F14
North Dandalup WA 106 G3
North Forest TAS 76 E6
North Fremantle WA 101 H1 102 J1
North Goonyella QLD 14 E6 21 C14
North Haven NSW 37 B14 39 K11
North Haven SA 81 C2 82 E1 86 G1
North Hobart TAS 68 B2
North Ipswich QLD 6 G2 10 C7
North Johnstone QLD 18 E4
North Karlgarin Nature Res WA 107 F14 110 D7 113 K8
North Lake WA 104 C4
North Lilydale TAS 75 D8
North Maclean QLD 11 D9
North Manly NSW 29 G13
North Melbourne VIC 53 F8
North Motton TAS 74 D2 77 H10
North Narrabeen NSW 29 D14
North Parramatta NSW 28 G6
North Perth WA 101 F4 102 E5
North Pinjarra WA 106 H3
North Plympton SA 84 D3
North Richmond NSW 34 B7
North Ringwood VIC 53 F14
North Rocks NSW 28 G6
North Rothbury NSW 33 A10 45 F4
North Ryde NSW 27 D4 29 H9 35 C11
North Scottsdale TAS 75 C10
North Shields SA 88 G3
North Shore VIC 56 F3
North St Ives NSW 35 C11
North Star NSW 13 K8 38 B6
North Stradbroke Island (Minjerriba) QLD 9 K13 11 B13 13 G14
North Strathfield NSW 29 K8 31 B8
North Sydney NSW 27 E5 29 J11 31 A11 35 D11
North Tamborine QLD 11 F11
North Tarin Rock Nature Res WA 107 J13
North Tivoli QLD 6 G3
North Toowoomba QLD 10 B1
North Turramurra NSW 27 C5 29 E10
North Wahroonga NSW 29 D9
North West Vernon Island NT 124 C4
North Willoughby NSW 27 D6 29 H11
North Wollongong NSW 35 K10
Northam WA 106 C6 110 C4 112 J6
Northampton WA 112 E3
Northbridge NSW 27 E6 29 H12
Northbridge WA 100 A2 101 F4 102 F5
Northcliffe WA 108 H6 110 J3
Northcote VIC 51 C4 53 F9 57 C8
Northdown TAS 74 D4 77 G13
Northfield SA 81 E5 82 H6 86 G2
Northgate QLD 5 H11
Northmead NSW 28 G6
Northville NSW 33 C13
Northwood NSW 29 J10 31 A10
Norton Summit SA 81 G7 85 C10 86 H4
Norval Park QLD 15 K12
Norway Range TAS 72 J7
Norwood SA 81 G5 84 C6 86 H3
Norwood TAS 73 A14 75 F8
Notley Hills TAS 74 E7
Notting Hill VIC 53 J12 54 A6
Notts Well SA 89 F11 98 B5
Nour Nour Nat Park QLD 13 B10
Nourlangie (Anlarrh) NT 123 D7 124 D6
Novar Gardens SA 81 H2 84 E3
Nowa Nowa VIC 65 H9
Nowendoc NSW 37 A11 39 K9
Nowendoc Nat Park NSW 37 A11 39 K9
Nowingi VIC 42 F3 62 C4
Nowley NSW 38 E3
Nowra NSW 37 K8 44 C6
Nowingi VIC 42 F3 62 C4
Nubeena TAS 69 J3
Nudgee QLD 3 C5 5 G11 9 K10
Nudgee Beach QLD 3 B5 5 G12 9 K10
Nudjabarra NT 127 E14
Nuga Nuga Nat Park QLD 12 A5 14 K7 21 H14
Nugent TAS 69 F4
Nukarni WA 107 A13
Nulawan NT 125 G10
Nulkaba NSW 33 C10 45 H4
Nulla Nulla NSW 39 H11
Nullagine WA 115 D10
Nullarbor Nat Park SA 96 E2 119 G2
Nullarbor Reg Res SA 96 D4 119 G7
Nullavale VIC 59 C13
Nullawarre VIC 58 H7 60 G4

Nullawil VIC 42 J5 62 G7
Numagalong NT 127 J8 129 A8
Numbla Vale NSW 44 H2 65 D11
Numbugga NSW 44 H4 65 D13
Numbulwar NT 125 F11
Numeralla NSW 44 G3 65 B12
Numinbah NSW 11 J11
Numinbah Valley QLD 11 H11 39 A13
Nummerloori NT 125 G10
Numurkah VIC 43 K9 63 H13 64 B1
Nunamara TAS 73 A14 75 E9
Nunawading VIC 53 G13
Nundah QLD 3 C4 5 J10
Nundle NSW 37 A10 39 K8
Nunga VIC 42 H4 62 E5
Nungarin WA 107 A13 110 B6 113 J8
Nungatta NSW 44 K3 65 F12
Nunjikompita SA 97 G12
Nuradidgee NT 127 H9
Nurina WA 119 F4
Nurinda QLD 8 F4
Nuriootpa SA 86 B6 89 F9 98 B3
Nurrabiel VIC 58 B4
Nutfield VIC 57 B9
Nuyts Archipelago Con Park SA 97 H10
Nuyts Archipelago Marine Park SA 97 J10
Nuyts Reef Con Park SA 97 K10
Nuytsland Nature Res WA 119 J2
Nyabing WA 110 G6
Nyah VIC 42 H5 63 E8
Nyah West VIC 42 H5 62 E7
Nyamup WA 108 F7
Nyapari SA 92 B3 128 K3
Nyarrin VIC 42 H4 62 E6
Nyikukura SA 92 A1 118 J7 128 K1
Nymagee NSW 41 H10 43 A10
Nymboi-Binderay Nat Park NSW 39 F11
Nymboida Nat Park NSW 39 E11
Nyngan NSW 36 A1 41 G12
Nyora VIC 57 J12 64 K2 66 G3
Nypo VIC 62 G4

O

O'Connell NSW 36 G6
O'Connor ACT 47 C5
O'Connor WA 101 J2 104 B3
O'Halloran Hill SA 84 J3
O'Halloran Hill Rec Park SA 86 K2 87 A5
O'Malley ACT 47 F4
O'Malley SA 96 C6
O'Sullivan Beach SA 87 B4
Oak Beach QLD 18 B3
Oak Forest QLD 18 D3
Oak Park NSW 45 C1
Oak Park VIC 52 D7
Oak Valley NT 129 G8
Oakbank SA 85 E14 86 J5
Oakdale NSW 37 H8 44 A6
Oakden SA 82 H7
Oakey QLD 13 G11
Oakey Creek NSW 36 A7 38 K4
Oakford WA 105 H8
Oakhampton NSW 33 A12
Oakhurst NSW 28 F1 35 C8
Oakland Park QLD 16 F6
Oaklands NSW 43 H10
Oaklands Junction VIC 52 A5
Oaklands Park SA 81 J3 84 F3
Oakleigh VIC 51 F5 53 J11 54 A5 57 E8
Oaks TAS 73 B13 74 G7
Oaks Estate ACT 47 F7
Oakvale VIC 42 J6 63 G8
Oakville NSW 28 B2 35 B8
Oakwood NSW 38 E7
Oakwood TAS 69 J4
Oaky Creek QLD 14 G7 21 E14
Oatlands NSW 28 G7
Oatlands TAS 69 C1
Oatley NSW 31 F8 35 E11
OB Flat SA 58 F1
Oban NSW 39 F9
Obanvale NSW 45 D1
Oberne NSW 43 H13
Oberon NSW 34 E1 36 G7
Obi Obi QLD 9 C8
Obley NSW 36 D4 41 J14 43 B14
Ocean Beach WA 109 K11
Ocean Grove VIC 56 H4 59 H12
Ocean Reef WA 101 A1
Ocean View QLD 9 H8
Oceana TAS 72 E4
Ockley NSW 45 D1
Oenpelli NT 124 C7
Offham QLD 23 E13
Officer VIC 55 F12 57 F11 64 J1 66 F2
Ogmore QLD 15 F9
Ogunbil NSW 37 A10 39 J8
Olary SA 89 A12 95 H12
Old Adaminaby NSW 44 F2
Old Andado NT 129 J10
Old Bar NSW 37 B13
Old Beach TAS 69 G1 71 D12
Old Birrimba NT 124 J5 126 A5
Old Bonalbo NSW 39 B11
Old Bowenfels NSW 34 C2
Old Dry River NT 124 H6
Old Gidgeon NSW 41 D11
Old Grevillea NSW 39 A12
Old Guildford NSW 28 K5 30 B5
Old Halls Creek NSW 117 H13
Old Koreelah NSW 10 K5
Old Mission NT 124 F1
Old Mount Peake NT 126 K7 128 C7
Old Noarlunga SA 87 C5

Old Quinyambie SA 40 D1
Old Reynella SA 84 K3
Old Silkwood QLD 18 J6
Old Tallangatta VIC 64 B7
Old Thorntonia QLD 16 H2
Old Toongabbie NSW 28 G5
Old Tyabb VIC 57 H9
Old Warburton VIC 57 C13
Oldbury WA 104 K7
Oldina TAS 77 G8
Olinda NSW 32 F1 36 E7
Olinda VIC 57 D10 64 H1 66 E2
Olio QLD 21 D8
Olive Island Con Park SA 97 J11
Olympic Dam SA 94 C5
Oman-Ama QLD 13 J10 39 A8
Ombersley VIC 59 G10 61 D11
Omeo VIC 64 E7
Ondit VIC 59 H10 61 E9
One Tree NSW 43 E8 63 A11
One Tree Hill SA 83 B11 86 F4
Ongerup WA 110 H7
Onkaparinga River Nat Park SA 87 C5
Onkaparinga River Rec Park SA 87 C4
Onslow WA 114 C4
Oodla Wirra SA 89 B9 95 J9
Oodnadatta SA 90 E2 93 E14
Oolambeyan Nat Park NSW 43 G9 63 C13
Ooldea SA 96 C7
Oolloo Crossing NT 124 F4
Oombulgurri WA 117 C13
Oombunghi QLD 18 E5
Oonah TAS 77 H8
Oondooroo QLD 20 D7
Oorindi QLD 16 K5 20 B5
Ootann QLD 17 E9
Ootha NSW 36 E1 41 K12 43 C12
Opalton QLD 20 E7
Ophir NSW 36 F5
Opossum Bay TAS 69 J2 71 E13
Ora Banda WA 111 A11 113 G11
Oran Park NSW 35 F8
Orange NSW 36 F5
Orange Grove WA 101 H7 103 J11
Orangeville NSW 34 G7
Oranmeir NSW 44 E4
Orbost VIC 65 H10
Orchard Hills NSW 34 D7
Orchid Beach QLD 13 A14 15 K14
Orchid Valley WA 109 E9
Ord River Nature Res WA 117 C14
Orelia WA 104 J4
Orford TAS 69 E4
Orford VIC 58 G5
Organ Pipes Nat Park VIC 52 B4 56 B6
Orielton TAS 69 G2 71 C14
Orkabie QLD 15 E8
Ormeau QLD 11 E11
Ormiston QLD 11 B11
Ormley TAS 75 H12
Ormond VIC 53 J10 54 A3
Orooroo SA 89 B9 95 J9
Orrtipa-Thurra NT 129 E11
Osborne NSW 43 H10 43 H11 63 F14
Osborne SA 81 C1 82 E1
Osborne Park WA 101 E2 102 D3
Osborne Village QLD 20 D4
Osmaston TAS 73 B11 74 G6 77 K14
Osmington WA 108 D2
Osterley TAS 71 A10 73 H12
Otago TAS 69 G1 71 D13
Otford NSW 35 H11 37 J9
Ottaba QLD 8 H4
Ottoway SA 81 D2 82 H3
Oura NSW 43 H13
Ourimbah NSW 33 H12 37 F10
Ournie NSW 43 J13 65 A8
Ouse TAS 71 B10 73 J11
Outer Harbor SA 81 B2 82 D2 86 F1 89 G8 98 C2
Ouyen VIC 42 G4 62 D5
Ovens VIC 64 C5
Overland Corner SA 89 F12 98 B5
Overlander Roadhouse WA 112 B3 114 K3
Ovingham SA 82 K4 84 B4
Owen SA 89 F8 98 B3
Owen Springs Reserve NT 128 F7
Oxenford QLD 11 F12 13 H14 24 B2
Oxford Falls NSW 27 C6 29 F12 35 B11
Oxford Park QLD 5 H8
Oxley ACT 47 H3
Oxley NSW 42 E7 63 A10
Oxley QLD 3 G2 7 F8 11 B9
Oxley VIC 43 K10 64 C4
Oxley Wild Rivers Nat Park NSW 39 H9
Oyster Bay NSW 31 G8 35 E11
Oyster Cove NSW 69 J1 71 F12
Ozenkadnook VIC 58 B2

P

Paaratte VIC 60 G5
Pacific Palms NSW 37 C13
Pacific Pines QLD 24 C2
Packers Crossing NSW 40 K3 42 B3
Packsaddle NSW 40 E3
Padbury WA 101 B2
Paddington NSW 26 D4 31 C12 35 D11
Paddington QLD 3 E3 7 B9
Paddys River NSW 36 K7 44 B5
Padstow NSW 27 H3 30 E7 35 E10
Padstow Heights NSW 27 H3 30 F7
Padthaway SA 98 G5
Padthaway Con Park SA 98 G5

Page ACT 47 C3
Pagett Nature Res WA 108 F3
Pagewood NSW 31 D12 35 E12
Paignie VIC 62 D4
Pakenham VIC 55 F13 57 F11 64 J2 66 F2
Pakenham South VIC 55 H14 57 G11
Pakenham Upper VIC 55 D14 57 F11
Palana TAS 78 A4
Palen Creek QLD 11 J8
Paleroo NSW 38 F5
Palgarup WA 108 F6
Pallamallawa NSW 38 D5
Pallara QLD 3 J3 7 H9
Pallarenda QLD 17 H12
Pallinup WA 109 E13
Palm Beach NSW 29 A14 33 K12 35 A12 37 Q10
Palm Beach QLD 11 H13 24 G6
Palm Cove QLD 18 C4
Palm Grove NSW 33 H11
Palm Island QLD 17 G12
Palmdale NSW 33 H12
Palmer River Roadhouse QLD 17 C9
Palmers Oakey NSW 36 F7
Palmerston ACT 47 A4
Palmerston NT 123 C1 124 C4
Palmgrove Nat Park (Scientific) QLD 12 A6 15 K8
Palmvale NSW 11 K13
Palmview QLD 9 D10
Palmwoods QLD 9 D9
Palmyra WA 101 J2 102 K2 104 A3
Paloona TAS 74 E3 77 H11
Paluma QLD 17 H11
Paluma Range Nat Park QLD 14 A4 17 H11
Palumpa NT 124 F2
Pamamaroo NSW 40 J4 42 A4
Pambula NSW 44 J5 65 E14
Pambula Beach NSW 44 J5 65 E14
Panania NSW 30 E6
Pandappa Con Park SA 89 C10 95 K10
Pandayal NT 124 D3
Panitya VIC 42 H1 62 E1
Panmure VIC 58 H7 60 F4
Pannawonica WA 114 C5
Pannikin Island QLD 11 C12
Panorama SA 81 J4 84 F5
Pantapin WA 107 E11
Pantijan WA 117 D9
Panton Hill VIC 53 A14 57 B9 64 G1 66 D2
Panuara NSW 36 F5
Paper Beach TAS 74 D7
Pappinbarra NSW 37 A13 39 K11
Pappinbarra Junction NSW 37 A13 39 J11
Papunya NT 128 E5
Para Hills SA 81 C5 82 F7 86 G3
Para Hills West SA 82 F5
Para Vista SA 81 D6 82 G7
Para Wirra Rec Park SA 86 E4
Paraburdoo WA 114 F7
Parachilna SA 95 E8
Paracombe SA 83 H11 86 G4
Paradise SA 81 E6
Paradise TAS 73 A9 74 F4 77 J12
Paradise Point QLD 11 E13 24 A4
Paradise Waters QLD 24 D5
Parafield SA 81 C5 82 E6 86 G2
Parafield Gardens SA 81 C4 82 D5
Paralowie SA 81 B4 82 D5
Parap NT 122 G2
Paraparap VIC 56 H2
Paratoo SA 89 B10 95 J10
Parattah TAS 69 D2 71 A13
Pardoo Roadhouse WA 115 A10 116 K2
Parenna TAS 78 D2
Parham SA 89 F8 98 B2
Parilla SA 42 H1 89 J12 98 D6
Paringa SA 42 F1 89 F13 98 B6
Park Beach TAS 69 H3 71 D14
Park Holme SA 81 J3 84 F3 86 J2
Park Orchards VIC 51 C7 53 F13
Park Ridge QLD 11 D10
Parkdale VIC 54 D4
Parkerville WA 103 A14 110 D3 112 K5
Parkes ACT 46 C3 47 E5
Parkes NSW 36 E3 41 K14 43 C14
Parkham TAS 73 A11 74 F5 77 J13
Parkhurst QLD 15 H10
Parkinson QLD 3 J4 7 J10
Parklea NSW 28 E3
Parkside SA 80 D3 81 G4 84 D6 86 J2
Parkside TAS 75 E14
Parkville VIC 53 F8
Parkwood QLD 11 F12 24 D3
Parkwood WA 101 J5 102 K7 104 A7
Parmelia WA 104 K4
Parnabal QLD 15 H8
Parndana SA 88 K6
Parnella TAS 75 E14
Parnngurr WA 115 E13
Parnta NT 126 F3
Paroo-Darling Nat Park NSW 40 E5
Paroo-Darling State Con Area NSW 40 F6
Parr State Con Area NSW 37 F9
Parramatta NSW 27 E2 28 H6 35 D10
Parrawe TAS 77 H8
Parrulyu (Mount Davidson) NT 126 J4 128 A4
Parry Lagoons Nature Res WA 117 D13
Parryville WA 109 J11
Parting Creek Reg Res TAS 72 D4
Paru NT 124 B3
Paruna SA 42 G1 89 G13 98 C6
Parwan VIC 56 C3 59 E12
Pasadena SA 84 F5
Pasco Group TAS 78 B3
Pascoe Vale VIC 52 D7 56 C7
Paskeville SA 88 E7 98 A2
Pata SA 89 G12 98 C6
Patchewollock VIC 62 E4

Pateena TAS 73 B14 75 G8
Paterson NSW 37 D11 45 E7
Patersonia TAS 75 E9
Patho VIC 42 J7 63 H11
Patjarr (Karilwara) WA 118 G4
Patonga NSW 33 K12 35 A11 37 G10
Patterson VIC 53 K10 54 B3
Patterson Lakes VIC 54 F6 57 F9
Paulls Valley WA 103 F14
Paupong NSW 44 H2 65 D11
Paupong Nature Res WA 44 H2 65 D10
Pawleena TAS 69 G3 71 C14
Pawpaw SA 92 D7
Pawtella TAS 69 C2
Paxton NSW 33 D10 45 K3
Payne QLD 14 G1 21 E9
Payneham SA 81 F5 82 K7 84 B7 86 H3
Payneham South SA 82 K7 84 B7
Paynes Crossing NSW 33 D8 37 E10
Paynes Find WA 112 F7
Paynesville VIC 65 H8
Peaceful Bay WA 109 K9 110 K5
Peachester QLD 9 E8
Peachna Con Park SA 88 F2
Peak Charles Nat Park WA 111 F11
Peak Crossing QLD 10 E7
Peak Downs QLD 14 F7 21 D14
Peak Hill NSW 36 D3 41 J14 43 B14
Peak Hill WA 113 A8 115 J8
Peak View NSW 44 F4 65 B13
Peake SA 89 J11 98 D5
Peake Creek Siding SA 90 F3
Peakhurst NSW 27 H3 30 F7
Pearce ACT 47 G3
Pearcedale VIC 55 K8 57 G9 64 J1 66 F1
Pearl Beach NSW 33 K12 35 A11
Pearsall WA 101 B3
Pearshape TAS 78 E1
Peats Ridge NSW 33 H11 37 F10
Pebbly Beach NSW 44 E6
Pechey QLD 8 J2
Peebinga SA 42 G1 62 D1 89 H13 98 C6
Peebinga Con Park SA
42 G1 62 D1 89 H13 98 C6
Peechelba VIC 43 K10 64 B4
Peel NSW 36 F6
Peel Island QLD 11 B12
Peelwood NSW 36 H6 44 A4
Peerabeelup WA 108 F4
Pegarah TAS 78 D2
Pekina SA 89 B8 95 J8
Pelaw Main NSW 33 B11 45 J5
Pelham QLD 16 H7
Pelham TAS 71 B11 73 K13
Pelican Waters QLD 9 E10
Pella VIC 62 G4
Pelton NSW 33 C10 45 J3
Pelverata TAS 71 F12
Pemberton WA 108 G6 110 J3
Pembrooke NSW 37 A14 39 K11
Pencil Pine TAS 72 B7 74 G2
Pendle Hill NSW 28 H4
Penfield SA 82 A5 86 E2
Penguin TAS 74 C2 77 G10
Penguin Island WA 106 F2
Penna TAS 69 G2 71 D14
Pennant Hills NSW 27 C3 29 F8 35 C10
Penneshaw SA 88 K7 98 E2
Pennington SA 82 H3
Penola SA 58 D1 98 H6
Penong SA 97 G10
Penrice SA 86 C7
Penrith NSW 34 D7 37 G9
Penshurst NSW 31 F8
Penshurst VIC 58 F5 60 B1
Pensioners Bush NSW 73 B12 74 G6 77 K14
Pentland QLD 14 C3 17 K10 21 A10
Penworthham SA 89 E9 98 A3
Penzance TAS 69 J4
Peppermint Grove WA 101 G2 102 H2
Peppers Plains VIC 62 H4
Peppimenarti NT 124 F2
Peranga QLD 13 F11
Percy Isles Nat Park QLD 15 E10
Percyville QLD 17 H8
Peregian Beach QLD 9 B10 13 E13
Perekerten NSW 42 G6 63 D9
Perenjori WA 112 F5
Perenna VIC 42 K3 62 H3
Perentie Bore SA 93 C9
Pericoe NSW 44 J4 65 F13
Perillup WA 109 H11
Peringillup WA 109 E13
Perisher Village NSW 43 K14 44 G1 65 C10
Peronne VIC 98 G7
Perponda SA 89 H11 98 C5
Perrederr NT 124 F2
Perseverance QLD 8 K2 10 A2
Perth TAS 73 B14 75 G8
Perth WA
100 B2 101 F4 102 F5 106 E2 110 D3 112 K5
Perthville NSW 36 G6
Petcheys Bay TAS 71 G11
Peterborough SA 89 C9 95 J9
Peterborough VIC 58 J7 60 H5
Peterhead SA 82 D2 82 G2
Petersham NSW 31 C10
Petersville SA 88 F7 98 B1
Petford QLD 17 E10
Petina SA 97 H12
Petrie QLD 5 C8 9 J9 13 F13
Petrie Terrace QLD 2 B1
Pettavel VIC 56 H2
Pheasant Creek VIC 64 G1 66 C2
Phegans Bay NSW 33 J12
Phillip ACT 47 F4
Phillip Bay NSW 31 F12 35 E12
Phillip Creek NT 127 G9

Phillip Island VIC 57 K9 59 J14 64 K1 66 H1
Phillott QLD 23 E13
Piallaway NSW 38 J6
Pialligo ACT 47 E6
Piambie VIC 42 G5 62 C7
Piangil VIC 42 G5 62 D7
Piccadilly SA 81 J7 85 E10 86 J4
Picaninny Bore NT 126 H2
Pickanjinnie QLD 12 E6
Pickering Brook WA 106 E4
Pickertaramoor NT 123 A1 124 B3
Picnic Point NSW 30 F6
Picola VIC 43 J8 63 G12 64 A1
Picton NSW 35 H8 37 H8 44 A6
Picton WA 108 B4 110 G3
Pidna Nat Park QLD 8 E1
Piedmont VIC 57 E14
Piednipple Hall SA 97 J12
Pier Millan VIC 42 H4 62 E6
Pierces Creek QLD 8 H2
Piesse Brook WA 103 G13
Piesseville WA 107 K9 109 A11 110 F5
Pigeon Hole Outstation NT 126 C4
Pigeon Ponds VIC 58 D3
Piggabeen NSW 11 H13 24 K6
Pikedale QLD 13 J10 39 B9
Pinehill QLD 14 H5 21 F12
Pilakatal NT 128 J2
Pilgna SA 92 D5
Pilliga NSW 38 F2
Pilliga Nature Res NSW 38 H4
Pilton QLD 10 E2
Pimpama QLD 11 E12
Pimpinio VIC 58 A5 62 K4
Pindar WA 112 E5
Pine Clump NSW 38 J1 41 F13
Pine Corner SA 88 D4
Pine Creek NT 123 G4 124 E5
Pine Hill NT 128 D7
Pine Landing TAS 70 A4 72 J6
Pine Lodge VIC 63 J13 64 C2
Pine Point SA 88 G7 98 B1
Pine Ridge NSW 37 A8 38 K6
Pine Ridge Con Park QLD 24 B4
Pinelands QLD 8 J1
Pinery SA 89 F8 98 B2
Piney Range NSW 36 G2 43 E13
Pingala NT 127 F8
Pingaring WA 110 E7
Pingelly WA 107 G8 110 E5
Pingrup WA 110 G7
Pinja NT 126 F3
Pinjarra WA 106 H3 110 E3
Pinjarra Hills QLD 3 G1 6 E6
Pinjarrega Nature Res WA 112 G5
Pinkawillinie Con Park SA 88 B3 94 J3
Pinkenba QLD 3 D6 5 J13 7 A13
Pinnaroo SA 42 H1 62 E1 89 J13 98 D6
Pinpirnga NT 128 E2
Pioneer TAS 75 C12
Pioneer WA 111 D12 113 K12
Pioneer Bay VIC 57 J11
Pipalyatjara SA 92 B1 118 J7 128 K1
Pipers Brook TAS 75 C8
Pipers Flat NSW 34 B1
Pipers River TAS 75 C8
Piries VIC 64 F3 66 B4
Pirlangimpi (Garden Point) NT 124 A3
Pirita VIC 42 F3 62 B3
Pirrinuan QLD 13 F10
Pirron Yallock VIC 59 H9 61 F8
Pitalu NT 128 J2
Pitfield VIC 59 F9 61 A9
Pithara WA 112 G6
Pitt Town NSW 35 B8
Pitt Water Nature Res TAS 69 G2 71 D14
Pittong VIC 59 E9
Pittsworth QLD 13 G11
Plainland QLD 10 C4
Planchonella Nature Res NSW 38 C7
Pleasant Hills NSW 43 H11
Pleasure Point NSW 30 F5
Plenty TAS 71 C11
Plenty VIC 51 A5 53 B11 57 B8
Plumpton NSW 28 F1 35 D8
Plumridge Lakes Nature Res WA 119 D3
Plympton SA 81 H3 84 E3 86 J1
Plympton Park SA 81 H3 84 E3
Pmara Jutunta NT 128 D7
Poatina TAS 73 D13 74 J7
Pocket Well SA 93 D8
Poeppel Corner NT QLD SA
20 K1 91 A8 129 K14
Point Addis Marine Nat Park VIC
56 K2 59 H12 61 F14
Point Arkwright QLD 9 B10
Point Bell SA 97 G10
Point Clare NSW 33 J12
Point Cook VIC 52 K3 56 E6 59 F13
Point Davenport SA 98 D1
Point Hicks Marine Nat Park VIC 65 H12
Point Labatt SA 97 K12
Point Leo VIC 57 K8
Point Lonsdale VIC 56 H5 59 H13
Point Lookout QLD 11 A13 13 G14
Point Nepean Nat Park VIC 56 J5
Point Pass SA 89 E9 98 A3
Point Piper NSW 29 K12 31 B12
Point Samson WA 114 B6
Point Souttar SA 88 G6
Point Talburpin QLD 13 G14
Point Turton SA 88 H6 98 C1
Poison Gate NSW 38 D3
Pokataroo NSW 38 D2
Pokolbin NSW 33 B10 45 H3
Police Point TAS 71 G11

Policeman Crossing NT 125 F11
Poltalloch SA 89 J10 98 D4
Pomborneit VIC 59 H9 60 E7
Pomborneit North VIC 59 H9 60 E7
Pomona QLD 9 A8 13 D13
Pomonal VIC 58 C6
Pompapiel VIC 63 J9
Ponto NSW 36 C4
Pontville TAS 69 F1 71 C12 73 K14
Pontypool TAS 69 D5
Poochera SA 88 B1 94 J1 97 J13
Pooginook Con Park SA 89 F11 98 A5
Poolaijelo VIC 58 C2
Poona Nat Park QLD 13 C13
Poona Point QLD 13 C13
Pooncarie NSW 42 D4
Poonindie SA 88 G3
Pooraka SA 81 D5 82 F6 86 G3
Pootilla VIC 59 D11
Pootnoura SA 93 G12
Poowong VIC 57 J13 64 K2 66 G3
Poowong East VIC 57 J14 64 K3 66 G3
Poowong North VIC 57 J13
Popanyinning WA 107 H8 110 E5
Popran Nat Park NSW 33 H11 37 F10
Porcupine Gorge Nat Park QLD
14 C1 17 K9 21 A9
Porepunkah VIC 64 D6
Pormpuraaw QLD 16 B5 19 J1
Porongurup WA 109 H14
Porongurup Nat Park WA 109 H13 110 J6
Port Adelaide SA
81 E2 82 H2 86 G1 89 G8 98 C2
Port Albert VIC 66 H6
Port Alma QLD 15 H11
Port Arthur TAS 69 K4
Port Augusta SA 88 A7 94 H7
Port Botany NSW 27 H6 31 F11
Port Broughton SA 88 D7
Port Campbell VIC 59 J8 60 H6
Port Campbell Nat Park VIC 59 J8 60 H5
Port Clinton SA 88 F7 98 B2
Port Darwin NT 122 J2
Port Davis SA 88 C7 94 K7
Port Denison WA 112 F4
Port Douglas QLD 17 D10 18 B3
Port Elliot SA 87 G7 89 J8 98 D3
Port Fairy VIC 58 H5 60 F1
Port Franklin VIC 66 H5
Port Gawler SA 86 E1
Port Gawler Con Park SA 86 E1
Port Germein SA 88 C7 94 J7
Port Gibbon SA 88 E5
Port Giles SA 88 H7
Port Gregory WA 112 D3
Port Hacking NSW 27 K4
Port Hedland WA 115 A8 116 K1
Port Hughes SA 88 E6 98 A1
Port Huon TAS 71 G11
Port Jackson NSW 27 E7 37 H10
Port Julia SA 88 G7 98 C1
Port Kembla NSW 35 K11 37 J9 44 B7
Port Kenny SA 88 C1 94 K1 97 K13
Port Latta TAS 76 E7
Port Lincoln SA 88 G3
Port Macdonnell SA 98 K6
Port Macquarie NSW 37 A14 39 K12
Port Melbourne VIC 51 E2 52 G7
Port Moorowie SA 88 H6 98 C1
Port Neill SA 88 E4
Port Noarlunga SA 87 B4 89 H8 98 D2
Port of Brisbane QLD 5 H14
Port Phillip Bay VIC 56 F6
Port Phillip Heads Marine Nat Park VIC
56 H5 59 G13
Port Pirie SA 88 C7 94 K7
Port Rickaby SA 88 G6 98 C1
Port Roper NT 125 G10
Port Smith WA 114 H5
Port Sorell TAS 74 D5 77 G13
Port Stephens NSW 37 E13
Port Stephens-Great Lakes Marine Park NSW
37 D13
Port Stewart QLD 19 G4
Port Victoria SA 88 F6 98 B1
Port Vincent SA 88 G7 98 C1
Port Wakefield SA 89 F8 98 B2
Port Welshpool VIC 66 H5
Port Willunga SA 87 C4
Portarlington VIC 56 G5 59 G13
Porters Retreat NSW 34 J1 36 H7
Portland NSW 36 F7
Portland VIC 58 H3 98 K7
Portland Roads QLD 19 C4
Portsea VIC 56 J5 59 H13
Postans WA 104 J4
Potts Point NSW 26 B4 29 K12 31 B12
Pottsville NSW 11 K14 13 J14 39 A14
Pound Creek VIC 66 H3
Powelltown VIC 57 D13 64 H2 66 E3
Powers Creek VIC 58 C2
Powlathanga QLD 14 B3 17 J11 21 A11
Powranna TAS 73 C14 75 H9
Prahran VIC 51 E4 53 H9 56 D7
Prairie QLD 14 C1 17 K9 21 B9
Prairie VIC 42 K7 63 J10
Prairiewood NSW 28 K3 30 B3
Precipice Nat Park QLD 13 B8
Premaydena TAS 69 J4
Premer NSW 36 A7 38 K5
Preolenna TAS 77 G8
Preston QLD 10 C1
Preston TAS 74 E2 77 H10
Preston VIC 51 B4 53 D9 56 C7
Preston Beach WA 106 J2 110 F3
Prestons NSW 30 E2
Pretty Beach NSW 33 J12
Prevelly WA 108 E1 110 H2

Price SA 88 F7 98 B2
Priestdale QLD 3 H6 7 G13
Prime Seal Island TAS 78 C3
Primrose TAS 72 D5
Primrose Sands TAS 69 H3
Prince of Wales Island QLD 19 B2
Prince Regent Nat Park WA 117 C10
Princess Charlotte Bay QLD 17 A8 19 H5
Princess River Con Area TAS 72 F6 74 K1
Princetown VIC 59 J8 60 J7
Princhester QLD 15 G9
Priors Pocket QLD 3 H1 6 G6
Professor Plateau TAS 72 E4
Propodollah VIC 62 J3
Proserpine QLD 14 C7 17 K14 21 A14
Prospect NSW 27 E1 28 H3 35 D9
Prospect SA 81 F4 82 J5 84 A5 86 H2
Prospect TAS 73 A14 75 F8
Prospect Hill SA 87 C7
Proston QLD 13 D11
Prubi QLD 20 D7
Pucawan NSW 36 J1 43 F12
Puckapunyal VIC 59 B14 66 A1
Pudman Creek NSW 36 K5 44 B3
Pukatja (Ernabella) SA 92 B7 128 K6
Pulbeena TAS 76 E5
Pullabooka NSW 36 G2 43 D13
Pullen Island SA 87 G7
Pullen Island Con Park SA 87 G7
Pullenvale QLD 6 E5 11 B8
Pullut VIC 62 H4
Pumphreys Bridge WA 106 H7
Punchbowl NSW 27 G3 30 D7 35 E10
Punchmirup WA 109 D12
Punmu WA 115 D14
Punritjanta (Bloods Range) NT 128 H1
Puntawarri WA 115 F12
Punthari SA 89 G10 98 C4
Pura Pura VIC 59 F8 60 A6
Pureba Con Park SA 88 A1 94 G1 97 G12
Purga QLD 10 D7
Purlewaugh NSW 38 J4
Purnim VIC 58 H6 60 E3
Purnong SA 89 G10 98 C4
Purnululu Nat Park WA 117 G13 126 C1
Purrembete South VIC 60 F7
Purrukuwurru NT 127 H11
Purrumbete South VIC 59 H8
Puta Puta NT 128 H2
Puta Puta SA 92 B2 128 K2
Putjamirra NT 124 A3
Putney NSW 29 J9 31 A9
Putty NSW 32 F5 37 E9
Putulu NT 126 K4 128 B4
Puyurru NT 126 K4 128 B4
Pwerte Marnte Marnte NT 129 G8
Pyalong VIC 59 C14
Pyap SA 89 F12
Pyengana TAS 75 E13
Pygery SA 88 C2 94 J2 97 J14
Pymble NSW 27 C5 29 F10 35 C11
Pymurra QLD 16 K4 20 B4
Pyramid Hill VIC 42 J7 63 H10
Pyramul NSW 36 E6
Pyrmont NSW 29 K11 31 B11

Q

Quaama NSW 44 G5 65 C14
Quail Island VIC 57 H10
Quairading WA 107 E10 110 D5 112 K7
Quakers Hill NSW 28 F3 35 C9
Qualco SA 89 F11 98 B5
Qualeup WA 109 D9
Quambatook VIC 42 J6 63 G8
Quambone NSW 41 E13
Quamby QLD 16 K4 20 A4
Quamby Bend TAS 73 A12 74 F6
Quamby Brook TAS 73 B11 74 G6
Quanda Nature Res NSW 41 G11
Quandialla NSW 36 H2 43 E13
Quangallin WA 109 B11
Quantong VIC 58 A4 62 K4
Quartz Ridge NT 126 J3 128 A3
Queanbeyan NSW 44 D3 47 G7 48 D6
Queen Victoria Spring Nature Res WA
111 A14 113 G14 119 E1
Queens Park NSW 31 C13
Queens Park WA 103 H8
Queenscliff NSW 29 G14 35 C12
Queenscliff VIC 56 H5 59 H13
Queensferry VIC 57 K11
Queensport QLD 5 K12 7 B12
Queenstown SA 82 H3
Queenstown TAS 72 F5
Queerah QLD 18 E4
Quellington WA 103 D8
Quilberry QLD 23 D13
Quilpie QLD 21 K9 23 C10
Quinalow QLD 13 F11
Quindalup WA 108 C2
Quindanning WA 106 K6 110 F4
Quindinup Nature Res WA 109 G9
Quinninup WA 108 G7
Quinns Rocks WA 106 C2 110 C2 112 J5
Quipolly NSW 37 A9 38 K6
Quirindi NSW 37 A9 38 K6
Quorn SA 88 A7 94 H7
Quorrobolong NSW 33 D11 45 K4

R

Rabbit Flat NT 126 H2
Raby NSW 30 H1 35 F9
Raby Bay QLD 11 B11

Raceview QLD 6 H2
Raglan QLD 15 H11
Raglan VIC 59 D9
Railton TAS 74 E4 77 J12
Rainbow VIC 42 J3 62 G4
Rainbow Beach QLD 13 C13
Rainbow Flat NSW 37 C13
Raine Island QLD 19 C5
Raine Island Nat Park (Scientific) QLD 19 C5
Rainworth QLD 7 C8
Raminea TAS 71 H11
Ramingining NT 125 C10
Ramornie Nat Park NSW 39 E11
Ramsay QLD 10 D1
Ramsgate NSW 31 F10 35 E11
Ranceby VIC 57 J14 64 K3 66 G3
Rand NSW 43 H11
Randalls Bay TAS 71 G12
Randwick NSW 27 G6 31 D12 35 D12
Ranelagh TAS 71 F11
Ranga TAS 78 D5
Rangal QLD 15 H8
Rankins Springs NSW 43 E10
Rannes QLD 15 J9
Ransome QLD 3 E7 7 C14
Rapid Bay SA 87 G1 98 D2
Rapid Creek NT 122 C4
Rapids Con Park WA 108 D2
Rappville NSW 39 C12
Rathdowney QLD 11 H8 13 H13 39 A12
Rathmines NSW 33 D13
Rathscar VIC 59 B9
Ravenhall VIC 52 E3
Ravensbourne QLD 8 K2 10 A2 13 F12
Ravensbourne Nat Park QLD 8 K3 10 A3
Ravensdale NSW 33 F11
Ravensdale TAS 69 D5
Ravenshoe QLD 17 F10 18 H3
Ravensthorpe WA 111 G9
Ravenswood QLD 14 B5 17 J12 21 A12
Ravenswood TAS 73 A14 75 F8
Ravenswood VIC 59 B11
Ravensworth NSW 37 D10
Rawdon Vale NSW 37 B11
Rawlinna TAS 69 A4 75 K12
Rawlinna WA 119 F3
Rawson VIC 64 J4 66 E5
Raymangirr NT 125 C11
Raymond Terrace NSW 33 A13 37 E11
Rayna TAS 72 D4
Rayners Hill Forest Reserve TAS 75 E13
Raywood VIC 63 J10
Razorback Nature Reserve NSW 36 H5
Red Banks SA 86 B2 89 D9 98 A3
Red Banks Con Park SA 89 D9 98 A3
Red Bluff WA 62 G1 89 K13 98 E6
Red Cap Creek VIC 58 D2
Red Cliffs QLD 13
Red Cliffs VIC 42 F3 62 B4
Red Hill ACT 47 F5
Red Hill QLD 2 A1 3 E3 5 K9 7 B9 11 A9
Red Hill VIC 57 J8
Red Hill WA 103 A13
Red Hill South VIC 57 J8
Red Hills TAS 73 B11 74 G5 77 K13
Red Rock NSW 39 F13
Redbank QLD 6 H5
Redbank VIC 59 B9
Redbank Plains QLD 6 J5 11 C8
Redcliffe QLD 5 B12 9 J10 13 F13
Redcliffe WA 101 F5 103 E8
Redesdale VIC 59 B12
Redfern NSW 27 F6 31 C11 35 D11
Redhead NSW 33 D14
Redhill SA 89 D8
Redland Bay QLD 11 C11 13 G14
Redlynch QLD 17 E11 18 D4
Redmond WA 109 J13
Redmond West WA 109 J12
Redpa TAS 76 F3
Redwood Park SA 81 C7 83 F9
Reedy Creek QLD 11 H12 24 G4
Reedy Creek SA 98 G5
Reedy Creek VIC 59 C14 64 F1 66 B1
Reedy Dam VIC 42 J4 62 G6
Reedy Flat VIC 65 G8
Reedy Marsh TAS 73 A11 74 F6 77 J14
Reefton NSW 36 H1 43 E12
Reefton VIC 57 B14 64 G3
Reekara TAS 78 B1
Reeves Beach VIC 66 H7
Reeves Plains SA 86 C2
Regatta Point TAS 72 G4
Regency Park SA 81 E3 82 H4
Regents Park NSW 27 F2 30 B6 35 D10
Regents Park QLD 3 K4 7 K10
Regentville NSW 34 D7
Reid ACT 46 A4 47 D5
Reid WA 119 F7
Reid River QLD 14 A5 17 J12
Reids Creek VIC 64 B5
Reids Flat NSW 36 H5 44 A3
Rekuna TAS 69 F2 71 C13
Relbia TAS 73 B14 75 F8
Rendelsham SA 98 H5
Renison Bell TAS 72 D5
Renmark SA 42 F1 89 F13 98 B6
Renmark North SA 42 G1
Renner Springs NT 127 E8
Rennie NSW 43 J10 64 A3
Renown Park SA 82 J4 84 A4
Research VIC 51 B6 53 C13
Reservoir VIC 51 B4 53 D9 56 C7
Retreat TAS 75 D8
Retro QLD 14 G6 21 E13
Revesby NSW 27 H3 30 E6 35 E10
Revesby Heights NSW 30 F6

Reynella SA 84 K3 87 B5
Reynolds Neck TAS 73 D11 74 J6
Rheban TAS 69 F4
Rheola VIC 59 A10 63 K9
Rhodes NSW 29 J8 31 A8 35 D10
Rhyll VIC 57 K10 64 K1 66 G2
Rhyndaston TAS 69 E2 71 B13
Rhynie SA 89 F9 98 B3
Riana TAS 74 D2 77 H10
Rich Avon VIC 42 K5 62 J6
Richardson ACT 47 J4
Richlands NSW 36 J7 44 A5
Richlands QLD 3 H2 6 G7
Richmond NSW 34 B7 37 G9
Richmond QLD 16 K7 20 R7
Richmond SA 81 G3 84 C4 86 H2
Richmond TAS 69 G2 71 C13
Richmond VIC 51 D4 53 G9 57 D8
Richmond Range Nat Park NSW 13 J13 39 B12
Rickeys WA 107 E8
Riddells Creek VIC 59 D13
Ridgehaven SA 81 D7 83 F9
Ridgelands QLD 15 G10
Ridgeway NSW 69 H1 71 E13
Ridgley TAS 74 D1 77 G9
Ridleyton SA 82 K4 84 A4
Rifle Creek QLD 20 B3
Rimbanda QLD 21 E8
Rinadeena TAS 72 G5
Ringarooma TAS 75 D11
Ringarooma Bay TAS 75 A12 78 J4
Ringwood VIC 51 D7 53 G14 57 D9
Rinyirru (Lakefield) Nat Park QLD 17 B8 19 J5
Ripley QLD 6 K3 11 D8
Ripplebrook VIC 57 H13 64 J2 66 F3
Risdon TAS 69 G1 71 D13
Risdon Vale TAS 69 G1 71 D13
Rittarangu (Urapunga) NT 125 G9
River Derwent Con Area TAS 71 D12
River Heads QLD 13 B13
Riverhills QLD 3 G1 6 F6
Riverside QLD 14 E6 21 C14
Riverside TAS 73 A13 75 F8
Riverstone NSW 28 D1 35 C8
Riverton SA 89 F9 98 B3
Riverton WA 101 G5 102 F7
Rivervale WA 101 G5 102 F7
Riverview NSW 29 J10 31 A10
Riverview QLD 6 G4 11 C8
Riverwood NSW 27 H3 30 E7 35 E10
Rivett ACT 47 F2
Rixs Creek NSW 45 D1
Roadvale QLD 10 F7
Rob Roy Nature Res ACT 47 K4 48 E5
Robbins Island TAS 76 D4
Robe SA 98 H4
Robertson NSW 37 K8 44 B6
Robertson QLD 3 G4 7 F11
Robertstown SA 89 E9 98 A3
Robigana TAS 74 E7
Robin Hood VIC 57 F14
Robina QLD 11 G12 24 G4
Robinvale VIC 42 F4 62 C6
Rochedale QLD 3 G6 7 F12 11 C10
Rochedale South QLD 3 H6 7 G13
Rocherlea TAS 73 A14 75 E8
Rochester VIC 43 K8 63 J11
Rochford VIC 59 C13
Rock Flat NSW 44 G3 65 C12
Rockbank VIC 52 D1 56 C5 59 E13
Rockbrae QLD 39 A10
Rockdale NSW 27 H4 31 E10 35 E11
Rockhampton QLD 15 H10
Rockingham WA 106 F2 110 D3 112 K5
Rocklands Reservoir VIC 58 C4
Rocklea QLD 3 G3 7 F9 11 B9
Rockleigh SA 86 J7
Rockley NSW 36 G6
Rocklyn VIC 59 D11
Rocksberg QLD 9 G8
Rocky Cape TAS 76 E7
Rocky Cape Beach TAS 76 E7
Rocky Cape Nat Park TAS 76 E7
Rocky Creek NSW 38 F6
Rocky Crossing ACT 48 G4
Rocky Dam NSW 13 K9 38 C7
Rocky Glen NSW 38 J4
Rocky Gully WA 109 G10 110 J5
Rocky Hall NSW 44 J4 65 E13
Rocky Hill QLD 8 E1
Rocky River NSW 39 G8
Rodd Point NSW 29 K10 31 B10
Rodinga NT 129 H8
Roebourne WA 114 B6
Roebuck Plains Roadhouse WA 116 G6
Roelands WA 108 B5
Rogans Hill NSW 28 E6
Roger River TAS 76 F5
Roger River West TAS 76 F5
Rogerville TAS 69 F1 71 C12
Rokeby TAS 69 H2 71 E13
Rokeby VIC 57 G11 64 J3 66 F4
Rokewood VIC 59 F10 61 B10
Roland TAS 73 A9 74 F3 77 J11
Roleystone WA 105 D13
Rolleston QLD 14 J7 21 G14
Rollingstone QLD 17 H12
Roma QLD 12 D5 21 K14
Romsey VIC 59 D13
Rookhurst NSW 37 B12
Rookwood NSW 28 K7 30 B7
Rooty Hill NSW 28 G1 35 D8
Ropely QLD 10 C4
Roper Bar NT 125 G9
Rorruwuy NT 125 C12
Rosa Glen WA 108 E2
Rosanna VIC 53 D10 57 C8
Rose Bay NSW 29 K13 31 B13 35 D12

Rose Bay TAS 68 A4
Rose Bay North NSW 29 K14 31 B13
Rose Park SA 84 C6
Roseberry VIC 62 G5
Rosebery NSW 31 D11
Rosebery TAS 72 D5
Rosebrook NSW 33 A11 45 F5
Rosebrook VIC 58 H5 60 F1
Rosebud VIC 56 J7 59 H14
Rosedale QLD 15 K12
Rosedale SA 86 C5
Rosedale VIC 64 J5 66 F6
Rosegarland TAS 71 C11
Rosehill NSW 27 E3 28 J7 30 A7
Roselands NSW 30 F7
Rosemeadow NSW 35 G9
Roses Gap VIC 58 B6
Rosevale QLD 10 E5
Rosevale TAS 73 A13 74 F7
Rosevears TAS 74 E7
Roseville NSW 27 D5 29 G11 35 C11
Roseville Chase NSW 29 G11
Rosewater SA 81 E2 82 H2
Rosewhite VIC 64 C5
Rosewood QLD 10 C6 13 G12
Roseworthy SA 86 C4 89 G9 98 B3
Roseworthy College SA 86 C3
Roslyn NSW 36 J6 44 B4
Roslynmead VIC 63 H11
Rosny TAS 68 B4
Rosny Park TAS 68 B4
Ross TAS 69 A2 75 K10
Rossarden TAS 75 H11
Rossbridge VIC 58 D7
Rossi NSW 44 E4
Rosslyn Park SA 85 C8
Rossmore NSW 35 F8
Rossmore WA 106 B7
Rossmoyne WA 101 H4 102 K5 104 A6
Rossville QLD 17 C10 19 K7
Rostrevor SA 81 F6 83 K8 85 B8 86 H3
Rostron VIC 59 A8 62 K7
Rothbury NSW 33 B10 45 G3
Rothwell QLD 5 B11 9 H10
Rothwell VIC 56 E3
Roto NSW 41 K9 43 C9
Rottnest Island WA 106 E1 110 D2 112 K5
Rouchel NSW 37 C10
Round Corner NSW 27 B2 28 D6 35 C9
Round Hill Nature Res NSW 41 K10 43 C10
Rouse Hill NSW 28 D3 35 C9
Rowella TAS 74 D7
Rowena NSW 38 E3
Rowland Flat SA 86 D6
Rowles Lagoon Nature Res WA 111 A10 113 G11
Rowley Shoals Marine Park WA 116 F1
Rowsley VIC 56 C3 59 E12
Rowville VIC 53 K14 55 B8 57 E9
Roxburgh Park VIC 52 A7
Roxby Downs SA 94 C5
Royal George TAS 75 J12
Royal Nat Park NSW 27 K3 30 J7 31 K8 35 G11 37 H10
Royal Park SA 81 E2 82 J2 84 A2
Royal Park VIC 53 F8
Royalla NSW 48 E5
Roydon Island TAS 78 B3
Roysalt WA 111 C12 113 J12
Royston Park SA 81 F5 82 K6 84 B6
Royston Range VIC 66 C4
Rozelle NSW 29 K10 31 B10 35 D11
Ruby VIC 57 K14
Ruby Gap Nature Park NT 129 F10
Rubyvale QLD 14 H6 21 F13
Rudall SA 88 D4
Rudall River (Karlamilyi) Nat Park WA 115 D13
Ruffy VIC 64 E2 66 A2
Rufus River NSW 42 E2 62 A2 89 F14 98 B7
Rugby NSW 36 J5 44 A3
Rules Point NSW 43 J14 44 E2
Rulla TAS 76 F7
Rumbalara NT 129 J9
Rumula QLD 17 D10 18 B2
Runaway Bay QLD 11 F12 24 B4
Runcorn QLD 3 H5 7 G11
Rundle Range Nat Park QLD 15 H11
Running Creek VIC 64 C6
Running Stream NSW 36 E7
Runnymeade VIC 63 J11
Runnymede TAS 69 F3 71 C14
Rupanyup VIC 58 A6 62 K6
Rupanyup North VIC 62 J6
Rurrangala NT 125 D12
Ruse NSW 35 G9
Rush Creek QLD 4 A4
Rushcutters Bay NSW 29 K12 31 B12
Rushworth VIC 63 K12
Rushy Lagoon TAS 75 A13 78 J5
Russell ACT 46 C4 47 E5
Russell Island QLD 11 C12 18 F6
Russell Lea NSW 29 K10 31 B9
Russell River Nat Park QLD 17 E11 18 F6
Russell Vale NSW 35 J10
Ruth Creek Hut QLD 17 C9 19 K6
Rutherford NSW 33 A11
Rutherglen VIC 43 J11 64 B4
Ryan NSW 43 H11
Ryans Creek VIC 64 D4
Rydal NSW 34 C1
Rydalmere NSW 27 E3 28 H7 35 D10
Ryde NSW 27 E4 29 H9 35 D11
Rye VIC 56 J6 59 H13
Rye Park NSW 36 J5 44 B3
Ryhope NSW 33 D12
Rylstone NSW 36 E7
Rythdale VIC 55 H13
Ryton VIC 66 H5

S

Sabina NT 124 F2
Sackville NSW 33 K9 35 A8
Sackville North NSW 33 K9 35 A8
Saddleworth SA 89 E9 98 A3
Sadleir NSW 30 D3
Sadliers Crossing QLD 6 H1
Safety Bay WA 106 F2 110 E3 112 K5
Safety Beach NSW 39 F12
Safety Beach VIC 56 H7
Saint Germains VIC 63 H13 64 B1
Sale VIC 64 J6 66 F7
Salisbury NSW 37 C11
Salisbury QLD 3 G4 7 F10
Salisbury SA 81 B5 82 D7 86 F3
Salisbury VIC 42 K3 62 J3
Salisbury Downs SA 81 B4 82 D6
Salisbury East SA 81 C6 83 E8
Salisbury Heights SA 81 B6 83 D8
Salisbury North SA 81 A5 82 C6
Salisbury Park SA 82 D7
Salisbury Plain SA 82 D7
Salisbury South SA 81 C5 82 E6
Salisbury West VIC 42 K6 63 J9
Sallys Flat NSW 36 E6
Salmon Gums WA 111 F12
Salt Creek SA 98 F4
Salt Lake NSW 22 K6
Salter Point WA 101 H4 102 J5
Saltern QLD 14 H2 21 F10
Saltwater Nat Park NSW 37 C13
Saltwater River TAS 69 J3
Samford QLD 13 F13
Samford State Forest QLD 3 C1
Samford Valley QLD 4 G5 9 K8 11 A8
Samford Village QLD 3 B1 4 G6
Sampson Flat SA 83 C12
Samson WA 101 J2 104 B3
Samsonvale QLD 4 D3 9 J8
San Marino Hut SA 93 F12
San Remo VIC 66 H2
Sanctuary Cove QLD 11 E12 24 A3
Sand Hill Siding WA 115 E9
Sandalwood SA 89 H11 98 C5
Sandfire Roadhouse WA 115 A11 116 K4
Sandfly TAS 69 H1 71 E12
Sandford TAS 69 H2 71 E14
Sandford VIC 58 E3
Sandgate NSW 33 B13
Sandgate QLD 3 A4 5 E10 9 J10
Sandilands SA 88 F7 98 B1
Sandon NSW 39 E13
Sandringham NSW 27 J4 31 G10
Sandringham VIC 51 G4 54 B2 56 E7
Sandsmere VIC 62 J2
Sandstone WA 113 D9
Sandstone Point QLD 9 G10
Sandy Bay TAS 68 D2 69 H1 71 E13
Sandy Beach NSW 39 F13
Sandy Bore SA 93 D8
Sandy Creek SA 86 D5
Sandy Creek Con Park SA 86 D5
Sandy Hill NSW 39 C10
Sandy Hollow NSW 37 C8
Sandy Point NSW 27 H2 30 F5
Sandys Hut SA 98 G5
Sangar NSW 43 J10
Sans Souci NSW 31 G9 35 E11
Santa Teresa (Ltyentye Apurte) NT 129 G9
Sapphire NSW 39 E8
Sapphire QLD 14 H6 21 F13
Saraji QLD 14 F7 21 D14
Saratoga NSW 33 J12
Sarina QLD 15 D8
Sarsfield VIC 65 H8
Sassafras NSW 44 D6
Sassafras TAS 74 E4 77 H13
Sassafras VIC 57 D10
Satur NSW 37 B9
Savage River TAS 72 B3 76 K6
Savage River Nat Park TAS 72 A4 76 H7
Savage River Reg Res TAS 72 A4 76 H6
Savernake NSW 43 J10
Sawtell NSW 39 G12
Sayers Lake NSW 40 K5 42 B5
Scabby Range Nature Res NSW 48 H2
Scaddan WA 111 G12
Scamander TAS 75 F14
Scamander Con Area TAS 75 F14
Scarborough NSW 35 H11 37 J9
Scarborough QLD 5 A12 9 H10
Scarborough WA 101 E2 102 C2 106 D2
Scarsdale VIC 59 E10
Scheyville NSW 28 A2 35 B8
Scheyville Nat Park NSW 28 A2 35 B8
Schofields NSW 28 E2 35 C8
School Hill VIC 56 K7
Schouten Island TAS 69 C7
Scone NSW 37 B9
Scopus TAS 76 E5
Scoresby VIC 51 E7 53 J14 55 A8 57 D9
Scotchtown TAS 76 E5
Scotia WA 113 G11
Scotland Island NSW 27 A7 29 B14
Scotsburn VIC 59 E11
Scott Con Park SA 87 F7
Scott Creek SA 85 J8 86 K3 87 A7
Scott Creek Con Park SA 85 K8 86 K3 87 B6
Scott Nat Park WA 108 F2 110 H2
Scotts Creek VIC 59 H8 60 G6
Scotts Flat NSW 33 A9
Scotts Head NSW 39 H12
Scottsdale TAS 75 D10
Scottville QLD 14 C6 17 K13 21 B13
Scullin ACT 47 C2
Sea Elephant TAS 78 C2

Sea Lake VIC 42 H5 62 F6
Sea View VIC 57 H14
Seabird WA 106 A1 110 C2 112 J5
Seabrook TAS 74 C1 77 F9
Seacliff SA 81 K2 84 G2 86 K1 87 A4
Seacliff Park SA 81 K2 84 H3
Seacombe VIC 64 J7
Seacombe Gardens SA 81 K3 84 G3
Seacombe Heights SA 84 H3
Seaford VIC 51 K6 54 G5 57 G8
Seaford SA 87 C4
Seaforth NSW 29 H12 35 C11
Seaforth QLD 15 C8
Seaham NSW 37 D11
Seahampton NSW 33 C12 45 J6
Seaholme VIC 52 H5
Seal Bay Con Park SA 88 K6
Seal Island SA 87 H6
Seal Rocks NSW 37 D13
Seaspray VIC 64 K6
Seaton SA 81 F2 82 J2 84 A2 86 H1
Seaton VIC 64 H5 66 E6
Seaview VIC 64 K3 66 G4
Seaview Downs SA 81 K2 84 H3
Sebastian VIC 36 J1 43 F12
Sebastopol VIC 59 E10
Second Valley SA 87 G2 98 D2
Sedan SA 89 G10 98 B4
Sedgwick VIC 59 B12
Sefton NSW 30 C6 35 E10
Sefton Park SA 82 J5 84 A5
Seisia QLD 17 A3
Selbourne TAS 73 A12 74 F7
Sellheim QLD 14 B4 17 J12 21 A12
Sellicks Beach SA 87 E4 89 J8 98 D2
Sellicks Hill SA 87 E4
Semaphore SA 81 D1 82 G1 86 G1
Semaphore Park SA 81 E1 82 H1
Semaphore South SA 82 G1
Sentinel Island TAS 78 A3
Seppeltsfield SA 86 C5
Serpentine VIC 42 K6 63 J9
Serpentine WA 106 F5
Serpentine Nat Park WA 106 G4 110 E3 112 K5
Serra Range VIC 58 C6
Serviceton VIC 42 K1 62 J1
Seven Hills NSW 27 D1 28 G4 35 D9
Seven Hills QLD 7 C11
Seven Mile Beach TAS 69 H2 71 D14
Seven Mile Beach Nat Park NSW 37 K9 44 C7
Sevenhill SA 89 E8 98 A3
Seventeen Mile Rocks QLD 6 F7
Seventeen Seventy QLD 15 J12
Severn River Nature Res NSW 39 D8
Seville VIC 57 C11 64 H2 66 D2
Seymour TAS 75 H14
Seymour VIC 59 B14 64 E1 66 A1
Shackleton WA 107 D11 110 D6 112 K7
Shadforth NSW 36 F5
Shailer Park QLD 3 J7 7 J14 11 C11
Shallow Inlet Marine and Coastal Park VIC 66 J4
Shanes Park NSW 35 C9
Shannon TAS 73 F12 74 K6
Shannon WA 108 H7
Shannon Nat Park WA 108 G7 110 J4
Shannons Flat NSW 44 F3 48 K3 65 A11
Shark Bay WA 112 A3
Shark Bay Marine Park WA 114 J2
Sheans Creek VIC 63 K14 64 D2
Shearwater TAS 74 D5 77 G13
Sheep Hills VIC 62 J5
Sheffield TAS 73 A9 74 E4 77 J12
Sheidow Park SA 84 K2
Shelbourne VIC 59 B11
Sheldon QLD 3 H7 7 G14
Shelford VIC 59 F11 61 C12
Shelley VIC 64 B7
Shelley WA 101 H4 102 J6
Shelley Beach NSW 33 H13
Shellharbour NSW 37 K9 44 B7
Shelly Beach QLD 9 E11
Shelly Beach TAS 69 E4
Shenton Park WA 101 F2 102 F3
Sheoak Hill Con Park SA 88 D5 94 K5
Sheoak Log SA 86 C5
Sheoaks VIC 56 D1 61 B13
Shepherds Hill Rec Park SA 86 J2 87 A6
Shepparton VIC 43 K9 63 J13 64 C1
Sheringa SA 88 E2
Sherlock SA 89 J11 98 D4
Sherwood NSW 39 J11
Sherwood QLD 3 F3 7 E8
Sherwood Hill Con Area TAS 71 F12
Sherwood Nature Res NSW 39 F12
Shoal Point QLD 15 D8
Shoalhaven Heads NSW 37 K9 44 C7
Shooters Hill NSW 34 G1 36 H7
Shoreham VIC 57 K8 59 H14 66 G1
Shorncliffe QLD 3 B5 5 F12 9 K10
Short Island QLD 11 D12
Shortland NSW 33 B13
Shotts WA 108 B6
Shutehaven QLD 15 B8
Sidmouth TAS 74 D7
Silkstone QLD 6 H3
Silkwood QLD 17 F11 18 J6
Silvan VIC 57 D11
Silver Sands SA 87 D4
Silver Spur QLD 13 K10 39 B8
Silverdale NSW 34 F7
Silverdale QLD 10 E5
Silverleaves VIC 57 K9
Silverton NSW 40 H1 42 A1 95 G14
Silverwater NSW 27 E3 28 J7 30 A7 33 E13
Silverwood QLD 10 K2
Simmie VIC 63 H12
Simpson VIC 59 J8 60 G7
Simpson Desert Con Park SA 20 K1 129 K14

Simpson Desert Nat Park
  see Munga-Thirri Nat Park
Simpson Desert Reg Res SA 90 C5 129 K12
Simpsons Bay TAS 71 H13
Single Nat Park NSW 39 F8
Singleton NSW 33 A8 37 D10 45 E1
Singleton WA 106 G2
Sinnamon Park QLD 3 G2 6 E7
Sir Edward Pellew Group NT 125 H12
Sir George Hope Islands NT 124 B6
Sir Graham Moore Islands WA 117 A11
Sir Joseph Banks Group NT 88 G4
Sir Joseph Banks Group Con Park SA 88 G4
Sir Joseph Banks Group Marine Park SA 88 F4
Sisters Creek TAS 77 F8
Skenes Creek VIC 59 K10 61 J10
Skipton VIC 59 E9
Skye SA 81 G6 85 C8
Skye VIC 51 K7 54 G7 57 G9
Slacks Creek QLD 3 J6 7 J13
Slade Point QLD 15 D8
Slaty Creek VIC 62 J7
Smeaton VIC 59 D11
Smeaton Grange NSW 35 G8
Smith Point NT 124 A5
Smithfield NSW 27 E1 28 K4 30 B4 35 D9
Smithfield QLD 17 D11
Smithfield SA 83 A8 86 E3
Smithfield Heights QLD 18 D4
Smiths Lake NSW 37 D13
Smithton TAS 76 E5
Smokers Bank TAS 76 E5
Smoky Bay SA 97 H11
Smythesdale VIC 59 E10
Snake Range Nat Park QLD 14 J6 21 G13
Snake Valley VIC 59 E9
Snapper Island QLD 18 A3
Snobs Creek VIC 64 F3 66 B4
Snowtown SA 89 E8 98 A2
Snowy River Nat Park VIC 44 J1 65 F10
Snug TAS 69 J1 71 F12
Sodwalls NSW 34 C1
Sofala NSW 36 E6
Solitary Islands Marine Park NSW 39 E13
Somers VIC 57 J9 64 K1 66 G1
Somersby NSW 33 H11
Somerset QLD 19 B2
Somerset TAS 74 C1 77 F9
Somerset Dam QLD 8 H6 13 F12
Somerset Hill WA 109 J11
Somerton NSW 38 H6
Somerton VIC 51 A3 52 A7 56 B7
Somerton Park SA 81 J2 84 F2 86 J1 87 A4
Somerville VIC 57 H9 64 J1 66 F1
Sommariva QLD 12 D1 21 K12 23 B14
Sorell TAS 69 G3 71 D14
Sorell Creek TAS 71 D12
Sorrento QLD 24 E4
Sorrento VIC 56 J6 59 H13
Sorrento WA 101 C1 106 D2
South Arm TAS 69 J2 71 F13
South Bank QLD 2 C2 7 C10
South Blackwater QLD 15 J8
South Brighton SA 84 G3
South Brisbane QLD 2 D3 E4 7 C10
South Bruny Island TAS 71 H13
South Bruny Nat Park TAS 71 J13
South Coogee NSW 27 G7 31 D13
South Copperfield QLD 14 G6 21 E13
South East Cape TAS 71 K10
South East Forest Nat Park NSW 44 H3 65 E13
South Elliott TAS 74 C1 77 G9
South Eneabba Nature Res WA 112 G4
South Forest TAS 76 E6
South Franklin TAS 71 F11
South Fremantle WA 101 J1 104 B1
South Glen QLD 13 F8
South Granville NSW 28 K6 30 B6
South Guildford WA 101 E6 103 D9
South Hedland WA 115 B8 116 K1
South Hobart TAS 68 D1
South Hurstville NSW 31 F9
South Johnstone QLD 17 F11 18 H6
South Kilkerran SA 88 F6 98 B1
South Kulin WA 107 H13
South Kumminin WA 107 F14 110 D7 113 K8
South Lake WA 101 K3 104 D5
South Maclean QLD 11 D9
South Melbourne VIC 50 D2 51 D3 53 G8
South Misson Beach QLD 18 K6
South Morang VIC 53 B11 57 B8
South Mount Cameron TAS 75 C12 78 K4
South Nanango QLD 8 D1
South Nietta TAS 73 A8 74 F7 77 J10
South Perth WA 100 D2 101 G4 102 G5
South Plympton SA 84 E4
South Preston TAS 74 E2 77 J10
South Quairading WA 107 F10
South Riana TAS 74 D2 77 H10
South Springfield TAS 75 D10
South Springvale VIC 54 C6
South Stradbroke Island QLD 11 E13 24 A5
South Tammin WA 107 D10
South Trayning WA 107 A11
South Turramurra NSW 27 D3 29 F9
South Wentworthville NSW 28 J5 30 A5
South West Cape TAS 70 K6
South West Rocks NSW 39 H12
South Yarra VIC 53 H9
Southbank VIC 50 D1
Southend QLD 15 H11
Southend SA 98 J5
Southern Brook WA 106 C7
Southern Cross QLD 14 B4 17 J11 21 A11
Southern Cross VIC 60 E2
Southern Cross WA 111 B8 113 J9
Southern Moreton Bay Islands Nat Park QLD 11 E13

Southern River WA 101 K6 105 C8
Southern Spencer Gulf Marine Park SA 88 J6
Southport QLD 11 F13 13 H14 24 D4
Southport TAS 71 J11
Southwest Con Area TAS 70 C3 72 K5
Southwest Nat Park TAS 70 G7
Southwood Nat Park QLD 13 G8
Sovereign Island QLD 11 E13
Sovereign Islands QLD 24 A4
Spalding SA 89 D8
Spalford TAS 74 D3 77 H11
Spargo Creek VIC 59 D11
Spearwood WA 101 K2 104 D2
Speed VIC 42 H4 62 E5
Speers Point NSW 33 C13
Speewa VIC 63 E8
Spence ACT 47 B3
Spencer NSW 33 J11
Spencer Gulf SA 88 E5 94 K6 98 A1
Spencers Brook WA 106 C6
Spicers Creek NSW 36 C5
Spinnaker Island ACT 46 B1
Spinning Gum Con Area TAS 69 E2 71 B14
Spotswood VIC 52 G6
Sprent TAS 74 E3 77 H11
Spreyton TAS 74 D4 77 H12
Spring Beach TAS 69 E4
Spring Creek QLD 10 F1
Spring Farm NSW 35 G8
Spring Hill NSW 36 F5
Spring Hill QLD 2 A2 3 E4 7 B10
Spring Mount Con Park SA 87 F5
Spring Ridge NSW 36 C6 37 A8 38 J6
Springbank Island ACT 46 B1
Springbrook QLD 11 J12 13 H14 39 A13
Springbrook Nat Park QLD
    11 H12 13 H13 24 K1 39 A13
Springdale NSW 36 J2 43 F13
Springdale TAS 71 D12
Springfield QLD 3 K1 6 J6 11 C8
Springfield SA 81 J5 84 E6
Springfield TAS 75 D10
Springfield Lakes QLD 3 K1 6 K6
Springhill Bottom TAS 69 E1 71 B13
Springhurst VIC 43 K11 64 B4
Springsure QLD 14 J7 21 G14
Springton SA 86 F7 89 G9 98 C3
Springvale VIC 51 G6 54 B6 57 E8
Springwood NSW 34 D5 37 G8
Springwood QLD 3 J6 7 H13 11 C10
Squeaking Point TAS 74 D5 77 H13
St Agnes VIC 3 D7 83 G9
St Albans NSW 33 H9 37 F9
St Albans VIC 51 C1 52 E4 56 C6
St Albans East VIC 52 E5
St Andrews NSW 30 H1
St Andrews VIC 57 B10 64 G1 66 D2
St Andrews Beach VIC 59 H13
St Arnaud VIC 59 A8 62 K7
St Clair NSW 35 D8 37 C10 45 B3
St Clair Island QLD 11 C12
St Fillans VIC 57 A12 64 G2 66 D3
St George QLD 12 H5
St Georges SA 84 D7
St Georges Basin NSW 44 D6
St Helena Island QLD 9 K11 11 A11
St Helena Nat Park QLD 9 K11 11 A11
St Helens TAS 75 E14
St Helens VIC 58 B6
St Helens Con Area TAS 75 E14
St Helier VIC 57 J12
St Ives NSW 27 C5 29 F10 35 C11
St Ives Chase NSW 29 E10 35 B11
St James VIC 43 K10 63 H14 64 B3
St James WA 102 H7
St Johns Park NSW 30 C3
St Johns Wood QLD 5 K8 7 B8
St Kilda SA 81 A3 82 C3 86 F1
St Kilda VIC 51 E3 53 H8 56 D7
St Kitts SA 86 A7
St Lawrence QLD 15 F9
St Leonards NSW 29 J11 31 A11 35 C11
St Leonards TAS 73 A14 75 F8
St Leonards VIC 56 G5 59 G13
St Lucia QLD 3 F3 7 D9 11 B9
St Marys NSW 35 D8
St Marys SA 81 J4 84 F4
St Marys TAS 75 G13
St Morris SA 82 K7 84 B7
St Patricks River TAS 75 E9
St Pauls QLD 19 A2
St Pauls Reg Res TAS 75 H12
St Peters NSW 31 D11 35 D11
St Peters SA 81 F5 82 K6 84 B6 86 H2
St Vidgeon NT 125 H9
Staaten River Nat Park QLD 16 D7
Stafford QLD 3 C3 5 J9 9 K9 11 A9
Stafford Heights QLD 5 H9
Staffordshire Reef VIC 59 E10 61 A10
Stalker VIC 59 J9 61 H8
Stamford QLD 21 C8
Stanage QLD 15 F9
Stanborough NSW 39 E8
Stanhope VIC 43 K6 63 J12
Stanhope Gardens NSW 28 E3
Stanley TAS 76 D6
Stanley VIC 64 C5
Stanley Island QLD 17 A9 19 H5
Stanmore NSW 31 C10
Stanmore QLD 8 E7
Stannifer NSW 39 E8
Stannum NSW 39 D8
Stansbury SA 88 G7 98 C1
Stanthorpe QLD 13 J11 39 B10
Stanwell QLD 15 H10
Stanwell Park NSW 35 H11 37 J9 44 A7
Stapylton QLD 11 D11
Starcke Nat Park QLD 17 B10 19 J6

Starling Gap VIC 64 H2 66 E3
Staughton Vale VIC 56 D2 59 F12 61 A14
Stavely VIC 58 E6
Staverton TAS 73 A9 74 F3 77 J11
Stawell VIC 58 B7
Steels Creek VIC 57 A10
Steels Hills TAS 73 K12
Steiglitz QLD 11 D12
Steiglitz VIC 56 D1 59 F11 61 B13
Steiglitz Historic Park VIC 56 D1
Stenhouse Bay SA 88 H5
Stephens NSW 33 E13
Stephens Creek NSW 40 H2
Stephens Island QLD 18 J7
Stepney SA 84 B6
Steppes TAS 73 F12
Stewarts Brook NSW 37 B10
Stieglitz TAS 75 E14
Stirling ACT 47 F3
Stirling SA 81 J7 85 F9 86 J3
Stirling VIC 65 G8
Stirling WA 101 D3 102 C3
Stirling North SA 88 A7 94 H7
Stirling Range Nat Park WA 109 F13 110 H6
Stockdale VIC 64 H6
Stockinbingal NSW 36 J2 43 F13
Stockleigh QLD 11 E10
Stockmans Reward VIC 64 G3 66 C4
Stockport SA 86 A3
Stockrington NSW 45 J7
Stockton NSW 33 B14 37 E11
Stockwell SA 86 B7
Stockyard QLD 10 D2
Stockyard Hill VIC 59 E9
Stokers Siding NSW 11 K12
Stokes Bay SA 88 J6
Stokes Nat Park WA 111 G11
Stone Hut SA 89 C8 95K8
Stonefield SA 89 F10 98 B4
Stonehaven VIC 56 G2
Stonehenge NSW 39 E9
Stonehenge QLD 21 G8
Stonehenge TAS 69 D3 71 A14
Stones Corner QLD 7 D10
Stonor TAS 69 D2 71 A13
Stony Batter Creek Nature Res NSW 38 G7
Stony Creek Nature Res ACT 47 E1 48 C3
Stony Crossing NSW 42 G6 63 D8
Stony Point VIC 57 J9
Stonyfell SA 81 G6 85 C8 86 H3
Stonyford VIC 59 H9 61 E8
Stoodley TAS 73 A10 74 F4 77 J12
Storm Bay TAS 69 K2 71 G14
Stormlea TAS 69 K4
Storys Creek TAS 75 G11
Stotts Creek NSW 11 J13
Stotts Island NSW 11 J13
Stowport TAS 74 C1 77 G10
Strachan WA 108 G7
Stradbroke VIC 64 K6 66 G7
Stradbroke Island Con Park QLD 24 A5
Stradbroke West VIC 64 K6 66 G7
Strahan TAS 72 G4
Strangways Springs SA 90 J5
Stratford NSW 37 C12
Stratford VIC 64 J6 66 E7
Strath Creek VIC 64 F1 66 B1
Strathalbyn SA 89 H9 98 D3
Stratham WA 108 B4
Strathblane TAS 71 H11
Strathbogie NSW 39 D9
Strathbogie VIC 64 B2 66 A3
Strathdownie VIC 58 F2 98 J6
Stratherne WA 107 H9
Strathewen VIC 57 A10
Strathfield NSW 27 F3 29 K8 31 B8 35 D10
Strathfield South NSW 31 C8
Strathfieldsaye VIC 59 A12 63 K10
Strathgordon TAS 70 D6
Strathkellar VIC 58 E5
Strathmerton VIC 43 J9 63 G13 64 A2
Strathmore VIC 52 E7
Strathpine QLD 3 A3 5 E8 9 J9 13 F13
Stratton WA 103 B12
Streaky Bay SA 97 J12
Streatham VIC 59 E8
Stretton QLD 3 J5 7 H11
Stretton WA 107 G11
Strickland TAS 71 A9 73 H11
Strike-A-Light Nature Res NSW
    44 F3 48 J6 65 A12
Stroud NSW 37 D12
Struan SA 58 C1 98 H6
Strzelecki VIC 57 J14 64 K3 66 G4
Strzelecki Nat Park TAS 78 D5
Strzelecki Reg Res SA 22 G2 91 H11 95 A12
Stuart Mill VIC 59 A8 62 K7
Stuart Park NT 122 G2
Stuart Town NSW 36 D5
Stuarts Point NSW 39 H12
Stuarts Well NT 128 G7
Studfield VIC 53 H14
Studio Village QLD 24 B2
Sturt SA 84 G4
Sturt Gorge Rec Park SA 86 K2 87 A6
Sturt Nat Park NSW 22 H5 40 B1 91 J14
Subiaco WA 101 F3 102 F4
Success WA 104 F5
Suffolk Park NSW 13 J14 39 B14
Sugarloaf QLD 10 D1
Suggan Buggan VIC 44 J1 65 E9
Sulphur Creek TAS 74 C2 77 G10
Summer Hill NSW 31 C9
Summerfield VIC 42 K7 63 J10
Summerholm QLD 10 C5
Summerland VIC 59 J14 66 H1
Summerland Point NSW 33 E13
Summerlands VIC 57 K9

Summertown SA 81 H7 85 E9 86 J4
Sumner QLD 3 G2 6 F7
Sunbury VIC 56 A5 59 E13
Sundown Nat Park QLD 13 K11 39 B9
Sunny Corner NSW 36 F7
Sunnybank QLD 3 H5 7 G11
Sunnybank Hills QLD 3 H4 7 G10
Sunnyside NSW 39 C10
Sunrise Beach QLD 9 A10
Sunset Cove Estate NT 122 D3
Sunshine NSW 33 E13
Sunshine VIC 51 D1 52 F5 56 C6
Sunshine Beach QLD 9 A10
Sunshine Coast QLD 9 C11
Sunshine North VIC 52 E5
Sunshine West VIC 52 F4
Surat QLD 12 F6
Surfers Paradise QLD 11 G13 13 H14 24 E5
Surges Bay TAS 71 G11
Surrey Downs SA 81 C7 83 E9
Surrey Hills TAS 72 B6 77 K8
Surrey Hills VIC 53 G11
Surry Hills NSW 31 C11
Surveyor Generals Corner NT SA WA
    92 A1 118 J7 128 K1
Surveyors Bay TAS 71 H12
Sussex Inlet NSW 44 D6
Sutherland NSW 27 J3 30 H7 35 F10 37 H9
Sutherland Creek VIC 56 F2 61 C13
Sutherlands SA 89 F10 98 B4
Sutton NSW 48 A6
Sutton VIC 62 G7
Sutton Grange VIC 59 B12
Swan Creek QLD 10 H2
Swan Hill VIC 42 H6 63 E8
Swan Island TAS 75 A13 78 H5
Swan Island VIC 56 H5
Swan Marsh VIC 59 H9 61 F8
Swan Reach SA 89 G10 98 B4
Swan Reach VIC 65 H8
Swan Reach Con Park SA 89 G10 98 C4
Swan Regional Park WA 101 D7
Swan Vale NSW 39 E8
Swan View WA 103 C12
Swanbank QLD 6 J3
Swanbourne WA 101 G1 102 G2
Swanfels QLD 10 H4
Swanpool VIC 64 D3
Swansea NSW 33 E13 37 E11
Swansea TAS 69 B5
Swanwick TAS 69 B6
Sweetmans Creek NSW 33 D9 45 J2
Swift Creek Con Area TAS 73 C8 74 G2
Swifts Creek VIC 65 F8
Sydenham NSW 31 D11
Sydenham VIC 52 D3 56 C6
Sydenham West VIC 52 C1
Sydney NSW 26 B2 27 F6 29 K11 31 B11
    35 D11 37 H10
Sydney Harbour Nat Park NSW 27 E7 29 H14
    35 C12 37 H10
Sylvania NSW 27 J4 31 G8 35 F11
Sylvania Waters NSW 31 G9
Sylvester Lake NT 127 F11
Symonston ACT 47 F6
Syndal VIC 53 J12

T

Tabacum QLD 18 E2
Tabbara VIC 65 H11
Tabberabbera VIC 64 G7
Tabbita NSW 43 E10 63 A14
Tabby Tabby Island QLD 11 D12
Table Top NSW 43 J11 64 A6
Tabor VIC 58 F5
Tabratong NSW 36 C2 41 H12 43 A12
Tabulam NSW 39 C11
Tacoma NSW 33 G13
Taggerty VIC 64 F2 66 C3
Tahara VIC 58 E4
Tahara Bridge VIC 58 E3
Tahara West VIC 58 E3
Tahmoor NSW 35 J8 37 J8 44 A6
Taigum QLD 3 B4 5 G10
Tailem Bend SA 89 H10 98 D4
Takalarup WA 109 H14
Takapimiliyi Outstation NT 123 A1 124 B3
Takenup NSW 109 J14
Takone TAS 77 G8
Talawa TAS 75 E11
Talbingo NSW 43 H14 44 E1
Talbot VIC 59 C10
Talbotville VIC 64 F6 66 C7
Talbragar NSW 36 C4 41 H14 43 A14
Taldra SA 42 F1 62 B1 89 F13 98 B6
Taleeban NSW 43 E11
Talgarno VIC 64 B6
Talia SA 88 C1 94 K1 97 K13
Talisker Con Park SA 87 H1
Tallaganda Nat Park NSW 44 D4 65 A13
Tallageira VIC 58 B1
Tallai QLD 11 G12 24 G2
Tallandoon VIC 64 C6
Tallangatta VIC 43 K12 64 B6
Tallangatta Valley VIC 64 B7
Tallaringa Con Park SA 93 G10
Tallarook VIC 59 C14 64 F1 66 B1
Tallebudgera QLD 11 H12 24 K5
Tallebudgera Valley QLD 11 H12 24 J4
Tallegalla QLD 10 C6
Tallimba NSW 43 E11
Tallong NSW 36 K7 44 C5
Tallygaroopna VIC 43 K9 63 H13 64 B2

Talmalmo NSW 43 J12 64 A7
Talmo NSW 36 K4 43 G14 64 C2
Talwood QLD 12 J7 38 A4
Tam O'Shanter Nat Park
    see Djiru Nat Park
Tamar River Con Area TAS 74 E7
Tamarama NSW 31 C13
Tamaree QLD 9 A10
Tambar Springs NSW 38 J5
Tambellin SA 86 D3
Tambellup WA 109 E12 110 H6
Tambo QLD 12 A1 14 K4 21 H11
Tambo Crossing VIC 65 G8
Tambo Upper VIC 65 H8
Tamboon VIC 65 H12
Tamborine QLD 11 E10 13 H13
Tamborine Nat Park QLD 11 E11 13 H13
Tamboy NSW 37 D12
Tamleugh VIC 63 K14 64 C2
Tammin WA 107 C10 110 C5 112 J7
Tampa WA 113 F12
Tamrookum QLD 11 H8
Tamworth NSW 38 F7
Tanah Merah QLD 7 K14
Tanawha QLD 9 D9
Tandarra VIC 42 K7 63 J10
Tangalooma QLD 11 B13 13 F14
Tangambalanga VIC 43 K12 64 B6
Tangmangaroo NSW 36 K4 44 B2
Tangorin QLD 14 E1 21 C9
Tanina TAS 71 C11 73 K13
Tanja NSW 44 H5 65 D14
Tanjil Bren VIC 64 H4 66 E5
Tankaanu SA 92 B3
Tankerton VIC 57 J10 64 K1 66 G2
Tannum Sands QLD 15 J11
Tannymorel QLD 10 J3
Tansey QLD 13 C11
Tantanoola SA 98 J5
Tanunda SA 86 C6 89 G9 98 B3
Tanwood VIC 59 B9
Tanybryn VIC 59 J10 61 H10
Taperoo SA 81 C2 82 F1
Tapin Tops Nat Park NSW 37 B12 39 K10
Taplan SA 42 F1 89 G13 98 C6
Tara NT 127 K8 129 B8
Tara QLD 13 E8
Taracumbi NT 124 B3
Taradale VIC 59 C12
Tarago NSW 44 C4
Tarago VIC 57 F14
Taragoola QLD 15 J11
Taralga NSW 36 J7 44 B5
Tarana NSW 36 G7
Taranna TAS 69 J4
Tarawi Nature Res NSW 42 D1 89 D14 95 K13
Tarcoola SA 97 C13
Tarcoon NSW 41 D11
Tarcowie SA 89 C9 95 J8
Tarcutta NSW 43 H13
Tardun WA 112 E5
Taree NSW 37 B13
Taren Point NSW 27 J4 31 H9 35 F11
Targa TAS 75 E9
Tarin Rock WA 107 K13
Tarin Rock Nature Res WA 107 K13 110 F6
Taringa VIC 59 D11
Taringa Nature Res NSW 38 C7
Tarlee SA 89 F9
Tarleton TAS 74 D4 77 H12
Tarlo NSW 36 K7 44 B5
Tarlo River Nat Park NSW 36 J7 44 B5
Tarnagulla VIC 59 A10 63 K9
Tarneit VIC 52 H1 56 D5
Tarnma SA 89 F9 98 B3
Tarnook VIC 63 J14 64 C3
Taroborah QLD 14 H6 21 F13
Tarome QLD 10 F5
Taromeo QLD 8 E3
Tarong Nat Park QLD 13 E11
Taroom QLD 12 B7
Taroon VIC 58 H7 60 F5
Taroona SA 69 H1 71 E13
Tarpeena SA 58 E1 98 J6
Tarra-Bulga Nat Park VIC 64 K5 66 G6
Tarragal VIC 58 H3
Tarraganda SA 44 H5 65 D14
Tarragindi QLD 3 F4 7 E10
Tarraleah TAS 73 H10
Tarrango VIC 62 B3
Tarranyurk VIC 42 K3 62 H4
Tarraville VIC 66 H6
Tarrawarra VIC 57 B11
Tarrawingee VIC 64 C4
Tarrayoukyan VIC 58 D3
Tarrington VIC 58 F5
Tarro NSW 33 B13
Tarvano QLD 21 C14
Tarwin Lower VIC 66 H4
Tarwin Meadows VIC 66 J3
Tarwin Middle VIC 66 H4
Tarzali QLD 18 G4
Tasman Island TAS 69 K5
Tasman Nat Park TAS 69 K3
Tasman Peninsula TAS 69 J4
Tatham NSW 39 C13
Tathra NSW 44 H5 65 D14
Tathra Nat Park WA 112 G5
Tatlows Folly TAS 76 E6
Tatong VIC 64 D3
Tatura VIC 43 K9 63 J13 64 C1
Tatyoon VIC 58 D7
Tatyoon North VIC 59 D8
Taunton Nat Park (Scientific) QLD 15 H8
Tawallah Range NT 125 J11 127 A11
Tawonga VIC 64 D6
Tawonga South VIC 64 D6

Tayena TAS 75 E10
Tayetea Bridge TAS 76 G6
Taylors Arm NSW 39 H11
Taylors Beach QLD 17 G11
Taylors Flat NSW 36 J5 44 A3
Taylors Hill VIC 52 D3
Taylors Lakes VIC 52 D4
Taylors Point NSW 29 B14
Tea Gardens NSW 37 D12
Tea Tree TAS 69 F1 71 C13
Tea Tree Gully SA 81 D7 83 G9 86 G4
Teddington WA 109 H12
Teddywaddy VIC 42 K5 63 H8
Teddywaddy West VIC 62 H7
Teepookana TAS 72 G5
Teerk Roo Ra Nat Park QLD 11 B12
Teesdale VIC 59 G11 61 C12
Teeta Bore SA 93 D8
Telangatuk East VIC 58 C4
Telarah NSW 33 A12
Telegraph Point NSW 37 A14 39 K11
Telfer Mine WA 115 C13
Telford VIC 64 B3
Telita TAS 75 D11
Tellaraga NSW 38 D4
Telopea NSW 28 H7
Telopea Downs VIC 42 K2 62 H2 98 F6
Telowie Gorge Con Park SA 89 C8 95 J8
Temma TAS 76 H3
Temora NSW 36 J2 43 F12
Tempe NSW 27 G5 31 D10
Tempe Downs NT 128 G6
Templers SA 86 B4
Templestowe VIC 51 C6 53 E12 57 C9
Templin QLD 10 F7
Tempy VIC 42 H4 62 E5
Tenambit NSW 33 A12
Tenby Pt VIC 57 K11
Teneriffe QLD 7 B10
Tenindewa WA 112 E4
Tennant Creek NT 127 G9
Tennyson NSW 27 E4 29 J9 31 A9 34 B7
Tennyson QLD 7 E9
Tennyson SA 81 F1 82 J1 84 A1 86 H1
Tennyson VIC 63 J11
Tent Hill NSW 39 D9
Tent Hill SA 88 A7 94 H7
Tenterden NSW 39 F8
Tenterden WA 109 G12
Tenterfield NSW 13 K11 39 C10
Tenthill QLD 10 C3
Teralba NSW 33 C13
Terang VIC 58 G7 60 E5
Teridgerie NSW 38 F4
Teringie SA 81 G7 85 C9
Terip Terip VIC 64 E2 66 A3
Termeil NSW 44 E6
Terowie NSW 36 C2 41 J13 43 B13
Terowie SA 89 C9 95 K9
Terranora NSW 11 J13
Terrey Hills NSW 27 B6 29 D11 35 B11
Terrick Terrick Nat Park VIC 42 K7 63 H10
Terrigal NSW 33 H13 37 F10
Terry Hie Hie NSW 38 E5
Terryvale TAS 75 E13
Tetoora Road VIC 57 H14
Teven NSW 13 K14 39 C13
Teviotville QLD 10 F7
Tewantin QLD 9 A9 13 D13
Tewantin Nat Park QLD 9 A9 13 D13
Tewkesbury TAS 77 H8
Texas QLD 13 K10 39 B8
Thalanga QLD 14 B3 17 J11 21 A11
Thallon QLD 12 J5 38 B2
Thane QLD 13 H11
Thangool QLD 15 K10
Tharbogang NSW 43 E10
Thargomindah QLD 23 F9
Tharwa ACT 44 E3 48 E4
The Basin VIC 57 D10
The Basin Nature Res NSW 39 F8
The Bump NSW 57 D13
The Cape NSW 39 B12
The Caves QLD 15 G10
The Channon NSW 39 B13
The Cove VIC 58 J7 60 G4
The Cross Roads NSW 30 E3
The Dutchmans Stern Con Park SA 88 A7 94 H7
The Entrance NSW 33 G13 37 F10
The Fisheries TAS 69 B6
The Gap QLD 3 D2 4 K7 6 B7 9 K9 11 A9
The Gap SA 88 F6 98 B1
The Gap VIC 56 A5
The Gardens NT 122 G2
The Gardens TAS 75 D14
The Glen TAS 75 D8
The Gulf NSW 39 D8
The Gums QLD 13 F8
The Gurdies VIC 57 J12
The Heart VIC 64 J6
The Hi-Way Inn Motel NT 124 K7 126 B7
The Knoll Con Park SA 86 J3 87 A7
The Lakes WA 106 D5
The Lakes Nat Park VIC 65 J8
The Lost City NT 123 E1 124 D3
The Meadows NSW 34 E1
The Monument NT 20 C3
The Narrows NT 122 F3
The Neck SA 90 H7
The Oaks NSW 34 G7 37 H8 44 A6
The Oasis Roadhouse QLD 17 G9
The Pages Con Park SA 98 E2
The Palms QLD 13 D12
The Risk NSW 39 A12
The Rock NSW 43 H12
The Rocks NSW 26 A2 29 K11 31 B11
The Sideling TAS 75 E9
The Sisters VIC 58 G7 60 E4

The Spectacles WA 104 J4
The Spit NSW 29 H12
The Spit QLD 24 C5
The Springs TAS 73 F11
The Three Sisters QLD 19 A3
The Triangle VIC 64 G3 66 D4
The Valley TAS 75 D11
The Vines WA 101 A7
Thebarton SA 81 G3 84 B4 86 H2
Theebine QLD 13 C12
Theodore ACT 47 K4
Theodore QLD 13 A8 15 K9
Theresa Park NSW 34 F7
Thevenard SA 97 G11
Thirlmere NSW 34 J7 37 J0 44 A0
Thirlmere Lakes Nat Park NSW 34 J7
Thirlstane TAS 74 D5 77 H13
Thirroul NSW 35 J10 37 J9 44 A7
Thistle Island SA 88 H4
Thomastown VIC 51 A4 53 C9
Thompsons Corner NSW 28 F7
Thooloora Island QLD 9 F10
Thoona VIC 64 C3
Thornbury VIC 51 C4 53 E9
Thorneside QLD 3 E7
Thorngate SA 80 A2 82 K5 84 B5
Thornlands QLD 11 C11
Thornleigh NSW 27 C3 28 F7 35 C10
Thornlie WA 101 J6 105 B8
Thornton NSW 33 B13 45 H7
Thornton QLD 10 E4
Thornton VIC 64 F2 66 B3
Thorny Passage Marine Park SA 88 H2
Thorpdale VIC 64 K3 66 G5
Thowgla VIC 65 B9
Thowgla Upper VIC 43 K13 65 C8
Thredbo Village NSW 43 K14 44 G1 65 C9
Three Bridges VIC 57 D13
Three Hummock Island TAS 76 B4
Three Moon QLD 13 A10 15 K11
Three Springs WA 112 F5
Three Ways NT 124 B3
Three Ways Roadhouse NT 127 G9
Throsby ACT 47 A6
Thrushton Nat Park QLD 12 G3
Thuddungra NSW 36 H3 43 E13 44 A1
Thulimbah NSW 39 B10
Thurgoona VIC 64 A6
Thuringowa QLD 14 A5 17 H12
Thurla VIC 42 F3 62 B4
Thurloo Downs NSW 40 B5
Thursday Island QLD 19 B2
Tiaro QLD 13 C13
Tibarri QLD 16 K5 20 B5
Tiberias SA 69 D2 71 A13
Tibooburra NSW 22 J6 40 B3
Tichborne NSW 36 F3 43 C13
Tickera SA 88 E7 98 A1
Tidal River VIC 66 K5
Tidbinbilla Nature Res ACT 48 E2
Tieri QLD 14 G7 21 E14
Tikkawoppa Plateau Reg Res TAS 72 C2
Tilba Tilba NSW 44 G5
Tilbaroo Crossing NSW 37 A13 39 K10
Tilley Swamp Con Park SA 98 F4
Tilmouth Crossing NT 128 E6
Tilpa NSW 40 F7
Timallallie Nat Park NSW 38 H3
Timbarra VIC 44 K1 65 F9
Timbarra Nat Park NSW 39 C11
Timber Creek NT 124 J3 126 A3
Timberoo VIC 62 E4
Timberoo South VIC 42 H3 62 E4
Timbillica NSW 44 K4 65 G13
Timboon VIC 59 J8 60 G5
Timor NSW 37 B10
Timor VIC 59 B10
Timor Sea NT 122 A1
Timor Springs NT 124 A6
Tin Can Bay QLD 13 C13
Tinamba VIC 64 J5 66 E7
Tinaroo Falls QLD 17 E10
Tincurrin WA 107 J11
Tindal NT 124 G6
Tinderbox TAS 69 J1 71 F13
Tinderry Nature Res NSW 44 E3 48 G6
Tindo QLD 14 C1 17 K9 21 B9
Tingalpa QLD 3 E6 7 C13 11 B10
Tingaringi NSW 44 J2 65 E11
Tingha NSW 39 E8
Tingoora QLD 13 D11
Tinnanbar QLD 13 C13
Tinonee NSW 37 B13
Tintaldra VIC 65 B8
Tintinara SA 89 K11 98 E5
Tipperary NT 123 G2 124 E4
Tirrannaville NSW 36 K6 44 C4
Titjikala NT 129 H8
Ti-Tree (Nturiya) NT 128 C7
Tittybong VIC 42 J5 63 G8
Tivoli QLD 6 G2
Tivoli Hill QLD 6 G2
Tiwi NT 122 B4
Tjintalka SA 92 B2 118 J7 128 K2
Tjirrkarli WA 118 J3
Tjukayirla Roadhouse WA 118 K1 119 A2
Tjukurla WA 118 G6 128 G1
Tjunti NT 118 G7 128 H2
Tjuntinanta NT 118 G7 128 H1
Tjuntjuntjara WA 119 D5
Tobermorey Station NT 20 D1 129 D14
Tocal QLD 21 F8
Tocumwal NSW 43 J9 63 G14 64 A2
Tods TAS 73 E12 74 K6
Tods Beach TAS 70 D6
Togari TAS 76 F4
Togganoggera NSW 44 E4
Toiberry TAS 73 B13 74 G7

Tolga QLD 17 E10 18 F3
Tollingo Nature Res NSW 41 J11 43 B11
Tolmie VIC 64 E4 66 A5
Tolmies QLD 14 H7 21 F14
Tom Gibson Nature Res TAS 73 C14 75 H9
Tom Groggin NSW 43 K13 44 H1 65 C9
Tom Price WA 114 E7
Tomago NSW 33 B13
Tomahawk TAS 75 B11 78 J3
Tomakin NSW 44 F5
Tomaree Nat Park NSW 37 E12
Tombong NSW 44 J2 65 E11
Tomerong NSW 44 C6
Tomewin QLD 11 J12
Tomingley NSW 36 D2 43 A13
Tonderburine NSW 38 J2
Tone Perup Nature Res WA 109 E8
Tonebridge WA 109 F8 110 H4
Tongala VIC 63 H12
Tonganah TAS 75 D10
Tonghi Creek VIC 65 G11
Tongio VIC 65 F8
Tongio West VIC 65 F8
Tonimbuk VIC 57 F13
Tooan VIC 58 A4 62 K3
Tooan East VIC 58 A4 62 K4
Toobanna QLD 17 G11
Toobeah QLD 12 J7 38 A5
Tooborac VIC 59 B13
Toodyay WA 106 C6 110 C4 112 J6
Toogong NSW 36 F4
Toogoolawah QLD 8 G4 13 F12
Toogoom QLD 13 B13
Toolamba VIC 43 K9 63 J13 64 C1
Toolangi VIC 57 A11 64 G2 66 C2
Toolern Vale VIC 56 B4 59 E13
Tooleybuc NSW 42 G5 63 D8
Toolibin WA 107 J11
Tooligie SA 88 E3
Toolleen VIC 59 A13 63 K11
Toolondo VIC 58 B4
Toolong VIC 58 H5 60 F1
Toolonga Nature Res WA 112 C4
Tooloom NSW 13 J12 39 B11
Tooloom Nat Park NSW 13 J12 39 A11
Tooma NSW 43 J13 44 F1 65 A9
Toombul QLD 3 C5 5 J11
Toomcul QLD 8 A4
Toompine QLD 23 D10
Toomulla QLD 17 H12
Toongabbie NSW 27 D1 28 H4 35 D9
Toongabbie VIC 64 J5 66 F6
Toongi NSW 36 C4 41 J14 43 B14
Toonpan QLD 14 A5 17 H12
Toonumbar NSW 39 B12
Toonumbar Nat Park NSW 13 J13 39 A12
Tooperang SA 87 E7
Toora VIC 66 H5
Tooradin NSW 55 K11 57 H10 64 J1 66 F2
Toorak VIC 51 E4 53 H9
Toorak Gardens SA 81 G5 84 C6
Tooraweenah NSW 36 A5 38 J2
Toorbul QLD 9 G10
Toorongo VIC 64 H3 66 E4
Tootgarook VIC 56 J6
Tootool NSW 43 H11
Toowong QLD 3 E3 7 C8
Toowoomba QLD 10 C1 13 G11
Toowoon Bay NSW 33 H13
Top Marshes Con Area TAS 73 F11
Topaz QLD 18 G4
Torbanlea QLD 13 B13
Torbay WA 109 K13
Torndirrup Nat Park WA 109 K13 110 K6
Toronto NSW 33 D13 37 E11
Torquay VIC 56 J2 59 H12 61 F14
Torrens ACT 47 G4
Torrens Creek QLD 14 C2 17 K10 21 B10
Torrens Island SA 81 C2 82 E2 86 G1
Torrens Island Con Park SA 81 B2 82 E6 86 F1
Torrens Park SA 81 J4 84 E6
Torrens Vale SA 87 F5
Torrensville SA 81 G3 84 C4
Torres Strait QLD 19 A1
Torrington NSW 39 D9
Torrington State Con Area NSW 13 K10 39 C9
Torrita VIC 42 H3 62 E4
Torrumbarry VIC 42 J7 63 H11
Torryburn NSW 39 G8 45 C6
Torwood QLD 7 C9
Tostaree VIC 65 H9
Tottenham NSW 36 C1 41 H12 43 A12
Tottenham VIC 52 F5
Tottington VIC 59 A8 62 K7
Tottness Rec Park SA 86 K5
Touckley NSW 33 G13
Towamba NSW 44 F5
Towaninny VIC 42 J5 63 G8
Towarri Nat Park NSW 37 B9
Tower Hill TAS 75 G12
Townson QLD 10 F4
Townsville QLD 14 A5 17 H12
Towong VIC 43 K13 65 B9
Towra Point Nature Res NSW 27 J5 31 G10
Towradgi NSW 35 K10
Towrang NSW 36 K7 44 B5
Trafalgar VIC 64 J3 66 F4
Tragowel VIC 63 G9
Trangie NSW 36 B3 41 H13 43 A13
Tranmere SA 81 F6 82 K7 84 B7
Traralgon VIC 64 J4 66 F6
Traralgon South VIC 64 K4 66 G6
Trawalla VIC 59 D9
Trawool VIC 64 E1 66 B3
Trayning WA 107 A11 110 B6 112 J7
Traysurin WA 107 J12
Trebonne QLD 17 G11
Treesville WA 106 K5 108 A7

Treeton WA 108 D2
Tregole Nat Park QLD 12 D2 21 K12
Tregony QLD 10 G4
Trenah TAS 75 E11
Trentham VIC 59 D12
Trentham East VIC 59 D12
Trephina Gorge Nature Park NT 129 F9
Tresco VIC 42 H6 63 F8
Trevallyn NSW 37 D11 45 D6
Trevallyn TAS 73 A14 75 F8
Trewalla VIC 58 H3
Trewilga NSW 36 D3 41 K14 43 B14
Triabunna TAS 69 E4
Trial Harbour TAS 72 E3
Triamble NSW 36 E2
Trida NSW 41 K8 43 C8
Trigg WA 101 D1 102 C1
Trigg Island WA 101 D1
Trigwell Nature Res WA 109 C8
Trinita VIC 42 G4 62 D5
Trinity Beach QLD 17 D11 18 C4
Trinity Gardens SA 81 F5 82 K7 84 B7
Trott Park SA 84 J3
Trowutta TAS 76 F5
Truganina VIC 56 D5
Trundle NSW 36 E2 41 K13 43 C13
Trunkey Creek NSW 36 G6
Truro SA 89 F9 98 B3
Truslove Townsite Nature Res WA 111 F12
Tryphinia QLD 15 H9
Tuan QLD 13 C13
Tuart Forest Nat Park WA 108 C3
Tuart Hill WA 101 E3 102 C4
Tubbul Road NSW 36 H3 43 E13
Tubbut VIC 44 J2 65 E10
Tucabia NSW 39 E12
Tuckanarra WA 113 C8
Tuckey SA 88 D4
Tudor WA 109 J12
Tuen QLD 23 G13
Tuena NSW 36 H6
Tugan QLD 11 H13
Tuggerah NSW 33 G12
Tuggeranong ACT 47 J4 48 D4
Tuggerawong NSW 33 G13
Tugun QLD 24 J7
Tugun Heights QLD 24 J6
Tulendeena TAS 75 D11
Tulka SA 88 G3
Tullagirie QLD 13 F8
Tullah TAS 72 C6
Tullamarine VIC 51 B2 52 C6 56 B6
Tullamore NSW 36 D2 41 J12 43 B12
Tullibigeal NSW 43 D11
Tullochgorum TAS 75 H12
Tully QLD 17 F11 18 K5
Tully Falls Nat Park QLD 17 F10 18 J3
Tully Gorge Nat Park QLD 17 F11 18 K5
Tully Heads QLD 17 F11
Tumbarumba NSW 43 J13 44 E1 65 A9
Tumbi Umbi NSW 33 H13
Tumblong NSW 43 G13 44 D1
Tumbulgum NSW 11 J13 39 A13
Tumby Bay SA 88 F4
Tumorrama NSW 43 G14 44 D1
Tumoulin QLD 17 F10 18 H3
Tumut NSW 43 H14 44 D1
Tunbridge TAS 69 B2
Tunbridge Tier Con Area TAS 69 B1
Tuncurry NSW 37 C13
Tungamah VIC 43 K10 63 H14 64 B3
Tungkillo SA 86 G7
Tunnack TAS 69 D2 71 A14
Tunnel Creek Nat Park WA 117 G9
Tunney WA 109 E11
Tupul SA 92 A5 128 K4
Tura Beach NSW 44 J5 65 E14
Turill NSW 36 C7
Turkey Beach QLD 15 J12
Turkey Lagoon NT 125 G9
Turlinjah NSW 44 F5
Turner ACT 47 D5
Turners Beach TAS 74 D3 77 G11
Turners Marsh TAS 75 E8
Turondale NSW 36 E6
Tuross Head NSW 44 F5
Turramurra NSW 27 C4 29 F9 35 C10
Turrawan NSW 38 G5
Turrella NSW 31 D10
Turriff VIC 42 H4 62 F5
Tusmore SA 81 G5 84 C7
Tutanning Nature Res WA 107 G9
Tutunup WA 108 C3
Tutye VIC 42 H2 62 E2
Tweed Heads NSW 11 H14 13 H14 39 A14
Tweed Heads West NSW 24 K7
Twelve Apostles Marine Nat Park VIC 59 K8 60 J6
Twelve Mile NSW 36 D6
Two Mile Flat NSW 36 C6
Two Peoples Bay Nature Res WA 110 K7
Two Rocks NSW 106 B2 110 C2 112 J5
Two Wells SA 86 D1 89 G8 98 B2
Tyaak VIC 59 C14 64 F1 66 B1
Tyabb VIC 57 H9 64 K1 66 G1
Tyagong NSW 36 H3 43 E14 44 A1
Tyalgum NSW 11 K11 39 A13
Tyalgum Creek NSW 11 K10
Tyalla VIC 62 E2
Tycannah NSW 38 D5
Tyenne TAS 71 C9
Tyers VIC 64 J4 66 F5
Tygalgah NSW 11 J13
Tylden VIC 59 D12
Tylerville QLD 11 J8 39 A12
Tyndale NSW 39 E12
Tyndall Reg Res TAS 72 E6
Tynong VIC 57 F12 64 J2 66 F3

Tynong North VIC 57 F12
Tyntynder South VIC 42 H6 63 E8
Tyraman NSW 45 C6
Tyrendarra VIC 58 H4 98 K7
Tyrendarra East VIC 58 H4
Tyringham NSW 39 F11
Tyrrell Downs VIC 42 H5 62 E7

U

Uarbry NSW 36 B7
Ubirr NT 123 C7 124 C7
Ubobo QLD 15 J11
Uglruuk TA3 73 D9 74 G4 77 K(12
Ukatjupa NT 92 A1 118 J7 128 K1
Uki NSW 11 K12 13 J14 39 A13
Ulamambri NSW 38 J4
Ulan NSW 36 C7
Ulandra Nature Res NSW 36 K2 43 G13
Ulaypai SA 92 A6 128 K5
Uley NSW 43 F11
Uleybury SA 86 E4
Ulidarra Nat Park NSW 39 G12
Ulinda NSW 36 A6 38 K4
Ulkiya (New) SA 92 B5
Ulladulla NSW 44 D6
Ullawarra WA 114 F5
Ullina VIC 59 C10
Ullswater VIC 58 B2 98 G7
Ulmarra NSW 39 E12
Ultima VIC 42 H5 62 F7
Ultimo NSW 26 D1 31 C11
Uluru-Kata Tjuta Cultural Centre NT 128 J4
Uluru-Kata Tjuta Nat Park NT 128 J4
Ulva WA 107 C13
Ulverstone TAS 74 D3 77 G11
Umagico QLD 19 B2
Umbakumba NT 125 F13
Umina NSW 33 J12
Uminyuluk NT 124 F2
Umpukulu SA 92 A4 128 K3
Umuwa SA 92 B7
Unanderra NSW 35 K10
Undandita NT 128 F6
Undara Resort QLD 17 F9
Undara Volcanic Nat Park QLD 17 G9
Undarana NT 128 F6
Undera VIC 43 K9 63 H13 64 B1
Underbool VIC 42 H3 62 E3
Underdale SA 84 B3
Underwood QLD 3 H5 7 G12
Underwood TAS 75 E8
Undina QLD 16 K5 20 B5
Ungarie NSW 43 D11
Ungarra SA 88 F3
Ungo QLD 14 K1 21 H9
Unicup Nature Res WA 109 F9
Unley SA 80 D2 81 H4 84 D5 86 J2
Unley Park SA 84 D5
Un-Marr NT 124 F2
Unumgar NSW 39 A12
Upolu Cay Nat Park QLD 18 C6
Upper Bingara NSW 38 F7
Upper Blessington TAS 75 F10
Upper Brookfield QLD 6 C5
Upper Caboolture QLD 9 H8
Upper Calder VIC 77 G8
Upper Castra TAS 74 E3 77 J11
Upper Colo NSW 32 K7 34 A7
Upper Coomera QLD 11 F11 24 A1
Upper Durogy NSW 11 J13
Upper Esk TAS 75 F11
Upper Ferntree Gully VIC 55 A9 57 E10
Upper Freestone QLD 10 H3
Upper Gulf St Vincent Marine Park SA 88 F7
Upper Hermitage SA 83 E10 86 G4
Upper Horton NSW 38 F6
Upper Kedron QLD 3 D1 4 J6 6 A6
Upper Manilla NSW 38 G7
Upper McDonald NSW 33 H8
Upper Mount Gravatt QLD 3 G5 7 E11
Upper Mount Hicks TAS 77 G8
Upper Myall NSW 37 C12
Upper Natone TAS 74 D1 77 H9
Upper Pilton QLD 10 F2
Upper Plenty VIC 59 D14 66 C1
Upper Scamander TAS 75 F14
Upper South East Marine Park SA 98 G4
Upper Spencer Gulf Marine Park SA 88 C7 94 K7
Upper Spring Creek QLD 10 F2
Upper Stone QLD 17 G11
Upper Stowport QLD 74 D1 77 G9
Upper Sturt SA 81 K6 85 G8
Upper Swan WA 106 D4 110 D3 112 K5
Upper Tallebudgera QLD 11 J12
Upper Tenthill QLD 10 C3
Upper Yarra Dam VIC 57 B14
Uraidla SA 81 H7 85 D10 86 J4 89 H9 98 C3
Uralla NSW 39 G8
Urana NSW 43 H10
Urandangi QLD 20 C1
Urania SA 88 F6 98 B1
Uranquinty NSW 43 H12
Urawa Nature Res WA 112 E5
Urbenville NSW 13 J12 39 A11
Urilpila NT 128 J3
Urisino NSW 23 J9 40 C6
Urlampe NT 20 E1 129 D14
Urlip QLD 15 D2
Urrbrae SA 81 H5 84 E7
Urunga NSW 39 G12
Useless Loop WA 112 B2 114 K2
Uxbridge TAS 71 D10

V

Vacy NSW 37 D11 45 D6
Vale Belvoir TAS 72 B7 74 G1 77 K9
Vale of Belvoir Con Area TAS 74 G2 77 K9
Vale Park SA 82 J6 84 A6
Vale View QLD 10 C1
Valentine NSW 33 D13
Valla Beach NSW 39 G12
Valley Heights NSW 34 D6
Valley View SA 81 D5 82 G7
Van Diemen Gulf NT 123 A4 124 B5
Vanderlin Island NT 125 J13 127 A13
Varley WA 111 F8
Varroville NSW 30 G1
Varsity Lakes QLD 24 G4
Vasey VIC 58 D4
Vasse WA 108 C2
Vaucluse NSW 27 F7 29 K13 31 B13 35 D12
Vectis VIC 58 A5 62 K4
Veitch SA 89 G12 98 C6
Venman Bushland Nat Park QLD 3 J7 11 C11
Ventnor VIC 57 K9 59 H14 64 K1 66 G1
Venus Bay SA 88 C1 94 K1 97 K13
Venus Bay VIC 66 H3
Venus Bay Con Park SA 97 K13
Verdon Rock QLD 16 H2
Verdun SA 85 F11 86 J4
Veresdale QLD 11 F9
Vermont VIC 53 H13 57 D9
Vermont South VIC 53 H13
Verona NSW 44 G4 65 C14
Verona Sands TAS 71 H12
Verran SA 88 E4
Vervale VIC 57 G12
Victor Harbor SA 87 G6 89 J8 98 D3
Victoria Park WA 101 G4 102 G6
Victoria Point QLD 11 C12 13 G14
Victoria River Research Station NT 124 J4 126 A4
Victoria River Roadhouse NT 124 H4 126 A4
Victoria Valley TAS 73 H11
Victoria Valley VIC 58 E5
Victory Well SA 93 D8
View Bank VIC 53 D11
Villawood NSW 27 F2 30 C5
Villeneuve QLD 8 F6
Vineyard NSW 28 C2 35 C8
Vinifera VIC 42 H5 63 E6
Violet Town VIC 63 K14 64 D2
Virginia NT 123 C2 124 E4
Virginia QLD 3 C5 5 G11 8 H2
Virginia SA 86 E2 89 G8 98 C3
Vista SA 81 D7 83 G10
Vite Vite VIC 59 F8
Vite Vite North VIC 59 F8 60 A7
Viveash WA 103 B10
Vivonne Bay SA 88 K6
Vivonne Bay Con Park SA 88 K5
Voyager Point NSW 30 E5
Vulkathunha-Gammon Ranges Nat Park SA 95 C10

W

WA/NT Border Quarantine Checkpoint WA 117 D14
Waaia VIC 63 H13 64 A1
Waarre VIC 59 J8 60 H6
Wabma Kadarbu Mound Springs Con Park SA 90 J5
Wacol QLD 3 H1 6 G6 11 C9
Wada Wadalla NT 125 J12 127 A12
Wada Warra NT 125 J12 127 A12
Wadbilliga Nat Park NSW 44 G4 65 C13
Waddamana TAS 73 F12
Waddi NSW 43 F10
Waddikee SA 88 C4 94 K4
Waddles Creek Con Area TAS 71 B11 73 J13
Wadeye (Port Keats) NT 124 F1
Waeel WA 107 C8
Wagaman NT 122 C5
Wagant VIC 42 G4 62 D5
Wagga Wagga NSW 43 G12
Waggon Flat VIC 62 G2 89 K14 98 F2
Wagin WA 109 B11 110 F5
Wahgunyah VIC 43 J10 64 A4
Wahgunyah Con Park SA 96 F7
Wahroonga NSW 27 C4 29 E9 35 C10
Waikerie SA 89 F11 98 B5
Wail VIC 62 J4
Wairewa VIC 65 H9
Waitara NSW 29 E8
Waitchie VIC 62 E7
Waitpinga SA 87 H5
Waitpinga Con Park SA 87 H3
Wakefield NSW 33 D13
Wakeley NSW 28 K3 30 B3
Wakerley QLD 7 C13
Wakooka QLD 17 A9 19 H6
Wakool NSW 42 H7 63 F10
Walalkara SA 92 C7
Walang NSW 36 F7
Walbundrie NSW 43 J11
Walcha NSW 39 H9
Walcha Road NSW 39 H8
Waldnarr NSW 125 E11
Walebing WA 110 A3 112 H5
Walga Gunya WA 113 C9
Walgett NSW 38 E1 41 C13
Walgoolan WA 110 C7 113 J8
Walgra QLD 20 D1
Walhalla VIC 64 H4 66 E5
Walkamin QLD 18 F3
Walitjara SA 92 B4 128 K4

Walkamin QLD 17 E10 18 F3
Walkaway WA 112 F4
Walker VIC 57 A14
Walker Channel TAS 76 C4
Walker Flat SA 89 D8 C4
Walkerston QLD 15 D8
Walkerville SA 81 F4 82 K6 84 A6 86 H2
Walkerville VIC 66 J4
Wall Creek NT 90 A1 93 A13 129 K9
Walla Walla NSW 43 J11
Wallabadah NSW 37 A9 38 K7
Wallabadah Nature Res NSW 37 A9 38 K7
Wallabi Group WA 112 E2
Wallabi Point NSW 37 B13
Wallaby Island QLD 19 F1
Wallace VIC 59 E11
Wallace Rockhole NT 128 G7
Wallacedale VIC 58 F4
Wallacia NSW 34 E7 37 H8
Wallaga Lake Heights NSW 44 G5
Wallal QLD 21 K11 23 C14
Wallalong NSW 33 A12 45 F7
Wallaloo VIC 58 A7 62 K6
Wallaloo East VIC 58 A7 62 K7
Wallan VIC 59 D14 66 C1
Wallan East VIC 59 D14 66 C1
Wallangarra NSW 13 K11 39 C10
Wallangra NSW 38 C7
Wallany SA 92 B6
Wallaroo NSW 47 A2
Wallaroo SA 88 E7 98 A1
Wallaville QLD 13 A11
Wallendbeen NSW 36 J3 43 F13 44 B1
Wallerawang NSW 34 B1 36 F7
Walleroobie NSW 43 F12
Walli NSW 36 G5
Wallinduc VIC 59 F9 61 B9
Wallingat Nat Park NSW 37 C13
Wallington VIC 56 H4
Walliston WA 103 H13
Walloon QLD 10 C7 13 G12
Walloway SA 89 B9 95 H9
Walls of Jerusalem Nat Park TAS 73 E9 74 K3
Wallsend NSW 33 C13 37 E11 45 K7
Wallumbilla QLD 12 E6
Wallundry NSW 36 J2 43 F13
Wallup VIC 42 K4 62 J5
Walmer NSW 36 D4 41 J14 43 B14
Walpa VIC 64 H7
Walpeup VIC 42 H3 62 E4
Walpole TAS 71 H11
Walpole VIC 59 J9 110 K4
Walpole Nornalup Nat Park WA 109 K8 110 K4
Waltara NSW 35 C10
Walu NT 118 G7 128 H2
Walungurru (Kintore) NT 118 E7 128 E2
Walwa VIC 43 J13 65 A8
Walyahmoning Nature Res WA 110 A7 113 H8
Walyinynga (Cave Hill) SA 92 A6 128 K4
Walytjatjata NT 92 A2 118 J7 128 K2
Walyunga Nat Park WA 106 C4
Wamberal NSW 33 H13
Wamboyne NSW 36 G1 43 D12
Wamindah NSW 38 E1 41 C14
Wammutta QLD 20 C4
Wamoon NSW 43 F10
Wampoony SA 42 K1
Wampoonya SA 98 F6
Wamuran QLD 9 G8 13 F13
Wamuran Basin QLD 9 G8
Wanaaring NSW 23 J10 40 C6
Wanagarren Nature Res WA 110 B2 112 H4
Wanakutja NT 124 A6
Wanbi SA 89 G12 98 D5
Wandana Nature Res WA 112 D4
Wandangula NT 125 J12 127 A12
Wandawuy NT 125 D12
Wandearah East SA 88 D7 94 K7
Wandearah West SA 88 D7 94 K7
Wandella NSW 44 G5
Wandering WA 106 H6 110 E4
Wandi WA 104 H6
Wandiligong VIC 64 D6
Wandin North VIC 57 C11
Wando Bridge VIC 58 D3
Wando Vale VIC 58 E3
Wandoan QLD 13 D8
Wandong-Heathcote Junction VIC 59 D14 66 C1
Wandoo Nat Park WA 106 E6 110 D4 112 K6
Wandsworth NSW 39 F9
Wangalinji NT 127 E13
Wangan QLD 18 H6
Wanganella WA 43 H8 63 E12
Wangara WA 101 B3
Wangarabell VIC 44 K4 65 G13
Wangaratta VIC 43 K10 64 C4
Wangary SA 88 F2
Wangetti QLD 18 C3
Wangi Wangi NSW 33 E13
Wangianna SA 90 K7 94 A7
Wangkari NT 128 J1
Wangkatjungka WA 117 H10
Wangoom VIC 58 H6 60 F3
Wanguri NT 122 C5
Wanilla SA 88 F3
Wanjarri Nature Res WA 113 C11
Wanko QLD 21 K11 23 B13
Wanmarri NT 124 J7
Wannamal WA 106 A5 110 B3 112 J5
Wannan WA 118 H5
Wanneroo WA 101 A3 106 D3 110 D3 112 K5
Wanniassa ACT 47 H4
Wannon VIC 58 E4
Wanora QLD 10 B6
Wansbeck QLD 8 B1
Wansborough WA 109 F13
Wantabadgery NSW 43 G13

Wantirna VIC 53 H14
Wantirna South VIC 53 H14
Wapengo NSW 44 H5 65 D14
Wapet Camp WA 114 B4
Warakurna WA 118 G6
Warakurna Roadhouse WA 118 G6
Waramanga ACT 47 G3
Warana QLD 9 D10
Waratah NSW 33 C13
Waratah TAS 72 A5 76 J7
Waratah Bay VIC 66 J4
Waratah North VIC 66 J4
Warburn NSW 43 E10
Warburton VIC 57 C13 64 H2 66 D3
Warburton WA 118 J4
Warburton East VIC 57 C13
Warby Range State Park VIC 64 B4
Wardell NSW 13 K14 39 C13
Wards Mistake NSW 39 F10
Wareemba NSW 29 K9 31 B9
Warialda NSW 38 D6
Warianna QLD 21 B8
Warilla NSW 37 K9 44 B7
Warkworth NSW 32 A7
Warlpeyangrere NT 129 D13
Warmun (Turkey Creek) WA 117 F13
Warncoort VIC 59 H10 61 E10
Warneet VIC 57 H10
Warneet East VIC 64 J1 66 F2
Warner QLD 4 E7
Warners Bay NSW 33 C13
Warnertown SA 89 C8 95 K8
Warnervale NSW 33 G12
Warooka SA 88 H6 98 C1
Waroona WA 106 J3 110 F3
Warra QLD 13 C9
Warra Nat Park NSW 39 F10
Warrabah Nat Park NSW 38 G7
Warrabillinna SA 93 B8
Warrabkook VIC 58 F5
Warracknabeal VIC 42 K4 62 H5
Warradale SA 81 J2 84 F3
Warraderry NSW 36 G3 43 D14
Warragamba NSW 34 E7 37 H8
Warragoon NSW 43 J10 64 A3
Warragul VIC 57 G14 64 J3 66 F4
Warrak VIC 59 C8
Warralakin NSW 110 B7 113 H8
Warrambine VIC 59 F10 61 B11
Warramboo SA 88 C3 94 K3
Warrandyte VIC 51 C7 53 D14 57 C9
Warrandyte South VIC 53 E14
Warrandyte State Park VIC 51 B7 53 D14 57 C9
Warranulla NSW 37 C12
Warranwood VIC 53 E14
Warrawee NSW 29 E9 35 C10
Warrayure VIC 58 E5
Warreah QLD 14 C2 17 K10 21 B10
Warrego NT 127 G8
Warrell Creek NSW 39 H12
Warren NSW 36 A2 41 G13
Warren Con Park SA 86 F5
Warren Creek NT 128 E4
Warren Nat Park WA 108 G5 110 J3
Warrenbayne VIC 64 D3
Warrenben Con Park SA 88 H5
Warrenmang VIC 59 B9
Warrentinna TAS 75 C11
Warriewood NSW 29 D14 35 B11
Warrigal QLD 14 C2 17 K10 21 B10
Warrill View QLD 10 E6
Warrimoo NSW 34 D6
Warrina SA 90 F3
Warringa TAS 74 E2 77 H10
Warrion VIC 59 G9 61 E9
Warrnambool VIC 58 H6 60 F2
Warrong VIC 58 G6 60 E1
Warroo NSW 36 F2 43 C12
Warrow SA 88 F2
Warrumbunge NSW 38 J2
Warrumbungle Nat Park NSW 38 J3
Warrupura NSW 38 H1
Warruwi NT 124 B7
Wartook VIC 58 B5
Warumbul NSW 31 J8
Warup WA 109 B11
Warwick QLD 10 J2 13 H11 39 A10
Warwick WA 101 C2 102 A3
Warwick Farm NSW 27 G1 30 D4
Wasaga QLD 19 B2
Washpool NSW 37 C12
Washpool Nat Park NSW 39 D10
Wasleys SA 86 B3 89 F9 98 B3
Watagan NSW 33 E10
Watagans Nat Park NSW 33 D11 37 E10 45 K4
Watalgan QLD 15 K12
Watanobbi NSW 33 G12
Watarrka Nat Park NT 128 G5
Watarru SA 92 D3 118 K7
Watchem VIC 42 K5 62 H6
Watchupga VIC 62 G6
Watdagawuy NT 125 B11
Waterbank WA 116 G5
Waterfall NSW 35 G10 37 H9 44 A7
Waterfall Gully SA 81 H6 85 D8
Waterford VIC 64 G6
Waterford WA 101 H4 102 J6
Waterhouse TAS 75 B11 78 K3
Waterloo NSW 31 C11
Waterloo SA 89 E9 98 A3
Waterloo TAS 71 G11
Waterloo VIC 59 D9
Waterloo WA 108 B4
Waterloo Bay NSW 88 H6
Waterloo Corner SA 81 A3 82 A4

Watermanis Bay WA 102 A1
Watermans Bay WA 101 C1
Waters Meeting TAS 69 A5 75 K13
Watersmeet TAS 73 F8
Waterview Heights NSW 39 E12
Watgania VIC 58 D6
Watheroo WA 110 A3 112 G5
Watheroo Nat Park WA 110 A3 112 G5
Watinuna SA 92 B7
Watson ACT 47 C5
Watson SA 96 C6
Watsonia VIC 51 B5 53 C11 57 C8
Watsons Bay NSW 27 E7 29 J13 31 A13 35 D12
Watsons Creek NSW 38 H7
Watsons Creek VIC 57 B9
Watsons Creek Nature Res NSW 38 H7
Wattamolla NSW 35 G11
Wattamondara NSW 36 H4 43 E14
Wattening WA 106 B6
Wattle Corner TAS 75 F10
Wattle Creek VIC 59 B8
Wattle Flat NSW 36 E6
Wattle Glen VIC 53 B13 57 B9
Wattle Grove NSW 30 E4 35 E10
Wattle Grove TAS 71 G11
Wattle Grove WA 101 H7 103 H11
Wattle Hill TAS 69 G3
Wattle Park SA 81 G6 85 C8
Wattle Range SA 98 H6
Wattleup WA 104 F3
Waubra VIC 59 D10
Wauchope NSW 37 A13 39 K11
Wauchope NT 127 J9 129 A9
Waukaringa SA 89 A10 95 H10
Wauraltee SA 88 G6 98 B1
Waurn Ponds VIC 56 H2 59 G12 61 D13
Wavell Heights QLD 3 C4 5 H10
Waverley NSW 27 F7 31 C13 35 D12
Waverley Downs NSW 40 B6
Waverton NSW 29 J11 31 A11
Wayatinah TAS 71 A8 73 H10
Waychinicup Nat Park WA 110 J7
Waygara VIC 65 H9
Wayililinypa NT 128 D5
Wayville SA 80 D2 81 G4 84 A4
Weabonga NSW 39 J8
Wearne NSW 38 B6
Wearne QLD 13 J8
Weasel Plains NSW 73 G13
Weaver SA 88 H7 98 C1
Webbs NSW 36 C3 41 H14 43 A14
Webs Creek NSW 33 J9
Wedderburn NSW 35 G9
Wedderburn VIC 42 K6 63 J8
Wedderburn Junction VIC 63 J9
Weddin Mountains Nat Park NSW 36 H3 43 E13
Wedge Island SA 88 H4
Wedin WA 107 J11
Wee Jasper NSW 43 G14 44 D2
Wee Jasper Nature Res NSW 44 D2
Wee Waa NSW 38 F4
Wee Wee Rup VIC 63 G10
Weegena TAS 73 A10 74 F4 77 K12
Weelaty TAS 75 E9
Weemelah NSW 38 C3
Weemol NT 125 E9
Weengallon QLD 12 H6 38 A3
Weerangourt VIC 58 F4
Weerite VIC 59 H8 60 E7
Weetah TAS 73 A11 74 F5 77 K13
Weetaliba NSW 36 A6 38 K4
Weetaliba Nature Res NSW 36 A6 38 K4
Weetangera ACT 47 C3
Weethalle NSW 43 E11
Weetulta SA 88 F7 98 B1
Wehla VIC 63 K8
Weilmoringle NSW 12 K2
Weipa QLD 19 E1
Weismantels NSW 37 C12
Weja NSW 43 D11
Welaregang NSW 43 J13 65 A9
Weldborough TAS 75 D12
Welere (Perety) NT 129 C10
Welford Nat Park QLD 21 H8
Welland SA 82 K4
Welland West SA 84 D4
Wellers Hill QLD 7 E10
Wellingrove NSW 39 E9
Wellington NSW 36 D5
Wellington SA 89 J10 98 D4
Wellington Nat Park WA 108 B5 110 G3
Wellington Point QLD 11 B11
Wellstead WA 110 J7
Welshmans Reef VIC 59 B11
Welshpool VIC 66 H5
Welshpool WA 101 G6 103 H9
Wembley WA 101 F3 102 E4
Wembley Downs WA 101 E2 102 D2
Wemen VIC 42 G4 62 C6
Wensleydale VIC 61 F12
Wentworth NSW 42 E3 62 A4
Wentworth Falls NSW 34 D5
Wentworthville NSW 28 H5
Werakata Nat Park NSW 33 B11 45 H4
Weranga QLD 13 F9
Werneth VIC 59 F10 61 B9
Werombi NSW 34 F7
Werrap VIC 42 J3 62 H4
Werribee VIC 52 K1 56 E5 59 F13
Werribee Gorge State Park VIC 56 B3
Werribee South VIC 56 F5
Werrikimbe Nat Park NSW 39 J10
Werrimull VIC 42 F2 62 B3
Werrington NSW 34 D7
Werris Creek NSW 38 J6
Wesburn VIC 57 C12
Wesley Vale TAS 74 D4 77 H12

West Beach SA 81 G2 84 D2 86 H1
West Bore No. 2 SA 92 C7
West Burleigh QLD 24 G5
West Cape Howe Nat Park WA 109 K12 110 K6
West Coast Bays Marine Park SA 97 J11
West Coast Range Reg Res TAS 72 G5
West Croydon SA 82 J4 84 A4
West End QLD 2 D1 3 E3 7 C9 11 B9
West Footscray VIC 52 F6
West Frankford TAS 69 E6 77 H14
West Gosford NSW 33 H12
West Hindmarsh SA 82 K4 84 B4
West Hobart TAS 68 C1
West Hoxton NSW 30 D1 35 E9
West Ipswich QLD 6 H1
West Island SA 87 H6
West Island Con Park SA 87 H6
West Kentish TAS 73 A9 74 F3 77 J11
West Killara NSW 35 C11
West Lakes SA 81 E1 82 J1 84 A2 86 H1
West Lakes Shore SA 82 H1
West Lindfield NSW 35 C11
West Macdonnell Nat Park NT 128 F6
West Melbourne VIC 52 F7
West Montagu TAS 76 A2
West Pennant Hills NSW 27 C2 28 F6
West Perth WA 100 A1 101 F3 102 F4
West Pine TAS 74 D2 77 G10
West Pyengana TAS 75 E12
West Pymble NSW 27 D4 29 G9 35 C10
West Richmond SA 84 D3
West Ridgley TAS 74 C1 77 G9
West Ryde NSW 27 E4 29 H8
West Scottsdale TAS 75 D10
West Swan WA 101 C6 103 A9
West Takone TAS 76 H7
West Wallsend NSW 33 C12 45 K6
West Wyalong NSW 36 H1 43 E12
Westall VIC 53 K12 54 B6
Westbourne Park SA 81 H4 84 E5
Westbrook NSW 45 C3
Westbury TAS 73 B12 74 G6 77 K14
Westby NSW 43 H12
Westby VIC 63 F9
Westdale WA 106 F6
Western Creek TAS 73 C10 74 G5
Western Flat SA 62 K1 98 F6
Western Junction TAS 73 B14 75 G8
Western Port VIC 57 H10
Westerway TAS 71 C10 73 K12
Westfield WA 101 K7 105 D10
Westgate QLD 21 K11 23 B14
Westlake QLD 6 E6
Westleigh NSW 28 E7
Westmar QLD 12 J7
Westmead NSW 27 E2 28 H5
Westmeadows VIC 51 A2 52 B6
Westmere VIC 59 E8
Westminster WA 101 D3 102 B4
Weston ACT 47 F3
Weston NSW 33 B11
Weston Creek ACT 47 F2 48 C4
Westonia WA 110 B7 113 J8
Westwood QLD 15 H10
Westwood TAS 73 A13 74 F7
Wetherill Park NSW 28 K3 30 B3 35 D9
Wewak SA 96 B7
Weyba Downs QLD 9 A10
Weymouth TAS 75 C8
Whale Beach NSW 33 K12 35 A12
Wharminda SA 88 E4
Wharparilla VIC 43 K8 63 H11
Wheeler Heights NSW 29 E13
Wheelers Hill VIC 51 F6 53 J13 54 A7
Wheeo NSW 36 J5 44 B3
Wherrol Flat NSW 37 B12
Whetstone QLD 5 K9 7 B9
Whicher Nat Park WA 108 D3
Whim Creek WA 114 B7
Whiporie NSW 39 D12
Whirily VIC 62 G7
White Beach TAS 69 K3
White Cliffs NSW 40 E5
White Flat SA 88 F3
White Gum Valley WA 101 J2 104 B2
White Hill Plain TAS 72 J7
White Hills TAS 73 B14 75 F9
White Hut SA 88 H5
White Mountains Nat Park QLD 14 C2 17 K10 21 A10
White Rock QLD 18 E4
Whiteford TAS 69 D2 71 A14
Whiteheads Creek VIC 64 E1 66 A1
Whiteman WA 101 C5 103 A8
Whitemark TAS 78 D5
Whitemore TAS 73 B13 74 G7
Whites Dam Con Park SA 89 E10 98 A4
Whiteside QLD 4 C6
Whitewood QLD 21 C8
Whitfield VIC 64 D4
Whitsunday Islands Nat Park QLD 15 B8
Whittingham NSW 32 A8
Whittlesea VIC 57 A8 59 D14 64 G1 66 C1
Whitton NSW 43 F10
Whitwarta SA 89 E8 98 A2
Whoorel VIC 59 H10 61 F11
Whorouly VIC 64 C5
Whorouly South VIC 64 C5
Whroo VIC 59 A14 63 K12
Whyalla SA 88 C6 94 K6
Whyalla Con Park SA 88 B6 94 J6
Whyte Island QLD 3 D7 5 J14 9 K11 11 A10
Whyte-Yarcowie SA 89 C9 95 K9
Wialki NSW 110 A6 113 H8
Wiangaree NSW 39 B12
Wicherina WA 112 F4
Wickepin WA 107 H10 110 E5
Wickham WA 114 B6

West Beach SA 81 G2 84 D2 86 H1
Wickliffe VIC 58 E7
Widden NSW 32 B2 37 D8
Widgelli NSW 43 F10
Widgiemooltha WA 111 C12 113 J12
Widgiewa WA 43 G10
Wietalaba QLD 15 J11
Wights Mountain QLD 4 H4
Wilandspey Con Park QLD 14 E4 21 C12
Wilberforce NSW 35 B8 37 G9
Wilburville TAS 73 F12 74 K7
Wilby VIC 64 B3
Wilcannia NSW 40 G5
Wild Horse Plains SA 89 F8 98 B2
Wildcat Bore SA 93 D9
Wiley Park NSW 31 D8
Wilga WA 108 C6
Wilgamar NSW 38 G4
Wilgarup WA 108 E6
Wilgi NT 124 B6
Wilgul VIC 61 B9
Wilkatana SA 88 A7 94 G7
Wilkawatt SA 89 J12 98 D5
Willa VIC 42 H3 62 F5
Willagee WA 102 K3 104 A3
Willalooka SA 98 F5
Willandra Nat Park NSW 41 K8 43 C8
Willangie VIC 62 F6
Willare Bridge Roadhouse WA 116 G7
Willatook VIC 58 G5 60 C5
Willaura VIC 58 E7
Willawarrin NSW 39 H11
Willawong QLD 3 H3 7 G9 11 C9
Willbriggie NSW 43 F10
Willetton WA 101 J4 102 K6 104 A6
Willi Willi SA 92 B2 118 J7
Willi Willi Nat Park NSW 39 J11
William Bay WA 109 K11
William Bay Nat Park WA 109 K10
William Creek SA 90 H4
Williams WA 106 K7 110 F4
Williamsdale NSW 44 E3 48 F5
Williamsford TAS 72 D5
Williamston SA 86 E5 89 G9 98 C3
Williamstown VIC 51 E2 52 J7 56 D7
Williamstown North VIC 52 J6
Williamtown NSW 33 A14 37 E11
Willis VIC 44 J1 65 E10
Willmot NSW 35 C8
Willochra SA 89 A8 95 G8
Willow Crossing VIC 43 K13 65 C8
Willow Grove VIC 64 J3 66 F5
Willow Tree NSW 37 A9 38 K7
Willow Vale NSW 37 J8 44 B6
Willowbank QLD 10 D6
Willowie SA 89 B8 95 J8
Willows QLD 14 H6 21 F13
Willows Gemfields QLD 14 H6 21 F13
Willowvale QLD 10 H2
Willowvale VIC 59 F9 61 A8
Wills Creek Con Park SA 88 F7 98 B2
Willung VIC 64 K5 66 G7
Willunga SA 87 D5 89 H8 98 D2
Willunga Hill SA 87 D6
Wilmington SA 89 B8 95 H8
Wilmores Lane TAS 73 B13 75 G8
Wilmot TAS 73 A8 74 E3 77 J11
Wilora NT 129 C8
Wilpena SA 95 F9
Wilson SA 95 G8
Wilson WA 102 J7
Wilson Nature Res WA 112 F4
Wilsons Promontory Marine Nat Park VIC 66 K5
Wilsons Promontory Marine Reserve VIC 66 K5
Wilsons Promontory Nat Park VIC 66 K5
Wilston QLD 5 K9 7 B9
Wilton NSW 35 J8 37 J9 44 A7
Wiltshire TAS 76 E6
Wiltshire-Butler Nat Park WA 108 E3
Wiluna WA 113 B10 115 K10
Wimba SA 95 J9
Wimbra VIC 61 H9
Winbin QLD 21 K9 23 C11
Winburndale Nature Res NSW 36 F7
Winchelsea VIC 59 G11 61 E12
Windarra WA 113 C13
Windella Downs NSW 45 G5
Windellama NSW 44 C5
Windera QLD 13 C11
Windermere TAS 74 E7
Windermere VIC 59 D10
Windeyer NSW 36 D6
Windjana Gorge Nat Park WA 117 F9
Windmill Flat NSW 42 D4
Windorah QLD 20 J7
Windsor NSW 35 B8 37 G9
Windsor QLD 3 D4 5 K10 7 A10
Windsor SA 89 F8 98 B2
Windsor VIC 53 H9
Windsor Downs NSW 35 C8
Windsor Downs Nature Res NSW 35 C8
Windsor Gardens SA 81 E5 82 H7
Windy Harbour WA 108 J6 110 J3
Winfield QLD 15 K12
Wingala NSW 27 D7 29 F13
Wingarnie WA 111 D12 113 K12
Wingaroo Nature Res TAS 78 A4
Wingeel VIC 59 G10 61 C11
Wingello NSW 36 K7 44 B5
Wingen NSW 37 B9
Wingfield SA 81 D3 82 G4 86 G2
Wingham NSW 37 B13
Winiam VIC 42 K3 62 J3
Winiam East VIC 62 J3
Winjallok VIC 59 A8 62 K7
Winkleigh TAS 74 E6 77 H14
Winmalee NSW 34 D6

Winnaleah TAS 75 C12
Winnambool VIC 62 D6
Winnap VIC 58 F2
Winnellie NT 122 F5
Winninowie SA 88 B7 94 H7
Winninowie Con Park SA 88 B7 94 J7
Winnunga NSW 43 D11
Winslow VIC 58 H6 60 E2
Winston Hills NSW 27 D2 28 G5 35 C9
Wintawatu SA 92 A5 128 K4
Winthrop WA 101 J3 102 K4 104 A4
Winton QLD 20 D7
Winton VIC 43 K10 64 C3
Winwill QLD 10 C3
Winya QLD 8 F6
Wirha SA 42 H1 89 H12 98 D6
Wirliyatjarrayi (Willowra) NT 126 K6 128 B6
Wirrabara SA 89 C8 95 J8
Wirragulla NSW 37 D11
Wirraminna SA 94 E4
Wirrate VIC 59 A14 63 K12
Wirrega SA 42 K1 98 F6
Wirrida SA 93 K13
Wirrimah NSW 36 H4 43 E14 44 A1
Wirrinya NSW 36 G2 43 D13
Wirrulla SA 97 H13
Wisemans Ferry NSW 33 J9 37 F9
Wishart QLD 3 G5 7 F12
Wishbone WA 109 B13
Witchcliffe WA 108 E2 110 H2
Withcott QLD 10 B2
Withersfield QLD 14 H6 21 F13
Witjira Nat Park SA 90 A3 93 A14 129 K11
Witta QLD 9 D8
Wittenoom WA 115 D8
Wivenhoe Pocket QLD 10 A6
Wiyarra QLD 10 J3
Woden ACT 48 C4
Woden Valley ACT 47 G4
Wodonga VIC 43 K11 64 B6
Woggoon Nature Res NSW 41 K11 43 B11
Wogyala NT 127 F10
Wokalup WA 106 K3 108 A5 110 F3
Woko Nat Park NSW 37 B11
Wokurna SA 88 D7 98 A2
Woldston QLD 14 B5 17 J12
Wolfdene QLD 11 E11
Wolfe Creek Meteorite Crater Nat Park WA 117 J12
Wollar NSW 36 C7
Wollemi Nat Park NSW 32 B5 34 A4 37 E8
Wollert VIC 57 A8
Wollman NT 124 D3
Wollombi NSW 33 D9 37 E10 45 K1
Wollomombi NSW 39 G10
Wollongbar NSW 39 B13
Wollongong NSW 35 K11 37 J9 44 B7
Wollstonecraft NSW 29 J11 31 A11
Wollumbin Nat Park NSW 39 A13
Wollun NSW 39 H8
Wolseley SA 42 K1 62 J1 98 F6
Wolumla NSW 44 H4 65 E14
Wombarra NSW 35 H11
Wombat NSW 36 J3 43 F14 44 B1
Wombelano VIC 58 B3 98 H7
Womboota NSW 42 J7 63 G11
Wombramurra NSW 38 A3 38 K7
Womikata SA 92 A7 128 K6
Wonboyn Lake NSW 44 K5 65 F14
Wondai QLD 13 D11
Wondalga NSW 43 H13 44 D1
Wondecla QLD 18 G2
Wondul Range Nat Park QLD 13 H9
Wonga QLD 17 D10 18 A2
Wonga Park VIC 57 C10 64 H1 66 D2
Wongaling Beach QLD 17 F11 18 K6
Wongamine WA 106 B6
Wongan Hills WA 110 B4 112 H6
Wongarbon NSW 36 C4
Wongarra VIC 59 J10 61 J10
Wongawallan QLD 11 E11
Wongi Nat Park QLD 13 B12
Wongoni NSW 36 B6
Wongoondy WA 112 E5
Wongwibinda NSW 39 F10
Wonnerup WA 108 C3
Wonthaggi VIC 66 H3
Wonwondah East VIC 58 B5
Wonwondah North VIC 58 B5
Wonwron VIC 64 K5 66 G6
Wonyip VIC 66 H5
Woodanilling WA 109 C12 110 G5
Woodberry NSW 33 B13
Woodbine NSW 30 J1
Woodbine QLD 10 E3
Woodbourne VIC 59 F11 61 A12
Woodbridge TAS 69 K1 71 G12
Woodburn NSW 13 K14 39 C13
Woodbury TAS 69 B2
Woodenbong NSW 10 K6 13 J12 39 A11
Woodend NSW 43 H11
Woodend QLD 6 G1
Woodend VIC 59 D12
Woodford NSW 34 D5
Woodford QLD 8 F7 13 F13
Woodforde SA 83 K8 85 B8
Woodgate QLD 13 A13
Woodhill QLD 11 F9
Woodhouselee NSW 36 K6 44 B4
Woodlands QLD 10 C4
Woodlands WA 101 E2 102 D3 109 H13
Woodleigh VIC 57 K12 64 K2 66 G3
Woodman Point WA 106 E2
Woodpark NSW 28 J4 30 A4 35 D9
Woodridge QLD 3 J5 7 H12 11 C10
Woods Point VIC 64 G4 66 D5
Woods Reef NSW 38 G7
Woods Well SA 89 K10 98 E4

Woodsdale TAS 69 E3 71 A14
Woodside SA 86 J5 89 H9 98 C3
Woodside VIC 66 H7
Woodside Beach VIC 66 H7
Woodstock NSW 36 G5
Woodstock QLD 14 A5 17 H12
Woodstock TAS 71 F11
Woodstock VIC 57 A8
Woodstock WA 115 C8
Woodstock Nature Res ACT 47 C1 48 B3
Woodvale WA 101 B2
Woodville NSW 33 A12 45 F7
Woodville SA 81 E3 82 J3 84 A3 86 H2
Woodville Gardens SA 82 H3
Woodville North SA 82 H3
Woodville Park SA 82 J3 84 A3
Woodville South SA 81 F3 82 J3 84 A3
Woodville West SA 82 J2 84 A2
Woodvine Nature Res TAS 69 G3
Woody Bay QLD 9 G11
Woody Island QLD 18 A3
Woody Point QLD 5 C12 9 J10
Woodycupaldiya NT 124 F2
Woogenellup WA 109 G13
Woogoompah Island QLD 11 E12
Woohlpooer VIC 58 D5
Wool Bay SA 88 G12
Wool Wool VIC 59 G9 61 E8
Woolamai VIC 66 H2
Woolaning NT 124 D3
Woolbrook NSW 39 H8
Woolgarlo NSW 36 K4 43 G14 44 C2
Woolgoolga NSW 39 F13
Wooli NSW 39 E13
Wooliana Tourist Park NT 124 E3
Woollahra NSW 31 C12 35 D12
Woolloomooloo NSW 26 C4
Woolloongabba QLD 7 C10
Woolner NT 122 G3
Woolomin NSW 39 J8
Woolooga QLD 13 D12
Woolooma NSW 37 B10
Woolloomooloo NSW 29 K12 31 B12
Woolooware NSW 27 K4 31 J9
Woolloowin QLD 5 J10 7 A10
Woolloweyah NSW 39 D13
Woolsthorpe VIC 58 G6 60 C2
Woolwich NSW 29 J10 31 A10
Woomargama NSW 43 J12 64 A7
Woomargama Nat Park NSW 43 J12 64 A7
Woombye QLD 9 C9
Woomelang VIC 42 J4 62 F6
Woomera SA 94 E5
Woondum Nat Park QLD 13 D13
Woongarra Marine Park QLD 15 K13
Woongoolba QLD 11 D12
Woonigan QLD 20 C3
Woonona NSW 35 J10
Woorabinda QLD 15 J9
Wooragee VIC 43 K11 64 B5
Woorak VIC 42 K3 62 J3
Wooramel Roadhouse WA 112 A3 114 J3
Wooreen VIC 64 K3 66 G4
Woori Yallock VIC 57 C11 64 H2 66 E2
Woorim QLD 9 G11
Woorinen VIC 42 H6 63 E8
Woorinen North VIC 63 E8
Woornack VIC 42 H4 62 E5
Woorndoo VIC 58 F7 60 B4
Woorndoo Upper VIC 60 A4
Wooroconda WA 114 E5
Wooroloo WA 106 D5 110 D3 112 K6
Wooroolin QLD 13 D11
Wooroonook VIC 42 K5 62 H7
Wooroonooran Nat Park QLD 17 E11 18 G5
Woosang VIC 42 K6 63 J8
Wootha QLD 9 D8
Wootton NSW 37 C12
Woowoonga Nat Park QLD 13 B12
Worimi Nat Park NSW 37 E12
Worlds End SA 89 E9 98 A3
Worongary QLD 11 G12 24 F3
Woronora NSW 27 J3 30 H7
Woronora Heights NSW 30 H6
Worsley WA 108 B5
Wotto Nature Res WA 112 G5
Wowan QLD 15 J10
Woy Woy NSW 33 J12
Wright Island SA 87 H6
Wroxham VIC 44 K4 65 G13
Wubin WA 112 G6
Wudadah NT 124 F2
Wudapuli NT 124 F2
Wudinna SA 88 C2 94 J2 97 J14
Wugularr (Beswick) NT 124 G7
Wujal Wujal QLD 17 C10 19 K7
Wulagi NT 122 C6
Wulgulmerang VIC 44 J1 65 E9
Wulkabimirri NT 125 C10
Wulkuraka QLD 6 H1
Wumajbarr NT 125 F11
Wumalgi QLD 15 F9
Wumirdin NT 124 F2
Wunara NT 127 H12
Wundowie WA 106 D5 110 C4 112 J6
Wunghnu VIC 43 K9 63 H13 64 B2
Wungong WA 105 F10
Wungu WA 117 H13
Wunjunga QLD 14 A6 17 J13
Wunkar SA 89 G12 98 B5
Wunnamurra NSW 43 H9 63 E14
Wurankuwu NT 124 B3
Wurarga WA 112 E5
Wurdiboluc VIC 59 H11 61 E12
Wurrkleni NT 124 H4
Wurruk VIC 64 J6 66 F7
Wurrumenbumanja NT 125 F12
Wurtulla QLD 9 D10

Wutan QLD 19 F1
Wutul QLD 13 F11
Wutunugurra NT 127 J10 129 A10
Wuyagiba NT 125 G11
Wy Yung VIC 64 H7
Wyalkatchem WA 110 B5 112 J7
Wyalong NSW 36 H1 43 E12
Wyan NSW 39 C12
Wyandra QLD 23 D13
Wyangala NSW 36 H5
Wybalenna TAS 78 C4
Wyberba QLD 39 B9
Wycarbah QLD 15 H10
Wycheproof VIC 42 K5 62 H7
Wychitella VIC 42 K6 63 H8
Wycliffe Well NT 129 A9
Wye River VIC 59 J10 61 H11
Wyee NSW 33 F12 37 F10
Wyee Point NSW 33 E13
Wyeebo VIC 43 K12 64 C7
Wyelangta VIC 59 J9 61 H8
Wyena TAS 75 D9
Wyening WA 106 A6
Wylie Creek NSW 13 J11 39 B10
Wylkatchem WA 107 A9
Wyllie QLD 5 D9
Wymah NSW 43 J12 64 A7
Wymlet VIC 62 D4
Wynarka SA 89 H11 98 D4
Wynbring SA 97 C11
Wyndham NSW 44 J4 65 E13
Wyndham WA 117 D13
Wynn Vale SA 81 C6 83 E8
Wynnum QLD 3 D7 5 K14 7 B14 11 A10
Wynnum West QLD 5 K13 7 B13
Wynyard TAS 77 F9
Wyola WA 107 C9
Wyoming NSW 33 H12 37 B12
Wyong NSW 37 F10 33 G12
Wyong Creek NSW 33 G12
Wyongah NSW 33 G13
Wyperfeld Nat Park VIC 42 H2 62 F3 89 K14 98 E7
Wyrrabalong Nat Park NSW 33 G13
Wyuna VIC 43 K8 63 H12

Y

Yaamba QLD 15 G10
Yaapeet VIC 42 J3 62 G4
Yabba VIC 43 K12 64 B7
Yabba North VIC 43 K9 63 H14 64 B2
Yabba Vale QLD 8 A7
Yabbra Nat Park NSW 13 J12 39 B11
Yabulu QLD 17 H12
Yacka SA 89 D8
Yackadunyah WA 119 E5
Yackandandah VIC 43 K11 64 B5
Yagga Yagga WA 118 B6
Yagoona NSW 30 C6 35 E10
Yakanarra WA 117 H9
Yalamurra QLD 21 K10 23 C12
Yalata SA 96 E7 96 F7
Yalbarrin WA 107 E13
Yalboroo QLD 14 C7 17 K14 21 B14
Yalbraith NSW 36 J6 44 A4
Yalgogrin NSW 43 E11
Yalgoo WA 112 E6
Yalgorup Nat Park WA 106 H2 110 F3
Yalkula QLD 18 C2
Yallambie NSW 33 E9
Yallambie VIC 53 D11
Yallaroi NSW 13 K8 38 C6
Yalleroi QLD 14 J3 21 G11
Yallingup WA 108 C1 110 G2
Yalliquin NT 125 C11
Yallock NSW 41 J8 43 A8
Yallock VIC 57 H12
Yallook VIC 63 J10
Yallourn North VIC 64 J4 66 F5
Yallunda Flat SA 88 F3
Yaloak VIC 56 B2
Yaloak Vale VIC 56 C2
Yalpara SA 95 H9
Yalwal NSW 44 C6
Yamala QLD 14 H7 21 F14
Yamanto QLD 6 J2 10 C7
Yamba NSW 39 D13
Yamba SA 42 F1 62 B1 89 F13 98 B6
Yambacoona TAS 78 B1
Yamboyna QLD 14 H7 21 F14
Yambuk VIC 58 H5
Yaminyi NT 125 C9
Yan Yean VIC 57 A8 59 E14 64 G1 66 D1
Yanac VIC 62 H2 98 F7
Yanac South VIC 42 K2 62 H2
Yanakie VIC 66 J5
Yanbakwa NT 125 F12
Yanchep WA 106 C2 110 C2 112 J5
Yanchep Nat Park WA 106 C2 110 C2 112 J5
Yanco NSW 43 F10
Yanco Glen NSW 40 G2
Yandaran QLD 13 A12 15 K12
Yanderra NSW 35 K8
Yandi WA 115 E9
Yandicoogina WA 115 E9
Yandina QLD 9 B9 13 E13
Yandinga SA 88 A2 94 H2 97 H14
Yandoit VIC 59 C11
Yanga Nat Park NSW 42 F6
Yanga Nature Reserve NSW 63 C9
Yanga State Con Area NSW 42 G6
Yangalake NSW 42 G6 63 C8
Yangan QLD 10 H3 13 H12 39 A10
Yangebup WA 104 E4
Yangena TAS 73 F13 74 K7

Yango NSW 33 E9
Yaninee SA 88 B2 94 J2 97 J14
Yankalilla SA 87 F3 89 J8 98 D2
Yankalilla Bay SA 87 F2
Yanmah WA 108 F5
Yannathan VIC 57 H12
Yanna QLD 23 C13
Yantabulla NSW 23 J11 41 B8
Yantanabie SA 88 A1 94 H1 97 H13
Yanununbeyan Nat Park NSW 44 E4
Yaouk NSW 44 E2
Yaouk Nature Res NSW 44 F2 48 K2 65 A11
Yaraka QLD 14 K1 21 H9
Yarck VIC 64 E2 66 B3
Yardanogo Nature Res WA 112 F4
Yarding WA 107 D12
Yaringa Marine Nat Park VIC 57 H9
Yaripilangu NT 128 D4
Yarlington TAS 69 E1 71 B13
Yarloop VIC 106 J3 110 F3
Yarra Creek TAS 78 D2
Yarra Glen VIC 57 B10 64 G1 66 D2
Yarra Junction VIC 57 C12 64 H2 66 E3
Yarra Ranges Nat Park VIC 57 B12 64 G3 66 D4
Yarrabah QLD 17 E11 18 D5
Yarrabandai NSW 36 E2 41 K12 43 C12
Yarrabin NSW 36 D6
Yarragon VIC 64 J3 66 F4
Yarralena WA 109 F11
Yarralin NT 124 K4 126 B4
Yarralumla ACT 46 C1 47 E4
Yarram VIC 66 H6
Yarramalong NSW 33 G11
Yarraman NSW 37 A8 38 K5
Yarraman QLD 8 E1 13 E11
Yarrambat VIC 53 A12 57 B9
Yarramony WA 106 B7
Yarranbah NSW 38 E3
Yarrangobilly NSW 43 J14 44 E2
Yarrara VIC 42 F2 62 B2
Yarraville VIC 52 G6
Yarrawarrah NSW 30 J6
Yarrawonga VIC 43 J10 64 A3
Yarriabini Nat Park NSW 39 H12
Yarrie Mine Camp WA 115 B10
Yarrock VIC 62 J2
Yarroweyah VIC 63 G14 64 A2
Yarrowitch NSW 39 J9
Yarrowyck NSW 39 G8
Yarto VIC 42 H4 62 F5
Yarwun QLD 15 H11
Yass NSW 36 K5 44 C3
Yatala QLD 11 D11
Yatala Vale SA 81 C7 83 E10
Yatchaw VIC 58 F5
Yathalamarra NT 125 C10
Yathong Nature Res NSW 41 J9 43 B9
Yatpool VIC 42 F3 62 B4
Yattalunga SA 86 E4
Yawalpa QLD 11 E12
Yea VIC 64 F1 66 B2
Yeagurup WA 108 G6
Yeal Nature Res WA 106 B3 110 C3 112 J5
Yealering WA 107 G11 110 E6
Yearinan NSW 38 J3
Yearinga VIC 62 J2
Yederr NT 124 F2
Yedikba NT 125 F12
Yednia QLD 8 D5 13 E12
Yeelanna SA 88 E3
Yeerongpilly QLD 3 F3 7 E9
Yelarbon QLD 13 J9 38 A7
Yelbeni WA 107 A11
Yeldulknie Con Park SA 88 D5
Yellabinna Reg Res SA 97 D9
Yellagonga Regional Park WA 101 B2
Yellangip VIC 62 H5
Yellingbo VIC 57 D11
Yellowdine WA 111 B9 113 J9
Yellowdine Nature Res WA 111 B9 113 J10
Yelta VIC 42 E3 62 A4
Yelverton WA 108 D2
Yelverton Nat Park WA 108 D1
Yenda NSW 43 E10
Yendon VIC 59 E11
Yengo Nat Park NSW 33 E8 37 E9
Yennora NSW 28 K5 30 B5 35 D10
Yenyening Lakes Nature Res WA 107 F9
Yeo Lake Nature Res WA 119 B2
Yeo Station WA 119 B2
Yeo Yeo NSW 36 J3 43 F13
Yeoval NSW 36 D4 41 J14 43 B14
Yeppoon QLD 15 G10
Yerilla WA 113 F12
Yering VIC 57 B10
Yerong Creek NSW 43 H12
Yeronga QLD 3 F3 7 D9
Yerranderie NSW 34 J4 37 H8 44 A6
Yerranderie Rec Park NSW 34 J5
Yerrinbool NSW 35 K8
Yetholme NSW 36 F7
Yetman NSW 13 K9 38 B7
Yikarrakkal NT 125 C8
Yilila NT 125 E11
Yilliminning WA 107 J9
Yin Barun VIC 64 D3
Yinguwunarri NT 124 K5 126 B5
Yinnar VIC 64 K4 66 G5
Yinnar South VIC 64 K4 66 G5
Yirrirra WA 118 G5
Yirrkala NT 125 C13
Yokine WA 101 E4 102 D5
Yolla TAS 77 G8
Yongala SA 89 C9 95 J9
Yoongarillup WA 108 D3
York WA 106 D7 110 D4 112 K6
York Plains TAS 69 C2
York Town TAS 74 D6 77 G14

Yorke Peninsula SA 88 G7 98 C1
Yorketown SA 88 H6 98 C1
Yorkeys Knob QLD 17 D11 18 D4
Yorkrakine WA 107 B10
Yornaning WA 107 H9 110 E5
Yornup WA 108 E6
Yoting WA 107 E10
You Yangs Reg Park VIC 56 E3
Youanmite VIC 63 H14 64 B2
Youndegin WA 107 D9
Young NSW 36 J3 43 F14 44 A1
Youngs Siding WA 109 K12
Youraling WA 107 F8
Yowah Opal Field QLD 23 F11
Yowie Bay NSW 27 K4 31 J8
Yowrie NSW 44 G4
Yudi Yudi NT 125 C12
Yuelamu (Mount Allan) NT 128 D6
Yuendumu NT 128 D5
Yugar QLD 4 F5
Yuleba QLD 12 E6
Yulecart VIC 58 E4
Yullundry NSW 36 E4 41 K14 43 B14
Yulte Con Park SA 87 F5
Yuluma NSW 43 G11
Yumali SA 89 J11 98 D4
Yumbarra Con Park SA 96 A2 97 F10
Yuna WA 112 E4
Yundamindera WA 113 F12
Yunderup WA 106 G3 110 E3
Yundi SA 87 F6
Yundool VIC 63 H14 64 B3
Yungaburra QLD 17 E11 18 F3
Yungera VIC 42 G5 62 C7
Yungngora WA 117 H9
Yunndaga WA 113 G11
Yunta SA 89 B10 95 H10
Yununbunbeyan Nat Park NSW 48 E7
Yununbunbeyan State Con Area NSW 48 F7
Yunyarinyi (Kenmore Park) SA 93 B8
Yurangka SA 92 B6
Yuraygir Nat Park NSW 39 E13
Yurgo SA 89 H11 98 D5
Yuroke VIC 59 E14
Yurol QLD 9 A8
Yuulong VIC 59 K9 61 J8
Yuwalki NT 128 F2

Z

Zanthus WA 113 H14 119 F1
Zeehan TAS 72 E4
Zeerust VIC 63 H13 64 B1
Zetland NSW 31 D11
Zillmere QLD 3 B4 5 G10
Zumsteins VIC 58 C3
Zuytdorp Nature Res WA 112 C3

List of Abbreviations

CBD	– Central Business District
Con Area	– Conservation Area
Con Park	– Conservation Park
CYPAL	– Cape York Peninsula Aboriginal Land
Nat Park	– National Park
Nature Res	– Nature Reserve
Rec Park	– Recreation Park
Reg Res	– Regional Reserve
Res	– Reserve

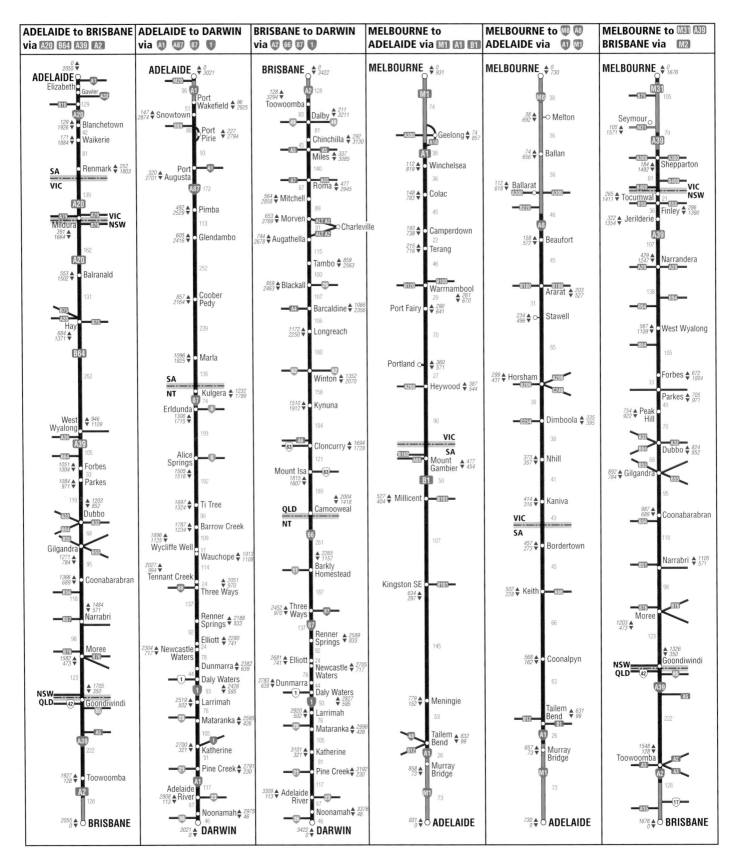

ADELAIDE to BRISBANE via A20 B64 A39 A2

ADELAIDE	0 / 2055 ▲
Elizabeth	A1
Gawler	A32
	B10
	129
Blanchetown	A20 · 129/1926 ▲
Waikerie	42 · 171/1884 ▼
	81
SA / VIC	Renmark · 252/1803
	A20 · 139
Mildura	A79 VIC / B79 NSW · 391/1664 ▼
	A20 · 162
Balranald	553/1502 ▲
	131
Hay	B75 A20 B75 · 684/1371 ▼
	B64 · 262
West Wyalong	946/1109 ▲
	A39
Forbes	B64 · 105 · 1051/1004 ▲
Parkes	33 · 1084/971 ▼
	119
Dubbo	A32 A32 · 1203/852 ▲
Gilgandra	B84 B55 B55 · 68 · 1271/784 ▼
	95
Coonabarabran	B56 · 1366/689 ▼
	118
Narrabri	B57 · 1484/571 ▲
	98
Moree	B76 B76 · 1582/473 ▼
	123
NSW / QLD	Goondiwindi · 42 · 1705/350 ▲
	85 A39 A5
	222
Toowoomba	1927/128 ▲
	A2 · 128
BRISBANE	2055/0 ▲

ADELAIDE to DARWIN via A1 A87 87 1

ADELAIDE	0 / 3021 ▲
	M20 · 96
Port Wakefield	A1 · 51 · 96/2925
Snowtown	B89 · 147/2874 ▲
Port Pirie	80 · 227/2794
	93
Port Augusta	A1 · 320/2701 ▲
	A87 · 172
Pimba	492/2529 ▲
	113
Glendambo	605/2416 ▲
	252
Coober Pedy	857/2164 ▲
	239
Marla	1096/1925 ▲
	136
SA / NT	Kulgera · 87 · 1232/1789 ▲
Erldunda	4 · 74
	199
Alice Springs	6 · 1505/1516 ▲
	192
Ti Tree	1697/1324 ▲
	90
Barrow Creek	1787/1234 ▲
	109
Wycliffe Well	1896/1125 ▲
	17
Wauchope	2027/994 ▲ · 1913/1108 ▼
	114
Tennant Creek	66 · 24
Three Ways	2051/970 ▼
	137
Renner Springs	2188/833 ▼
	92
Elliott	2304/717 ▲ · 2280/741 ▼
Newcastle Waters	24
Dunmarra	78 · 2382/639 ▼
	1 · 44
Daly Waters	1 · 93 · 2426/595 ▼
Larrimah	2519/502 ▲
	20 · 76
Mataranka	2595/426 ▼
	105
Katherine	1 · 2700/321 ▲
	91
Pine Creek	21 · 2791/230 ▼
Adelaide River	A1 · 117 · 2908/113 ▲
	23 · 67
Noonamah	36 · 46 · 2975/46 ▲
DARWIN	3021/0 ▼

BRISBANE to DARWIN via A2 66 87 1

BRISBANE	0 / 3422 ▲
	A2 · 128 / 3294
Toowoomba	128/3294 ▲
	83
Dalby	49 49 · 211/3211 ▼
	81
Chinchilla	292/3130 ▼
	45
Miles	A5 A5 · 337/3085 ▼
	140
Roma	A7 A55 · 477/2945 ▼
	87
Mitchell	564/2858 ▲
	89
Morven	653/2769 ▲
Augathella	744/2678 ▲ · Charleville (ALT A2 ALT A2)
	115
Tambo	859/2563 ▼
	100
Blackall	26 · 959/2463 ▲
	107
Barcaldine	A4 · 1066/2356 ▲
	106
Longreach	1172/2250 ▲
	180
Winton	62 62 · 1352/2070 ▼
	158
Kynuna	1510/1912 ▲
	184
Cloncurry	83 · A6 · 1694/1728 ▼
	121
Mount Isa	83 · 1815/1607 ▼
	189
Camooweal	2004/1418 ▲
QLD / NT	
	66 · 261
Barkly Homestead	2265/1157 ▲
	187
Three Ways	11 · 2452/970 ▲
	87 · 137
Renner Springs	87 · 2589/833 ▼
	92
Elliott	2681/741 ▲
	24
Newcastle Waters	2705/717 ▼
	78
Dunmarra	2783/639 ▼
	1 · 44
Daly Waters	1 · 2827/595 ▼
	93
Larrimah	2920/502 ▲
	24 · 76
Mataranka	2996/426 ▼
	105
Katherine	3101/321 ▲
	91
Pine Creek	23 · 3192/230 ▼
Adelaide River	1 · 117 · 3309/113 ▲
	23 · 67
Noonamah	35 · 46 · 3376/46 ▲
DARWIN	3422/0 ▼

MELBOURNE to ADELAIDE via M1 A1 B1

MELBOURNE	0 / 931 ▲
	M1 · 74
Geelong	A300 A10 · 74/857 ▲
	A1 · 38
Winchelsea	112/819 ▼
	36
Colac	148/783 ▼
	45
Camperdown	193/738 ▼
Terang	215/716 ▼
	46
Warrnambool	B120 B100 · 290/641 ▲
Port Fairy	29 · 261/670
	70
Portland	360/571 ▲
	27
Heywood	A200 · 387/544 ▼
	90
VIC / SA	Mount Gambier · B160 A66 · 477/454 ▲
	B1 · 50
Millicent	B101 · 527/404 ▲
	107
Kingston SE	B101 · 634/297 ▲
	145
Meningie	779/152 ▲
	53
Tailem Bend	A8 B12 A1 · 832/99 ▲
	26
Murray Bridge	A1 · 858/73 ▲
	73
ADELAIDE	M1 · 931/0 ▲

MELBOURNE to ADELAIDE via M8 A8 A1 M1

MELBOURNE	0 / 730 ▲
	M8 · 38
Melton	38/692 ▲
	36
Ballan	74/656 ▲
	38
Ballarat	A300 A300 · 112/618 ▲
	A8 · 46
Beaufort	158/572 ▲
	45
Ararat	B180 B180 · 203/527 ▲
	31
Stawell	234/496 ▲
	65
Horsham	A200 B200 C240 · 299/431 ▲
	36
Dimboola	C234 · 335/395 ▲
	38
Nhill	373/357 ▲
	41
Kaniva	414/316 ▲
	43
VIC / SA	
Bordertown	457/273 ▲
	45
Keith	A66 · 502/228 ▲
	66
Coonalpyn	568/162 ▲
	63
Tailem Bend	B12 B1 · 631/99 ▲
	A1 · 26
Murray Bridge	A1 · 657/73 ▲
	M1 · 73
ADELAIDE	730/0 ▲

MELBOURNE to BRISBANE via M31 A39 M2

MELBOURNE	0 / 1676 ▲
	M31 · 105
Seymour	B75 · 105/1571 ▲
	M31 · 79
	A39
Shepparton	A300 A300 · 184/1492 ▼
	81
Tocumwal	B400 B400 · 265/1411 ▲ · **VIC / NSW**
Finley	B59 · 21 · 286/1390 ▼
Jerilderie	36 · 322/1354 ▲
	A39 · 107
Narrandera	A20 A20 · 429/1247 ▲
	138
West Wyalong	B94 B94 · 567/1109 ▼
	105
Forbes	B64 · 672/1004 ▲
	33
Parkes	A32 A32 · 705/971 ▼
	49
Peak Hill	B84 B84 · 754/922 ▲
	70
Dubbo	824/852 ▼
	68
Gilgandra	B55 · 892/784 ▲
	95
Coonabarabran	B56 · 987/689 ▲
	118
Narrabri	B51 · 1105/571 ▲
	98
Moree	B76 B76 · 1203/473 ▼
	123
NSW / QLD	Goondiwindi · 42 85 · 1326/350 ▲
	A39 A5
	222
Toowoomba	A2 A3 A3 · 1548/128 ▲
	A2 · 128
	A15 17
BRISBANE	1676/0 ▲

BRISBANE RIVER, BRISBANE (2 C2)

PHOTO: LESLEY DOWNIE

YARRA RIVER, MELBOURNE (50 C3)

PHOTO: ISTOCK.COM/ROSS KUMMER

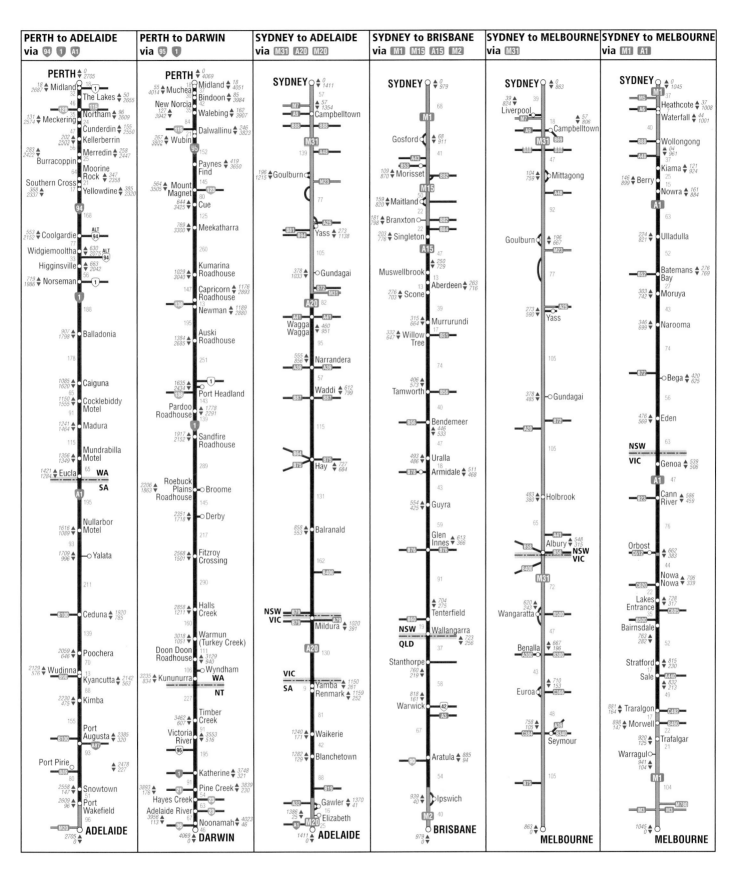

PERTH to ADELAIDE
via 94 1 A1

PERTH ▼ 0 / 2705
18 / 2687 ▲ Midland 18
The Lakes ▲ 50 / 2655
131 / 2574 ▲ Meckering 46 / Northam ▲ 96 / 2609
Cunderdin ▲ 155 / 2550
47 / 2503 ▲ Kellerberrin 56
Merredin ▲ 258 / 2447
283 / 2422 ▲ Burracoppin 25
Moorine Rock ▲ 347 / 2358
21
Southern Cross ▼ 368 / 2337 17
Yellowdine ▲ 385 / 2320
168
553 / 2152 ▲ Coolgardie 77
Widgiemooltha ▼ 630 / 2075 ALT 94
33
Higginsville ▲ 663 / 2042
56
719 / 1986 ▲ Norseman
188
907 / 1798 ▲ Balladonia
178
1085 / 1620 ▲ Caiguna
65
1150 / 1555 ▲ Cocklebiddy Motel
91
1241 / 1464 ▲ Madura
115
1356 / 1349 ▲ Mundrabilla Motel
65
1421 / 1284 ▲ Eucla   WA / SA
195
1616 / 1089 ▲ Nullarbor Motel
93
1709 / 996 ▲ Yalata
211
Ceduna ▲ 1920 / 785
139
2059 / 646 ▲ Poochera
70
2129 / 576 ▲ Wudinna 13
Kyancutta ▲ 2142 / 563
88
2230 / 475 ▲ Kimba
155
Port Augusta ▲ 2385 / 320
93
Port Pirie
80
2558 / 147 ▲ Snowtown 51
2609 / 96 ▲ Port Wakefield
96
ADELAIDE
2705 / 0 ▼

PERTH to DARWIN
via 95 1

PERTH ▼ 0 / 4069
Midland ▲ 18 / 4051
55 / 4014 ▲ Muchea
Bindoon ▲ 85 / 3984
New Norcia
127 / 3942 ▲ Walebing ▲ 162 / 3907
84
Dalwallinu ▲ 246 / 3823
267 / 3902 ▲ Wubin
152
Paynes Find ▲ 419 / 3650
145
564 / 3505 ▲ Mount Magnet
80
644 / 3425 ▲ Cue
125
769 / 3300 ▲ Meekatharra
260
Kumarina Roadhouse
1029 / 3040 ▲ 147
Capricorn Roadhouse ▲ 1176 / 2893
13
Newman ▲ 1189 / 2880
195
1384 / 2685 ▲ Auski Roadhouse
251
1635 / 2434 ▲ Port Headland
143
Pardoo Roadhouse ▲ 1778 / 2291
139
1917 / 2152 ▲ Sandfire Roadhouse
289
2206 / 1863 ▲ Roebuck Plains Roadhouse
Broome
145
2351 / 1718 ▲ Derby
217
2568 / 1501 ▲ Fitzroy Crossing
290
2858 / 1211 ▲ Halls Creek
160
3018 / 1051 ▲ Warmun (Turkey Creek)
111
Doon Doon Roadhouse ▲ 3129 / 940
106
3235 / 834 ▲ Kununurra   WA / NT
Wyndham
227
3462 / 607 ▲ Timber Creek
91
Victoria River ▲ 3553 / 516
195
Katherine ▲ 3748 / 321
3893 / 176 ▲ Pine Creek ▲ 3839 / 230
91
Hayes Creek
63
Adelaide River
3956 / 113 ▲ Noonamah ▲ 4023 / 46
67
DARWIN
4069 / 0 ▼

SYDNEY to ADELAIDE
via M31 A20 M20

SYDNEY ▼ 0 / 1411
57
57 / 1354 ▲ Campbelltown
139
196 / 1215 ▲ Goulburn
77
378 / 1033 ▲ Gundagai
105
Wagga Wagga ▲ 460 / 951
95
555 / 856 ▲ Narrandera
57
Waddi ▲ 612 / 799
115
858 / 553 ▲ Hay ▲ 727 / 684
131
162
NSW / VIC
Mildura ▲ 1020 / 391
130
VIC / SA 9
Yamba ▼ 1150 / 261
Renmark ▲ 1159 / 252
81
1240 / 171 ▲ Waikerie
42
1282 / 129 ▲ Blanchetown
88
1386 / 25 ▲ Gawler ▲ 1370 / 41
16
Elizabeth
25
ADELAIDE
1411 / 0 ▼

SYDNEY to BRISBANE
via M1 M15 A15 M2

SYDNEY ▼ 0 / 979
68
68 / 911 ▲ Gosford
41
109 / 870 ▲ Morisset
22
159 / 820 ▲ Maitland
22
181 / 798 ▲ Branxton
203 / 776 ▲ Singleton
47
Muswellbrook
250 / 729 ▲
13
276 / 703 ▲ Scone
Aberdeen ▲ 263 / 716
39
315 / 664 ▲ Murrurundi
17
332 / 647 ▲ Willow Tree
74
406 / 573 ▲ Tamworth
40
Bendemeer ▲ 446 / 533
47
493 / 486 ▲ Uralla
18
Armidale ▲ 511 / 468
43
554 / 425 ▲ Guyra
59
Glen Innes ▲ 613 / 366
91
704 / 275 ▲ Tenterfield
NSW / QLD 19
Wallangarra ▲ 723 / 256
37
Stanthorpe
760 / 219 ▲
58
818 / 161 ▲ Warwick
67
Aratula ▲ 885 / 94
54
939 / 40 ▲ Ipswich
40
BRISBANE
979 / 0 ▼

SYDNEY to MELBOURNE
via M31

SYDNEY ▼ 0 / 863
39 / 824 ▲ Liverpool 39
18
Campbelltown
47
104 / 759 ▲ Mittagong
92
Goulburn
77
273 / 590 ▲ Yass
105
378 / 485 ▲ Gundagai
105
Albury ▲ 548 / 315
NSW / VIC
72
Wangaratta
47
620 / 243 ▲ Benalla ▲ 667 / 196
43
Euroa
710 / 153 ▲
48
758 / 105 ▲ Seymour
105
MELBOURNE
863 / 0 ▼

SYDNEY to MELBOURNE
via M1 A1

SYDNEY ▼ 0 / 1045
37
Heathcote ▲ 37 / 1008
Waterfall ▲ 44 / 1001
40
Wollongong ▲ 84 / 961
Kiama ▲ 121 / 924
15
146 / 899 ▲ Berry Nowra ▼ 161 / 884
63
224 / 821 ▲ Ulladulla
52
Batemans Bay ▲ 276 / 769
303 / 742 ▲ Moruya
43
346 / 699 ▲ Narooma
74
Bega ▲ 420 / 625
56
476 / 569 ▲ Eden
63
NSW / VIC
Genoa ▲ 539 / 506
47
Cann River ▲ 586 / 459
76
Orbost ▲ 662 / 383
44
Nowa Nowa ▼ 706 / 339
22
Lakes Entrance ▲ 728 / 317
35
Bairnsdale
52
763 / 282 ▲ Stratford ▲ 815 / 230
17
Sale ▲ 832 / 213
49
881 / 164 ▲ Traralgon
17
898 / 147 ▲ Morwell ▲ 860?
22
920 / 125 ▲ Trafalgar
21
Warragul
941 / 104 ▲
104
MELBOURNE
1045 / 0 ▼

Freeway; Divided Highway

Autobahn
Autoroute; route rapide à chaussées séparées
Autostrada; superstrada
Autosnelweg; hoofdweg met gescheiden rijbanen

Freeway – future

Autobahn – im Bau
Autoroute – en construction
Autostrada – in costruzione
Autosnelweg in aanleg

Major Highway – sealed; unsealed

Durchgangsstraße – befestigt; unbefestigt
Route principale – revêtue; non revêtue
Strada di grande comunicazione – pavimentata;
non pavimentata
Hoofdverbindingsweg – verhard; onverhard

Major Road – sealed; unsealed

Hauptstraße – befestigt; unbefestigt
Route de communication – revêtue; non revêtue
Strada principale – pavimentata; non pavimentata
Belangrijke weg – verhard of onverhard

Minor Road – sealed; unsealed

Nebenstraße – befestigt; unbefestigt
Autre route revêtue; non revêtue
Altra strada – pavimentata; non pavimentata
Secundaire weg – verhard of aardeweg

Track, four-wheel drive only

Piste, nur mit 4-Rad-Antrieb befahrbar
Piste, utilisable pour véhicule à 4 roues motrices
Pista, praticabile solo con trazione integrale
Piste, uitsluitend voor 4 x 4

Rough Track, four-wheel drive only

Piste (unwegsam), nur mit 4-Rad-Antrieb befahrbar
Piste rugueux, utilisable pour véhicule à 4 roues motrices
Pista greggio, praticabile solo con trazione integral
Piste moeilijk berijbaar, uitsluitend voor 4 x 4

Walking Track; Gate

Wanderweg; Tor
Sentier; barrière
Sentiero; cancello
Wandelweg; gate

★ 44 ★   ↗ 20 ↗ 24 ↗
Total Kilometres   Intermediate Kilometres

Entfernung (total) in km   Teildistanz in km
Distance totale en km   Distance partielle en km
Distanza totale in km   Distanza parziale in km
Totale afstand in km   Gedeeltelijke afstand in km

National Route Number/
National Highway Number

Nummer Nationalstraße/ Nummer nationale
Durchgangsstraße
Numéro de route nationale/ de route rapide
Numero della strada nazionale/ Numero della
strada di grande comunicazione
Wegnummers op nationale/ wegen en expresswegen

State Route Number

Staats-Straßennummer
Numéro de route d'Etat
Nùmero della strada dello stato
Staatswegnummer

Tourist Route

Touristische Route
Route touristique
Strada turistica
Toeristische route

Railway – in use; disused

Bahnlinie – in Betrieb; stillgelegt
Chemin de fer – en service; abandonné
Ferrovia – in esercizio; interrotto
Spoorweg – in gebruik; buiten gebruik

Ferry Route

Fährverbindung
Route de traversier
Traghetto rotta
Veerdienst

State/ Territory Border

Staats-/ Territoriengrenze
Frontière d'Etat/ territoire
Stato/ territorio di confine
Staats-/ Territorygrens

Pest Free Area

Pest Freie Zone
Zone de ravageur franche
Zona parassiti franca
Pestvrij gebied

Fruit Fly Exclusion Zone

Fruchtfliegen Ausschluss Zone
Zone exclusive de la mouche des fruits
Zona esclusiva della mosca della frutta
Fruitvliegvrij gebied

National Park

Nationalpark
Parc national
Parco nazionale
Nationaal park

Other Parks & Nature Reserves

Sonstige Parks und Natur Reservate
Autre parks et réserve naturelle
Altri parchi e riserve
Andere parken en natuurreservaten

Resources Reserve

Ressourcen Schutzgebiet
Zone protégée de ressources
Zona protetta di risorse
Ontginnings Reservaat

Scientific Reserve

Naturwissenschaftliches Schutzgebiet
Zone protégée scientifique
Zona protetta scientifica
Wetenschappelijk Reservaat

State Forest & Timber Reserve

Staatsforst & Holz Reservat
Forêt domaniale
Zona protetta di risorse
Staatsbos en bosbouw reservaat

Aboriginal Land

Aborigines-Gebiet
Région d'aborigènes
Regione d'aborigeni
Gebied van de aborigines

World Heritage Area

Weltkulturerbegebiet (UNESCO)
Site du patrimoine mondial
Luogo dell' patrimonio mondiale
Wereld Beschermd Gebied

Marine Park

Meeresschutzgebiet
Parc marin
Parco marino
Zeereservaat

Prohibited Area

Sperrgebiet
Zone interdite
Area vietata
Afgesloten gebied

Lake or Reservoir

See oder Reservoir
Lac ou réservoir
Lago o lago artificiale
Meer of waterreservoir

Intermittent or Salt Lake

Periodischer oder Salzwassersee
Lac périodique ou d'eau salée
Lago periodico o salato
Periodiek of zoutwatermeer

River – perennial;
non-perennial

Fluß – dauerhaft; periodisch
Rivière – constant; périodique
Fiume – constante; periodico
Rivier – altijd; periodiek

Saline Coastal Flat

Wattgebiet
Salines côtières
Salino castiero platts
Zeekust vlakte

Swamp

Sumpf
Marais
Palude
Moeras

Subject to Inundation

Überschwemmungsgebiet
Sujet aux inondations
Soggette a inondazioni
Kan onderwater lopen

Sandridges

Sanddüne
Dune de sable
Dune de sabbia
Zandruggen

Mangroves

Mangroven
Mangroves
Mangrovie
Wortelbomen

Built up area

Bebaute Fläche
Zone construite
Costruito nell'area
Bebouwde kom

● BRISBANE
Capital City

Hauptstadt
Capitale
Capitale
Hoofdstaad

● **Cairns**
City

Grossstadt
Ville importante
Città grande o importante
Stad of hoofdplaats

● **Gympie**
Large Town

Stadt
Ville
Città
Stad

● **Tully**
Medium Town

Mittelgroße Stadt
Ville moyenne
Città de medie
MIddelgrote Stad

● Samford
Small Town

Kleinstadt
Ville petite
Piccola città
Kleine Stad

▪ Ayton
Locality

Gegend
Localité
Località
Plaats

▪ 'Rostock'
Homestead

Gehöft
Ferme
Masseria
Hofstede

◉ Doomadgee   ⊙ Urlampe
Aboriginal Community –
major; minor

Aborigines Gemeinde – groß; klein
Communauté d'aborigènes
Comunità d'aborigeni
Gebied van aborigines – groot; klein

+ *Mount James*
Mountain/ Hill

Berg/ Hügel
Montagne/ colline
Monte/ colle
Bergen/ heuvel

● *Fruit Bat Falls*
Tourist Point of Interest

Sehenswürdigkeit
Curiosité touristique
Curiosità turistica
Toeristische bezienswaardigheid

● *Lindeman's*
Hunter Valley
Winery

Weinkellerei
Établissement vinicole
Cantina
Wijnmakerij

⚓   ✧
Shipwreck   Lighthouse

Schiffswrack   Leuchtturm
Naufrage   Phare
Naufragio   Faro
Schipwrak   Vuurtoren

⚡   ▲
Tower   Hut

Turm   Hütte
Tour   Hutte
Torre   Capanna
Toren   Hut

—40—
Distance from GPO (km)

Entfernung zum Hauptpostgebäude (km)
Distance par la route du bureau de poste général (km)
Distanza dalla strada da General Post Office (km)
Afstand uit de algemene postkantoor (km)

Camping Area (with facilities)

Camping (mit Einrichtungen)
Camping (avec équipement)
Campeggio (con equipaggiamento)
Campingplaats (met voorzieningen)

Rest Area (with toilet)

Rastplatz (mit Toilette)
Aire de repos (avec Toilettes)
Area di riposo (con Gabinetto)
Rustplaats (mel toilet)

… with overnight camping

Rastplatz (Toilette)
...mit Camping (nur 1 Nacht)
Aire de repos (Toilettes)
...et camping (seulement 1 nuit)
Area di riposo (Gabinetto)
...e campeggio (solo 1 notte)
Rustplaats (toilet)
...en Campingplaats (één overnachting)

…with overnight camping (no toilet)

Rastplatz (ohne Toilette)
Aire de repos (sans Toilettes)
Area di riposo (senza Gabinetto)
Rustplaats (zonder toilet)

Picnic Area/ Rest Area (no facilities)

Picknickplatz / Rastplatz (ohne Einrichtungen)
Place pique-nique / Aire de repos (sans equipment)
Picnic / Area di riposo (senza equipaggiamento)
Piknikplaatsen / Rustplaats (zonder voorzieningen)

Accredited Visitor Information Centre

Akkreditiertes Besucher Informationszentrum
Accréditée centre d'information touristique
Accreditato visitatore centro di informazione
Officieel touristenkantoor

⛳
Golf Course   Caravan Park

Golfplatz   Wohnwagen-Park
Terrain de golf   Terrain pour caravanes
Campo da golf   Area per Camper/Roulotte
Golfbaan   Het karavaan park

Boat ramp   Lookout

Bootsrampe   Aussichtspunkt
Rampe   Point de vue
Barca rampa   Belvedere
Boothelling   Uitkijk

⛽   ⛽
24 Hour Fuel   Diesel

Tankstelle 24 Std.   Diesel erhältlich
Station-service ouverte 24h   Diesel disponible
Stazione di servizio aperta 24h   Diesel disponibile
24 uur benzene   Diesel beschikbaar

Outback Fuel (Diesel and Unleaded)

(not shown in region pages)
Diesel u. bleifreies Benzin bzw.
Diesel et carburant sans plomb
Diesel e benzina senza piombo
Diesel en loodvrij

⛽
Opal (unleaded replacement)

Opal Bezin erhältlich
Opal disponible
Opale disponibile
Opal

Airport; International Airport

Flughafen; Internationaler Flughafen
Aéroport; Aéroport international
Aeroporto; Aeroporto internazionale
Vlieghaven; Vlieghaven internationaal